FITS, TRANCES, & VISIONS

Ann Taves

FITS, TRANCES, & VISIONS

Experiencing Religion and Explaining

Experience from Wesley to James

PRINCETON UNIVERSITY PRESS

PRINCETON, NEW JERSEY

Library of Congress Cataloging-in-Publication Data

Taves, Ann, 1952–
Fits, trances, and visions : experiencing religion and explaining experience from Wesley to James /
Ann Taves.
p.   cm.
Includes bibliographical references and index.
ISBN 0-691-02876-1 (hardcover : alk. paper). — ISBN 0-691-01024-2 (pbk. : alk. paper)
1. Experience (Religion)—History—18th century. 2. Psychology, Religious—History—18th century.
3. Methodism—History—18th century. 4. Experience (Religion)—History—19th century. 5. Psychology, Religious—History—19th century. 6. Methodism—History—19th century. I. Title.
BL53.T38 1999
291.4'2—dc21   99-29754 CIP

This book has been composed in Berkeley Book typeface

The paper used in this publication meets the minimum requirements
of ANSI / NISO Z39.48-1992 (R1997) (*Permanence of Paper*)

http://pup.princeton.edu

Printed in the United States of America
2   3   4   5   6   7   8   9   10

TO MY PARENTS

C O N T E N T S

LIST OF ILLUSTRATIONS

ACKNOWLEDGMENTS

THIS BOOK, more than any other I have written, integrates my long-standing interest in the both the theory and practice of religion and my institutional involvement with both the academic study of religion and theological education, commitments which at times have seemed hopelessly at odds with one another. In many ways, it is rooted in my experiences in Claremont as an undergraduate in the early 1970s and as a professor in the 1980s and 1990s. It has many spiritual parents. Robert Voelkel, my undergraduate advisor at Pomona College, William Scott Green, my informal advisor while I was a student at Colgate Rochester Divinity School, and Lee Cormie (then) at the University of Chicago awakened and nurtured my love of the theory of religion. Jerald Brauer, my advisor at the University of Chicago, introduced me to Protestant revivalism and to piety and practice as ways to approach American religious history. President Richard Cain invited me (as a non-Methodist) to teach the required course in Methodist history when I began teaching at the School of Theology in 1983. Almost ten years later, Dean Marjorie Suchocki encouraged me to teach theory of religion courses for the Religion Department at the Claremont Graduate University.

This project took initial form while I was studying psychology at California Family Studies Center in 1990–91. Certain key ideas crystalized in a long conversation with my friend and colleague Karen Torjesen on a train trip to Mazatlan that December. The outline of the book acquired much of its present shape during 1993–94. Conversations with Thomas Tweed and other contributors to the "Narratives Project" during the fall pushed my ideas in a more historical direction. Nathan Hatch's presidential address to the American Society of Church History at the 1993 meeting convinced me how central Methodists were to the story I was piecing together. Tom Tweed was a faithful email conversation partner and my most helpful critic as I outlined the book and wrote the first chapters during the following spring. Grey Gundaker and others connected with the Center for the Study of American Religion at Princeton University played a similar role as I completed the manuscript during the 1997–98 academic year.

Numerous people have read all or part of the manuscript over the past five years. Leigh Schmidt, Greg Schneider, Thomas Tweed, and an anonymous reader read and commented on the whole manuscript. Steven Cooley, Paul Croce, Lori Anne Ferrell, Tamar Frankiel, Rebecca Gould, David Griffin, Grey Gundaker, David Lamberth, Henry Mitchell, Karen Torjesen, and David Wills read and commented on various chapters, as did several anonymous readers, my parents, and many of my students. The members of the Religion and American Culture Workshop at Princeton and the History of Christianity Colloquium at Claremont discussed the introduction. I am grateful to these readers for their encouragement and critical feedback. Many others have helped as well. The staff of the Interlibrary Loan Office at Honnold Library supplied me with a seemingly endless stream of obscure books. Lester Ruth, Ian Straker, Leigh Schmidt, David Wills, Albert

ACKNOWLEDGMENTS

Raboteau, Stephen Cooley, Stephen Prothero, Wayne Warner, and Grey Gundaker all provided me with primary materials related to their own research. Lynn Euzenas provided invaluable research assistance for several years, including reading through years of Spiritualist periodicals on microfilm. Olga Morales provided cheerful and prompt secretarial support.

I would like to thank the Claremont School of Theology, especially President Robert Edgar and Dean Suchocki, for the combination of sabbatical and leave time during the academic years 1993–94 and 1997–98 that allowed me to write the book. The Association of Theological Schools provided a grant that made the first leave possible and the Center for the Study of American Religion at Princeton University funded the second. I would like to thank Robert Wuthnow, John Wilson, Al Raboteau, and Anita Kline for making my stay in Princeton such a pleasant one. I am also grateful to my colleagues at the School of Theology and in the Religion Department, especially Tamar Frankiel, Bob Edgar, and Jack Coogan, for filling in for me in various ways while I was gone. My editors at Princeton University Press, first Ann Wald and then Deborah Malmud, have been a continual source of support and encouragement. Last I am grateful to my family and friends, who have put up with, even supported, the absences that went into making this book a reality. I dedicate the book to my parents, Don and Ellen Taves, who take great delight in aiding and abetting the disparate creative passions of their grown children.

ABBREVIATIONS

AFLA	*The Apostolic Faith* (Los Angeles). Reprinted in E. Myron Noble, ed. *Like As of Fire: Newspapers from the Azusa Street World Wide Revival.* Washington, DC: Middle Atlantic Regional Press, 1995.
BL	*The Banner of Light.*
SPR	Society for Psychical Research
CC	*Cambridge Companion*
DSM-IV	American Psychiatric Association. *The Diagnostic and Statistical Manual of Mental Disorders*, 4th ed. Washington, DC: American Psychiatric Association, 1994.
JAAR	*Journal of the American Academy of Religion*
JE	*The Works of Jonathan Edwards.* New Haven: Yale University Press, 1957–.
JPPSM	*Journal of Philosophy, Psychology, and Scientific Methods*
JW	*The Works of John Wesley.* Oxford: Clarendon Press, 1975– (Oxford Edition); Nashville: Abingdon Press, 1984— (Bicentennial Edition).
ME	John Fanning Watson. *Methodist Error.* 1814; rev. ed., Trenton: D. & E. Fenton, 1819.
PSPR	*Proceedings of the Society for Psychical Research.*
QM	Horatio W. Dresser, ed. *The Quimby Manuscripts.* 1921; reprint ed., New Hyde Park, NY: University Books, 1961.
SH	Mary Baker [Glover] Eddy. *Science and Health.* Various editions.
STSR	Charles Chauncy. *Seasonable Thoughts on the State of Religion in New England.* Boston, 1743; reprint ed., Hicksville, NY: Regina Press, 1975.
ST	*The Spiritual Telegraph*
VRE	William James. *Varieties of Religious Experience.* Ed. John Smith. Cambridge, MA: Harvard University Press, 1985.

FITS, TRANCES, & VISIONS

THIS BOOK is about the interplay between experiencing religion and explaining experience. It is mostly about Anglo-American Protestants and those who left the Protestant fold beginning with the transatlantic awakening in the early eighteenth century and ending with the rise of the psychology of religion and the birth of Pentecostalism in the early twentieth. It focuses on a class of seemingly involuntary acts alternately explained in religious and secular terms. These involuntary experiences include uncontrolled bodily movements (fits, bodily exercises, falling as dead, catalepsy, convulsions); spontaneous vocalizations (crying out, shouting, speaking in tongues); unusual sensory experiences (trances, visions, voices, clairvoyance, out-of-body experiences); and alterations of consciousness and/or memory (dreams, somnium, somnambulism, mesmeric trance, mediumistic trance, hypnotism, possession, alternating personality).

Those who experienced religion, not surprisingly, explained their experience in religious terms. Those who appear in this narrative typically did so in terms of the "power" or "presence" or "indwelling" of God, or Christ, or the Spirit, or spirits. Typical expressions include "the indwelling of the Spirit" (Jonathan Edwards), "the witness of the Spirit" (John Wesley), "the power of God" (early American Methodists), being "filled with the Spirit of the Lord" (early Adventists), "communing with spirits" (Spiritualists), "the Christ within" (New Thought), "streams of holy fire and power" (Methodist Holiness), "a religion of the Spirit and Power" (the Emmanuel Movement), and "the baptism of the Holy Spirit" (early Pentecostals). Biblical imagery figured prominently in the explanations of Protestants and ex-Protestants. Pentecost, in which the disciples received the Holy Spirit, runs as a leitmotif throughout. Some early-nineteenth-century Methodists believed the disciples shouted at Pentecost. Some mid-nineteenth-century Spiritualists held that the disciples were inspired by spirits. Some late-nineteenth-century Methodists insisted that the disciples were sanctified at Pentecost, while early-twentieth-century Pentecostals argued that the crucial event was speaking in tongues.

Those who challenged such claims typically characterized their opponents as "enthusiasts" or "fanatics" and offered naturalistic or secularizing explanations of their experiences. Depending on the era, critics framed their explanations in terms of the imagination, animal spirits, animal magnetism, mesmerism, hysteria, hypnosis, subconscious automatisms, and suggestion. Those who explained such experiences in this way were not necessarily outsiders to the traditions in question, nor were they necessarily opposed to all claims of religious experience. Regardless of where they positioned themselves, however, they explained claims they regarded as false in naturalistic or secularizing terms. Some who experienced religion, such as the Spiritualists, challenged the dominant tendency to dichotomize religious experience and naturalistic explanation. Committed to reconciling science and religion, they insisted on explaining their experience in religious *and* naturalistic terms.

   Much of the writing on this topic has either taken the critics' charges of enthusiasm or fanaticism at face value or has focused exclusively on those who claimed
to have experienced religion. These histories generally dichotomize explanation
and experience, on the one hand, and intellectual abstraction and cultural embeddedness, on the other, and then ascribe these characteristics to different strata
within society. The result is that educated elites are typically depicted as explaining (away) religious experience in abstract terms, while ordinary people,
embedded in traditions of faith and practice, are depicted as having them. In an
attempt to undercut the stereotyped narrative in which educated secularizing
elites combat the superstitions of ordinary people, I have placed those experiencing religion and those explaining experience, ordinary people and elites, in the
same narrative and made the interaction between them the focus.[1]
   In doing so, I have not assumed that ordinary people were the only ones experiencing religion and elites the only ones explaining experience. As I hope this
book will amply demonstrate, claims about religious experience were consistently
contested at a grassroots level and significant theoretical explanations of experience were generated by the self-educated as well as by intellectual elites. Conversely, while the experience of religion was integrally bound up with traditions
of discourse and practice, those who explained such experiences by abstracting
and comparing them to other things were also bound up in other, often competing, communities of discourse and practice. By recontextualizing explanations of
experience in their own traditions of discourse and practice, we can see something
of what was at stake for both those experiencing religion and those explaining
experience in the period from Wesley to James.
   The book is divided into three parts. Each reflects significant changes in discourse, practice, and social location of the experiences in question. Part I , "Formalism, Enthusiasm, and True Religion, 1740–1820" highlights the politically
charged interpretations of Anglo-American evangelicalism promulgated during
the eighteenth century against a backdrop of established churches, Enlightenment
thought, and a legacy of religious warfare. The focus of debate was dreams,
trances, visions, and various involuntary vocalizations and bodily movements,
referred to as fits, falling as if dead, bodily exercises, crying out, and shouting.
The discourse of formalism, enthusiasm, and true religion extended into the early-
nineteenth century and informed the development of American Methodism in the
decades immediately after the Revolutionary War.
   Part II, "Popular Psychology and Popular Religion, 1820–1890," highlights the
widespread interpretive creativity unleashed in the United States during the middle decades of the nineteenth century with the disestablishment of the churches,
the decline of Calvinist orthodoxy, the continued expansion of Methodism, and
the birth of new religious movements. Wheras in the previous period, fits, bodily
exercises, trances, and visions seemed to occur spontaneously, the new psychology of animal magnetism provided people with a means of inducing what seemed
like similar experiences in themselves and others. During the nineteenth century,
many began thinking of these experiences as evidence of special mental states.
The range of experiences associated with these mental states expanded to include

clairvoyance, healing, automatic writing, and mediumship as well as fits, trances, and visions. By the end of the period covered by Part II, trance was the umbrella term most commonly used to designate these experiences collectively, and debate correspondingly focused on whether or not trance should be interpreted in religious or secular terms.

Part III, "Religious Experience and the Subconscious, 1886–1910" highlights the professionally charged character of the interpretive field at the turn-of-the-century as psychology emerged as an academic discipline and psychotherapy as a formal clinical practice. At the end of the nineteenth century, elites—clinicians, psychologists, and psychical researchers—transformed the popular psychology of animal magnetism into the new experimental psychology of the subconscious, granting it a new respectability. The pre-Freudian concept of the subconscious mind replaced that of mental states, while the language of hypnosis, hysteria, dissociation, automatisms, and suggestion replaced that of fluids, electromagnetism, and sympathy. The range of experiences associated with the subconscious expanded beyond fits, visions, clairvoyance, healing, automatic writing, and mediumship to include conversion, mysticism, and speaking in tongues. During this period, debate focused on the subconscious and its implications for the understanding of religious experience. By 1910, the concept of the subconscious was largely discredited in academic circles.

Three figures—the enthusiast, the clairvoyant somnambule, and the multiple—provide the foils in relation to which religious experience was constructed in each of these three periods. The enthusiast, understood as falsely inspired; the clairvoyant somnambule, thought to enter a special mental state in which the mind passed beyond the external senses; and the multiple, believed to manifest co-conscious secondary personalities, provided the chief means of explaining religion and the chief challenge to those who claimed to have experienced it. The emergence of the enthusiast is discussed in the Introduction to Part I; the clairvoyant somnambule in the Introduction to Part II; and the co-conscious multiple in the Introduction to Part III.

From chapter to chapter, my goal is to construct an interconnected narrative that tracks the unfolding and interaction of particular "chains of interpretation."[2] Although the primary focus of the book is on the United States, the narrative moves back and forth across the Atlantic in order to locate these claims in relation to chains of interpretation that showed no particular respect for national boundaries. Within the Protestant tradition, Methodists provide the central narrative thread, since they and their heirs in the Adventist, Holiness, and Pentecostal movements embraced religious experience in greater numbers and with greater enthusiasm than most other Protestants. As Protestants embrace new religious movements—Spiritualism, Christian Science, New Thought, and Theosophy—that wrestle directly with matters of experience and explanation, they in turn are woven into the narrative. The naturalistic or secularizing explanations of experience in Part I are drawn from medicine or philosophy (although they are often recognizably psychological in retrospect) and from psychology, psychopathology, and neurology in Parts II and III. But again when the narrative thread demands it, sociology and anthropology also make appearances.

This book is constructed around three chains of interpretation. The first two stand in opposition to one another and run the whole length of the book. The first, running from the seventeenth-century polemic against enthusiasm through the rise of mesmerism and hypnosis to the twentieth-century Protestant modernists, constituted these experiences in natural terms, usually in relation to secularizing theories of mind. The second, running from John Wesley and the transatlantic awakening of the early eighteenth century to the independent Holiness and Pentecostal churches of the early twentieth century, constituted the experiences in question in supernatural terms. The third line of interpretation, which appears midway through the book, attempted to mediate between the other two lines of interpretation. Running from German romanticism through the Spiritualist movement to the flowering of the subconscious, the mediating tradition interpreted these phenomena as both natural and religious.

Readers may rightly wonder why a book mostly about Protestants and ex-Protestants would play with the ideas of "religion" and "religious experience" in its subtitle, as if the experiences of Protestants could be equated with religious experience in general. The short answer is that "religion" and "religious experience" were the terms used by the subjects of this book. By sticking to their terms we can see how explanations of the experiences of Protestants and former Protestants informed explanations of religion in general.[3] Eighteenth-century thinkers commonly used "false religion" to refer to particular forms of Protestantism. But the desire to discredit "false" forms of Protestantism by comparing them to non-Protestant phenomena led to the expansion of the idea of "false religion" and the development of more-comprehensive explanatory theories. Midway through the book, mediators emerge to claim that what had been deemed "false religion" was in fact "true religion." For the mediators, "true religion" *was* "religion-in-general" and authentic religious experience and naturalistic theories of religion were not incompatible. By tracking how the concepts of religion and religious experience developed in a particular historical context, we can gain a fresh perspective on the way in which Protestant and anti-Protestant modes of thought have informed the academic study of religion.

While the subtitle "Experiencing Religion and Explaining Experience" reflects the subjects' usage in this book, the phrases are also meant to conjure up contemporary debates within the academic study of religion. Contemporary theorists of religion tend to view experiencing religion and explaining experience as antithetical. Many prominent theorists of religion argue that the primary task of scholars of religion is to explain religion as opposed to "defending" their own or others' experience of it. Whether these theorists depict the "wrong-headed" scholar of religion as a "religionist" or a closet "theologian," they tend to depict the situation in dualistic terms.[4] In the conclusion, I argue that a threefold typology, based on the three chains of interpretation outlined in the book, does more justice to the cultural legacy that has informed and in many ways continues to inform such quarrels within academic study of religion than does a dualistic formulation.[5]

This third or mediating tradition relied upon and contended for a distinction between the "natural" and the "secular," which will be honored throughout the book. For them, "natural" designated the opposite of "supernatural," while "secular" designated the opposite of "religious." Given this distinction, a "natural" explanation could be either religious or secular and religious naturalism was not a contradiction in terms. Their religious naturalism targeted supernaturalism for attack, not religion in general. Their stance presupposed the availability of definitions of religion that were not based on supernaturalism.[6]

Methodologically, the book posed two significant challenges. The first was to describe the subject of the book without doing violence to my sources and their categories. The second was to figure out my place in the narrative, particularly in relation to William James and the other early psychologists of religion. Solving these methodological problems backed me, through sheer necessity, into thinking explicitly about problems of comparison in the study of religion, historical or otherwise. In retrospect it is clear, not only that these methodological challenges were linked, but that my interest in James and the early psychologists of religion was rooted in a shared fascination with theories of mental dissociation and their implications for understanding religious experience. Such theories, first developed in the 1880s, were repopularized in the 1980s in conjunction with a proliferation of cases of "multiple personality disorder."

This book had its origins in my readings in the psychiatric literature on multiple personality disorder during the late 1980s. Those readings led me to the anthropological literature on shamanism and trance and to the conversations between psychiatrists and anthropologists about dissociative disorders that antedated the 4th edition of the American Psychiatric Association's *Diagnostic and Statistical Manual* (*DSM*-IV).[7] At some point in the process, I realized that this literature might make some sense of the early Methodists about whom I had been teaching for so many years. Initially, I thought I was going to write a book about "dissociation" or "trance" among Protestants. As it became clear that these terms were used by my sources, usually to explain and often to discredit the experiences of others, I began to say that the book was about "religious experience." In doing so, I switched to the language of those experiencing religion, but implied that the subject matter under discussion was always viewed as religious, which obviously was not the case. Then for a while, to get everyone in the picture, I said the book was about "contested experience." Although overly vague, this way of viewing what I was writing about both focused my difficulties and forced me to think explicitly about problems of comparison.

Over time, I became aware that specifying the kind of experiences I wanted to discuss posed challenges precisely because of their contested character. Various academic disciplines have developed distinctive discourses to designate the general sort of experience in question. Psychiatrists most commonly refer to dissociation (or more distantly hysteria); anthropologists to trance, spirit possession, and altered states of consciousness; and religionists to visions, inspiration, mysticism, and ecstasy. These discourses are not simply descriptive, but rather reflect the various historical and explanatory commitments of the disciplines themselves.

Use of any one of these terms thus tacitly positions us both in relation to disciplinary subject matters (e.g., religion, culture, or psychopathology) and explanatory commitments and in doing so theoretically constitutes the experience about which we are speaking in particular ways.[8]

Mikkel Borch-Jacobsen makes this point quite forcefully. When asked to speak on the topic of "hypnosis," he pointed out that calling "this phenomenon 'hypnosis' immediately exposes us to many methodological difficulties, for 'hypnosis' is only one name among many that designate the elusive 'X' we are trying to grasp." After considering the terms used by psychiatrists, anthropologists, and theologians, he concluded that "each of these ways of naming brings with it not only a different *theory* but also a different *phenomenon*, as if the most remarkable property of our 'X' was not to have any property and to vary in accordance with the discourse brought to bear upon it."[9]

Not only does this naming position us in relation to contemporary disciplines, it also positions us as scholars in relation to our historical subjects. Each of these terms carries with it presuppositions and associations that may be at odds with, and thus distort, the experience of our historical subjects. In seeking to identify what the experiences that form the subject matter of this book hold in common, I am not looking for universal or objective categories or essences, but rather a tentative and particularistic starting point for comparative work. Comparison by definition "lifts out and strongly marks certain features within difference as being of possible intellectual significance, expressed," as Jonathan Smith says, "in the rhetoric of their being 'like' in some stipulated fashion." Smith emphasizes the scholar's agency in this process. "Comparison," he stresses, "provides the means by much *we* 're-vision' phenomena as *our* data in order to solve *our* theoretical problems."[10] My concerns in re-visioning this diverse set of phenomena are both pragmatic and theoretically driven. Pragmatically, I want to identify a specific feature that these experiences have in common as a means of saying what the book is "about" and, at least as crucially, as a means of identifying such experiences in the context of historical research. Since I am interested in the contestations that arose around such experiences, I want to define this comparative field so as to mark what the experiences share without obscuring their differences.

Once we begin to think in terms of delineating a comparative field and identifying relevant instances in the context of historical research, the difficulties attached to the various terms currently in use become even more apparent. While scholars working with non-English-speaking subjects must figure out how to translate (and in the process operationalize) concepts such as trance, ecstasy, or dissociation, scholars working with English-speaking subjects face the fact that our subjects also use these terms, but not necessarily in the same way. The solution, I believe, is to move away from single terms to more extended descriptive statements that identify common features in a way that is simultaneously intelligible across disciplines—religious, anthropological, and psychotherapeutic—and workable in terms of designating comparable subject matters at the level of lived historical experience. By workable, I mean language that, while perhaps striking those within these various interpretive traditions as awkward and overly general, allows us to engage phenomena across traditions of interpretation without unduly violating the lived experience of those within them.[11] Here I aim to avoid, as much as I can, what Wayne Proudfoot has termed "descriptive reduction" by specifying the experiences in question "under a description that can plausibly be ascribed to the person to whom we attribute the experience."[12]

As anthropologist Michelle Stephen points out, many of the terms we use to refer to these contested experiences are problematic precisely because they obscure the subjective experience of the native actor, that is the lived experience of persons within traditions of interpretation.[13] The crucial element of the experience for the "native actor," according to Stephen, is its "self-alien" or, in the terms used here, its involuntary aspect, that is, the sense that "I" am not the agent or cause of "my" experience.[14] To put it more precisely, the historical sources I discuss in this book depict subjects whose usual sense of themselves as embodied agents is altered or discontinuous. Their experiences includes include the loss of voluntary motor control, unusual sensory perceptions (kinesthetic, visual, auditory, and tactile), and/or discontinuities of consciousness, memory, and identity.[15] If we equate our "usual" sense of ourselves with our ordinary waking consciousness, the most common human experience of a discontinuity in consciousness is the discontinuity between waking and dreaming.[16]

We can find classic illustrations of such modifications and disruptions of a person's usual sense of embodied selfhood in the New Testament. Thus, for example, when the Apostle Paul said "it is no longer I who live, but Christ who lives in me" (Gal. 2:20), he described an experience in which his usual identity was disrupted (it is no longer I, but Christ). When he said "whether [I was] in the body or out of the body I do not know" (2 Cor. 12:2), he described a modification of his usual kinesthetic or bodily sense of himself. When he said he saw "a great light from heaven" or "heard a voice saying . . . 'Saul, why do you persecute me?'" he was describing unusual visual or auditory experiences (Acts 22:6–9). If, when he "fell to the ground" after seeing the great light, he did so involuntarily, it would provide an example the loss of voluntary muscular control. If he had fallen to the ground in a trance, it would illustrate both the loss of voluntary muscular control and a modification of consciousness.

In reopening the comparison between religious and psychological or psychopathological phenomena, I am picking up the questions that fascinated William James and, to a lesser extent, the other early psychologists of religion. In making such comparisons, how we think about the relationship between experience and explanations of experience becomes particularly crucial. The usual course, as I have indicated, has been to divorce explanation and experience, on the one hand, and intellectual abstraction (theory) and cultural embeddedness (practice), on the other. Upon close scrutiny, these dichotomies break down. Narratives of experience cannot avoid implicit theoretical and explanatory commitments.[17] Theories of experience, while abstracted from the practices they are objectifying, are not abstracted from practice in general. It is more accurate, in other words, to assume that narratives of experience contain theoretical and explanatory commitments, however rudimentary, and that theories of experience, however abstract, are nonetheless constituted within their own (e.g., academic or intellectual) traditions of discourse and practice.[18]

A distinction between narratives of experience and theories of experience is more useful. The important thing about narratives of experience is that they retain the marks, bodily and social, of the contexts in which they were constituted and within which they normally are reproduced, whereas theories of experience usually do not. Narratives, cast in the first person, are usually concrete and particular and provide clues to the bodily knowledges that inform particular traditions of experience. Bodily knowledge, what Pierre Bourdieu refers to as habitus and Paul Connerton as habit, manifests itself in the ability to *do* something, that is, in the practical mastery (Bourdieu) or skilled performance (Connerton) of the socialized human agent. While this bodily knowledge is acquired, acquisition does not necessarily occur consciously. As long as the work of education is not institutionalized with specialized agents and occasions, "practical mastery is transmitted in practice, in its practical state, without attaining the level of discourse." Every society, according to Bourdieu, provides "*structural exercises* tending to transmit this or that form of practical mastery." These exercises range from "apprenticeship through simple familiarization . . . [to] explicit and express transmission by precept and prescription." The narratives of involuntary experience presuppose bodily knowledges that people acquire in part "insensibly and unconsciously," in the way that an apprentice acquires "the principles of the 'art' and the art of living—including those which are not known to the producer of the practices or works imitated."[19]

If narratives of experience presuppose certain bodily knowledges that are acquired and assumed in practice, the marks of this knowledge are lost when experiences are abstracted from practice and constituted as "theory." Narrating and theorizing, thus, represent two different genres, typically reliant on very different sorts of practices. Both may, indeed often do, take place within a particular tradition, although some traditions may emphasize one over the other. Some individuals easily switch from one genre to the other. Jonathan Edwards and John Wesley are two good examples of persons who theorized about experience (as Christian theologians), narrated their own experiences, and passed on the narratives of others. In this book, Chapters One and Seven focus on theories about experience (experience-in-theory) and tease out their authors' practical commitments. Chapters Three, Five, and Eight focus on narratives of experience (experience-in-practice) and tease out their implicit theory and explanation. Chapters Two, Four, and Six include sections on both.

While, for the sake of clarity, I emphasize narrative or theory at any given point, my overall aim is to highlight the complex interplay between experiencing religion and explaining experience over time. In doing so, I assume that the process whereby theorists abstract experiences from narratives is only one example of a larger process whereby experience is extracted from one context and reconstituted in another. Narrators of experience may switch from one narrative to another (e.g., through conversion). Theorists may abstract from their own experience or from the experience of others (e.g., as theologians or secular theorists). Narrators may recount their narratives and theorists disseminate their theories in service of a variety of ends, including the promotion, transformation, or eradication of particular forms of experience. Oftentimes, critics attempt to discredit one form of experience as a means of advancing another. To understand how experience has been variably constituted in a particular swath of history, we must be willing to follow the process whereby interpreters make and remake specific experiences by extracting them from one community of discourse and practice and reconstituting them in another.

Although I find the comparative universe constructed by the early psychologists of religion fascinating and have constructed a comparative field very similar to theirs, I do not think they have been read with enough attention to this process. As theorists, they abstracted the experiences in question from the contexts in which they were originally constituted for their own reasons and in doing so constituted something new. I, of course, cannot claim to stand outside such processes myself. In tracing these processes of making and remaking, I too am involved in extracting these experiences from their initial communities of discourse and practice and re-constituting them within the pages of this book. In the process, the experiences inevitably become something other than what they originally were. Nonetheless, by creating historical representations of traditions in which experience was constituted and from which experiences were abstracted and remade, I hope to level the playing field somewhat between those who experienced religion, those who explained it in secular terms, and those who mediated between them.[20]

The underlying approach to my subject matter involves an intellectual movement in and out of competing communities of discourse and practice. Although an ability to sympathetically enter into diverse points of view is generally valued by historians, religious and secular perspectives on these sorts of experiences are rarely juxtaposed in an even-handed way. My own adoption of such an approach reflects both my commitments as a historian and my own experience of moving between communities, both secular and religious. This movement, which is not unlike a movement between cultures, is increasingly common in religiously and culturally pluralistic societies. I expect this methodology will appeal most to those accustomed to that sort of movement.

There is a vast literature on religious experience within the field of religious studies, much of it theological and/or philosophical. There also are numerous historical studies of particular forms of religious experience in specific historical contexts. Although some attention has been given to the relationship between psychological theories and religious experience, relations between psychologists of religion, on the one hand, and theologians and phenomenologists of religion, on the other, have been rather strained, to say the least.[21] Even as the history of dynamic psychology prior to Freud has attracted much recent interest, the range of significant interactions between psychology and religion in this era have only begun to be mapped. Those who have ventured into this historical territory have done so under a variety of rubrics, including the cure of souls, consciousness, and miracles.[22] While there is some overlap between our studies, this study is distinguished by its focus on the category of "experience," scrutinized historically.

Within an overarching narrative that runs from the more radical Puritans to Pentecostals, on the one hand, and the early psychologists of religion, on the other, the Methodist tradition, known for its emphasis on religious experience, stands out. Although it was the largest nineteenth-century Protestant denomination in the United States, Methodism was until very recently one of the least studied by historians outside the denomination.[23] Not only were Methodists numerous, they were also diverse in terms of race and class. A focus on Methodism and its offshoots and competitors in the realm of religious experience allows us to examine claims about religious experience from a variety of perspectives at a grassroots as well as a more elite level.

I hope this study of the interplay between experiencing religion and explaining experience will contribute to our understanding of what anthropologists refer to as "trance" and psychiatrists as "dissociation." Anthropologists have long been fascinated by the role of trance in so-called "primitive" cultures. Since the early 1970s, there has been a resurgence of popular and academic interest in dissociation and trance states in the Anglo-American context. This interest has led to studies of spiritualism, psychical research, and multiple personality in the Victorian era and studies of the role of hypnosis in the emergence of dynamic psychiatry. Although Christianity is often given credit for the apparent aversion to "trance" or "dissociation" in the West, little effort has been paid to how or why mainstream Protestants marginalized the more extravagant forms of religious experience. By focusing on historical explanations of involuntary phenomena among American Protestants, I hope this book will contribute to a broader understanding of the role of involuntary experience in human culture.

Finally, I hope to enhance our methodological sophistication in the comparative study of religious experience and our critical self-awareness as scholars of religion. Although most scholars view the academic study of religion as a child of the Enlightenment, only a few studies have attempted to root the discipline historically. Significant advances have been made in our understanding of the relationship between the emergence of the discipline and the "discovery" of the non-Western world. In this quest for disciplinary self-understanding, the relationship between the rise of the study of religion and elite engagement with the Protestant "other" within Anglo-American culture—those whose religious experiences were variously disparaged as enthusiastic, fanatical, hysterical, or popular—has been largely ignored. By turning our attention inward, I hope to enhance our awareness of the political dimensions of explanation within a Western cultural context and also enrich our understanding of the history of difference. Contemporary historians of difference are preoccupied with matters of race, gender, and sexual orientation, but they rarely attend to the parallel processes by means of which religious difference or identity was (and is) constructed. As I hope this study will make clear, competing claims about the authenticity of religious experiences were also claims about identity.

PART ONE

Formalism, Enthusiasm, and True Religion, 1740–1820

1. William Hogarth, "Enthusiasm Delineat'd" (c. 1760). Courtesy of the British Museum. A satirical depiction of Methodist "enthusiasm." The puppets suggest the literal manner in which the preacher (modeled on George Whitefield) employed metaphors. The two thermometers register the loudness of the preacher and the reaction of the congregation. The latter ranges from the "Luke Warm" midpoint to the extremes of "Madness," "Prophesy," and "Revelation" at top and bottom. The congregational thermometer rests on the "Methodist brain." The woman at the left has reached the "Convulsion Fits" stage and is being offered smelling salts (Ronald Paulson, *Hogarth's Graphic Works*, 3rd ed. [London: The Print Room, 1989], 175–77).

Two Camisard prophets arrived in London in 1706 and created an immediate stir with their inspired prophecies of the imminent Second Coming of the Lord. The Camisards, or French Prophets as they came to be known in England, were a radicalized remnant of the French Calvinist Huguenots. With the revocation of the Edict of Nantes in 1685, Protestantism was outlawed in France, public worship was forbidden, schools were closed, pastors exiled, and the people forced either to convert to Catholicism or emigrate. Those who stayed maintained traditional forms of private and family devotion in secret. In this context, the Huguenot remnant turned to the prophetic books of the Bible and to direct inspiration. Inspired lay persons (*inspiré*), often young women, sometimes fell into "Natural Lethargy, . . . without any appearance of a violent motion"; other times they were wracked by convulsions. Most often they fell or fainted or swooned (*évanouir*). They would then "Prophesie and Preach in their Sleep," typically without remembering what they said once they "awoke."[1] An English critic provided the following description of the French Prophets soon after they arrived in London:

> . . . their Countenance changes, and is no longer Natural; their Eyes roll after a ghastly manner in their Heads, or they stand altogether fixed; all the Members of their Body seem displaced, their Hearts beat with extraordinary Efforts and Agitations; they become Swelled and Bloated, and look bigger than ordinary; they Beat themselves with their Hands with a vast Force, like the miserable Creature in the Gospel, cutting himself with Stones; the Tone of their Voice is stronger than what it could be Naturally; their Words are sometimes broken and interrupted; they speak without knowing what they speak, and without remembering what they have Prophesied.[2]

Promptly repudiated by the more moderate Hugenots who had emigrated earlier, the French Prophets epitomized "enthusiasm" for many early-eighteenth-century Anglo-Americans.

The specter of the French Prophets haunted the transatlantic awakening of the 1730s and 1740s. Opponents of the revivals in Great Britain and the American colonies compared the bodily agitations of the French Prophets with those of Presbyterians, Congregationalists, and Methodists. In Scotland, opponents of the revivals circulated the writings of the French Prophets to make the comparison obvious. In 1742, "anti-enthusiasticus," probably the American Congregationalist minister Charles Chauncy, published a tract subtitled *A Faithful Account of the French Prophets, their Agitations, Extasies, and Inspirations* in both Glasgow and Boston. An appendix explicitly compared the French Prophets to the "Enthusiasts" of New England. George Lavington, an Anglican bishop, brought out what he took to be the unfortunate similarities between Methodists, the French Prophets, and Roman Catholics in *The Enthusiasm of Methodists and Papists Compared* (1749). Leading spokesmen *for* the transatlantic awakening emphatically rejected the charge of enthusiasm. They did so, not by defending the French Prophets, but by repudiating them. Whatever their differences, those who weighed in for and against the revival agreed that the French Prophets were "enthusiasts" and that "enthusiasm" was bad. Only John Wesley, of all the prominent Methodist and Reformed leaders, evidenced any ambivalence in this regard.[3]

While Wesley emphatically opposed enthusiasm, he was himself more regularly painted with the brush of enthusiasm than most of the moderate revival leaders and more open than they to finding something of true religion in those usually designated as enthusiasts. In January 1739, having "long been importuned" to do so, Wesley went with several friends from the Fetter Lane society to visit the French Prophet Mary Plewit. Wesley reports that "two or three of our company were much affected [by her prophesying] and believed that she spoke by the Spirit of God." As for himself, he said, "this was in no wise clear to me."[4] While John Wesley did not actually conclude that Plewit was speaking by the Spirit of God, he at least seemed open to the possibility.[5] When an anonymous Anglican critic argued that Wesley's claims regarding the "perceptible inspiration" of the Holy Spirit were "never maintained but by Montanists, Quakers, and Methodists," Wesley did not respond defensively, already having indicated to Smith that "if the Quakers hold the same perceptible inspiration with me I am glad."[6]

In 1750, twelve years after his initial contacts with the French Prophets, Wesley read one of their books, John Lacy's *The General Delusions of Christians of with Regard to Prophesy* (1713). Although critics had circulated the book widely in order to discredit the revival, Wesley was convinced by Lacy, "of what [he] had long suspected," that the Montanists, to whom both the French Prophets and the Methodists had so often been compared, "were real, scriptural Christians." Moreover, he concluded, "the grand reason why the miraculous gifts were so soon withdrawn, was not only that faith and holiness were well nigh lost; but that dry, formal, orthodox men began even then to ridicule whatever gifts they had not themselves, and to decry them all as either madness or imposture."[7]

The shifting patterns of accusation and counter-accusation reveal the contested space in which religious experience was constituted. As these vignettes are meant to suggest, the language of religious experience developed, not in isolation, but hand-in-hand with the language of enthusiasm and formalism. Both enthusiasm and formalism were epithets used to disparage what their beholders viewed as false forms of Christianity. Neither concept was new in 1740 or even 1640, but they derived much of their eighteenth-century meaning from the events of a hundred or so years earlier, specifically the rise of Puritanism within the Church of England and the outbreak of the English Civil War. Thus, from the mid-seventeenth century at least, a "formalist" was understood as one who had the form of religion without the power, while an "enthusiast" was understood as one who falsely claimed to be inspired.[8] Both terms came to the fore with the Puritan emphasis on "inward" or "heart" religion. Puritans used the word "experience" to talk about this dimension of inwardness. One mid-seventeenth-century Puritan autobiographer referred to "experience" as "the inward sense and feeling of what is outwardly read and heard; and the spirituall and powerfull enjoyment of What is believed." Another described it as "truth brought home to the heart with life

and power." As these definitions' references to "power" suggest, Puritans disparaged the absence of experience as "formalism." Conversely, non-Puritans disparaged the "inward sense and feeling," that is the "experience," of the Puritans as
"enthusiasm."[9]

While both "enthusiasm" and "formalism" were epithets, enthusiasm was by
far the more potentially damaging of the two insults. The emotional freight
attached to the term went back to what were for many the dual traumas of the
mid-seventeenth century—regicide and republicanism. It is hard to appreciate
the passions aroused by the specter of enthusiasm through the eighteenth and
into the nineteenth century unless we understand the word as one associated
with wounds deep in the Anglo-American psyche. Modern historians have been
at times too quick to recapitulate a theological reading of the history of enthusiasm, tracing it back, following seventeenth- and eighteenth-century thinkers, to
the Anabaptists or the Montanists. In so doing they have essentialized and decon-
textualized our understanding of anti-enthusiastic rhetoric, ensnared us in fruit-
less attempts to separate real enthusiasts from those falsely accused, and made it
difficult to understand how persons could be both opposed to and accused of
enthusiasm.[10]

As late as the 1640s, the term "enthusiasm"—derived from the Greek *en theos*,
meaning to be filled with or inspired by a deity—was simply an attribute, albeit
a negative one, often associated with Puritans. With the publication of *The Anatomy of Melancholy* in the 1620s, Robert Burton introduced long-standing medical
discussions of the religious symptoms of melancholics into the realm of religious
polemics. "Enthusiasts" appeared in lists of persons prone to religious melancholy,
as in "Hereticks old and new, Schismaticks, Schoolmen, Prophets, Enthusiasts,
& c."[11] Many in England came to identify "Religious Melancholy," which Burton
constituted as a "distinct species" of the more traditional medical malady "Love-
Melancholy," with Puritanism.[12] Opponents of Puritanism began to associate "Enthusiasms and Revelations," both synonyms for inspiration, "with mental and
emotional derangement."[13]

During the 1640s, with religious toleration and the lifting of censorship, religious literature, including radical religious pamphlet literature, burgeoned.[14]
Many of these radical publications were spiritual autobiographies; among them
were the first religious titles containing the word "experience."[15] Although numerous publications appeared at this time condemning sects, sectaries, schismatics,
errours, heresies, and blasphemies, their titles did not refer to enthusiasts or enthusiasm.[16] It was during the 1650s, with the publication of Meric Causaubon's
Treatise Concerning Enthusiasme (1655) and Henry More's *Enthusiasmus Triumpha-
tus* (1656), that enthusiasm took on new prominence as a negative catchall term
for what had been formerly conveyed by schismatic, sectarian, and heretic.[17]

In contrast to sectarian and schismatic, which were linked to false ecclesiology,
and heresy, which was linked to false doctrine, enthusiasm defined illegitimacy
in relation to false inspiration or, more broadly, false experience. Enthusiasm,
unlike schism or heresy, located that which was threatening not in challenges to
ecclesiology or doctrine but in challenges to that most fundamental of Christian

categories—revelation.[18] As such it lifted up the Puritan claim to access God in relatively direct fashion through a combination of spirit, word, and ordinance (baptism and the Lord's supper). The precise mix of factors was a matter of considerable controversy among Puritans with opinion ranging from the relatively traditional emphasis of Presbyterians on the inspiration of the spirit in a context of fixed liturgies and clerically interpreted scriptures to the radical Quaker principle of the "Spirit in every man." It was this Puritan desire to access God directly that, as Peter Lake points out, linked moderate and radical Puritanism before and after 1640 and was, in his words, "arguably . . . a central strand in the events that produced the regicide [the beheading of Charles I] and the republic, the protectorate and, indeed, the restoration [of the monarchy]."[19]

While, generally speaking, "enthusiasm" challenged Puritan claims to access God directly, anti-enthusiasts saved their greatest fury for those who emphasized the revelatory power of dreams, visions, and audible voices, an emphasis particularly marked in the new literature of "spiritual experience" published by the more radical Puritans.[20] The same desire to access God directly was apparent almost a century later in Jonathan Edwards' claim that the "Spirit of God" dwells in all true saints and in John Wesley's expectation that every true Christian would receive "the witness of God's Spirit with his spirit, that he is a child of God." It was these claims, so central to the theology of each, that opened Edwards and Wesley to charges of "enthusiasm." As in the mid-seventeenth century, the claims to see the action of God in dreams, visions, and involuntary bodily movements on the part of eighteenth-century evangelicals invited the most hostile attacks.

Enthusiasm, unlike formalism, was more than just an epithet used by critics to denigrate the claims of their opponents. It was additionally, and more precisely, a theoretically laden epithet that had the effect of recasting the theological claims of one's opponents as "delusions" that could be explained in secular, scientific terms. Causaubon and More, both Anglicans and royalist in their sympathies, wrote their influential works on enthusiasm in the second decade of republican rule and were part of the growing backlash against the democratic vision of radical Puritans that led to the protectorate and the restoration.[21] In elevating the concept of enthusiasm as a catchall term for religious dissent, "Enlightened" Anglicans drew upon Robert Burton's *Anatomy of Melancholy*, which, following medical and philosophical tradition, associated enthusiasm with madness or pathological religious despair. In doing so, they recast the problem of religious dissent in terms of mental illness rather than heresy. By associating that which was problematic—indeed that which had produced regicide and republic—with false inspiration rather than false doctrine, enthusiasm could be explained in scientific rather than theological terms. Recast as delusion or madness, political and religious radicalism was more easily contained.

The anti-enthusiasts' case against democratic radicalism was further strengthened by the creation of a comparative history of enthusiasm that overlapped with and, in Anglo-American Protestant circles, often superseded the history of heresy. Causaubon describes his twofold purpose as first, "by examples of all professions in all ages, to show how men have been very prone upon some grounds of nature

. . . to deem themselves divinely inspired" and, second, to discover "reasons, and probable confirmations of such natural operations, falsely deemed supernatural."[22] The quest for *explanations* of "divine inspiration" upon "grounds of nature," that is, for "reasons" that would account for "natural operations, falsely deemed supernatural" was central to the development of Enlightenment thought. With the Restoration of the monarchy, the enlightened fear of enthusiasm was coupled with a desire for an end to religious disputes. As one contemporary put it, "since the *King's* return, the blindness of the former *Ages* and the miseries of this last, are vanish'd away: now men are generally . . . satiated with *Religious* Disputes: . . . Now there is an universal *desire*, and *appetite* after *knowledge*, after the peaceable, the fruitful, the nourishing *Knowledge*: and not after that of antient Sects, which only yielded hard indigestible *arguments*."[23] In this quest for an end to religious dispute, enthusiasm (along with superstition) held pride of place as the enemy of reason.

All the moderate leaders of the early-eighteenth-century revival, therefore, took aggressive action to distance themselves from the threat of enthusiasm. Most of the moderates, including George Whitefield and Charles Wesley, actively discouraged bodily manifestations while they were preaching. Others, such as Jonathan Edwards in New England and James Robe in Scotland, not only discouraged these bodily manifestations, they joined with ministerial critics of the revivals, such as Charles Chauncy, and Enlightened skeptics, such as David Hume, in actively seeking to explain them. While Edwards, Chauncy, and Hume disagreed sharply in their understandings of "true" religion, their views when it came to enthusiasm or "false" religion were not nearly so far apart.

Evangelical leaders, while distancing themselves from charges of enthusiasm, continued the tradition of disparaging their critics as mere "formalists." Nonetheless, the concerted effort to explain enthusiasm or false religion had a profound effect on evangelical Protestant understandings of true religion. Caught between the specter of enthusiasm, on the one hand, and formalism, on the other, evangelical moderates, such as Jonathan Edwards and John Wesley constituted religious experience in significantly different ways in practice. These differences gave a different shape to "experience" in the two traditions throughout the course of the nineteenth century.

The three chapters that make up Part I unfold in a discursive arena defined by the concepts of formalism, enthusiasm, and true religion. Chapter 1 locates an emergent psychology of religious experience in the efforts of Reformed clergy (such as Charles Chauncy, James Robe, and Jonathan Edwards) and Enlightened skeptics (such as David Hume) to explain "enthusiasm." Chapter 2 explores the making of evangelical religious experience in the wake of Enlightenment attacks on enthusiasm. It compares the ideas about religious experience held by Jonathan Edwards and John Wesley and the working out of those ideas in practice in the Reformed and Methodist traditions. Chapter 3 examines tensions between "formalists" and "enthusiasts" within early American Methodism in the context of interracial revivals and camp meetings.

CHAPTER ONE

Explaining Enthusiasm

DAVID HUME looms large in the philosophy of religion and in recent histories of the modern academic study of religion, but little attention has been paid to the role of enthusiasm in his thinking about religion.[1] In relation to the academic study of religion, Hume's theory of religion is typically linked, not implausibly, with superstition. Without detracting from that reading, we may also locate Hume and the emergence of the modern study of religion in relation to a narrative oriented toward the history of psychology and the engagement with enthusiasm. Framed in this way, Frank Manuel's observation that the study of psychology emerged in England, not as a dispassionate science of human nature, but as "the newest handmaiden of true religion" becomes particularly pertinent. As the handmaiden of true religion, psychology's initial task was to explain and thus discredit enthusiasm.[2]

Building on this, I argue that in the wide-ranging struggle against enthusiasm, as in their engagement with superstition, promoters of the Enlightenment forged weapons that became standard tools of the academic study of religion. Foremost among them was the power to explain religion in secular terms. Here, however, the development of secular explanations was not the straightforward result of conflict between moderates and radicals or the enlightened and the orthodox. In contrast to the engagement with the "other without," stalwart defenders of orthodoxy such as Jonathan Edwards played as important a role as enlightened skeptics such as Hume. All participants in the conversation—revivalist, anti-revivalist, and skeptic alike—framed their attacks in terms of true religion and enthusiasm. The attack on enthusiasm so narrowed the evidences for true religion that in the end little was left tangibly present in the world that could reliably count as true religion.

The context of this chapter is the transatlantic awakening or revival of the 1730s and 1740s. The revival encompassed Pietists in Germany, the Methodist movement within the Church of England (in both its Calvinist and Wesleyan variants), and the Reformed (Congregationalist and Presbyterian) revivals in Scotland and the American colonies. All the authors I consider—Charles Chauncy (New England Congregationalist minister and anti-revivalist), Jonathan Edwards (New England Congregationalist minister and moderate defender of the revivals), James Robe (Scottish Presbyterian minister and moderate defender of the revivals), and David Hume (one-time Scottish Presbyterian layman turned Enlightened skeptic)—wrote on enthusiasm between 1740 and 1743, as the awakening peaked in Scotland and New England and Methodism began its rapid expansion in England. My discussion extends beyond the peak years of the awakening to include

Jonathan Edwards's *Treatise Concerning the Religious Affections* and David Hume's *Natural History of Religion*.

During the peak years of the revival, the pace was intense and events intertwined. Note, for example, that Hume had a spiritual crisis of sorts in 1734, Edwards in 1737, and the Wesleys in 1738. Benjamin Colman's abridgment of Edwards's *Faithful Narrative of the Surprising Work of God* appeared in 1736. From 1738 to 1741, George Whitefield, the awakening's preeminent preacher, published his *Journal* in a series of six installments. In 1739, Hume published *A Treatise on Human Nature* and Whitefield left the Wesleys in England for his first preaching tour of the American colonies. Whitefield's *Short Account* of his life and the first of John Wesley's *Journals* appeared in 1740. In September 1741, Edwards preached his famous sermon on the "Distinguishing Marks of a Work of the Spirit of God" at Yale in the wake of the radical preacher James Davenport's departure from New Haven. Hume's *Essays: Social and Political* were published in Edinburgh the same year, including one titled, "Of Superstition and Enthusiasm." In 1742 revival broke out in the Scottish towns of Cambuslang, outside Glasgow, and Kilsyth, outside Edinburgh. Five months later, Whitefield arrived in Scotland for a preaching tour. That same year, James Robe, minister at Kilsyth, having read Edwards's "Distinguishing Marks," published his *Narrative* of events in Scotland. Shortly thereafter, and during James Davenport's visit to Boston, Charles Chauncy, minister in that city, preached "Enthusiasm Described and Cautioned Against," following the next month with "A Letter . . . to Mr. George Wishart," principal of Edinburgh University, Hume's alma mater. Just after Davenport reached what some called the "zenith of fanaticism," Edwards published *Some Thoughts Concerning the Revival of Religion in New England*, which was countered six months later by Chauncy's *Seasonable Thoughts* on the same subject. After this flurry of activity, things quieted down. Edwards's most significant thoughts on the awakening, his *Treatise Concerning the Religious Affections*, did not appear until 1746. The first volume of Hume's *History of Great Britain* was published in 1754 and his *Natural History of Religion* in 1757.

Given the flurry of overlapping and sometimes repetitious writing in the early 1740s, I do not proceed in a strictly chronological fashion. I begin with the writings of Charles Chauncy, the leading anti-revivalist among the Protestant clergy, and as such the theologian with the greatest investment in explaining enthusiasm. I then turn to Jonathan Edwards, foremost among the moderate defenders of the revival, and, in passing, his Scottish colleague, James Robe. I conclude by locating the work of Hume in relation to the problem of enthusiasm and efforts to explain it.

CHARLES CHAUNCY ON ENTHUSIASM

The Puritan tradition to which the eighteenth-century awakening was heir expected individuals to undergo a process of conversion. From a distance, this process can be understood as one in which individuals internalized basic Calvinist doctrines and thereby were transformed both internally and in relation to God.

The classic Puritan conversion account can be broken down into two movements. The first centered on the internalization of the Calvinist view of God as judge and humans as totally sinful or depraved, in need of salvation, and yet unable to save themselves. Fears of damnation and feelings of terror or despair often accompanied this "downward" movement. This movement typically ended as individuals "let go" of efforts to save themselves, resigned themselves to the will of God (whatever that might be), and acknowledged their total dependence on God's grace. The second movement centered on the internalization of the Calvinist view of God as gracious and loving. This "upward" movement was often accompanied by feelings of hope that one might indeed be saved, moments of intimate communion with a loving God, and feelings of joyous assurance.[3] The behaviors that Chauncy viewed as enthusiastic in the context of the New England awakening were linked to these two movements.[4] With respect to the first, he was disturbed by the appearance of "*strange Effects* upon the *Body*" and, with respect to the second, the appearance of "raptures," "extasies," "visions," "trances," and "revelations."

Under the heading of "*strange Effects* upon the *Body*," he described "*swooning away* and *falling to the Ground*, where Persons have lain, for a Time, speechless and motionless; bitter *Shriekings* and *Screamings*; *Convulsion-like Tremblings* and *Agitations*, *Strugglings* and *Tumblings*." These "Effects," he indicated, were not "peculiar to some *particular Places* or *Constitutions*; but have been common all over the Land." People had different subjective experience while undergoing these "strange Effects upon the Body." Some, Chauncy said, reported that they were "insensibly wrought upon, they can't tell how." Others were presented with "a Sight of their Sins," while still others saw devils "ready to . . . draw them away to Hell" or saw Hell itself and "felt as they were about to fall in." Generally speaking, according to Chauncy, persons experiencing these bodily effects were "fill'd with great Anxiety and Distress, having upon their Minds an over-powering Sense of Sin, and Fear of divine Wrath."[5]

Those who experienced the assurance of salvation, Chauncy reported, were almost universally given to "*Raptures and Transports*." Many "shew[ed] this Joy by *clapping of Hands*, by *jumping up and down*, by *Congratulations in the Way of Kissing*, by breaking out into *hearty loud Laughter*." Others manifested it through "*Swoonings*, and *Out-cries*, and *Screamings*, so like to these same Effects under *Terror*, that it han't been known, whether persons were in *Joy* or *Sorrow*." The expression of joy did not stop there. In "too many Instances," according to Chauncy, "*Raptures and Extasies*" gave way to "*Visions*, and *Trances*, and *Revelations*" (*STSR*, 126–27).

Although Chauncy said he could "fill many Pages with the Accounts I have had of the *Trances* Persons have been in," he recounted only one in detail. In this instance, "two Women . . . fell into a Trance together" while at a "private Fast, kept by a Number of the New-Light Party [i.e. the pro-revival faction among the Congregationalists]." There, Chauncy recounted, the women were "exceedingly fill'd with Zeal, and their Affections rais'd very high: They were, in some Degree, depriv'd of their bodily Strength; but yet, were by Turns able to speak, which they did, in Addresses and Exhortation to, and Prayers for, those present, who they supposed were unconverted." The following evening "they fell down unable to walk . . . [and] continued in a Sort of Extasie, either lying as though in a Sleep, or uttering extatic Expressions of Joy, of the Love of Christ, and of Love to him; of Concern for the Souls of Sinners, and the like." Many came to see them. The women prayed for those who came "with great Earnestness" and addressed them with "awful Warnings, moving Perswasions, and pathetic Exhortations, in which they use some Expressions, from whence it seem'd that they suppos'd themselves to have a special Commission, or endow'd with some special Authority . . . and indeed many People, especially those of their Party, seemed verily to believe they were inspir'd" (STSR, 128–29).

Chauncy's explanations of these phenomena, largely derived from other thinkers, fall under two broad headings. While both types of explanations can be considered at least nascently psychological, the first, which was rooted in physiology, is more individualistic; while the second, rooted in epidemiology, was more social. Among his earlier writings, "Enthusiasm Describ'd and Cautioned Against" (1742) reflected this more individualistic viewpoint, while "A Letter . . . Mr. George Wishart," written shortly thereafter reflected the more social.

Internal Dynamics

From the psycho-physiological vantage point, enthusiasm was above all the result of an overactive imagination. As Chauncy explained, "the enthusiast mistakes the workings of his own passions for divine communications, and fancies himself immediately inspired by the Spirit of God, when all the while, he is under no other influence than that of an over-heated imagination." Chauncy proffered various theories to account for the overheating of the imagination, all physiologically based. At one point, he claimed that the cause of enthusiasm is "bad temperament of the blood and spirits." At another point, he averred that it is "properly a disease, a sort of madness," to which none are more susceptible than "those, in whom *melancholy* is the prevailing ingredient in their constitution." At yet another point, he seemed to contradict himself by stating that the majority of enthusiasts "act [not] so much under the influence of a *bad mind*, as a *deluded imagination*."[6] As we shall see, those with bad temperaments, weak minds, or melancholic dispositions were ultimately the most susceptible to delusion.

Psychological theorizing about enthusiasm started with the simple observation that, when frightened by natural phenomena, such as earthquakes, people often experienced bodily effects much like those seen in religious contexts. Theorizing began, in other words, with comparison. The anti-enthusiasts' disproportionate emphasis on the role of terror (and a deluded imagination) in inducing bodily effects reflected the seeming aptness of their comparisons and their resulting explanatory confidence about what caused physical disturbances at the outset of the conversion experience. While no less confident that a deluded imagination could account for the raptures, ecstasies, and visions associated with the second phase of the conversion experience, the thinness of explanations at this point reflected a general inability to account for involuntary sensory phenomena in any detail.

Chauncy thus focused on the first stage of the conversion experience, reminding his readers that "the Passion of Fear may be excited, not only from a just
Representation of Truth to the Mind by the SPIRIT of GOD, but from the natural
Influence of awful Words and frightful Gestures." Fear, even fear of "the Torments
of another World," may be excited, he says, by "a mechanical Impression on
animal Nature" (STSR, 80). He did not go so far as to claim that *all* of the conversions with bodily effects should be explained by such mechanical impressions nor
did he claim that the presence of natural effects *necessarily* invalidated a conversion. He did, however, argue that the majority of the alleged converts were
wrought upon, not by "the proper Influence of Truth," but by "a sudden and
strong Impression on the animal Oeconomy" (STSR, 80). Even in those unusual
cases where lasting change, and thus genuine conversion, had been effected in
those who "have been frighten'd into Shrieks and Fits," he argued, their experience
did not differ significantly from that of those who were genuinely converted in
response to such natural phenomena as "a terrible Clap of Thunder, or the Shock
of an Earthquake" (STSR, 109).[7]

For Chauncy, the clergy and the lay exhorters produced these effects through
the use of "awful words and frightful gestures." He quoted "a Friend in the Country," who provided a graphic description of their "boisterous and shocking" manner, a manner adapted, he said, "to the best of their Skill to alarm and surprize
the Imagination and Passions." On one occasion, the preacher was only a short
way into his sermon when "there began to be some Commotion among the *young
Women*." This, the writer said, "inspired him with new Life," such that "[h]e lifted
up his Voice like a Trumpet, plentifully pouring down Terrors upon them." Half
a dozen of the "young Women were presently thrown into *violent histeric Fits*"
(STSR, 94–95).

Chauncy also cited an account published in the Boston *Post-Boy* in which the
content of the terrifying rhetoric was spelled out. According to this source, the
itinerant preachers were telling congregations "that God is doing *extraordinary*
Things in other Places, and that they are some of the last hardened Wretches that
stand out; that this is the last Call that ever they are likely to have; that they are
now hanging over the Pit of Destruction, and just ready, this Moment, to fall into
it; that Hell-fire now flashes in their Faces; and that the Devil now stands ready
to seize upon them, and carry them to Hell!" And they will often, the writer
concluded, "repeat the awful Words, *Damn'd! Damn'd! Damn'd!* three or four
Times over" (STSR, 96). Here, using a technique we will encounter again, the
preacher created a vivid verbal picture of hell, into which he rhetorically placed
his listeners. While Chauncy did not identify the rhetorical strategy involved, he
and many of his informants clearly recognized the impact of this kind of preaching
on lay audiences.

Chauncy argued that "true joy" was the result of regeneration made evident in
a "*renewed Heart* . . . [and] *in Newness of Life*" (STSR, 120–21) and "false joy" the
result of "*meer sensitive Passion*" or "*sudden Impressions*" (STSR, 123). He did not,
however, offer compelling examples of naturally induced "raptures and trances"
to complement his examples of naturally induced bodily effects. He assumed on

theological grounds that "true joy" resulted in a lasting change of heart manifest in discernable alterations in behavior. Thus, only in retrospect did some come to realize that "their Joy was nothing more than a meer *sensitive Passion*, and have own'd they were under a Delusion, while they imagin'd it was of a divine *Origin*." Others, he said, "have made it evident by their after-Lives, that their Joy was only a *sudden Flash*, a *Spark of their own kindling*" (*STSR*, 121). While Chauncy placed the far more troubling "Visions, and Trances, and Revelations" under the rubric of "Impulses and Impressions," his explanation was limited to deploring the "Aptness [of persons] to take the Motion of their own Minds for something divinely extraordinary, or to put those Constructions upon common Occurances, which there is no Ground for but in their own Imagination" (*STSR*, 189).

Theoretical Background

Chauncy's psycho-physiological explanation of enthusiasm reflected both his reading of earlier theorists of enthusiasm and the general scientific thought of his era. Three broad layers of thought informed his psycho-physiological explanation. The oldest layer, dating back to the classical era, was that of the tripartite psyche or soul that informed traditional scientific thought into the Reformation period. The second layer was the Cartesian science of "mechanical Impressions" and "animal spirits" that displaced Scholasticism at colonial universities, such as Harvard, during the latter third of the seventeenth century.[8] The third, and most "modern," layer was the post-Lockean science of nerves and nervous disorders.

PSYCHES/SOULS

Renaissance philosophers and scientists used the newly minted Latin term *psychologia* to designate a subfield within natural philosophy concerned with the philosophical study of the soul. They approached the study of the soul, as they did the other subfields within natural philosophy, through the work of Aristotle. Most specifically, then, we can say that the term *psychologia* designated the traditional complex of problems associated with Aristotle's *De Anima* and the *Parva naturalia*.[9]

Aristotle and his followers defined the soul as the life principle and thus that which differentiated living from nonliving things. In this tradition, the soul was divided into three parts—the natural or vegetative, characteristic of plants; the sensitive or animal, characteristic of animals; and the intelligent or rational, characteristic of humans—in an ascending hierarchy of complexity. The natural soul of plants, being without parts, was the simplest. The sensitive soul of animals contained two parts, one natural (as in plants) and one sensitive. The intelligent soul of humans contained three parts, natural (as in plants), sensitive (as in animals), and intelligent (unique to humans). The plant and animal parts of the human soul together were referred to as the "organic soul" and contrasted with the higher or "intellective soul."

Faculties, from whence comes the term "faculty psychology," were associated with each of these parts of the human soul. Faculties of nutrition and generation common to plants, animals, and humans were associated with the natural part of the human soul, while the higher functions of sensation, emotion, imagination, and memory understood to be common to animals and humans were attributed to the sensitive part of the soul. The will and the understanding or intellect were attributed to the intelligent or rational part of the soul. The organic soul was responsible for all functions that were inextricably linked to the body; the intellective soul for those functions that, in the view of most philosophers, did not require physical organs for their operation. Because it did not require the physical body to function, philosophers believed the intellective or rational part of the soul capable of surviving the death of the body and thus making it alone "immortal."[10] In this schema, both biology and psychology were subsumed under the heading of natural philosophy. *Psychologia,* with its concern for the principles governing animate bodies (as opposed to plants), was both the culmination of natural philosophy and the foundation for a number of other disciplines including theology, metaphysics, and medicine.[11]

The seventeenth-century debates among New England Puritans over the relationship between the will and the intellect raised long-standing questions regarding the nature of the will (Is it really a "rational appetite"? Could it be confined to the "rational soul"?) that had consequences for locating the passions. This debate carried over into the eighteenth-century awakening with Chauncy taking the "intellectualist" and Edwards the "voluntarist" positions. Although both positions were represented in Scholastic thought, the roots of the intellectualist position were in classical philosophy and the voluntarist in Augustine. As an intellectualist, Chauncy held that the will was a rational appetite that could be confined to the rational soul and that the passions were sensitive appetites located, logically enough, in the sensitive or animal part of the soul. In this understanding, the will as the rational appetite was to govern "the lower sensitive appetites, though . . . unruly vehement sensitive appetites, or passion, [might] carry one forward independently of intellect and will, anticipating and obscuring rational judgment."[12]

Thus when Chauncy referred to "animal nature" or the "animal Oeconomy," he was referring to what would traditionally have been called the "sensitive" part of the soul. It would have been understood even in a post-Cartesian world as that aspect of the person which animals and humans have in common. Chauncy located fear or terror, like all the other passions, within this animal-like part of the human. The placement of the imagination in the sensitive or animal part of the soul, alongside the passions, explains the close connection in Chauncy's mind between the "workings of the passions" and the "over-heated imagination" of the enthusiast. And it is evident, given this understanding, why he complained about preachers who "aimed at putting their (hearer's) Passions into a Ferment, [rather] than filling them with such a *reasonable* Solicitude, as is the Effect of a just Exhibition of the Truths of GOD to their Understandings" (*STSR,* 93).

Since the views of Edwards and Chauncy on the passions have been overly polarized at times in the past,[13] it is important to point out that Chauncy did not condemn the passions. Indeed, in "Enthusiasm Describ'd," he indicated that the passions were inevitably excited "in the business of religion: And 'tis proper they shou'd [be]." The function of the passions, he said, was to "awaken the *reasonable powers*" of the rational part of the soul such that "the *understanding* [was] enlightened, the *judgment* convinc'd, the *will* perswaded [sic], and the *mind* intirely [sic] chang'd." It is only when "transports of affection" did not lead to the "awaken[ing] of the reasonable powers" that individuals were in "great danger of being carried away by [their] imaginations" and thus, into enthusiasm. The key to avoiding enthusiasm lay not in the denial of the passions, but in keeping them "in their proper place, under government of a well informed understanding."[14] The passions could and should *awaken* the reasonable powers, but they could not and should not *rule* them.

ANIMAL SPIRITS

Descartes challenged traditional philosophy at a number of important points. Most crucially, for our purposes, he made a new distinction between life (which he equated with the body and motion) and soul (which he equated with the mind and thought). The divide between the living body and the thinking soul followed the old line of demarcation between the organic and intellective souls. In his "Treatise on Man," Descartes compared the body to a machine and ascribed to this self-moving machine or "automaton" all the functions traditionally attributed to the vegetative and sensitive parts of the soul, including the "internal movements of the appetites and passions, and . . . the external movements of the limbs." To explain these functions, he stated that "it is not necessary to conceive of this machine as having any vegetative or sensitive soul or other principle of movement and life, apart from its blood and its spirits, which are agitated by the heat of the fire burning continuously in its heart—a fire which has the same nature as all the fires that occur in inanimate bodies."[15] The crucial points, here, were (1) that plants and animals no longer had souls; and (2) that the functions once assigned to the souls of animals and plants, and to the corresponding parts of the human soul, now could be accounted for mechanistically in terms of blood and spirits.

Animal spirits were simply a rarefied portion of the blood. They were produced by the heat of the heart and likened by Descartes to "a very lively and pure flame." Animal spirits, unlike "less fine" parts of the blood, could pass from the bloodstream into the nervous system, by way of the pineal gland ("situated near the middle of . . . the brain"). From the pineal gland, they gained access to the cavities of the brain and ultimately the nerves. By traveling through the nerves ("little threads or tubes"), the animal spirits could then affect muscles throughout the body.[16] Although the soul was joined to the whole body, it exercised its functions most directly through the pineal gland ("the principal seat of the soul"). The pineal gland was suspended in the passageway between the anterior and posterior cavities of the brain, an area suffused with animal spirits. It was here, above all, that body (animal spirits) and soul (rational mind) affected one another. Thus, as described by Descartes, "the slightest movements on the part of the gland may alter very greatly the course of these spirits, and conversely any change, however slight, taking place in the course of the spirits may do much to change the movements of the gland."[17]

Descartes used the example of a "strange and terrifying" shape to illustrate the way in which different passions (e.g., anxiety, courage, terror) are aroused in the soul, "depending upon the particular *temperament* of the body or the *strength* of the soul."[18] While the temperament effected the deployment of the animal spirits and consequently the movements of the body, the strength of the soul determined the soul's ability to "conquer the passions and stop the bodily movements which accompany them." Descartes explicitly recast the traditional conflict between the sensitive and rational parts of the soul (or "between the natural appetites and the will") in terms of conflicts "between the movements which the body (by means of its spirits) and the soul (by means of its will) tend to produce at the same time in the [pineal] gland."

In this contest between the spirits and the will, it is the "strongest souls" that conquer, while the "weakest souls . . . constantly allow [themselves] to be carried away by present passions." In asserting that "the Passion of Fear" could be excited by the "mechanical impression" of "awful words and frightful gestures" on the "animal nature," Chauncy was stating a commonplace of Cartesian thought. Moreover, that those "whose preaching has been *most remarkably* accompanied by those *Extraordinaries,* . . . [preach] in such a Manner, as *naturally* tends to put *weaker* Minds out of Possession of themselves . . . 'tis too well known [Chauncy said] to need much to be said upon it" (*STSR*, 94). Enthusiasts, thus, were those who by virtue of "bad temperament of the blood and spirits" and/or "weak minds" were least able to "conquer" the passions aroused by the "new Method" of preaching.

Although Chauncy, in keeping with the leading thinkers of his time, assumed a connection between the imagination and the passions aroused by the animal spirits, debates raged during this period over the precise nature of their interaction. In fact by 1740, there had been so much controversy about animal spirits specifically in relation to the physiology of the imagination that literary satires started to appear and a few scientists rejected the idea of animal spirits altogether.[19] For our purposes, the details of such controversies are unimportant. What is crucial is that in eighteenth-century Europe and America many came to accept that scientists could provide mechanistic explanations for the functions of the sensitive part of the soul, including its higher sensory and imaginative functions, and that for much of the eighteenth century these *scientific* explanations involved animal spirits. As a result, until well into the nineteenth century the mere mention of animal spirits in religious circles signaled the user's belief that an alleged religious phenomenon was inauthentic and could be better accounted for in scientific (i.e., secular) than religious terms.

NERVES

What we might call the sociology of "weak-mindedness" is the third, and most modern, layer of thought that informed Chauncy's understanding of enthusiasm. As Chauncy's references to enthusiasm as "properly a disease, a sort of madness" and to "young women . . . thrown into violent histeric fits" suggest, Chauncy understood some as more prone to enthusiasm than others. According to Chauncy, "the Weakness of their Nerves, and from hence their greater Liableness

to be surpris'd, and overcome with Fear," explains why "*Women* [are more] generally the Persons thrown into these *Agitations* and *Terrors* [than men]" (*STSR*, 105).

The cultural histories of physiology, disease, and gender meet in these references. Nerves, already important in Descartes, took on even greater significance
after the English physician Thomas Willis published his physiological texts on the
brain during the latter part of the seventeenth century. There Willis argued that
the soul is located in and, moving beyond Descartes, limited to the brain. The
nerves, understood as hollow tubes that could carry the animal spirits, became
the *only* means of connecting the soul and the body. Following Willis and his
student Locke, human nature was understood as essentially "nervous." This shift
laid the groundwork for such eighteenth-century developments as the "science of
man," an emphasis on "sensibility" in literature, and a new conception of madness
as a *nervous* disorder.[20]

Hysteria had been known and discussed since the classical era. In the medieval
period hysteria had theological connotations and demonic associations. It was
medicalized and secularized early in the seventeenth century. Its causes, however,
remained elusive and its somatic associations shifted with changes in medical
theory. By the early seventeenth century, physicians, following Greek precedent,
linked hysteria with the "wandering womb," an organ related through "the power
of sympathy" to the animal part of the soul, especially the imagination, the senses,
and involuntary movement. Melancholy was the corresponding male disease. The
gendered character of such diseases was captured, according to G. S. Rousseau,
in seventeenth-century drama, where "virgins and widows frequently found themselves cast as hysterics while clerics and students were depicted as melancholics."[21]

The English physician Thomas Sydenham was largely responsible for severing
the direct biological link between women and hysteria. Writing in the 1680s, he
was, in Rousseau's words, "the first . . . to claim that no single organ was responsible [for hysteria] but a combination of 'mental emotions' and 'bodily derange-
ments' working through the nerves and the then all-important animal spirits."[22]
Sydenham claimed that "the radical mood swings of women—spasms, swoonings,
epilepsies, convulsions, sudden fits—were also known among men, especially, as
he wrote, 'among such male subjects as lead a sedentary or studious life, and grow
pale over their books and papers.' " Shifting the cause of hysteria from the womb
to the nerves did not equalize the prevalence of hysteria among women and men
as much as it shifted the biological foundation of gender differences. Thus, as
Rousseau puts it, "if hysteria was more prevalent and more severe among women
than men, it was because their anatomic nervous constitutions were weaker."[23] By
the early eighteenth century, educated persons thus associated weak minds and,
in the most advanced formulation, weak *nerves*, with women and, in the extreme
case, with madness.[24]

This profound shift would reverberate through the next few centuries. Eighteenth-century Enlightenment thought, "one magisterial footnote on nervous
physiology" in Rousseau's fitting phrase,[25] attributed the "otherness" of women to
"a defect—discursively represented as an inherent weakness, a lingering form of
exhaustion, a fundamental lack of tonic vigour—in female nerves and fibres."

Around this alleged anatomic disparity, Rousseau adds, male scientists spun a "new mythology about inherent male vigor and defective female frailty, all lodged in the nerves: a web of representational 'otherness' newly wedged between the sexes and claimed to be absolute, unchanging, eternal now that it had been discovered."[26] Thus, Chauncy reflected the assumptions of the Enlightened thinkers of his day when he argued that it is "the Weakness of their [women's] Nerves" that best explained why "[men] should be, as it were, overlook'd" by the Holy Spirit when it comes to these allegedly supernatural "*Agitations* and *Terrors*" (*STSR*, 105).

Social Dynamics

Throughout "Enthusiasm Describ'd" Chauncy's focus was on the enthusiast as an individual and enthusiasm as the result of individual defects—mistaken understanding, bad temperament, or most extremely, a diseased mind. From some of the examples cited so far, it is apparent that Chauncy's psychological theory, especially as it is applied, was not as individualistic as such explanations might suggest. The social dimension of Chauncy's understanding of enthusiasm is evident in an often quoted paragraph from his "Letter to Wishart," published in 1742. Here, having described how under the influence of George Whitefield's preaching the "*sensible Perceptions* [of the 'Multitudes'] arose to such a Height, as that they *cried out, fell down, swooned away,* and, to all Appearance, were like Persons in *Fits*," he offered the following explanation:

> [T]o a Person in possession of himself, and capable of Observation, this surprising Scene of Things may be accounted for: The *Speaker* delivers himself, with the *greatest Vehemence* both of *Voice* and *Gesture,* and in the most *frightful Language* his Genius will allow of. If this has its intended Effect upon *one* or *two weak Women,* the Shrieks catch from one to another, till a great Part of the Congregation is affected; and some are in the Thought, that it may be too common for those *zealous in the new Way to cry out themselves,* on purpose to move others, and bring forward a *general Scream. Visions* now became common, and *Trances* also, the Subjects of which were in their own Conceit transported from Earth to Heaven, where they saw and heard most glorious Things; conversed with *Christ* and *Holy Angels;* had opened to them the *Book of Life,* and were permitted to read the names of persons there, and the like.[27]

In contrast to the individualistic emphasis in "Enthusiasm Describ'd," this passage depicts significant social interactions between the preacher and the congregation and between the congregants themselves. There is a notable *lack* of interaction between the observer and the participants. In light of Chauncy's belief that preaching of this sort "*naturally* tends to put *weaker* Minds out of Possession of themselves" (*STSR*, 94), it is significant that Chauncy described the observer as "a Person in possession of himself." From what has been said so far, it is clear that the aroused animal spirits seek to possess the rational mind, and only by conquering them can the strong mind engage in *reasoned* observation and explanation.

Physiological and sociological dynamics came together for Chauncy at this point. By besting the aroused animal spirits, the strong-minded observer could resist the preacher's attempt to influence him *and* rationally observe the preacher's effect on others, especially on his antitype—the "weak Woman" who shrieks. Rational observation and consequently the ability to accurately discern the action of God, thus, were rooted in "self-possession." In the words of Shaftesbury, "to judge the spirits whether they are of God, we must antecedently judge our own spirit, whether it be of reason and sound sense; whether it be fit to judge at all, by being sedate, cool, and impartial, free of every biassing passion, every giddy vapour, or melancholy fume."[28]

We can also see that the "weak Women" played a pivotal role in the unfolding of this "surprising Scene." If they shriek, "the Shrieks catch from one to another, till a great Part of the Congregation is affected." The endpoint was visions and trances in which members of the congregation were "transported from Earth to Heaven" where, most crucially, they were permitted to read the names of persons recorded in the *Book of Life*. They were given, that is to say, knowledge of who was saved and who was damned. Such knowledge gave the visionary power, and this new power was an important source of the social consequences—challenges to traditional relationships of authority, to the established church, and ultimately to the entire political order—that Chauncy deplored.

The idea that the "Shrieks catch from one to another, till a great Part of the Congregation is affected" was rooted in what Shaftesbury referred to as a "panic."[29] Passions aroused in an individual became a "panic" when it was "raised in a multitude and conveyed by aspect or, as it were, by contact of sympathy." Drawing on infectious diseases as a metaphor, Shaftesbury, indicated that when people are "in this state their looks are infectious." Passions fly "from face to face; and the disease is no sooner seen than caught." Panics may arise from a variety of sources. Fear is a common source of panics, he said, but religion can also give rise to a panic, especially "when enthusiasm of any kind gets up, as oft, on melancholy occasions, it will."[30]

Chauncy held the new style preachers largely responsible for initiating such "panics." He acknowledged that outcries sometimes arose in response to preachers who were not known for "the *Loudness of their Voice,* or the *Boisterousness of their Action*" (STSR, 100). But, he suggested that in those rare instances where "moderate Preachers" seemed to evoke such effects, there were always previous influences that come into play. In some such cases, he indicated, the congregation had already become alarmed by word of such "extraordinary Effects" occurring elsewhere and had concluded "it was necessary they also should be in like Circumstances." In other cases, one or two cried out and influenced the rest of the congregation. The one or two who started things off, said Chauncy, were "*accustomed* to the Way of *screaming out.*" And, he asked, "were they not, *at first*, brought to it, under a more terrible Kind of Preaching?" (STSR, 100).[31]

Chauncy also thought that preachers subtly communicated what they wanted to their congregations and that the congregants tended to respond as the preachers desired. Chauncy described a minister he observed who "[gave] the People a plain

Intimation of what he wanted . . . [by telling] them of the *wonderful Effects* [pre-viously] wrought by the Sermon, he was then preaching; how in *such* a Congrega-tion, they were all melted and dissolved, and in another so over-poured, that they could not help *screaming out*, or *falling down*, as though they had been *struck dead*" (*STSR*, 93–94). The converse was also true, Chauncy believed. No matter how distinguished a minister might be, "if he wan't before known to have been a *Favourer* of these *Outcries*, he has not produced them: Nor do I believe, an Instance can be given in the Country, of their being brought forward by any Minister, of whom the People had a Suspicion, that he did not like them" (*STSR*, 101).

Chauncy indicated that the preachers had the power to modulate the congrega-tion's response while they were preaching. Quoting from one of his correspon-dents, he reported that:

> When he [the preacher] grew calm and moderate in his Manner, tho' the Things deliv-ered were equally Awakening, they [the congregation] by Degrees grew calm and still; when he again assum'd the *terrible*, and spake *like Thunder*, the *like violent Strugglings* immediately returned upon them, from Time to Time. Sometimes he put a mighty Em-phasis upon little unmeaning Words, and delivered a Sentence of no Importance with a mighty Energy, yet the sensible Effect was as great as when the most awful Truth was brought to View (*STSR*, 95).

Such effects were not only produced by ministers, but also, Chauncy believed, "in more numerous Instances" by exhorters. The exhorters, to quote his rather famous description, were "Men of all Occupations, . . . who, though they have no Learning, and but small Capacities, yet imagine they are able, and without Study too, to speak to the spiritual Profit of such as are willing to hear them: Nay, there are among these Exhorters, *Babes* in *Age*, as well as Understanding." Indeed, he said, the exhorters were "chiefly . . . *young Persons*, sometimes *Lads*, or rather *Boys*: Nay, *Women* and *Girls*; yea, *Negroes*, have taken upon them to do the Business of *Preachers*" (*STSR*, 226).

The two women who fell into trance together, described earlier, provide a more detailed picture of how one became an exhorter. These women, although deprived of their bodily Strength ". . . were [yet] by Turns able to speak, which they did, in Addresses and Exhortation to, and Prayers for, those present, who they sup-posed were unconverted." According to Chauncy's correspondent these women claimed "that they had been to Heaven, had seen the Book of Life, the Names of many Persons of their Acquaintance wrote in it." It was there, we may presume, that they also noted names that were missing and thus unconverted. It was this knowledge that allowed them to suppose themselves "to have a *special Commission*, or endow'd with some *special Authority*," and these visions that led "many People . . . to believe they were inspir'd" (*STSR*, 129). Visions and trances, and especially the visionary transports "from Earth to Heaven" to read the "Book of Life," gave even the most ordinary persons the authority to exhort the unsaved.

Chauncy believed that Whitefield through his preaching and writings propa-gated this *"fanciful Disposition* to others," especially the radical preachers and the laity. Specifically, Chauncy says, "[Whitefield] so frequently [wrote] after such a Manner, as to lead People to think, he imagined he was under the *immediate, extraordinary* Guidance of the Holy Ghost, . . . [that] I was always afraid, lest People, from him, should learn to give Heed to *Impulses* and *Impressions,* and by Degrees come to *Revelations,* and other *Extraordinaries,* in this Kind." Moreover, in his preaching on "*inward Feelings* . . . he totally neglected giving People warning of the Danger of a *deluded,* or *over-heated Imagination;* which I could not but wonder at, considering how many, in all Ages, have impos'd themselves thinking they *felt* the *Divine SPIRIT* acting in them, when it was apparent to every one else, that it neither was, nor could be any other than the *Motions* of their own *Fancies,* or the *Suggestions* of *Satan*" (*STSR,* 181–82).

Following "after the Example of the Preachers they admire," the common people not only mistook "the Motions of their own Minds for divine Suggestions," but they also began to demand new forms of pastoral leadership from the clergy. Many people, Chauncy indicates, developed "a low Opinion of *studied Sermons,* . . . while gladly hear[ing] any who will venture to speak to them without *previous Preparation,* whether *learned* or *unlearned* (if converted)." Not only did they "see *Visions* and *hear Voices*"; they also were able to discern "the *internal* State of others . . . whether *Ministers,* or *People,* and speak of them, and act towards them accordingly." Most dangerously, their view of "the Spirit's *Influence*" was such, in many cases, as to "reflect great Dishonour on the *written Word*" (*STSR,* 216).

Although he didn't make the connection directly, it was clearly the knowledge of the conditions of others' souls, acquired in this fashion, that led to the "*Spirit of rash, censorious and uncharitable Judging,* which has been so prevalent in the Land," and which Chauncy found so appalling (*STSR,* 140). Here again he cited the preachers—Whitefield, Tennent, and above all Davenport—as the offending parties and held them responsible for propagating this attitude among "the *common People.*" The effects were seen through out the social order, such that Chauncy claimed "there never was a Time, since the *Settlement of* NEW-ENGLAND, wherein there was so much *bitter* and *rash Judging;* Parents condemning their Children, and Children their Parents; Husbands their Wives, and Wives their Husbands; Masters their Servants, and Servants their Masters; Ministers their People, and People their Ministers" (*STSR,* 169–70). He gave as illustration a young woman of about fifteen years, who exhorted with such a "bitter and rash" spirit for about four hours. "[S]he began," he said, "with her Father, and told him, she could see the Image of the Devil then in his Face, and that he was going Posthaste down to Hell; and that all the Prayers he had ever made in his Family [were] nothing but Abomination in the Ears of the Almighty, and that all the Counsels he had ever given her, had no better a Tendency than to instruct her, how she should please the Devil; and that both he, and his Wife, were no better than the Devil" (*STSR,* 169 [note]). While there was no indication of how she acquired her knowledge of the condition of her parents' souls, this account clearly illustrates the threat which such knowledge posed to the traditional hierarchical relations of authority and deference that structured New England society.

JONATHAN EDWARDS ON ENTHUSIASM

Moderate supporters of the transatlantic awakening, such as James Robe, Charles Wesley, George Whitefield, and Jonathan Edwards, shared Chauncy's fear of enthusiasm, concern for social order, and commitment to an established church. While Chauncy provided the most sustained attempt to explain enthusiasm, Robe and Edwards also drew upon naturalistic explanations in their attempt to guide their followers between the twin dangers of indifference and enthusiasm. Before turning to the issues that divided Chauncy and Edwards, I want to make it clear that Reformed clergy, such as Edwards and Robe, were willing to concede at least as much to naturalistic explanation as Chauncy.

Jonathan Edwards preached the "Distinguishing Marks of a Work of the Spirit of God" as the commencement address at Yale in September 1741, immediately after James Davenport, a leading radical Congregationalist, left town. While Davenport may have been the precipitating cause of the address, anxiety had been building along with the revival since the visits of George Whitefield and Gilbert Tennent the previous fall and the publication of Whitefield's journal, with its disparaging comments on some of the New England clergy, shortly thereafter. Davenport visited Whitefield and the Tennents in Philadelphia and began itinerating in southern Connecticut two months earlier. All three stimulated the revival and aroused fears that it was spinning out of control.[32]

Edwards's primary aim in "The Distinguishing Marks" was to provide scripturally based theological criteria for distinguishing the true Spirit of God from its counterfeits. He assumed that both visions, which he refers to tellingly as "impressions on the imagination," and bodily effects could be accounted for in naturalistic terms, and he recognized that both had been associated with what he deemed "enthusiasm." Nonetheless, anticipating Chauncy's criticisms, he argued that the presence of either did not rule out the operation of the Spirit of God. Both bodily effects and visions might be accidental effects or indirect consequences, albeit not distinguishing marks, of the work of the Spirit of God.

Edwards believed that "crying out" and other such bodily effects were only natural when people were faced with a strong sense of their own "wickedness and God's anger." In a passage reminiscent of his famous sermon, "Sinners in the Hands of an Angry God," he stated:

> If we should suppose that a person saw himself hanging over a great pit, full of fierce and glowing flames, by a thread that he knew to be very weak . . . and saw nothing within reach that he could take hold of to save him; what distress would he be in? How ready to think that *now* the thread was breaking; *now, this minute*, he should be swallowed up in these dreadful flames? And would not he be ready to cry out in such circumstances? How much more those that see themselves . . . held over it in the hand of God, who at the same time they see to be exceedingly provoked? No wonder they are ready to expect every moment when this angry God will let them drop; . . . and no wonder that the wrath of God when manifested but a little to the soul, overbears human strength" (JE 4:231–32).

Again, anticipating Chauncy, he argued that preachers' insistence on the "terrors of God's holy law" was not, to his way of thinking, an argument against a true awakening. For if there really was a hell, then he insisted, it was proper for preachers "to take great pains to make men sensible of it" (JE 4:246–47). It was, he said, a "reasonable thing to endeavor to fright persons away from hell . . . [just as] 'tis a reasonable thing to fright a person out of a house on fire." While it was inappropriate to stir up groundless fears, preachers had an obligation to arouse "a just fear . . . though it be very great" (JE 4:248).

Nor, said Edwards, were ecstatic experiences, including visions wherein people were seemingly transported to heaven, an argument against this being a work of the Spirit of God. Again, he argued that such phenomena were a natural result of the "intense exercises and affections of mind" in persons of "particular constitutions." According to Edwards, " '[t]is no wonder that when the thoughts are so fixed, and the affections are so strong, and the whole soul so engaged and ravished and swallowed up, that all other parts of the body are so affected as to be deprived of their strength, and the whole frame ready to dissolve; I say, 'tis no wonder that in such a case, the brain in particular (especially in some constitutions) . . . should be overborne and affected, so that its strength and spirits should for a season be diverted, and so taken off from impressions made on the organs of external sense, and wholly employed in a train of pleasing delightful imaginations" (JE 4:237). Here, in what was in effect a short aside, Edwards not only prefigured much of what Chauncy later argued, but provided a more detailed explanation of the connection between the imagination and the animal spirits. Indeed, his notion of "fixed thoughts" prefigured late nineteenth-century discussions of the role of "fixed ideas" in hysteria and hypnosis.

James Robe, having read Edwards's "Distinguishing Marks," and possibly Chauncy's "Letter to Wishart," followed Edwards in conceding the naturalness of the bodily effects that accompanied the conversions of many of his Scottish congregants. For him, the willingness to accept a naturalistic explanation was a means of differentiating his people from real enthusiasts, such as the "Camizars" or French Prophets, who claimed that *their* ongoing "bodily agitations" and their prophesies had a supernatural source. Where the "Camizars" oftentimes neither "understood . . . what they uttered" nor "remember[ed] it afterwards," Robe's people never "pretended in the least to inspiration." Unlike the "Camizars," "they give a rational account of themselves, now and remember what they say and do." Moreover, he stated, "[t]he Camizars continued many years under their bodily agitations whenever their pretended inspirations seized them, and these did not proceed from any apprehension of the wrath of God due to them because of their sins." His people, again by way of contrast, were "delivered from their bodily distresses, which do not return upon them again, when they [were] delivered from their fears."[33]

In modern terms, Robe was saying that the French Prophets exhibited bodily agitations in conjunction with ongoing ostensibly supernaturally inspired speech, often accompanied by glossolalia and amnesia; while some, but not all, of the Presbyterian laity exhibited one-time naturally induced bodily agitations due to fear arising in the process of conversion. For Robe, traumatically induced motor dissociation was acceptable and understandable among his followers as long as it was manifest only in conjunction with conversion and no claims were made for supernatural inspiration. Given that both his followers and the French Prophets experienced involuntary bodily effects and visions, the crucial difference between the two groups, for Robe, lay in their interpretations of the phenomena. As we will see in the next chapter, this difference had tremendous pastoral implications for the making of what the moderate evangelical clergy viewed as authentic religious experience.

While Robe viewed bodily exercises and visions as natural phenomena and made allowances for them as such in the context of conversion, Edwards's understanding of them grew more complex over time. Against critics, such as Chauncy, Edwards consistently maintained that both bodily effects and visions, while not distinguishing marks, might well be accidental effects or indirect consequences of the work of the Spirit of God. In contrast to Robe, who attempted to distinguish between the phenomena associated with revival converts and French Prophets, Edwards rejected the comparative enterprise altogether and devoted his energies to developing a theological perspective that could account for the appearance of similar phenomena in conjunction with either true or false religion. Thus, he said, "some err in making history and former observation their rule to judge of this work." Such persons compared "some external, accidental circumstances of this work, with what has appeared sometimes in enthusiasts; and as they find an agreement in some such things, so they reject the whole work . . . concluding it to be enthusiasm" (*JE* 4:313).

Edwards developed the theoretical underpinnings for explaining why these phenomena should appear in conjunction with both true religion and enthusiasm in *Some Thoughts Concerning the Revival of Religion* (1743) and *A Treatise on the Religious Affections* (1746). The two key components of his explanation were his "voluntarist" view of human nature and his "new spiritual sense." In *Some Thoughts* Edwards directly challenged Chauncy's "intellectualist" view of human nature for the first time. He rejected the view that associated the affections or passions solely with the body (i.e., with the "animal nature") and divorced them from anything distinctively human. Adopting the "voluntarist" stance characteristic of Augustine and the contemporary British moralists, Edwards argued that the higher affections were associated with the "noblest part of the soul" and indeed could not be separated from the will. It was thus, he resoundingly asserted, "false divinity to suppose that religious affections don't appertain to the substance and essence of Christianity: on the contrary, it seems to me that the very life and soul of all true religion consists in them" (*JE* 4:297).

Edwards, however, made this claim only for the *religious* affections. Indeed, he conceded that "there are many exercises of the affections that are very flashy, and little to be depended on; and oftentimes there is a great deal that appertains to them, or rather that is the effect of them, that has its seat in animal nature, and is very much owing to the constitution and frame of the body" (*JE* 4:297).[34] Thus, while Edwards and Chauncy disagreed about where to locate the "high and raised affections," they both located the lower, more "flashy" affections in the body. Edwards did not tackle the difficult question of how exactly one distinguished between the religious and nonreligious affections, leaving the task, at that point, simply to "the skill of the observer" (*JE* 4:297). Differentiating the two depended on his "new spiritual sense" and was the subject of *Religious Affections*, his most psychologically oriented work.

Edwards's interest in advising ministers with regard to these phenomena was also very evident in *Some Thoughts*. In helping the clergy understand and guide parishioners caught up in the awakening, Edwards revealed both his unparalleled gift for observation and analysis and his willingness to embrace secular explanations. This was perhaps nowhere more apparent than in his insightful discussion of the "secret and unaccountable influence that custom has upon persons." By custom, Edwards said he "mean[t] both a person's being accustomed to a thing in himself, in his own common, allowed and indulged practice, and also the countenance and approbation of others amongst whome he dwells, by their general voice and practice" (*JE* 4:472). Although he was unwilling to ascribe "all the late uncommon effects and outward manifestations of inward experiences to custom and fashion," he said it was "exceedingly evident . . . that custom has a strange influence in these things." Like Chauncy, he observed that when a preacher "countenances and encourages such kind of outward manifestations of great affections, they naturally and insensibly prevail, and grow by degrees unavoidable; but when they [parishioners] come under another kind of [ministerial] conduct, the manner of external appearances will strangely alter." Yet he moved beyond anything Chauncy offered when he added that the alterations seemed to be "*without any proper design or contrivance* of those in whom there is this alteration." It was evident, he concluded, "that example and custom has some way or other a secret and unsearchable influence on those actions that are involuntary, by the difference that there is in different places and in those same places at different times, according to the diverse examples and conduct they have" (*JE* 4:472–73, emphasis added). Further development of this insight into mimetic action awaited the development of more sophisticated theories of magnetic and then unconscious interaction.

In "Distinguishing Marks," Edwards acknowledged that many of the revival phenomena could be explained naturalistically, and he sharply challenged Chauncy's intellectualist psychology in *Some Thoughts*. He did not tackle the difficult issue of distinguishing religious and nonreligious affections nor did he confront the related issue of whether one could have a *direct* experience of God or the Holy Spirit until he wrote *A Treatise on the Religious Affections*. By locating all the affections in the body, Chauncy was able to avoid the problem of religious affections entirely. Moreover, when he criticized George Whitefield for giving people the impression that he thought he was under "the *immediate, extraordinary* Guidance of the Holy Ghost," Chauncy ruled out direct religious experience as well. "I doubt not," he stated, that "the Spirit *may be felt*, i.e. Christians may have an *inward real Perception* of those Things which are the *Effects* of the SPIRIT's *Influence*; but this quite differs from an *immediate Feeling of the SPIRIT himself*" (STSR, 182). Chauncy's point was that a "inward real Perception," like a Lockean idea, was not the same as the object itself, in this case the Holy Spirit. And while the "inward real Perception" corresponded, although not infallibly, with an external object whose essential nature was beyond human understanding, its existence could be inferred only through the effects of its influence.[35]

Although there has been considerable controversy over Jonathan Edwards's debt to Locke, recent scholarship has emphasized Edwards's metaphysical repudiation of Locke at precisely this point.[36] As James Hoopes points out, "orthodox Puritans were not enthusiasts and did not usually claim to have received explicit messages from God, but they did believe that they had direct experience in their souls of the saving presence of the Holy Ghost. This belief, as well as Antinomianism, was put on trial by Locke's implication that we have no empirically verifiable knowledge of anything divine."[37] While Chauncy accepted the idea that all knowledge of God comes through secondary causes and hence found Locke's views congenial, Edwards, like Wesley, wanted to make a case for direct religious experience while at the same time repudiating that which he viewed as enthusiasm.

To make his case, Edwards found it necessary to engage on three fronts. Against the intellectualist psychology of the revival's critics, Edwards articulated a voluntarist psychology with roots in Augustinian theology, Puritan piety, Cambridge Platonism and, most immediately, the British sentimentalist moral philosophy exemplified by Shaftesbury. Against the British moral philosophers' movement toward a secularized understanding of the affections grounded in an innate "moral sense," Edwards grounded what he deemed to be specifically religious, that is God-given "gracious" affections, in a new "spiritual sense."[38] Finally, with respect to those he deemed enthusiasts, Edwards argued that this spiritual sense was so obscured by sin in this life that behavior, rather than experience, must be the ultimate test of assurance.[39]

Edwards described the new spiritual sense using the language of Paul's Letter to the Galatians. Arguing that the "Spirit of God" dwelt in true saints, he added that "Christ by his Spirit not only is in them [the saints], but lives in them; and so that they live by his life; so is his Spirit united to them, as a principle of life in them; they don't only drink living water, but this living water becomes a well or fountain of water, in the soul."[40] While the Spirit of God may "influence natural men," they were only acted upon, not "dwelt in." As long as the Spirit acted on the essentially passive soul from without rather than manifesting itself as an "active principle" dwelling within, a person remained natural and not spiritual (*JE* 2:201).

Salvation gave to the saints "a new inward perception or sensation in their minds, entirely different in its nature and kind, from anything that ever their minds were the subjects of before they were sanctified." This was not, Edwards said, arguing with Locke, a mere "exalting, varying or compounding of that kind of perceptions or sensations which the mind had before." Rather it was equivalent to "what some metaphysicians [such as Locke] call a new simple idea."[41] In other words, this new spiritual sense was not a new thing perceived by the senses, but an altogether new sense. It was not "a new faculty of understanding, but . . . a new foundation laid in the nature of the soul" (*JE* 2:205–6).[42] This new spiritual sense thus provided the theoretical foundation for direct religious experience, but because, as Chamberlain points out, Edwards viewed the new sense as obscured by sin, direct experience could *not* be trusted to provide assurance of one's salvation.

While the Spirit of God operated *directly* through its indwelling in the new spiritual sense of the saints, the Spirit, "in all his operations upon the minds of natural men, only moves, impresses, assists, improves, or some way acts upon natural principles" (*JE* 2:206). Thus while the Spirit of God operated as a "first cause" with respect to spiritual persons, the Spirit operated only as a "second cause," that is, through natural means, with respect to natural persons.[43] This meant that for Edwards with respect to natural persons *everything* could be explained (in theory anyway) in natural terms. This did not rule out, of course, the possibility of either God or Satan acting through natural processes to achieve some end, but it did extend the realm of the natural even more radically than in Chauncy. Thus, while Edwards made this radical distinction between natural and religious experience in order to build his case for the radical newness of the religious sense, his argument required a correspondingly radical naturalistic understanding of the natural order. In service of this end, Edwards here made, as Hoopes points out, "the frankest and fullest use of empirical psychology in any of his works published in his lifetime."[44] The upshot was that while Edwards *repudiated* Locke when it came to authentic religious experience, he *followed* Locke when it came to enthusiastic and counterfeit religious experience. Thus, authentic "spiritual understanding" consisted, for Edwards, "in a divine supernatural sense and relish of the heart," while enthusiasm consisted in "impressions on the imagination [resulting from] . . . the exciting [of] external ideas in the mind" (*JE* 2:285–86).

Impressions on the imagination, according to Edwards, could account not only for "a very great part of the false religion that has been in the world, from one age to another," but also for "the religion of the many kinds of enthusiasts of the present day" (*JE* 2:286–87). "[F]or the sake of the common people," he explained exactly what he meant by "impressions on the imagination." Imagination, he said, was "that power of the mind, whereby it can have a conception, or idea of things of an external or outward nature, . . . when those things are not present, and be not perceived by the senses." Everything perceived by the five "external senses . . . are external things." Images in the mind of external things when they were not actually there constituted "imaginary ideas." When such ideas were "strongly impressed upon the mind . . . almost as if one saw them . . . that is called an impression on the imagination" (*JE* 2:210–11). Recognizing that the common people often viewed such impressions as "spiritual discoveries," he explained that imaginary ideas were still external ideas. "These external ideas," he said, "though their coming into the mind is sometimes unusual, yet . . . they are still of no different sort from what men have by their senses" (*JE* 2:214). Drawing on the verities of post-Cartesian science, he went on to say, that "these ideas [external or, more narrowly, imaginary ideas] may be raised only by impressions made on the body, by moving the animal spirits, and impressing the brain" (*JE* 2:215–16).

Although there is nothing here that he or Robe or Chauncy had not said before, Edwards then observed that the "imagination or phantasy [thus] seems to be . . . the devil's grand lurking place," and more importantly, that it was "very much to be doubted whether the devil can come at the soul of man . . . *any other way*, than by the phantasy" (*JE* 2:288, emphasis added). Because the "[animal spirits] have no other medium of acting on other creatures or being acted on by them, than the body," he concluded that "it is not to be supposed that Satan can excite any thought, or produce any effect in the soul of man . . . [other] than by some motion of the animal spirits, or by causing some motion or alteration in something which appertains to the body" (*JE* 2:288). If it was indeed the case that "the devil can't produce thoughts in the soul immediately, or any other way than by the animal spirits, or by the body; then it follows, that he never brings to pass anything in the soul, but by the imagination or phantasy, or by exciting external ideas" (*JE* 2:288–89). Satan, although himself supernatural, could act only by means of natural causes. Satan, unlike the Spirit of God, could not impinge directly on or take up residence in the soul. Satan, and by extension, false religion, could be accounted for *only* in naturalistic terms.

For Edwards, then, the operation of the imagination provided the primary means of explaining false religion, including the enthusiasm of his own time. The presence of imaginary ideas, as he was quick to point out, could not be taken, however, to mean that a feeling was *not* spiritual, since humans were such that they "can scarcely think of any thing intensely, without some kind of outward ideas." In the end, it came down to a question of origins. Thus, he claimed, "there is a great difference between these two things, viz. lively imaginations arising from strong affections [produced by the direct action of the Spirit of God indwelling in the soul], and strong affections arising from lively imaginations [produced naturally or by means of God or Satan acting through natural means]." While true spiritual affections were independent of the imagination, imaginary ideas might arise as an "accidental effect, or consequent of the affection, through the infirmity of human nature" (*JE* 2:291). Bodily effects and visions, while always products of a lively imagination, might arise either as an accidental effect of the indwelling Spirit of God arousing *authentic* religious affections *or* as the result of external ideas creating *counterfeit* religious affections by means of impressions on the imagination.

By locating the higher, spiritual passions in the soul and by postulating a new spiritual sense through which God could act directly on the soul, Edwards could provide separate explanations for the genesis of true and false religion. By establishing two different routes through which the imagination might be aroused, a spiritual pathway through the soul and a natural pathway through the body, he could account for the appearance of bodily effects and visions in conjunction with both true and false religion without discrediting the former.

Elegant as Edwards's solution was, it hung—to use his metaphor—by the thread of his "new spiritual sense." Were that thread to be cut, God, like Satan, would be reduced to acting through natural means in a natural world devoid of evident supernatural presence. Or as Hoopes put it, a bit less dramatically, "Edwards's philosophical and psychological theories . . . [while] a brilliant defense of heart religion, . . . also conceded something to empiricism." The challenge of the scientific revolution, as Hoopes points out, was "not atheism but the gradual elimination of God's special providence." By narrowing the scope of religious experience such that "no experience of the natural senses, however miraculous, ha[d] any special claim," proponents of the awakening such as Edwards and Robe unintentionally furthered the naturalistic study of religion in their attempt to protect the awakening from charges of enthusiasm.[45]

Maintaining the thread was to prove nearly impossible. Although Edwards had read of the British moralists prior to writing the *Religious Affections*, he did not read the work of its premier spokesperson, Francis Hutcheson, until afterward. According to Norman Fiering, "Edwards could only have been amazed and dismayed when he first read Hutcheson's *Inquiry* and discovered in it arguments for a natural and universal moral sense that paralleled almost exactly what Edwards had been claiming exclusively for spiritual sense." In the works of Hutcheson and his disciples, "there were dozens of . . . passages, ascribing to nature what Edwards for years had been insisting belonged to grace alone."[46]

DAVID HUME ON ENTHUSIASM

While Hutcheson and his disciples argued for a moral sense that paralleled Edwards's spiritual sense, Hume extended the thought of Locke, Shaftesbury, and Hutcheson to locate not only morality, but also the most basic assumptions about reality within the realm of human feeling or sentiment.[47] Belief in such fundamentals as cause and effect were constituted, according to Hume, not through reason, but through the nonrational faculty he variously referred to as the "imagination" or "instinct."[48] Although Hume's views on the origins of "true religion" remained somewhat obscure, the origins of false religion (superstition and enthusiasm) and, in his later writings, "religion as it has commonly been found in the world," were clearly, for Hume, products of the imagination as informed by the passions.

Raised within the Presbyterianism of the Scottish state church, Hume, by his late teens, had become a skeptic not only with regard to the truth of religion but with respect to the power of reason as well.[49] In *A Treatise of Human Nature*, written in his twenties, Hume compared the insufficiencies of human reason for the philosphical task to that of a man, who having once "narrowly escap'd shipwreck . . . put[s] out to sea in the same leaky weather-beaten vessel, and even carries his ambition so far as to think of compassing the globe under these disadvantageous circumstances." The thought of embarking on the philosophical journey in such an unseaworthy vessel filled him "with melancholy" and he could not, he said, "forbear feeding [his] despair."[50]

His despair was grounded in the limitations of reason and his conviction that human understanding in its first principles, as, for example, in the fundamental relations between cause and effect, "lies merely in ourselves, and is nothing but that determination of the mind, which is acquir'd by custom."[51] Belief in such basic matters-of-fact as cause and effect were, for Hume, the product of the imagination, shaped by "habit" and "custom."[52] All the basic operations of the mind—memory, sense, and understanding—were dependent, in his view, on the imagination.[53] His insights into the arbitrary way in which fundamental beliefs are formed and his contemplation of "the manifold contradictions and imperfections in human reason . . . heated [his] brain, . . . [to the point that he was] ready to reject all belief and reasoning, and . . . look upon no opinion even as more probable or likely than another."[54] The result, as he indicated, was melancholy or, as it was sometimes called, "the disease of the learned." Melancholy, as we have seen, was associated with enthusiasm and Hume, in fact, viewed himself as susceptible to a form of philosophic enthusiasm.

In a letter written to his physician in 1734, Hume averred that his sufferings were "pretty parralel [sic]" to that found in "the Writings of the French Mysticks, & in those of our Fanatics here." He found the parallel particularly in their descriptions of "a Coldness & Desertion of the Spirit, which frequently returns, & some of them, at the beginning, have been tormented with it many Years." He did not, of course, either explain or resolve his crisis of the spirit in the same way as the "Mysticks" or "Fanatics," but rather embarked on a lifelong regimen in which he successfully balanced his scholarly pursuits with more mundane activities (e.g., exercise and conviviality) to keep the "warmth or Enthusiasm" of his devotion to scholarship from overheating his brain and "discompos[ing] the Fabric of the Nerves."[55]

For Hume, unrestrained skepticism was simply enthusiasm in another guise. Two years before the publication of the *Treatise* he indicated to a friend that he was "at present castrating [his] Work, that is, cutting off its noble Parts . . . [so] as to give as little Offence as possible." The "noble Part" was an attack on miracles and, while he viewed its excision as "a Piece of Cowardice," he stated, "I was resolv'd not be an Enthusiast, in Philosophy, while I was blaming other Enthusiasms."[56]

In an essay published in 1741, Hume discussed superstition and enthusiasm as "two species of false religion" that proceeded from different states of mind or temperaments. Both, however, were rooted in the imagination. Superstition, he said, arose from "certain unaccountable terrors and apprehensions, issuing either from the unhappy situation of private or public affairs, from ill health, from a gloomy or melancholy disposition, or from the concurrence of all these circumstances." Prefiguring his argument in the *Natural History of Religion*, he stated that the soul, lacking "real objects of terror . . . finds imaginary ones" and then devised methods—ceremonies, observances, mortifications, sacrifices—to appease them. The mind of the enthusiast, by way of contrast, was "subject to an unaccountable elevation and presumption, arising from prosperous success, from luxuriant health, from strong spirits, or from a bold and confident disposition." Enthusiasm, however, was also rooted in the imagination, such that when the imagination was given full reign, it gave rise to "raptures, transports, and surprising flights of fancy." At the summit of enthusiasm these transports were "attributed to the immediate inspiration of that Divine Being," such that the inspired person regarded himself as "a favorite of the Divinity" and "every whimsy [as] . . . consecrated."[57]

Superstition and enthusiasm were central to Hume's analysis of religion in the context of English history and politics. Volume one of his *History of Great Britain* (1754) was preoccupied with the twin dangers of superstition and enthusiasm. The first volume, which was chronologically also the last, dealt with the reigns of James I and Charles I. The entire projected history thus ended with the "tragical death" of the pious Charles I amidst various "consecrated whimsies" or supernatural sanctions—Cromwell's tongue cleaving to the roof of his mouth, a Herfordshire woman receiving a revelation, and miraculous answers to prayer—entrusted to his executioners.[58] Hume's sympathy for Charles I was evident and his contempt for those who "imagined, that, in the acts of the most extreme disloyalty to their prince, consisted their highest merit in the eyes of Heaven" was barely concealed. His deepest sympathy, however, was not with the monarch *as* monarch but with the mixed constitution and limited monarchy to which Charles had consented and from which the parliamentary radicals were in retreat.[59]

Hume's *History* embedded a political theory which, in turn, was grounded in his philosophical conviction that moral, social, and political relations were all human constructs. To Hume's way of thinking, superstition and enthusiasm could be linked not only to emotional dispositions, but to political dispositions as well. Thus, he associated superstition with Catholicism, High Church Anglicanism, old-fashioned Toryism, absolutism, and divine-right monarchism, and enthusiasm with Puritanism, personal autonomy, individual rights, and the absence of mediating factors between God and man.[60] Hume understood his political writings, including his history of England, as "political *acts*" intended to shape "the opinions or beliefs that in turn shaped politics and society."[61] By analyzing the consequences of superstition and enthusiasm in English history, Hume attempted to encourage a public commitment to a middle ground, a "mixed constitution" as it were, in political life.

Some clergy accused Hume of irreligion after the first volume was published. Hume attributed this to the fact that, as he put it, "I run over all the sects successively, and speak of each of them with some mark of disregard, the reader, putting the whole together, concludes that I am of no sect; which to him will appear the same thing as the being of no religion."[62] In an unpublished preface to the second volume of the history, Hume explained why false religion figured so much more prominently in his history than true. "The proper Office of Religion," according to Hume, was to reform men's lives, enforce moral duties, and secure obedience to the law. "[I]ts operations, tho' infinitely valuable, are secret & silent; and seldom come under the Cognizance of History." It is only the "adulterate Species" of religion, "which inflames Faction, animates Sedition, & prompts Rebellion, [that] distinguishes itself on the open Theatre of the World."[63] True religion, because it pursued its "useful Purposes" secretly and silently, was hidden from history, playing its part behind the scenes of the "Theatre of the World." Here, as with Edwards, we see the realm of true religion dramatically reduced, in this case to the point of public invisibility.

John Gaskin makes a persuasive case that Hume was not being disingenuous in his references to true religion, citing not only his several published references to it, but also his statement to Boswell on his deathbed that " 'he had *some* belief' but . . . kept to his earlier 'Objection both to Devotion & Prayer & indeed to every thing we commonly call Religion, except the Practice of Morality, and the Assent of the Understanding to the Proposition *that God exists.*' "[64] Assuming Hume to be sincere in his distinction between true and false religion, I think it is fair to say that *in his writings on religion*, Hume, like Chauncy and Edwards, was still only attempting to explain (an admittedly all-encompassing) "false religion" or "religion as it has commonly been found in the world." I do not think this means that Hume was necessarily reluctant to explain true religion in terms of his science of man. Insofar as true religion was indistinguishable from the practice of morality, he had indeed already done so.

While enthusiasm loomed large in Hume's "factual" history of England, Hume gave the negative emotions—anxiety, fear and terror—primacy when discussing the origins of religion. Thus, while he stated in the *Natural History* that the origins of religion lay in the "hopes and fears, which actuate the human mind," it was especially "the anxious concern for happiness, the dread of future misery, the terror of death, the thirst of revenge, the appetite for food and other necessaries" that led people to see "the first obscure traces of divinity."[65] While he conceded that "*any* of the human affections may lead [to religion]," he noted that "men are much oftener thrown to their knees by the melancholy than by the agreeable passions." Moreover, in the *Dialogues*, Hume stated outright that "terror is the primary principle of religion."[66]

As Peter Harrison explains, "natural histories" were "conjectural" as opposed to "factual" or "accidental" histories. A natural history of religion was intended to provide a theoretical account of the unimpeded development of a particular institution, in this case, religion. Such a history was considered natural, "because it attempt[ed] to penetrate the veil of historical accidents to uncover the true object of study."[67] The emphasis on superstition and the primacy of fear in the *Natural History* suggests that enthusiasm, for Hume, was more "accidental" than "natural." Thus, even when he discussed superstition and enthusiasm as ostensibly balanced ideal types, superstition took primacy over enthusiasm by virtue of its tendency to generate rituals and institutions (for the purpose, of course, of assuaging terror). As he stated in the *Essays*, enthusiasm, while initially "more furious and violent," lost its initial ardor because it had "no rites, no ceremonies, no holy observances, which may enter into the common train of life, and preserve the sacred principles from oblivion."[68] Enthusiasm, it would seem, must wind up as superstition, if it was not simply to disappear. While a balanced typology was necessary in the context of English history (i.e., "accidentally") in order to define a middle way between the two extremes of high church monarchicalism (superstition) and Puritan republicanism (enthusiasm), superstition could subsume enthusiasm in a "natural" or theoretical history of religion.

Reading the *Natural History* in isolation not only obscures the role of enthusiasm in Hume's thought, it also leaves his theory of religion looking somewhat more narrowly individualistic than it really was. If we locate Hume's theory of religion in relation to his larger theory of the role of the imagination *informed by habit and custom* in forming belief, it is clear that this was not a *purely* individualistic psychological theory, but rather a social psychology. Religion, like other beliefs, may have been all in the mind for Hume, but the mind did not stand in isolation.[69]

CONCLUSION

The efforts of revivalists, anti-revivalists, and Enlightened skeptics to explain enthusiasm in naturalistic terms highlight the role that "false religion" played in the rise of the study of religion. This was not, of course, accidental. Opponents used naturalistic explanations to account for the origins, persistence, and appeal of false religion in order to undercut the supernaturalistic explanations offered by believers. Opponents *wanted* to discredit false religion, and their explanations, as a result, were inevitably political in the broad sense of the term. Whereas false religion cried out for explanation, "true religion" by definition, did not. While some enlightened thinkers rejected all supernaturalistic explanations and argued that natural religion was the only true religion, more traditional thinkers embraced supernatural explanations for that which they deemed true and naturalistic explanations for that which they deemed false.

A comparative method undergirded the search for naturalistic explanations and formed the bedrock of the attack on false religion. When the bodily exercises of the transatlantic awakening were compared with the bodily exercises of such evidently false manifestations of religion as the Montanists, the French Prophets, or the Quakers, this undermined the credibility of the revival phenomena. Comparison of Protestant bodily exercises to the "fits" of the mentally ill had much the same effect. Christian thinkers in this period tended to assume that authentic supernatural revelation was (by doctrinal definition) "unique" and thus incomparable, while false revelation was in some sense all "the same" and, thus, comparable. Comparable phenomena, it was assumed, shared a common naturalistic explanation, whether or not science was yet able to provide it. If some found animal spirits uncompelling as an explanation of such phenomena, that did not make the "fits" of Methodists, French Prophets, and the insane any less comparable.

Protestant defenders of bodily exercises, such as Edwards and Robe, resisted the simplistic comparisons of the revivals' detractors. Robe responded by making subtler distinctions and, thus, more nuanced comparisons. Edwards's elaborate theological system was designed in part to make such comparisons meaningless by redefining the similarities as "externals," epiphenomena of both true and false religion. While neither Robe nor Edwards wanted to discredit bodily exercises or visions entirely, both understood them as at best incidental accompaniments of authentic conversion. In defending the revivals of religion from charges of enthusiasm, they, like Chauncy, conceded considerable ground to the Enlightenment attack on the supernatural. Moreover, as we shall see in the next chapter, their attack on false religion disseminated the sorts of naturalistic theories that were to characterize the emergent academic study of religion as represented by David Hume.

Most people associated true religion with order and false religion, especially enthusiasm, with disorder. Politically, anti-enthusiasts tended to be moderate or conservative in their views. Chauncy, Edwards, and Hume all sought a middle way between monarchy and radical republicanism. None advocated disestablishment of the church and all associated enthusiasm with social chaos and tacitly with "radical" democratization. Tensions between order and disorder in a hierarchically ordered society were mirrored by tensions within a hierarchically ordered self. Insofar as anti-enthusiasts embraced the theory of animal spirits, they adopted a worldview in which the "will" sought to control the chaotic and ultimately perhaps revolutionary impulses of the "spirits." The triumph of the will was a triumph of dispassionate "strong-minded" and "self-possessed" reason over that which sought to dispossess it. When the animal spirits gained ascendancy over the "weak-minded," they dispossessed the rational soul or "self." In the language of animal spirits, we hear the lingering resonances of the language of possession by demons or Satan, and indeed for Edwards the animal spirits constituted the pathway through which Satan operated. This physiological theory took on explicit social form, moreover, with the assumption that some constitutions, particularly those of women, were "weaker" than others and thus more prone to dispossession by animal spirits.

Looking back, it is clear that thinkers of this era contributed more to the modern study of religious experience on the level of incidental observation than grand theory. A number of theoretical insights stand out, including recognition of the subtle dynamics between preacher and congregation, the impact of clergy attitudes on a congregation, the importance of habit and custom, and the effects of "terror" and "fixed thoughts" on the body. Later thinkers developed all of these insights more fully. In terms of my argument in this book, it is perhaps most important to highlight Hume's observation that in the end enthusiasts were not much of a threat, because direct inspiration (in the absence of rites, ceremonies, and holy observances) had no way of entering into "the common train of life" and, thus, preserving itself from "oblivion." Although I think Hume was right in claiming that direct inspiration survives only when it is supported by a sacred mythos embedded in sacred practices, it survived to varying degrees in both the Reformed and the Methodist traditions. In the next chapter, I explore how the Enlightenment attack on enthusiasm shaped the construction of religious experience in both of these traditions.

CHAPTER TWO

Making Experience

WE CAN talk about the making of evangelical religious experience on two levels, the level of theories about religious experience and the level of personal narratives of religious experience; at the level, that is, of theology or of testimony. There are definite connections between theories *about* religious experience and narratives *of* religious experience, but the latter, unlike the former, are not constituted simply by means of discourse, although discourse may play an important part in the process. The process whereby experience is constituted is, for the most part, neither conscious nor spontaneous. Rather a mythic worldview is inscribed on the body of the individual and/or group as people gain mastery of practices in ritual contexts wherein the mythic discourses, images, and/or structures are embedded. As Bourdieu has written, "it is in the dialectical relationship between the body and a space structured according to the mythico-ritual oppositions that one finds the form par excellence of the structural apprenticeship which leads to the em-bodying of the structures of the world." The sacralization of experience thus involves cultivating and maintaining those practices through which a community understands, locates, and experiences the sacred. The relationship between "experiences" and "practices" is necessarily dynamic and interdependent. Persons with experience—that is, with practical mastery—endow practices with meaning and value. Practices in turn structure experience and provide the occasion for developing practical mastery.[1]

The Reformation and the Enlightenment both intervened in the process of making Christians. Protestants and purveyors of the Enlightenment each attempted in their own way to reinterpret the Christian myth and remap the way in which the bodies of individual Christians and the collective Christian body as a whole were constituted. Although inward religion predated the Enlightenment attack on enthusiasm, it is only a slight exaggeration to say that in this period "religious experience" was the name Protestants gave to that which survived the attacks of the Enlightenment.[2] From an evangelical Protestant perspective, experience was constituted not only in relation to enthusiasm (excessive or false experience) but also in relation to formalism (the alleged absence of experience). Caught between these two unacceptable alternatives, evangelical moderates, such as Jonathan Edwards and John Wesley, constituted theologies of experience that had much in common.

Edwards and Wesley shared considerable common ground on the level of theological ideas, yet Wesley and the Methodist tradition were markedly more open to manifestations of the supernatural than were Edwards and the moderate Reformed tradition. Whereas Edwards sought to avoid enthusiasm by promoting a clerically led effort to naturalize much of Christian experience, Wesley sought to avoid enthusiasm through lay-led small-group processes. As a result, they promoted very different models of and for religious experience within very different ecclesiastical structures. Where the philosophically inclined Edwards mounted a sophisticated defense of experimental religion, the more practically oriented Wesley launched a brilliantly orchestrated, experientially based popular religious movement.

THE IDEA OF EXPERIENCE

> Experience is the life of a Christian. What is all knowledge
> of Christ without experience?
> —*Richard Sibbes, 16—*[3]

In keeping with recent studies that have emphasized the importance of viewing the revivals in colonial America, Great Britain, and on the Continent as aspects of a broader transatlantic awakening, several scholars have called for a recognition of the similarities between Jonathan Edwards's and John Wesley's understandings of "religious experience."[4] For our purposes, it is enough to recognize several broad points of agreement between Edwards and Wesley. First, both Edwards and Wesley defined true religion in opposition to both formalism and enthusiasm. Second, they both equated true religion with vital or heart religion as manifest in conversion and a continuing process of sanctification. Third, they both defended the possibility of a direct or immediate experience of the Spirit of God and they both argued that authentic experience must be tried and tested in practice. They differed somewhat in their terminology, with Edwards preferring the phrase "experimental religion" and the "indwelling of the Spirit of God" and Wesley "true Christian experience" and the "witness of the Spirit of God."

Jonathan Edwards

Edwards refered to "experience" and "experimental" sparingly in his earliest accounts of the awakening in New England. "Christian experience" appeared, seemingly without qualification, as a synonym for "heart religion" and "vital and experimental religion" (*JE* 1:101, 114). He also refered to persons "giving an account of their experiences" (*JE* 1:126) or more specifically, relating their "experience of a work of conversion" (*JE* 1:121).[5] In his *Faithful Narrative of the Surprising Work of God in the Conversion of Many Hundreds of Souls* . . . (1737), he provided two narratives of individuals' "experiences" of conversion in order to give "a clearer idea of the nature and manner of the operation of God's Spirit" (*JE* 1:191).

By the early 1740s, "experience" was a more loaded term and Edwards's view of it more chastened. Caught between "Old Light" clergy for whom any mention of experience smacked of enthusiasm and radical "New Lights" whose appeals to experience Edwards viewed as enthusiastic, he tried to articulate a middle ground. Preaching his sermon on the "Distinguishing Marks of a Revival of Religion" at the Yale commencement in 1741, soon after James Davenport had left the campus totally divided, Edwards both defended the revival and distanced himself from the radicals' unqualified view of experience. "[T]here is a great aptness in men," he admonished, "that think they have had some experience of the power of religion, to think themselves sufficient to discern and determine the state of others' souls by a little conversation with them; and experience has taught me that this is an error." Acknowledging that the "heart of man" was far more un-searchable than he had heretofore imagined, he added, "I find more things in wicked men that may counterfeit, and make a fair shew of piety, and more ways that the remaining corruption of the godly may make them appear like carnal men, formalists, and dead hypocrites, than once I knew of" (*JE* 1:285).[6] A year later, in *Some Thoughts on the Revival of Religion* (1742), he was still pondering how best "to judge of experience," especially given both the "unheeded defects" and the tendency to degenerate that one finds even in "the experiences of true Christians" (*JE* 1:462, 466).

By the time he wrote his *Treatise on the Religious Affections* (1746), he was clear that to separate experience and practice was to court the twin dangers of formal-ism and enthusiasm. Thus, he explained, there are two things to watch out for.

> There is a sort of external religious practice [formalism], wherein is no inward experi-ence; which no account is made of in the sight of God; but it is esteemed good for nothing. And there is what is called experience that is without practice [enthusiasm], being neither accompanied, nor followed with a Christian behavior; and this is worse than nothing. (*JE* 2:452)

Authentic experience, by way of contrast, must be tried in practice. It must be experimentally tested. "This," Edwards said, "is properly Christian experience, wherein the saints have opportunity to see, by actual *experience* and *trial*, whether they have a heart to do the will of God, and to forsake other things for Christ, or no." Authentic experience and authentic practice were conjoined for Edwards under the heading of experimental religion. Just "as that is called experimental philosophy, which brings opinions and notions to the test of fact, so it is properly called experimental religion, which brings religious affections and intentions to like test" (452). True religion, in Edwards's view, is best understood as experimen-tal religion. Edwards's disciple, Joseph Bellamy, neatly summed up the Edward-sean position in the title to his frequently reprinted book: *True Religion delineated; or, Experimental Religion, as distinguished from Formality on the one Hand, and Enthu-siasm on the other, set in a Scriptural and Rational Light* (1750).[7]

The Life of David Brainerd, edited by Edwards and published in 1749, exempli-fied the devotional ideal embraced by the moderate Reformed wing of the revival and, as one of the most popular devotional books of the nineteenth century, the ideal that came to typify much of middle-class Protestantism in the next century. It was the popular capstone to the series of treatises on the revivals published by Edwards since 1736 and the only one devoted almost entirely to narrative exposi-tion (*JE* 7:1–6; 37–51). In his concluding observations on Brainerd's religion,

Edwards addressed in turn those who opposed the revival, those who were caught up in it and fell away, and those who zealously embraced it.

To the opponents of the revival, Edwards said that Brainerd's *Life* demonstrated that "there is indeed such a thing as true experimental religion, arising from immediate divine influences, supernaturally enlightening and convincing the mind, and powerfully impressing, quickening, sanctifying, and governing the heart" (*JE* 7:520). While some, he said, may argue that any such experience is enthusiasm, he listed the fruits of Brainerd's religion and averred that "if all these things are the fruits of enthusiasm, why should not enthusiasm be thought a desirable and excellent thing?" (*JE* 7:521). To those who had fallen away, he pointed out that Brainerd's work in the "business of religion" did not begin and end with his conversion. Even when religion "decayed" in the wake of the revival, "his experiences were still kept up in their height . . . wherever he was and whatever his circumstances were" (*JE* 7:500–502). Finally, he pointed out to the zealous "high pretenders to religion" all that Brainerd's religion did *not* include. Edwards's list was quite long, but in sum, he noted the absence of bodily sensations, strong impressions on the imagination (i.e., visions or voices), and claims to "immediate witness of the Spirit." "[I]f we look through the whole series of his experiences, from his conversion to his death, we shall find none of this kind. I have had occasion to read his diary over and over, and . . . I find no one instance of a strong impression on his imagination through his whole life [and] [no] supposed immediate witness of the Spirit" (*JE* 7:503–4).

John Wesley

John Wesley started using the term "experience" later than Edwards and with less ambivalence. Indeed, it was not until 1746, when Edwards was giving clear precedence to "experimental religion" in his *Treatise on the Religious Affections*, that Wesley made his first references to "what the children of God experience" and to "the experience of all real Christians" in a sermon entitled "The Witness of the Spirit, I."[8] The sermon was based on Romans 8:16 ("The Spirit itself bears witness with our spirit, that we are the children of God"), a passage that had been at the core of his understanding of a renewed religion of the heart since the 1730s. The idea of "real Christian experience" remained central to his thinking and to the Methodist movement more generally. It achieved its fullest statement in *A Collection of Hymns for the use of the People called Methodists* (1780). Wesley stated in the preface to the collection that "[t]he hymns are not carelessly jumbled together, but carefully ranged under proper heads, according to the experience of real Christians."[9] The witness of the Spirit, the idea upon which Wesley built his theological understanding of real Christian experience, was central to the hymn-book and, in Wesley's view, comprised the heart of the distinctively Methodist message.

The idea of the witness of the Spirit appeared in Wesley's writings beginning in the early 1730s. It was connected to his understanding of both conversion and sanctification, experiences that he tended to conflate in his early thinking. It appeared, although it was not centrally featured, in a sermon he preached in 1733 that he later described as containing "all that I now teach concerning [holiness, that is] salvation from all sin, and loving God with an undivided heart" (*JW* 1:398, 406, 411). In February 1736, the witness of the Spirit moved to center stage when the Moravian pastor August Spangenberg asked Wesley if he had "the witness [of the Spirit] within [him]self" and Wesley was unsure how to respond.[10] Wesley's "heart was strangely warmed" two years later at a meeting of a religious society in Aldersgate Street. He understood that occasion, in keeping with Moravian theology, as the point at which "sin had no more dominion over him" and he became a Christian, in what he took to be the true sense of the word.[11] Looking back on that day six months later, he wrote his older brother, Samuel, that he had not yet received "this witness of the Spirit . . . but . . . patiently wait[s] for it." He said that he "know[s] many who have already received it, more than one or two in the very hour we were praying for it." He added that "those who have not yet received joy in the Holy Ghost, the love of God, and the *plerophory* [full assurance] of faith (any or all of which I take to be the witness of the Spirit with our spirit that we are the sons of God [Rom. 8:16]), I believe to be Christians in that imperfect sense wherein I call myself such" (*JW* 25:577). In *The Character of a Methodist* (1742), Wesley wrote that the Methodist is defined as "one who has 'the love of God shed abroad in his heart by the Holy Ghost given unto him.' "[12]

In his lengthy exchange of letters with the anonymous Anglican cleric, "John Smith," in the mid-1740s, Wesley put it a little differently. Accepting Smith's contention that the doctrines that distinguish Methodists could be summed up in the phrase "perceptible *inspiration*," he wrote "[f]or this I earnestly contend; and so do all who are called Methodist preachers" (*JW* 26:181–82). He went on to elaborate, saying that what Methodists mean by "perceptible inspiration" is the

> inspiration of God's Holy Spirit whereby he fills us with righteousness, peace, and joy, with love to him and all mankind. And we believe it cannot be, in the nature of things, that a man should be filled with this peace and joy and love by the inspiration of the Holy Ghost without perceiving it, as clearly as he does the light of the sun. This is (so afar as I understand them) the main doctrine of the Methodists. This is the *substance* of what we all preach. And I will still believe, none is a *true Christian* till he experiences it. (*JW* 26:181–82)

A few sentences later, he repeats himself, saying:

> 'No man can be a *true Christian* without such an inspiration of the Holy Ghost as fills his heart with peace and joy and love; which he who perceives not, has it not.' This is the point for which alone I contend. And this I take to be the very foundation of Christianity. (*JW* 26:182)

The witness of the Spirit remained central to Wesley's understanding of what was distinctively Methodist. Some twenty years later, in a revised version of his original sermon on the witness of the Spirit ("The Witness of the Spirit, II" [1767]), Wesley maintained that "[i]t more clearly concerns the Methodists, so called, clearly to understand, explain, and defend this doctrine [the witness of the Spirit], because it is one grand part of the testimony which God has given them to bear to all mankind." He added that "[i]t is by his [the Spirit's] peculiar blessing upon them in searching the Scriptures, confirmed by the experience of his children, that this great evangelical truth has been recovered, which had been for many years well-nigh lost and forgotten" (*JW* 1:285–86).

Although Wesley did not give the kind of attention to philosophical matters that Edwards did, they both relied on an intuitionist epistemology with respect to true religion that was grounded in a "spiritual sense" and shared a concern for identifying the distinguishing marks of the Spirit. In his first sermon on "The Witness of the Spirit" (1746), Wesley indicated that although we do not really know *how* the Spirit bears witness with our spirit that we are the children of God, we do know *that* the Spirit does it. For the believer, this knowledge was self-evident. "[T]he fact [that] we know," he said, the believer can no more doubt "than he can doubt of the shining of the sun while he stands in the full blaze of his beams" (*JW* 1:276). At this point, according to Albert Outler, Wesley presupposed a "whole theory of knowledge with its notion of a 'spiritual sensorium' analogous to our physical senses and responsive to prior initiatives of the Holy Spirit." In the early 1730s, well before his conversion experience, Wesley distinguished between natural perception known through the natural senses and spiritual perception known through a "spiritual sense." Thus, Wesley wrote, "[the natural man] 'receiveth not the' words 'of the Spirit of God', taken in their plain and obvious meaning. 'They are foolishness unto him; neither' indeed 'can he know them, because they are spiritually discerned:' they are perceivable only by that *spiritual sense* which in him [the natural man] was never yet awakened" (*JW* 1:402, emphasis added).[13]

When Wesley turned to the tricky question of how the witness of the Spirit might be "clearly and solidly distinguished from the presumption of a natural mind, and . . . the delusion of the devil," Wesley, again like Edwards, identified distinguishing "marks." But at precisely the point where Edwards expended enormous philosophical energy attempting to distinguish between natural and spiritual affections, that is, in effect attempting to distinguish between the psychological and the religious, Wesley turned away from philosophy to identify theological marks derived, he said, from scripture.[14] Claiming that "the Holy Scriptures abound with marks whereby the one [presumptions and delusions] can be distinguished from the other [the joint testimony]," he listed such marks as repentance, being born of God, and the fruits of the Spirit (meekness, patience, gentleness, and long-suffering). Ultimately, he admitted that the distinction must be intuitively grasped by "rightly disposed . . . spiritual senses." Deflecting further inquiry, he said that "[t]o require a more minute and philosophical account . . . of the *criteria* or intrinsic marks whereby we know the voice of God, is to make a demand which can never be answered; no, not even by one who has the deepest knowledge of God" (*JW* 1:277–78, 282).

Just as dreams, visions, and involuntary bodily movements came to the fore in the context of Reformed discussions of the "indwelling of the Holy Spirit," they were also never far from the surface of Methodist discussions of the "witness of the Spirit." These phenomena were intimately, if not always positively, bound up with the experience of the new birth for both Wesley and Edwards. Both Edwards and Wesley agreed on two fundamental points regarding these phenomena: first, that they were no sure sign or evidence of salvation and, second, that the witness of the Spirit (experience) must be tested by the fruits of the Spirit (practice).

John Wesley emphasized both these points in a letter to his brother Samuel in April 1739 and later quoted from the letter in his journal, where he refered to the passage as the "sum of [his] answer" to those cautioning him against taking such phenomena as signs of salvation.

> What I have to say touching visions or dreams is this: I know several persons in whom this great change [the new birth] was wrought, in a dream, or during a strong representation to the eye of their mind, of Christ either on the cross or in glory. This is the fact; let any judge of it as they please. And that such a change was *then* wrought appears (not from their shedding tears only, or falling into fits, or crying out: these are not the fruits, as you seem to suppose, whereby I judge, but) from the whole tenor of their life, *till then* many ways wicked; *from that time* holy, just, and good. (JW 19:59–60)

Wesley emphasized that the visions, dreams, and "falling into fits" were *not* the same thing as "the fruits." Dreams, visions, and involuntary movements might be marks of adoption (as children of God) or they might not. They might simply be marks of enthusiasm, i.e., an imagined witness of the Spirit and an imagined adoption or new birth. As he wrote to Elizabeth Hutton in 1744, "Dreams and visions were never allowed by us to be certain marks of adoption. . . . Neither did we ever allow the falling into fits (whether natural or supernatural) to be a certain mark."[15] Such experiences must be judged by their fruits. The fruits were evidenced in practice, specifically through a transformation that encompassed the whole tenor of a person's life, a transformation that Wesley summed up in the phrase "*till then* many ways wicked; *from that time* holy, just, and good."

In his "Witness of the Spirit" sermons, Wesley emphasized the clear distinction between the witness of the Spirit confirmed by the experience of the children of God and the fruits of the Spirit that followed from it (JW 1:274–75, 289–90). Experience, however, could not stand alone. Experience (the witness of the Spirit) was always, for Wesley, in dynamic relationship with practice (the fruits of the Spirit). Wesley concluded his second "Witness of the Spirit" sermon with the two inferences he wanted his listeners to draw from his sermon: "The first: let none ever presume to rest in any supposed testimony of the Spirit which is separate from the fruit of it. . . . The second inference is: let none rest in any supposed fruit of the Spirit without the witness" (JW 1:297–98).

Wesley's discussion of true religion, like that of Edwards, was explicitly situated in opposition to both enthusiasm and formalism.[16] The 1746 version of "The Witness of the Spirit" sermon opened with the acknowledgment many "vain men" have misunderstood Romans 8:16 to the destruction of their souls. It is they, he said, who "have mistaken the voice of their own imagination for this 'witness of the Spirit' of God, . . . [who] are truly and properly *enthusiasts*" (JW 1:269 [emphasis in original]). Given the enthusiasts, he said, "who can then be surprised if many reasonable men, seeing the dreadful effects of this delusion, and labouring to keep at the utmost distance from it, should sometimes lean toward the other extreme?" Wesley explicitly attempted to "steer a middle course" between these two extremes (*JW* 1:270). In the 1767 version he identified "a danger on the right hand and on the left." The former, he said, is "mere formality," the latter is "the wildness of enthusiasm" (*JW* 1:285). The 1780 *Collection of Hymns* was organized in order to highlight the distinction between "formal Religion" and "inward Religion." Part II of the hymnal was devoted to hymns describing formal and inward religion, while Parts III and IV were devoted to acquiring (hymns for "mourners"), regaining (hymns for "backsliders"), and deepening (hymns for "believers") inward religion. This knowledge culminated in sanctification or "full redemption," that is, at the point when the heart was released from the power of "inbred sin" and became a fit dwelling place for the Spirit of God.

Charges of enthusiasm dogged Wesley through most of his career precisely because the witness of the Spirit—a doctrine particularly associated with the more radical Puritans and Pietists—was at the heart of what he understood as true religion.[17] Acknowledging the phenomenological similarity between what Wesley espoused as true religion and what he condemned as enthusiasm, both Henry Rack and Stephen Gunter refer to Wesley as a "reasonable enthusiast." I think that this sells Wesley short. While Wesley did not spell out his views as systematically or as explicitly as Edwards did in his *Treatise on the Religious Affections*, I think that theologically they distinguished between true religion and enthusiasm on similar grounds. Thus, as both Outler and Gunter have argued, Wesley's "witness of the Spirit" was linked (like Edwards's "indwelling of the Spirit") to the presence of a "spiritual sense" in the spiritual, but not the natural, man. The presence or activation of the spiritual sense (a result of the new birth) enabled converts to intuitively apprehend the witness of the Spirit with their spirit that they were children of God (the experience of the new birth). Because the alleged spiritual sense might be nothing more than the natural senses caught up in their own vivid imaginings (enthusiasm), none could presume to rest in any supposed testimony of the Spirit separate from the fruits of the Spirit.

Following this logic, the distinction between enthusiasm and an authentic experience of the new birth rested on the distinction between the natural and the spiritual senses, and ultimately, of course, on belief in the objective reality of the Spirit itself. What Wesley held to be true cannot be distinguished from what he or others refered to as enthusiasm on the basis of its reasonableness or any other ordinary criteria we might dream up. The distinction between true Christian experience and enthusiasm was not a matter of empirical substance open to the view of "natural men." It was a matter of spiritual substance, grounded in the presence of a spiritual sense and available only to those who had an authentic experience of the new birth. This logic was admittedly circular. If one could not see the distinction, one by definition had not had the experience.[18] But its circularity should not blind us to the point that Wesley, like Edwards, recognized that "natural men" had no basis upon which to distinguish between true Christian experience and enthusiasm.

Those whom Wesley viewed as formalists, i.e., nonevangelical Protestants, shared the evangelical belief in the objective reality of the Spirit, but did not believe that the Spirit witnessed in the present other than through the standing testimony of Scripture. As a result, they denied the objective reality of the Spirit's perceptible presence in the present and had no basis for distinguishing between inward religion, as understood by Wesley, and enthusiasm. Thus, Wesley forthrightly told his rationalist critics in *An Earnest Appeal to Men of Reason and Religion* (1743) that they could not tell the difference between the two because their own "faith (so called)" was merely formal.[19] By extension, if we as modern scholars are by Wesley's definition "natural men," we should not expect to be able to find any discernible difference between what Wesley called true Christian experience and what he and others called enthusiasm.

While, according to Wesley, "natural men" were trapped in (natural) senses that by definition could not see any distinction between true Christian experience and enthusiasm, the experience of the children of God served to confirm, in equally circular fashion, the doctrine of the witness of the Spirit. While the idea that experience could confirm doctrine was implicit in the ceaseless recounting of and testifying to experience on the part of the Wesleys and their followers, Wesley made this claim explicit in his second sermon on the witness of the Spirit when he claimed that "[e]xperience is sufficient to *confirm* a doctrine which is grounded in Scripture" (*JW* 1:297). But he did not mean by this that *any* experience was sufficient. It was quite specifically the experience of the children of God that served to confirm this doctrine, that is, the experience of those who had been born anew and had the requisite spiritual sense to intuitively apprehend the witness of the Spirit.

This theory of knowledge was reflected clearly in the 1780 *Collection of Hymns*. Hymn 94 (in the section "Describing Inward Religion") stated for all to sing that the "foolish world" could not distinguish between enthusiasm and real divine work.

> The same in your esteem
> Falsehood and truth ye join,
> The wild enthusiast's idle dream,
> And real work divine;
> The substance or the show,
> No difference you can find:
> For colours all, full well we know,
> Are equal to the blind. (*JW* 7:199)

In Hymn 93, the believer sang of knowledge gained through the witness of the Spirit:

> We by his Spirit *prove*
> And *know* the things of God; . . .
> His Spirit to us he gave,

And dwells in us, we *know*;
The witness in ourselves we have,
And all his fruits we show. (*JW* 7:197, emphasis added)

If we simply focus on the ideas that Edwards and Wesley had about religious experience, we can find a great deal of common ground between them. The most significant difference, for our purposes, is that, although Edwards and Wesley were both concerned to identify "marks" of the Spirit, Edwards did so on the basis of psychological criteria, whereas Wesley did not. Edwards differentiated between natural and supernatural affections in order to isolate the supernatural affections as the true distinguishing marks of the Spirit, but Wesley held to a strictly theological set of marks (repentance, being born of God, and exhibiting the fruits of the Spirit) that were not premised on such a distinction. This meant that Edwards was much more concerned to distinguish in practice between primary causation (effects arising directly from supernatural action) and secondary causation (effects arising naturally as indirect effects of supernatural action) than was Wesley. Thus, in the context of narratives of religious experience, Edwards not only routinely distinguished between the two, he increasingly privileged that which he understood to be the direct result of divine action (primary causation) to the exclusion of that which he deemed secondary or indirect. As we will see in the next section, if Edwards referred to visions or involuntary bodily movements at all, he did so in naturalistic terms.

Wesley, by way of contrast, did not make a rigorous distinction between primary and secondary causation nor privilege one over the other in the context of narrative. Thus, where David Brainerd's experience was exemplary in Edwards's eyes because it did *not* include phenomena he deemed natural (i.e., bodily sensations, strong impressions on the imagination, and claims to the "immediate witness of the Spirit"), Wesley freely depicted the Spirit of God acting through these very phenomena when he narrated what he took to be an authentic Christian experience. More specifically, in addressing the "high pretenders to religion," Edwards was pleased to note that Brainerd's "first experience of the sanctifying and comforting power of God's Spirit did *not* begin in some bodily sensation, any *pleasant warm feeling in his breast* that he (as some others) called the feeling the love of Christ in him, and being full of the Spirit" (*JE* 7:503–4, emphasis added). Wesley, of course, made precisely this claim, and not only for his followers, but above all for himself. Significantly, when Wesley edited Edwards's reflections on Brainerd's life, he left in the remarks directed to the opponents of the revival and to those who had fallen away, but deleted those addressed to the zealous "high pretenders."[20]

Edwards downplayed the phenomena that he counted as "no sure signs" of true religion; Wesley did not. Because they were, in his view, so manifestly biblical, Wesley refused to reject phenomena simply because they could be "perverted." Thus, he conceded to Samuel that to pray for the "witness of the Spirit" did encourage visions and dreams but "that it does this accidentally, or that weak minds may pervert it to an ill use, is no reasonable objection against it for so they may pervert every truth in the oracles of God." He specifically cited in this regard the "dangerous doctrine of Joel, cited by St. Peter," a passage whose references to prophesy, visions, and dreams Wesley presumably viewed as having been "perverted" by "weak minds" at numerous points in the history of the church. Although he told Samuel that he rejected "idle visions and dreams," he insisted that the existence of such does not mean "that visions and dreams in general are bad branches of a bad root[.] God forbid! This would prove more than you desire" (*JW* 25:594).[21] A few months later, he vehemently reasserted his central claim: "God *does now, as aforetime, give remission of sins and the gift of the Holy Ghost, even to us and to our children; yea, and that always suddenly, as far as I have known, and often in dreams or in the visions of God*" (*JW* 19:59–60). So too, when he wrote Mrs. Hutton that he did not believe that "the falling into fits" was a certain mark of adoption, he added that he did "believe that the Spirit of God, sharply convincing the soul of sin, may occasion the bodily strength to fail" (*JW* 26:113).

Looking back twenty years later, he commented that he had "generally observed more or less of these outward symptoms to attend the beginning of a general work of God . . . [b]ut after a time they gradually decrease, and the work goes on more quietly and silently."[22] Methodist historians, wanting to downplay the role of these "outward symptoms" in the Methodist movement, have wanted to read *disappear* where Wesley wrote *decrease*, but in fact these "outward symptoms" continued for decades.[23] In light of their general decrease, however, Wesley shifted his approach. In the past, he wrote, "[t]he danger *was* to regard *extraordinary* circumstances too much, such as outcries, convulsions, visions, trances, as if these were *essential* to the inward work, so that it *could not* go on without them. Perhaps [now] the danger *is* to regard them too little, to condemn them altogether, to imagine they had nothing of God in them and were an hindrance to the work." Although Wesley moved from emphasizing that these phenomena were not *essential* to emphasizing that there was something of God in them, he presumed throughout that such phenomena were desirable (*JW* 21:234).[24]

He offered his fullest summary of his views in response to those who regarded them too little, stating that, whereas they believe there is nothing of God in them,

> the truth is (1) God suddenly and strongly convinced many that they were lost sinners, the *natural* consequences whereof were sudden outcries, and strong bodily convulsions. (2) To strengthen and encourage them that believed, and to make his work more apparent, he favoured several of them with divine dreams, others with trances and visions. (3) In some of these instances, after a time, nature mixed with grace. (4) Satan likewise mimicked *this work of God* in order to discredit the *whole work*.[25]

This statement is entirely in keeping with what Wesley had been saying for two decades and clearly reflects the differences between Edwards and himself. Where he, like Edwards, described the outcries and convulsions as secondary causes of divine action in this instance, he broke with Edwards in viewing some dreams, trances, and visions as divine. Moreover, even though he viewed outcries and convulsions as natural, they, like dreams, visions, and trance were narratively linked to God's action. Satan might mimic God's work; in "some few cases," there might even be some "dissimulation," such that "persons *pretended* to see or feel what they did not and *imitated* the cries or convulsive motions of those who were really overpowered by the Spirit of God." Yet, he said, "even this should not make us either deny nor undervalue the real work of the Spirit. The shadow is no disparagement of the substance, nor the counterfeit of the real diamond" (*JW* 21:234–35).

EXPERIENCE-IN-PRACTICE

When we turn to the level of lived experience, the picture becomes more complex. The impact of the Enlightenment attack on enthusiasm on the formation of experience can be seen in the ways those seeking to cultivate experience sought to avoid enthusiasm, on the one hand, and to constitute authentic religious experience, on the other. Although the two processes were intimately related, for the sake of clarity, I treat each in turn. I argue that Edwards sought to avoid enthusiasm by promoting a clerically led effort to naturalize through education much that others viewed as supernatural in Christian experience, while Wesley sought to avoid enthusiasm through regulating lay-led small groups. These divergent strategies for avoiding enthusiasm emerged from and perpetuated very different traditions of practical mastery and consequently very different models of and models for experience-in-practice.

Avoiding Enthusiasm

CONGREGATIONALISTS AND PRESBYTERIANS

In using education as a means of avoiding enthusiasm, Edwards assumed the traditional role of the minister as teacher and drew upon the traditional authority vested in his office. The legitimacy of his office rested, in turn, on his and his fellow ministers' ability to delegitimate the experientially based authority of their radical challengers. Through his writings, Edwards provided moderate Congregationalist clergy in particular, and evangelical clergy in general, with the intellectual and pastoral tools for the task. He approached this from two different, but mutually reinforcing, directions. He shored up clerical authority by discouraging public lay leadership and he taught clergy and laity to distinguish "correctly" between the natural and the supernatural and in so doing undermined the authority of the radicals.

Congregationalists of this era distinguished between three different types of religious practice: public worship, social worship, and private (that is, "secret" or "closet") devotions. Public worship, normally on Sunday, was composed of prayer, singing, and preaching. On some Sundays, the "sacrament of the Holy Supper" was administered as well. Sermons and devotional literature elaborated the traditional Puritan understanding of conversion and sanctification. Notes on sermons and devotional books provided a theological filter through which scripture was engaged in the context of private devotions. Spiritual diary-keeping, which emerged as a replacement for oral confession to a priest especially within the Puritan wing of the Church of England, was the primary means of self-examination and the foundation of private devotion.[26] Social worship, that is weekday meetings for various purposes, had a venerable history in Puritan weekday lectures by an ordained teaching minister or meetings in congregants' homes to discuss the week's sermon.

The emergence of numerous public lay exhorters who made claims to authority based on their experience dramatically expanded the opportunities for lay-led social worship and posed a challenge to the authority of the clergy. James Davenport was credited with greatly encouraging, if not initiating, the rise of the public exhorters, that is exhorters who traveled from place to place speaking publicly to groups (specifically, exhorting them to repent) outside the context of Sunday worship. The number of lay exhorters rose sharply during the early 1740s—they sprang up, said one minister, "like *Mushrooms in a Night*"—and bore much of the responsibility for the spread of the revival. These gatherings were a matter of considerable concern to the regular clergy, many of whom viewed the exhorters as a threat to their authority and to public order. Jonathan Parsons, writing to a fellow minister, indicated that Davenport's practice of "encouraging persons in a *Lay* Capacity to set up as Heads of public Assemblies," was one of his most hurtful and divisive.[27]

The meeting, described by Charles Chauncy in which the two young women were in trance, was a New Light gathering for prayer and fasting. Specifically, it was "a *Conference Meeting*, or *private Fast*, kept by a Number of the *New-Light* Party (as it was said) to pray that the *general Council of Ministers*, who were then sitting at Guilford, might be restrained from doing any Thing that should be detrimental to the *Work of God*, or (should I be too uncharitable, if I say) in other Words, to their *Cause*" (STSR, 128). One of the things the young women were doing in trance was exhorting and praying for those at the gathering. Joshua Hempstead left a report of another such meeting in his diary. According to Hempstead:

> Mr. Allin of New London [a Congregationalist minister sympathetic to the revival] was to come & failed them & after Long waiting the young men 2 of them Newlight Exhorters begun their meeting & 2 or 3 Women followed both at once & there was Such medley that no one could understand Either part untill near night Mr Fish [another minister sympathetic to the revival] came amongst them and Soon began to Pray & one of the Women Speakers kept on praying and Exhorting at the Same time for Several minutes till at Length She grew Silent and Mr fish had all the work to himself who made a short Discourse & So Dismist us.[28]

The exhorters could "spring up" in the context of a revival because exhorting was a familiar, yet flexible concept that encompassed a range of extemporaneous performances, from the commonplace, informal "exhortation" of one lay person by another to the public exhortation of a group by a layperson. In the first instance, exhorting was a species of earnest conversation; in the last, it approached, and at times could not be distinguished from, preaching or teaching, both roles that were reserved for the ordained ministry. Jonathan Edwards spoke for the moderate clergy when he upheld the obligation of lay Christians to exhort one another, while at the same time upholding the prerogatives of the clergy.

It took Edwards several tortured pages, however, to explain how he thought teaching and exhorting in the manner reserved for the clergy should be distinguished from "exhorting in a way of Christian conversation" (*JE* 4:483). The general rule, he said, is that "lay persons [except for male heads of families in their own homes] ought not to exhort one another as [if] clothed with authority," through their words, their manner, or the circumstances in which they speak. They definitely were not to exhort and teach as a calling. Speaking in a "time of conversation, or a time when all do freely converse with one another . . . to none but those that are near 'em and fall in their way," even if it happened to be in a meetinghouse, was acceptable, as long as the "public service and divine ordinances" were over (*JE* 4:483–88).

As a further safeguard against inappropriate lay exhorting, Edwards urged the clergy to discourage people from speaking out during both regular Sunday worship or weekday social worship. His expressed aim was to help the laity avoid the impulse to exhort by creating a climate in which it would be "unbecoming" to do so. Thus, he stated, "if it [speaking out] was disallowed, and persons at the time that they were thus disposed to break out had this apprehension that it would be a very unbecoming, shocking thing for 'em so to do, it would be a help to 'em as to their ability to avoid it." He made a similar suggestion with respect to people speaking out loudly when emotionally aroused. If such an ethos was not established, Edwards said, people would become louder and louder, "till it becomes natural . . . to scream and halloo" (*JE* 4:488–89). The upshot was that while persons could, and indeed were supposed to, engage in "mutual religious conversation," this was to occur informally and not in the context of worship, whether Sunday or weekday social worship. Lay people had no official religious roles, apart from the father's role as "teacher and governor" of the family (the "little church") (*JE* 4:487). Thus, while people might have intense experiences in the context of Sunday worship or at a meeting for social worship, they were expected to keep silent about them until after the meeting, at which time they were encouraged to converse freely with others.

As we saw in the last chapter, Edwards, more than anyone else in his era, was sensitive not only to the effects of custom and fashion in the development of religious experience, but to the involuntary and "secret" or, in modern terms, unconscious dimensions of this process. Because "example and custom" have, as he said, this "secret and unsearchable influence on those actions that are involuntary," Edwards advised the clergy to provide "gentle restraint" and "prudent care" for persons in the throws of extraordinary experiences. Such persons, he indicated "should be moderately advised at proper seasons, not to make more ado than there is need of, but rather to hold a restraint upon their inclinations; otherwise extraordinary outward effects will grow upon them, they will be more and more natural and unavoidable." Unrestrained, such "persons will find themselves under a kind of necessity of making a great ado . . . till at length almost any slight emotion will set them going" (*JE* 4:473). He, thus, encouraged his fellow ministers to actively create an ethos, in effect "counter-customs," within their congregations that would subvert the unconscious tendency to normalize what Edwards viewed as enthusiasm.

This more restrained ethos provided the context in which theologically trained clergy could effectively teach the laity to distinguish "correctly" between the natural and supernatural when recounting their religious experiences. While Edwards, as we have seen, discussed the principles underlying this distinction at length in his writings, he also provided four in-depth narratives of religious experience as examples. The first two—Abigail Hutchinson and Phebe Bartlet—were included in *A Faithful Narrative* before the problem of enthusiasm had become a major issue. The other two—Sarah Pierpont Edwards in *Some Thoughts* and the *Life of David Brainerd*—both illustrated how one should make these distinctions in practice. Thus, when Sarah Edwards's experiences were at their most intense, they were, according to her husband, "frequently attended with very great effects on the body." Edwards emphasized, however, that it was "*nature*" that "often [sank] under the weight of its divine discoveries" and the "*animal nature*" that was "often in great emotion and agitation" (*JE* 4:332, emphasis added). Additionally, when her soul "seemed almost to leave the body," Jonathan Edwards pointed out that this occurred "without [her] being in any trance, or being at all deprived of the exercise of the bodily senses" (*JE* 4:332). The "trances and visions" experienced by many of the more radical New Light converts were natural, while her experience evidently, in his mind, was not.[29]

Sarah Edwards's own account indicated that many of her more intense experiences took place in public, either in the meetinghouse or in gatherings for social worship at the Edwards's house. In both contexts it is evident that she had internalized a clear sense of what was and was not appropriate. While during a sermon her soul was "overwhelmed" and her "bodily strength" taken away by the presence of God in the congregation, there is no evidence that she cried out or in any way disrupted the sermon. She did, however, remain "in the meeting-house about three hours, after the public exercises were over . . . convers[ing] with those who were near [her], in a very earnest manner." On numerous occasions, she reported that she was so "impressed with the love of God" that she was able to refrain "from rising in [her] seat, and leaping with great joy" only with great difficulty. While she lost her strength regularly, she consistently restrained herself from "leaping with transports of joy" or "expressing [her] joy aloud, in the midst of the service."[30]

Brainerd, also evidencing the clear benefits of Jonathan Edwards's mentoring, was able to specify, in keeping with the *Treatise on the Religious Affections*, that the "unspeakable glory" that opened to his soul at the time of his conversion was "a new inward apprehension" and not a sensory perception or an impression on his imagination.

> By the glory I saw I don't mean any external brightness for I saw no such thing, nor do I intend any imagination of a body of light or splendor somewhere away in the third heaven, or anything of that nature. But it was a new inward apprehension or view that I had of God; such as I never had before, nor anything that I had the least remembrance of it. (138; mss ver)

Brainerd also taught Edwards's views on the natural and supernatural affections to his Indian converts. Walking the fine Edwardsean line, Brainerd recounted how he attempted to "rectify [his Indian converts'] notions about religious affections: showing them, on the one hand, the desirableness of religious affection, tenderness, and fervent engagement in the worship and service of God, when such affection flows from a true spiritual discovery of divine glories" and, on the other, "the sinfulness of seeking after high affections immediately and for their own sakes." Brainerd reported that "this appeared to be a seasonable discourse, and proved very satisfactory to some of the religious people who before were exercised with some difficulties relating to this point" (JE 7:399–400).

Likewise James Robe, after reading Edwards's *Distinguishing Marks*, took up the task of teaching his congregation how to interpret their experiences correctly. At the outset of the revival, Robe instructed his congregation "in the expressest, strongest, plainest manner [he] could, That Jesus Christ in the body cannot be seen by any with their bodily eyes in this life." If they thought they saw such sights, he let them know "that it was owing only to the strength of their imagination, to the disorder of their head, and of the humours of their bodies at that time: and that it was not real."[31]

Robe also engaged his parishioners individually with respect to these issues. Of the "many hundreds" he talked to, he said there was "only one who said, she thought she saw hell open as a pit to receive her." He told her that this vision "was owing to her imagination: and, that she must see [instead] the wrath of God, due to her for her sins, in the threatening of the law." Three others, a woman and two girls, said they saw "Jesus Christ," according to Robe. But when he "met with them afterwards, and examined into it, and they appeared to be ashamed of it, and were convinced that they had really seen nothing." On another occasion, he reported, three women "thought they saw a great and glorious light, for a very short time. But when I examined into the circumstances, I found that their eyes had been shut at the time, and so easily convinced them, that it was not real, but imaginary, and that no weight was to be laid upon it by them." He also said he had "a few instances" of persons "who alleged that they had been frighted with the appearance of the devil." But this, he said, did not "appear strange" to him "among country people, who are from their infancy bred up, with stories about frightful appearances, especially in their present situation, when the arrows of the Almighty were within them." According to Robe, his parishioners were agreeable to his instruction. He found none, he said, who were not "easily persuaded that no weight was to be laid upon any of these things." He also recognized that his aggressive instruction was "possibly . . . one reason why there was so little of this [visions, voices, and revelations] to be observed here."[32]

The commitment of the evangelical Presbyterian clergy to strong pastoral guidance was also evidenced by their readiness to edit their parishioners' accounts of their spiritual experiences prior to making them public. Robe's colleague, the Rev. William McCulloch, minister at Cambuslang, outside Glasgow, collected numerous such accounts during the revivals of the 1740s. While, as Leigh Schmidt has pointed out, the immediacy of the accounts suggests that they were fairly direct transcriptions of the words of the laity, McCulloch and other clergy later went through the manuscripts bracketing material they thought should be excised prior to publication.[33] According to Schmidt, the excised material was comprised almost entirely of references to "ecstatic religious experience, such as visions, voices, and trances."[34] The pastors, whether face-to-face or through the publication of edited testimonies, emphasized the point that visions, voices, and trances were natural phenomena and thus could not to be construed as evidence of the supernatural.

METHODISTS

Ironically, Wesley and the Methodist tradition embraced as integral to the task of reforming the church and spreading scriptural holiness precisely the things that Edwards and the Reformed tradition viewed as the *cause* of enthusiasm and thus sought to avoid. Wesley not only eschewed any rigorous distinction between natural and supernatural, he also built the Methodist movement by mobilizing a vast network of lay leaders with no formal training and creating innumerable lay-led small groups. Since the ultimate criterion for judging experience was the "fruits of the Spirit," he sought to avoid enthusiasm by formalizing his use of lay leadership and small groups and providing them with strict standards and practical guidelines.[35]

Small groups emerged as a means of intensifying devotion within both the Church of England and the Lutheran Church in Germany during the seventeenth century. These small groups or "societies" formed the basis for the Pietist movement in Germany beginning in the seventeenth century and the Methodist movement in England in the eighteenth.[36] The formation of societies within the Lutheran Church drew its inspiration from Philipp Spener's *Pia Desideria* (1675). Spener, believing that public preaching was "not always fully and adequately comprehended" and that private reading of scripture did not always "provide the reader with sufficient explanation," encouraged Lutheran pastors to "reintroduce the ancient and apostolic kind of church meetings" described in the Letters of Paul. Clergy would organize and lead such meetings, but they would not preach. In them, lay persons "who have been blessed with gifts and knowledge" would be encouraged to speak and "present their pious opinions on the proposed subject to the judgment of the rest."[37]

The Moravians, as they were known in England, were a radical pietist group from Eastern Europe who found refuge at Herrnnut in Germany under the leadership of Count Nikolaus Ludwig von Zinzendorf. The community at Herrnhut was divided into "choirs" composed of men and women of all ages, both single and married, that were similar in many ways to Wesley's later "societies." Additionally, there were small voluntary groups of five to ten people at the same stage of spiritual development called "bands," upon which Wesley modeled his "bands" and "class meetings." The Moravians also celebrated an Agape meal of bread and water that was taken up as the Methodist "love-feast" and, as inveterate hymn-singers, the Moravians also provided many of the hymns that fueled the Methodist movement, especially in its early stages.[38]

Religious societies intent on revitalizing devotion within the Church of England emerged in the late seventeenth century. By 1700 there were more than forty of these "little devotional cells" in London and the surrounding towns. According to John Walsh, they pursued " 'real holiness of heart and life' by a regimen of self-examination, fasting, attendance at church and sacrament, and weekly meetings for 'pious conference', often in church vestries." These cells were strictly confined to members of the Church of England and were normally presided over by a clerical spiritual director.[39] When John Wesley returned from Georgia and his encounter there with the Moravians, he and James Hutton formed the religious society that met at a house on Fetter Lane. This, and the religious society founded by Hutton on Aldersgate Street shortly thereafter, were simplified versions of the Anglican religious societies. They differed primarily in avoiding a set-pattern of devotion and in their inclusion of Moravians and other non-Anglicans. Both societies were later divided into "bands" following the Moravian model (*JW* 9:6–7). According to Walsh, the rapid growth of early Methodism was due in large part to its ability "to cannibalize the religious societies of London, Bristol and elsewhere" for Methodist purposes.[40]

Wesley wrote the first set of "Rules of the Band Societies" in 1738, soon after his return from visiting the Moravians in Germany. The meetings of the "band societies" were centered on confession and prayer. They opened with singing and prayer, followed by the confession of faults to the group, and concluded with "prayer, suited to the state of each person present." Members were instructed "to speak, each . . . in order, freely and plainly the true state of our souls, with the faults we have committed in thought, word, or deed, and the temptations we have felt since our last meeting." While the meetings were not intended as a substitute either for private and family prayer or for formal confession in the context of the liturgy, the "band societies" provided the primary locus for intimate, personal confession for those not accustomed to keeping a spiritual diary.

In addition to outlining the purposes and procedures of the "band societies" (later called "class meetings"), the rules provided a series of questions that persons had to answer before being admitted to the group. A number of the questions related to the person's readiness to engage in the group process. Thus, questions inquired about their willingness to "speak everything that is in [their] heart" and to hear of their faults, even if in doing so "we should cut to the quick, and search your heart to the bottom." Other questions probed their experiential readiness, embedding matters at the heart of Wesley's theology at the center of Christian practice. Here the crucial questions were: "Have you the forgiveness of your sins? Have you peace with God? . . . Have you the witness of God's Spirit with your spirit that you are a child of God? Is the love of God shed abroad in your heart? Has no sin, inward or outward, dominion over you?" (*JW* 9:77–79).

Within another year, John Wesley and George Whitefield formed the first specifically Methodist society in Bristol. "The society" soon came to designate the basic Methodist organizational unit (within the Church of England) in a given locale. Bands and, within a few years, class meetings were subgroupings within the societies designed to facilitate the spiritual growth of their members. During the 1740s, Wesley encouraged the proliferation of small groups, each serving specialized needs. "Select societies" encouraged the most spiritually advanced within the bands to "press after perfection." Other specialized subgroups were established in some locations for "backsliders" who had repented. While bands were maintained in some of the larger societies, class meetings in time superseded all other small groups as the basic small group within the society. Leadership of the bands and classes was provided by lay leaders, recruited from among the membership, and originally appointed by Wesley (JW 9:10–14, 269–70).

Eventually Wesley appointed lay preachers (referred to in English Methodism as "assistants") who traveled from society to society preaching and were charged with visiting the classes and bands and overseeing their leaders (JW 9:270–71). At the start, however, Wesley did all of this himself. For our purposes, the key feature of this oversight process was that it entailed, as Wesley put it, the separation of "the precious from the vile." To this end, he says:

> I determined, at least once in three months, to talk with every member myself, and to inquire at their own mouths, as well as of their leaders and neighbors, whether they grew in grace and in the knowledge of our Lord Jesus Christ. . . . To each of those of whose seriousness and good conversation I found no reason to doubt I gave a testimony under my own hand, by writing their name on a *ticket* prepared for that purpose. . . . By these it was easily distinguished when the society were to meet apart [from the larger church], who were members of it and who not.

The tickets, which endured for some generations within Methodism, supplied Wesley with (as he put it) "a quiet and inoffensive method of removing any disorderly member" from the Methodist society and the primary means by which he could protect the societies from the threat of enthusiasm (i.e., experience without "fruits" or "growth in grace"). Tickets were reissued quarterly and if a person had "no new ticket at the quarterly visitation . . . it [was] immediately known that he [was] no longer of this community." Numerous members were expelled using this system, especially in the early years (JW 9:265, 11).

Narrating Experience

MODERATE CONGREGATIONALISTS

The moderate Reformed understanding of experience was developed and promoted in the context of parish-based, clerically supervised revivals. Within the narrowly defined range of authentic experience, an experience of conversion and continuing experiences of the "operations of the Spirit of God" were expected. As Edwards made clear in his commentary, Brainerd's life exemplified the moderate Reformed ideal because (1) he had a "*clear work* of saving conversion," (2) "his experiences [of the "operations of the Spirit of God"], rather than dying away, were evidently of an increasing nature," and (3) his experience did not consist of "strong impressions on his imagination" [i.e., visions or voices] or "supposed immediate witness of the Spirit" (JE 7:500–505).

Certain distinctive phrases were used in the narratives to describe these "operations of the Spirit of God," which, while not "signs" or "marks" of authenticity in a theological sense, can be considered signs of authenticity in a literary sense. Entries in David Brainerd's diary that describe his Indian converts' response to his preaching suggest the language and range of expression appropriate to those under conviction. Congregants were, he said, "melted into tears," "wept aloud," and "appeared earnestly concerned." An assembly could demonstrate "a very considerable moving and affectionate melting" or a "tenderness and melting engagement." According to Brainerd, "very desirable . . . effects of the Word" included: "an earnest attention, a great solemnity, many tears and heavy sighs," as long as such expressions were "modestly suppressed in a considerable measure, and appeared unaffected and without any indecent commotion of the passions" (JE 7:375, 378–80).

Brainerd limited communion, following traditional Congregational practice, to those who had demonstrated convincing evidence of salvation. Following a day of "solemn prayer and fasting"— including prayers that God's divine presence might be with them at the table, a sermon on the Lord's Supper, and catechesis of those preparing to partake—Brainerd administered the sacrament to them for the first time.

> The ordinance was attended with great solemnity, and with a most desirable tenderness and affection. . . . The affections of the communicants, although considerably raised, were notwithstanding agreeably regulated and kept within proper bounds. So that there was a sweet, gentle, and affectionate melting, without any indecent or boistrous commotion of the passions.

Conversing with the communicants in their homes afterwards, he "found they had been almost universally refreshed at the Lord's table." The "appearance of Christian love" among them was such that "nothing less could be said of it than that it was 'the doing of the Lord' " (JE 7:383–87).

The personal narratives of Abigail Hutchinson, Sarah Edwards, and David Brainerd all included these experiences of "sweetness" and being "refreshed," as well as more intense experiences of being "swallowed up" or "ravished" by God. Edwards said of his wife, for example, that her soul frequently dwelled "in such views of the glory of the divine perfections, and Christ's excellencies, that the soul . . . has been as it were perfectly overwhelmed, and swallowed up with light and love . . . that was altogether unspeakable." He said that her soul "more than once" continued in this fashion "for five or six hours together" and while it "dwelt on high, and was lost in God," Edwards said, it "seemed almost to leave the body" (JE 4:332).[41] At the height of his conversion experience, David Brainard recounted: "My soul was so captivated and delighted with the excellency, the loveliness and the greatness and other perfections of God that I was even swallowed up in him, at least to that degree that I had no thought, as I remember at first, about my own salvation or scarce that there was such a creature as I" (*JE* 7:138–39 [mss. version]).[42]

Many moderate Congregationalists probably experienced their most intense religious emotions, both at the time of conversion and beyond, in the context of secret or closet devotions. The diary upon which Edwards's *Life of Brainerd* was based was written during these times of private devotion, as were most Congregationalist spiritual diaries. This kind of devotional practice presupposed, not only literacy, but engagement with a tradition of biblical interpretation spelled out in devotional guides. Devout Congregationalists internalized the tradition by chronicling their spiritual progress in their diaries.[43] The Puritan tradition was "undogmatic" regarding the particular setting and posture for such devotions, but secret devotions were associated with solitude and the absence of sensory stimulation. Moreover, whether one lay down, sat, stood, or walked while engaging prayer and meditation, one's posture was to be "reverent," that is "composed to rest and quiet."[44]

Of all the practices that constituted Brainerd's secret devotions, Edwards singled out one—fasting—for special attention. Edwards noted a close correlation between Brainerd's secret fasts and the special blessings he received from God. "Among all the many days he spent in secret fasting and prayer that he gives an account of in his diary," Edwards said, "there is scarce an instance of one but what was either attended or soon followed with apparent success and a remarkable blessing in special incomes and consolations of God's Spirit; and very often before the day was ended" (*JE* 7:531). In fact, Edwards went so far as to suggest that Brainerd's dedication to "secret prayer and fasting . . . kept [his experiences] up in their height" even after "religion decayed again" in the wake of the revival and thus, that secret prayer and fasting, more than anything else, revealed "the right way of practicing religion" in order to obtain an abiding change of nature (*JE* 7:502).

Although Edwards noted a correlation between Brainerd's days of "secret fasting and prayer" and his reception of "remarkable blessings . . . of God's Spirit," even referring to fasting as "the right way of practicing religion in order to obtain the ends of it," Edwards, good Calvinist that he was, did not grant fasting causal efficacy in this regard. Indeed the relationship of practices, even such highly touted practices as fasting, to the longed-for blessings of God's Spirit was a paradoxical one. The thoroughgoing internalization of Calvinist theology meant that Reformed Protestants, more than other evangelicals, insisted that the *means* of grace could not and did not cause the *experience* of grace. The paradoxical relationship between means and experience is illustrated in the conversion of David Brainerd.

Brainerd's conversion turned on the insight that "there was no necessary connection between my prayers, and the bestowment of divine mercy, that they laid not the least obligation of God to bestow his grace upon me, for I never intended his glory in them, and that there was no more virtue or goodness in my praying than there would be in my paddling with my hands in the water" (*JE* 7:134 [mss version]). Ironically, however, the way in which all his efforts were "rendered odious" was through a vision that Jonathan Edwards excised from the published text. The vision was of "a stately house" against which Brainerd had been "heaping up dirt, filth, and rubbish . . . supposing [he] was doing the building some service." In the vision, he realized that the building "did not need the assistance of any of [his] pile of dirt" and that he was "eclips[ing] the glory of the building by throwing rubbish against it" (*JE* 7:134–35 [mss version]). "The application" of the vision, he added, "was instantly this, that I had been heaping up my devotions before God, fasting, praying, etc., pretending and indeed really thinking that at some times I was aiming at his glory, when I never once intended his honor and glory but only my own happiness" (*JE* 7:135–36 [mss version]). With this he reached the depths of self-abasement, concluding that all his efforts were "nothing but self-worship and a horrid abuse of God" (ibid., 137). It was shortly thereafter, during an early morning walk in which he was "endeavoring to pray" that " 'unspeakable glory' seemed to open to the view and apprehension of [his] soul."

Like other Reformed editors of experiential narratives, Edwards edited Brainerd's diary before he published it. He excised this vision and generally suppressed the "vitality" of Brainerd's prose. The David Brainerd who emerged from Edwards's hand was, to paraphrase Norman Pettit, a far less imaginative and less desperate man than the one who appeared in the original diary (*JE* 7:81–82). In large measure, Edwards's editing furthered his expressed goal of demonstrating to the "high pretenders to religion" that inward vital religion need not involve strong impressions on the imagination. Ironically, the manuscript evidence contradicts Edwards's claim that in reading Brainerd's "diary over and over . . . [he found] no one instance of a strong impression on his imagination."

RADICAL (SEPARATE) CONGREGATIONALISTS

Although their opponents preserved many secondhand accounts of direct religious experience among the separate Congregationalists, the radicals published few first-person accounts. This absence likely marks the radicals' shift away from recording their experiences in diaries in the context of secret devotions to narrating their experiences aloud in the context of separatist meetings. Nathan Cole, a Connecticut layman whose narrative of his "Spiritual Travels" was never published, provides one of the few surviving first-person accounts of Separate Congregationalist experience. It mirrors and breaks with Brainerd's narrative in significant ways.

Cole's conversion began when he heard Whitefield preach in 1740. After two years of distress in which "hell fire was most always in [his] mind," the turning point came for Cole, as for Brainerd, in a vision. At his lowest point, when he was ready to "creep into that fire and lye there and burn to death and die forever," he wrote:

> God appeared unto me and made me Skringe [sic]: before whose face the heavens and
> the earth fled away; and I was Shrinked into nothing; I knew not whether I was in the
> body or out, I seemed to hang in open Air before God, and he seemed to Speak to me

in an angry and Sovereign way what won't you trust your Soul with God; My heart
answered O yes, yes, yes; before I could stir my tongue or lips. . . . Now while my Soul
was viewing God, my fleshly part was working imaginations and saw many things which
I will omitt to tell at this time. When God appeared to [me] every thing vanished. . . .
But when God disappeared or in some measure withdrew, every thing was in its place
again and I was on my Bed.[45]

As a result of the vision, he said: "I was set free, my distress was gone, and I was
filled with a pineing desire to see Christs own words in the bible." Opening to
John 15, "Christs own words . . . spake to my very heart . . . and I believe I felt
just as the Apostles felt the truth of the word when they writ it, every leas[t] line
and letter smiled in my face; I got the bible up under my Chin & hugged it; it
was sweet and lovely; the word was nigh me in my hand, then I began to pray
and to praise God. . . . I was swallowed up in God."[46]

Cole's account, like the accounts discussed by Edwards, was shot through with
Calvinist theology. Like Brainerd and many others, Cole described himself as
"swallowed up in God." For the most part, however, it is the differences between
Brainerd and Cole that are instructive. Not only was Cole obviously less literate
than Brainerd, his style was very different as well. In Cole's account we surely
have what Jonathan Edwards would have called an "impression on the imagination" and possibly a "trance and vision" as well. Here, in contrast to Brainerd's
Life or any other narrative utilized by Edwards, God appeared to Cole face to face
and spoke to him. God and Nathan Cole then engaged in a dialogue. Cole's vivid
and graphic prose, reads more like a story than an entry in a spiritual diary.

Where scripture was mediated for Brainerd by a written interpretive tradition,
Cole's engagement was more direct. As a result of his vision, "the word," literally
and figuratively, became the focus of Cole's attention and desire. Cole anthropo-
morphized literal words and letters and the words and letters assumed a mystical
agency totally absent from Brainerd's account. "Christs own words . . . spake" and
"every leas[t] line & letter smiled in my face." Cole's emphasis on the Word, his
devotional engagment with the words as words, and the bible as object ("I got the
bible up under my Chin & hugged it"), suggest, on the one hand, a theology that
emphasized an unmediated reading of the sacred text, and, on the other, a relatively uneducated man unhabituated to the interpretive traditions that Brainerd
took for granted.

Finally, where Brainerd struggled with the question of assurance throughout
his life, Cole received "the sealing evidence" of assurance by means of another
vision: "It seemed as if I really saw the gate of heaven by an Eye of faith, & the
way for Sinners to Get to heaven by Jesus Christ; as plain as I ever saw anything
with my bodily eyes in my life."[47] Although he distinguished between the "bodily
eyes" and the "Eye of faith" in a way that Robe would have appreciated, both the
fact of his visions and their content would have been problematic in the eyes of
the moderate Congregationalist clergy.

Visions of heaven, and especially visions in which the visionary was allowed to
read from the Book of Life, were common among Separates. An Anglican mission-

ary described the typical Separate conversion experience as a two-part drama: "The tragic scene is performed by such as are entering into the pangs of ye New Birth; the comic by those who are got thro' and those are so truly enthusiastic, that they tell you they saw the Joys of Heaven, can describe its situation, inhabitants, employments & have seen their names entered into the Book of Life & can point out the writer, character & pen."[48] Seeing one's name written in the Book of Life was about as concrete and graphic an answer as one could expect to the question of whether or not one was saved. This was, of course, the sort of solution to the problem of assurance that left all but more radical sorts crying out about enthusiasm and antinomianism.

The moderate Congregationalist polemic against speaking out in public worship suggests that those with a more radical or Separatist orientation encouraged people to express intense religious feeling in the context of public worship. While people were generally quite restrained when George Whitefield preached, certain elements in his style of preaching undoubtedly encouraged the new trend. In his recent biography of Whitefield, Harry Stout describes Whitefield's emphasis on the feelings attendant to the new birth. "Repeatedly," Stout says, "he asked his listeners to imagine a different state of being, to imagine being birthed into a new creature." Most distinctive, however, was not the emphasis on the affections, but the way he "performed" his sermons. Specifically, according to Stout, Whitefield inserted his body into his discourse.

> Even though his sermons were written out in classic Anglican fashion, his body did not—could not—remain still in the prescribed fashion. From the start of his preaching, apparently without premeditation or guile, he evidenced a dramatic manner that remained a hallmark of his preaching style throughout his career. A sarcastic account . . . called attention . . . to . . . his bodily manner: 'Hark! he talks of a Sensible New Birth— then belike he is in Labour, and the good Women around him are come to his assistance. He dilates himself, cries out [and] is at last delivered.'[49]

It does not seem farfetched to suggest that Whitefield's graphic enactment of new birth may well have sparked some of the more graphic enactments of the same by lay people, both in private, as in the case of Nathan Cole, and in public, as in the case of James Davenport and those he inspired.

Davenport apparently was so taken with Whitefield's manner of preaching that he followed him to New York and Philadelphia in order to learn to imitate him.[50] Contemporary descriptions suggest not only that he exaggerated Whitefield's dramatic delivery but that he did so in order to elicit a response from the congregation. Looking back on the awakening, the moderate Congregationalist minister Joseph Fish indicated that Davenport gave

> an unrestrained liberty to *noise* and *outcry*, both of *distress* and *joy*, in time of divine service, . . . promot[ing] *both* with all his might—by extending his own voice to the highest pitch, together with the most violent agitation of body, even to the distorting of his features and marring his visage. . . . And all this, with a strange, unnatural *singing* tone, which mightily tended to *raise* or *keep up* the affection of the weak and undiscern-

ing people, and consequently, to heighten the confusion among the *passionate* of his hearers. Which odd and ungrateful *tuning* of the *voice*, in exercises of devotion, has, from thence, been propagated down to the present day [1765], and is become *one* of the characteristics of a *false spirit*, and especially of a *separate*; that *sect* almost universally distinguished by such a *tone*.[51]

Davenport's style of preaching—his bodily movements and the tone of his voice—promoted "distress and joy [in the congregation] in time of divine service." His preaching, in other words, promoted the experience of conversion *in the context of divine worship*. The noise, outcry, and confusion were the sounds of people "experiencing" in the context of public worship. There is also evidence that alongside the "strange, unnatural *singing* tone" used in preaching, Davenport also encouraged a new style of highly repetitious congregational singing, in which he, according to one diarist, "Called the people to Sing a New Song & forevere 30 or 40 times or more & yn Something Else & then over with it again."[52]

Davenport and other radical Congregationalists encouraged the proliferation of lay public exhorters. The exhorters often led meetings for social worship where they exhorted and prayed for those they believed unsaved. Radicals also encouraged people to experience and express feelings associated with conversion in the context of both public and social worship. Institutionally, they separated from the established Congregational Church in order to create what they hoped would be purer congregations comprised only of the converted, while still maintaining the Congregational practice of infant baptism. Caught between the idea of an established, territorial church and the idea of a church for believers only, the Separate Congregationalists did not survive long as a distinct body.[53] The more traditional among them were absorbed back into established (nonseparating) Congregationalist congregations, while the more radical either formed or joined Baptist churches, where adult baptism became the primary ritual marker of their conversion experience.[54] The trances, visions, and distinctive practices of the Separate Congregationalists were preserved and elaborated by the Separate Baptists.

The Separate Baptists experienced their most remarkable growth, not in New England, but in the South. Shubal Stearns, converted by Whitefield during his second visit to New England in 1745, was the leading Separate Congregationalist missionary to the South and the founding father of the Separate Baptists. He, along with others, carried the distinctive Separatist style of worship to the South, where "the strange, unnatural singing tone" continued as "an unmistakable mark of a man who spoke as a mouthpiece of the Holy Spirit."[55] In conjunction with the late-eighteenth-century revivals in Virginia, the Separate Baptists played a significant role in the development of the shout tradition.

METHODISTS

The Methodist movement, premised on the proliferation of biblically informed but theologically unsophisticated lay leaders and lay-led religious groups, embraced Wesley's tendency to blur the distinction between the natural and supernatural. Methodists developed and promoted Wesley's narrative tendency to attribute all "outward symptoms" of true Christians to the power of God in contexts where narratives were socially enacted and orally narrated. This style of narrative was present from the start of the movement and, while particularly well suited to persons lacking in education or even basic literacy, was never limited to them.

To take a paradigmatic instance, Wesley reported in a journal entry dated January 1, 1739, that he and five other university-educated clergy, including George Whitefield and his brother Charles, were present "at our love-feast in Fetter Lane, with about sixty of our brethren."

> About three in the morning, as we were continuing instant in prayer, *the power of God came mightily upon us,* insomuch that *many cried out for exceeding joy,* and *many fell to the ground.* As soon as we were recovered from shock and amazement at the presence of his majesty, we broke out with one voice, 'We praise thee, O God; we acknowledge thee to be the Lord.' (*JW* 19:29 emphasis added)

This narrative, like Brainerd's description of his Indian congregants, described a collective experience. The language, however, was strikingly different. Here "the power of the God came mightily upon us" and "many cried out for . . . joy" and "many fell to the ground." God was quite definitely present and people cried out and fell to the ground when the power of God came upon them. Moreover, this took place, not in a preaching or communion service or in private devotions, but at a "love-feast," the Agape meal of "plain cake and water" adapted from the Moravians (*JW* 9:267–68).

This sort of language came to characterize Methodist experience narratives. In an entry dated April 17, 1739, Wesley described a meeting in Bristol in which a young woman named Hannah Cornish "(to our no small surprise) cried out aloud, with the utmost vehemence, even as in the agonies of death." On April 21, "a young man was suddenly seized with violent trembling all over, and in a few minutes, 'the sorrows of his heart being enlarged', sunk down to the ground." By April 26, Wesley simply wrote: "Immediately one and another and another sunk to the earth: they dropped on every side as thunderstruck" (*JW* 19:49–51). Understood in relation to the individual, the "sinking to the ground" often signaled the onset of the experience of new birth. Writing to his brother Samuel in May 1739, Wesley gave a fuller description:

> While we were praying at a society here . . . , the power of God (for so I call it) came so mightily among us that one, and another, and another fell down as thunderstruck. In that hour many that were in deep anguish of spirit were all filled with peace and joy. Ten persons till then in sin, doubt, and fear, found such a change that sin had no more dominion over them; and instead of the spirit of fear they are now filled with that of love, and joy, and a sound mind. (*JW* 25:646)

In some instances, crying out or falling to the ground was understood as confirmation of scripture or doctrine. Although Wesley indicated that he was surprised when Hannah Cornish cried aloud, Wesley had actually just called for such a "sign." After preaching on Acts 4, Wesley said, "We . . . called upon God to confirm his word [that 'signs and wonders may be done by the name . . . of Jesus']."

It was then that Hannah Cornish cried out, soon followed by three others. These persons were, for Wesley, "living witnesses" whose experiences confirmed God's word. From this, he concluded, quoting Acts 4:30, that "[God's] hand is *still* stretched out to heal, and that signs and wonders are even *now* wrought by his holy child Jesus" (*JW* 19:49, emphasis in original). On April 26, Wesley, in a similar fashion, called upon God to "bear witness" to the truth of his repudiation of the Calvinist doctrine of predestination. He stated: "I was sensibly led, without any previous design, to declare strongly and explicitly that God 'willeth all men to be *thus* saved' and to pray that if this were not the truth of God, he would not suffer the blind to go out of the way; but if it were, he would bear witness to his Word." Immediately thereafter people again began falling to the ground.

Wesley did warn his followers in these early years that "dreams, visions, or revelations," as well as "tears or any involuntary effects wrought upon their bodies[,] . . . were in themselves of a doubtful, disputable nature: they *might* be from God and they *might not*, and were therefore not simply to be relied on (any more than simply condemned) but to be . . . brought to the only certain test, 'the law and the testimony.' " Such cautions, however, did not cause these phenomena to subside. In this instance, as he was cautioning them, "one . . . dropped down as dead, and presently a second and a third." Within the next half hour, "five others sunk down . . . , most of whom were in violent agonies" (*JW* 19:73).

Wesley indicated in these early journal entries that while everyone witnessed the "signs and wonders (for so I must term them), yet many would not believe." Skeptics did not deny that the "involuntary effects" were occurring; they simply attempted, as Wesley said, to "*explain* them away" (*JW* 19:60). According to Wesley,

> Some said, 'These were purely *natural* effects; the people fainted away only because of the heat and closeness of the rooms.' And others were sure 'It was all a cheat: they might help it if they would. Else why were these things only in their private societies? Why were they not done in the face of the sun?' (*JW* 19:60)

Then in a tone that would echo through countless later Methodist narratives, Wesley responded: "Today, Monday [May] 21, our Lord answered for himself. For while I was enforcing these words, 'Be still, and know that I am God', he began to make bare his arm, not in a close room, neither in private, but in the open air, and before more than two thousand witnesses. One and another and another was struck to the earth, exceedingly trembling at the presence of his power" (*JW* 19:60).

This is a quintessential example of the use of a sacralizing narrative to counter secularizing explanations. Modeled on biblical narrative, it placed "our Lord" as a character in the narrative of events ("our Lord answered"). It juxtaposed challenging explanations proffered by skeptical humans ("heat," "closeness of the rooms," and fraud conducted in private) with a divine response ("our Lord . . . began to make bare his arm") that negated the explanations ("in the open air" and "before . . . witnesses"). The many who fell were tacitly cast as testifying through their trembling bodies to "the presence of [God's] power."

A month later, Wesley confessed that he and others had been having doubts about these phenomena and that as a result God had "withdrawn his Spirit" from them. Their "unfaithfulness," he said, was manifest "above all by blaspheming [God's] work among us, imputing it either to nature, to the force of imagination and animal spirits, or even to the delusion of the devil." Wesley was not only aware of the competing naturalistic explanations, the explanations were compelling enough to lead him to doubt that the phenomena in question were the work of God. He viewed his doubts as a sign of his lack of faith and proceeded to confess them.

In resisting naturalistic explanation, Wesley chose a different route than did Edwards or Robe. While he did not always resist naturalistic explanations of such phenomena this sharply and at times acknowledged such phenomena as natural responses to the work of God, he continued, as we have seen, to leave room for viewing them within a sacred narrative of the work of God. In doing so, Wesley did not simply override his doubts. He put them to the test, but he did so within the scripturally grounded mythic framework he and his followers were developing. Thus, as in the previous example, their faith was vindicated, when, after they confessed their doubts, the bodily phenomena once again resumed.

Five years later, Wesley wrote to Mrs. Hutton that the "fits (as you term them) are not left off. They are frequent now, both in Europe and America, among persons newly convinced of sin. I neither forward nor hinder them" (JW 26:113). Wesley was correct that "fits" were still frequent both in Europe and America in 1744, but they would soon subside, as would the revivals themselves, in Reformed strongholds, such as New England and Scotland. Both the revival and the related dreams, visions, and involuntary bodily movements endured for decades under Methodist auspices. In a refreshingly frank discussion of Methodist historiography, Stephen Gunter indicates that "for two centuries students of the Methodist revival have tended to 'play down' Wesley's emphasis on . . . miraculous intervention." The fact is, he writes, that "[Wesley] searched incessantly for testimonies of conversion experiences which would substantiate the validity of his claim that human experience was a form of proof for divine activity." According to Gunter,

> Even Charles, who was more resistant to this emphasis than John, requested the converts to provide written accounts of their conversion experiences. Scores of letters by converts were sent to Charles fulfilling this request, many of which have been preserved. A reading of these accounts will destroy the myth that this emphasis was short-lived.[56]

The tendency to minimize the supernatural aspects of these accounts, as Gunter suggests, "can probably best be accounted for by recognizing a personal aversion to such phenomena on the part of scholars themselves."[57]

For our purposes, the crucial point is that Wesley's narrative tendency to attribute all "outward symptoms" of true Christians to the power of God was developed and promoted in classes, bands, and love-feasts, that is, in what some referred to collectively as Methodist *experience-meetings.* These meetings were intended, as Wesley said, "to encourage free and familiar conversation in which every man, yea and every woman, has liberty to speak whatever may be to the glory of God."[58]

Such meetings, in the words of John Walsh, made room "for plebeian spontaneity and for orality as well as literacy in the life of the societies."[59] They provided the context, in other words, in which experience was socially enacted and given form as oral narrative. They also provided the occasion for recounting (or witnessing to) one's experience and thus provided models of authentic experience for others. Unlike private devotions, which were not social, and public worship, which was not personal, experience-meetings gave voice to the individual within the society. As one unsympathetic Anglican priest complained: "I have great objection to 'experience meetings' . . . they are a short sermon upon the little word 'I.' "[60]

Although the Reformed tradition developed voluntary societies, their purpose was not to foster the spiritual development of the laity. Hymns were sung in church and piety was practiced in private. Methodism changed all that. The Methodist tradition encouraged, indeed demanded, that its members participate in small groups designed to foster their spiritual development. These groups required lay people intent on "fleeing the wrath to come" and "going on to perfection" to do so in a semipublic setting. In the context of class meetings, bands, love-feasts, and watch nights, Methodists sang the hymns of Christian experience written by Charles Wesley and testified to their own "experience." By locating experience in this context, Methodists did two things that set them apart from their Congregationalist and Presbyterian contemporaries. First, they created a quasi-public space in which they expected that they might physically experience the power of God. Second, by locating such experiences in communal, lay-led spaces and linking authenticity with observable "fruits" rather than nuanced philosophical distinctions, they democratized the process whereby such experiences were authenticated. Both developments were relative and should be hedged with qualifications. Nonetheless, the location of religious experience in a relatively democratic quasi-public space laid the groundwork for the further elaboration of the Methodist experience of the power of God and the further elaboration of spaces in which this power might be known in the decades that followed.

CHAPTER THREE

Shouting Methodists

AMONG THE camp-meeting songs that have come down to us from the early-nine-teenth century is one titled simply "The Methodist." From it we learn not only that Wesley's followers in America were "despised . . . because they shout and preach so plain," but also that they proudly referred to themselves as "shouting Methodists."[1] Because the tradition of "shouting" was developed and passed on by means of embodied performance, the sources do not tell us what it meant to "shout" in any systematic fashion. We get glimpses of what it meant and how it changed over time from the letters and journals of participants in early American Methodist revivals and from camp-meeting songs preserved in later collections of black and white spirituals. Perhaps the single most helpful source, and one to which I return frequently throughout this chapter, was written by John Fanning Watson, a lay Methodist from Philadelphia alarmed by the ritualistic elaboration of shouting in the context of public worship.

Watson's book, titled *Methodist Error; or, Friendly Christian advice to those Methodists who indulge in extravagant emotions and bodily exercises*, was published anonymously in 1814.[2] In it, Watson emphasized that he was not opposed to extravagant emotions and bodily exercises at the time of conversion or in private devotion, but on the part of converted Christians in the context of public worship.[3] Reflecting the standards disseminated among Methodists through Wesley's editions of Edwards's writings, Watson argued that such exercises were appropriate in "closet" devotions because it was there, rather than in public or social worship, that persons "enter more peculiarly into the very presence of Deity" and because there persons might be "as vehement" as they liked "without offense to others" (ME-1819, 27).

Watson framed the practices he found objectionable as "enthusiasm," providing numerous extracts on the subject from the writings of John Wesley, John Fletcher, Adam Clarke, Jonathan Edwards, and John Locke in his introduction and appendices. In the main body of the work, he specified the practices he deplored and the scriptural passages used by Methodists to legitimate them. He anticipated that his "exposures" would lead "some well-meaning Methodists" to conclude that he had betrayed their cause through indiscretion. But he justified his forthrightness on the grounds that such exercises were prejudicing their fellow Philadelphians against them (ME-1814, 13) and he addressed Methodists with the evident hope that "respectable" Philadelphians would be reading, so to speak, over his shoulders. Drawing these onlookers in, he admitted to them what "we [Methodists] have all long known," that is, "that there has been considerable division of sentiment among us, respecting the *character* of our religious exercises." While the majority of Methodists were, he claimed, "sober and steady" and desired decent and orderly worship, "the minor part, have been, on the contrary, very zealous for . . . outward signs of the most heedless emotion" (*ME*-1814, 7). It was this "minor part" of Methodism that had given it a reputation that was, in his view, undeserved.

Watson marginalized these more "zealous" Methodists by positioning them as a minority and marking them both in terms of race and class. Those, he wrote, who "learn a *habit* of vehemence [are] . . . mostly persons of credulous, *uninformed* minds; who, before their change to grace had been of rude education, and careless of those prescribed forms of good manners and refinement, of which polite education is never divested—and which, indeed, religion ought to cherish. They fancy that all the restraints of conduct, viz. 'sobriety, gravity and blamelessness,' is a formality and resistance of the Spirit;—and so to avoid it, they seem rather to go to the other extreme, and actually run before it" (*ME*-1814, 10). He noted, too, that the new songs, "often miserable as poetry, and senseless as matter, . . . [are] most frequently composed and first sung by the illiterate *blacks* of our society" (*ME*-1814, 15). After describing the noisiness of a service at Bethel, the "mother" church of African Methodism, he stated that "they have now parted from us [the MEC], and we are not sorry" (*ME*-1814, 13).

In his preface to the "improved edition" of 1819, he reported that Methodism had gone up in the eyes of outsiders as a result of his book, "because they now perceive that the excesses *of a few*, were never the acts *of the whole*." He made it clear that he had written with the interests of "the great 'substantial middle class' " in mind, those who, in his words, "were too often offended in their instinctive sympathies, tastes and feelings, to come enough among us, to be profited by the soundness of our general doctrine." Because Methodists taught that "Christ died *for all*[,] . . . to be content with any partial success, or to regard the poor, or illiterate, as their only hope, or only accountable charge, would be neither Scriptural, nor politic; and certainly contrary to obvious fact" (*ME*-1819, v). Not only were the "excesses of the few" firmly identified with the poor and illiterate, but in a new footnote he also took pains to locate the origins of these "errors" elsewhere. "It began," he said, "in Virginia, and as I have heard, among the blacks" (*ME*-1819, 27 [note]).

While Watson was forthcoming in his examples and free with his opinions in a way that clearly made the Methodist clergy uncomfortable,[4] he provided historians with an invaluable resource. His descriptions of worship at the Bethel Church in Philadelphia and of singing and dancing at camp meetings in the area by blacks and whites provide some of the earliest Protestant accounts of the call-and-response style in worship, the spirituals, and the ring shout. In his discussions of exegesis, we have clues as to the biblical typologies that informed the emergent camp-meeting tradition and the later interracial Holiness and Pentecostal movements. In short, Watson provided us with evidence to suggest that a new style of public worship had already emerged among Methodists by the first decades of the nineteenth century and that this form of worship had it roots in Virginia.

As Methodist itinerant George Roberts stressed, what reformers found most offensive about this new style of worship was not "the involuntary loud hosannas of . . . pious souls, [but] . . . forming jumping, dancing, shouting, &c. into a *system*, and pushing our social exercises into those extremes."[5]

In this chapter, I focus on the emergence of "shouting Methodists," what Watson referred to as "Methodist enthusiasm and errors," and more specifically the process whereby "jumping, dancing, [and] shouting" were formed into "a system" in the context of public worship. In the previous chapter, I emphasized the role of narratives in the construction of British Methodist experience in class meetings, bands, love-feasts, and watch nights. This chapter emphasizes the way in which "shouting Methodists" utilized biblical narratives and bodily knowledges handed down from Europe and Africa to elaborate on the narratives of their British counterparts and constitute a distinctively American Methodist experience of the power and presence of God in new public spaces. These new publics spaces—the quarterly conferences of the late-eighteenth century and the camp meetings of the early-nineteenth century—emerged as primary contexts in which Methodists might expect to see the power of God manifest through bodily experience.

I argue that shouting Methodists elaborated on the experience of their British counterparts in two ways: by pushing the Methodist performance tradition in a more interactive direction and by interpreting their bodily experiences in light of biblical typologies. The chapter is divided into two parts. The first part surfaces the idioms of the shouting Methodists as they emerged in the interracial revivals in Virginia in the 1770s and 1780s, in the Mid-Atlantic in the 1790s, and in the camp meetings of the early 1800s. I locate what I take to be the shouters' central interpretive act—the association of weeping, crying out, falling to the ground, and shouting for joy with the presence of the power of God—in relation to grassroots pressures to make preaching and worship more interactive. The shouters' attempts to push the Methodist tradition in a more interactive direction were contested by others. Analysis of these controversies suggests that the shouters presupposed a bodily knowledge, derived from the African performance tradition, which insisted that the presence and power of God was most fully realized in the dynamic interaction of the group.

In the second half of the chapter I analyze the idioms of the shouting Methodists as they surfaced through songs, autobiographies, journals, and diaries, focusing on the way shouters used the biblical narrative to sacralize their bodily experiences and the space of the camp. They did so, I argue, through the typological exegesis of scripture, that is, by casting themselves as the "new Israelites" and the camp as "Zion." While the use of typology was not new, scholars have largely missed the way that typological exegesis was employed at the grassroots level, especially in contexts where it was enacted rather than preserved in written commentaries on scripture.[6] The emergence of "shouting Methodists" and the development of the camp-meeting tradition more generally illustrate the role that typological interpretation played in the construction of religious experience at a grassroots level. More comprehensively, analysis of the shouting Methodists allows us to see the way in which early American Methodists narratives of experience drew upon bodily knowledges and biblical narratives, which they both acquired and assumed in practice. These narratives of experience in turn constituted the bodies of believers and the spaces in which they experienced religion in the distinctive form that later generations referred to as "old-time Methodism."

THE SHOUT AS INTERACTIVE PERFORMANCE

Scholars generally trace the origins of the shout tradition back to the revivals of the late-eighteenth century, note its connection with the camp meetings of the early-nineteenth century, and acknowledge its continued existence within the Sanctified, Holiness, and Pentecostal churches of the early-twentieth century.[7] Although most scholars agree that the shout tradition has both European and African roots, recent scholarship, relying on primary sources from the late-nineteenth and early-twentieth centuries, has emphasized the African and Baptist side of that heritage.[8] Relatively little attention has been paid to the emergence of the shout tradition in the context of the late-eighteenth-century revivals.[9] These revivals took place in the region surrounding the Chesapeake Bay in the 1760s, 1770s, and 1780s. While the revivals of the 1760s took place among Baptists and Presbyterians, Baptists and the newly arrived Methodists dominated the revivals of the 1770s and 1780s.[10]

As Russell Richey has pointed out, the historic roots of American Methodism lie in the areas surrounding the Chesapeake Bay: the Delmarva Peninsula, the Western shore from Baltimore to Washington, D.C., and eastern Virginia and northeastern North Carolina.[11] Methodism's rapid rise to become the nation's largest Protestant denomination began with the revivals of the mid-1770s and late 1780s. In the 1770s, growth was most rapid in Virginia and neighboring North Carolina, in part due to the involvement of Devereux Jarratt, an Anglican priest and Methodist sympathizer, whose parish lay within the boundaries of the famous Brunswick circuit near Petersburg, Virginia. Between 1774 and 1777, the Brunswick circuit went from 218 members to 1,360, with its newly formed daughter circuits (Amelia, Sussex, and North Carolina) claiming an additional 2,277 members. Membership again jumped dramatically in a number of circuits in the mid-to-late 1780s. In this period, too, growth was most dramatic on the Brunswick and adjacent circuits.[12]

Components of the Tradition

While Methodists played a considerably larger role in the creation of the shout tradition than has been recognized and provided some of the best documentation for the early period, I do not mean to suggest that they did so alone. Surviving sources suggest that both Separate Baptists and Methodists played a significant role. Nor was shouting mostly a "white" or European American phenomenon. Black membership in the Methodist Episcopal Church was disproportionately concentrated in the Chesapeake Bay region. Although one-fifth of the total denomination was of African descent in 1790, a third or more of Methodists were of African descent in many of the circuits around the Chesapeake. In Virginia, nearly half the population was of African descent as of the late 1780s.[13] By the 1790s, somewhere between a quarter and a third of the Separate Baptists and Methodists in Virginia were black. The revivals of the 1770s and 1780s in Virginia, thus, were thoroughly interracial affairs and the shout tradition was, to paraphrase Mechel Sobel, a tradition "they [Europeans and Africans] made together."

My aim in discussing the shout tradition as a Methodist or, more broadly, a Protestant phenomenon is not to obscure its Africanness, but to document the sacralization of certain kinds of experience within *Christianity* in an interracial and more importantly a *multicultural* context.[14] In order to give a clearer sense of this multicultural mix, I will briefly discuss some of the key ingredients: first, those derived from broad differences in African and European performance styles and, second, specific contributions of the Separate Congregationalists (turned Separate Baptists) and the English Methodists.[15]

EUROPEAN AND AFRICAN PERFORMANCE STYLES

Two very different performance styles—the African and European—met in the context of the Virginia revivals. The most notable differences involved the relationship between music and worship and the interaction between leader and people. Where European worship, especially in the Protestant traditions, placed the emphasis on the word, whether spoken or sung, African worship placed the emphasis on rhythmic interaction, whether spoken or enacted in bodily movements. Where the former encouraged a relatively static relationship between leader and people structured around the formal preaching and singing of the word, the latter emphasized a dynamic interaction between leader and people structured by means of music. The effect of this confluence of styles was apparent in singing, preaching, the use of the body, and the level and meaning of interaction in worship.

Whereas the words of the eighteenth-century hymns were largely derived from Isaac Watts and Charles Wesley, the wandering choruses and spiritual songs were most likely a product of the (interracial) late-eighteenth-century revivals and the early-nineteenth-century camp meetings. The specifically African, as opposed to European or interracial, character of the sung tradition lies in the condensation of meaning,[16] repetition of musical phrases, and marked changes in performance style. Such changes included an emphasis on the improvisation of words and melodies, call-and-response, multiple rhythms operating simultaneously (polyrhythm), and the use of hand-clapping for percussion, all of which are among the most basic and widespread features of African music.[17]

The impact of the African musical tradition reached well beyond singing, in the conventional Western sense of the term, to preaching and dance. In the African context, speech and music were frequently integrated, running on a continuum from speech, recitative, and chant to song. Songs might move into speech and vice versa during the course of a performance, and the entire performance could be shot through with the rhythms of call-and-response or verse and chorus.[18] That the African musical tradition influenced the black preaching styles of the nineteenth and twentieth centuries is widely recognized. LeRoi Jones, for example, describes "the long, long, fantastically rhythmical sermons of the early Negro Baptist and Methodist preachers." Shaped by the traditional African call-and-response song, "the minister would begin slowly and softly, then built his sermon to an unbelievable frenzy with the staccato punctuation of his congregation's answers."[19] We will see that there was considerable congregational pressure on eighteenth-century Methodist preachers to develop a more interactive preaching style. This congregational pressure most likely had its roots in the call-and-response styles to which Africans were accustomed.

Movement and music were also integrated in the African context. Movement was typically an integral part of the music-making process, such that dancers and musicians were often one and the same.[20] African dancing was typically circular. Some early observers commented on a "predilection for 'principally confining [movement] to the head and upper parts of the body' and for 'scarcely moving their feet' or using a shuffle like step." Musicians were often placed in the center of the ring.[21] The ring shout, a circular dance, frequently described in post–Civil War accounts of slave religion has been widely interpreted as an African dance of this sort.[22] Some of the earliest American accounts of such circular dances appear in conjunction with Methodist camp meetings.

Overall, and perhaps most crucially, the nature of African music was interactive. As John Miller Chernoff points out, African music, because of its emphasis on polyrhythm and call-and-response, is always the product of a group interaction. A focus on African rhythms encourages us to shift our mode of viewing away from the actions of individuals—the preacher, the convert, the shouter—to the *interaction* among people in a group. Oddly enough, such an approach brings us back full circle to Chauncy and Edwards's observations about the *interaction* between preacher and congregation. This time, however, such interaction, and indeed the constructedness of the rhythmic interaction, is not a means of *explaining away* the action of the Spirit, but precisely the means whereby the dynamic rhythmic interconnection of individuals-within-a-group emerges and the Spirit is known.[23]

SEPARATE BAPTIST

While Methodism in its British phase constituted a largely separate cultural as well as religious world, this was not the case for indigenous American denominations, such as the Separate Baptists. As descendants of the radical wing of the Great Awakening, the Separatist tradition, as Albert Raboteau and David Wills have shown, was multi-ethnic (European, Indian, and African) in its make-up and probably to some extent multicultural in its practices from the start.[24] Thus, while it is clear that the Separate Baptists carried the distinctive forms of worship and religious experience of the radical wing of the New England awakening into the South, the radicalness of such practices in a transatlantic perspective may be due, at least in part, to Indian and African involvement beginning in New England.

Unfortunately for the historian, the Separate Baptist commitment to direct religious experience was linked to an unwillingness to put things down on paper. This unwillingness extended even to confessional statements. Where Regular (that is, firmly Calvinist) Baptists, in keeping with the Baptist Association of Philadelphia, adopted the London Confession of Faith (1689), the Separates, to the consternation of the Regulars, adhered simply to the Bible, fearing, in the words of one early historian, that "a confession of faith . . . would lead to formality and deadness."[25] Given this fear, as well as their general lack of literacy, it is not surprising that few descriptions of their experiences come to us by way of their own first-person accounts.[26] Most of the early accounts are histories written by Baptist clergy, most notably, Morgan Edwards, John Leland, Robert Semple, and David Benedict, after the Separate Baptists had merged with the Regular Baptists.[27]

According to Morgan Edwards, Separate Baptist "ministers resemble[d] . . . [the radical Congregationalists of New England] in tones of voice and actions of body; and the people in crying-out under the ministry, falling-down as in fits, and awaking in extacies; and both ministers and people resemble those in regarding impulses, visions, and revelations."[28] Leland indicates that "the Regulars were orthodox Calvanists [sic], and the work under them was solemn and rational; but the Separates were the most zealous, and the work among them was very noisy."[29] Robert Semple describes "most of the *Separates*" as having "strong faith in the immediate teachings of the spirit," but does not give specific instances of this.[30] David Benedict indicates the Separates held in their early years to "nine Christian rites, viz. *baptism, the Lord's supper, love-feasts, laying-on-of-hands, washing feet, anointing the sick, right hand of fellowship, kiss of charity, and devoting children*," based on their reading of scripture. Again, presumably in attempt to follow scriptural precedent, the Separates not only appointed men as elders and deacons, but also women as "eldresses" and "deaconesses."[31]

The Separate Baptists' penchant for developing a ritual life directly derived from their reading of scripture without the benefit of mediating theological, devotional, or confessional traditions, was undoubtedly a stimulus to what scholars have called an "iconic" or "pictorial" reading of scripture, in which biblical "scenes" are reenacted in the present. This approach to scripture will characterize the shout tradition more broadly, and is specifically attacked by John Watson in *Methodist Error*. Moreover, one of these practices, the giving of the "right hand in fellowship," still survives in black Baptist churches. In some post–Civil War accounts of ring shouts in slave communities, the giving of the right hand of fellowship marked the transition from the "praise meeting," devoted to singing, praying, and preaching, and the "ring shout."[32]

John Williams, an unusually bookish convert to the Separate Baptist ministry, provided our only first-hand account of Separatist ritual practice. In his journal, he gives a detailed description of a "great meeting" held in Virginia on June 25, 1771, in which the ministers proceeded through cycles of preaching, exhorting, and the taking of experience, punctuated by the "ordinance" of footwashing, and culminating in baptism.[33] The Baptists' ritual focus on baptism by immersion, often in rivers, was as many have noted a key point of contact for European and African Baptists. The River Jordan, a very prominent image in the spirituals associated with the shout tradition, does not come to the fore in Methodist sources and probably reflects the emphasis on baptism on the Baptist side of the shout tradition. Both Methodists and Baptists, however, testified to their experience. In post–Civil War accounts of black Christian practice under slavery, there are numerous references to shouting at "experience meetings."[34]

Separate Baptist preachers also were known for a distinctive preaching style that, like the sermons of Whitefield and Davenport, was extemporaneous and musically inflected. Morgan Edwards described the voice of Shubal Stearns, a Whitefield convert from New England and the "father" of the Separate Baptist movement in the South,[35] as "musical and strong." Stearns managed his voice "in such a manner as . . . to make soft impression on the heart, and fetch tears from the eyes in a mechanical way; and anon, to shake the very nerves and throw the animal system into tumults and perturbations." Moreover, according to Edwards, all the Separate ministers copied him "in tones of voice and actions of body; and some few exceed[ed] him."[36] "Old-time" black Baptist preachers preserved much of the flavor of Separate Baptist preaching. According to William Montgomery, the greatest asset of successful Baptist preachers was their language skills, including their ability to create vivid word pictures and "their feel for the rhythms that evoked bodily responses."[37]

There is also evidence, as we have seen, that the repetitive spiritual songs that John Watson deplored had roots in the New England awakening as well. While the hymns of Isaac Watts were the general standard for Virginia's Baptists, Leland noted that they did not confine themselves to them. "Any spiritual composition," he reported, "answers to their purpose." Leland also commented that with respect to the "great meetings" of the 1780s, "in some places, singing was more blessed among the people than the preaching was. . . . At meeting, as soon as preaching is over, it is common to sing a number of spiritual songs; sometimes several songs are sounding at the same time, in different parts of the congregation."[38]

ENGLISH METHODIST

In contrast to the Separates, the Methodists in England and the colonies demonstrated a penchant for writing letters, keeping journals, and compiling statistics. The documentation of the revivals in Virginia under the auspices of the Methodists in the 1770s and 1780s was correspondingly richer. Early Methodists, while not particularly well educated on average, reflected a wider range of educational backgrounds than did the Separate Baptists, ranging from the university-educated Wesleys to illiterate slaves. John Wesley himself has been described as "a cultural middleman" and early English Methodism as a movement that "established deep roots in popular culture but did not surrender to a purely magical framework."[39] The Methodist emphasis on written as well as oral narrative gave rise to a rich collection of early African American accounts of their "gospel labors," beginning with John Marrant and flowering in the writings of early-nineteenth-century Methodist preachers, such as Richard Allen, George White, Zilpha Elaw, and Jarena Lee.

In addition to a habit of writing things down, English Methodists also brought distinctive forms of organization and practice to the colonies. The distinctive organizational structure developed by Wesley in England was transported largely intact to the American colonies. Early on Wesley began delegating some of the responsibility for preaching to lay preachers who traveled from society to society. In the American colonies, these traveling preachers, known as itinerants, were assigned to "circuits" that included a number of Methodist societies. Local preachers and exhorters, none of whom itinerated, assisted the itinerant preachers with the task of conversion at the local level. The societies were divided, as in England, into small groups called "class meetings" and in some instances "bands" of about twelve persons each. Each class or band had its own leader, responsible, like the exhorters and local preachers, to the itinerant assigned to the circuit (*JW* 9:1–23).

The whole structure was arranged hierarchically. Although ultimate authority for Methodism in the colonies rested with John Wesley in England, it resided more immediately in the traveling (i.e., itinerant) preachers meeting in annual conference.[40] At the annual conference, business was conducted and the general assistant, as Wesley's designated representative, assigned the itinerants to circuits for the coming year. With the constitution of the Methodist Episcopal Church as an independent American body in 1784, some of the itinerants were ordained as "elders," circuits were clustered under the supervision of "presiding elders," and Francis Asbury and Thomas Coke were "set apart" as general superintendents or, in common parlance, bishops. The bishops and the itinerants constituted the upper strata of the Methodist system. The local preachers, exhorters, and class leaders, none of whom were members of annual conference, comprised a second tier of leadership within the system.

Each society met together as a whole for preaching services on Sundays and, on other occasions, when an itinerant was present. The societies on a circuit met together quarterly, at what were known as quarterly conferences. In the early years in America, when few itinerants were ordained and thus able to administer the sacraments, quarterly conferences were major occasions, not only for conducting the business of the circuit, but in the religious life of the people. Everyone who could attended—the local preachers, exhorters, class leaders, and the members of the societies, as well as the presiding elder and the itinerants assigned to the circuit. Quarterly conferences lasted several days and typically included preaching, exhorting, a love-feast, and the Lord's Supper. While all Christians were welcome at the Lord's Supper, the love-feasts were limited to class members in good standing, and as in England, involved prayer and song, witnessing to experiences of conversion and sanctification, and sharing an agape meal of bread and water.[41]

With respect to religious practice, it is important to note that although Wesley claimed that his teaching on sanctification never changed, few, if any, English Methodists had "instantaneous" experiences of sanctification distinct from conversion during the first twenty years of the movement. Claims to such, according to Henry Rack, "erupted in profusion" between 1758 and 1763. Wesley published his *Thoughts on Christian Perfection* in 1759 and republished it with some earlier writings in 1767 as his *Plain Account of Christian Perfection*. According to Rack, Wesley was stimulated to define the experience of sanctification by the perfectionist revivals in England during the late 1750s and 1760s. The doctrine was controversial, and although Wesley attempted to present it "reasonably," scandal broke out in 1762 when two English Methodist preachers of long-standing, Thomas Maxfield and George Bell, not only encouraged the sanctification-related visions of their followers, but granted them special status as marks of perfection.[42] Such claims reinvigorated fears of Methodist enthusiasm, alienated the more Calvinistic-Methodists of the Countess of Huntington Connexion, and occasioned vigorous satire from the pens of the learned.[43]

Although Maxfield and Bell were expelled, Wesley did not retreat from the idea of sanctification as a distinct second experience in the life of the converted Christian, nor were visions expunged from the repertoire of phenomena that might accompany such an experience.[44] The introduction of a second experience, linked with visions and bodily effects, beyond that of conversion had significant implications for the development of the shout tradition. Specifically, it provided a theologically grounded rationale for such phenomena beyond the point of conversion and created an expectation that they would continue to manifest themselves among those already saved. The fact that the emphasis on sanctification blossomed in England in the late 1750s and 1760s, just prior to the arrival of the first Methodist itinerants in the American colonies, ensured the centrality of the sanctification experience in the early years of American Methodism.

The published experiences of Thomas Rankin, who was converted and sanctified in England in 1761 and appeared on the scene in Virginia about a decade later, provides a basis for comparing English and later American accounts of conversion and sanctification. In Rankin's conversion account we find references to "sinking down in despair" in view of the "wrath of God" while under conviction and a lengthy account of an experience of "trance" (his word) in which it seemed as if "[his] soul [was] near entering into the world of the spirits." These experiences took place while he was alone and there were no references to shouting. Sometime after his conversion, Rankin went to hear Wesley preach for the first time. "When we came within the sound of your voice," he wrote Wesley, "I was so struck with the power of God, that if I had not held fast by Dr. Watson's arm, I should have fallen to the ground."[45]

While engaged in prayer and song with "some Christian friends," following a discussion of sanctification, Rankin's "mouth was stopped" and he was "overpowered with the love of God." When one of his friends asked him afterwards, " 'If I thought, God had given me that blessing?' I replied, 'I cannot tell what God hath done for me; but I never felt such close fellowship with God the Father, and with his Son Jesus Christ, since first I knew redeeming love.' " While he was "afraid to say that God had purified his heart," a common enough disclaimer, he did say to them, "I experienced such communion with the Father of spirits, as I never imagined was to be found on this side of eternity." He went on to add in his written account: "I did, with Enoch, walk with God! my conversation was indeed in heaven; and I sat with Christ Jesus in heavenly places!"[46]

References to sanctification are common in the Methodist accounts of the revivals in Virginia and at early-nineteenth-century camp meetings.[47] As in Rankin's account, Methodist sources from the Virginia revivals and the early camp meetings typically link the experience of sanctification with the experienced reality of heaven *in the present*. In contrast to Baptists, who generally referred to heaven as an *anticipated*, rather than *present*, reality, the felt-presence of heaven took on special prominence among Methodists in conjunction with the doctrine of sanctification.

Preachers and People in the Virginia Revivals

Many of the accounts of the Virginia revivals during the mid-1770s describe individual sinners who, as in the transatlantic revivals of the 1740s, fell to the floor and then rose up praising God. In the Virginia revivals, many of the converts were said to have praised God with a "shout." Here, however, it is evident that not only newly converted sinners "shouted." This is evident in the few surviving descriptions of Separate Baptist religious gatherings. Describing the baptism at the great meeting on Cub Creek, Virginia, in 1771, Baptist John Williams wrote, "*the Christians* [fell] to shouting, sinners trembling & falling down convulsed."[48] Referring to the revival that began at James River some fourteen years later, Leland described the "heavenly confusion among the preachers" and the "celestial discord among the people" at Associations and great meetings. "This exercise," he said, "is not confined to the newly convicted, and newly converted, but *persons who have been professors a number of years*, at such lively meetings, not only jump up, strike their hands together, and shout aloud, but will embrace one another, and fall to the floor."[49] Although Leland's references to "heavenly confusion among the preachers" and "celestial discord among the people" were rather cryptic, they were clearly linked to professed Christians jumping up, clapping their hands, and shouting aloud. The far more numerous Methodist sources allow us to explore the social dynamics of such "heavenly" meetings in more detail.

A striking feature of the Methodist accounts was their continual reference to manifestations of the power of God or the outpouring of the Spirit. In his "Brief Narrative of the Revival of Religion in Virginia," Devereux Jarratt said that as early as "the year 1765, the power of God was . . . sensibly felt by a few." In 1770 and 1771, there was "a more considerable outpouring of the Spirit." With the arrival of Methodist itinerant Robert Shadford in the winter of 1776, "the Spirit of the Lord was poured out in a manner we had not seen before." Over and over, Methodists' accounts of revivals in the 1770s and 1780s refer to the power of God being manifest in their assemblies. Falling to the ground, crying out, and shouting for joy came to be identified by many as specific manifestations of God's presence in their midst. Thus, Jarratt stated:

> Some of our assemblies resembled the congregation of the Jews at laying the foundation
> of the second temple in the days of Ezra—some wept for grief; others shouted for joy;
> so that it was hard to distinguish one from the other. So it was here: the mourning and

distress were so blended with the voice of joy and gladness, that it was hard to distinguish the one from the other, till the voice of joy prevailed—the people shouting with a great shout, so that it might be heard afar off.[50]

The same spirit was evident in the account of Thomas Rankin, newly appointed by Wesley to oversee the work in America, on his first visit to Boisseau's chapel, near Petersburg, Virginia, in 1776. Preaching to a congregation "full of white and black," he reported that the power of God descended as he began to apply his words "to the present." "Now when such power descended," he said, "hundreds fell to the ground, and the house seemed to shake with the presence of God." Both he and Mr. Shadford were, he said, "so filled with the divine presence, that we could only say, This is none other than the house of God! This is the gate of heaven!"[51]

Many accounts from the revival of 1787 have much the same tone. Richard Garrettson, a local preacher living in Petersburg, described class meetings in which "saints were praising God aloud, and mourners crying for mercy as from the depth of hell; so that the noise of the people could be heard afar off." At another meeting, he said, "the sight of the mourners penetrated my heart with the greatest view of hell that I ever had; likewise the saints struck my mind with the deepest views of heaven, and the love of God to man." He reported that on another occasion, "hundreds of saints were so overcome with the power of God, that they fell down as in a swoon. . . . During this time, they were happy beyond description; and when they came to themselves, it was with loud praises to God, and with tears, and speeches enough to break a rock, or melt the hardest heart."[52]

Philip Bruce, presiding elder for the circuits near Norfolk, Virginia, described the work on the Portsmouth circuit in terms similar to Garrettson's, reporting that in many places, "as soon as the preacher begins to speak, the power of GOD appears to be present; which is attended with trembling among the people, and falling down; some lie void of motion or breath, others are in strong convulsions: and thus they continue, till the Lord raises them up, which is attended with emotions of joy and rapture." He added, "when one gets happy, it spreads like a flame: so that one after another, they arise to join in the praises of their loving Redeemer."[53] The same sense of collective joy was evident in the report of Methodist preacher James Meacham, dated August 1789, to the effect that "the dear black people was filled with the power & spirit of God and began with a great Shout to give Glory to God."[54]

In these passages, some of which referred to shouting explicitly and some of which did not, both "sinners" and "saints" fall to the ground. Mourners (persons convinced of their sinfulness who have yet to experience conversion) weep and cry out, and the saved (those who have "gotten happy") praise God with loud voices and shout for joy. Joy is so contagious that it "spreads like a flame" and gives rise, in some cases, to what is called "a great shout." In each instance, these religious expressions were intimately associated with the presence of the power of the Lord *in the congregation*. This latter point cannot be stressed too highly, for it is the association of these actions *on the part of congregants* with the power of the Lord that lay at the root of the shout tradition. Not everyone, however, interpreted the actions of the people in the same way and, indeed, how one interpreted the people's response appears to have been related, at least in part, to one's place in the Methodist system.

Devereux Jarratt commented that during the revival the work of God was especially evident in the "meeting of the classes," and people "flocked to hear, not only me and the traveling preachers, but also the exhorters and [class] leaders." Jarratt added that "whether there was preaching or not, [God's] power was still sensible among the people . . . at their meetings for prayer." These prayer meetings, he said, were "singularly useful in promoting the work of God."[55] Jarratt's comments on the prayer meetings held by the classes suggest that the main source of religious energy fueling the revivals lay in the small groups located at the most grassroots level of the Methodist system. In the context of the Virginia revivals, it seems clear that the classes and their leaders, above all, were responsible for associating falling and shouting with the manifestation of God's power.

The itinerants were least comfortable equating the physical manifestations of the revival with God's presence. Jarratt "disliked . . . [the] loud outcries, tremblings, fallings, [and] convulsions" that accompanied the revival and was "pain[ed]" by the "confusion" created by people in the congregation praying aloud and exhorting during the preaching service. He was more or less reconciled to both by reading Jonathan Edwards's defense of such phenomena, concluding that it "requires much wisdom to allay the wild, and not damp the sacred fire."[56] Many of the itinerants quickly realized, however, that to embrace this association without qualification was to relinquish control of their meetings. The differing views of the itinerants and the people frequently led to struggles over the direction their meetings should take.

When Rankin preached at Boisseau's chapel, for example, his voice was drowned out once the house began to "shake with the presence of God" and he had to sit down, unable to continue his sermon. From that point on the congregation was in charge of the meeting. As he described it:

> Husbands were inviting their wives to go to heaven, wives their husbands: parents their children, and children their parents: brother[s] their sisters, and sisters their brothers. In short, those who were happy in God themselves, were for bringing all their friends to him in their arms. This mighty effusion of the Spirit continued for above an hour; in which time many were awakened, some found peace with God [conversion], and others, his pure love [sanctification].

Rankin and Shadford repeatedly tried to regain control of the congregation by speaking or initiating a song, "but no sooner we began than our voices were drowned." In the end, "with much difficulty," they simply persuaded the people to go home.[57]

When Rankin returned to Boisseau's chapel two weeks later, the conflict between preacher and people became overt. According to the newly sanctified Jesse Lee, later a prominent itinerant and American Methodism's first historian, Rankin "tried to keep the people from making any noise while he was speaking, and at the close of the meeting, he thanked the people for their good behaviour, told them he was much better pleased with them at that time, than he was when among them before." He then left the chapel to have dinner (the noon meal) at a friend's house before preaching again in the afternoon. As soon as he was gone, according to Lee, "the people felt at liberty, and began to sing, pray and talk to their friends, till the heavenly flame kindled in their souls, and sinners were conquered, and twelve or fifteen souls were converted to God, before the preacher returned from his dinner." In fact, Lee reported, *"many of the people were sorry that he returned at all,* knowing that he was not fond of so much noise."[58]

In the wake of this powerful noontime prayer meeting, Rankin "prevailed on them to be quiet enough for him to preach . . . with much difficulty." Rankin's sermon was good, according to Lee, but "the people did not hold in till he was done." When he tried to stop them from crying out and praying aloud, he failed, as he had two weeks earlier. In contrast to that occasion, this time, however, he asked Shadford to take over the preaching. According to Jesse Lee, "Mr. Shadford, who had been preaching among them for some months before[,] . . . did [so] with pleasure, and in a little time cried out in his usual manner, 'Who wants a Saviour? the first that believes shall be justified.' In a few minutes the house was ringing with the cries of broken hearted sinners, and the shouts of happy believers."[59]

Garrettson recorded similar struggles between preachers and people in the 1787 revival. At one meeting, he reported, "the Preachers all came up together; and by the time we got within half a mile of the Chapel, we heard the people praising God." They tried to "silence them" once they got there, but could not be heard. "Then," he said, "we sent some to go through the people, to try to stop them, to have preaching; but we found it was all in vain. . . . All the preachers could do, was to go among the distressed, and encourage them."[60] When Garrettson preached on another occasion, he had to beg the converted to "be still for the sake of the rest that wanted to hear preaching." He reported that "[s]ome were so full, that the rest held them down fast on their seats, knowing that if they looked up, and saw others in like heavenly frames, they must inevitably cry aloud, so that the people could not hear preaching." One person, unable to resist, "broke out in praises," setting off the rest of the congregation. At the "height of this stir," Garrettson reported, "eleven rafters of the house broke down at once, with a dreadful noise; and what was amazing, not one person seemed to hear it, so mighty was the power of God among the people."[61]

In Philip Bruce's description of "a night-meeting for the negroes in the *Isle of Wight* county," the people quickly drowned out the preaching and again reorganized the dynamics of the meeting. According to Bruce, "those who were happy, would surround those who were careless, with such alarming exhortations, as appeared sufficient to soften the hardest hearts." If the sinners responded to their exhortations, "they would begin to shout and praise GOD, and the others would soon begin to tremble and sink." Bruce said he saw "a number (some who at first appeared to be most stubborn) brought to the floor, and there lie crying till most of them got happy."[62]

In all these instances, congregations—one black and the rest interracial—refused to sit quietly until the preacher finished delivering his sermon. The struggle between preachers and people was rooted in different understandings of the power of God. If the power of God was manifest solely through the preached word, the people could be expected to be quiet, orderly, and passive. If the power of God was manifest in the congregation's response, the people had the power to silence the preacher. If the power was to be located somewhere in between, a new style of preaching, prefigured in Shadford's dialogue with his shouting congregation, would have to emerge. Where one located the power of God in such a situation—whether in the preacher's sermon or the congregational response or a combination of the two—directly affected the balance of power between the preacher and the people. If the itinerant's authority was rooted in the annual conference, the authority of the people, and their understanding of God, was rooted in the more egalitarian dynamics of the class meeting. The people's response to the itinerants could be interpreted as an attempt to incorporate that understanding into the preaching service.

Although historians usually give the itinerants credit for promoting the revival, leaders that were situated locally, such as Garrettson (a local preacher) and Devereux Jarratt (an Anglican priest), stressed the role of the classes and prayer meetings. Garrettson described how, when the "power came down" in a class meeting and it was no longer possible to speak to the class, the class leaders would open the doors and let everyone in. The noise of the people "induced numbers of people to come, so that in places where we used to have but twenty or thirty on a week day, now there will be a thousand, and sometimes more." According to Garrettson, "prayer-meetings are now used in every place; five, eight, and ten are often converted at one meeting, *where there are no Preachers* [and] the meetings often hold six or seven hours together." Classes, he added, frequently held prayer meetings prior to preaching services, which undoubtedly explains why the power so often came down before the preachers arrived. In the prayer meeting *prior to the sermon*, he said, the people "got their souls glowing with love to God," so that when the preaching was over, "one and another would break out and pray in the congregation."[63] Viewed locally, the prayer meetings of the classes appear to have been the engine of the revivals. Conversions apparently proceeded apace even in the absence of preachers, and preachers seemed to have particular difficulty silencing congregations when their sermons had been preceded by a successful prayer meeting.

Shouters and Formalists in the Mid-Atlantic

While tensions between itinerant preachers and people were evident in the accounts of the revivals in Virginia, tensions surfaced in accounts of Methodist gatherings to the north between shouters and opponents of "noisy" worship, later dubbed "formalists." As further south, the most ardent advocates of shouting could still be found among the local Methodist leadership—the class leaders, exhorters, and local preachers—both white and black. Among the societies' membership, however, opinions were increasingly divided along racial and class lines.[64] Many of the itinerants, led by Asbury's example, attempted to mediate the emerging extremes of opinion so as to maintain the unity of Methodist worship, whatever their personal sympathies.

William Colbert, assigned to the Calvert circuit on Maryland's western shore in 1789, described racially charged white opposition to shouting. When he arrived, the Calvert circuit had almost equal numbers of black and white members and the highest black membership of any circuit (just over nine hundred). Colbert, who opposed slavery, was attentive to the circuit's black membership, and perhaps not overly sensitive to the whites' concerns. The statistics for the year he itinerated there show a loss of over a hundred white members and a gain of more than two hundred blacks. Colbert's journal indicated that classes on the Calvert circuit were racially segregated and that, although blacks and whites both attended preaching services, they were generally separated in some way. Colbert met regularly with the classes, both black and white, and gave details of a number of preaching services.[65]

It is clear from his descriptions that the black class meetings were "noisier" than the white, that blacks were more likely than whites to shout both at class meetings and preaching services, and that some whites were offended by the shouting. At a preaching service on Easter Sunday, he reported that

> for a conciderable [sic] time the people were attentive, to ward [sic] the last I endeavourd to cry aloud and spare not, the black people that stood out of doors began to shout aloud—two of them fell to the ground and began to wallow whilest others were praying for them, and I have no reason to doubt but the power of God was manifest in the house among the white people. One of the white society was much opposd to the noise and was for going away, but was prevented by a power that came on him, and was so wrought on that he took hold on one of his brothers that stood by to keep from falling. Capt John Hughs's wife another of the white society began to cry as she was standing, and as suddenly deprivd of the use of limbs fell on the floor but soon recoverd.

On Easter the shouting began among the blacks with the whites joining in, albeit in some cases reluctantly, but the white reaction was more hostile at his next preaching stop. There Colbert preached at the door of the partition dividing blacks and whites, with the blacks behind him and the whites in front. He wrote: "I wanted to see a move among them, therefore I exerted myself, and sure enough, there was a move for the blacks behind the partition began to shout aloud and jump and fall." The whites, however, began "to look wild, and go off." One young woman said that "she would come no more, and that she believed I should kill myself." The meeting, needless to say, did not last long and Colbert lamented the fact that "prejudice moved so many." Colbert indicated too that a reluctance to alienate whites kept many from assisting him in the work of revival. "Our friends here," he wrote, "were fearful that the noice [sic] would prevent the people [presumably white people] from coming in the future."[66]

Although he recognized the whites' prejudice, Colbert attributed their hostile reaction partly to his own youth and inexperience. His comment that he was "not guarded enough" in his approach suggests he imagined that a more experienced itinerant, one more circumspect, could have avoided provoking such controversy. Whether or not that would have been the case, it is significant that Colbert held this up as an ideal, for the inclination to moderate conflict, such that Methodists could continue to worship together, seems to have been a goal of Asbury and many of Colbert's fellow itinerants. Two controversies, one in New York and the other in Philadelphia, can be reconstructed sufficiently to illustrate the complex dynamics surrounding shouting in the last decade of the eighteenth century. Benjamin Abbott, the premier exemplar of the shout tradition, played a role in both.

Abbott grew up in New Jersey and Pennsylvania well before Methodism arrived in the American colonies. Orphaned at a young age, he spent most of his life farming in New Jersey, professing himself a Presbyterian until his conversion to Methodism in 1772 at the age of forty. He had two striking dreams seven years prior to his conversion, one in which he died and went to hell and another in which he journeyed to heaven. These were called to mind when he heard his first Methodist preacher. He described the preacher as "much engaged" and indicated his surprise at seeing "the people . . . crying all through the house . . . for I never had seen the like before." The preacher's words on the reality of heaven and hell threw Abbott into a state of conviction. His distress was accompanied by fainting fits, crying out for mercy at meetings, levels of pain and anxiety that almost drove him out of his body, and an inability to eat that only more Methodist meetings seemed to alleviate. There he would shake and tremble and try not to cry out. Finally, Christ appeared to him in a dream and he experienced salvation. Dreams also guided his decision to become a Methodist and his informal attempts at preaching. He helped form the first class meeting in the area and was appointed to lead it. He experienced sanctification shortly after being told about it by an itinerant. When the itinerant prayed for him to receive it, "the Spirit of God came upon [him] in such a manner, that [he] fell on the floor." He lay there half an hour with his wife and children crying while "[he] felt the power of God running through . . . [his] soul and body, like fire consuming the inward corruptions of fallen depraved nature."[67] Abbott spent most of his ministerial career as a local preacher, itinerating only after the death of his wife in 1789 until his own death in 1796.

Most itinerants' accounts of their conversion and sanctification, even when dramatic, pale in comparison with Abbott's. In fact, his account of his life and experiences reads more like accounts of later African American local preachers, such as Zipha Elaw and George White, for whom he may have been a model. Moreover, Abbott's fifteen years as a local preacher, in which he did a remarkable amount of "unofficial" traveling, prefigure what we see in the later autobiographies of Methodists who functioned as local preachers or exhorters, whether officially licensed or not. Abbott was well known in his day and remembered, not always positively, long after his death. Robert Southey, in his famous *Life of Wesley*, published in 1820, describes Benjamin Abbott as "a sincere and well-meaning enthusiast, upon the very verge of madness himself."[68] Richard Allen described him as "one of the greatest men" he ever knew, adding, that he "seldom preached but what there were souls added to his labor."[69]

Southey, drawing on the medicalized language of the enlightened polemic against enthusiasm, indicates that Abbott "not only threw his hearers into fits, but often fainted himself through the vehemence of his own prayers and preachments." Abbott himself, drawing upon the biblical imagery that undergirded the shout tradition, reported that under his preaching "many fell under the mighty power of God, like dead men." Abbott utilized a wide range of shout-related terminology. Often he refered to the fallen as having been "slain" and on numerous occasions noted that "the slain lay all over the house." Numerous people fell, as he did when he was sanctified, and then rose praising God. He also repeatedly referred to having "a shout in the camp of Israel."[70]

Abbott brought all this with him when he joined the ranks of the itinerants. At the love-feast held at the annual conference in New York City in 1790, Abbott, venerable in years and reputation but still a neophyte among the itinerants, shared his experience on the heels of the most senior leaders and, as often seemed to be the case with shouters, took over the meeting. As he recounted it,

> Bishop Asbury opened the love feast; then brother Whatcoat [a presiding elder and future bishop] spoke; and when he had done, I arose and told them my experience: the people gave great attention, and when I came to the account of my sanctification, down dropped one of the preachers, and did not rise until the Lord sanctified his soul. I then claimed the promises [of sanctification], and in a moment the house was filled with cries and screeches, and wonderful shouts! Several went among the people, to those whom they found in distress, to admonish, exhort, and pray with them. Afterwards, six told me, that God had sanctified them; and I think, seven, that God had justified them. Three had to be carried home that evening, who were not able to go of themselves.[71]

Not until the following year did he learn that "there were but a few," in the words of his presiding elder, who liked the way the love-feast had gone. At the 1791 meeting, elder Robert Cloud brought the matter "on the carpet." According to Abbott:

> He said that I hallooed and bawled, and cried Fire, Fire! and scared the people. Then brother G[arrettson] got up, and seconded him, and opposed the work with all the powers he had; brother J[esse] Lee said he was happy in the love feast. The bishop [Asbury] said he did not want to hear them halloo, and shout, and bawl; but he wanted to hear them speak their experiences.[72]

The opposition of both Bishop Asbury and Freeborn Garrettson seems somewhat out of character given their positive references to shouting on other occasions. Three years earlier, on Christmas Day 1787, Asbury noted a dream in his journal in which he prayed for sanctification and "God very sensibly filled me with love, and I waked shouting glory, glory to God! My soul was all in a flame. I had never felt so much of God in my life." He also recorded meetings where "there was a shouting among the people" or "a small shout in the camp of Israel" and contrasted the "cries of precious souls struggling into life" with "the shouts of the redeemed captives." Likewise, Freeborn Garrettson recounted with satisfaction meetings in which the "power of God came down," including the one and only meeting of the ill-fated "Methodist Council" in 1789. There he reported "the whole congregation [was] agitated" and numbers of people were converted and sanctified.[73]

The key to their seeming inconsistency probably lies elsewhere. In his journal, Asbury barely mentioned the love-feast that so engaged Benjamin Abbott. His concern was with a Mr. Hammett whose sermon, "aimed at our zealous men and passionate meetings, . . . was not well received."[74] William Hammett was a reasonably prominent British Methodist minister who defected from the church early the following year, taking with him a significant number of Methodists from Charleston, South Carolina, Methodists. Speculation had it that he left because he was not appointed to be general assistant of the West Indies by the British Conference and because he was "fearful of being brought to answer for some malicious and ill-natured reflections, not founded in truth, which he had spoken against Mr. Asbury and the preachers in general." According to Thomas Morrell, those who followed him were "unawakened persons," the sort, he said, who "have always kept the Society here in dispute." Hammett, said Morrell, "is for money, show, and a worldly church."[75] Although it is impossible to know, I suspect that the leadership was caught between the zeal of Abbott for a thoroughly converted and sanctified church and the vehement scorn of the visiting Hammett. Aware of the divided opinions within the ranks of both the itinerancy and the people, Asbury and leading itinerants apparently attempted to rein in *both* Abbott and Hammett.

Abbott seems also to have been involved in bringing the shout tradition to public worship at St. George's Church in Philadelphia. According to Watson, sober and orderly worship in the style of the Church of England was the norm at St. George's through the early 1790s. The Reverend Mr. Willis, who was assigned there through 1794, not only "wore a black silk gown, which gave offense to many," he also "*read* prayers . . . from Mr. Wesley's Liturgy . . . previous to the sermon."[76] The traditional worship was "first broken in upon by a Mr. Chambers, from Baltimore, who, with a sharp penetrating voice and great energy of manner, soon produced a kind of revolution in the form of worship." About the same time, he wrote:

> the far-famed (among Methodists) Benjamin Abbott, from Salem country, New Jersey, used to "come over and help" to keep alive the new fire which had been kindled in "the church at Philadelphia." He was at the time an old man, with large shaggy eye-brows, and eyes of flame, of powerful frame, and great extent of voice, which he exerted to the utmost, while preaching and praying, which, with an occasional stamp with his foot, made the church ring. It was like the trumpet sounding to battle, amidst shouts of the victorious and the groans of the wounded. His words ran like fire sparks through the assembly, and "those who came to laugh" stood *aghast* upon the benches—looking down upon the slain and the wounded, while, to use a favourite expression of his, "The shout of the king was in the camp."[77]

Benjamin Abbott spent a year on the Salem circuit in New Jersey, leaving there for the Eastern Shore of Maryland in the fall of 1793. This suggests that this incident occurred at St. George's prior to the founding of the Bethel Church in the summer of 1794.[78] In his autobiography, Richard Allen suggested that the famous incident in which the white trustees of St. George's pulled him and other black members from their seats in the new galleries in the midst of prayer, precipitating the "walk-out" from St. George's and ultimately the formation of the Bethel Church, occurred in 1787. Scholars have been aware for some time that the "walk-out" must have occurred later, since the galleries were not completed until the late spring or early summer of 1792, not long before Abbott was appointed to the Salem circuit. We also know that the conference and the itinerant assigned to St. George's, presumably Willis, initially opposed the formation of a separate black congregation, but made an unexplained turn-about at the end.[79] We can also surmise, given Allen's highly positive comments about Abbott in his autobiography, that Allen and his followers would have responded favorably to Abbott's preaching. It is worth speculating whether the transformation of worship at St. George's might have polarized the membership of St. George's and left some whites more eager to see the black members depart.

Six year later, another controversy broke out among the Methodists in Philadelphia, resulting in the departure of about a hundred of the wealthiest and most "respectable" white members to form a lay-led congregation at the nearby Academy building. Ezekiel Cooper, who was appointed to Philadelphia to head the Book Concern throughout this period, described the controversy in social terms. According to Cooper, the controversy pitted "the wealthy and respectable minority" against the "poor majority." The itinerant appointed to the circuit, Lawrence McCombs, took the side of the wealthy, as did a few of the local preachers. Matters came to a head when McCombs "broke" several class leaders "who differed with him in opinion." The presiding elder, viewing this as "a stretch of power" on McCombs's part, removed him in the middle of the year. Cooper attempted to remain neutral, believing there were "wrongs on both sides." But when the "respectable party" refused to compromise, rejected the authority of the newly assigned itinerant, Richard Sneath, and "gave way to . . . an abusive practice of evil-speaking and persecution," Cooper threw his weight "in favor of the poor, and as they [the "respectable party"] called them, the ignorant part of the Society."[80]

Doris Andrews's research indicates that Cooper's characterization of the two parties was accurate. According to Andrews, the Academy's membership had a high percentage of merchants and wealthy artisans, while those who stayed at St. George's were mostly artisans of more modest means and journeymen, laborers or other unskilled workers often not listed in city directories. The group that departed was not only disproportionately wealthy, it was also disproportionately male. The great majority of women remained at St. George's. While this schism at St. George's involved whites, the whites were polarized along lines of class and gender. Those who remained at St. George's were persons of the "lower" and "middling" classes, the same sort of folk, in terms of class, as could be found in the two black Methodist congregations, Bethel and Zoar.[81]

It is also clear that the "respectable" and "poor" parties were divided in their attitudes toward revivals and, we can surmise, toward shouting. Cooper noted that in the midst of the controversy, "a work of religion broke out among us, which the others [the respectable party] opposed with much severity, and endeavored to make it be believed that it was a delusion, etc." Cooper also indicated that "the work of religion . . . went on gloriously" after the respectable party departed, such that the church's membership increased dramatically in 1801, despite the schism.[82] The revival in 1800 had been preceded by a revival two years earlier that resulted in a lesser but still dramatic increase in membership in 1799, two years before the controversy broke out.[83]

Although newly converted whites swelled the ranks of St. George's and blacks joined class meetings at Bethel or Zoar, there is evidence to suggest that many of the new members, white and black, were converted at interracial meetings at Bethel and Zoar. Richard Allen described the revival of 1798 in a letter to Bishop Asbury in February of that year. According to Allen:

> there has a very great Revival taken place in our Churches & is still Encreasing & Spread-ing. Our evening meetings mostly Continue untill 10 or 12 oclock & from 4 to 8 Con-vinced and Converted of a night Whites and Blacks. Our Churches ar [sic] Crouded particularly Bethel. . . . it is at Bethel the work is in General. for at Prayermeetings the House is Crouded & persons under Conviction for Weeks Come there to get Con-verted. . . . At our Love faste [sic] on the 16th inst the House weas Crouded & Continued untill after 12 Oclock[.] . . . Our Class meetings are Crouded & Remarkably lively, in short we have no Barren meetings. . . . Our Congregations Nearly Consist of as many Whites as Blacks. Many that Never attended any place of Worship come Some through Curiosity & many of them are awakened & join the Society So that Nearly as many Whites as Black are Convinced and Converted to the Lord.[84]

It is not clear from the letter itself whether Allen's use of "our" refers to our "African" churches (Bethel and Zoar) or our "Methodist" churches (Bethel, Zoar, St. George's, and Ebenezer). If one assumes that he is referring in every case to all the Methodist churches in Philadelphia, black and white, it might be possible to assume that blacks were being converted at Bethel and whites elsewhere.

Two entries in William Colbert's journal make it clear that this was not the case. On February 15, 1798, he wrote: "I rode to Philadelphia and met brother Cavender at Richard Allen's and at night preached to the black people and a good many white people . . . bro. Cavender gave an exhortation we had a shout and many appeard to be happy." A month later, he wrote: "I have rode . . . to Philadel-phia, where I met Charles Cavender, and heard him preach at night at Bethell the black peoples house to a large congregation of black and whites . . . I gave an exhortation after him a great shout broke out and I am told that 8 souls got converted."[85] Allen's letter taken together with Colbert's journal entries suggest that in 1798 the Bethel Church was at the center of a revival that drew almost equal numbers of blacks and whites and added a number of previously un-churched whites to the Methodist roles at St. George's.[86] The meetings lasted well into the night, experience-meetings played a pivotal role in promoting conver-sions, and shouting was very much in evidence.

Richard Sneath, who took over for McCombs in 1800, indicated that the reviv-als of that year began at Zoar, "the African Church, in the Northern Liberties, *tho'*

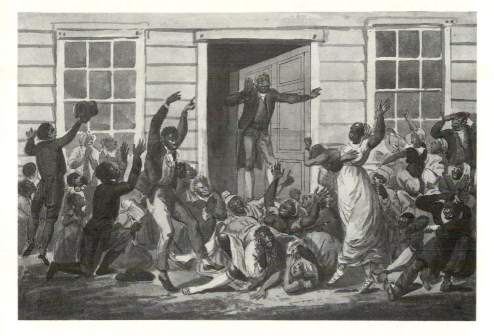

2. Shouting Methodists as depicted by visiting German painter, John Lewis Krimmel (c. 1810), in a watercolor titled: "Negro Methodists Holding a Prayer Meeting in Philadelphia." Courtesy of the Metropolitan Museum of Art, Rogers Fund, 1942. (42.95.19)

chiefly among the Whites, who crowded the place at almost every meeting." He added that "[a]t Bethel, another African preaching-house, numbers of White people came there, and found the Lord" and that subsequently "[t]he work spread to St. George's in Fourth-street, and to Ebenezer in Southworks, so that a general alarm went thro' the city."[87] We know too that in 1801, Richard Allen published a hymnal for the Bethel Church. The first hymnal published under African American auspices, it contained the vibrantly popular sorts of hymns from which the words of the black spirituals were derived as well as the new "wandering choruses" that were to characterize the camp-meeting hymn.[88]

It is clear that the "respectable party" opposed the revival of 1800, attempted to convince others "that it was a delusion," and withdrew to worship separately with their own local preachers and members once the itinerant who supported them was removed.[89] As at St. George's six years earlier, issues of race and class came to a head with respect to worship. In 1800, revivals were widespread throughout Methodism and the shout tradition was in the ascendant. Bethel and Zoar formed the leading edge of the revival in Philadelphia, and the success of the African congregations in appealing to whites as well as blacks was such that this time the "respectable" white elite walked out.

Their withdrawal was only temporary, however, and conflicts over worship did not end in 1800. The shout tradition continued to dominate worship at the Bethel

Church for some years thereafter. One Sunday in 1809, Freeborn Garrettson made the rounds of Philadelphia's Methodist churches, preaching at "the Ecaoomy [Academy] Church" in the morning, St. George's in the afternoon, and at Bethel in the evening. He described his visit to Bethel in a letter to his sister.

> Mr. Allin, the African Minister sent his Coach for me and took me to the New African Church, a stately building, a large Congregation [of about 700 members] and much in the power of *God*. Several they say were Converted during the meeting. When I left the Congregation they were shouting, jumping, Clapping, and praising *God*.[90]

Some white itinerants even learned to use the call-and-response style preferred by its members. According to Watson:

> The Rev. R. S——, when stationed in Philadelphia, after preaching through much acclamation, came down to the altar, saying he had some thing special to communicate. He thus hushed them:—after proceeding a little, a rising murmur, began to drown his voice—he would appease them again and again in this way—'Stop, stop, my honies, not now! bye and bye!' then they would bridle in, and so he and they alternately drew in and let out, till he showed the sign of ending, by waving his handkerchief with the word *now!* Then the whole church was in a instant uproar, jumping and shouting, till 'they made the welkin ring.' (*ME*-1814, 13 [note])

Watson indicates that this style of worship was so important to the congregation that an itinerant who believed "that such religion was greatly mechanical . . . dared not to teach such people the errors of their fancies" (ibid.).[91]

Watson's attacks on the worship of the Bethel Church and his attempt to show that those engaged in bodily exercises were in the minority in 1814 should be read against the backdrop of the controversies of 1800. While Watson was glad that Philadelphia's black Methodists were *en route* to forming their own denomination, the camp meetings that had become increasingly common in the Philadelphia area since 1800 were still interracial affairs. At the time he wrote *Methodist Error*, it was the excesses of the camp meeting that bothered him most.

Mourners and Shouters

One of the most frequently quoted passages in *Methodist Error* describes what came to be called the "ring shout." In it Watson told how "the colored people get together, and sing for hours together, short scraps of disjointed affirmations, pledges, or prayers, lengthened out with long repetition *choruses*." With each word, he continued, "they have a sinking of one or other leg of the body alternately, producing an audible sound of the feet at every step, and as manifest as the steps of actual negro dancing in Virginia, &c. If some in the mean time sit, they strike the sounds alternately on each thigh" (*ME*-1814, 16). Many scholars have commented on the similarities between this and traditional circular dances in Africa. Scholars have attended less to the fact that this circular dance occurred in the blacks' quarter at a camp meeting outside Philadelphia. As a result, we know little about the meaning and purpose of this circular dance in the context of Protestant ritual.

Ezra Stiles Ely, the Presbyterian editor of the *Quarterly Theological Review* and, like Watson, a thorough-going "formalist," offered another description of a circular dance performed at a Methodist camp meeting in his favorable review of *Methodist Error*:

> In the lowest part of the consecrated enclosure, we saw about fifty persons in various stages of prostration. Some were lying on their backs, some on their faces, some on their sides, some on their knees and elbows, some with half the body elevated from the ground, at an angle of about thirty degrees; while others were on their bended knees; and about the whole of this convicted group, a file of new converts was marching, in a circle, hand in hand, with black and white commingled. The persons wheeling around in Indian file, were singing several different airs, to different words, and shouting and praying all at once. Some of them we distinctly heard saying, more than once, 'Well, well, Lord, I guess you are doing the job for them now.' . . . [When] the trumpet blew for public preaching[,] lo! all the prostrate persons, who had fallen, because they could not help it, being weighed down by the powerful conviction of their sins [except three or four] . . . marched off to the remote part of the camp, to hear the discourse. . . . After the sermon was ended, the same scene of a prayer meeting was acted over again. One after another drew near, to form the dancing circle of new converts, while others prostrated themselves within this living palisade.[92]

Ely does not give either the date or the location of the Methodist camp meeting he visited, but his visit must have occurred prior to the publication of his review in 1819 and, more likely than not, since Ely lived in Philadelphia, somewhere in that vicinity.

The similarities and differences between the Watson and Ely accounts are instructive. In both cases we have dances, presumably circular. In the dance described by Ely, blacks and whites march hand in hand in a circle, "Indian file," singing several different "airs" to different words, and shouting and praying all at once. In the dance described by Watson, which he never actually says is circular, we have "a sinking of one or other leg of the body alternately, producing an audible sound of the feet at every step," which he compares with "the steps of actual negro dancing in Virginia, &c." and to "Indian dances." While both integrate singing and dancing, we get a much more nuanced picture of how singing, music-making, and movement were integrated in the Watson account. In neither case was dancing limited to blacks. Blacks performed the first dance in the "black's quarter," but it nonetheless visibly affected some whites. Blacks and whites performed the second dance in an open part of the camp. Both can be located in relation to the regularly scheduled "exercises" of the camp meeting. The dance described by Ely took place in the middle of the day and was interrupted by a trumpet blowing for public preaching and resumed after the sermon ended. The dancing described by Watson often took place, he said, in a crowded tent "after public devotions [were] closed, and there continue the whole night."

Ely provides us with a clue that I believe is the key to understanding these circular dances within a Protestant context. In his account, he explicitly stated that the dancers were encircling a group of *mourners* prostrate on the ground. The dancers, themselves already converted, were simultaneously shouting, praying, and singing. The connection between the ring shout and the conversion of mourners is reinforced by two roughly contemporary, but undated, descriptions of "old-time" Methodist camp meetings on the Delmarva Peninsula.

In the first instance, Robert Todd reported that "great crowds of slaves were wont to assemble [at Garrison's chapel]; and, while the white members, on protracted meeting occasions, rallied around the altar within, the sable soldiers of the cross [i.e., converted Christians] would repair to the open air, build a camp-fire; and, under the starry canopy of the heavens, form a circle for a holy shout." Within this circle, he indicated, there were "weeping penitents." Todd's second account was embedded in a detailed description of a prayer meeting in the black section of a camp meeting. It bears resemblance to both the services at Boisseau's chapel in Virginia in 1776 and the worship services decribed by anthropologist Walter Pitts in his study of African American Missionary Baptist churches in Texas.[93]

As described by Todd, the prayer meeting began with a "solemn hymn . . . sung to a melancholoy minor, in the slowest time possible, and slurred and tremoloed into all sots of fantastic shapes." This hymn was followed by a lengthy prayer that began "in slow and measured sentences, in indistinct monotone, . . . ris[ing] by degrees from apparent formalism to warmth; from warmth to earnestness; from earnestness to intense enthusiasm and excitement. . . . The prayer and the responses struggled with each other for the master in the midst of a confused babel of flowing metaphor and red-hot exclamation; and the conflict was finally terminated by the surrender of the tired lungs and wrecked voice of the leader, to the overpowering noise of superior numbers."[94]

This "surrender," like the silencing of the preachers in the Virginia revivals, signaled the triumph of the congregation and the beginning of the "jubilant" era of the meeting. The transition was marked by a shift in musical key and "significant glances" that directed the "men-singers and women-singers" one by one into position in a "hollow circle facing inward." Todd wrote, "the space thus inclosed was devoted to penitent; and there, kneeling on the bare ground—ofttimes prostrate in the dust—many a wounded spirit, from the double bondage, human and satanic, found the liberty of Christ and the 'balm in Gilead.' " Here too, the circle surrounded penitents. The circle was located in the "jubilant" second half of the meeting, following a first half devoted to a solemn, melancholy hymn and a lengthy prayer, better described as a chanted sermon.[95]

These accounts suggest a theological continuity between the ring shout at Methodist camp meetings and earlier accounts of converted Christians surrounding mourners to pray, sing, and shout in an effort to bring them through to conversion. The connection between the ring shout and the conversion of mourners is further reinforced by evidence, discovered by Lester Ruth, indicating that the practice of circling the mourners was ritualized by the early-nineteenth century as a "praying circle" or "social ring." A camp-meeting hymn entitled "A Call to form the Praying Circle," published in 1818, stated:

> 1. Come, and let us form the circle,
> With the mourners let us pray,
> They are griev'd and broken-hearted,
> And they know not what to say.
>
> 2. Have you faith to pray for mourners?
> Come and form the social ring;
> They with deep distress are groaning,
> While they hear their neighbours sing.[96]

Nor were these "praying circles" simply static "rings" around the mourners. Billy Hibbard, an itinerant assigned to a circuit in the New York district, referred to "praying circles" in conjunction with a Methodist camp meeting held in Croton, New York, in 1805, which he claimed to have improved on by introducing "the practice of marching around a praying circle to sing." Instructing people to march around a praying circle, he said, "diverted the multitude from crowding on those that were praying in the circle."[97]

The ring shout as it appeared in Protestant contexts was, like the shout tradition as a whole, a tradition that Africans and Europeans made together. The evidence suggests that it developed in stages, beginning with converted Christians surrounding mourners to pray, sing, and shout in order to bring them through to conversion. These gatherings around mourners were evidently formalized as "praying circles" or "social rings" by the early-nineteenth century. Evidence of formal movement around the mourners appeared as early as 1805 and in the early, but undated, descriptions provided by Ely and Watson. Watson's account, which doesn't actually mention mourners, makes the most explicit references to the early incorporation of African rhythms and styles of dance.[98]

As we have seen, the practice of shouters surrounding mourners in order to pray for their conversion often disrupted eighteenth-century Methodist preaching services. By the early-nineteenth century, innovations had been introduced that effectively moved prayer for mourners out of the midst of the congregation and made the preaching service more orderly. Chief among these was the practice of setting aside a special place for mourners to go during the preaching service. Traditionally, according to Todd, "the custom seems to have been for them [mourners] to pray as best they could, wherever they might happen to be seated; or, perchance to kneel in their place; or, if mightily convicted, to fall upon the floor, writhing and wailing in the agony of their penitential sorrow." It was the Reverend Chandler, Todd says, who in 1799 first "invited awakened sinners to leave their places in the congregation, and to come forward and kneel at the 'altar' or communion rail." The result, he says, was highly practical, "the interest became concentrated; penitents were much more conveniently counseled; [and] the meetings became more orderly."[99]

Formal seating in front of the preaching stand and the creation of a special place for mourners reduced the amount of crying out and shouting during the camp-meeting sermon and moved the engagement between mourners and shouters to other arenas. Zilpha Elaw, at a camp meeting near Burlington, New Jersey, in 1821 described how, after "high and low, rich and poor, white and coloured, were all melted like wax" by a presiding elder's sermon, people in distress collected at their tent. "We engaged in fervent prayer with and for them; and a great noise being made from the mingling of so many voices, and of such various tones of sorrow and rejoicing, of despair and exultation, of prayer and praise hundreds were attracted to the place, and came round to witness the scene, and ascertain what was going forward."[100] In other contexts, to extrapolate from the accounts of Ely and Hibbard, believers (sometimes black and white together) formed prayer circles around penitents between sermons, leaving as the trumpet called and returning again after the next sermon was over. In meetings where white and black were segregated, convicted whites might gather around the altar to be prayed over, as in Todd's account of the protracted meeting at Harrison's chapel, while blacks went elsewhere to form a "circle for a holy shout" around the black penitents.

The pattern of shouters praying for mourners after the sermon provides a context for reexamining Methodist (A.M.E.) Bishop Daniel Alexander Payne's famous encounter with the leader of a "singing and clapping ring" later in the century. When, after his sermon, Payne attempted to stop the "singing and clapping ring," the leader responded:

> "Sinners won't get converted unless there is a ring." Said I: "You might sing till you fell down dead, and you would fail to convert a single sinner, because nothing but the Spirit of God and the word of God can convert sinners." He replied: "The Spirit of God works upon people in different ways. At camp meeting there must be a ring here, a ring there, a ring over yonder, or sinners will not get converted."[101]

Here it is significant, first of all, that the exchange took place in the context of a Methodist camp meeting, presumably A.M.E. and, second, that the ring formed *after the sermon*. The argument between Payne and the leader of the ring was specifically focused on *how sinners get converted*. Given that the lay leader's argument that "at a camp meeting there must be a ring here, a ring there, a ring over yonder, or sinners will not get converted," it makes sense to suppose that for the lay leader the only way to ensure the conversion of mourners in the wake of the sermon was to form "a singing and clapping ring" around them.[102]

Post–Civil War accounts suggest that the ring shout was performed both outside the church, especially at camp meetings, and inside the church, most often after a preaching service. Under slavery, ring shouts were often held at the "praise-house," a cabin in the slave quarters, following "praise meetings," consisting of singing, preaching, and prayer.[103] Bishop Payne wrote that "in some cases it was the custom to begin these dances after every night service and keep it up until midnight." James Weldon Johnson, writing in the 1920s, reports that he saw the ring shout many times when he was a boy, but that he did "not recall ever seeing a 'ring shout' except *after* the regular services."[104] Although preaching often was accompanied by shouting without a ring, the circular or danced shout consistently *followed* the preaching service. It was set apart, I am suggesting, not because it was *African,* but because praying over mourners had long since been moved out of the preaching service. Preaching led sinners to conviction; the Afro-Protestant ring shout that followed was traditionally intended within Christian contexts to lead mourners to conversion.

Shouters, like many of their British predecessors, linked the physical manifestations of the revival—weeping, crying out, falling to the ground, and shouting with joy—with the presence and power of God. In the interracial revivals in Virginia in the 1770s and 1780s, in the Mid-Atlantic in the 1790s, and in the camp meetings of the early 1800s, shouting Methodists went beyond their British counterparts by pushing the Methodist performance tradition in a more interactive direction. Two types of interaction shaped the emergence of the shout tradition—the interaction between preachers and people and the interaction between mourners and shouters.

The evidence from the Virginia revivals suggests that the latter interaction, rooted in the prayer meetings of the laity, was the more fundamental. Preachers recognized the importance and ubiquity of the prayer meetings conducted by the classes and acknowledged that the power of God often "came down" in the prayer meetings even before the preachers arrived. Preachers lost control of preaching services, not simply because people cried out or shouted, but because the people transformed them into prayer meetings, turning their attention away from the preacher to pray for family and friends in the throes of conviction. Although we can see the definite development of and numerous variations in the way that shouters prayed for mourners, shouters assumed that mourners needed their prayers in order to be saved. This assumption was congruent with both the Wesleyan emphasis on spiritual development as a communal (rather than a solitary) process and the traditional African emphasis on knowing the Spirit through the dynamic rhythmic interaction of individuals within a group.

The shouters brought this assumption into the preaching service, where preachers often found it disruptive. While many preachers responded by asserting their desire for a "sober and rational" as opposed to "noisy" preaching service, others interacted with the people to create new styles of Protestant worship in which the "shouts" of the people formed a counterpoint to the words of the preacher. We see this in the services of the Separate Baptists, in Shadford's dialogue with his shouting congregation in the 1770s, in the interaction between William Colbert and his black congregants, and in the itinerants' engagement with the Bethel Church congregation in 1800s. In Todd's account of black worship at an early camp meeting, the competitive engagement between preacher and congregation was fully ritualized. Not only did the leader and people interact through call-and-response, but Todd described the interaction as a struggle for mastery that was terminated by the surrender of the leader to the "overpowering noise of superior numbers." The leader's surrender marked the shift from worship that centered on the interaction between the preacher and the people to worship that centered on the interaction between mourners and shouters.

Methodist reformers opposed to noisy worship attributed these developments to the uneducated and especially to "illiterate blacks," but recognized (and attempted to counter) its appeal to whites as well. In the emergence of an interactive style of worship, we see clear evidence of an insistent bodily knowledge regarding the presence and power of God that was both derived from and amplified by the African performance tradition. This knowledge was acquired and assumed in practice by shouting Methodists and other proponents of what came to be known as "old-time religion."

THE SHOUT AS BIBLICAL INTERPRETATION

When critics such as John Fanning Watson referred to shouting as "noise" and linked it to "extravagant emotions" or "a habit of vehemence," they obscured what shouting meant to shouters. Shouting did not simply involve performance, it also involved narrative, sometimes in the context of performance and sometimes after the fact. Such narratives were not simply individual accounts, but located the individual in relation to the group. They did so by constituting personal experience in the idioms of the biblical narrative, that is, by placing the individual within the collective narrative of the people of God. Many of the biblical idioms that shouters used to characterize their experience surfaced in accounts of the late-eighteenth-century revivals; the interpretive process was most fully realized, however, in the context of the nineteenth-century camp meeting.

The continuous line of development from the late-eighteenth-century Methodist quarterly conferences to the early-nineteenth-century Methodist-dominated camp meetings has been obscured by a traditional emphasis on the camp meeting's roots in Presbyterian sacramental meetings, its emergence in the context of the Kentucky revival, and its links with the frontier and/or the South.[105] Since my concern here is with religious experience, claims to primacy are less important than the traditions of practice and experience that converged in the camp meeting. Although references to "camp meetings" *per se* are rare before 1800, large outdoor gatherings of various sorts were common in a number of Protestant traditions during the eighteenth century. The three most important were the Presbyterian sacramental meetings, the Methodist quarterly conferences, and the Separate Baptist "big" or "great" meetings.[106] The Red River meeting in Kentucky, sometimes designated as the first camp meeting, represented the confluence of Presbyterian and Methodist traditions and illustrates the interplay between bodily knowledge and interpretation in the construction of religious experience.

Accounts indicate that the Red River meeting was jointly organized by four Presbyterians, James McGready, John Rankin, William Hodge, and William McGee, all with experience of sacramental meetings; and John McGee, a Methodist elder with experience at quarterly conferences in the Carolinas, Tennessee, and

Kentucky. John McGee reported that on the third day of the meeting, while he was preaching, the "glory of God" broke out among the people. In the familiar idiom of the shout tradition McGee reported that "some fell to the floor, screaming and praying for mercy, while others shouted aloud the praises of God." McGee, who almost fell himself, "went through the house shouting and exhorting with all possible ecstasy and energy, and the floor was soon covered with the slain."[107] The Presbyterian ministers, not knowing what to make of this, turned to the Methodist for guidance. John Rankin later wrote that "on seeing and feeling his [John McGee's] confidence, that it was the work of God, and a mighty effusion of his spirit, and having heard that he was acquainted with such scenes in another country, we acquiesced and stood in astonishment, admiring the wonderful works of God."[108] McGee here passed on a tradition of interpretation extant among Methodists "in another country" (i.e., back east) to the Presbyterians in Kentucky. Without McGee's confident interpretation of this performance as "the work of God," it would have been incomprehensible to the Presbyterian ministers.

For several years after this meeting, Presbyterians, Methodists, and to a lesser extent Baptists, held "General Meetings" or "General Camp Meetings" in the West and deep South in which Presbyterians invited Methodists and Baptists to their sacramental occasions and Methodists invited Presbyterians and Baptists to their quarterly conferences.[109] Russell Richey emphasizes Francis Asbury's role in promoting camp meetings among Methodists. In an episcopal directive issued in December 1802, Asbury bestowed his blessing on the (general) camp meetings in the Carolinas and Georgia (in which "hundreds have fallen and have felt the power of God") and called for a (denominational) camp meeting to be held in conjunction with a conference outside Baltimore.[110] By 1802, a rising tide of opposition to camp meetings among the more conservative Baptist and Presbyterian ministers in the South and West led many of the more revivalistically oriented Presbyterians to join the Cumberland Presbyterian Church, the "Christian" movement, or in a few cases, the Shakers.[111] By 1804, the cooperative arrangements had largely broken down and the Methodists had embraced the camp meeting as their own.[112]

Letters from Methodist itinerants reflected both the Methodist embrace of and the Calvinist retreat from camp meetings. Through 1802 the preachers' letters referred to quarterly conferences and general (i.e., multidenominational) camp meetings in the West and the South. After 1803, the letters regularly referred to Methodist, but rarely multidenominational, camp meetings, not only in the deep South and West, but in Virginia and Maryland as well.[113] The first Methodist camp meeting in the New York City area was held in 1804 and on the Delmarva Peninsula in 1805.[114] Camp meetings under Methodist auspices, as Richey makes clear, were not simply associated with the frontier, but took place in the established heartlands of Methodism from New York to Georgia. There were undoubtedly many reasons why the Methodists took on the camp meeting as their own. One reason was that the Methodists extended the narrative embedded in the shout tradition from the body of the believer to the space of the camp and in doing so constructed the camp meeting as a public space with sacred significance. Just as shouting for shouters was not just noise, the camp was not just a collection of tents, but the new Zion where the people of God recognized the presence of God by shouting with joy.

Methodists of various sorts described their experiences at early-nineteenth-century camp meetings. A number of them record how the meeting ground itself was laid out. Itinerant Samuel Coate described a three-day Methodist camp meeting held "in a grove or forest" near Baltimore in 1803. "A stand [was] erected in the midst of a piece of ground containing three or four acres; and round this, the tents, waggons, carts, coaches, stages, and the like were arranged in a circular form; and fires were kindled at the front of the tents to accommodate those who lodged in them." Jesse Lee described the layout of the typical Methodist camp meeting as an "oblong square," and indicated that some had two preaching stages, one at either end of the area bounded by the tents. Zilpha Elaw, who attended Methodist camp meetings in New Jersey a decade or so later, described the typical camp meeting, like Coate, as circular. "A large circular inclosure of brushwood is formed; immediately inside of which the tents are pitched, and the space in the centre is appropriated to the worship of God, the minister's stand being on one side, and generally on a somewhat rising ground." In contrast to later camp-meeting observations, none of these early Methodists note any area being set apart for mourners.[115]

Like quarterly conferences, camp meetings were interracial events. How relations between the races were configured spatially seems to have varied. In his history of the camp meeting, Kenneth Brown indicates that in the deep South, "black Christians had to conduct their own services, with their own preachers, in their own quarters; in effect, they had to hold their own separate camp meeting." Segregation was apparently also the norm on the Delmarva Peninsula from an early date. Robert Todd, referring to the "old-time" camp meetings, states that "a portion of the circle to the rear of the preacher's stand [was] . . . invariably set apart for their [the 'colored people's'] occupancy and use," with a plank partition separating the white and colored sides of the encampment. Segregation may not have been the custom everywhere, however. Although Jesse Lee mentioned separate seating for men and women in his general description of the layout of Methodist camp grounds, he made no reference to race. Nor did Zipha Elaw, in her descriptions of meetings in New Jersey in the 1810s and early 1820s, give the impression that she as a free black woman was encamped or seated in a distinctive space. The only seating she mentioned (and she was seated) was located "in the space before the platform."[116]

Coate, Elaw, and Lee offered similar descriptions of the "religious exercises" that structured the camp meeting. The two itinerants, Coate and Lee, used much the same language to describe these exercises, although Lee went into considerably more detail. In Jesse Lee's words:

> soon after the dawn of day, a person walks all round the ground in front of the tents, blowing a trumpet as he passes; which is to give the people notice to rise; about ten minutes after the trumpet is blown again with only one long blast upon which, the

people in all their tents begin to sing, and then pray, either in their tents, or at the door of them, as is most convenient. At the rising of the sun a sermon is preached, after which we eat breakfast. We have preaching again at 10 o'clock, and dine about one. We preach again at 3 o'clock, eat supper about the setting of the sun, and have preaching again at candle light. We generally begin these meetings on Fridays, and continue them until the Monday following about the middle of the day.[117]

While Zilpha Elaw described the same basic format, the language she used to do so differed sharply from that of Jesse Lee and Samuel Coate. Where in Lee's account a person awakened the people by blowing a trumpet, in Elaw's "watchmen proceed round the inclosure, blowing with trumpets to awaken every inhabitant of this City of the Lord." Where Lee indicated that "we have preaching again at 10 o'clock," Elaw wrote,

At ten o'clock, the trumpets sound again to summon the people to public worship; the seats are all speedily filled and as perfect a silence reigns throughout the place as in a Church or Chapel; presently the high praises of God sound melodiously from this consecrated spot, and nothing seems wanting but local elevation to render the place a heaven indeed. It is like God's ancient and holy hill of Zion on her brightest festival days, when the priests conducted the processions of the people to the glorious temple of Jehovah.[118]

Richey argued that, in the Methodist context, the camp meeting "recalled the memory of intense community and the dramatic revivalistic response at Methodist conferences—quarterly and annual," while at the same time permitting a separation of the business of the denomination from the business of revival.[119] It did this, I agree, but it also did more. In separating business and revival, Methodism took the final step in a process of creating a *public* time and place where (to paraphrase Watson) "the very presence of the Deity" was manifested in and through the bodily exercises and extravagant emotions of the faithful. In the words of Zilpha Elaw we get a glimpse of the biblical idioms involved in the sacralization of the camp. For shouters, the sacralization of the body, the sacralization of the camp, and the passage from sin to salvation were intimately linked through a series of biblical typologies.

The Sacralization of the Body

Like quarterly conferences, early descriptions of camp meetings drew on the language of the shout tradition. As in the earlier accounts, sinners falling and saints shouting were linked with the felt power or presence of God, most typically in association with prayer or singing. James Jenkins, wrote regarding a camp meeting on the Bladen circuit near Wilmington, North Carolina, in 1804: "We began the exercises after breakfast, and continued nearly till night, with very little stir; but under the last prayer *the power of God came down* among the people. The saints began to shout aloud and praise God. And sinners began to cry for mercy. In a little time, there were many agonizing on the ground." Thomas Sargent used similar language to describe a camp meeting near Baltimore the same year: "Our strong lunged men exerted themselves until the whole forest echoed, and all the trees of the woods clapped their hands. *God came near*, sinners fell in abundance, christians rejoiced and shouted, and a glorious sacrifice of praise ascended to God."[120]

FALLING

As John Watson indicated, the shout tradition was steeped with biblical allusions. Ezekiel and Matthew provided the biblical underpinnings for falling. According to Watson, the words of Ezekiel 21:7—"and every heart shall melt, and all hands shall be feeble, and every spirit faint, and all knees shall be weak as water"—were "so very characteristic of some people's notions of religious emotion now a days, that they have again and again been pressed into the service of such" (*ME*-1819, 61*). This passage falls in the midst of a prophesy regarding the "sword of God," also referred to as "the sword of the slain." Ezekiel's prophesy, "I have set the point of the sword against all their gates, that their heart may faint" (Ezek. 21:14–15), links falling to the ground as dead with being "slain" by the "sword of God."

In addition to the imagery of hearts melting, spirits fainting, and persons being slain, there were also frequent allusions to the axe being "laid unto the root of the trees." At a "memorable watch-night" in 1791 at the Bowery Church in New York, George White indicates that "under the preaching of the Rev. Mr. Stebbens, from 'the axe is laid unto the root of the trees,' . . . I experienced such a manifestation of the Divine power, as I had before been a stranger to: and under a sense of my amazing sinfulness in the sight of God, I fell prostrate on the floor, as one wounded or slain in battle; indeed I was slain by the law, that I might be made alive by Jesus Christ." Looking back to the revival on the Brunswick circuit in 1787, William McKendree recalled that "frequently while he [Mr. Easter] was preaching the foundations of the place would seem to be shaken and the people to be moved like the trees of the forest when shaken by a mighty tempest. Many were 'the slain of the Lord,' and many were made spiritually alive."[121]

Not only sinners fell, however. Nicholas Snethen, an itinerant who had "always doubted . . . that the power of divine love [could without injury] deprive a man of the exercise of his rational powers in an instant," wrote that at a camp meeting in Maryland he was overcome by "a display of redeeming love, [too mighty] for my mortal frame to bear. My body sunk under it; or rather, was overcome, and suddenly deprived of its animal functions. Had I judged myself to be falling into the abyss, I could have made no kind of resistance." A Presbyterian investigating the Kentucky revival "conversed with many who fell under the influence of *comfortable* feelings" and was surprised by the orthodox account "they [gave] of their exercises as they lay entranced." Their minds, he said, "appeared wholly swallowed up in contemplating the perfections of God, as illustrated in the plan of salvation; and while they lay apparently senseless, and almost lifeless, their minds were more vigorous and their memories more retentive and accurate than they had ever been before." With evident satisfaction, he goes on to state: "I have heard men of respectability assert, that their manifestations of gospel truth were so clear, as to require some caution when they began to speak, lest they should use language which might induce their hearers to suppose they had seen those things with their bodily eyes." Nonetheless, in fashion that would have made Robe or Edwards proud, they insisted that "they had seen no image nor sensible representation, nor indeed any thing besides the old truths contained in the Bible."[122]

Most Methodist accounts did not conform so closely to the Reformed or Edwardsean ideal. Indeed, the falling of converted Methodists was often linked to visionary experiences of sanctification in which the fallen journeyed to heaven, journeys recounted in the language of the Pauline epistles or the Book of Revelation. Details of such visions appear in the autobiographies of a number of early-nineteenth-century Methodists who preached without formal denominational recognition. These preachers, many of them African American women, were similar in some ways to their predecessor, Benjamin Abbott, and certainly stand with him as later exemplars of the "shout tradition."[123]

George White, an African American who was eventually licensed as a local preacher, and Fanny Newell, a Euro-American woman who preached with her itinerant husband, had the most graphic visions of heaven. White reported that "in the month of May, 1806, at a [class] meeting held in my own house [in New York], I fell prostrate upon the floor, like one dead. But while I lay in this condition, my mind was vigorous and active; and an increasing scene of glory, opened upon my ravished soul; with a spiritual view of the heavenly hosts surrounding the eternal throne, giving glory to God and the Lamb."[124] Fanny Newell, who was "caught up to the third heaven" after a "spark of divine power . . . took away all [her] bodily strength," said she was "transported by bright Angels . . . upward to the paradise of God." As she entered "the celestial city," she said she saw "God and his throne, and . . . countless armies of shining spirits, who were praising God, and giving glory to the Lamb."[125] In their linkage of heaven and the presence of God with giving praise and glory, these visions, inspired by Paul's journey to the third heaven and the visions of the celestial city in the Book of Revelation, went to the heart of the shout tradition.

SHOUTING

For participants in the shout tradition, shouting was above all about praising and glorifying God. This is evident not only in early prose descriptions of Methodist camp meetings,[126] but also in the spiritual songs of the camp meetings. Watson decried the emergence of these spiritual songs, while at the same time providing some of our earliest descriptions of them. Such songs, he said were "*merry* airs, adapted from old *songs*, to hymns of our composing: often miserable as poetry, and senseless as matter, and most frequently composed and first sung by the illiterate *blacks* of our society." The songs, "ordinarily sung in most of our prayer and camp meetings," aroused "musical feelings, and consonant animal spirits," and often led to persons "stepping the merry strains with all the precision of an avowed *dancer*" (*ME-1819*, 15–16). At camp meetings, he said he had seen "from fifty to sixty people croud [sic] into one tent, after the public devotions had closed, and there continue the whole night, singing tune after tune, (though with occasional short episodes of prayer) scarce one of which were in our hymn books." These songs, made up of "very long repetition choruses and short scraps of matter," were "composed as sung" and were, in Watson's words, "almost endless" (*ME*-1814, 16).

As an example of the nonsensical character of these songs, he cited two phrases: "Touch but one string, 'twill make heaven ring" and " 'Go shouting all your days,' [sung] in connexion with 'glory, glory, glory,' in which go shouting is repeated six times in succession" (*ME*-1819, 28 [note]). "Go shouting all your days," which appeared as a hymn chorus in Richard Allen's 1801 hymnal and as a spiritual in *Slave Songs of the United States* (1867), provides an early illustration, according to Eileen Southern, of the link between the "wandering chorus" attached to the hymns of Wesley or Watts and improvised spirituals.[127] Watson's other song fragment also appeared in *Slave Songs* in the following verse from the spiritual *King Emmanuel*:

> If you touch one string,
> Den de whole heaven ring.
> Sing glory be to my King Emmanuel.

The song fragments preserved by Watson thus link, on the one hand, shouting and glory and, on the other, glorifying "King Emmanuel" and heaven.

Although there has been much controversy over the origins of the "white spirituals" that appeared in the shape-note songbooks of the 1840s and 1850s and the "black spirituals" that appeared in post–Civil War collections, several points can be made with some confidence. First, the two traditions were most similar in terms of words and most different in terms of music and performance. Second, the words to many of the songs in both traditions were based on the hymns of Watts and Wesley; others were folk compositions rooted in the camp-meeting tradition.[128] Although they cannot be dated with any precision apart from references such as Watson's, these camp-meeting spirituals are, as Dickson Bruce has argued, among the best sources of the practical theology of the camp meeting. The bulk of these songs fall squarely in the interracial shout tradition.[129]

Comparison of the references to shouting in collections of white and black spirituals reveals a more explicit connection between shouting and glorifying God in the white spirituals. There, *what* one is to shout was almost always spelled out, as for example, "When we all get to Heaven, We will shout aloud and sing, [Chorus] Shout glory, halle, hallelulujah"; or "Streams of mercy never ceasing, Call for songs of loudest praise. [Chorus] Shout, oh, glory, glory, glory"; or the oft-repeated "shout, oh, glory!"[130] Where meaning was spelled out in the white tradition, it was typically condensed in the black, as for example, in the spirituals "Going to Shout all Over God's Heaven" and "Listen to the Angel's Shoutin.' "[131] This compression or abbreviation of meaning, a general characteristic of black spirituals, might lead us to assume that references to "shouting" and the "shout tradition," as opposed to "shouting glory," reflected the more African American, rather than European American, side of the tradition.

This, I think, would be to oversimplify the early tradition.[132] Three songs, two in "white" collections and one in a "black" collection, linked Methodism in particular with camp meetings and shouting.[133] *There's a Meeting Here Tonight*, a black spiritual, linked the camp meeting with the Methodists: "Camp meeting in the wilderness / I know its among the Methodes' / My father says it is the bes' / To live an' die a methodes.' "[134] It was the "white" song tradition, however, that preserved the lines: "They are despised by Satan's train / Because they shout and preach so plain. / I'm bound to march in endless bliss, / And die a *shouting* Methodist."[135]

The shout tradition's answer to John Fanning Watson was preserved by the "white" spiritual tradition in the dialogue song "A Methodist and a Formalist." Sung at camp meetings with verses alternating between the "Methodist" and the "Formalist," it reenacted the visit of a Formalist to the Methodist camp meeting. The song opened with the Methodist asking the Formalist, addressed as "Brother Pilgrim," if he was "trav'ling to Zion" and if he had "a desire that burns like a fire, and longs for the hour when Christ shall appear?" The Formalist responded that he had just come for the day and was returning home "little better than when he first came." He added:

> Such groaning and shouting, it sets me to doubting,
> I fear such religion is only a dream.
> The preachers were stamping, the people were jumping,
> And screaming so loud that I nothing could hear,
> Either praying or preaching—such horrible shrieking!
> I was truly offended at all that was there.

The Methodist asked in response if perhaps, while everyone was praying, "he sat and considered, but prayed not at all." The Formalist responded that the camp meeting was "no place for reflection," that he was "filled with distraction," and that "if this be religion," he was sure that it was not the religion of scripture. After a lengthy exchange on the last subject, the contest was resolved emotionally by the Formalist's admission that the sight of Methodists "lying and rolling prostrate on the ground" had left him "fearful that [he'd] be the next that would come tumbling down." And, of course, in his final verse, the Formalist proclaimed, "My heart is now glowing! I feel his love flowing! Peace, pardon, and comfort I now do receive!"[136]

The Methodist and the Formalist provides our fullest surviving articulation of the theology of the shout tradition and, indeed, was a direct theological response (or provocation) to *Methodist Error*. In many ways they provide a study in contrasts, both claiming the mantle of authentic Methodism and both devoting much attention to scripture. Although both readings of scripture were infused with the presuppositions of their respective traditions—"enthusiastic" and "enlightened"—their respective depictions of the scriptural passages that informed the shout tradition were largely in agreement.

In two lengthy verses, *The Methodist and the Formalist* alluded to six passages from scripture, all of which had some connection to falling or shouting (or at least praising with a loud voice): David dancing before the ark, the Jewish nation weeping and praising at the rebuilding of the Temple, Ezekiel smiting with the hand and bidding the people to repent, Jesus telling the Pharisees upon entering Jerusalem that if the disciples "cease from praising" the stones will cry out, the descent of the Spirit at Pentecost, and Jesus' return in "power and glory."[137] The passage from Ezekiel, already cited, linked the wrath of God with persons "melting" and being "slain." The ark was brought to the Temple in Jerusalem "with shouting and with the sound of the trumpet." When Jesus entered Jerusalem, the disciples "rejoice and praise God with a loud voice." In Revelation, John "beheld . . . the voice of many angels round about the throne [of the Lamb] . . . saying with a loud voice, Worthy is the Lamb that was slain to receive power . . . and glory, and blessing" (Rev. 5:11–13 [KJV]).

The connections between shouting and the other two passages—the rebuilding of the Temple and Pentecost—require more commentary, in the first case, because the connections were so obvious and in the second case, because they were not. Indeed, the rebuilding of the temple was, so to speak, the foundation stone of the shout tradition. On that occasion, the people of Israel not only sang, praised, and gave thanks to the Lord, they also "shouted with a great shout, when they praised the Lord . . . [M]any . . . wept with a loud voice; and many shouted aloud for joy: So that the people could not discern the noise of the shout of joy from the weeping of the people: for the people shouted with a loud shout, and the noise was heard afar off" (Ezek. 3:11–13 [KJV]). This is the passage that Devereux Jarratt paraphrased in his description of the Virginia revivals of 1776 and, as we have seen, there were numerous, albeit more cryptic, allusions to "shouting for joy" or "shouting with a great shout" or "a shout that might be heard afar off" in subsequent accounts of Methodist conferences and camp meetings. Even Watson conceded that "Nehemiah and Ezra, give a case, more apparently like some of our more moving meetings, than any thing else I know of" (*ME*-1819, 69).

The story of Pentecost was another matter. Accounts of conferences and camp meetings frequently alluded to the power of the Spirit and shouting in the same breadth, but Watson's exegesis was to the point when he observed that when the "first christians" are all *filled* with the Holy Ghost . . . none scream, nor shout nor jump" (*ME*-1819, 89). *The Methodist and the Formalist* in fact seemed to consciously rectify this situation in rendering the Pentecost story:

> The Spirit descended and some were offended,
> And said of these men, "They're filled with new wine."
> *I never yet doubted that some of them shouted,*
> *While others lay prostrate, by power struck down;*
> *Some weeping, some praising,* while others were saying:
> "They're drunkards or fools, or in falsehood abound."[138]

Here the shouters interpreted the "founding of the church," as Pentecost was popularly understood, as the antitype of the rebuilding of the Temple. Using the Old Testament to interpret the New, as opposed to the other way around, the shouters recast the descent of the Spirit in the idiom of the shout tradition.

Watson criticized the exegesis of the shouters, not because it was typological, but because he thought their typological exegesis was sloppy. Although the shouting Methodists presented the Old and New Testaments as providing unified support for their point of view, Watson argued that the Old Testament provided support only if interpreted out of context, while the New Testament provided none at all. His exegesis rested primarily on his concern for public worship, and he challenged any "sober reader" to come up with an instance of shouting in public worship in the New Testament (ME-1819, 86). Pentecost, understood as the founding of the church and its public worship, was thus a crucial test of his interpretation. Ironically, considering later developments, he nailed down his case against the shouters by pointing, not only to the absence of shouting at Pentecost, but also to the presence of something for which they had evidently made no claim, that is, "speak[ing] with other tongues, as the spirit gave them utterance." Because, he added with emphasis, "We have no gift of *tongues,*" it is "idle to attempt to use such a case for our precedent" (ME-1819, 89).

Watson used a distinction between poetic and literal meaning and an insistence on interpreting passages in context to argue against the meaning attributed to Old Testament texts by the shout tradition (ME-1819, 42, 50–51, 57 [note]). He objected, as he put it, to the use of "scraps, picked here and there from a bible dictionary" to prove a point, and sought to model a more "rational" form of exegesis that progressed in an orderly fashion from Old to New Testament (ME-1819, 66). Throughout, he evinced the disdain of the enlightened for religion that appealed to the external senses and the progression from Old to New Testament was, in his view, a movement from the gross and external to the refined and internal. Thus, he denigrated the Jews, or more accurately the ancient Israelites, and by extension the shouters, as "a gross people in many things; their religion too was addressed to the external senses, and with all they were an illiterate people."

The six biblical passages to which *The Methodist and the Formalist* alluded provide a thumbnail sketch of the theology of the shouters. First, it was centered on the presence of the Lord in the holy city of Jerusalem, as presented sequentially in six images: the ark (in which the Lord is present) being returned to Jerusalem, Ezekiel prophesying the fall of Jerusalem due to Israel's sinfulness, the rebuilding of the Temple (the house of the Lord) in Jerusalem, Jesus' triumphal entry into Jerusalem, the coming of the Holy Spirit to the first Christians at Pentecost in Jerusalem, and the new Jerusalem of John's vision in which the "temple is the Lord God and the Lamb." The presence of the Lord was manifest chronologically in the Ark, the Temple, the Messiah (the body of Christ), the Church (the bodies of believers), and in Heaven. The presence of the Lord was manifest simultaneously in the Ark, in the Temple, in the holy city of Jerusalem, and in the holy land of Palestine. This sequence prefigured the manifestation of the Spirit of God in the Messiah (the body of Christ), the Church (the people of God and bride of Christ), and the new heavenly Jerusalem. Their theology was rooted in a typological exegesis centered on the presence of God in the Old and New Testaments. The Old Testament type (the presence of God in the Ark, the Temple, Jerusalem, and Canaan) prefigured its New Testament antitype (the presence of God in Christ, the Church, and in Heaven).

Second, the proper response of God's chosen people when in God's presence was to shout. Thus, the people of Israel danced and shouted before the ark as it entered Jerusalem; the faithful remnant of Israel shouted with a great shout when the foundation of the Temple was laid; the disciples rejoiced and praised with a loud voice when Jesus entered Jerusalem; the first Christians shouted and praised at Pentecost; and the angels and saints shouted and gave glory to God and the Lamb in heaven.

Third, it was to be expected that the shouts of God's people would elicit criticism and opposition. Saul's daughter saw David "leaping and dancing before the Lord; and she despised him in her heart" (II Sa. 6:14–15). The Pharisees asked Jesus to rebuke his noisy disciples. Many present at Pentecost mocked the first Christians as drunkards. And, of course, the new heaven and new earth were to emerge from the apocalyptic encounter with the ultimate opponent, Satan.

The Sacralization of the Camp

Underlying the image of the holy city of Jerusalem was the image of the Israelites encamped in the wilderness. Although not specifically mentioned in *The Methodist and the Formalist,* the prominence of Moses, Joshua, the River Jordan, the Battle of Jericho, and Canaan in other spirituals makes it clear that the sacred narrative did not begin in Jerusalem, but with Moses and the people camped in the wilderness. It was in the wilderness that Moses commanded the people to build the ark and its tabernacle (Ex. 35–40) and arranged their tents around it (Num. 2). It was in the wilderness that the "glory of the Lord fill[ed] the tabernacle" or "tent of the congregation" (Ex. 40:34). The people of Israel then miraculously crossed the River Jordan with the priests bearing the ark of the covenant under the leadership of Joshua (Josh. 3), conquered the city of Jericho (Josh. 6), and ultimately the land of Canaan (Josh. 11). Under the prophetic leadership of Samuel, Israel again encamped to battle the Philistines and the ark of the covenant was brought into the camp of Israel (I Sam. 4). Finally, David brought the ark of the Lord into the tabernacle in Jerusalem, the Temple was built, and the people of Israel were planted in a place of their own and "move[d] no more" (II Sam. 6–7).[139]

Methodists routinely described the camp-meeting ground as sacred space. In 1804, George White attended one of the first camp meetings held in the New York district. "A large concourse of people, of all descriptions," he wrote, "convened on the occasion, of which, many were made the subjects of saving grace, and believers were filled with perfect love. . . . I left the hallowed place with a glow of heavenly joy, which none but God himself can inspire." A lay woman wrote itinerant James Jenkins "that if she ever saw a specimen of heaven on earth, it was at the Hanging Rock [camp meeting in North Carolina], when there were so many Christians praising God, with a feeling, joyous sense of his presence in their souls." One itinerant said the camp meeting was "like a heaven on earth," another that "every foot of ground seemed to [him] sacred," and another referred to its "sacred groves."[140]

In describing the camp as "heaven on earth," Methodists extended the typological interpretation of scripture beyond the bounds of scripture itself. If the presence of God in the camp meeting made the camp a type of heaven, Methodists were then free to envision the heavenly camp in light of the Old Testament types. Thus the form of camp, both in terms of its layout and ritual practice, was modeled on the Israelites encamped with the tabernacle in the wilderness and the Temple in Jerusalem. As Zilpha Elaw put it, when the trumpets summon people to public worship, "it is like God's ancient and holy hill of Zion on her brightest festival days, when the priests conducted the processions of the people to the glorious temple of Jehovah." The camp-meeting ground was the new *public* place of worship wherein the very presence of the deity was to be expected and where Methodists gathered to glorify God with shouts of praise.[141]

Itinerant Samuel Coate described groups within the camp in similar terms. "I could have led . . . you," he wrote Coke and Asbury, "to a place where the divine blessing was manifested similar to the glory which appeared in the tabernacle of the congregation, when the wandering Israelites fell down upon their faces and shouted; it was a tent filled with happy souls, to the number of fourteen or fifteen, who had either been converted, sanctified, or had received some remarkable blessing that day." The singing from such tents, he said, was such "that for a few minutes, you would be so absorbed in contemplation, and lost in the vision of God's presence, that you would imagine yourself already in Paradise."[142]

Benjamin Abbott's oft-repeated references to "a shout in the camp" or "a shout in the camp of Israel" is early evidence of a conceptual link between shouting Methodists and the people of Israel encamped for battle, shouting in response to the presence of the Lord. His reference was to I Samuel 4:5–7, which reads:

> And when the ark of the covenant of the Lord came into the camp, all Israel shouted with a great shout, so that the earth rang again. And when the Philistines heard the noise of the shout, they said, "What meaneth the noise of this great shout in the camp of the Hebrews." And they understood that the ark of the Lord was come into the camp. And the Philistines were afraid, for they said, God is come into the camp.

In the black spiritual "There's a Great Camp Meeting [in the Promised Land]," heaven was envisioned as a great camp meeting. In this spiritual, as in others especially in the black spiritual tradition, the major devotional modes of the camp meeting—mourning, praying, singing, and shouting—were lifted up in successive verses or refrains. In the final verse of this song, shouts in the camp in the promised land of Canaan prefigured shouts in the great camp meeting in Heaven.[143]

Nowhere was the typological relationship between the camp meeting and Zion more clearly realized than in the songs and rituals associated with circling the camp. When Zipha Elaw described the person who, in Jesse Lee's words, "walks all round the ground in front of the tents, blowing a trumpet as he passes" as a "watchman," that is one who "proceed[s] round the inclosure, blowing with trumpets to awaken every inhabitant of this City of the Lord," she not only sacralized the wake-up call, but sacralized the camp as the "City of the Lord."[144] Watson listed passages from the prophets Isaiah, Ezekiel and Joel that the shout tradition used to connect "watchman" and the "trumpet" with Zion and Jerusalem (*ME-1819*, 60, 63–64). As depicted in Ezekiel 33, it was the duty of Zion's watchman to watch for the coming of the sword of the Lord and notify the people so that they might repent (Ezek. 33:1–3).

While the watchman circled the camp throughout the meeting to waken the people and call them to worship, on the last morning of the camp meeting, following a love-feast, the tents were struck and ministers "form[ed] themselves in procession and march[ed] round the encampment; the people falling into rank and following them." After circling the camp a number of times, "the ministers turn aside from the rank, stand still, and commence singing a solemn farewell hymn; and as the different ranks of the people march by, they shake hands with their pastors, take an affectionate farewell of them, and pass on in procession, until the last or rear rank have taken their adieu." While songs such as the "Minister's Farewell" were undoubtedly examples of the "solemn farewell hymn" referred to by Elaw, songs such as "Zion's Walls" and "Heavenly King" were likely sung by ministers and people as they marched around the encampment.[145]

In the segregated "old-time" Methodist camp meetings described by Robert Todd on the Delmarva Peninsula, only the blacks participated in the grand march around the encampment at the end of the meeting. The last night of the camp meeting blacks were allowed to "praise and sing" throughout the night. According to Todd, dawn was signaled, "by the sound of hammer and axe [as blacks] knock[ed] down the plank partition walls separating the white and colored precincts; and, in a few moments, the grand 'march 'round de 'campment' was inaugurated, accompanied with leaping, shuffling, and dancing, after the order of David before the ark when his wife thought he was crazy; accompanied by a song appropriate to the exciting occasion." The song Todd cited as an example had as its chorus, "O come an' jine de army; An' we'll keep de ark a movin'; As we goes shoutin' home!"[146]

In the context of a segregated camp meeting in which the dividing partition had just been broken down, the verses describing an army marching into Canaan's land and storming Jericho's walls provided suggestive social commentary. When the walls of Jericho fall, "We's all united heart an' hand; An' fully able to 'sess de land. . . . When we gits dere we'll all be free; An' oh, how joysome we shall be!"[147] Here black shouting Methodists were the children of Israel. Shouting through the night led to the tearing down of the wall that divided the camp. Only when the walls fell were all united and only then did all have access to the holy land, the land where all were free.

Shouters sacralized their bodily experiences and the space of the camp through the typological exegesis of scripture, that is, by casting themselves as the "new Israelites" and the camp as "Zion." Just as shouters prayed for mourners in a variety of ways, so too there were variations in the ways that shouters depicted themselves typologically. Where African as well as European cultural traditions influenced how shouters and mourners interacted, slavery and segregation influenced how the shouters read their experiences typologically. While these differences are significant, we should not allow them to obscure the two key features that characterized the shout tradition as a whole. First, shouters linked "extravagent emotions and bodily exercises" with God's power and presence in the context of group interaction and, second, they used biblical typology to locate the body of the believer and the space of the camp within the collective narrative of the people of God.

Although the legitimacy of shouting as a regular part of public worship was contested from the start, shouters created a relatively congenial home for themselves in the camp meeting. In doing so, they created a new public space in which God's presence and power might be known. In setting the camp meeting (for revival) apart from the quarterly conference (for business), Methodists located that public time and place *outside the formal structures of Methodism*. Thus, while shouters endowed the camp meeting with a rich tradition of biblical theology and sacred practice, those traditions never became an official part of the Methodist Episcopal or African Methodist churches, either in terms of hymnody or polity.[148] The camp meeting existed along side the Methodist denominations, where it was increasingly viewed as a manifestation of "old-fashioned" or "old-time" Methodism.

In Chapters Six and Eight, we will return to the camp-meeting tradition to consider how the Holiness and Pentecostal movements of the late-nineteenth century built upon the foundations laid down by the shouters to articulate their experience of God's presence. The next chapter is structured around two figures— La Roy Sunderland and Ellen G. White—each of whom was formed by and in turn reconstituted the shout tradition, albeit in very different ways. Sunderland sought to explain his experiences as a Methodist revival preacher in psychological terms, while Ellen White sought to elaborate the shout tradition in light of her belief in the imminence of the Second Coming. In both cases, their reconstitution of the tradition was mediated by the new psychology of animal magnetism.

PART TWO

Popular Psychology and Popular Religion,

1820–1890

3. Animal Magnetism: The operator putting his patient into a crisis. From E. Sibly, *A Key to Physic and the Occult Sciences* (1814).

IN SEPTEMBER 1837, Colonel William L. Stone, editor of the *New York Commercial Advertizer*, explained to the physician Amariah Brigham that he was not, as Brigham had suggested, "a convert to Animal Magnetism." Rather, he said, "I have recently beheld phenomena, under circumstances where collusion, deception, fraud, and imposture, were alike out of the question, . . . which have brought me from the position of a positive skeptic to a dead pause." Based on the evidence he had seen, he continued, he could neither deny nor explain "the extraordinary phenomena produced by the exertion of the mental energy of one person upon the mind of another, while in a state of what is termed magnetic slumber." During the previous months, Stone and most of the reading public in New England had become acquainted with the subject of animal magnetism through newspaper accounts of the lectures of the Frenchman Charles Poyen and his assistant, Cynthia Gleason, America's first clairvoyant somnambule. Poyen's demonstrations made an unusually strong impact in Providence, Rhode Island, where "men of science and learning," including numerous physicians, philosophers, and theologians, began conducting their own experiments using local subjects.[1]

Stone's initial skepticism was challenged only after an Episcopal priest from Providence invited him up from New York to see one of their most remarkable subjects for himself. The person in question, a young woman who had been blinded by a head injury, was first placed in a "magnetic sleep" by Dr. George Capron, "a physician of established reputation" in Providence. Capron reported that the woman, Loraina Brackett, manifested several different kinds of "somnambulic" or "magnetic phenomena," the "first and most obvious," he said, "is what the French term *clairvoyance*—clear-sightedness, mental vision, or vision without the use of the visual organs." Numerous detailed accounts, including Capron's and Stone's, documented her ability to see objects when magnetized that she could not see when awake and to respond accurately to the unspoken will of the magnetizer. People were most astounded, however, at her ability to "[transport] herself in imagination from one place to another, no matter how distant, and [to view] objects and scenes which she had never seen or heard described, and [to give] correct accounts of them."[2]

The response of Providence's "men of science and learning" was unusual, as was Stone's change of heart. Elites were more likely to share Stone's original impulse to satirize the new movement. They commonly assumed, as Stone had initially, that "Mesmer was an imposter, that his followers were enthusiasts, and his patients affected, if at all, only through the workings of their own imaginations." The skepticism, even scorn, with which elites viewed animal magnetism left itinerant practitioners as its chief promoters. Elites distanced themselves from animal magnetism in different ways and for different reasons, but the range of reasons they offered—mental excitement, sympathy, delusion, extreme sensibility, disease of the nervous system—were in keeping with the explanations of enthusiasm offered by eighteenth-century philosophers and physicians. In fact, both Brigham and Stone (prior to his about-face) compared those who had been magnetized to stock examples of enthusiasm, such as the French Prophets, as well as to the "various religionists in Kentucky, some thirty or forty years ago."[3]

Stone's turnabout signals the conceptual shift that informs Part Two. Initially, Stone viewed animal magnetism as a form of enthusiasm, compared it to various well-known examples of false religion, and explained them all as products of the imagination. After observing Loraina Brackett, he viewed "magnetic slumber" as a distinctive "state" in which "the mental energy of one person [acts] upon the mind of another," although he could not explain how. This postulated "state" with its accompanying powers or abilities played a central role in both constituting and explaining religious experience at a popular level during the nineteenth century. Established physicians and academics, for the most part, did not take this state seriously until the 1880s, at which point they reconstituted it as hypnotism in order to divest it of its popular connotations.

The histories of American psychology and psychiatry by and large reflect the attitudes of the established academics and physicians. The history of American psychology between Jonathan Edwards and William James, for example, has traditionally been written as the history of the moral or mental philosophy taught in colleges and theological schools during the nineteenth century. The subject matter of mental philosophy was "the mind, its faculties, its operations, and its laws." Many, if not most, academic mental philosophers in the American context were clergymen who viewed mental philosophy as foundational to a broader theological agenda.[4] This tradition was heavily influenced by the Scottish philosophy of mind as articulated by Thomas Reid and Dugald Stewart. Both drew on the work of Hume, but moderated his skepticism through their insistence on rooting philosophy in "common sense." Stewart, building on earlier explanations of enthusiasm offered by British moralists such as Shaftesbury, explained both enthusiasm and animal magnetism in terms of sympathetic imitation and the imagination.[5]

Two academic mental philosophers, Thomas Upham, a Congregationalist who taught at Bowdoin College, and Asa Mahan, a Presbyterian who taught at Oberlin College, paid particular attention to "the psychology of Christian experience."[6] Both also played notable roles in the rise of the mid-century holiness and perfectionist movements. In 1839, Upham was the first non-Methodist to experience sanctification at Methodist Phoebe Palmer's famous "Tuesday Meeting[s] for the Promotion of Holiness." Asa Mahan and revivalist Charles Finney were the major architects of "Oberlin perfectionism," a movement that emphasized holiness within the Reformed tradition. Taken together, Palmer, Upham, Mahan, and Finney represent a confluence of strands within the Methodist and Reformed traditions around a common interest in an eminently respectable, bourgeois form of holiness. While Upham discussed both animal magnetism and visions in his popular *Elements of Mental Philosophy*, he did so, like most academic moral and mental philosophers, under the heading of disordered mental action. Following Dugald Stewart, Upham explained the phenomena associated with animal magnetism and "religious assemblies" in terms of sympathetic imitation.[7]

American psychiatry emerged out of the nineteenth-century asylum movement. The Association of Medical Superintendents of American Institutions for the Insane, the forerunner of the American Psychiatric Association, was formed in 1844. Amariah Brigham, superintendent of the New York State Lunatic Asylum at Utica, New York, edited the related professional journal, the *American Journal of Insanity*. Although asylum physicians relied heavily on the moral philosophers, just as the British moralists drew extensively from the literature of medical physiology, the asylum superintendents focused on the etiology and treatment of insanity. Asylum physicians assumed that insanity was a somatic disease that involved lesions of the brain. Although insanity was an organic disorder, its origins could be behavioral, environmental, or hereditary.[8]

In his *Observations on the Influence of Religion upon the Health and Physical Welfare of Mankind* (1835), Brigham explained how this worked in the case of religion. Quoting extensively from Dugald Stewart's discussion of enthusiasm and animal magnetism, Brigham used the general principles of imagination and sympathetic imitation to explain how "religious excitement" could have a potentially damaging effect on the brain and nervous system. When clergy "strongly excite the feelings of their hearers," he explained, "they excite and increase the action of one of the most delicate and important organs of the body,—one on which all the manifestations of the mind are dependent,—and one exceedingly liable to be injured by excitement." Giving illustrations from the Methodist camp-meeting literature, he deplored the fact that "[l]ong accounts of nervous diseases are published and attributed to the *influence of the Holy Spirit*."[9] The asylum physicians rejected animal magnetism because they viewed the loss of a subjective sense of personal agency and a tendency toward involuntary actions as characteristics of mental and moral decay *and* of those most easily magnetized. Asylum physicians stressed the moral treatment of the insane because they felt that treatments rooted in mesmerism merely exploited and intensified the morbid subjectivity and moral depravity of the mentally disturbed.[10]

Moral philosophers and asylum physicians, virtually all of whom were Protestants, held common assumptions about the value of human agency that came to characterize respectable nineteenth-century Protestantism more generally. The moral philosophy of the Scottish Enlightenment, especially its emphasis on the intuitive power of consciousness, played an important role in undercutting the pessimistic view of human agency traditionally embraced by the Reformed tradition. Conscious conviction, as James Hoopes has argued, provided a new basis for assuring Protestants that they had experienced salvation and encouraged Calvinists to adopt a more positive view of human nature and the efficacy of the will.[11] Moral philosophy and asylum medicine both assumed not only that a highly developed personal sense of human agency was good but that this sense could be lost or impaired. Asylum physicians viewed its loss as one of the chief characteristics of mental illness. Although they rooted agency in the faculties of the mind, damage to the brain resulted in the impairment of the faculties.

This understanding of human agency informed how many respectable Protestants viewed both religious enthusiasm and animal magnetism. Environments that might overexcite and thus potentially damage the brain, including camp meetings and revivals, were a recognized cause of insanity. Persons whose nerves were weak to begin with were particularly susceptible, not only to religious excitement, but also to animal magnetism. Both played upon the faculties of imitation and the imagination, carrying them to dangerous extremes. Asylums removed the insane from these damaging environments and offered them forms of moral treatment designed to foster personal agency and self-control. Asylum physicians rejected the healing methods pioneered by animal magnetizers because, in their view, the use of such techniques would further impair rather than heal those susceptible to them. Although animal magnetism and asylums were new developments, most respectable Protestants assimilated them into an outlook that was relatively traditional. Although updated, it shared much in common with that of Charles Chauncy.[12]

In the last twenty years, animal magnetism has found a place in histories of psychotherapy or psychodynamic psychology. As historians have looked beyond Freud, they have recognized the importance of animal magnetism both theoretically and practically in the history of mental healing. Following the lead of historian Henri Ellenberger, several such histories begin with Anton Mesmer and the history of animal magnetism.[13] The significance of the interplay between animal magnetism and popular religion in nineteenth-century America has been recognized as well. Following nineteenth-century precedents, however, historical studies have focused almost exclusively on the role of animal magnetism in relation to religious healing and the cure of souls.[14]

Animal magnetism, however, can also be viewed as popular psychology.[15] Although it was marginalized by elites, it went head to head with less established forms of religion, where it functioned both as a means of explaining and constituting religious experience. Where asylum physicians, following the academic theologians and philosophers, maginalized animal magnetism, animal magnetizers engaged directly with the shout tradition and with new movements, such as Seventh-day Adventism, Spiritualism, Christian Science, and Theosophy. These movements in turn responded to the challenge and opportunity posed by animal magnetism. Where Thomas Upham stands out among the academic mental philosophers, others, including La Roy Sunderland, an ex-Methodist minister and self-taught mental philosopher; James Monroe Buckley, a Methodist editor and clergyman; and George M. Beard, a well-known neurologist, engaged directly with popular psychology and popular religion.[16]

Viewed from a less elite perspective, the historical picture looks rather different. First, contrary to the academic tradition, non-elites did not necessarily write trances, visions, voices, and so on out of the realm of legitimate religious experience. Second, contrary to the medical tradition, non-elites did not necessarily view mesmeric abilities as a sign of mental or moral degeneracy, but often embraced them as a valuable asset. Indeed, at this level, there was a lively preoccupation with precisely those subjects the academic and medical establishments had already decided—namely, those dealing with the loss of one's subjective sense of personal agency.

Three incidents from the late-eighteenth century provide a more detailed look at the new mesmeric psychology and the shift it inaugurated in both theory and practice. The first is the famed rivalry between Mesmer and the Roman Catholic priest and exorcist Joseph Gassner. Gassner, a successful popular healer, used the traditional techniques of exorcism to heal persons he believed to be possessed. After Gassner cured a nun who was suffering from "convulsive fits," a commission called to investigate him invited Mesmer, who was also gaining a reputation for performing marvelous cures, to demonstrate the powers of "animal magnetism." Mesmer obliged by demonstrating his ability to make symptoms, including convulsions, come and go through a touch of his finger.[17] While Gassner and Mesmer were both able to make convulsions come and go in their patients, Gassner believed he effected his cures through taming and then casting out demons, while Mesmer claimed he effected his cures through the manipulation of magnetic fluids. According to Mesmer, magnetic fluid filled the universe and formed a connecting link between humans and between humans and the cosmos. Persons became ill when their fluids were depleted or imbalanced. Persons, such as Mesmer, with an abundant supply of this fluid could restore the depleted or imbalanced fluids of their patients. The movement of the fluids into the patient or within the patient's body was signaled by a "crises," the French word for a "fit" or "attack."[18]

This rivalry highlights two basic similarities between the discourse of enthusiasm and the discourse of mesmerism. Both were concerned with involuntary bodily movements and both were secularizing discourses. Where enthusiasm was used to disparage claims to inspiration, so too mesmerism, at least in the early years, was used to disparage claims of demonic possession and priestly exorcism. While the disparaged claims differed in their specifics, both ascribed religious meaning (i.e., sacred inspiration or demonic possession) to the bodies of the faithful. The discourses differed most significantly, not in the objects of their attention, but in their approach to it. While anti-enthusiasts *explained* involuntary bodily movements that appeared spontaneously, mesmerists also *induced* them. Anti-enthusiasts and mesmerists were both comparativists, but mesmerists were often *experimentalists* as well. Anti-enthusiasts articulated a rudimentary theory; mesmerism denoted both a theory and a *practice*.

In 1784, when Mesmer was at the height of his success, the French government appointed a commission from the Royal Academy of Sciences and the Paris Faculty of Medicine to bring experimental methods to bear on mesmeric practices. The Report of the Commissioners provides a second key moment in the early history of mesmerism. The report provided descriptions of the "crisis" phase in the mesmeric cure and accounts of experiments conducted by the commissioners. Patients were typically treated as a group at a "clinic." At the clinic investigated by the commissioners, that of Mesmer's pupil Charles d'Eslon, the patients' reactions to treatment ranged from calm tranquility to agitated convulsions. Symptoms often spread like a contagion among the patients and altered in response to music. Thus, they noted, "the changing of the key and the time, in the airs played upon the piano forté has an effect upon the patients; so that a quicker motion agitates them more, and renews the vivacity of their convulsions."[19] When they found that skeptics and children were less likely than others to respond to magnetization, they carried out a series of experiments in which they attempted to magnetize some persons without telling them and told others they were being magnetized when they were not. On the basis of these experiments, they concluded that there was no evidence of a magnetic fluid and that the sensations reported by magnetized subjects, including their convulsions, were the product of imagination and "mechanical imitation."[20]

While the theories of both Mesmer (magnetic fluid) and the commissioners (imagination and imitation) were not unlike the theories of animal spirits and the imagination used to explain enthusiasm, the Commissioners' Report provided further experimental evidence that "fits" and "convulsions" could be induced. In contrast to Mesmer, however, the commissioners suggested that induction occurred not by magnetizing people, but by leading people to *believe* that they had been magnetized. The report was widely circulated in both Europe and the United States following its publication in 1784. Thomas Upham and Amariah Brigham both followed the lead of Dugald Stewart and quoted extensively from the Commissioners' Report.

The third important incident concerned Mesmer's most important student, the Marquis de Puységur, and Puységur's most important patient, Victor Race. Its repercussions were not felt in the United States until after Poyen began his lecture tour in 1837. Race, a young peasant, suffered from an inflammation of the lungs. After being magnetized by Puységur, he fell into what seemed like a sleep and then began talking about his domestic problems. Puységur tried to stop his "disagreeable" ideas and "inspire more cheerful ones." By having him imagine himself engaging in a variety of pleasurable activities ("shooting at a target, dancing at a festival, and so on"), Puységur was able to "produce[] in him an abundant sweat." "After an hour of crisis," says Puységur, "I calmed him down and left the room. He was given a drink, and . . . I made him some soup. The following day, being unable to remember my visit of the previous evening, he told me of his improved state of health."[21]

Here Puységur moved to what we would think of as a more genuinely psychological engagement with his patient. It is significant that this engagement took place while the patient was in a sleeplike state, described by Puységur as a "crisis," and that when it was over Race had no memory of what had occurred. According to mesmeric doctrine, one entered into the "crisis" state because one's magnetic fluids were depleted or imbalanced. Just as the "bodily exercises" were supposed to end with conversion, so too once cured, patients were no longer expected to go into "crisis." This, however, was not the case with Victor Race. It soon became evident that while in this sleeplike state of crisis (soon renamed the "somnambulic" state), Race was able to do remarkable things. He conversed in what was considered an unusually fluent and elevated manner for a peasant and diagnosed, prescribed for, and predicted the course of his own and other's illnesses. Throughout his crises, he was in close "rapport" with Puységur and able to do whatever Puységur silently willed.

Others persons, mostly women, turned out to be equally good "clairvoyant somnambules."[22] According to one first-hand observer, these persons appeared as if they were asleep. "The[ir] physical faculties seem suspended, but to the advantage of the intellectual ones." While asleep, they had a "supernatural power," which they used to identify diseased organs and "indicate . . . the proper remedies." When they were awakened, they "remember[ed] nothing at all."[23] Here, with the discovery or invention of somnambulism, animal magnetism took on a new form. This "waking sleep," in which people spoke without remembering and saw with their eyes closed (i.e., "clairvoyantly") what others cannot see at all, generated tremendous popular interest throughout the nineteenth century.

The figure of the clairvoyant somnambule informed the way people experienced religion and explained experience in the period covered by Part Two. In Chapter Four, I consider the challenge that the clairvoyant somnambule posed to visionary experience, particularly to the claims of Methodists and early Adventists prior to 1848. In Chapter Five, I focus on the Spiritualists' transformation of the clairvoyant somnambule into the trance medium during the 1850s and 1860s and the wide-ranging implications of this transformation for the psychology of religious experience and the study of religion. In Chapter Six, I discuss the backlash against the Spiritualists' spiritualized understanding of trance and somnambulism in the 1770s and 1780s and the resultant splitting of the clairvoyant somnambule into the neurologically impaired somnambule and the conscious clairvoyant.

The life and experience of one-time shouting Methodist La Roy Sunderland runs as a thread through much of Part Two. During the 1830s, while still a Methodist minister, Sunderland read of the Commissioners' Report and attended Charles Poyen's lectures. In the early 1840s, he induced a state of waking sleep in willing Methodists and used his experiments to explain their visionary experiences. During the forties, the belief that mesmerically induced somnambulism could lead to visionary experiences was so widespread that those, such as the early Adventists, with a stake in visions had to prove that they had not been mesmerized. The mesmeric lecturers and clairvoyant somnambules of the 1840s set the stage for the Spiritualist trance mediums of the 1850s and 1860s. Sunderland became a Spiritualist in the early 1850s and died a skeptic in the 1880s. During the 1860s, he used his experiences as a Methodist and a Spiritualist and his knowledge of moral philosophy to formulate an original psychology of religious experience. In the 1870s and 1880s, neurologists, new religious movements, and mainstream clergymen challenged the spiritualized understanding of trance and somnambulism. New religious movements, such as Theosophy and New Thought, continued to rely upon the concepts of clairvoyance and suggestion by cultivating them as conscious states and divorcing them from the liabilities they had come to associate with somnambulism and trance. Part Two closes at the point when the medical profession, in an attempt to further strip mesmerism of its religious overtones, rebaptized it as "hypnotism" and granted it something of the legitimacy it had long sought.

CHAPTER FOUR

Clairvoyants and Visionaries

La Roy Sunderland and Ellen Harmon (later Ellen G. White), the two principals around whom this chapter is built, were both New Englanders who left the Methodist Episcopal Church in 1842. Both would have been understood in their day as "come-outers," that is persons who "came out" from a denomination over an issue they deemed to be of utmost importance. Although Sunderland and Harmon "came out" over different issues, the former over the abolition of slavery and the latter over the second advent (i.e., the second coming) of Christ, both bore the marks of the shout tradition. Both were converted at camp meetings and both for a time embraced the shout style of worship, Sunderland as a preacher and Harmon as a lay person. Although what we know about this part of their lives is limited, it is clear that their early embrace of the shout tradition provided the foundation upon which their later, very disparate, careers were built.

La Roy Sunderland (1802–1885) may have been raised as a Baptist. He was converted at a revival meeting in 1822, probably under Methodist auspices. Within a year, he experienced sanctification and received a call to the Methodist ministry. For ten years, from 1823 to 1833, he, in his words, "exercised the functions of a revival preacher."[1] From 1833 until 1843, Sunderland was known in Methodist circles as a reformer. In 1833, he organized the "Junior Preachers' Society," and at their request wrote an "Essay on Theological Education," the first call for such among American Methodists. The cause of theological education remained a burning issue for Sunderland during his second ten years in the ministry and aroused considerable controversy within the church, although never as much as his efforts on behalf of abolition. He took up the latter cause in 1834, by writing an "Appeal to the Members of the New England & New Hampshire Conference of the M. E. Church." The appeal was signed by Sunderland and others and distributed throughout the two conferences. From 1836 to 1842, he edited the Methodist Episcopal Church's only abolitionist paper, *Zion's Watchman*.

Ellen Gould Harmon (1827–1915), twenty-five years Sunderland's junior, was raised in the Chestnut Street Methodist Church in Portland, Maine, where her father was an exhorter. Sometime during her childhood, a conflict erupted between advocates of "shouting" and advocates of instrumental music, which was won by the latter. The Harmons most likely sympathized with the shouters, but did not withdraw from the church.[2] Harmon heard William Miller lecture on the imminent second coming of Christ in Portland in 1840. Harmon was deeply impressed by Miller's warnings and she brought her newly awakened anxiety with her to a Methodist camp meeting, where she began to "seek the Lord." Shortly thereafter, she experienced conversion at a prayer meeting. Sometime in her twelfth year, she was baptized, presumably after the traditional six months of probation, and became a formal member of the Methodist Church. After attending Miller's second course of lectures in Portland in 1841, Harmon decided she was "not ready for Christ's coming" because, in her words, she had not experienced "the soul-purifying [i.e., sanctifying] effects of the [advent] truth." For the next year or so, she attended both adventist meetings and Methodist class meetings and experienced no contradiction in doing so. She described herself as all the while "hungering and thirsting for holiness of heart," suggesting that she did not distinguish between the purification of soul that she sought in preparation for the second coming and the Methodist experience of sanctification.

The abolitionist and the Millerite (or adventist[3]) movements followed parallel courses in the late 1830s and early 1840s. Leaders of both movements worked within the churches, the former preaching the sinfulness of slavery and the latter the imminent second coming of Christ, in an attempt to convert their fellow Protestants to their views.[4] Abolitionists and Millerites both found ardent followers as well as fierce opponents in the churches of the northeast. In the face of opposition, both developed their own associational structures and many within both movements urged their followers to abandon denominations that refused to embrace their views.[5] The annual conferences of the Methodist Episcopal Church (M.E.C.) in New England were particularly hard hit by both movements.

La Roy Sunderland, Orange Scott, and George Storrs were the three most prominent leaders of the abolitionist movement within the M.E.C., and Sunderland helped create the associational structures dedicated to promoting abolition within that body. In addition to editing Zion's Watchman, he presided at the first meeting of the New England Methodist Antislavery Society in 1834 and chaired the first two meetings of the M.E.C. Antislavery Convention in 1837 and 1838. Sunderland's outspoken advocacy was opposed by numerous powerful bishops intent on preventing a schism over the issue of slavery. He was tried on, and generally acquitted of, various charges related to his abolitionist work in seven ecclesiastical trials between 1835 and 1840.[6] The abolitionists were repeatedly frustrated in their attempts to bring their cause to the floor of the annual and general conferences of the M.E.C.[7] At the 1840 conference, widely viewed as the great test of Methodist antislavery principles, the bishops successfully thwarted abolitionist efforts at every turn.[8] Their energies exhausted in what seemed to be a hopeless cause, Sunderland, Scott, and Storrs all left the M.E.C. within the next two years. George Storrs became a leading preacher of the second advent.[9] Scott and Sunderland, along with Jotham Horton, issued a call for a new abolitionist Methodist church in November 1842. The call precipitated a large-scale exit from the M.E.C. and the formation of the Wesleyan Methodist Church a year later.[10] Orange Scott chaired the convention that constituted the new church; La Roy Sunderland was appointed secretary, pro tem.[11]

Millerism was a subject of great concern in the Methodist conferences of the northeast during the early 1840s as well. It came up at the Maine annual conference in both 1842 and 1843. By the end of 1843, records of the Maine conference indicate that eight or ten ministers in full connection and three on trial were reproved by the conference and told to abstain from advocating "the peculiarities

of Millerism." Portland was the center of advent-oriented Methodism in the conference. Gerschom Cox, Harmon's former minister at the Chestnut Street church,
was the most prominent adventist in the conference. As presiding elder of the
Portland district and editor of the *Maine Wesleyan Journal*, he was in a position
both to promote and protect the Millerite movement in the Portland area.[12] By
1842, Cox's efforts were so successful and, in the eyes of the conference, so detrimental to the church that he was appointed to Orrington, a town outside Bangor.
There, a Methodist source recounts, he continued to teach "the doctrines of Miller,
to the damage of the strong and flourishing society in that place."[13] The removal
of Cox as presiding elder led to the expulsion of Harmon and other Portland-area
Millerites from the Methodist church in 1842.

While events related to adventism and abolition continued to unfold in tandem,
Sunderland and Harmon took increasingly divergent paths in relation to them. In
1843, while Scott and Sunderland were forming the Wesleyan Methodist Church,
Harmon and other adventists, relying on calculations based on biblical prophesy,
were eagerly awaiting the second coming predicted for later that year. When the
end didn't come as anticipated in 1843, adventists reassessed their calculations,
adjusted for differences in ancient and modern calendars, and set the new date
for October 22, 1844. In 1844, Methodists watched as the M.E.C. split over slavery, despite the exodus of the denomination's most committed abolitionists two
years earlier, and the adventists, sure that they had it right this time, reeled with
disappointment when October 22 came and went without incident. Although
Harmon was at the center of radical adventist attempts to make sense of the "Great
Disappointment," Sunderland, already deeply involved in his new career as a
"mental philosopher," was only half-heartedly involved in the formation of the
Wesleyan Methodist Church and soon severed his connections with Methodism
altogether.

As we have seen, mesmeric practice made its swift, albeit somewhat belated
appearance, on the American scene during the late 1830s and early 1840s. By
1843, K. Dickerson, a self-described "practical magnetizer," could confidently
state that those who "successfully magnetize in the United States are so numerous
that their names would fill a volume."[14] Dickerson discussed five American-born
promoters of mesmerism with La Roy Sunderland, "a [conspicuous] writer on
Mesmerism," heading the list.[15] He noted that Sunderland's monthly periodical,
The Magnet, had "done much to diffuse a knowledge of the laws of Mesmerism"
and indeed was "one of the best and most philosophical periodicals published in
America."[16] Dickerson spoke highly of Sunderland, but he also lavished praise on
Robert Collyer, an Englishman viewed by many as "the Champion of Mesmerism
in America." Collyer, not shy when it came to self-promotion, claimed much of
the credit for the proliferation of American magnetizers, saying that "the discoveries which I made, and the philosophy of science which I explained fully in my
lectures, induced hundreds of ignorant mechanics, carpenters, painters, furriers,
scavengers, barbers, and other 'unlettered cubs,' who having power to produce
by mechanical labor, the unconscious state, attempted to lecture and explain the
phenomena to the public; and a pretty mess they made of it."[17]

Although all these "professional magnetizers" viewed themselves as descendants of Mesmer and Puységur, they engaged in freewheeling theoretical speculation with so little restraint (or scientific training) that they soon generated a plethora of new terms to distinguish their efforts from that of Mesmer or Puységur and their contemporary rivals. Although their theories and thus their vocabularies differed, the most notable were engaged to varying degrees in three activities: public lecture-demonstrations, private healing sessions with patients, and/or writing. The backgrounds of the better-known magnetizers varied. Some identified themselves as professors or former professors, some as physicians. Others were ministers or former ministers. Whatever their background or training, most were free-lance professionals.[18] The professional magnetizers of the 1840s varied in the amount of attention they accorded to religion. The ministers and former ministers were clearly the most interested. John Bovee Dods, a Universalist minister, and La Roy Sunderland were the two most prominent minister-magnetizers in the United States during the 1840s.

Armchair comparisons between mesmeric and revival phenomena were increasingly common during the 1830s and 1840s, but Sunderland was the only mesmerist who published accounts of what were, in effect, rudimentary controlled experiments on religious subjects to see if muscular rigidity and visions could be artificially induced through mesmeric means. Sunderland was able to make these contributions owing to, not despite, his twenty years in the Methodist ministry. While a minister, Sunderland witnessed phenomena that he later explained in terms of a state of "induced sleep," and for at least ten years he enthusiastically promoted them as signs of the presence of God. Referring to his unique position, he wrote: "I am not aware that anyone connected with the clerical profession, ever before attempted to account for these things on pure psychological principles. . . . Certainly, no clergyman has attempted this, who, himself, was in the habit of inducing these results."[19]

Not only did Sunderland explain revival phenomena in psychological terms, he also used what he came to view as his experience "inducing" mental phenomena in believers as a basis for criticizing mesmeric theory and practice. In contrast to many of his contemporaries in the profession, Sunderland, when he finally took to the lecture circuit, did not rely upon a "clairvoyant somnambule" to demonstrate his methods and theories. Rather, in the manner of a preacher, he invited entranced subjects from his audience onto the stage, demonstrating, in doing so, that neither specific techniques, particular persons, nor special fluids were necessary to induce or account for these mental phenomena.

Although few of the professional mesmerizers devoted as much time to explaining religious phenomena in mesmeric terms as did Sunderland, the adventist movement of the 1840s amply demonstrates that most people in the northeastern United States had heard of mesmerism. Indeed, adventist use of mesmerism as an epithet to discredit "fanatics" within their own ranks during the 1840s indicates that they too understood mesmerism as means of explaining claims they deemed to be false in naturalistic terms. The religious experiences of the early adventists, specifically the bodily exercises and visions rooted in their Methodist heritage, were particularly vulnerable to mesmeric explanation.

This chapter explores the role of the magnetic state in thinking about visions and other revival phenomena. In the first half of this chapter, I focus on the emergence of the experimentally induced "magnetic state" as a means of explaining visions. I look at the early "armchair" comparisons of mesmeric and revival phenomena, particularly as they influenced Sunderland's development from Methodist revival preacher to mental philosopher; the emergence of the idea of a "magnetic state" and the new magnetic histories based upon it; and Sunderland's private and public experiments with religious subjects. After a brief excursus on the fate of experience among the emerging Methodist middle class, I focus, in the second half of the chapter, on the challenge that mesmerism posed for the radical adventists. I highlight the importance of Methodist-style religious experience for adventist radicals in Maine in the mid-1840s; examine the role of visions in the making of Ellen G. (Harmon) White as the prophetess of Seventh-day Adventism; and discuss the place of mesmerism in the Seventh-day Adventist cosmos. I argue that the clairvoyant somnambule, as a naturally induced analog to the visionary, provided a more convincing means of demonstrating the natural character of involuntary sensory phenomena than had been available to eighteenth-century anti-enthusiasts. Radical adventists, recognizing the threat that mesmerism posed to their vision-based movement, responded by integrating it as a demonic element into their cosmology.

EXPLAINING VISIONS

Animal Magnetism and the Shout Tradition

The shout tradition entered New England in the 1790s under the pioneering efforts of itinerant Jesse Lee. Methodism was from the outset an upstart, populist presence in New England. It was known for its enthusiastic worship, its uneducated preachers, and its all-round lack of respectability. Although details are sketchy, the shout tradition seems to have flowered particularly amidst the Methodist revivals of the early 1820s under the leadership of itinerants, such as La Roy Sunderland.[20] The challenge to the respectable revivalism of the Congregationalists and Presbyterians continued with the birth of Presbyterian Charles Finney's "new-measures" revivalism in the towns of upstate New York shortly thereafter.[21]

In response to the challenge posed by these more "enthusiastic" forms of revivalism, New England Congregationalists and "Old School" Presbyterians looked back to the colonial awakening in New England, appropriating Jonathan Edwards as the father of a tradition of "sober, clerical-directed, local revivals." This one-sided interpretation of Edwards cast him as the staunch opponent of "enthusiasm" and revivalistic "excesses," or, in the language of the early national period, as an unequivocal opponent of "fanaticism." The tradition of "respectable" revivalism was thus defined in relation to, and in turn created associations between, those

CAMP MEETING AT EASTHAM, MASS

4. Mourners praying at a camp meeting in New England. Courtesy of Corbis Images.

branded as "fanatics." As memories of the French Prophets faded, James Davenport was held up as the exemplary "fanatic" to whom the "disorderly" revivals on the Kentucky frontier, the camp meetings of the Methodists, and ultimately the "new-measures" of Charles Finney were assimilated.[22] This perspective on Edwards and the colonial awakening was institutionalized at Andover Theological Seminary, the first and for a time most influential postgraduate theological school in America, and widely disseminated by its graduates. The triumph of Andover's "New England theology" effectively established a sober, learned, and professional Jonathan Edwards as America's foremost theologian and created a revival tradition that ran from one New England awakening to the next, effectively obscuring the more "fanatical" revivals that swept the South and the West during the late-eighteenth and early-nineteenth centuries.[23]

During the late 1820s, Congregationalists seized on the Commissioners' Report on animal magnetism as a further means of discrediting the excesses of "fanaticism." Grant Powers, a Congregationalist minister from New Hampshire, tackled the question of the "influence of the imagination on the nervous system" and its implications for religion at the behest of his ministerial association. He apparently first learned of the Commissioners' Report through entries on "Imagination" and

"Imitation" in "Dr. Rees' Cyclopedia." In light of the conclusions of the Commission regarding, in his words, "the astonishing influence of the imagination," he invited his readers to participate in a thought experiment in which he linked the bodily exercises associated with revivals with animal magnetism.

> Let us suppose that Mesmer and Deslon has been ecclesiastics; that they had inculcated the idea on this class of person, that religion, in a high degree, produced similar effects on the human body; and that without religion they must be damned;—suppose they had endeavored by all possible means to excite their apprehensions, to raise their animal feelings, and by hurried, boisterous, and long addresses, they had kept their minds strained intensely for hours in succession, yea, whole days and nights;—and have we not reason to believe, that similar effects would have followed? and when one had exhibited these symptoms, another, and another, would do the same?

These effects would be reinforced, "if when one arose from the paroxysm, he was taught by those whom he considered his superiors, to believe that he emerged from a state of endless condemnation to a state of justification, life, and peace; should hear his conversion proclaimed by a multitude of voices, and should join his own, also, to the quire in a song of praise for his deliverance." Because these feelings would be "involuntary and real effects, the subjects of them would ascribe them to the supernatural influence of the spirit of God, and the deception might be fatal."[24]

Although John Fanning Watson had already concluded privately that animal magnetism might explain the "circumstances of camp meetings,"[25] Powers was the first, so far as I know, to make the connection, in print, between revival phenomena and animal magnetism.[26] Methodism figured prominently in Powers's discussion. Although he cited a variety of authors both medical and religious, including Edwards, Whitefield, M'Nemar on the Kentucky revivals, and Southey's *Life of Wesley*, he relied more heavily on Watson's *Methodist Error* than on any other source.[27] Methodists not only supplied most of Powers's examples, they were notably absent from the long list of divines—Anglican, Calvinist, and Lutheran— whom he claimed shared his naturalistic understanding of these phenomena.[28] In fact, he noted that John Wesley, unlike his brother Charles, "was greatly inclined to attribute all appearances which he could not explain to a supernatural influence, either good or bad."[29]

Others made the connection between Methodism and mesmerism in the 1820s and 1830s as well. In addition to Amariah Brigham, who included a chapter on camp meetings in his *Observations on Religion*, John Bovee Dods also made a brief foray into explaining Methodism. Dods did so not because he, as a Universalist, had a personal interest in or animus against the Methodists, but because "[e]ver since that class of Christians had a religious existence in the United States, persons have fallen down in a species of trance" and been wrongly stigmatized as a result. In an attempt to "remove . . . [this] stigma on a large and respectable denomination," he explained to his readers that what is going on among Methodists is not a matter of "delusion" or "deception," but rather a manifestation of "the magnetic state—or more properly . . . the spiritual state."[30]

La Roy Sunderland made the connection between the Methodist shout tradition and animal magnetism by reading Powers's book. In contrast to Powers, Dods, and Brigham, however, Sunderland was a revival preacher who was intimately involved with the phenomena he sought to explain. During his first ten years in the ministry, Sunderland "attended camp-meetings, conferences, class-meetings, love-feasts, four-days' meetings, field-meetings, &c."[31] He described meetings in which "the audience were completely convulsed with emotions, so much so that I left the pulpit, and stood within the altar, which was immediately surrounded by the people pressing 'forward for prayers;' some wringing their hands, and smiting their breasts in agonies of grief; others prostrate and groaning upon the floor; while others, in a state of trance and ecstatic joy, were clapping their hands, and shouting aloud 'the praises of the Lord.' " While he was preaching on another occasion, "[people] wept, fell upon the floor, become cold and rigid in their muscular systems; their eyes were closed, or elevated and set; some of them fell into a state of trance, and all the singing, praying, rejoicing and other manifestations which took place during that sermon, we supposed to have been produced by the 'power of the Holy Ghost,' operating on the minds of the people."[32]

Sunderland apparently had his doubts about these phenomena even as they occurred. In fact, he indicated "that his mind was more or less unsettled" with respect to them until he read Powers's book. He did so in 1834, a year after "his zeal in public [had] so much exhausted his strength that he lost the use of his vocal powers." Perhaps his doubts undermined his zeal and contributed to his collapse. Whatever the cause, he was "compelled to give up the labors of a pastor" in 1833 on account of losing his voice and retired, as a result, to Andover, Massachusetts, home of Andover Theological Seminary, to spend three years reading and writing.[33]

While in Andover, he radically remade his approach to ministry. He arrived, a preacher in the shout tradition who had lost his voice, and left with interests in psychology and mental phenomena, a commitment to a formally educated ministry, and an ardent advocate of abolition. From 1835 to 1842, Sunderland served as editor of *Zion's Watchman* and devoted most of his energies to abolition. His interest in psychology was not entirely abandoned, however. Two years after reading Powers's essay, Sunderland went to hear Monsieur Poyen, and he later told James Monroe Buckley that he "soon found that he could equal the Frenchman."[34] Sunderland witnessed his first " 'Mesmeric' operation" at his home in New York in 1839, at what would have been the height of the conservative attacks on him for his abolitionist work. Following the setbacks at the General Conference of 1840, Sunderland focused his attention on his psychological interests. In 1841, he began a series of experiments on mental phenomena, the results of which he published in *Zion's Watchman*. In July 1842, he discontinued publication of *Zion's Watchman* and began a new paper, *The Magnet*, devoted to "the Investigation of Human Physiology," which he continued to publish for about two years.[35] Relying heavily on material that had already appeared in *The Magnet*, he published *Pathetism*, his first book on "mental or nervous phenomena" in 1843.

The Magnetic State

The postulation of special mental states, initially designated as "magnetic" and later as "trance" or "dissociative" states, played a central role in psychological theorizing about religion during the course of the nineteenth century. The newly discovered "clairvoyant somnambule," the exemplar of this state, provided a humanly induced analogue to religious visionaries. Where the fits and convulsions of hysterics, epileptics, and persons terrorized by natural phenomena provided eighteenth-century theorists with examples of naturally induced involuntary motor phenomena, the "clairvoyant somnambule" provided a means of demonstrating the natural induction of involuntary *sensory* phenomena that the eighteenth-century theorists lacked.

The Magnet played a crucial role in disseminating information about this state in the American context. In contrast to the writings of Powers and Brigham, which relied on the older Commissioners' Report, *The Magnet* facilitated the dissemination of the Puysegurian tradition introduced by Poyen in the late 1830s and, thus, represented the latest thinking on animal magnetism. Where the Commissioners' Report explained the "fits" and "convulsions" of magnetized subjects as products of imagination and imitation, the Puysegurian tradition promoted the idea that magnetizers could induce a sleep-like state with unusual properties in receptive subjects. The only American periodical devoted to the topic of animal magnetism, *The Magnet* served as clearinghouse not only for accounts of American attempts to induce and work with the state, but also for European literature on the subject. For a number of years, Sunderland was, as he said, "in the habit of importing about every thing published in England and France upon this philosophy."[36] In the pages of the *Magnet*, we see the confluence of European and American thinking about this state, the variety of terms used to name it, and the way that Sunderland and others defined related terms, such as ecstasy and trance.

In the first number of *The Magnet*, Sunderland referred to "Mesmerism," "Living Magnetism," "coma," and "sleep." In the second issue, he introduced the terms "sleep-waking," "somno-vigilium," and "somnambulism" in conjunction with a lengthy excerpt on "Sleep-Waking" taken from British physician John Elliotson's textbook on human physiology.[37] Sunderland introduced the selection by saying that "the term sleep-waking, or somno-vigilium, has been used to signify a partial sleep, of a peculiar kind, in which persons have a sense of hearing and seeing, without the use of the common organs of these exercises." He added, "the term somnambulism is sometimes applied to such cases, though, indeed, the patient does not walk at all."[38] Neither "sleep-waking" nor "somno-vigilium" gained much currency in either England or America. Somnambulism, Sunderland's objections not withstanding, was the most widely used term for this state during the 1840s.[39]

While Elliotson tried to popularize the English term "sleep-waking" as a corrective to the French term *somnambulisme*, the New York physician Samuel Mitchill, according to Sunderland, introduced the term "somnium" as an alternative to "sleep-waking." Somnium, according to Mitchell, was "a state in which persons, in a peculiar state of sleep, perform acts of which they are, at the time or afterwards, wholly unconscious."[40] Mitchill was well known for his account of Rachel Baker, the "sleeping preacher," published in 1814. Baker was a young Presbyterian woman who rather regularly lost consciousness and, while lying still with her eyes closed, would "fall into a devotional exercise." According to Mitchill, the exercise consisted of three parts: "an opening prayer to God, similar to those of our reformed preachers; . . . an address or exhortation as to a human audience present, and listening to her; and . . . a closing supplication to the Supreme being resembling in its principle [sic] points the final offering of confession and thanksgiving from the pulpit."[41] Elliotson was rather more to the point when he described her as "preach[ing] during her sleep, performing regularly every part of the Presbyterian service, from the psalm to the blessing."[42]

Mitchill compared Baker's "paroxysms" to those of hysterics and epileptics, noting that as with hysterics and epileptics, she lost all "recollection of occurrences during the fit." In contrast to them, he said that while in this state, "she exercises the faculty of invention, by combining her ideas in new ways, by pronouncing discourses infinitely diversified amidst the sameness of topics, and of uttering some phrases and metaphors that are peculiar to herself." Perhaps, the most extraordinary feature, he added, was "the readiness and aptness" with which she answers the questions of bystanders.[43] After pointing out several similar cases, Mitchill suggested that her case should be explained neither in terms of the supernatural nor of imposture. Rather, he located it in relation to the third of the "three states of animal existence. *Wakefulness, Sleep,* and *Vision* or *Dream*." He indicated that this third state, that of "Vision or Dream," was not as well understood as the first two and that "perhaps another term might be chosen to signify this intermediate and peculiar modification of the organs of sense." He indicated that he would refer to this third state "under the latin name of somnium."[44]

Although Sunderland and others used the terms "trance" and "ecstasy" more or less interchangeably during the 1840s, they did not equate them with the magnetic state. Thus, referring to trance, Sunderland wrote: "this term has long been used to signify a state, in which the soul seems to have passed out of the body into the celestial regions." As an illustration, he excerpted liberally from the life of the early-eighteenth-century Presbyterian revivalist William Tennent, adding that "some . . . believe that he actually died and went to heaven, in the trance narrated below."[45] A month later, he wrote that the term "ecstasy . . . has been used to signify a fixed state, or trance, in which . . . the functions of the senses are suspended by the contemplation of some extraordinary or supernatural object." He indicated that a case of this kind, that of William Tennent, was described in the last issue.[46] This traditional use of trance as a synonym for ecstasy, independent of the magnetic state, undoubtedly reflected the King James Version's translation of the Greek *ecstasis* as "trance" and the use of the word *ecstasis* in conjunction with Peter's visions in the Book of Acts.[47]

Some months later Sunderland confronted the problem of terminology head on. "[E]very person familiar with the phenomena described in this work," he wrote, "has felt the want of suitable terms, by which to designate them; and some terms we have been in the habit of using, have not been understood by all, and others, it is well known,—such, for instance, as 'somnambulism,' have been used in a sense widely different from what their radical meaning would justify." Not only was the root meaning of somnambulism inappropriate, it made no reference to "the manner in which it [a state of sleep] may have been brought on." Sunderland, desirous of a "term suitable for designating the state of *induced* sleep," proposed "somnipathy," that is "sleep from *sympathy*." Nor in his view were the terms "Mesmerism" and "Magnetism" any more apt designations for "the *process* for producing sleep by *sympathy*." For that, Sunderland proposed the term "pathetism," which he defined as the "agency by which one person, by manipulation, produces emotion, feeling, passion, or any physical or mental effect, in the system of another." To "pathetise" someone was to induce in them this peculiar state of sleep.[48]

Despite his forceful promotion of "pathetism" and its derivatives as substitutes for "mesmerism" and "magnetism," his terminology never really caught on.[49] Sunderland himself was satisfied with the term and continued to use it throughout his career. During the 1840s, sleep-related terminology—somnambulism, somnium, somnipathy, and induced sleep—dominated, but never completely prevailed, as a means of designating the "mesmeric state." As Sunderland conceded, "the truth is, many of the phenomena common to a state of induced sleep, are so new and unaccountable, that language does not seem to have afforded the necessary terms for designating them all."[50] Sunderland's own hesitancies were reflected in *Pathetism*'s subtitle, where he avoided designating the state itself, referring simply to the "laws which induce somnambulism, second sight, sleep, dreaming, trance, and clairvoyance." In a similar fashion, he titled a chapter in *Pathetism*: "Somnium, Trance, [and] Somnambulism." Although trance at this point denoted a particular form of Christian experience, Sunderland decided in another ten years that "trance," understood abstractly, provided a more accurate designation for the magnetic state than any of the sleep-related derivatives. His last book, titled *The Trance and Correlative Phenomena* (1868), reflected this shift in nomenclature.

Whether theorists recognized a magnetic state and, if they did, the way in which they designated it were not inconsequential matters. Classifying animal magnetism as a form of enthusiasm and explaining it in terms of imagination and imitation left animal magnetism without explanatory power in its own right. As a mental state, it acquired explanatory power. How this mental state was conceptualized in turn affected the kind of explanatory power it might convey. When the state was designated with sleep-related terminology, theorists located potential explanations in relation to the familiar continuum between sleeping and waking. Conceptualized in this way, it was not simply another manifestation of enthusiasm easily imbued with pathological overtones, but a new potentially nonpathological explanation for "enthusiasm."[51] Understood as a state, animal magnetism provided a new basis for wide-ranging comparisons of religious and nonreligious phenomena and resulted in magnetic histories of false religion that vastly superseded the earlier histories of enthusiasm.

Magnetic Histories

Sunderland opened his first book on pathetism with the wide-ranging historical assertion that "it is now generally admitted, that some knowledge of Pathetism prevailed in Egypt, more than three thousand years ago." In addition to the ancient Egyptians, he noted that "it is said, that the priests of Chaldea practiced pathetism as a medicinal agent" and he adds that "almost every sect of enthusiasts has had its records of cures performed, not, indeed, by miracle, but in some instances, it may have been by the touch or friction of the human hand; as it is well known that similar means were recommended for the cure of diseases, long before the days of Mesmer."[52] In making these claims, Sunderland rehearsed the outlines of the history of animal magnetism found in the *Dictionnaire des Science Médicales*. John Elliotson recommended the entry on "Magnétisme Animal" as the best single source for a complete history of the subject.[53]

As Alan Gauld points out, many of the mesmerists of this era searched through historical works and travelers' journals seeking examples of mesmeric phenomena in other times and places. In this way, he says, they built up "a kind of mesmeric perspective on history," a precursor of what "now would be called social anthropology."[54] Such histories also built on earlier histories of enthusiasm and prefigured later more extensive histories of religion. Although all these histories tended to range widely in their search for comparable phenomena, John Elliotson explained that they approached the phenomena in two very different ways, with different implications for explaining the origins of false religion.

Some, according to Elliotson, "ascribe all to imagination, consider the agitations and prophecies of the Delphian priestess of Apollo and the Sybils[;] . . . the ecstacies of Dervishes and Santons, and of Shakers and Quakers, Irvingites, and of all ridiculous enthusiasts [;] . . . and the pretended miraculous cures of all ages . . . as only a piece with mesmerism, showing how strongly fear or enthusiasm will work upon the brain and all the other organs."[55] These authors viewed mesmerism as being of a piece with false religion. In their view, both mesmerism and false religion had their origins in the power of fear and enthusiasm to act upon the imagination.

Others, according to Elliotson, contended that "magnetic influence has always been acknowledged," although not always, of course, by that name. "They believe," he said, that "mesmeric operation[s]" can be identified in ancient healing practices "and consider them, and all the oracles, visions, prophecies, magic, and miracles of the pagan world . . . the result of this mighty power." Moreover, he stated, "those mesmerizers who are deists consider even the alleged supernatural things of the Jewish and Christian world, as not supernatural, but [as] the result of [mesmeric operations]."[56] These authors viewed mesmerism or mesmeric operations as a power in its own right, as in effect a distinctive mental state. As such it was *not* of a piece with false religion and indeed could be used to account for its origins.

Elliotson's distinction between mesmerizers who were deists and those who were not highlighted the fact that these mesmeric histories, like the earlier histories of enthusiasm, were still histories of *false* religion. While Christian mesmerizers explained the supernatural things of the pagan world in terms of mesmerism, only deists were willing to explain the "alleged supernatural things of the Jewish and Christian world" in naturalistic terms. As was the case with histories of enthusiasm, many of the magnetic histories distinguished between true and false forms of Christianity. Thus, for example, Joseph Ennemoser, in his *Geschichte des thierischen Magnetismus* (1844), linked the "religious visions and ecstasies" of various religious traditions, including Christianity, with what was "formerly called magical" but should now, he argued, be understood as "magnetic."[57] He included visionaries and ecstatics in his history of magic, but he excluded saints and prophets. The latter, he said, "do not belong to the history of magic, but of religion." Disparaging both the "Brahmanic seers" and the Eastern Orthodox "hermits of Mount Athos," Ennemoser, presumably a German Protestant, identified visions and ecstasy with reliance on such "artificial means" as monasticism and asceticism. In contrast to visionaries and ecstatics, "the true prophet makes use of no artificial means; he repeats the word directly received from God, without preparation or mortification of the flesh." While "[t]he magical seer lives in the intoxication of his own visions; the prophet lives in faith; and actions, not visions, are signs of holiness."[58]

Not everyone associated magnetism with false religion either in Europe or America. During the early part of the nineteenth century, the German Romantics made important links between magnetism and what they understood to be true religion. Jung-Stilling's *Theorie der Geisterkunde* (1808), excerpted in *The Magnet* in 1842, was the principal means by which the mystical ideas, such as those of Swedenborg and Boehme, were fed into the magnetic movement.[59] Jung-Stilling's ideas were reinforced by Justinus Kerner's case histories of magnetic somnambules. The most famous of these, Friedericke Hauffe, known as the "Seeress of Prevorst," delivered cosmological and theological teachings while in the somnambulistic state and attracted numerous distinguished visitors. The writings of Jung-Stilling and Kerner led to a flowering of interest in "mystical magnetism" in Germany during the 1820s and 1830s.[60]

While Jung-Stilling's views on the soul and life after death prefigured, and indeed influenced, those of mid-century Spiritualists, he was rather more skeptical than they regarding human ability to reliably connect with that spirit world during this life. Thus, Sunderland quoted Jung-Stilling to the effect that "when a person falls into fits, either with or without convulsions, so that he loses his consciousness, and see visions, associates with spirits, and utters the sublimest things . . ., it must not on no account [sic] be regarded as anything divine, but as a real disease, and as an aberration of nature from her regular and prescribed path." Everything such a person said and did must be "rationally examined." Even if a person predicted future things and they came to pass, that did not prove that they were divine revelations. As long as the "soul is still attached to the body," Jung-Stilling wrote, "the connexion [between the soul and the spiritual world] is not perfect" and individuals cannot reliably "distinguish the images of [their] own imagination from spirits."[61]

Although Sunderland undoubtedly excerpted Jung-Stilling more for his cautionary remarks than his theological speculations,[62] some Americans, perhaps influenced by the spread of German ideas, shared Jung-Stilling's mystical views. K. Dickerson, an avid reader of *The Magnet*, may have been paraphrasing Jung-Stilling when he wrote that "mesmerism . . . exhibits a development of the mind heretofore unknown—it tells us plainly that the mind, freed from the 'husk of organization,' becomes immortal; that when this physical organization decays, that the immaterial principle expands its powers, and exists in another sphere."[63] Lecturing in the late 1840s, the Univeralist minister-magnetizer John Bovee Dods described mesmerism in a similar fashion as a long-dormant "power basined up in the fountains of the soul."[64] For most of the 1840s, however, such views were uncommon. During this period, magnetic theories were less often viewed in relation to the alleged powers of the soul than as a challenge to claims of direct religious experience.

It is against the backdrop of the magnetic histories of "false" religion, not the nascent spread of mystical magnetism, that we can understand Sunderland's sweeping claim that Pathetism could account, not only for revival phenomena, but also for "those curious *sympathetic imitative* results produced among the *Hindoos, Mohammedans, Anabaptists, French Prophets, Roman Catholics, Shaking Quakers, Mormons, Methodists,* and other *sects,* which have by ignorant fanatics been thought superhuman or miraculous."[65] Sunderland did not offer evidence to support this claim nor did he attempt to produce a full-scale magnetic or "pathetic" history of his own. Like Powers and Brigham, Sunderland was, however, responsible for disseminating magnetic interpretations of revival phenomena and giving American examples of magnetic phenomena a prominence they did not have in the European-authored histories of magnetism.[66]

Neither Sunderland's lists of historical examples, examples not unlike those of Powers and Brigham, nor his introduction of personal examples, which others might have supplied, were particularly original. What stood out was his claim that, based on unspecified experiments of his own, "there is a most striking similarity, between this state [of induced 'magnetic sleep'] and that into which the nervous system seems to be thrown, when persons are said to 'lose their strength,' under great religious excitement."[67] These experiments, although not "controlled" in any technical sense, were inherently comparative when performed on Methodist subjects who had lost their strength or had visionary experiences in the context of Methodist revivals. It was this double layer of experience that allowed both Sunderland *and his experimental subjects* to compare their experiences of induced "magnetic sleep" with experiences they had had in the context of Methodist revivals.

Magnetic Experiments

Looking back on his career later in life, Sunderland liked to think of himself as having begun his experiments while preaching revivals in the 1820s. "[D]uring all that time," he wrote, "I was (in some sense), unconsciously to myself, yet nevertheless performing what were really 'experiments' upon the nervous systems of my auditors; but, like the multitudes who have since operated under the name of 'Mesmerism,' &c., I did not fully comprehend how the strange results were brought about." So too, later in life, he would single out the "first 'Mesmeric' operation" he ever witnessed and credit it with supplying "the germ" about which his "new theory was formed." A fellow Methodist minister and his wife performed this experiment at Sunderland's home in 1839. We have three accounts of the experiment with Mrs. M'Reading, all late.[68]

Sunderland lifted up these earlier "experiments" in his later writings, but he began his first formal series of experiments in the summer and fall of 1841 with the help of a physician, Dr. Sherwood, and a noted phrenologist, Mr. Fowler. The experiments, conducted with the cooperation of a blind clairvoyant somnambule referred to simply as Mary, consisted of tests of her clairvoyant abilities while in the magnetic state.[69] The results of this series of experiments were published in *Zion's Watchman* between August 1841 and July 1842. Sunderland continued to experiment, informally with persons who came to him for treatment (since all such treatments were in effect experimental) and formally in the presence of small groups of observers. Starting in 1843, he began experimenting in public using subjects from his audiences to demonstrate his theories. Accounts of some of these later experiments were published in *The Magnet* in 1842 and 1843 and some materials related to his early experiments were reprinted or referred to in his later books.

The earliest available accounts of his experiments suggest, first, that they were not purely magnetic experiments, but combined phrenology and magnetism.[70] Second, while religious phenomena appear in many of them, the experiments were performed, for the most part, not to explain religious phenomena, but to understand the magnetic state and its possible uses.[71] Third, although he made any number of comments regarding the power of magnetism (or pathetism) to explain fanaticism, his primary practical interest at this time was not the psychology of religion, but "the cure of disease, and the relief of human suffering."[72] That his experiments on Methodist subjects were largely incidental, an artifact as it were of his situation, does not detract from their significance. Indeed, as we will see in the next chapter, Sunderland himself came to view them as increasingly significant as his theory matured.[73] In the early 1840s, however, Sunderland's primary aim, understandable enough in light of his problems with Methodism, was to establish himself in a new career as a mental philosopher and healer.

The earliest published account I have been able to find of an experiment on a Methodist subject appears as one in a series of medical cases that Sunderland published in *The Magnet* in 1842 to demonstrate the "therapeutic efficiency of Human Magnetism." This case, which appeared under the heading of "Monomania," reads as follows:

> A lady in A——, had been quite zealous in religion, a few years ago, and, during that time, she was known frequently to 'lose her strength,' as it is called, when she would appear to be exceedingly happy, and remain hours in a state of apparent catalepsy. But, sometime since, she sunk into a state of mental *despair*, and supposed herself abandoned of God and doomed to perdition. On putting her to sleep, (she had been magnetised

before) we not only removed her despair, but by exciting some of the organs, she declared herself perfectly happy, and what is remarkable, when we excited a particular organ she instantly lost her strength and her limbs became rigid, precisely as she was formerly affected, under religious excitement. Indeed, she declared the two states to be *precisely the same.*[74]

The ostensible point was the cure of a case of religious "monomania" or "mental despair," but the subtext was an experimental comparison of losing one's strength and becoming happy in the context of religious "excitements" and losing one's strength and becoming happy in the context of a phreno-magnetic treatment. As he would do in other accounts, Sunderland emphasized that the subject herself "declared the two states to be *precisely the same.*"

A second account of this sort, explicitly labeled as an experiment, took place in Sunderland's office on February 15, 1843. This and two other experiments were described by a witness, the unnamed editor of the *American Millenarian*. He wrote:

The first experiment was on an intelligent Christian lady of about twenty six. Mr. Sunderland stood behind her chair, and placing one finger on each side of her head, her eyes closed in a few minutes; and to all appearance, she was in a sound sleep, with this exception, that she seemed partially conscious of what was said in her presence, but she manifested great unwillingness to talk. She described her state, as one of complete *abstraction,* her mind, she said, seemed elevated far above the body, and the things of this world. Her countenance assumed a most expressive and heavenly appearance, and she declared that her perceptions of the spiritual world, and the happiness of its inhabitants was as real as any thing she had ever seen with her eyes.[75]

Here again, the state was induced using a phreno-magnetic technique. This time it was Sunderland, according to the witness, who declared that "this state . . . was, as far as he could judge, *identical* with that called *Trance* or *Ecstasy,* having, as he said, seen and examined, many cases, of this state, into which persons of a peculiar temperament have been known to fall, especially under religious excitement." The witness commented that "Mr. Sunderland thinks this *susceptibility,* and the *agency,* by which he produces these results . . . are destined to throw great light on . . . the various fanatical delusions which have done so much mischief in the world."[76]

Although our accounts of the "first 'Mesmeric' operation" that Sunderland ever witnessed, the experiment with Mrs. M'Reading in 1839, appeared much later, they were similar in many respects to the ones just described. In all the versions, Sunderland described Mrs. M'Reading as having been "entranced," in the first instance by a sermon he had delivered in 1824 and in the second instance in his home in 1839.[77] In each case, the two states were compared and their identity proclaimed. In the 1868 version, he indicated that the identity of " 'the state' brought on by the 'Mesmeric' processes of her husband . . . with that produced by [his] sermon . . . [was elicited] by free conversation with that excellent lady."[78] In his interview with James Monroe Buckley, the editor of the Methodist *Christian Advocate,* Sunderland gave the following account of the interchange:

> I had a visit from two Methodist friends, the Rev. C[harles] M['Reading] and his wife. I recognized her as one of my "converts" who had been entranced under a sermon I had preached in 1824. Hence, when the opportunity came, I asked Mrs. M['Reading] if she had heard of M. Poyen and the entrancement of Miss Gleason? "O, yes," she said; "and I have often been entranced in the same way by my husband." At this statement I was much surprised, and said to her that I would feel much obliged if she would allow me to see her in that state.[79]

The incident, as recalled by Sunderland, suggests that he was not alone among the Methodist clergy in his interest in animal magnetism. Not only had the M'Readings heard of Poyen and Gleason, but the Rev. M'Reading had already been experimenting with his wife. Presumably due to the experimentation, Mrs. M'Reading was already able to "entrance" herself.

When Sunderland asked if he could see her in that state, "she immediately complied, and, leaning back in her chair, she closed her eyes in a state of trance." "In a few moments," according to Sunderland,

> she appeared to be in a state of ecstatic joy, when she grasped my hand and said: "O, Brother Sunderland, this is the happiest state I was ever in. It is heaven. And do you remember how I went into this state under that powerful sermon you preached in our church in Scituate Harbor years ago? I was then 'caught up to Paradise,' as St. Paul was, and where I saw Jesus and all the angels so happy. Yes, Brother Sunderland, and this is the same heaven—the same as when my soul was converted and filled with the love of God."[80]

Here again, two states were compared, the state induced by preaching in 1824 and the self-induced trance in 1839. The first was a visionary experience in which Mrs. M'Reading had been "caught up to Paradise." She declared to Sunderland, that the self-induced trance reproduced that happy state and indeed in it, she experienced "the same heaven"—the same heaven as when her soul was converted and filled with the love of God, that is, sanctified.

As in the case of the "intelligent Christian lady," Sunderland described Mrs. M'Reading as being in a "state of trance" or "ecstatic joy." Neither he nor the M'Readings, however, explicitly described Mrs. M'Reading as clairvoyant, although they do refer to her as being entranced in the same fashion as Miss Gleason. The only Methodist that Sunderland explicitly described as a clairvoyant somnambule was a sixteen-year-old who fell into "a state of *trance,* as her religious friends call it[,] . . . soon after she had been much *excited,* and had professed to become completely sanctified." The young woman's friends referred to her as being in "a state of trance," using trance in the traditional, nontechnical sense of the term. Sunderland, although not changing the word's referent, relocated it as a subset of somnium. Trance, he said, "seems to differ from the ordinary states of somnium, merely in the degrees of abstraction of the mind to which it is carried, and in respect to the locomotion of the patient." Though some of the young woman's friends thought her experience "quite *miraculous,*" Sunderland concluded that hers was, "undoubtedly, a case of somnambulism."[81]

He added that persons in trance were "sometimes . . . remarkably clairvoyant; they [often] describe with accuracy persons and places, without the use of the external senses." This young woman, Sunderland said, was just such a case. Like the clairvoyant somnambules of the day, but also like the two young female exhorters described by Charles Chauncy, and Rachel Baker, the sleeping preacher described by Samuel Mitchill, this young Methodist woman interacted with others while in trance. According to Sunderland,

> She has, occasionally, a correct perception of the characters of different persons who enter he room, and will address them in reproofs, or exhortations to prayer and praise, according to their various characters, though she is said to have had no previous knowledge of them beforehand. When one enters her room who is pious, or is believed to be so by her, she clasps her hands into the form of what she calls 'a crown,' and places them upon his head; and the statements she makes about the characters, views, and feelings of those who have been to see her, are considered by her friends as the miraculous interpositions of the Divine Being.[82]

The behaviors described here—falling unconscious, out-of-body experiences, and engagement with visitors while in trance—combine elements we have seen. What was new was the terminology of "somnambulism" and "clairvoyance" and Sunderland's conviction that he had artificially induced this visionary state. Charles Chauncy, Dugald Stewart, and Amariah Brigham could explain involuntary sensory phenomena in terms of the imagination and sympathetic imitation, especially in the context of the crowd, but they did not attempt to test their theory by inducing such phenomena in susceptible subjects. Based on his experiments, Sunderland could say to one of the young woman's friends that he "had put persons into a state precisely similar, in which they had made descriptions of the characters of strangers, every way as correct and remarkable as in the present case."[83]

Clairvoyance was a controversial subject in the early 1840s. Letters to *The Magnet* often expressed the writers' desire for reliable information. A letter from Skaneateles, New York, referred to the "thousand marvelous stories" kept in circulation by the newspapers of the day and opined "that the popularity and success of [Sunderland's paper would] in great measure, depend upon his speedily disabusing the public mind of the impositions of quackery and villainy, and honestly teaching the truth—what is really known and what is merely conjectured." Sunderland was very aware of the problem that the circulation of "these marvelous stories" posed to science and he repeatedly reminded his readers "how easy it is to make persons of certain temperaments, see *any thing*, in the magnetic sleep."[84]

Although Sunderland placed little or no confidence in most of the stories that were circulated about clairvoyance, he nonetheless had witnessed numerous "demonstrations of the clairvoyant power" that led him to be "just as certain of its reality as I am of any other function of the nervous system."[85] He considered this clairvoyant power an extension of the magnetic sense awakened in the magnetic state. This "independent sense . . . sometimes takes accurate knowledge of things present and absent . . . and yet, at the same time, . . . may be deceived, so that the person may fancy he sees or tastes, or even does things, which have no existence except in his own apprehension."[86] In his cautious affirmation of clairvoyance as an independent sense awakened in the magnetic state, Sunderland lifted up the most distinctive and most controversial feature attributed to the magnetic state. The clairvoyant abilities of the somnambule raised the possibility of an experimentally accessible special sense that allowed the mind to pass beyond the external senses.

When he began his series of experiments in 1841, Sunderland's aim was to test the truth of theories that went under the heading of Mesmerism and Magnetism. By the time he published his book on pathetism two years later, he had rejected significant aspects of both the theory and the technique of animal magnetism. While maintaining something akin to Puységur's concept of "rapport," Sunderland followed the Commissioners' Report in rejecting magnetic fluids as an explanation of these phenomena. Sunderland was, as a result, something of an anomaly on the lecture circuit. Other lecturers postulated various sorts of fluids or currents to explain the state they induced, but Sunderland, in the words of a reporter from Providence, "goes dead against 'Mesmerism,' 'Neurology,' and other theories which have evidently been tried, and . . . found wanting."[87] A Boston paper described his lectures as "quite original," adding that "he does not follow or seem to agree with the lecturers on what is called 'Neurology,' or 'Mesmerism,' inasmuch as he rejects the idea of a fluid, said to be transmitted from the operator into the patient, by which the various phenomena have been said to be produced, under the name of 'Animal Magnetism.' "[88]

The elaborate procedures used by the mesmerizers to induce their results went by the wayside as well.[89] Although he provided instructions for pathetising in his book, his lecture demonstrations were notable, as Gauld points out, for their apparent lack of attention to method. In contrast to other magnetizers, the early newspaper accounts indicate that Sunderland did not travel the lecture circuit with a gifted somnambule. Nor did he go out of his way to make sure that there were experienced subjects in the audience upon whom he could demonstrate his points. Instead, in the words of a reporter, "he brought his process to bear on the entire assembly; and not withstanding the excitement and confusion which proceeded in the vast crowd, it was soon found, that some eight or ten persons were in a state of real somnambulism, and four of them, we were assured, were new subjects, never having been put to sleep before."[90]

One reporter recounted that Sunderland elicited such behavior by telling the audience, in a tone of voice "well calculated to produce sleepy inclinations[,] . . . to fix their eyes upon him," adding that "he was sure some of them would fall asleep!" That evening in Providence, the reporter said:

> We looked intently, but without any very decided effect. While gazing intently, we were told there was a lady in our vicinity fast asleep. Our attention was attracted to this *susceptible* subject, and sure enough there was every appearance of the same effects which we have seen produced by mesmerism.

The woman, seated in the back of the hall, soon moved from her seat, walked up to the stage, and there sat down.[91]

Looking back a decade later, Sunderland credited his rejection of traditional mesmeric methods to his previous experience as a minister. As he put it, "I, of course, felt no need of the 'passes' and 'efforts' by the 'will,' as I had been in the habit of inducing those very results long before without any 'passes,' or any specific efforts of the *will*."[92] Like a preacher, Sunderland brought his process to bear on the entire assembly, lecturing in such a way as to inform them directly and indirectly of what he expected would happen. Some people fell "asleep," just as in earlier years people had been convicted of sin. Then, like sinners responding to an altar call, the susceptible subjects proceeded to the stage where Sunderland would then engaged them as experimental subjects. As in the case of revivals, there were numerous tales of skeptics who succumbed to the "mesmerizing" effects of his lectures. In Boston, at his first lecture, five gentlemen unknown to Sunderland fell into "a state of real somnambulism" while Sunderland was lecturing. One of the men, a Baptist clergyman, "on being restored to a state of wakefulness, declared that he came to the lecture with no faith at all on the subject; and yet the Rev. Gentleman was so deeply impressed that he left his seat while asleep, and walked up to Mr. Sunderland at the desk."[93]

Although the experiments Sunderland performed on his entranced subjects varied, the content of the experiments, in many cases, extended the revivalistic comparison. The first person to take a seat on the stage during the Providence lectures, for example, "soon began to talk about angels, and to say she was in a very bright place and saw angels, while snatches of sacred music were chanted by her in a very sweet voice." A Mr. Snyder soon joined her. He too began to "talk about angels and sing songs."[94] Two young women were described as having ecstatic visions of heaven at one of Sunderland's Boston lectures. Before he had a chance to propose any experiments,

> one of the young ladies [on stage] began to rub her hands in great ecstacy, and turning her face towards the ceiling overhead, explained 'Oh! how beautiful, *beautiful*, BEAUTI-FUL!' 'What is so beautiful?' said the lecturer. 'Oh! those lights! how beautiful!' 'What else do you see? Be so kind as to tell me?' 'Oh! I see Heaven, and my father—glorious. Oh! how glorious!' Immediately after this dialogue was finished, she commenced singing a revival melody, and the other lady who had remained quiet until now, joined in and sung the second.

A bit later the second woman, "with an expression of delight upon her countenance which almost baffle[d] description," engaged in a similar dialogue with Sunderland in which, while staring at the ceiling, she saw "[her] Saviour" and her brother. The two women concluded with another duet.[95]

In his lecture-demonstrations, Sunderland's explicit aim was to demonstrate that mesmeric or magnetic phenomena could be explained in psychological terms. Convinced by his reading and experimentation that magnetic effects could be produced without recourse to special methods of induction and explained without recourse to special fluids, he used his skills as a revival preacher to demonstrate the power of "sympathy" to induce somnambulistic "sleep" in susceptible subjects. In replicating the form of a Methodist revival in his lectures and experimenting with subjects who experienced religious visions, Sunderland's demonstrations offered not only explicit explanations of magnetic phenomena, but implicit explanations of revival phenomena as well. Those familiar with revivals did not miss the comparison, often telling Sunderland "how much the nervous 'exercises' of those 'influenced' in [his] lectures resembled what they had seen in religious meetings among the different sects."[96]

In his use of sympathy to explain how he induced somnambulistic sleep in his subjects, Sunderland drew from a long tradition in moral and mental philosophy. In presuming that he was inducing a somnambulistic state, he allied himself with the magnetic tradition descended from Puységur. In affirming, however cautiously, that an independent sense was at times awakened in the magnetic state, Sunderland lifted up the most intriguing and the most controversial aspect of the magnetic state. In doing so, he stood in opposition not only to those who made supernatural claims regarding their experiences but to the academic tradition in moral philosophy as well.

AN EXCURSUS ON RESPECTABLE EXPERIENCE

Phoebe Palmer, the person typically given credit for initiating a decades-long revival of interest in holiness in both the Methodist and Reformed traditions, intervened paradoxically into the polarized debates over the authenticity of experience. Motivated by the absence of experience rather than its presence, she articulated a theology of experience that accorded well with what the academic moral philosophers could, and did, embrace. Palmer's distress, from childhood, stemmed from the fact that she did not experience "what she conceived to be the manner of the Spirit's operation on the hearts of others."[97] Her altar theology, as Stephen Cooley has pointed out, "represented a breakthrough for Palmer and others like her who seemed unable to experience revivalism's 'outward exhibitions,' its 'overwhelming manifestations of feeling,' or its 'luminous manner of assurance.' " Her famous "shorter way" to holiness was comprised of a series of steps, beginning with consecration ("laying all upon the altar" in the manner of Abraham's sacrifice of Isaac). Consecration was followed by the recognition of God's promises in scripture, the acceptance of God's promises for oneself, and public testimony to one's acceptance of the promises. The crucial twist was her determination to "*take God at his word* [in scripture], whatever her emotions might be." Indeed, she determined "that if . . . denied all outward or inward manifestations to an extent before unheard of, . . . she would still, through the power of the ALMIGHTY, . . . journey onward through the pilgrimage of life—*walking by faith.*"[98]

The paradoxical quality of Palmer's experience of sanctification was similar in some respects to David Brainerd's experience of conversion. Where the Edwardsean tradition emphasized the paradoxical relationship between the means of grace and the experience of grace, Palmer emphasized the paradoxical relationship between feeling and faith. In her words, her "error . . . during the whole of her former pilgrimage in the heavenly way, had been . . . [to require] *feeling,* the *fruit* of faith, previous to having exercised faith."[99] Where traditionally Methodists had testified to the witness of the Spirit, Palmer now encouraged them to make their testimony based on "the naked promises." Some critics sympathetic to the emphasis on holiness feared, according to Melvin Dieter, that reliance "upon a simple statement of faith . . . endangered the concept of the 'witness of the Spirit' that constituted the ground for assurance . . . in historical Wesleyanism."[100]

Ultimately, God did not actually deny Palmer the witness of the Spirit. It came, however, after she had offered herself to God on the altar in faith and it was manifest when she was assailed by doubts that her offering of herself had simply been "the work of [her] own understanding—the effort of [her] own will." Then, "the SPIRIT . . . bore full testimony to her spirit, of the TRUTH of THE WORD! . . . her very existence seemed lost and swallowed up in God; she plunged, as it were, into an immeasurable ocean of love, light, and power, and realized that she was encompassed with the 'favor of the Almighty as with a shield.'"[101] As in the case of Wesley, the Spirit witnessed to the truth of the Bible and manifested itself in opposition to the Satanic temptations of rationalism. The Spirit did so, however, in the idiom of authentic experience characteristic of the Edwardsean tradition, that is, not through visions, voices, trances, or even strangely warmed hearts but by swallowing her up in God. As argued earlier, the differences between Edwards and Wesley were subtle and there was considerable overlap between them. Where old-fashioned "shouting" Methodists embodied the differences between Wesley and Edwards, Phoebe Palmer occupied the common ground between them.

Palmer's ability to bridge the two traditions was aptly illustrated in her relationship with Thomas Upham, a Congregationalist minister and professor of mental and moral philosophy at Bowdoin College, who experienced sanctification in conjunction with Palmer's Tuesday meetings in the winter of 1839–40. Although Upham, like Palmer, experienced the witness of the Spirit, he too encouraged Christians to claim sanctification based on the promises rather than awaiting the witness of the Spirit as a sign of special assurance. Palmer and Upham agreed, according to Darius Salter, that "if the grace of God enabled a person to give his all and a person could be conscious that his all had been given, that person would be considered sanctified." Palmer, however, made this argument from scripture, while Upham made it from his understanding of the mind, specifically the intuitive powers of consciousness, derived from Scottish common-sense philosophy. Indeed, according to Salter, the Reformed theologians associated with the holiness movement—Upham, Asa Mahan, and Charles Finney—substituted the testimony of consciousness in place of the direct witness of the Spirit or Scripture as evidence of sanctification.[102]

In substituting consciousness of giving one's all for the witness of the Spirit, both Palmer and Upham downplayed the role of "sensible" experience in relation to assurance. This shift in emphasis allowed Upham to connect Wesleyan holiness with the Edwardsean tradition of "disinterested benevolence" and the Catholic mystical tradition of "indifference," found especially in the Quietists and Madame Guyon. Upham was known in holiness circles not only for his devotional works, *The Interior Life* (1843) and *The Life of Faith* (1845), but also for his biographies of two devout Catholic women, Catherine of Adorna and Madame Guyon. The latter was by far the most influential. Although extracts from Guyon's autobiography had been published in England and America previously, Upham was her chief popularizer. Upham interpreted her spiritual autobiography in such a way as to make her a "living example . . . of holiness" in a tradition that included both Catholics and Protestants.[103] Upham's positive interest in Catholic mysticism resulted, as Melvin Dieter has indicated, in the permanent infusion of "a deep sense of experiential kinship" between at least some portions of the American holiness tradition and Catholic mystics, such as Guyon. In fact, Upham regarded Palmer herself as a genuine mystic, although she rejected the comparison and criticized Upham for his turn to Catholic writers.[104]

As Upham stated in his preface to the *Life of Madame Guyon*, the point of connection between Guyon, her mentor Fenelon, and the Protestant holiness tradition lay in the belief that the "sanctification of the heart essentially consists . . . in the experience of . . . pure or unselfish love."[105] To love God unselfishly, Guyon, in Upham's rendering, encouraged the more advanced soul to "suffer whatever He requires you to suffer" with resignation and patience and "with inward submission and quietness . . . [to] wait the return of the Beloved." In this way, she said, "you will demonstrate, that *it is God himself alone* and his good pleasure which you seek, and *not the selfish delights of your own sensations*." This was done through "abandonment," that is, through resigning or consecrating oneself entirely to God. The consecration of the soul was continually tested through tribulations, of which Madame Guyon's life provided many illustrations. Nonetheless, the soul that perseveres was "astonished to find God gradually taking possession of its whole being."[106] In a similar vein, Upham wrote in his *Life of Faith* that "the state of mind . . . which is most favorable to . . . the constant indwelling and operation of the Holy Spirit, is that of inward meekness or quietness." "A quiet spirit," he said, "is one, in which the natural desires, in distinction from God's desires and will, no longer exist."[107] According to Upham, "one of the most decisive marks of the presence of the Holy Ghost in its fulness [sic], is a resigned and peaceful state of the spirit, originating in perfect faith in God."[108]

He contrasted the state of mind most favorable to the constant indwelling of the Holy Spirit—quietness, calm, resignation, peace—with the state of mind that he considered least favorable—excitement. In the former, Upham said, "there seems to be an entire subsidence or withdrawal of that natural excitability which is so troublesome to the Christian."[109] This polarity between peace and excitement informed Upham's psychology. Or, more precisely, Upham's understanding of authentic Christian experience was built upon a mental philosophy that associated peace with ordered mental action and excitement with disordered mental action, i.e., nervous disease. Upham's underlying mental philosophy provided a basis for explaining what he took to be inauthentic religious experience, i.e., "visions, voices, trances and physical agitations," in terms of "natural causes or disordered mental action, especially of the senses."[110]

The association between false religious experience and disorder, whether emotional or social, was, as we have seen a longstanding one, and Upham did not spend much time developing it. Indeed, he argued that "the decisive circumstance, unfavorable to this form of christian [sic] experience, if by courtesy we may call it such, is . . . *that, in itself considered, it is wholly intellectual.*" On its face this is a rather odd assertion, but, as it turns out, one grounded in Upham's threefold division of the faculties into intellect, sensibilities (feelings), and will and his evangelical commitment to a religion of the heart, that is, to experience grounded ultimately in feeling rather than intellect. Although Upham contended that the experiences in question could be explained in terms of the disordered mental action of the intellectual faculty, the particulars were not important, because, in his view, nothing that arose solely from the intellectual faculty could be considered as religion. In his words, "visions, trances, revelations, and all other things, which are exteriorly imparted without being inwardly and operatively experienced, communicating new and perhaps remarkable views without changing the dispositions of the heart, are just what they are and just what their names indicate; *but they are not religion.*"[111]

Both animal magnetism and somnambulism had a place, of sorts, in Upham's philosophy of mind. Both, as we might expect, were forms of disordered mental action. More intriguing, however, is the fact that Upham apparently saw no theoretical relationship between them. Somnambulism, like the senses and, significantly, like dreaming, was an "intellectual state of external origin." The main difference between dreaming and somnambulism was that in the latter case the dreaming mind retained its "power over the muscles." While in most cases of somnambulism, Upham said, the senses were "locked up," there were, he acknowledged, a few "extraordinary" cases where "perceptions of sight increased much above the common degree." For such cases, he said, there was no satisfactory explanation. Indeed, it is not even clear from his account how such persons entered the somnambulistic state. However it occurred, we can assume it had nothing to do with animal magnetism. Animal magnetism in Upham's system was a product of "sympathetic imitation," which was classified among the "sensitive states of the mind or sentiments." It had to do, in other words, with feelings, not the intellect. His discussion of animal magnetism was taken from Dugald Stewart, including excerpts from Stewart's discussion of the Commissioner's Report.[112]

Although the absence of any theoretical connection between somnambulism and animal magnetism is not surprising in Upham's early works, revised editions of his textbooks give no indication that his views changed over the next thirty years. Although he cut the sections on somnambulism and animal magnetism altogether from the *Abridgement of Mental Philosophy* (1861), his popular college textbook, he retained both sections unchanged in later editions of *Outlines of Imperfect and Disordered Mental Action* (1868). While the popular psychologists were busily using animal magnetism to induce a somnambulistic state in experimental subjects, academic psychology slept as it were under "a heavy blanket of philosophical orthodoxy" that relied heavily on Reid, Stewart, and Locke. Until the 1890s, academic psychology was a subset of philosophy. Unlike popular psychology, it had little use for experimentation. As a prominent systematizer and popularizer of academic mental philosophy, Upham provided respectable Protestants with a synthesis of theology and philosophical psychology that explained and discredited both the enthusiasm of the camp meetings and the investigations of the animal magnetizers.[113]

The standard histories of holiness in the American Methodist tradition view Palmer as reviving interest in holiness in the wake of an extended decline. I think it would be more accurate to describe her, along with Upham and the Oberlin Perfectionists, as reworking the popular Methodist understanding of sanctification to enhance its appeal both to middle-class elites within Methodism and to solidly middle-class Congregationalists and Presbyterians.[114] Traditional histories of holiness overlook the importance of sanctification for early American Methodists, especially for the side of the tradition so often deemed "enthusiastic." While efforts to make Methodist camp meetings more "orderly" in the late 1810s and 1820s may have led to a decrease in "visible" experiences of conversion and sanctification,[115] Palmer and her generation grew up with the earlier ideal. The new understanding of holiness promoted by Palmer and Upham did not simply reflect the experiential difficulties of a few individuals or the absence of interest in sanctification. Rather, it reflected their need to reformulate the tradition (and reconstitute religious experience) in ways that spoke to the sensibilities of an emerging Methodist middle class.[116] This new understanding, although not totally eschewing more visible forms of religious experience, made them, as had Edwards, incidental to authentic experience and relegated them to the private realm. This move by Palmer distanced her understanding of holiness from the more visible sanctification experiences traditionally associated with camp meetings and laid the groundwork for a rapprochement between Methodist elites and the Reformed tradition in relation to holiness.

Upham's views on visions, trances, and revelations were rooted in contemporary developments as well. In fact, he described "the love of manifestations, of that which is visible and tangible, . . . [as] one of the evils of the present age." He contrasted the love of manifestations with the love of holiness and claimed that people would rather "have God in their hands, . . . than in their hearts. They would set him up as a thing to be looked at . . . on the precise principles of heathenism; because, being weak in faith, they find it difficult to recognize the existence, and to love and to do the will of an *'unknown God.'* "[117] While Upham can certainly be read as infusing a long overdue apophatic strain into the Wesleyan holiness tradition, he can also be read in relation to the dynamics of religion and class in southern Maine in the early 1840s.

As a Congregationalist, a graduate of Dartmouth College and Andover Theological Seminary, and a professor at Bowdoin College in Brunswick, Maine, Upham represented one end of the spectrum in terms of religion and class. His best-known works—both psychological and devotional—were published in the 1830s and early 1840s. The *Life of Faith*, from which the passage just cited was taken, appeared in 1845. As the remainder of the chapter illustrates, Maine was rife with itinerant visionaries and mesmerists in the mid-1840s. In their desire to know more than Upham thought possible through extraordinary means, both visionaries and mesmerists expressed a desire for visible and tangible manifestations.

While adventist visionaries and mesmerists went head to head in southern Maine, Upham sought to distance himself and respectable Protestantism from both.

The Millerite expectation that Jesus would return at a specified date in 1843, later revised to 1844, epitomized the desire for visible and tangible manifestations. Moreover, both before and after the Great Disappointment of 1844, adventists in Upham's part of Maine, the young Ellen Harmon among them, were known for their visionary experiences and disparaged *even within* adventist *circles* for their "fanaticism." For Palmer and Upham, the great test of faith, and thus the sine qua non of holiness, came at the point when God was experienced as absent. Adventists, by way of contrast, expressed their desire for sanctification not in relation to an "unknown" and, presumably unknowable, God but in relation to the graphic expectation of Jesus' imminent and very tangible return.

EXPERIENCING VISIONS

Methodists and Adventists

Between 1842 and 1844, adventist lecturers, known up until that time primarily for their rationalistic exposition of the prophetic texts of the Bible, turned, like Sunderland, to the Methodist revival tradition as a means of proclaiming their message. By 1842, a year before the predicted Second Coming, the ranks of both believers and opponents had grown dramatically. The growing opposition within the denominations made it more difficult to hold meetings in churches, while burgeoning numbers made it harder to find rental halls suitable for the largest adventist gatherings. At the adventist General Conference held in Boston in 1842, the Millerites, a majority of whom were by that time come-outers from Methodism, voted to adopt the camp meeting as a means of holding large gatherings and effectively spreading the advent message.[118]

In recasting the camp meeting for their own purposes, adventists downplayed communion and love-feasts, potentially divisive rituals in a movement of that had come out from a variety of Protestant traditions, and substituted the by-then traditional adventist lecture, with its detailed exegetical charts for the traditional camp-meeting sermon. Despite adventist leaders' efforts to avoid any hint of enthusiasm, Millerite camp meetings did not lack for emotion. While adventist lectures were rationalistic in tone, their content evoked strong emotional responses.[119] Indeed, while the Millerites' rationalistic exegesis, precise predictions, and premillennial eschatology were novel, their effect was to intensify and often revitalize traditional evangelical fears of damnation and longings for the felt-presence of God and heaven.[120]

Adventist emotions were caught up in camp-meeting hymns and spiritual songs, rapidly amended and abridged where necessary to reflect adventist theology.[121] In many cases little adaptation was needed. Much of the practical theology and ritual of the Methodist camp meeting was appropriated without change. Millerite camp meetings, for example, continued the shout tradition's focus on Jerusalem, the Jerusalem prefigured in the camp and the new heavenly

Jerusalem soon to come. As adventists circled the camp before departing, they typically sang the traditional camp-meeting spiritual "Jerusalem." A song of longing and expectation, tinged with this-worldly sorrow and otherworldly hope, it played off inverse images of departing the camp to return to the world and departing the world for heaven. In the interplay of images, the sorrow of departure from the camp was transformed into longing for the second coming where "we shall our Jesus meet, / And never, never part again." The longing and hope were caught up in the concluding lines of the chorus in a call and response dialogue ("What, never part again? No, never part again.") popular among both Millerites and Methodists.[122]

Conversion and sanctification remained central to the adventist camp meeting, the urgency of both only enhanced by the advent message. As at Methodist camp meetings, convicted sinners came forward to the mourner's bench or the anxious seat and were directed from there to prayer tents after the sermon was over.[123] Those already converted sought sanctification or, as they more commonly put it, to "consecrate" themselves more fully in preparation for the coming advent. Historian Milton Perry argues that the adventist camp meetings were less emotional, and in particular gave less evidence of "physical exercises," than Methodist camp meetings. Nonetheless, he presents considerable evidence to the contrary. At a camp meeting in Kentucky in 1844, for example, the newspaper reported that "the mourners or converts, of whom there were a very large number, threw themselves in the dust and dirt around the pulpit, and for nearly an hour, men and women were praying, singing, shouting, groaning, and weeping bitterly."[124] In the prayer tents, in particular, there was seemingly little restraint. There, the *New York Herald* reported, "men and women [were] down in the straw lying and sitting in every conceivable posture; praying, shouting, and singing indiscriminately with all their might."[125] The power of God manifested itself at smaller meetings as well. Hiram Edson reports that a meeting in his home in 1844 a number of people were "so deeply convicted" that they attempted to leave before succumbing to the advent message. While two left, "the third one fell upon the threshold; the fourth, the fifth, and son on, till the most of the company were thus slain by the power of the God." All then lay on the floor, uttering "agonizing cries and pleading for mercy."[126]

In light of the antipathy of the movements' most prominent leaders toward any displays of Methodist-style "enthusiasm," Perry evinces some puzzlement in the face of the abundant evidence of "emotional and ecstatic experiences" among the Millerites.[127] I suspect that he is right in finally attributing the prevalence of such experiences to the disproportionate numbers of Methodist preachers and people in the ranks of the Millerite movement. But, knowing that not all Methodists were "shouters," we might also speculate that adventism, especially after it appropriated the camp-meeting tradition, had a disproportionate appeal to those Methodists most steeped in the shout tradition. Ruth Alden Doan has emphasized the supernaturalism inherent in the Millerite movement. "For most Millerites," she points out, "mention of 1843 served as a reminder of a supernatural order so real as to be almost palpably, physically present."[128] For "shouting Methodists," early adventism undoubtedly aroused or intensified traditional longings for the felt-presence of Jesus-in-heaven and precipitated renewed attention to sanctification as a means of preparing for his imminent return. Viewed in light of their intense concern for sanctification, adventist come-outers from Methodism had features in common with both "respectable" holiness advocates, such as Phoebe Palmer, and the more radical holiness "come-outers" of the late-nineteenth century.[129]

The early religious experiences of Ellen Harmon make a great deal of sense when viewed in relation to the Methodist shout tradition. Although some scholars have questioned her mental health, her religious experience was not unlike that of Benjamin Abbott.[130] In both cases, dreams and trance played a significant role. Where Abbott had a long and tortuous conversion experience accompanied by significant dreams and a relatively unanguished trance-based sanctification experience, Harmon's conversion was relatively uneventful and her experience of sanctification long and tortuous. The latter process was accompanied by dreams and ended in trance. Her experiences presupposed and elaborated upon the shouter's typological reading of the Bible.

Harmon's first dream was set in the heavenly temple in the new Jerusalem. All who entered the temple were expected to "come before the lamb and confess their sins, and then take their place among the happy throng who occupied the elevated seats." In her dream, Harmon was "slowly making [her] way . . . to face the lamb, when the trumpet sounded, and the building shook, and shouts of triumph went up from the saints in that building" and she was left "alone in the place in great darkness."[131] Here imagery prominent in the shout tradition—the temple, the trumpet, and shouts of triumph—blended with the adventist imagery of an imminent end.

In the second dream, she met face to face with Jesus, again it seems within the heavenly temple.

> As I entered I saw Jesus, so lovely and beautiful. His countenance expressed benevolence and majesty. I tried to shield myself from his piercing gaze. I thought he knew my heart, and every circumstance of my life. I tried not to look upon his face but still his eyes were upon me. I could not escape his gaze. He then, with a smile, drew near me, and laid his hand upon my head, saying, 'Fear not.' The sound of his sweet voice, caused me to feel a thrill of happiness I never before experienced. I was too full of joy to utter a word. I grew weak, and fell prostrate at his feet. And while lying helpless, scenes of glory and lasting beauty passed before me. I thought I was saved in heaven. At length my strength returned. I arose upon my feet. The loving eyes of Jesus were fixed upon me still, and he smiled upon me. His presence filled me with such holy awe that I could not endure it.[132]

Here we have an encounter with Jesus that begs to be described as "mesmerizing." The effect of Jesus' gaze stands out. It pierced her heart and seemed to know every circumstance of her life. She tried to shield herself from it, to turn herself away from his face, but his eyes did not leave her and she could not escape it. He broke the spell with a smile and a touch. Harmon, thrilled by the sound of his voice, filled with joy, and unable to utter a word, responded to his presence in the manner of the shout tradition. She fell prostrate and lay helpless while scenes of heavenly glory passed before her eyes.

Shortly after recounting these dreams to her mother and a Methodist minister, who was preaching to "the Advent people in Portland," she experienced sanctification at a prayer meeting. There, apparently for the first time, she entered into trance and "the burden and agony of soul" that she had so long felt finally left her. As she described it:

> Wave after wave of glory rolled over me, until my body grew stiff. Everything was shut out from me but Jesus and glory, and I know nothing of what was passing around me. I remained in this state of body and mind a long time, and when I realized what was around me, everything seemed changed. Everything looked glorious and new, as if smiling and praising God.[133]

Here again in its language and imagery and in its use of trance, Harmon's experience of sanctification was entirely in keeping with the Methodist shout tradition.

Although White would not have denied her Methodist heritage, it was largely presupposed in her account. She emphasized the importance of her faith in the imminent second coming of Christ, and indeed her "Methodist" narrative was infused with this expectation. Harmon's expulsion from her Methodist class meeting was precipitated by her refusal to abandon her adventist understanding of her sanctification experience. After testifying in her class meeting shortly after Gershom Cox left Portland for Orrington, her new presiding elder asked Harmon "if it would not be more pleasant to live a long life of holiness here, and do others good, than to have Jesus come and destroy poor sinners." Harmon responded by expressing her longing for the second advent, adding that then "sin would have an end, and we should enjoy sanctification forever."[134]

Although this exchange prefigured later controversies over the meaning of holiness, it was only after she left Methodism that Harmon faced opposition as a "shouter." The "shouting Methodist" in Ellen Harmon, in other words, stands out in sharpest relief for us, as indeed it did for her, not while she was among Methodists, where it was still reasonably well accepted, but in adventist meetings filled with "come-outers" from a variety of other Protestant denominations. In a section of her *Experience and Views* titled the "Opposition of Formal Brethren," White recounted the conflict that emerged between herself and the adventist "formalists" at the Portland adventist meetings in 1842. Here, in the unmistakable cadences of the shout tradition, she wrote:

> At times the Spirit of the LORD rested upon me in such power that my strength was taken away. This was a trial to some of those who had come out from the formal churches. . . . They did not believe that any one could be so filled with the Spirit of the LORD as to lose their strength. . . . But soon one of the family which had been most forward in opposing me, while praying fell prostrate like one dead. His friends feared he was dying; but . . . he regained his strength to praise GOD, and shout with a voice of triumph. . . . While attending an evening meeting I was much blessed, and again lost my strength. Another of the family mentioned, said he had no faith that it was the Spirit

of GOD that was upon me. . . . Bro. R. was immediately prostrated, and as soon as he could give utterance to his feelings, declared that it was of GOD.[135]

As Malcolm Bull and Keith Lockhart have noted, "the intense desire for experience of the divine presence is an aspect of Mrs. White's experience that is often over-looked."[136] Bull and Lockhart look to St. Teresa and the Catholic mystical tradition for a point of comparison, but it was Methodism, and above all the Methodist shout tradition, that provided Ellen Harmon with an initial sense of the form that an experience of the divine presence might take.

Fanatics

Although many outsiders viewed the Millerites as fanatics, most adventists did not view fanaticism as a serious threat to their movement until after the Great Disappointment. After October 22 passed, seemingly without event, many left the movement. Those that remained were divided and confused. Within a month prominent leaders, such as Joshua V. Himes, publicly admitted not only that their calculations had been wrong, but that they had erred in attempting to antici-pate a definite date.[137] The radicals who rejected this conclusion were typically branded as "fanatics" by the more moderate adventists who renounced dates. The radicals, while remaining committed to the idea of a definite date, differed with respect to particulars. Some sought new dates; others sought to find meaning in the apparent uneventfulness of October 22. Between November 1844 and April 1845, moderates and radicals battled for the loyalties of those who remained in the movement.[138]

In April 1845, probably in response to widely publicized reports of fanaticism in Maine, the moderates held a convention and formed a new denomination, the Advent Christian Church. The new denomination abandoned camp meetings and revivals and denounced the fanaticism of their opponents.[139] They specifically rejected the practices associated with the radicals, stating "we have no confidence in any new messages, visions, dreams, tongues, miracles, extraordinary revela-tions, impressions, discerning of spirits, or teachings not in accord with the un-adulterated word of God."[140]

While the moderates returned to a more traditional understanding of the sec-ond coming, the radicals forged ahead in their efforts to understand the signifi-cance of October 22. Relying on biblical exegesis and visions, the radicals did not suffer for lack of creative insights into the Great Disappointment. Indeed their problem, as the moderates clearly discerned, was that they had too many solutions and no way to adjudicate between them. Ellen G. White emerged out of this period of exegetical and visionary "enthusiasm" as the prophetess of a new denom-ination, the Seventh-day Adventists.

This did not happen over night. At first the unmarried Ellen Harmon was only one among a number of radical adventist visionaries attempting to make sense of what had occurred. By the late 1840s or early 1850s she may have been the only active adventist visionary, yet sabbath-keeping or sabbatarian adventists had reached no consensus regarding the significance of her visions.[141] These were, in fact, so troubling to many that in 1851 her husband, James White, editor of a widely distributed sabbatarian adventist paper, decided to suspend printing his wife's visions to avoid arousing further controversy. It was not until 1855, at a general meeting of the sabbatarian leadership, that James White was replaced by a new editor and Ellen White's visions were again featured in the paper. Although James was not the only champion of Ellen White's visions prior to 1855, the move to a new editor signaled a more general acceptance by sabbatarian adventists of the authority of Ellen White's visions and of her status as a prophetess of the movement. Those who granted her this status and thus viewed her visions as authoritative began the process of forming the Seventh-day Adventist Church under her visionary leadership six years later.[142]

The official writings of Ellen G. White and other early sources uncovered by Adventist historians portrayed the process of "prophet-making" rather differently, but both acknowledged the challenge that mesmerism presented to that process. The many volumes of Ellen G. White's writings published by the Review and Herald Publishing Association, historically useful as they are, remain documents of the church. These documents, including White's narratives of her life experience and her visions, were all edited to a greater or lesser extent by Ellen and James, and after James's death by Ellen alone. They reflect their faith that she was called by God as a prophet to the faithful remnant in the wake of the Great Disappointment, challenged by Satan in the guise of mesmerism, and opposed by both nominal adventists and fanatics.[143] Historical sources discovered by Adventist historians in the last twenty years provide a view of the young Ellen Harmon only hinted at in the official writings. These sources indicate that she was one among a number of adventist visionaries who surfaced in Maine in early 1845, and that she participated fully in the fanaticism from which she would later want to distance herself.[144] Taken together, they illustrate how early Seventh-day Adventists "made" a prophetess by demonizing mesmerism. In doing so, Seventh-day Adventists both neutralized mesmerism and inscribed it at the heart of the Seventh-day Adventist cosmos.

Visionaries

Visionaries were common in Maine both before and after October 22. Referring to the earlier period, M. F. Whittier, a non-adventist observer, wrote that among Portland's "children of light . . . nothing was more common than visions." He described a teenage girl at one adventist meeting in Portland prior to the Great Disappointment, who "descanted upon a sort of vision she had had the night before in which she had seen the awful scenes of the judgment enacted."[145] In fact, Portland's adventists were notorious in Millerite circles for what Joshua Himes described as their "*continual* introduction of *visionary nonsense*." Combing through secular newspapers published after 1844, Adventist historian Frederick Hoyt identified at least five radical adventist visionaries active at the time in addition to Ellen Harmon—William Foy, Emily Clemons, Dorinda Baker, Phoebe Knapp, and Mary Hamlin.[146] According to historian Ingemar Lindén, "women served in leading positions as 'exhorteresses,' teachers and visionaries" in the informal shut-door "bands."[147]

New sources documenting the events of this period have proved disconcerting for many Seventh-day Adventists, but they do not so much undercut a careful reading of White's most detailed accounts of this period, as heighten our understanding of the crisis of authority radical adventists faced at this time. The most startling new document is a reporter's transcript of the trial of a radical adventist from Atkinson, Maine, named Israel Dammon. Ellen White discussed this incident in the 1860 edition of her "Experience and Views," indicating that she was present at the meeting, and indeed speaking, when "Elder Damman" [sic] was arrested. Not only was her depiction of Elder Dammon sympathetic, the story she told about his arrest was cast in the idiom of the shout tradition. When two officers broke into the meeting, she said, "the Spirit of the Lord rested upon him [Elder Dammon], and his strength was taken away, and he fell to the floor helpless." "The power of God," she continued, "was in that room, and the servants of God with their countenances lighted up with his glory, made no resistance." Nonetheless, the officers could neither lift the prostrate Dammon, nor "endure the power of God," present in the room. Miraculously, Elder Dammon was "held by the power of God about forty minutes," such that, even with ten additional officers present, they were unable to move him.[148]

What Adventists find disconcerting in the newspaper account are details that White left out or glossed over. These details do not so much contradict what White said as force modern Adventists to read her writings differently. Thus, for example, while it is clear from White's description of Dammon's arrest that she viewed him sympathetically, the fact that Dammon is understood by Adventists as one of the more extreme "fanatics" has led them to downplay White's positive assessment of him in her 1860 account. White's elimination of references to Dammon in later versions of her "Experience and Views" assisted in this process. The transcript of the trial, however, undercuts any effort to distance the young Ellen Harmon from Israel Dammon and clearly establishes that when Ellen Harmon spoke at the meeting in Atkinson, it was not to condemn Dammon as a fanatic.[149]

Both White's "Experience and Views" and the trial transcript indicate that Ellen Harmon was traveling from band to band throughout the region in order to relate her December vision.[150] Ellen White's later attempts to distance herself from fanaticism and her negative comments in later writings about "shouting and hallooing" and "noisy" meetings led Adventists to imagine the young Ellen Harmon calmly entering "into vision" at such meetings surrounded by respectful listeners. If any hints of fanaticism were to surface, modern Adventists typically expect that she would have condemned them, given her later outspoken opposition to such things. Adventists also have tended to discount the fact that "nominal Adventists," by White's own account, reckoned her not only as a fanatic, but as the leader of the fanatics. The trial transcript, however, makes clear that the meeting in Atkinson was "noisy," due to singing and shouting, and involved a number of practices—footwashing, rebaptising, hugging and kissing, and crawling on the floor—

that most modern Adventists would imagine Ellen White condemning as fanaticism. Probably most shocking to Adventist sensibilities, all who testified, both for the prosecution and for the defense, depict Ellen Harmon lying on the floor in the trance, with James White at times holding her head in his lap.[151]

Finally, and perhaps most significantly, White's "Experience and Views" was written in such a way as to give the impression that she alone was having visions. Although she made numerous references in her account of her travels to the "impressions and burdens" of fanatics, modern Adventist readers typically have not interpreted these as references to the visions of other radical adventists. The trial transcript is, thus, startling in its references to the *two* "vision women"—Sister Dorinda Baker of Orrington and Sister Ellen Harmon of Portland—who spent much of the meeting in trance. In the witnesses' descriptions of Harmon and Baker, we can see evidence of both the development of the visionary currents within the shout tradition and what La Roy Sunderland would have called clairvoyant somnambulism.

The witnesses all agreed that the two women spent much of the meeting lying on their backs on the floor "in a trance." One witness, Isley Osborn, described the vision women as "los[ing] their strength and fall[ing] on the floor."[152] William Crosby described Harmon "occasionally arous[ing] up and tell[ing] a vision which she said was revealed to her." Jacob Mason described her as "in a vision, part of the time insensible." According to Joel Doore, "the vision woman would lay looking up when she came out of her trance—she would point to some one, and tell them their cases, which she said was from the Lord." Numerous witnesses testified to their belief in the authenticity of both women's visions. As Joel Doore said: "We believe her (Miss Baker's) visions genuine. We believe Miss Harmon's genuine—t'was our understanding that their visions were from God."[153]

What the witnesses referred to as "revealing" or "describing out their cases" is reminiscent of the young Methodist woman, described by Sunderland as a clairvoyant somnambule, who just a year earlier had been correctly perceiving "the characters of different persons who enter[ed] the room, and . . . address[ing] them in reproofs, or exhortation to prayer and praise" while in trance. In the adventist band, the witnesses indicated that what was revealed to the women in their visions had to do with the "cases" of band-members, that is with their faith and practice. Harmon apparently informed two young women that if they were not rebaptized they would go to hell. They were rebaptized later that evening. George Woodbury said he "believe[d] in Miss Harmon's visions, because he told my wife's feelings correctly." Harmon, according to Woodbury, told his wife and daughters that "if they did not do as she said, they would go to hell."[154] Sister Baker, according to Loton Lambert, said that Joel Doore "had doubted, and would not be baptized again—she said Br. Doore don't go to hell." Joel Doore testified that she gave him the message that he had "thought hard of her," which he acknowledged was the case. Both Lambert and Doore indicate that Doore confessed his error and that Baker and Doore "kissed each other with the holy kiss."[155]

Several of the witnesses testified to their faith that the world would end shortly. George Woodbury said he believed that the world would come to an end "within two months," that this was what Dammon preached, and that it was, in his view, "the faith of the band." He also indicated that Dammon advised them not to work, because they had "enough to live on until the end of the world."[156] Lindén describes many of these practices—rebaptism, footwashing, the salutation kiss, and not working—as tests that the radical adventists introduced in order to qualify not only for membership in the band but for inclusion in the select remnant destined for salvation.[157] The vision women's "telling out" of band-member's "cases" based on "revelation" pressured band-members to bring not only their behavior but also their thoughts and feelings into conformity with group norms.

If we read Ellen G. White's later account of her visits to the various advent bands in Maine and New Hampshire in light of this contemporary account, the presence of conflict between competing visionaries and within groups becomes evident. In Exeter, for example, "a heavy burden" rested upon her until she related what she had been "shown concerning some fanatical persons present, who were exalted by the spirit of Satan." She did not go into detail about the beliefs or practices of these "fanatical persons," but she did say that "they trusted every impression, and laid aside reason and judgment."[158] She also indicated that there was "fanaticism" present in the band that met at her parents' house in Portland. Two rival visionaries followed "impressions and burdens, which led to corruption, instead of purity and holiness." Ellen apparently challenged them and while her parents remained loyal to her, she says that "J[oseph]. T[urner]. labored with some success to turn my friends, and even my relatives, against me . . . [b]ecause I had faithfully related what was shown me respecting his unchristian course."[159]

Adventists and Mesmerism

It was in this context that charges of mesmerism started to be bandied about. As White explained in her later writings, "if the Spirit of the Lord rested upon a brother or sister in meeting, and they glorified God by praising him, some raised the cry of mesmerism. And if it pleased the Lord to give me a vision in a meeting, some would say, 'it is excitement and mesmerism.'"[160] Adventists in Maine probably knew of mesmerism by word-of-mouth and through notices and discussions of mesmeric lectures in the newspapers. Phineas P. Quimby, who later gained recognition for his cure of Mary Baker Eddy, was one of the better known mesmerizers performing "public experiments" in Maine during this period. He grew up in the town of Belfast, a few miles south of Bangor, and learned of mesmerism from Charles Poyen when he lectured there in 1838. After some searching he found a sensitive subject, Lucius Burkmar, who readily assumed the role of clairvoyant somnambule. Together they traveled throughout Maine and New Brunswick from 1843 to 1847. In 1847, Burkmar left Quimby to accompany Universalist minister John Bovee Dods on the lecture circuit.[161]

In 1845, Ellen Harmon was confronted directly by "a physician who was a celebrated mesmerizer." He told her "that [her] views were mesmerism, that [she] was a very easy subject, and that he could mesmerize [her] and give [her] a vision." She responded by telling him "that the Lord ha[d] shown [her] in a vision that mesmerism was from the devil, from the bottomless pit, and that it would soon go there, with those who continued to use it."[162] Although the physician proved unable to induce a vision, people continued to ascribe her visions to "excitement and mesmerism." Despondent in the face of such charges, she went off to pray alone. There too she found that "JESUS seemed very near" and "the sweet light of heaven" would shine around her and she would enter into a trance. When she pointed out that she had solitary visions, people told her that "[she] mesmerized [her]self, and that those who lived the nearest to God were most liable to be deceived by Satan." She argued that "according to this teaching, our only safety from delusion was to remain quite a distance from God." These charges of mesmerism, she recounted, "wounded [her] spirit, and wrung [her] soul in keen anguish, well nigh to despair." "Many," she said, "would have [her] believe that there was no Holy Spirit, and that all the exercises that holy men of God have experienced, were only mesmerism or the deception of Satan."[163]

While struggling with these doubts, she continued to receive visions spelling out the errors of other radical adventists. When she passed the messages on to God's "erring children" as instructed, many of them "wholly rejected the message" and charged her with "conforming to the world." While White positioned herself in her later accounts as an opponent of fanaticism, during the 1840s moderates (whom she referred to as "nominal Adventists") charged *her* with fanaticism. Some, she says, even "falsely . . . represented [her] as being the leader of the fanaticism that [she] was laboring to do away."[164] The editor of the leading moderate newspaper, the *Advent Herald*, was, she said, among those who believed her visions "to be 'the result of mesmeric operations.' "[165]

It was in this "confusion," as she called it, that she was "sometimes tempted to doubt [her] own experience." The crisis came to a head one morning at family worship as "the power of God began to rest upon [her]." When "the thought rushed into [her] mind that it was mesmerism," she was immediately "struck dumb." Like John Wesley, who concluded he had sinned in attributing bodily exercises to animal spirits, so too Ellen White saw her "sin in doubting the power of God." When, as she predicted, her tongue was "loosed" less than twenty-four hours later, she "shout[ed] the high praises of God."[166] Both John Wesley and Ellen White rejected natural explanations of their experiences and continued to attribute them to the "power of God." Knowing full well that many believed them deluded, both Wesley and White continued to find God's presence in or through involuntary experiences.

The gap between the trial transcript and the "Experience and Views" of Ellen G. White reveals something of the process through which Ellen Harmon, initially one of several radical adventist visionaries, became Ellen G. White, the prophetess of Seventh-day Adventism. The trial transcript helps us to see more clearly the crisis of authority generated by the radical adventists' reliance on visionary solutions to the Great Disappointment. Although many of the radicals agreed that something momentous had occurred on October 22 and that the door of salvation had been shut to those who did not believe, they depended on visionaries for details of what had occurred. Without the interpretive limits and powers of enforcement typically vested in ecclesiastical institutions, visionary solutions rapidly resulted in competition and conflict. While some radicals backtracked once they experienced the hermeneutical chaos, those who were to found the Seventh-day Adventist Church forged ahead. Having opened the door to visions early on, they solved the problem of multiple solutions by granting one of the many visionaries the status of prophetess and interpreting her prophetic visions, not as new revelation, but an authoritative guide to scripture.[167] In retrospect, we can see the synergistic relationship between the formation of the denomination, given its early commitment to visionary experience, and the emergence of a prophet, that is, an authoritative visionary.

This is not the only way it could have gone. Instead of creating *an* authoritative visionary or prophet, the sabbatarian adventists could have created an authoritative *set* of visions, that is a canon, generated by more than one visionary. Had they chosen the latter route, it would suggest, as in the case of early Christianity, that no one (visionary) interpretation was sufficient or otherwise strong enough to win out over its competitors. The fact that an authoritative visionary did emerge suggests that Ellen White brought something more to the task than her competitors. Two factors come immediately to mind, both speculative, given the current state of the historical research. First, I think it is likely that White's visions spoke more consistently to the needs of the movement both in terms of content and timing than did those of her competitors.[168] Second, and at least as important, the "symbiotic relationship" between Ellen and James White, to borrow Jonathan Butler's phrase, provided Ellen White and her visions with a forceful promoter that the other visionaries lacked.[169] It was James's belief in his wife's visions that made the early 1850s such a crucial period of transition. By keeping Ellen's visions out of his paper, he in effect pulled back, allowing other sabbatarian adventists an opportunity to decide whether they wanted to proceed with or without a prophet. Their assent was crucial, for without them Ellen and James could not have cofounded a church.

"Fanaticism" and "mesmerism" came to symbolize the two primary threats Ellen Harmon White faced as she made the passage from adventist visionary to Adventist prophetess. "Fanaticism" represented the threat of competing visionaries and "mesmerism" the threat of natural explanations of visionary experience. In his introduction to the first published edition of his wife's "Experience and Views," James White confronted these two primary threats directly. In 1851, three years after the first spirits "rapped" in upstate New York, James White wrote:

> We are well aware that many honest seekers after truth and Bible holiness are prejudiced against visions. Two great causes have created this prejudice. First, fanaticism, accompanied by false visions and exercises, [and] [s]econdly, the exhibition of mesmerism, and what is commonly called the 'mysterious rapping.'

Fanaticism with its counterfeits, he argued, was always with us, while mesmerism, he correctly implied, was a newer phenomenon. With respect to the latter, he said, "we," presumably referring to himself and Ellen, "have ever considered it dangerous [and] therefore have had nothing to do with it." To distance them farther, he added, "We never even saw a person in mesmeric sleep and know nothing of the art by experience."[170] The subtext here was clear. Unlike (say) the Rev. and Mrs. M'Reading, James and Ellen White had *not* been experimenting with mesmerism. The reader was to understand, without it having to be said, that James White was not a mesmerist and Ellen White was not a clairvoyant somnambule.

The historical newness of mesmerism did not detract from its cosmic significance. Indeed, like the Methodists who believed the disciples must have shouted at Pentecost, Ellen White believed that opponents of adventism would have accused even Jesus of fanaticism and mesmerism. Referring to the dispute over the disciples praising God "with a loud voice" as Jesus entered into Jerusalem (a key passage in the shout tradition), Ellen White commented:

> A large portion of those who profess to be looking for Christ would be as forward as the Pharisees were to have the disciples silenced, and they would doubtless raise the cry, 'Fanaticism! Mesmerism! Mesmerism!' And the disciples, spreading their garments and branches of palm trees in the way, would be thought extravagant and wild. But God will have a people on the earth who will not be so cold and dead but that they can praise and glorify Him.[171]

While adventists, like the disciples, were falsely accused, "true" fanatics and mesmerizers were demonized. Just as fanatics were "exalted by the spirit of Satan" and those who did not heed her visions were destined for hell, so it was revealed to her in a vision that "mesmerism was from the devil" and that those who used it would be damned. White expanded on these views in her first extended statement on psychology, published in the *Review and Herald* in 1862. There she described the way that Satan was using "the science of the human mind" to make "the miracles and works of Christ" look as if they were "the result of human skill and power." "The sciences of phrenology, psychology, and mesmerism are the channel," she said, "through which he [Satan] comes more directly to this generation and works with that power which is to characterize his efforts near the close of probation." Imperceptibly, Satan was gaining access to human minds through these sciences, and eventually would "destroy faith in Christ's being the Messiah, the Son of God."[172] Although not a particularly sophisticated attack on either fanaticism or mesmerism, demonization effectively neutralized both threats for those willing to accept White's prophetic authority.

The mesmerists' attempts to explain adventist visionary experiences and the early Adventists' attempts to neutralize the mesmerists' explanations illustrate both recurrent themes and new developments. As was the case with the shouting Methodists and their formalist opponents, conflict over the legitimacy of religious experience took place at a grassroots level. In both cases, believers incorporated their opponents' explanations of their experience into their own self-presentation. In doing so, they both acknowledged the force of the critique and sought to neutralize it. Millerites and early Adventists appropriated significant aspects of the shout tradition, although neither shouting nor enthusiasm played a central role in efforts to explain or discredit the adventist movement. For adventists, the salient issues were fanaticism and mesmerism.

Both fanaticism and mesmerism broke with the past in significant ways. Fanaticism largely superseded enthusiasm as a means of designating false religion, but it did not speak as directly to the matter of experience—whether true, false, or absent—as had formalism and enthusiasm. Mesmerism, in attempting to explain many of the same phenomena as enthusiasm, did so rather differently. While formalists, such as John Fanning Watson, attempted to discredit the experience of shouting Methodists by criticizing their exegesis, mesmerists attempted to discredit visionaries by replicating their experiences in mesmerized subjects.

If fanaticism and mesmerism were the chief threats leveled against adventists during the 1840s, they faced a new challenge from the Spiritualist movement in the 1850s. As a new religious movement, Spiritualism positioned itself very differently with respect to mesmerism and the rise of psychology. Where Adventists demonized mesmeric psychology, the Spiritualists embraced it. Where Ellen White disavowed any similarity between herself and clairvoyant somnambules, the Spiritualists recognized a clairvoyant somnambule as the forerunner of their movement and understood their own trance mediums as but a more "developed" version of the older figure.

Embodying Spirits

MOST SPIRITUALISTS and most historians of Spiritualism date the beginnings of the Spiritualist movement to the rappings in the Fox home in Hydesville, New York, in 1848. Spiritualism did not, however, arrive in the world fully formed on March 31, the day the first raps were heard. It took a few years for a relatively coherent religious movement to emerge. This movement, known as "modern Spiritualism," interpreted the raps in light of the writings of the clairvoyant somnambule Andrew Jackson Davis and induced further raps and other related phenomena through the practices of animal magnetism. At the core of Spiritualism as a popular movement lay the blending of the belief in spirits of the dead with the ideas and practices of animal magnetism. Out of this blending emerged the basic Spiritualist idea that animal magnetism and, eventually and more specifically, trance states could provide access to the spirit realm. This idea was embodied in the most basic Spiritualist concepts and practices: the circle, the spiritual telegraph, and the medium. It gave rise to questions about the relationship between spirit communication and Christianity (especially Jesus and the Bible) and other religions and to questions about where the human psyche ended and the spirits began. Not all Spiritualists pondered these questions at length, but they were nonetheless basic questions that any nominally (or formerly) Christian participant in a circle was likely to raise. The formation of this core idea and its implications for understanding religion and religious experience are the subject of this chapter.[1]

Spiritualism stands at the center of a "historical hourglass" with respect to the subject matter of this book.[2] With the rise of Spiritualism and the idea of animal magnetism (and more narrowly, trance) as a doorway to the other world, the boundaries between believers and skeptics, practitioners and observers, and thus those who experience religion and those who explain it in naturalistic terms become blurred. Here experiencers and explainers—both mediums and investigators—fall along a variety of continua. Insofar as both drew on a Christian belief in souls and an afterlife, where they fell on a continuum between orthodox Christianity and post-Christian Spiritualism depended on their understanding of the nature and scope of revelation. Insofar as both drew on psychological theory and viewed intercourse with spirits as "natural" rather than "supernatural," where they fell on a continuum from credulity to skepticism depended on how and where they drew the line between psyche and spirit or this and the other world.[3] Insisting that animal magnetism provided a natural doorway to the other world, Spiritualists articulated a "religious naturalism" that claimed common ground with both science and religion, while provoking strong reactions from both materialistically oriented scientists and supernaturally oriented religionists.[4]

As religious naturalists, Spiritualists blurred the boundary between popular psychological theory and religious revivals in ways we have not seen before. Emma Hardinge Britten, renowned medium and the movement's first major historian, concluded that modern Spiritualism had two well-defined antecedents: first, "Religious Revivals" and isolated incidents of "haunting phenomena" and, second, animal magnetism.[5] Although Britten was referring to England, her conclusion was appropriate to the United States as well. Spiritualism, in other words, represented not only a popular psychological movement, but also a religious revival on the margins of Protestantism. Like the Methodist movement within Anglicanism or the holiness movement within the Methodist Church, the Spiritualist revival attacked the "formalism" of the churches and promoted its own version of "experimental religion" through circles, Sunday lectures, and camp meetings. Like their evangelical counterparts, Spiritualists also debated whether or not they should "come out" from the churches. In contrast to much of evangelical revivalism, the Spiritualist revival had its center in the more liberal denominations—the Unitarians, the Quakers, and above all the Universalists—although it spilled over into others as well. Finally, Spiritualists differed from evangelicals in that they fervently rejected orthodox Christian theology and firmly identified themselves with "free" or "liberal" or "progressive" religion.[6]

The Spiritualists' religious naturalism had far-reaching implications for the modern study of religion. Their view of trance as a common or universal doorway to the other world provided a new basis for interpreting the Bible, the history of Christianity, and the various religions of the world. As a universal doorway to the other world, animal magnetism laid the foundation for a new understanding of the essence of religion. The view of trance as a potential, but not in every case an actual, doorway to the other world provided a seemingly empirical basis, grounded in psychology rather than theology, for talking about religious experience. As a psychologically grounded and seemingly empirically verifiable doorway between the human and the spirit realm, animal magnetism laid the foundation for a more complex psychology of religion.

SPIRITS AND ANIMAL MAGNETISM

That there was a connection between Spiritualism and animal magnetism is a commonplace in the histories of Spiritualism authored by both Spiritualists and non-Spiritualists. In her history of the first twenty years of the movement, Emma Hardinge Britten acknowledged that "mesmerism has performed an important part in ushering in the more comprehensive movement of Spiritualism." Itinerant magnetizers, she says, spread knowledge of mesmerism to cities and towns throughout the U.S. Their exhibitions led to experiments "in the home circle . . . and the phenomena of animal magnetism became familiarly known to the most progressive classes of the community." In the end, she says, "magnetism became a fashion, and its legitimate claim to be considered as a science was at length fully established."[7]

Nor was the connection between them recognized only by historians. Spiritualists frequently were involved with mesmerism, either as mesmerizers or as mesmeric subjects, before and after becoming Spiritualists. "Thousands," Britten reports, were "first attracted to the subject [of Spiritualism] by their interest in magnetism." Throughout the country, "gentlemen distinguished for their literary abilities, progressive opinions, or prominence in public affairs, have graduated from the study of magnetism and clairvoyance to become adherents to the cause of Spiritualism, whilst many of the best mediums—especially the trance speakers and magnetic operators—have taken their first degree in Spiritualism, as experimentalists in the phenomena of mesmerism."[8]

Without denying the continuities between animal magnetism and Spiritualism, Britten wanted, nonetheless, to maintain a distinction between them both historically and theoretically. Spiritualism, which, in her words, "first began to assume the form of a concrete movement at Rochester in 1848," is, she said, "the more comprehensive movement." Britten described Andrew Jackson Davis as the John the Baptist of the Spiritualist movement. Picturing two epochs, the first dominated by animal magnetism and the second by Spiritualism, she placed Davis in the "interregnum" between them, "connecting both, yet standing alone."[9] There is much of interest in this analogy, not the least of which is her implicit comparison of the rappings to the coming of Jesus. For now, I want to highlight Britten's mythic depiction of the difference and continuity between animal magnetism and Spiritualism (the two epochs) and her sense that Davis, like John the Baptist, "prepared the way" and yet was not the messiah.

The Poughkeepsie Seer

Andrew Jackson Davis "prepared the way" for modern Spiritualism by both modeling the transformation from clairvoyant somnambule to seer and providing a conceptual framework for understanding it.[10] Davis first learned of animal magnetism from the itinerant magnetizer, J. Stanley Grimes, in 1843, when he was a young shoemaker's apprentice in Poughkeepsie, New York. In his autobiography, Davis presented himself as ripe for the encounter. As a child, he said he had a "tendency to spontaneous somnambulism" and "an ear for what [he] then called imaginary voices." He also had an "unconquerable dread of death" and a fear of damnation that was heightened by an itinerant revivalist's inquiries not long before Grimes came to town. Terrified, a "voice—soothing and loving like [his] mother's—repeat[ed] in minor tones: 'Be—calm! Jackson. The—pastor—is—wrong; you—shall—see!'"[11]

Davis attributed his interest in mesmerism, at least in part, to a first-hand awareness of the limitations of a purely religious (or as he later put it "superstitious") interpretation of clairvoyant phenomena, which he gained from observing his mother. Davis's parents were poor and uneducated. His father was an alcoholic and his mother, who also had clairvoyant abilities, was emotionally unstable. As a child, he chose to spend much of his time with his mother, " 'hanging,' as [his] father sneeringly said, 'to [her] apron-string.' " At the time, he thought she acted "queer." As an adult, he concluded that her inability to distinguish between the real and the imaginary on the basis of psychological principles "greatly increased her unhappiness and despondency." She had, he thought, "real clairvoyance, and, as I think, real spirit intercourse. But not being able to distinguish between fact and fancy, her life became a meandering stream of trial, sadness, and nervous apprehension." Soon after the voice like his mother's told him the pastor was wrong about damnation, striking "show-bills headed 'Mesmerism' " announced that "Professor Grimes" was conducting "experiments at the Village-Hall."[12] In contrast to both La Roy Sunderland and Ellen White, mesmerism provided Davis with a means of explaining his natural clairvoyant abilities and, at the same time, experiencing religion in a newly liberating way.

Although Stanley Grimes found Davis an unexceptionable mesmeric subject, the local tailor successfully magnetized him after Grimes left town. Davis quickly demonstrated "powers of clairvoyance" and, after a variety of "tests" to establish the "reality of the clairvoyant state," he embarked on a career as a clairvoyant healer.[13] Around 1845, Davis made the transition from an "ordinary medical clairvoyant" to "a prophet and seer." How this occurred is contested. Davis himself dates the transition to the appearance of the spirits of Galen and Emanuel Swedenborg to him while in a "strange abnormal state."[14] Grimes, an inveterate "explainer" of Spiritualism, attributed it to the influence of Davis's new managers, the Universalist clergyman and editor Samuel Brittan and his brother-in-law Dr. Lyon, a professional magnetizer.[15] Given Davis's negative encounters with more conservative clergy, the two explanations were probably not incompatible. In 1845, Davis, accompanied by Dr. Lyon, moved to New York City, where he dictated a series of lectures after being magnetized by Lyon. The lectures were recorded by another Universalist clergyman, William Fishbough, and published in 1847 as *The Principles of Nature, her Divine Revelations, and a Voice to Mankind*.[16]

In contrast to the visions of Ellen G. White, Davis's understanding of his "revelations" was firmly grounded in the "science known as Animal Magnetism." Fishbough explained the procedure by which Davis was magnetized in his introduction and described the characteristic way in which Davis entered into the magnetic state. At its deepest, according to Fishbough, Davis's body "becomes cold, rigid, motionless, and insensible to all external things. The pulsations become feeble, the breathing is apparently almost suspended, and all the senses are closed entirely to the external world. This condition, according to his own explanation, corresponds almost precisely to that of *physical death*."[17]

In the *Principles*, Andrew Jackson Davis explained this deathlike state as the fourth and highest of the magnetic states. Included in Davis's four states, we find most of the phenomena with which we have been concerned. Persons in the first state, he said, "lose none of their senses, but are susceptible to all external impressions. They have also the full power of muscular action; and if situated nearly midway between the first and second states, they are inclined to happy feelings." In the second state, "the patient still manifests his intellectual faculties, but is deprived of all muscular power. . . . In the latter part of this state all sensation and feeling is destroyed, so that any surgical operation can be performed

without giving pain." In the third state, "the patient is . . . placed in an unconscious condition" relative to the external world. This state is analogous to "natural
somnambulism." Although many suppose this to be "the *clairvoyant* state," Davis
said, it is not. It is only in the fourth state, wherein the mind is freed "from all
inclinations which the body would subject it to, and only sustains a connexion
[to the body] by a very minute and rare medium, the same that connects one
thought with another," that the mind becomes "capable of receiving impressions
of foreign or proximate objects." In this stage, he says, "the body is dormant and
inactive in all its parts." The fourth stage is analogous to "that natural state of
physical disunion known as *death*."[18] It was while in this last state that Davis
acquired the knowledge that formed the substance of his "revelations."

Similarities between the revelations of Davis and Swedenborg were quickly
recognized. George Bush, a professor at New York University and a noted Swedenborgian, attended many of Davis's lectures. Recognizing the similarities with
Swedenborg's thought, he dismissed the idea that Davis had plagiarized Swedenborg, given Davis's lack of education and the difficulty of acquiring Swedenborg's philosophical writings at that time. Bush devoted an appendix to his
book *Mesmer and Swedenborg* published in January 1847, to a discussion of Davis's
visionary lectures. Bush concluded, based on Davis's initial lectures, that some of
his revelations originated through "intercourse" with the "disembodied spirit" of
Emmanuel Swedenborg while in the mesmeric state.[19]

Davis's later lectures were directed more specifically toward theological matters.
They were critical in their assessment of orthodox Christianity, discussed the formation of the biblical canon as a means of undercutting the authority of the Bible
and orthodox theology, and read the biblical books themselves (which he referred
to as the "Primitive History") as "a history of mythology, ancient theology, false
and imaginary deities." In his approach to the Bible, a topic to which we shall
return, Davis broke with Swedenborg and alienated George Bush. In September
1847, just before the *Revelations* appeared in print, Bush published a pamphlet
entitled, *Davis' Revelations Revealed*, in which he cautioned people against being
deceived by Davis's revelations, which he now attributed, at least in part, to unin-
structed and deceiving spirits.[20]

While Bush's response to Davis was not entirely positive, they both viewed
mesmerism as the gateway to the highest spiritual states, played a significant role
in introducing Americans to the thought of Swedenborg, and drew upon the
works of German authors, such as Heinrich Jung-Stilling's *Pneumatology* and Justinus Kerner's *Seeress of Prevorst*, to support the idea of spirit communications.[21]
The first history of Spiritualism, published in 1850, used this complex of ideas,
together with prophetic statements extracted from the writings of Davis and Swedenborg, to interpret the raps as efforts on the part of disembodied spirits to
initiate a communications breakthrough between this world and the next.

Initially, however, those inclined toward a spiritual interpretation understood
the raps not in relation to spirits but in relation to the popular lore of ghosts or
poltergeists. On the evening when the raps commenced late in March 1848, it
was established that their source was the ghost of a dead peddler who had suppos-

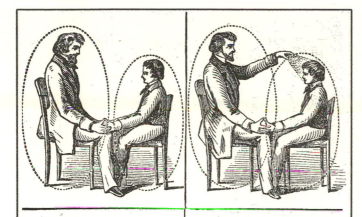

No. 1.

The Ordinary State.

SEPARATE PERSONAL
SPHERES.

The above represents the
operator and subject beginning
the magnetic process.

No. 2.

The Psychological State.

PARTIAL BLENDING OF
SPHERES.

The above condition is favorable to sympathetic and
transitional phenomena.

No. 3.

The Somnambulic State.

COMPLETE BLENDING OF
SPHERES.

The above state brings out
excursional, examining, and
medical clairvoyance.

No. 4.

The Superior Condition.

MENTAL SPHERES SEPA-
RATED.

The above state leads to independent clairvoyance and in-
tuitional wisdom.

5. Stages of develop-
ment in the magnetic
process, from the ordi-
nary state (far left) to
the superior condition
(far right). From
Andrew Jackson
Davis, *The Magic Staff*
(1864).

edly been murdered in the Fox's house in Hydesville, New York (near Rochester) some years previously and buried in the cellar.[22] This information was elicited by directing questions to the "ghost," who responded either with more raps (yes) or silence (no).[23] Not until four months later did the Fox sisters develop a communication system sophisticated enough to establish that they were not dealing with an isolated "ghost" but with a whole "host of spirits" eager to communicate. By soliciting raps from the spirits in response to the letters of the alphabet, the Fox sisters learned that the spirit communication was produced through "the forces of spiritual and human magnetism . . . [and] that the magnetic relations necessary to produce phenomena were very subtle, liable to disturbance, and singularly susceptible to the influence of emotions."[24]

The Spiritual Telegraph

Sometime during this early period, Spritualists made an analogy between communicating with spirits and telegraphy, comparing the raps to the taps of the telegraph key and the force or fluid that informed animal magnetism to electricity. The image of the "spiritual telegraph" represented the complex of ideas that informed the emergent movement in a manner easily accessible to the ordinary Spiritualist. Promoted by Davis and his followers, as well as many others, this image provided the name for the leading Spiritualist periodical of the early- to mid-1850s and served, during this early period, as a kind of conceptual "icon" for the movement as a whole.

Spiritualists developed the basics of modern Spiritualist practice—communication with spirits through circles—in relation to this image and in so doing infused their practice with the underlying theory of electrically based animal magnetism. According to Hardinge, "the spirits chiefly concerned in the inauguration of this telegraphy were philosophic and scientific minds, many of whom had made the study of electricity and other imponderables a specialty in the earth-life." Hardinge reprinted letters from this early period that illustrate how Spiritualists reconceptualized the clairvoyant as a human telegraph in order to access spirits. In one, Nathaniel Draper put his wife, Rachel, who was "susceptible to magnetic influence, . . . into a clairvoyant state in order to see what might be presented in relation to it." Mr. Draper recorded the dialogue that ensued between himself and the spirit of Benjamin Franklin, as it was relayed through his "magnetized" wife. Franklin's spirit indicated, in response to questioning, that "communications between two distant points by means of these rappings" was eminently "practicable" and designed an elaborate "test" to be conducted in the presence of witnesses. In describing the test, Draper indicated that "the sounds were . . . heard . . . exactly similar to the sound heard in the telegraph office." When "the telegraphic sounds" were repeated unusually loudly, it was learned through Mrs. Draper that Franklin's spirit was "trying the batteries." Eight witnesses recounted the results of the test in a signed letter to the editor of the Rochester *Daily Magnet*.[25]

The interpretive shift from poltergeist to spiritual telegraph was analogous in some ways to the shift from enthusiasm to animal magnetism. Both enthusiasm and poltergeists were theories used to explain unusual phenomena, but neither involved much in the way of practices. Few had the ability or the desire to "induce" enthusiasm or poltergeists.[26] The idea of the telegraph, by way of contrast, implied not only communication, but, more crucially, *two-way* communication. The spiritual telegraph, like animal magnetism, offered not only an explanation of unusual phenomena, but a means of initiating the phenomena as well. As the example of Mrs. Draper indicates, however, the relationship between the spiritual telegraph and animal magnetism did more than parallel one another in their relationship to the phenomena they sought to explain. Additionally, and quite crucially, it was the theoretical reliance of both animal magnetism and mechanical magnetism on electricity that gave the analogy between the spiritual and mechanical telegraphs its power.

Ideas of spirit communication also fused with ideas of animal magnetism in practice. Mr. Draper was able to contact the spirit world because his wife was "susceptible to magnetic influence" and could enter a "clairvoyant state." Eliab Capron, writing in 1850, "conceded that thus far the sounds have *generally* been freer in presence of known clairvoyants." Why this should be the case, was not immediately obvious to people. As Capron indicated, "The question has often been asked of spirits why this [the association between raps and clairvoyants] was so, and we received the following answer: 'They (clairvoyants) have the full power of sympathy with the spirits through the medium of the nervous fluid or electricity which is the only medium of communication between spirits in and out of the body."[27] Insofar as modern Spiritualism entailed not just a belief in spirits but an ability to communicate with them, "Spiritualism" did not simply appropriate "animal magnetism" as an explanatory theory. Rather modern Spiritualism *per se* was constituted through the fusion of *ideas* about spirits of the dead and the *practices* of animal magnetism. Neither, in themselves, would have been sufficient.

The association of the magnetically induced clairvoyant state with a world of spirits ready to communicate opened the door for a variety of new ways in which the spirits might manifest themselves beyond the "mysterious noises" and other physical phenomena traditionally associated with poltergeists. Initially the situation was quite chaotic. Hardinge indicates that "[i]n some of the circles . . . , the wildest scenes of confusion would often prevail . . . [and] all the crudities of impressible minds, stimulated half to frenzy by the contagious excitement of the times, were set down as direct communications from exalted ancients."[28] Eliab Capron reported not only chaos and improbable claims, but also described a variety of modes of communication in nearby Auburn, New York. Spirits, he said, "communicate their ideas by causing the feet or hands to rap on the floor or table; or by using their organs of speech—the words coming from the mouth with a convulsive force; or by writing with the hand." Many, he added, "also became clairvoyants."[29]

The formation of the Apostolic Brotherhood in Auburn under the leadership of James Scott, a former Seventh-day Baptist minister, and Thomas Lake Harris, a former Universalist minister, illustrates the alternatives that faced the early Spiritualists. Influenced by Adventist ideas, James Scott responded to the proliferation of claims by establishing an authoritative channel of inspiration through a Mrs. Benedict, much as James and Ellen White had responded to the claims of rival visionaries in the aftermath of the Great Disappointment. After they relocated to Mountain Cove, Virginia, in October 1850, Capron reported that "Mrs. Benedict's services were dispensed with, and Mr. Scott asserted that he was *divinely inspired* and especially chosen of God as the instrument to reveal His plenary will."

This desire to establish an authoritative channel of communication, evident in both Seventh-day Adventism and the Mountain Cove community, did not come to typify the Spiritualist movement more generally.[30] Eliab Capron and Henry Barron's *Explanation and History of the Mysterious Communion with Spirits* (1850), published shortly before the departure of Scott and his followers, was instrumental in setting an alternative course for the burgeoning Spiritualist movement. Their efforts rooted the movement more firmly in "psychological science" and, thus, grounded access to the spirits in psychological abilities available to many rather than in a supernatural status granted only to a few.

Given the heated atmosphere in Auburn, Capron and Barron began by emphasizing that they had "no desire to feed the popular credulity, or to excite the wonder-loving faculties of the ignorant and superstitious." Such persons, they said, "have already been made the prey of artful and designing men too long, and we are more desirous of stripping nature of the *super*naturalism which has been thrown around her by the crafty plunderers of the ignorant, than to have their superstitions wrought up to a still higher state of excitement." To that end, they continued, "we deem it important that a full explanation of the facts embodied in this work should be made, and a reasonable and *natural* explanation be given of these phenomena."[31]

In marked contrast to most others we have encountered who offered "reasonable and natural explanations" of seemingly supernatural phenomena, Capron and Barron did not want to explain the spirits away. Instead of attacking the idea of spirits, they launched into a critique of "the vast and entire separation . . . between spirit and matter" presupposed by the old philosophy and theology. Just because people "could not . . . see the more refined substance to which we give the name spirit . . . in a normal state," theologians falsely concluded that the spirits of the dead were "something beyond, and *entirely separate* from matter." Contrary to such views, they argued that "Clairvoyance and Psychological science, have convinced many of the skeptics in regard to future existence, that there is a positive identity of spirits of persons who have passed on beyond this state of existence."[32] Spirits, in other words, were composed of refined matter (not unlike the animal spirits of old) that could not be seen in a "normal state." They could only be seen in the "abnormal" (that is, Clairvoyant) state newly discovered by "Psychological science."

The significance of this move has been debated by a number of scholars. R. Laurence Moore has argued that Spiritualism "appealed not to the inward illumination of mystical experience, but to the observable and verifiable objects of empirical science." In seeming contradiction, Robert C. Fuller emphasized the continuity between the Spiritualists and Edwards, Emerson, and James insofar as each "connect doctrines of theological immanence with some prerational dimension of human personality."[33] The partial truth in both views is evident if we recognize that through the revelations of Davis, most American Spiritualists came to understand animal magnetism as *both* religious *and* scientific. Spiritualists, following Davis, understood the "empirical science" of animal magnetism as the natural (as opposed to supernatural) gateway to the other world. While this form of religious naturalism did characterize Emerson and James, the same cannot be said for Edwards. Edwards, like Wesley, grounded authentic religious experience in a new *supernatural* sense. In contrast to Edwards and Wesley, the blending of the psychological science of animal magnetism with theological beliefs regarding spirits and life-after-death in modern Spiritualism created a naturalistic (and seemingly empirical) basis for understanding religious experience. It also marked the popular advent of "religious naturalism" on the American scene.

Although much of Capron and Barron's book was devoted to descriptive testimonial, they also included a chapter devoted to showing the "very plausible, and to us very philosophical reasons [that] can be given for our spiritual theory." Their reasons fell under three headings: historical, prophetic, and empirical. The presence of *three* types of philosophical evidence for the "spiritual theory" suggest that from an early date Spiritualists were interested in more than just empirical evidence. Historically, Capron and Barron were eager "to show that the foregoing narrative is not wholly without a parallel in the world's history." Toward that end, they extracted from letters and other documents quoted in Adam Clarke's *Memoirs of the Wesley Family* detailing the Wesley family's transaction with a ghost they referred to as "Jeffrey." They then referred to the accounts of "precisely similar occurrences" that took place in Germany in the 1820s, as detailed in Justinus Kerner's *Seeress of Prevorst.*[34] In making these historical links, Capron and Barron followed the line of reasoning put forth by William Fishbough, erstwhile promoter of Andrew Jackson Davis and an editor of the by-then defunct paper devoted to Davis's teachings, the *Univercoelum.*[35]

Capron and Barron also referred to the prophecies of Davis and Emmanuel Swedenborg, both made "while in the Clairvoyant state." They singled out Davis's prophesy that the "TRUTH [that spirits communicate with the living] WILL ERE LONG PRESENT ITSELF IN THE FORM OF A LIVING DEMONSTRATION." They expected that this demonstration would usher in an "era when the interiors of men will be opened, and the spiritual communion will be established such as is now being enjoyed by the inhabitants of Mars, Jupiter, and Saturn, because of their superior refinement."[36] They claimed that "the testimony of clairvoyants almost without number . . . in private circles" was likewise a strong reminder of "Swedenborg's prophesy, that the year 1852 would be one that would decide the fate of his church or his doctrines." Based on the latter prophecy, they anticipated that Swedenborg's "general spiritual theory" would soon "be very generally received."[37]

William Fishbough endorsed the rappings as spirit manifestations in 1849, but A. J. Davis held off for another year. Having received letters for months requesting his views regarding the "mysterious noises," he was "impressed" to visit Stratford,

Connecticut, to witness the phenomena occurring there in the home of a Presbyterian minister, the Reverend Phelps.[38] The result of his investigation, titled *The Philosophy of Spiritual Intercourse* (1851), interpreted the raps within the framework of the Harmonial Philosophy and provided a philosophical framework for understanding spiritual communication.

Davis wanted his readers to view spiritual communication as an illustration of an underlying "world-revolutionizing philosophy" rather than as "an astounding effect of some hidden and mysterious causes." To this end, he, like Capron and Barron, sought to explain "the conditions and principles" by means of which the spirits communicated. Their method of communication, he said, could be readily understood "because those conditions are no more complicated or wonderful than the principles upon which the magnetic telegraph is daily operating along our great commercial avenues."[39] Davis explained that the analogy between the spiritual and the magnetic telegraph rested on the "electrical relations" between all created things, such that "all *higher* forms of development sustain *positive* [electrical] relations to all *lower* forms." The "*spirit-world*," being a higher form of development, "sustains a *positive* electrical relation to the *natural world*." The difference in the "electrical relations" allows the "negative physical system of the medium" to become a "receptacle for the influx of . . . spiritual electricity which the spirits discharge . . . to the *location* where they intend the sounds . . . shall be heard by the circle on earth." Thus, he said, "the inhabitants of the spirit-world have the *power*, when natural conditions are complied with, to communicate electrically with their friends in the body."[40]

Davis also provided guidelines so that circles could "avoid misapprehension and discord." Conceiving of the circle as the analogue to the telegraphic battery, he instructed his readers to organize their circles "upon *positive* and *negative* principles." Positive energy, according to Davis, was male, or more precisely masculine, and negative energy, feminine. Acknowledging that such traits were not necessarily distributed according to biological sex, he said that six of the twelve the members of the circle "should possess *feminine* attributes of character . . . and the others should be decidedly *masculine*." In 1851, he positioned the six "feminine principles" on one side of the circle and the six "masculine principles" on the other. Two years later, to better "accumulate, refine, and concentrate the vital electricity of the circle," he recommended placing "the males and females (the positive and negative principles) . . . *alternately*; as so many zinc and copper plates in the construction of magnetic batteries."[41]

In 1851, a number of prominent New Yorkers—including Judge J. Edmonds, the merchant Charles Partridge, Professor George Bush, and former *Univercoelum* editor-in-chief, Samuel Brittan—formed the "New York Circle." The group decided to establish a weekly "conference" wherein experiences could be exchanged and persons visiting from a distance might report on happenings elsewhere. In the circular advertising the first meeting, persons who shared the group's sentiments were invited to attend "to ascertain whether anything, and what, can be done by associative action in reference to the advancement of harmonious and profitable intercourse with the world of the spirits."[42]

As the number of out-of-town visitors increased the "New-York Conference for the investigation of Spiritual Phenomena" became, in Hardinge's words, "a focal point, where all the radiating lines of wide-spread interest could converse." The Conference sent out a circular to various parts of the country "calling for facts and requesting the narration of experiences in different States." A committee was also formed to facilitate the formation of daughter circles in the city of New York. Subscriptions were raised from the members to aid in the publication of pamphlets on Spiritualism. A series of public lectures on Spiritualism was delivered in February 1852. In May 1852, the conference initiated its most ambitious undertaking, the publication of the weekly paper, the *Spiritual Telegraph* under the editorial direction of Charles Partridge and Samuel Brittan.[43]

In the *Spiritual Telegraph*, which remained in print from 1852 to 1857, many of these interpretive currents coalesced. The paper's title reflected the grassroots analogy between the human and the spiritual telegraph. One of its two editors was an associate of Andrew Jackson Davis and former editor-in-chief of the *Univercoelum*. The paper advertised books on topics related to Spiritualism and in doing so gave intellectual direction to the movement. The first issue advertised Bush's new edition of Jung-Stilling's *Theory of Pneumatology* alongside numerous works of Andrew Jackson Davis and two books by an American medium. A year later, the advertisement for Partridge and Brittan's newly conceived "Spiritual Library" included a much wider selection of books. In addition to the works of Davis and Jung-Stilling, the list contained a new translation of Justinus Kerner's *Seeress of Prevorst,* numerous works on mesmerism and animal magnetism, a vastly expanded selection of writings by American mediums, and last, but not least, the *Spirit-Minstral*, "a collection of Ninety familiar Tunes and Hymns, appropriate to Meetings for Spiritual Intercourse."[44]

The Medium

As we have seen, the spirits, when asked to explain the close association between the rapping sounds and clairvoyants, referred to "the nervous fluid or electricity as the only medium of communication between spirits in and out of the body." Initially, "the nervous fluid or electricity" was the "medium" through which clairvoyants were in "sympathy with the spirits." In *The Principles of Spiritual Intercourse*, A. J. Davis described the Fox sisters as "mediums, because the electrical atmosphere which emanates from their systems contains but little gross electricity." In *The Principles*, Davis often placed the word "medium" in quotes when referring to a person, as if to suggest that the usage was not yet a familiar one. Nor was the relationship between the "medium" and the "clairvoyant" at all clear in these early publications. In his directions for the formation of circles, Davis had a role for both a medium and a clairvoyant. He defined the "medium" (in quotes) as the one "through whom 'sounds' are made" and the clairvoyant (without quotes) as one "who can discern spirits." By the end of the decade, however, the clairvoyant was largely subsumed by the concept of the "medium."

This concept gave order to much of the chaos of the early period by means of two ideas: first, that there were a variety of different types of media and, second, that all media went through a developmental process as they learned to communicate with the spirits. In 1853, Davis assisted this process along by constructing an elaborate "Table of Media" designed to show that "in the midst of apparent chaos, a beautiful harmony reigns." He discussed twenty-four different kinds of "spirit-media" from the "vibratory" or quaking medium to the "impressional" medium.[45] His descriptions, taken from historical and contemporary accounts of persons in various religious traditions, recatalogued a variety of familiar phenomena as stages in the development of a medium and constituted a veritable proto-Jamesian "varieties of mediumistic experience."

At the lower stages of development, "invisible powers" acted through the bodies of "vibratory," "motive," and "gesticulating" media. Such phenomena, Davis noted, were common in many traditions and he offered the Shakers and French Prophets as examples. The "manipulating" or healing medium was somewhat more developed. Davis expressed considerable enthusiasm for healing media, indicating that "all ancient records are explicit on the utter practicability of working so called 'miracles,' in this manner."[46] Fourteenth in the list were the psychologic media, "known to history as . . . mystics and revelators—individuals, seemingly under the direct inspiration of the Most High." Although he conceded that the visions and dreams of the psychologic medium were fraught with interest, he encouraged the developing medium to aim for higher and more reliable states.[47] Among the highest forms were the telegraphic media, the speaking media, the clairvoyant media, and the impressional media. In the last case, he said, "when the control [of the spirit] is perfect, the medium is annihilated, so to speak, so far as individualism of character is concerned, and the impressions truly are just what the *controlling* power desires."[48]

Spiritualists did not make such elaborate distinctions in everyday practice, although they did distinguish between varieties of media. Writing in 1854, the Reverend H. Mattison, a critic of the movement, provided descriptions of rapping media, writing media, speaking media, and, least common, dancing media.[49] While the "lists of mediums" published in the *Banner of Light* in the late fifties still included a range of types of mediums from the "clairvoyant healing medium" to the versatile "test, rapping, writing and trance medium," the vast majority described themselves as either "trance-speaking mediums" or "trance-speaking and healing mediums."[50]

By the late 1850s, the "medium" had largely subsumed the range of phenomena formerly associated with the clairvoyant. Healing and especially "trance-speaking" mediums rapidly superseded rapping and writing mediums. Moreover, with the disappearance of rapping and writing, the "trance medium" replaced the telegraphic metaphor for spirit communication as the key to understanding spirit communication.[51] As the new image gained in prominence, it precipitated an underlying theoretical shift away from an electrical or fluid-based animal magnetism toward a state or trance-based psychology.[52] By the late 1860s, the *Banner* had replaced the list of mediums with a list of lecturers. Trance, however, was still a key concept. About half the lecturers described themselves as "trance speak-ers" and the other half as "inspirational lecturers."[53]

As we have seen, during the 1840s, the term "trance" was used interchangeably with "ecstasy," primarily in relation to visions. In the late 1840s, La Roy Sunder-land began to use "trance" rather than sleep-related terminology to refer to the underlying magnetic state.[54] Sunderland carried this usage into the Spiritualist movement in the early 1850s. During his visit to Auburn during the tumultuous summer of 1850, the spirits told Sunderland that "they had often been present at [his] lectures, in Boston, Philadelphia, New York, Providence, and other places; attracted by the approach of those spirits whom [he] had pathetized into a state of TRANCE." The spirits assured him that "[t]his state of trance, . . . that very state of trance, into which [he] had pathetized thousands who had attended [his] lectures in different parts of the country, was the *nearest possible approach to the spirit world*."[55]

Dr. John F. Gray, a homeopathic physician and a regular at the "New-York Conference," also asserted that "the state of trance, near akin to dreaming, night-mare, etc., pertains to all shades of mediumship." According to the conference report, "[t]he doctor described the physical signs of the trance state, and main-tained that these signs were detectable in every exercise of true mediumship, especially in the temperature of the skin of the medium, in the state of the muscu-lar system as to voluntary motion, and in the condition and action of the pupils and balls of the eyes. Even in the rapping medium, he thinks these signs are observable to some slight degree."[56]

Although Sunderland and Gray made theoretically significant use of the term, most other psychologically oriented thinkers did not. References to trance, much less theories built on the concept, were still infrequent enough at mid-century to suggest that the shift in terminology was practically, rather than theoretically, driven. Divergent descriptions of Mrs. Conant, the *Banner*'s resident medium, suggest that mediums themselves may have played a role in this shift. As evi-denced by her advertisements at the back of the paper, Mrs. Conant described herself, from the start of the paper's publication, as a "trance medium." The paper's editors, however, appeared reluctant to adopt this designation. For the first year of publication, they published "communications . . . given us through the medi-umship of Mrs. J. H. Conant" in a weekly column. In April 1858, they added the communications are spoken "while she is in what is usually denominated 'The Trance State.' " Six months later, the editors finally adopted her self-designation, referring to her simply as "Mrs. J. H. Conant, Trance Medium."[57]

The shift in mediums' self-descriptions suggests that this may have been a "mar-ket-driven" change. Mediums advertised their services through the Spiritualist periodicals. As they moved from rapping to more efficient and potentially more ordinary modes of communication, such as writing and speaking, they needed a way to signal that it was not they who wrote and spoke, but the spirits who wrote and spoke through them. Neither the idea of a spiritual telegraph nor the associated electrically based theory of spirit communications provided an ade-quate means of differentiating the speaking and writing of the spirits from the ordinary speech and writing of humans. The word "trance," like "somnabulistic" or "magnetic," signaled the medium's ability to enter a special, nonvolitional state that clearly differentiated "normal" from "spirit" communications. Mediums who described themselves as "trance speaking mediums" or "trance lecturers" advertised their ability to enter into this non-ordinary state and thus their ability to serve as an authentic medium for spirit communications.

"Trance" may have caught on as the designation for this state because the word had both growing scientific legitimacy and popular resonance. "Trance," as the traditional Christian term for visionary experiences (*ekstasis*), was a word everyone knew. In designating themselves as "trance mediums," Spiritualists appropriated the largely positive connotations of the traditional term, while at the same time broadening its meaning to include the full range of mediumistic phenomena. In doing so, Spiritualists gave "trance" its modern breadth of psychological meaning, while retaining its traditional spiritual depth. In the hands of Spiritualists, "trance" became the psychological entryway into the spiritual realm.

Spirits and History

If mediumship was first of all a natural entryway into the spirit realm, it was understood by extension as a *common* or *universal* entryway. Spiritualists tended to assume that all persons had mediumistic abilities, albeit not equally developed, and thus the potential at least for direct access to the spirit realm.[58] They also assumed, in keeping with older magnetic histories, that evidence of Spiritualism could be found in all times and places in human history. Spiritualism, as a result, gave rise to historical claims about the role of spirits in other times and places, to Spiritualist histories of *true* religion built on the older magnetic histories of *false* religion, and, most broadly, to what was, in effect, a Spiritualist theory of religion.

Spiritualist claims about history varied in their depth and scope. While A. J. Davis, William Howitt, and James M. Peebles provided extended discussions of historical matters, many others simply made historical claims or allusions by implication or in passing. Some, such as Davis, focused primarily on the Bible or "Primitive History," as he called it, while others, such as Howitt and Peebles, gave more extended attention to the history of Christianity. While Spiritualists, most of whom were either heterodox or former Christians, focused most of their historical energies on Christianity, they did not neglect other religions. Indeed, their belief in the universality of spirit manifestations in all times and places led to reinterpretations of Christianity that, much to the chagrin of the orthodox, placed it on a more equal footing with other religions.

Armed with a belief in "mediums" and "spirits" as the common basis of true religion, Spiritualists were able to claim history and comparison as their own. For the first time, we have historical and comparative works on "true religion" that build on and incorporate the histories of enthusiasm and magnetic histories of magic. The Spiritualists' psychologically oriented reading of religion in general and Christianity in particular laid the foundation for the later, more respectable, theories of scholars such as William James. More immediately, it influenced the formation of Edward Tylor's "materialist" theory of religion and led to the founding of the nascent science of anthropology on an eerie theoretical inversion of Spiritualist assumptions about religion.

Primitive History and Ancient Spiritualism

In 1860, Elizabeth D. Schull, a member of the congregation of Charles Finney, well-known Presbygational minister, evangelist, and college president, in Oberlin, Ohio, was charged with not attending church for two years, denying the "divinity of Christ and the doctrine of the atonement," and "embracing modern Spiritualism." In her reply to the church's charges, Schull stated:

> I do believe in modern Spiritualism, and also in ancient Spiritualism, which I believe to be one and the same thing, differing only in degree of development in accordance with the advancement of the age. I believe God's laws are unchangeable, and that the same law that allowed Peter and John to see Moses and Elias, and John the Revelator to converse with angels, stands unrepealed to-day. I believe God commissions my angel friends as ministering spirits to commune with me, and I have tangible evidence of their presence, encouraging me to a nobler, purer, and higher life, and strengthening me to bear, unmoved, the scoffs and rebukes of the time-serving.[59]

Although Finney reportedly denied that "there was [any] such thing as ancient Spiritualism," the idea that "primitive Christianity," as it was more commonly known, differed only in degree from "modern Spiritualism" was a commonplace of modern Spiritualist thought. The equation of biblical "angels" with Spiritualist "spirits" was one of the building blocks of the Spiritualist reading of the Bible. This reading was undergirded by the idea of unchangeable law, simultaneously divine and natural, that allowed both biblical figures, such as Peter and John, and modern Spiritualists, such as Elizabeth Schull, to see and converse with the dead. Andrew Jackson Davis, although never enthusiastic about equating primitive Christianity and modern Spiritualism, laid the groundwork for this interpretation in his early writings.

SPIRITUALISTS AND THE BIBLE

In the lectures that made up the *Principles of Nature*, A. J. Davis made a number of moves that informed the later Spiritualist equation of the "Primitive History" with "ancient Spiritualism." First, and in keeping with the scientific biblical criticism of his day, he relentlessly privileged history over theology and reason over superstition. He attacked what he identified as the "four pillars upon which the [Christian] theological superstructure is sustained [Original Sin, the Atonement, Faith, and Regeneration]" and directed his readers to pay particular attention to this attack, "because it may be that it will demolish the whole system and leave nothing of it but a mass of disgusting rubbish."[60]

Second, he desacralized the Bible by pointing to the historical process by which it was canonized and placed the Christian Bible and Jesus more or less on a par

with the "Bibles" and founders of other religious traditions. He reminded his readers they were "merely reading a book pronounced the word of God by three
hundred exasperated bishops, and sealed by their emperor Constantine!" An understanding of the formation of the canon would, he believed, remove "at once
all that superstition concerning it, and all those ideas of its supernaturalness, that
have preserved it in the bosom of fanaticism from the period of its origin to the
present day." He reminded his readers that other traditions have scriptures that
they value as much as Christians do theirs and, while he recognized "the revelations made by Jesus as more useful, more truthful, and more natural" than any
others, he acknowledged the many revelations evident in other traditions. He
mentioned particularly Confucius, Brama, Zoroaster, Mohammed, Galen, the Ger-
mans (making particular note of the Seeress of Prevorst), the French (particularly
Charles Fourier), and Swedenborg.[61] He summed up his views on the Bible by
saying that while "the 'Primitive History' is useful as a history of mythology," it is
useless as a guide to theology. "Viewed in the light of *history*, I say, its writers
should be respected, and its contents preserved. But as a *theological* book it should
not be read."[62]

In freeing the Bible from a theological tradition that elevated it above all other
scriptures and Jesus above all other holy persons, he freed the religious imagination of his readers to read early Christian literature in search of the Jesus of "history." Whereas the quest for the historical Jesus has typically been understood as
a preoccupation of nineteenth-century Protestant scholars, the quest for the Jesus
of the New Testament also preoccupied the radical wing of Protestantism. Holding
firmly to the Protestant principle of *sola scriptura*, this wing of the tradition sought
a Jesus uncorrupted by the creeds and dogmas of later centuries. We have seen
these exegetical sensibilities at work among Baptists, Methodists, and Adventists,
but they were present also among the Protestant denominations for which Spiritualism had the greatest appeal—Quakers, Unitarians, and above all Universalists.

Davis made a number of moves that undoubtedly appealed to the exegetical
imaginations of his scripturally oriented readers. First, he did not reject the Bible
as history and indeed expressed a desire to "rescue its teachings . . . from *falsifica-
tions*." To this end, he spent some seven pages outlining "a true history of JESUS,
from his birth to his death." At first glance, his conclusion that "Jesus was a good
man, a noble and unparalleled Moral Reformer," suggests a forerunner of the
liberal Protestant Jesus of the late-nineteenth century. A closer reading, however,
suggests a Moral Reformer who healed by virtue of his superior "mental faculties"
and taught a harmonial philosophy not unlike Davis's own. According to Davis,
Jesus "spen[t] a large portion of his time in the visitation of the diseased, de-
pressed, disconsolate, and suffering inhabitants in various portions of the land."
Although his biographers represent him as performing "miracles," he was, according to Davis, "A TYPE OF PERFECT MAN" and not, he implied, a supernatural miracle worker.[63]

Second, Davis highlighted contradictions between the New Testament and orthodoxy that, while intended as a means of undercutting orthodoxy, had the
unintended effect of stimulating the imaginations of many Spiritualists. Thus, he

lifted up the passage from Mark in which the signs that will follow those who believe are listed, so as to point out that such signs (casting out devils, speaking with new tongues, healing the sick, etc.) were not to be found among the orthodox. While signs were absent among the orthodox, Davis could not resist pointing out that "the followers of two new faiths"—the Mormons and Shakers—*were* manifesting them. Although his tone suggests that he put little faith in any signs of this sort, he argued that the reasonable person ought to esteem all such miracles equally whether they were recorded in the book of Mark or in the writings of the "heathen, ancient, Chinese, Persianic, or Mohammedan" or among Mormons and Shakers. "Certainly," he concluded, "modern credulity is as much to be respected as ancient. . . . [W]hy confine belief [in miracles to the Bible], when external evidences of true faiths exist about and among us in abundance[?]"[64]

Although Davis differentiated his Harmonial Philosophy from the Spiritual Manifestations, he stressed their compatibility during the 1850s and 1860s. In *The Present Age and Inner Life* (1853) he summarized the key tenet of the Harmonial Philosophy, i.e., that "NATURE, REASON, and INTUITION . . . are . . . the only infallible mediums of revelation—the only CHURCH, CREED, and RELIGION *natural* to the mind of man." Orthodox Christianity, with its unnatural dogmas, blocked "the spontaneous development of Nature's own Religion." The Spiritual Manifestations, though not equivalent to the Harmonial Philosophy, were "a 'living demonstration' of many truths unfolded by the Philosophy; [just as] . . . the miracles recorded in the New Testament were *illustrative* of the doctrines and principles developed by that important Dispensation." Strictly speaking, he added, "these modern manifestations are no miracles." Rather, "like all other events called miracles, they are the incipient workings of *new laws* belonging to man in his present and future state of being." In the progressive unfolding of the new theology, "man, . . . as a physical and spiritual being, . . . [is] a medium or mediator between the Ideal and the Actual, between Heaven and Earth." Man, according to Davis, is "the pneumatic bridge over which every thing travels into this world."[65]

Davis and the many Spiritualists who adopted his approach were viewed by non-Spiritualists as "degrading" the Bible. The Reverend H. Mattison, writing in 1855, quoted from a number of books ostensibly written by spirits that claimed that the Bible itself was "nothing more than a book written through mediums." Mattison concluded, with obvious disgust, that "the Bible is [thus] degraded to a level with the infidel ghost-books from which we are now making extracts."[66] Some Spiritualists viewed other Spiritualists as degrading the Bible as well. At a meeting of the New-York Conference in 1854, William Fishbough stated that the resolutions and speeches of a recent Spiritualist convention "seem to have been mainly intended to degrade the Bible to the level of any other book containing the records of an 'unprogressed age,' interspersed with accounts of spiritual manifestations." Fishbough confessed that his views had grown more conservative. "At one state of his progress in the investigation of Spiritualism," according to the minutes, "he was not disposed to regard the Bible as a peculiarly divine revelation, more than some other books," but now, he had been convinced through "the instrumentality of Spiritualism that the god of the Bible is the true God."[67]

The charge that Spiritualists "degraded" the Bible was partly a matter of theology and partly a matter of tone. Theologically, Spiritualist views of the Bible reflected their understanding of revelation. The range of Spiritualist views fell along a continuum with Nature as the (sole) source of all revelation at one end and the Bible as the sole source of revelation at the other. At the radical end of the spectrum were those Spiritualists who focused solely on "Nature" and paid little or no attention to the Bible, except perhaps to state that it was no different from any other "unprogressed" book. More moderate than this were the Spiritualists, who, while viewing Nature as the ultimate source of all revelation, understood the Bible as a subsidiary source, since "Nature" encompassed everything.[68] Closest to orthodoxy, and the most conservative among the Spiritualists, were those, such as Fishbough, who made no mention of Nature and linked the revelatory claims of the Bible and spirit communications. Since orthodox Protestants viewed the Bible alone as revelation and left no room for spirit communication in the present, Spiritualists could approach, but never entirely reach the "orthodox" end of the spectrum.[69]

Mr. Finney and Mr. Lockwood, Spiritualist lecturers who spoke in Ohio in 1854, illustrate the shift in emphasis and tone that distinguished the more radical from the more moderate Spiritualists during the mid-1850s. According to J. D. Cox, both Finney (no relation to Charles) and Lockwood reflected "that particular phase of Naturalism which has been taught by A. J. Davis under the name of the Harmonial Philosophy." Mr. Lockwood, the more moderate of the two, regarded "Spiritualism as an advance upon Christianity, but admitted the value and purity of *both* the scriptural dispensations, the Mosaic as well as the Christian. He declared that modern Christendom had become enslaved to forms and creeds, and possessed little or no spiritual life."[70]

Finney's "opposition to the churches of the present day," according to Cox, "was much more vehement than that of Mr. Lockwood, and his invectives against the 'book religion' learned from the Bible were often exceedingly bitter." For the more radical Mr. Finney, Christianity was simply one among the many religions of the world. According to Cox, "[h]e classed the Scriptures with the Koran and the Zendavista, and would allow to the books of the Bible, their writers, and the men presented by them as saints, no superiority over the holy books and reputed holy men of heathen nations."[71]

The *Banner of Light*, as the most widely read of the Spiritualist periodicals, favored the moderate Spiritualist position. It avoided bitter attacks on orthodoxy and did not routinely equate Christianity with other religions. *The Banner's* editors waxed enthusiastic about mediums, such as Thomas Gales Forster, who effectively appealed to the "thinking mass[es]" looking for a "pure and spiritual religion" to replace the "meaningless forms and ceremonies" found in the churches. Forster, the son of a Unitarian minister and the medium for the spirit of a Universalist minister, took the irenic, yet still markedly heterodox, attitude toward the Bible that characterized the moderate Spiritualists. Acknowledging that the concern that "Spiritualism . . . attempts to refute the positions of the Bible" is "honestly raised," he responded evenhandedly, saying that while many had perhaps "reverenced that book too much," others had not paid it the respect it was due. Modern Spiritualism, he continued, "is sustained by this book, but it does not adhere to the facts [of spirit intercourse], . . . *because* they are in the Bible; it only brings in the Bible as an adjunct, relying on a more forcible and truthful basis." While not "mean[ing] to be disrespectful to the [Bible], or the truths contained in it," he asserted that the more truthful basis of revelation is Nature. "Nature [too] presents a book to humanity—a broader book."[72]

The editors hoped through this more moderate rhetoric to liberalize the churches. To this end, they encouraged their readers not to "come out" from the churches but to "remain at their posts," where they could serve as "instruments of spiritualizing the present unmeaning forms of the churches."[73]

James Martin Peebles, like many other Spiritualist leaders, a "come-outer" from the Universalist ministry, adopted a similarly conciliatory approach while serving as Western Editor of the *Banner* in the late 1860s. According to his biographer, "his uniform attitude was well calculated to attract the general public, interlarding his discourses on the one hand with just enough of Christian Spiritualism to interest and hold those who were beginning to emerge from the bondage of creeds; and [on the] other hand scrupulously avoiding anything like sensational ranting against prevailing religions, doctrines, and social usages."[74]

The range of attitudes toward revelation and toward orthodox Christianity illustrate why it was confusing then and now to designate some Spiritualists as "Christian" and others as not. Spiritualists such as Fishbough viewed themselves as a minority within the Spiritualist movement and were the ones most likely to be designated by themselves and others as "Christian Spiritualists." Spiritualists such as Lockwood, Forster, and Peebles, who viewed Nature as the ultimate source of revelation, but who nonetheless saw value in the Bible when interpreted from a Spiritualist perspective, were exceedingly common and exemplified, if anyone did, the "mainstream" of the Spiritualist movement. Although they did not necessarily refer to themselves as "Christian Spiritualists," they commonly embraced the "teachings of Jesus" as central to their self-understanding. As the Spiritualist movement became more polarized in the late 1860s, there was increased pressure to define oneself as "Christian" or "anti-Christian." Peebles, who resisted this trend, was castigated by Spiritualist reviewers of his book, *Seers of the Ages* (1869), for being, on the one hand, "too Christian for an infidel Spiritualist's fellowship" and, on the other, "too infidel for a Christian Spiritualist's approval." When they characterized themselves, they were most likely to describe themselves as "free" or "liberal" in matters of religion.[75]

Spiritualists were regularly accused of degrading the Bible, but many, especially of this moderate sort, saw themselves as rescuing it. Contrary to those who claimed Spiritualists "trample[d] under foot the Bible and its teachings," a Mrs. Hyser argued in the pages of *The Banner* that Spiritualism "comes forth to rescue the past, and to give the right language to the records of the past, and thus harmonize the past with the present, so that humanity may be blessed." In fact, she insisted, "[t]he past is more valuable to us than it is to any other," because, through intuition and reason, the Spiritualist is able to grasp its true import. Others used the parables to illustrate their belief that Jesus himself "referred [his listeners] to a future day and state in which they would better understand," because then "the *Spirit*-powers would convey the meaning."[76]

Spiritualists were not simply interested in illuminating the true meaning of scripture for its own sake, they also believed that the Bible, correctly interpreted, provided one of the best arguments for Spiritualism and against orthodoxy. In arguing from spirit communication in the Bible (which the orthodox were sometimes willing to concede) to spirit communication in the present, Spiritualists made yet another assault on Protestant efforts to limit revelation, miracles, and other forms of direct religious experience to the Bible. Some of the impulses behind Spiritualist biblical interpretation were not unlike those that drove other radical Protestant groups. Like them, Spiritualists who turned to the Bible were looking for "primitive Christianity," that is, the "true Christianity" undefiled by clergy, canon, and creed. Like other radical Protestants, they also assumed that their experience in the present could and should mirror what they saw in the past. Unlike them, however, the Spiritualists' blending of belief in spirits with the psychology of animal magnetism provided them with a basis for explaining the Spiritualistic phenomena they found in the Bible in naturalistic terms. The result was a naturalistic reading of Christian origins that has features in common with the work of some contemporary scholars.[77]

SPIRITUALISTS ON CHRISTIAN ORIGINS

The foundation of Spiritualist exegesis was the equation of spirits and angels. Spiritualists could rattle off a litany of spirit manifestations in both the Old and New Testaments. Angels or spirits appeared to Abraham, Lot, Hagar, Jacob, and Joshua. They appeared to Joseph, Peter, Paul, and John. Angels or spirits appeared at Jesus' birth, while he was in the desert, when he suffered in the garden, and to the women at his tomb. Columns in the *Banner of Light* waxed eloquent in this regard. According to one, "from Genesis to Revelations [sic], every act is participated in by angels—every word is at the dictation of a spirit. . . . In a word, the Bible will be found to be a record of angel visitations to mankind; of spirits encouraging the lovers of truth and the workers in its broad fields." Another, focusing on Jesus, proclaimed: "From the conception to the crucifixion of Christ; from his resurrection to the end of Revelation through St. John the Divine; his birth; his life; his death and his spirit after death—all are replete with the manifestation of spirit power."[78]

Among the biblical evidences for Spiritualism, one author listed "trances, visions, interpositions of angels, spirit voices, and healings of the sick" as the most prominent. Others professed to see evidence of mediumship, clairvoyance, and trance. The medium R. P. Ambler pointed out that "the seers and prophets whose names are mentioned in the primitive history were mediums." A *Banner* correspondent referred to the "physical manifestations of spirit power, through the mediumship of Paul and Peter, Silas and John." A Spiritualist in Louisville identified numerous examples of "clairvoyance and the spirit traveling from the body" and pointed out that "John [was] in trance under spirit direction" and "Paul [was] a developing medium." *The Banner*'s editors argued that, "if Paul was not entranced when he spoke, some of the most important lessons taught the apostles, were taught in the 'trance' state."[79]

In addition to noting the presence of psychological states in the Bible, some used them to explain biblical miracles. The spirit of William Ellery Channing explained through a Dr. Bristol how Lazarus was raised from the dead. "The spirit of Lazarus had not entirely left the body; he was in a trance. Christ in his superior condition saw this, and by his magnetic power restored the action of the system. The same was done at the restoration of the maid." The editors of the *Banner of Light* advanced a similar theory with respect to the Transfiguration in a dispute with the editor of the Universalist *Christian Freeman*. "We think," they wrote, "it is stated that the two disciples who accompanied Jesus at the Transfiguration, were afflicted with drowsiness. We have a right to determine the nature of this sleep for ourselves . . . and we might possibly think it was somnambulic, considering that in it they saw the spirits of two of the old prophets."[80] Many Spiritualists also rejected the idea of the resurrection of Jesus' "earthly body" as contrary to natural law, insisting that Jesus appeared to the disciples after his death as a spirit or in a "spirit body," that is in the same way that spirits were appearing to modern Spiritualists.[81]

Mrs. Henderson, speaking in trance, summed up the Spiritualists' naturalistic approach to miracles in response to a question put to her by a clergyman:

> Q. Were miracles wrought by God or man? A. Both. *Science* may work the same kind that Christ wrought. Q. In what do miracles consist? A. Philosophically there is *no miracle*. It is Nature's operation. Q. What is meant by Christ's 'walking on the water?' A. It was no miracle, except as an appearance of deviation from the ordinary operations of laws. Christ was a *great medium*. Q. Was the resurrection of Christ a miracle? A. No, *all* men rise—*all* have spiritual bodies—all *live* as immortal. Q. Was the rising of Lazarus according to natural law? A. Yes. He only *sleepeth*. Decomposition or death had not occurred. His magnetic will could bring him forth.[82]

Spiritualists' views of Jesus, like their views of revelation, fell along a continuum. The issue that divided Spiritualists was not so much the matter of Jesus' divinity, but the extent to which he should be set apart from other human beings. Just as Spiritualists could interpret revelation broadly (Nature) or narrowly (the Bible), so they could view Jesus' relationship to God, divinity, or the Spirit as exceptional or (relatively) ordinary. The more ordinary it was, the more like everyone else Jesus became. Critics, such as the Reverend Mattison, accused Spiritualists of "degrad[ing] the Redeemer of the world," just as they had degraded the Bible. Spiritualists who rejected orthodox theology might still refer to Jesus' divinity or to Jesus as savior or to the Christ-presence, but if they did so they viewed such qualities as accessible to other human beings as well.[83]

Mediums expressed this in different ways. According to Thomas Forster, "Jesus was divine, but not in the sense that we have been taught to believe." Rather, "he was actuated and governed [in his material life] by the fundamental principle of spirituality, Divinity," in the same way that modern Spiritualists were. In fact, it was by and through him that the "first principles of Spiritualism" were developed. L. K. Conley viewed Jesus as an "elder brother" and told his listeners that they could "[b]ehold in his life the capacity of [their] own souls, [and their] mediumistic powers." In his lecture, he tried "to show what principles made him a Savior, and how we all, like him, may be saviors." Mrs. Henderson saw in Jesus the victory of the "Christ principle . . . over Jesus the man," but while the orthodox viewed the incarnation as a unique event, Mrs. Henderson could "see no reason why there may not be myriads of them [Christs on earth]." The anonymous Spiritualist from Louisville thought that Jesus' "manifestations of divinity . . . made him the great medium for immortal truth, and in that sense the Mediator for mankind." This did not set him apart, however, since, as s/he went on to say, "[m]ediumship is the common heritage of humanity, accessible to all."[84]

However divergent their ways of expressing it, the underlying image that connected Jesus with his fellow humans was that of the mediumistic mediator between this world and the next. Joel Tiffany, a medium from Ohio who often appeared in columns of *The Banner*, left a more detailed record of his view of Christian origins than most Spiritualists. Like the Spiritualists just quoted, he believed that "Christ and his apostles really taught the spiritual truth and the doctrine of spiritual communication" and that they "were inspired with the same inspiration, in kind, which is attainable in these days by a cultivation of man's spiritual nature."[85] Tiffany, however, not only connected the past and the present, he explained why Christ was necessary.

According to Tiffany, Christ came in order to "change the character of the communications" between heaven and earth.[86] This change was initiated through Christ's earthly interaction with his disciples, but could not be completed until Jesus had ascended to heaven. Tiffany described the relationship between them in the mesmeric language characteristic of the Spiritualist circle. While on earth "Christ . . . established in the hearts of his disciples an affinity and bond of affection, which should bind them to him after he had gone into the spirit sphere." With the establishment of this bond, he completed the "work his father had given to him to do in this sphere." He went away so that he could "instruct them in the higher truth for which they were prepared." After his crucifixion, "the spirit of Jesus was emancipated from the body, so that he could come spiritually into *rapport* with them, and make them understand by impression and impulse." This laid "a foundation upon which spirits of the better spheres might work . . . [and] as soon as their minds became calm, after his death and resurrection, when they came into such a quiet state that spiritual influence could act upon them, *Christ appeared to them*."[87]

Pentecost marked the final step in the process of change initiated by Christ and the beginning of the new dispensation in which communications could flow freely between heaven and earth. Tiffany cast Pentecost in distinctly Spiritualist terms. According to Tiffany, "[t]he inspiration upon the day of Pentecost was not the inspiration of the Divine Father, but of spirits. The Holy Ghost . . . was the good Spirit without which the Christian dispensation could not be taught." The baptism of the spirit on Pentecost was manifested through fire ("tongues of flame") and "inspired men talked in divers tongues."[88] According to Tiffany, evidence that one had "received the Spirit truth" was manifest through the performance of "outward signs" of the spirit's power. Picking up on Davis's suggestion, Tiffany quoted Mark 16:

> And these *signs* shall follow them that believe: In my name they shall cast out devils; they shall speak with new tongues; they shall take up serpents; and if they drink any deadly thing it shall not hurt them; they shall lay hands on the sick and they shall recover.' . . . The gifts of the spirit were to follow, because they could not understand without them. Only thus could the connection with heaven be kept open, and the divine communications come down into the soul.[89]

Tiffany's interpretation may seem idiosyncratic, but there is considerable evidence to suggest a tradition of "signs and wonders" within the mainstream of the Spiritualist movement. This is only surprising if we lose sight of the fact that Spiritualism was both naturalistic *and* religious. Signs and wonders were explained naturalistically, but they were not explained *away*. Philosophically, Spiritualists understood signs and wonders, like the "miracles" of Jesus, as neither supernatural nor miraculous, but that did not make them any less important. Thus, we find a *Banner* correspondent quoting Corinthians to the effect that "all mediums have their various gifts—some one only, and some more." Among the gifts listed were "the gift of healing, . . . the working of miracles, . . . discerning of spirits, . . . divers kinds of tongues, [and] the interpretation of tongues." Mediums were encouraged to "take up their cross and follow in the footsteps of their divine predecessor, Christ." Then, the correspondent concluded, "the water would again be turned to wine, the sick healed, the dead would be raised, and God's name glorified through the mediums of the present age." Referring to this same list of spiritual gifts, the editors of the *Banner* indicated in another context that, "[a]s at the introduction of Christianity, so now, spiritual gifts are being imparted by this laying on of hands. Medium power is developed by it, and all the gifts alluded to are conferred."[90]

The case of the Reverend B. S. Hobbs, a Universalist clergyman in Webster, New York, provides an example of signs and wonders or mesmerism run amock, depending on your point of view. In 1857, Hobbs withdrew from the ministry because, as he concluded, spirits kept seizing control of his voice while he was praying and preaching. In a letter to the Universalist *Ambassador*, he wrote: "I was obliged in spite of all my *efforts* to prevent it, to exhibit the character of the speaking medium in full, by addressing an audience on two different occasions. . . . This has continued for a few months past . . . and from Sabbath to Sabbath I am acting, not as a Gospel minister, but as a spirit medium."[91] The

Universalist *Christian Freeman* used the occasion of the Reverend Hobbs's difficulties to express their concerns regarding Spiritualist trance lecturers. *The Banner of Light* printed extracts from both Hobbs's letter and the *Christian Freeman* and then offered an editorial response in the antiformalist spirit of John Wesley and Ellen G. White:

> Ah, it is a sad thing for the worshippers of dead forms and ceremonies, and mummied creeds, and the priests at the altars of such, to find that 'men speak with other tongues as the spirit (or spirits) give them utterance;' a sad thing, indeed, for the doctors and apothecaries, . . . when men and women, untaught of books and unskilled in the art and science of the schools in Cambridge, 'lay hands on the sick and they recover.' But Christ said, 'these things shall follow them that believe.' The editor of the *Freeman* professes to believe in Christ, yet when the very things occur which Christ said should occur as proof of our belief, he denounces it all, and warns mankind against even looking at them. . . . Had he published the *Christian Freeman* in Jerusalem in the year 33, he might have called the apostles, as he does those of the same class today, 'self mesmerising speakers traversing the country,' and Christianity he might have charged with being, as he does Spiritualism now, a 'perverted mesmeric and psychologic concern.'[92]

Ten years later, James M. Peebles editorialized in the columns of the *Banner* that "modern Spiritualism in many respects is but a revivification of primitive Christianity, with the attending signs, gifts, trances, visions, dreams, prophecies, tongues, healings, &c." Moreover, "those professed Christians who, through ignorance or bigotry, oppose the central fact, are undermining their own foundations, and recklessly hurling deistical and atheistical javelins at the temple of Christianity itself!"[93]

If Spiritualists could find modern Spiritualism in primitive Christianity, the converse was also true. The presence of signs and wonders in both the ancient and modern worlds was only the tail end of the comparison. It began with Andrew Jackson Davis, whom Emma Hardinge described as the John the Baptist of the Spiritualist movement. The editors of the *Banner of Light* continued the comparison when they declared that "[t]he Christ of Spiritualism—born in the manger at Rochester—came with healing, teaching, clairvoyance, clairaudience, and the Pharisees hated it without cause. They wondered at its vast and rapid spread, and would not recognize the fact that it was the Christ of the first century returned to quicken the Christ *within*, to bring forth higher germs, and to teach us what Christianity was, devoid of formality."[94]

Spiritualist Universalism

The parallels between modern Spiritualism and primitive Christianity were easily explored by any Spiritualist with access to a Bible. Evidence that spirits played a role in times, places, and traditions outside the Bible, and thus were truly universal, came both from historical sources and through the testimony of spirits. Through reflection on history and the testimony of the spirits, the initial tendency to view universality as a degrading lack of uniqueness gradually shifted to a view of universality as persuasive testimony to truth. As a universal doorway to the other world, animal magnetism laid the foundation for a new understanding of the essence of religion.

THE EVIDENCE OF HISTORY

Although they were nowhere near as common as Spiritualist litanies of spirit manifestations in the Bible, Spiritualists did occasionally recite lists of spirit-related historical phenomena. At the meeting of the New-York Conference in 1854 where he brought up the issue of trance and mediumship, Dr. John Gray cited the "oracular responses through the pythonesses and sibyls" as evidence that "the trance state [was] . . . a characteristic condition in all mediumship." He then added that this could also be seen in "the spiritual exercises and their trance results in Ignatius Loyola, and his disciples of the Jesuits; the ecstasies of Madame Guyon, and her disciples, including Fenelon; the experience in clairvoyance and trance-speaking of Geo. Fox and the Quakers of all kinds; the proceedings of John of Munster, and the trances of the Methodists of our own times." Speaking at a "Free Convention" in Rutland, Vermont, in 1858, A. J. Davis also turned to history, claiming that "it seem[ed] to be an undeniable historic fact that there have always been, at intervals, religious interior awakening, who internal influence has shown itself in external manifestations." The truth of Spiritualism, he said, "harmonizes with all history of the past and present. . . . From the days of Confucius, to those of Theodore Parker, there has been made manifest this unseen reality of spirit-power." He referred specifically to Pythagoras, Jesus, Martin Luther, John Wesley, and Swedenborg.[95]

In Gray's list, in particular, we have for the first time a list of traditional "enthusiasts"—George Fox, John of Munster, and the Methodists—enlisted in the cause of true religion. In both lists, we see comparisons across traditions—Catholic and Protestant, Christian and non-Christian—again in support of true religion. Some of these comparisons may have been drawn from Joseph Ennemoser's *Geschichte des thierischen Magnetismus*, which was translated into English by the British Spiritualist William Howitt and published as *The History of Magic* in 1854. Ennemoser himself, as noted in the previous chapter, equated magic, magnetism, and false religion, nonetheless his vast compendium provided a wealth of information for Spiritualists intent on demonstrating the presence of spirit communications in all times and places.

This task was first taken up in a serious way by William Howitt, who published his two-volume *History of the Supernatural* in 1863. Howitt, a self-described "Christian Spiritualist" who defined "Spiritualism . . . [as] but another term for the belief in the Supernatural," had several aims in writing the book. Negatively, it was a sustained attack on Protestantism and the Enlightenment for their abandonment of the miraculous. Positively, it was an attempt to convince Spiritualists that Spiritualism did not begin in America in 1848, and, most crucially, to make the case that Spiritualism was "a universal faith," evident, as the subtitle proclaimed "in all ages and nations, and in all churches, Christian and pagan."[96]

In a chapter on "the supernatural in the Bible," Howitt discussed the impact of the Enlightenment on biblical interpretation, pointing above all to Hume and his essay on miracles as the culprit. The extreme skepticism of the Enlightenment in which "[t]he churchman, the sectarian, the professor and the preacher, the man of literature and the man of science, are all educated," was not, for Howitt, the ultimate root of the problem. The problem, he argued, "came in with Protestantism, *and exists only in Protestantism*," because Protestantism constituted itself through an attack on miracle in "the Church of Rome." The Protestant embrace of the Enlightenment and its attack on miracle was not, in his view, a radical change of direction, but rather the unfolding of a prior predisposition rooted in the nature of the Protestantism itself. The result, he said, was that "[i]n endeavouring to pull up the tares of false Roman miracle, they have . . . pulled up the root of faith in miracle, and in the great spiritual heritage of the Church with it."[97]

If American Spiritualists in their instinctive turn to the Bible in search of "primitive Christianity" displayed their radical Protestant affinities, Howitt displayed a rather more Catholic disposition in his turn to "tradition," broadly defined. English Spiritualists, like their American counterparts, "almost universally . . . regarded [Spiritualism] as an entirely new phenomenon . . . originating in America within the last ten years." Howitt wanted to demonstrate that this was not the case. "Nothing," he said, "can be more self-evident than that American Spiritualism is but the last new blossom of a very ancient tree, coloured by the atmosphere in which it has put forth, and somewhat modified in its shape by the pressure of circumstances upon it." While American Spiritualists, through their discovery of "the telegraphy of rapping, and the further development of mediumship, . . . inaugurated a new era of spiritualism," this was not the first manifestation of the "power of spiritualism itself. That power," he argued, "is the all-time inheritance of the human race."[98]

Howitt defined Spiritualism as "the revival of the universal faith . . . in the communion of God and his angels with the spirit of man." That, he said, was "the essential, the substantial principle of Spiritualism," which he intended to demonstrate, "on historic evidence, to be as old as the hills, and as ubiquitous as the ocean." Spiritualism is, he said, "independent of all times, all people, and even of its own varying phenomena. It is, in itself, specifically and permanently the influx of divine angelic agency into and upon the human soul."[99] This "influx of divine angelic agency into . . . the human soul" is the essential feature of Spiritualism, the "universal faith" proclaimed "in all ages and nations, and in all churches, Christian and pagan." Here we have a notion of religion-in-general ("a universal faith" evident in all ages and nations and all "churches, Christian and pagan") and a theory of what constitutes it ("the influx of divine angelic agency into . . . the human soul").

Howitt ranged widely in an effort to demonstrate that Spiritualism was a "universal faith," drawing upon both the histories of enthusiasm and the magnetic histories of magic. His first attempt to demonstrate this point was published in the *Spiritual Telegraph* in the mid-1850s, where, ironically enough, he used "the wonderful story of the Prophets of the Cevennes," that is the French Prophets, "to demonstrate, that . . . the [Spiritualist] principle is universal, and belong[s] to all times and nations."[100] Howitt opened his full-length history of the supernatural with four chapters on late-eighteenth and early-nineteenth-century "Spiritualists" in Europe, focusing on Jung-Stilling, Justinus Kerner, along with Swedenborg, Ennemoser, and numerous others. He then devoted three chapters to the supernatural in the Bible, eight chapters to the supernatural in "ancient nations," e.g., Assyria, Egypt, India, China, Greece, Rome, and Scandinavia. After a chapter on the supernatural among the American Indians, he turned to the history of the Christian church with seventeen chapters devoted to such topics as the early fathers, the neo-platonists, the Roman Catholic Church, the Eastern Orthodox churches, the "so-called" medieval "heretics" and mystics, Martin Luther and the Protestant reformers, the Church of England, the Dissenters, the Quakers, the Jansenists (known in the histories of enthusiasm as the "Convulsionaires of St. Medard"), the French Prophets, and the Methodists. Out of the whole only two chapters were devoted to modern Spiritualism in England and North America.

Two American histories of Spiritualism were published at the end of the decade: James M. Peebles's *Seers of the Ages* (1869) and Emma Hardinge's *Modern American Spiritualism* (1869). Although both were moderate Spiritualists, they took rather different approaches in their histories. Peebles, like Howitt, evinced the sensibilities of an historical theologian and Hardinge, those of a church historian. Peebles, in fact, relied heavily on Howitt, infusing his universalist historical framework with a highly developed moderate Spiritualist theology. Hardinge took a very different tack, writing a detailed history of the first twenty years of the Spiritualist movement in the United States with the stated aim of preserving much of the movement's primary documentation. While Hardinge's work is of great value to the historian, Peebles's volume further developed the universalizing impulses evidenced by Howitt.

Like Howitt, Peebles believed that Spiritualism, under various names and in a variety of forms, "constituted the basic foundation, and has been the motive force of all religions in their incipient stages."[101] Peebles, again like Howitt, devoted considerable attention to the history of Christianity, but in contrast to Howitt, Peebles made a far sharper distinction between the primitive Christianity of the early church and the post-Constantinian Christianity that followed it. For Peebles, the high points of the church in the latter era were George Fox, William Blake, John Wesley, Ann Lee, Swedenborg, and John Murray, the founder of Universalism. He reinterpreted each from a Spiritualist perspective. With respect to early Methodism, for example, he said that "[d]uring the sermons, and especially in the prayer circles of the Wesleys, the more susceptible became sufficiently spiritually influenced to manifest symptoms of violent spasms and convulsions. Similarly wrought upon in our day, Methodists have 'fallen with the power,' and seen visions—all phases of Spiritualism." The denomination as a whole, he said, has lost its "angelic ministers and spiritual gifts. . . . The soul-fire of their primitive forces are dying under church formalisms and mocking sanctities."[102]

He broke with Howitt in his depiction of primitive Christianity, differentiating, not always clearly, between the "theologic Jesus" of the church fathers; the "mythic

Christ" of the Gospels, copied from "the Chrisna of India"; and the "natural Jesus, an enthusiastic Spiritualist of Judea."[103] Peebles argued that the "close and almost *perfect* parallelism between the Chrisna of the Bhagavat-Gita, and the Christ of the Gospels, was of itself sufficient evidence to show that one was borrowed from the other; or that they were both copies from some older myth."[104] Howitt, in his review of Peebles's book, was most disturbed by Peebles's comparison between "Chrishna of India and Christ of Syria."[105] Howitt made the usual charges of degradation, to which Peebles responded by saying that "few men know better than 'W[illiam] H[owitt],' " that the truths Jesus spoke "were the frequent enunciations of that common consciousness which relates to the universal religion of the races." Referring to a variety of canonical and noncanonical Christian gospels and to the Mahabarata, Peebles argued that there were "remarkable similarities in [all] those teachers."[106]

Having argued that the mythic Christ was derived from ancient myths, he argued that the historical Jesus was a Spiritualist. Peebles's Spiritualist reading of Jesus, like that of other moderates, portrayed Jesus as a medium. The spirit descended upon Jesus, like other mediums, at baptism. He healed under spirit influence, walked on water upheld by spirit-hands, exercised clairvoyant gifts, discharged "electro-spirit batteries" at his crucifixion, and appeared thereafter as "the Christ-spirit." At Pentecost, Jesus manifested himself to his followers "when they are all of 'one accord' in a spiritual circle . . . [and] confer[ed] upon them 'the gifts of the Spirit.' "[107] In *Jesus: Myth, Man, or God*, Peebles moved beyond the basic comparison between primitive Christianity and modern Spiritualism to argue that Jesus the Spiritualist embodied the "positive or universal religion" at the heart of all religions. This "universal religion" was characterized by belief in "the divine Fatherhood of God, the universal brotherhood of man, the perpetual ministry of angels and spirits, and the absolute necessity of toleration, charity, forgiveness, love—in a word, *good works*." This, he said, was the "inborn religion of all men."[108]

TESTIMONY OF THE SPIRITS

While Howitt and Peebles were among Spiritualism's intellectual elite, there is much to suggest that this universalizing process was not a product of scholarly studies, but of Spiritualist circles. In fact, Peebles and other Spiritualists attributed it to the testimony of the spirits. If we step outside the Spiritualists' own frame of reference, we can think of mediumship as providing an opportunity for imaginative speech in a voice that was, by definition, not one's own. Viewed in that light, it is clear that the Spiritualist movement allowed mediums to express a range of views that they may or may not have held consciously or wanted to express publicly. The Spiritualist movement provided investigators with an opportunity to engage with the views of these (imagined) others in the context of lectures and circles, without having to claim such views as their own. In doing so, it provided a context in which people could experiment with and become accustomed to ideas that they and others might otherwise have deemed unacceptable.[109]

When it came to theology, the spirits not only attacked orthodoxy, they also attested to the truth of universal salvation and wrestled with the leading theological questions of their day. They explained biblical and other miracles in scientific terms, pondered the relationship between Christianity and other religions, and sought to identify an "essence of religion" that underlay all the traditions. As the spirits who spoke through American mediums became more and more diverse, Spiritualists also began to express through them an interest in religious traditions other than their own.[110]

The preponderance of Universalists and former Universalists in the Spiritualist movement undoubtedly accounts for the large number of spirits who expressed support for the doctrine of universal salvation. While many who did so were the spirits of dead Universalists, there were many others, who presumably would not have looked kindly upon Universalist doctrines while living, that apparently changed their mind once they entered the spirit realm. From the spirits of Benjamin Franklin and Thomas Paine, on the rationalistic side, to the spirits of John Wesley and many lesser known Methodist and Baptist preachers on the evangelical side, the spirits of the dead returned to acknowledge the truth of Spiritualism, in general, and universal salvation, in particular. In doing so, the spirits of dead undermined the exclusivity of their own tradition relative to other Christian traditions or other religions more generally. Thus, the spirit of John Wesley wrote through the hand of a Mr. Boynton in Waterford, New York, to reject the orthodox conception of Jesus and depict him as no more "than any good man." Elder John Colby, a prominent Freewill Baptist revivalist, spoke through a Mr. Clark of Charlestown, Massachusetts, to retract the views he had once held on salvation in favor of the "great doctrine of universal salvation."[111]

As both colonial expansion and Protestant missionary efforts were building toward a peak at the turn of the century, the spirits evinced remarkable equanimity about Christianity's failure to convert the world. When one medium was asked why no more than "one-third of the race believed in Christ," the spirits responded that "the name is nothing." It was the "the acceptance of the Christ-principle" that mattered.[112] In a similar vein, another medium was asked why, if the Bible was a revelation intended for all, "so many nations [were] so ignorant of its meaning?" The spirits responded that

> [all nations] have their own peculiar conditions, states and revelations. The germs of revelation are the same with all nations. There are peculiarities of clime, of hemisphere, as well as of constitutional organism. Yet the substantial principles, as embodied in the writings of Confucius, in the Koran, and the various religions, are very similar. Among different Seers we observe the same grand principle evolved. Mediumistic powers have ever been adapted to localities and conditions, among the Jews, the Chinese, the Persians and others. The *appearances* of the *letter* have differed, yet been adapted. Still all their Seers have shadowed forth something Divine.[113]

The Spiritualist reading of Christianity wherein the "Christ-principle" could manifest itself under various names flowed logically into the view that mediumistic powers were operative in all times and places, "shadow[ing] forth something Divine." Spirit testimony to the idea that Spiritualist principles informed all the world's religions was not uncommon in the 1850s, but some spirits viewed the present-day manifestations of those faiths and creeds as having degenerated from their spirit-influenced origins. Spirits who spoke through Emma Hardinge, for example, while declaring "all religions . . . beautiful" if traced to their source, lamented the way in which "belief in the Great Unseen [had] degenerated into merest idolatry" in the various "creeds and sects" of the world.[114] Occasionally, in the early 1850s, spirits from other traditions gave their views on these matters. An Arabian prophet, "Axzas Zebah," declared that "angels ministered to him [Jesus] in his mission; but he is not the only son of man which they have ministered unto. We are all ministering spirits sent forth to be guardians of mankind."[115]

The most significant group of non-Christian spirits to appear during the 1850s and 1860s were those of Native Americans. "Nearly every medium," Hardinge said, "is attended by one of these beneficent beings" and they played, in her words, "a prominent and most noble part in the Spiritualism of America." From Hardinge's description it would appear that Indian spirits provided extensive testimony to the horrors that orthodox Christians, both as soldiers and missionaries, had wrecked on their people. They also, as spirits, "practically adopt[] the neglected duties of true Christianity, and by deeds of love and mercy show[] the white man how to prove the truth of his creed." While their presence, in and of itself, could be expected to have an expansive effect, it is clear that some (imagined) aspects of Native American practice were also transferred via the spirits. Foremost, in this regard, were healing practices. Hardinge indicated that among healing mediums, Indian spirits were the most esteemed, and that they used "their peculiar knowledge of herbs, plants, and earthly productions, to suggest rare and invaluable medicaments for the cure of disease."[116]

Hardinge also indicated that "many noble and distinguished Indians, both male and female, claim to see and hold converse with the spirits of departed friends and kindred; and the faith in immortality, and the presence and ministry of ancestral spirits as guardians to mortals, might well put to shame . . . many professing churchmen." Nonetheless, Hardinge did not simply equate Native American religions with modern Spiritualism. Rather she identified "phenomena which find no parallel or analogy amongst the records of modern Spiritualism." This led Hardinge into a lengthy discussion of "Asiatic and East Indian Spiritualism or magic," wherein she also found essential differences and characteristics that were "equally repulsive and incomprehensible to the American Spiritualist [as among the American Indians]."[117] Hardinge embraced the Western occult or magical tradition and Asian religions with a great deal more enthusiasm in the next decade. Nonetheless, the fact that she and other Spiritualists were engaged with non-Euro-American spirits and comparing Native American and Asian "Spiritualism" with "modern Spiritualism" during the 1850s and 1860s is highly significant.[118]

James Burns, an English Spiritualist, thought that the influence of Indian spirits had had a transforming effect on American Spiritualists. Writing in 1870, he stated:

> The more we see of American mediums and Spiritualists, and the deeper we dive into their psychological experiences, the more are we impressed by the fact, that the unsectarian, natural, free influence of the Indian spirits has much to do with the broad liberality

and untrammeled love of spiritual truth which characterizes advanced Americans; and the work is yet going on, intensifying from year to year. And, as new means of communication open up between the various countries of the earth, we shall behold a wider extension of this great principle of psychological action, which we believe is the great modifier of humanity.[119]

Burns wrote this while reflecting on the career of James Peebles, a man who, in his view, epitomized this "liberality and untrammeled love of spiritual truth." Peebles, it turns out, not only had an Indian spirit, Powhattan, who communicated with him through various mediums, he also established contact, beginning in the 1860s, with "a very ancient band of spirits," most of whom were of Asian origin. Peebles's interest in Asian religion was sparked while he was traveling in California in 1861. In a letter home, he described a life-changing encounter in which he "talked with a learned Chinaman [named Le Can] upon theology and the sacred books of the Chinese." Le Can, he said, "made me ashamed of our boasted American civilization and religion, when we claim, as we have, that it is so superior to the ancients." Peebles concluded that he had to "travel in Oriental lands, to learn the rudiments of Spiritualism."[120] From that time on, Peebles was in contact with two bands of spirits, the modern band, including Powhattan and numerous Euro-American spirits, with whom he had been in communication for some time and this "very ancient band of spirits." Indicative of primitive Christianity's position in all this is his biographers' report that "the beloved John [the disciple of Jesus] . . . formed a connecting link" between the two bands.

Under the tutelage of these ancient spirits, Peebles began to explore various non-Christian religions and to question his era's unequivocal embrace of the progress and development of civilization. His friend and biographer, the former Universalist minister J. O. Barrett, recalled that "up to 1864, Mr. Peebles, like the rest of us, maintained that the age in which we live casts all other ages into the shadow of its knowledge. Everywhere he was grandiloquent about the 'greatness of the nineteenth century.' " After learning more about ancient traditions of the east, Peebles cautioned: "Let no one presume originality. Let us pierce the inflated balloons of Bros. Davis, Brittan, Denton, Tuttle, Owen, Howitt, and Peebles especially; sit at the feet of the Neo-Platonists, Hindoo Gymnosophists, Egyptian Hierophants, Persian Magi, Chinese Philosophers, and learn wisdom; for 'of such is the kingdom of heaven.' "[121]

It was, moreover, at the instigation of this "ancient band" that Peebles resigned his position as Western Editor of the Banner of Light in 1869 soon after publishing Seers of the Ages in order to travel around the world learning about other religions.[122] Peebles followd this developmental trajectory to its logical conclusion. Two decades later, he described himself as a veritable "Parliament of Religions."

Briefly put, I am a Christian, a Spiritualist, a Buddhist, a Freethinker. . . . When traveling around the world I worshiped with the Brahmins in India, the Buddhists in Ceylon, the Parsees in Bombay, the Mohammedans in Cairo, and in God's first temples, the evergreen groves of the South Sea Isles, I myself constitute a Parliament of Religions.[123]

As a result of his travels, Peebles was able to provide Helena Blavatsky and Henry Olcott, the founders of the Theosophical Society, with key contacts that allowed them to successfully establish the Society in India during the 1870s. Even though Blavatsky did not think much of Peebles's universalistic Spiritualism—referring to it, after a few months in India, as "so broad as to be useless"—the Theosophical Society owed a considerable debt to Spiritualism. According to Paul Johnson, "while disparaging his [Peebles] concept of Universal Spiritualism, HPB applied it by developing Theosophy into a competitive movement which bridged the gap between Eastern and Western religion far more successfully than Spiritualism could ever have done."[124]

Thomas Tweed's research suggests that Spiritualism provided a path that allowed numbers of Americans to engage more fully with Buddhism during the 1870s. Tweed distinguishes between three types of Euro-American Buddhist sympathizers and adherents in the period between 1875 and 1912: esoteric, rationalist, and romantic. The esoteric Buddhists, shaped by "Neoplatonism, Theosophy, Mesmerism, Spiritualism, and Swedenborgianism," probably made up the majority of sympathizers and adherents, according to Tweed. Their Buddhism was characterized "by an emphasis on hidden sources of religious truth and meaning and by belief in a spiritual or nonmaterial realm that is populated by a plurality of nonhuman or suprahuman realities that can be contacted through one or another practices or extraordinary states of consciousness."[125]

Tweed indicates that interest in Buddhism prior to the 1870s was limited to Transcendentalists, Unitarians, and Free Religionists. While not wanting to downplay the contributions of these groups, I want to suggest that the Spiritualist movement of the 1850s and 1860s—the Transcendentalism of the "common man"— played an as yet unrecognized, but still crucial, role in popularizing attitudes that underpinned what Tweed refers to as esoteric Buddhism. While the emphasis on the "esoteric" or "occult" was more characteristic of Spiritualists and others during the 1870s and 1880s, the Spiritualist movement of the 1850s and 1860s paved the way for the emergence of "esoteric Buddhism" by promoting the idea that there was a spiritual realm populated by spirits of the dead that could be contacted through mediums in trance. Spiritualism, according to Spiritualists, was the universal religion that underlay all other religions. As such, Spiritualists could sympathize with or even adhere to Buddhism as an extension of their own Spiritualist beliefs. From a Buddhist perspective, they would indeed, as Tweed has argued, have been "esoteric Buddhists."

Primitive Animism

In claiming that all religions were based on Spiritualist principles, Spiritualists articulated a theory of religion. Communication with spirits through mediums was, we could say, the essence of their religion and, to their way of thinking, the essence of all other religions as well. As Spiritualists looked to the past, and especially to histories of enthusiasm and magic, to find evidence of Spiritualism in all times and places, they entered into highly contested terrain. Although they sought evidence of the universality of Spiritualist thought and practice, the attempt to secure legitimacy through comparisons with ancient cultures ran counter to the evolutionary and progressive presuppositions of their day and could be turned easily to other ends. Edward Tylor, the father of anthropology, asked the obvious question raised by their wide-ranging comparisons. "Do the Red Indian medicine-man, the Tatar necromancer, the Highland ghost-seer, and the Boston medium, share the possession of belief and knowledge of the highest truth and import, which, nevertheless, the great intellectual movement of the last two centuries has simply thrown aside as worthless? Is what we are habitually boasting of and calling new enlightenment, then, in fact a decay of knowledge?"[126] His answer, not surprisingly, was no.

Tylor rejected the idea of decay and embraced a model of evolutionary development that left modern Spiritualism as a mere survival of "savage philosophy and peasant folk-lore," yet he and the Spiritualists shared a similar theory of religion. Like them, he argued that religion could best be defined in terms of "the belief in Spiritual Beings." He identified "two great dogmas" that formed "the groundwork of the Philosophy of Religion, from that of savages up to that of civilized men." The first, he said, concerned the "souls of individual creatures, capable of continued existence after the death or destruction of the body" and the second, "other spirits, upward to the rank of powerful deities." These two dogmas emerged, he claimed because "thinking men, as yet at a low level of culture, were deeply impressed by two groups of biological problems." The first pondered "the difference between a living body and a dead one" and asked "what causes waking, sleep, trance, disease, death?" The second pondered the transition between sleeping and waking and "what are those human shapes which appear in dreams and visions?"[127]

Tylor referred to this type of religion—"which embodies the very essence of Spiritualistic as opposed to Materialistic philosophy"—as "Animism." He conceded that it could more logically be designated as "Spiritualism," but rejected that designation because of its use by "a particular modern sect, who indeed hold extreme spiritualistic views, but cannot be taken as typical representatives of these views in the world at large." While Tylor viewed the animism of primitive cultures as rational, given their stage of development and "the very evidence of their senses," he viewed the "animism of civilized men . . . [as] in great measure only explicable as a developed product of the older and ruder system."[128]

Tylor was not only aware of modern Spiritualism, he had, as historian George W. Stocking has discovered, spent some time investigating it. In fact, according to Stocking, Tylor developed his concept of animism in a series of papers written between 1866 and 1869 while keeping notes of his visits to Spiritualist seances. His ideas about religion were rooted in older discussions of fetishism in the writings of Comte and deBrosses (and behind them, Hume), but they moved away from those roots, as Stocking has shown, as a result of Tylor's "increased interest in modern spiritualist analogues."[129] Moreover, according to Stocking, Tylor's notes indicate that he found Spiritualism more compelling than his published writings would suggest. The most disconcerting aspect of Spiritualism for Tylor was, according to Stocking, "that people who theoretically should not have believed were in fact believers." His theory of survivals predicted that vestiges of animistic religion would continue among the lower classes, but not among the educated and well-bred. If this threw a disquieting wrench in his theory, Tylor did not let it show. As was the case with those who saw evidence of Spirits, Tylor's preexisting commitment to a evolutionary scheme that "explain[ed] away the apparently irrational or supernatural" influenced the conclusions he drew from his investigations of Spiritualist phenomena.[130]

SPIRITS AND RELIGIOUS EXPERIENCE

Spiritualists fell along a continuum ranging from credulity to skepticism depending on where they drew the line between psyche and spirit. Whereas believers and skeptics often looked at the same evidence and came to different conclusions, the Spiritualist understanding of the trance state allowed considerable room for doubt in relation to any particular spirit manifestation. If the trance state, as a descendent of the magnetic state, was a *natural* and *universal* entryway into the spiritual realm, it was also, at least for the majority of Spiritualists, only a *potential* entryway. Most Spiritualists had no trouble with this idea. They were quite aware that some alleged spirit communications were not in fact authentic and that discernment was always necessary. The difficult issue for Spiritualists, as for evangelicals, was distinguishing between psychological impressions and authentic spiritual manifestations.

Mediums and Investigators

The problem was apparent to many from the start. In his discussion of the varieties of media mentioned earlier, A. J. Davis provided a table detailing the causes of mediumistic phenomena as a means of explaining any "incongruities" that people might encounter. These causes, ranging from "voluntary deception" through various psychological causes to "departed spirits," occurred with varying frequencies. According to Davis, "when the unprejudiced eye scans the whole field . . . the mind cannot resist the conclusion that full forty per cent. of all and every description of the manifestations *are truly spiritually originated;* that about thirty per cent. is epidemical psychology; about twenty-five per cent. sympathy and misapprehension; and the remainder six per cent. is simple deception or voluntary imitation, by persons fond of attention or approbation."[131]

Davis's developmental schema provided a way of identifying the more developed, and thus presumably more reliable mediums, and a rationale for sheltering less developed mediums within private circles until they were likely to make a good impression. Davis indicated, for example, that there was "nothing in simple *gesturing* manifestations adapted to the public mind" and advised the medium at the gesturing stage to "remain in quiet circles, and allow himself to be further developed, before appearing among skeptical minds." The "neurologic" and "sympathetic" media could be particularly problematic. Both, Davis said, were in a transitional stage between normal and spirit-influenced habits of mind and typically did little to convince skeptical investigators of the truth of spirit communication. "[A] medium of this description," Davis cautioned his readers, "should be further advanced before reported as a real medium."[132]

While Davis's discussion seemed to link authenticity, or at least reliability, with the medium's level of development, other Spiritualists developed more refined criteria. Joel Tiffany, for example, argued that anti-Spiritualist psychological lecturers, such Stanley Grimes, knew "better than to pretend that there is no difference between the so-called spiritual phenomena, and that which results from his psychological experiments." Tiffany, who claimed to be familiar with "both classes of phenomena," said they were "as dissimilar as . . . the substance from the shadow—the real from the imaginative—and no one familiar with both classes can mistake the one for the other." The key difference, according to Tiffany, was that "psychologic impressions never continue or appear to be real beyond the duration of the influence making the impression." Spiritual phenomena, by way of contrast, he said, "seem to be real to the mediums and others, after the influence has passed away."[133]

Dr. John Gray, one of the more skeptical believers, would not have agreed with Tiffany that the two could be so easily distinguished. Given the nature of trance, Gray argued that "it is impossible for us to know whether they [the pronouncements of mediums] are simply spiritual or simply natural in their authorship, or a mixture from both sources." In his view, such pronouncements should "be received *only for the sake of the truths they manifestly contain*; precisely as we judge of the value of what we hear or read from any anonymous source." Others who attended the New-York Conferences shared Gray's skepticism. When discussion ensued regarding the appearance of the spirits of Henry Clay and William Shakespeare at a meeting, several expressed their doubts about the claims and especially about the wisdom of making such claims in public. Ira B. Davis said, "The question with him was not, 'Did Shakespeare and Henry Clay speak?' but, 'Was there any thing valuable in what the young lady and boy said?' "[134]

During the 1850s and 1860s La Roy Sunderland took a position on Spiritualism that placed him among the more skeptical believers. As we might expect from what we have seen of his earlier life, he did not arrive at this point in a straightforward fashion. In the late 1840s, Sunderland read widely in the writings of Swedenborg and followed the development of A. J. Davis's career closely. As indicated already, he visited Rochester, Auburn, and Stratford in the summer of 1850 and was told by the spirits that they had been present at his earlier lectures. His daughter, Margaretta Sunderland Cooper, was the first medium to create much of a stir in the Boston area, and Sunderland was the editor of an early, albeit short-lived, Spiritualist periodical, the *Spiritual Philosopher*. In 1851, he received a letter ostensibly written by an illiterate woman asking him to consult the spirits regarding her daughter. Sunderland did so, only to learn that the letter was a hoax written to expose the movement. This incident apparently had a sobering effect on Sunderland, and over the next twenty years his confidence in the authenticity of Spiritualist phenomena gradually waned.[135]

In his *Book of Human Nature* (1853), Sunderland estimated that "perhaps more than seven-eighths of all that has occurred . . . may be satisfactorily accounted for by the laws of psychology." Fifteen years later in *The Trance and Correlative Phenomena* (1868) he still maintained that he had witnessed "a variety of physical phenomena, represented by the so-called 'Mysterious Rap,' that cannot be accounted for by Pathetism." His book, however, focused not on these "mysteries," but on "the examination of phenomena that are merely human, or Psychological."[136] As of the early 1870s, Sunderland held to a mediumistic interpretation of both Christianity and Spiritualism, but believed that the "highest good is in the love of Virtue . . . for its own sake, and [that] for the development of this good . . ., no form of mediumistic revelation is necessary." By the time he died in 1885, he had abandoned belief in the afterlife altogether and, according to Buckley's obituary, "the atheist editor of an atheist paper" spoke at his funeral.[137]

The Psychology of Religious Revivals

Sunderland renounced orthodox Christianity at mid-life and Spiritualism sometime before he died, but his commitment to psychology remained constant and his interest in the psychology of religion only increased as he grew older. His experiments on Methodist subjects in the 1840s were more an artifact of his situation than the product of a focused interest in the psychology of religion, but this was not the case in the 1850s and 1860s. In the two works on psychology published in this period—*The Book of Psychology* (1853) and *The Trance and Correlative Phenomena* (1868)—the psychology of religion was central.

Sunderland's thinking about psychology and religious experience became progressively clearer as he began to integrate his own experiences with Methodism and Spiritualism with his psychological thinking and experimentation. In the *Book of Psychology*, he included a retrospective section which, for the first time, made reference to his career as a Methodist minister. There he acknowledged that "allusions have often been made, in my public Lectures throughout the country, and also in the accounts that have been published of them, to the *strange* results which took place under my Theological discourses, some thirty years ago."[138] Here too, for the first time, he described the experiment performed with Mrs. M'Reading. In *The Trance*, Sunderland expanded this historical section, placing it at the beginning of the book and developed the significance of the M'Reading experiment more fully. He opened the book with the statement: "My recollections of the nervous phenomena peculiar to sectarian revivals extend back to the year 1808." Looking back over the past sixty years, he located the origins of his thinking about "trance" in the "nervous phenomena" that accompanied Methodist revivals. He identified the experiment with Mrs. M'Reading as the turning point in his thinking and the "hint" around which "the germ of the new [psychological] theory was formed."[139]

Sunderland's psychology of religion was built on a comparison of the "nervous phenomena" associated with the two "revivals of religion" he knew best—Methodism and Spiritualism. Drawing on his experience with both, he described Spiritualism as having "all the elements of a true revival, (excepting an angry, vindictive God, hell and the devil)." Spiritualism, he said, "is characterized by precisely the same changes in the conduct of men, the same nervous phenomena which characterize sectarian revivals, more or less, always and everywhere."[140]

Although he described the "nervous phenomena" as "the same," he was not oblivious to the differences between Methodists and Spiritualists. In speaking, for example, of cures in a variety of contexts, he recognized that Catholics typically attributed the cures to relics of a saint, Spiritualists to the influence of a departed spirit, "sectarians" to the power of the Holy Spirit, "Mesmerists" to the will power of the operator, and the "pill men" to some "wonderful 'new medical discovery'" (*Trance*, 146). Sunderland was also well aware that not only the ideas about experience but the experiences themselves differed from one context to another.

> "[R]evivals of religion" have always have certain *characteristics*, depending on the *views* of the leaders by whom they were "got up." Thus, persons who were "converted" under the preaching of John Wesley, generally went through a certain routine of "feelings" and "exercises," as all have done, who have been since converted under the labors of Wesley's followers. But those attracted by the writings of Swedenborg are "converted" by a different process; and a similar remark might be made of "revivals" among the "Baptists," "Presbyterians," and "Mormons." . . . Hence, we may see John Wesley in a Methodist "revival." We see George Fox in the Quaker meeting and costume; Ann Lee, in the Shaker habits, and the preacher, or founder of the *sect*, always, in his followers, and in the "experience," the views and feelings of all who are converted by their labors. (*Trance*, 97–98)

To explain these differences Sunderland retained the traditional concepts of "sympathy" and "habit" that had been central both to his understanding of "Pathetism" and to eighteenth-century explanations of "enthusiasm." Where eighteenth-century explanations of enthusiasm focused on the role of sympathy and habit in creating impressions on the imagination, Sunderland emphasized their role in the generation of distinctive "mental states," which he now referred to collectively as "the Trance." Sunderland defined "sympathy" as the "tendency of one thing to act upon another." He defined Pathetism, which he coined from the same Greek root (*pathos*) that informed sympathy, as "the Philosophy of Influences, in, or upon, the Human Mind." Whereas Pathetism referred to "abnormal, induced, or artificial nervous phenomena," trance encompassed both spontaneous and induced mental states. He drew on the familiar concept of "sympathetic imitation" to explain mental phenomena that occurred seemingly spontaneously within crowds and then spread "contagiously" from one to another. In the context of revivals, panics, and political excitements, he said, "the sight of one person entranced, 'impresses,' 'influences,' another; and thus 'men go mad in crowds,' while one by one they awake from the extremes of delusion into which the excitement had carried them" (*Trance*, 49, 71, 75–76, 100–104).

The moral philosophers used the concept of sympathetic imitation to explain human behavior in crowds, whereas Sunderland drew on the "laws of association" to explain how sympathy and habit could produce specific mental states. Though sympathy and habit both implied relationships, it was the "associations" between things, whether mental or physical, that connected them. Thus, Sunderland said, "the sight of one object calls up another, with which it had become associated." So, too, "persons injured by fright, in cases of fire, or great danger are sometimes alarmed on hearing similar sounds." In general, he said, "the sight of any place where the mind has been peculiarly impressed, revives the same feelings, and we live over again the scenes which, otherwise, had remained entirely obliterated from recollection" (ibid., 104–5, 107–8).

Nervous phenomena or mental states, though "the same" in theory, were distinguishable in practice by virtue of the ideas and processes that were "associated" with them and which brought them on. Sunderland claimed that regular induction of a given mental state depended on the establishment of a relationship (an "association") between the mental state and a process believed to induce it. It does not matter, he said, "what the process is; when the Relation is once fully established, the process, (a look, a word, a sign, a particular time or place, a touch of the hand, a letter, a coin, a piece of paper or charcoal,) whatever it may be, (if not offensive,) will suggest the trance to the mind of the patient, and bring on the state with which it is associated." Thus, he said, "when the Idea of 'spirits' having the power to cause 'mediums' to fall into a state of trance, and to write, or speak, or to cure disease, once gets full possession of the mind, this *idea* or *belief will set the machinery of certain temperaments to work.*" Like the Commissioners' Report on Animal Magnetism, Sunderland believed that it was the *idea* that spirits could cause a medium to fall into trance that precipitated the trance rather than actual spirits. "Habit," according to Sunderland, gives *"Force* to the *Laws of Association* by which the Trance comes on, and thus it is that it [the trance] comes on when that state is associated with Religion, 'Spirits,' 'Magnetic passes,' or whatever else may have preceded the state, as the suggestive, or producing cause" (*Trance*, 72, 75, 108).

Although he acknowledged the importance of social factors, such as sympathy and habit, Sunderland broke with both academic and popular psychology when he argued that trance was, in the final analysis, self-induced. Contrary to popular understanding, Sunderland argued that the source of the trance lay in the mind of the individual not in the will of the mesmerist. Contrary to the academic moral philosophers, he argued that the induction of trance could not be explained solely in terms of the laws of association or the principle of sympathetic imitation, but must be understood in relation to the power of attention.

Sunderland defined trance as "a state of the nervous system, in which the mind is said to pass beyond the use of the external senses; a condition in which the mind is more or less active, without the normal consciousness of the external world." He located trance in relation to states of mind, such as dreaming, reverie, and mild insanity, that were not necessarily linked to groups or crowds and indicated that all these states "appear to be traceable to similar conditions of the nervous system." He described "ecstasy" as "the highest state of trance" and indicated that it is rare, "being mostly confined to religious exercises." Though "all human beings may be entranced," just as all may dream or become insane, some temperaments, he said, are more disposed to trance than others. Most significantly, he argued that the "immediate cause of trance, whether spontaneous or artificially produced, is always in the mind, or in the nervous system of the patient." Trance, in other words, is always "self-induced" (*Trance*, 109–10).

The "power of self-induction," according to Sunderland, is a "force . . . inherent in all minds . . . by which the mind *entrances* and *withdraws itself* from the consciousness of pain." This inherent power of self-entrancement or self-induction is, he said, "far greater than . . . any power known under the name of 'Mesmerism,' or which the will of one man can exercise over another." Pathetism, he added, "may assist you in calling it into exercise, as it may, indeed, be aroused by a word, a look, or by any event which may be design or incidentally arrest your attention, and set this mighty Force in motion" (*Trance*, 136–37). The idea of self-induction ultimately located the source of the trance in the individual and not in the "will" of the preacher, mesmerist, or physician.

Nor was self-induction, in Sunderland's view, a particularly unusual phenomenon. In its more everyday forms, he said, this "Principle of self-induction is in constant operation in and upon us." Drawing from the discussions of attention and memory among the academic moral philosophers,[141] he asked his readers:

> How else is it that events transpire before your eyes daily that you do not see, sounds are made near to you that you do not hear, and you are often touched when you do not feel. The clock ticks, and strikes the hours, but you do not hear it, until, some time afterwards, it may be, you *remember* even what you did not hear (or hearing, you did not notice) at the time. (*Trance*, 162)

When "our minds are self-inducted, entranced, diverted, by some other object . . . [w]e cease, for the time being, to hear, see, feel." In this manner, he said, "each of our external senses is suspended every day, and any number of times during the day."

Sunderland theorized, in other words, that focusing the attention led to the suspension of the external senses. Trance, in the formal sense, was thus simply an intensified form of ordinary mental processes. Whereas arresting or focusing of the attention could be considered a conscious volitional act, the suspension of the external senses and, thus, the mental state itself arose involuntarily. It was from this state, in which the external senses were suspended, that, as Sunderland put it, "the mind [was] said to pass beyond the use of the external senses."

Sunderland offered more sophisticated explanations of three aspects of religious experience. First, he used the traditional "law of association" to explain the relationship between trance as a generic "mental state" and the associated religious ideas that gave "trance" its particular forms. Second, in his discussion of the self-induction of mental states, Sunderland moved beyond the traditional mesmeric paradigm of mesmerist and patient to explain how involuntary experiences could be self-induced. This allowed him to explain experiences that occurred when people were alone. Third, he located trance, understood in terms of the suspension of the external senses, along a continuum of experiences ranging from the mundane to the unusual. Although the boundary between trance and insanity overlapped, Sunderland did not view trance as inherently pathological.

Despite Sunderland's theoretical advances and the Spiritualists' willingness to interpret Jesus and his miracles using the psychology of animal magnetism, neither attempted a psychological explanation of the experiences that were central to the self-understanding of mainline Protestants. They did not tackle Paul's statements that "it is not I that do it, but sin which dwells in me" and "it is no longer I who live, but Christ who lives in me." Neither their understanding of trance nor the religious phenomena with which they were primarily concerned—catalepsy or falling as if dead, visions, automatic writing, and trance mediumship—exactly fit the experiences Paul described. In contrast to the experiences described by Paul, the experiences most commonly discussed under the heading of trance involved the loss or restriction of normal consciousness. Sunderland defined trance as "a condition in which the mind is more or less active, *without the normal consciousness* of the external world" and the self-induction of trance as a process whereby "the mind entrances and *withdraws itself from the consciousness* of pain."[142] Where the typical entranced person either could not remember what occurred while entranced or remembered only after they "awoke," the Pauline writings, by way of contrast, articulated a full-blown language of *conscious* possession in which the "I" acknowledged its "possession" (by sin or Christ) in the present tense.[143]

Sunderland's definition of trance involved not only the loss or restriction of consciousness of the external world, but also "a state of the nervous system, in which the mind is said to pass beyond the use of the external senses." Here, as with the mesmeric tradition more broadly, we see a fusion of two phenomena under the heading of trance that would soon be distinguished. In the coming years, neurologists attempted to base their emergent discipline on the claim that "trance," understood as *the narrowing of consciousness* and the consequent loss of volition, was pathological and not spiritual. At the same time, new religious movements sought to distance themselves from "trance" by cultivating states in which the mind passed beyond the use of the external senses *while retaining full consciousness.* In doing so, they began to cultivate religious experiences that more closely approximate the Pauline ideal. The next chapter examines how neurologists and Theosophists reconstituted the experience of clairvoyant somnambules and trance mediums as the hypnotic trance of the hysteric and the conscious clairvoyance of the religious adept or healer.

CHAPTER SIX

Explaining Trance

DURING THEIR first two decades, the Spiritualists claimed a sizable chunk of intellectual turf. Their central experiential claim—that animal magnetism opened a psychologically grounded and empirically verifiable doorway between the human world and a world of spirits—faced challenges from a variety of directions during the 1870s and 1880s. Anglo-American neurologists, intent on establishing themselves as a recognized subspecialty within the medical profession, attacked Spiritualism in a largely successful bid to secure a secularized understanding of trance as a foundation for their own neurological science. New religions, such as Christian Science, Theosophy, and New Thought, while building on key elements of the Spiritualists' worldview, consistently rejected the Spiritualist understanding of trance. The emergence of Protestant faith healing in the early 1880s provided an occasion for mainstream Protestant clergy to employ psychological explanations to discredit a movement within their own ranks. The Methodist camp-meeting tradition and the related Wesleyan holiness movement were largely sheltered from this sort of scrutiny until holiness preachers began holding urban revivals and attracting newspaper coverage in the late 1880s. Maria Woodworth, dubbed the "trance evangelist," became a focal point for competing interpretations of the experiences associated with the old-time Methodist camp meeting. The Society for Psychical Research (SPR), founded in England in 1882, put Anglo-Americans in touch with the latest neurological and psychological developments in France and took popular religious phenomena as one of their primary objects of study. In 1890, William James, who helped form the American branch of SPR in 1884, called for "a comparative study of trance" that took both French studies of hysterics and Anglo-American studies of Spiritualist mediums into account.

Through the 1880s, the language of animal magnetism and an increasingly secularized concept of trance dominated both popular and scientific discussions of religious experience in the Anglo-American context. During the two decades under consideration, new religious movements claiming direct experiential access to spiritual truths wrestled with the psychology of animal magnetism, either appropriating it or demonizing it, while at the same time replacing the Spiritualists' practice of unconscious trance with an emphasis on conscious clairvoyance and/or suggestion. Protestants, both liberal and conservative, resisted the idea of allying mesmeric psychology and religion during this period and continued to use it primarily to discredit the religious experience of others, whether inside or outside the Protestant fold. The SPR, like some of the new religions, attempted to bridge the worlds of popular religion and medical science. Refusing to assume a materialist stance *a priori*, the psychical researchers formed a tenuous bridge between popular religion, neurology, and the new frontiers of psychological research.

James's call for a "comparative study of trance" went largely unheeded, however, as the discursive ground upon which psychological theory rested shifted once again. Thus, by the 1890s, animal magnetism was superseded by the more reputable concept of "hypnosis" and interest in trance was largely eclipsed by a preoccupation with the subconscious mind. This shift in psychological discourse, which emerged in the 1880s but was not widely adopted until the 1890s, marks the transition from Part II to Part III.

NEUROLOGY AND TRANCE

For much of the nineteenth century, the standing of physicians depended on their family background, their access to higher education, and the status of their patients. Physicians, as a result, included an elite that had graduated from medical schools in the U.S. and Europe, a majority that had served apprenticeships and perhaps completed a course of lectures or a short-term medical degree, and a "lower-class" of self-taught practitioners.[1] Approaches to medicine proliferated during the early and middle decades of the nineteenth century, resulting in what one historian has described as "a growing sectarianism," especially at the popular level. During the 1870s and 1880s, the emergence of medical specialties led to increased cooperation among the better educated physicians and to the reinstatement of medical licensing. Licensure enhanced professionalization by establishing standards and reducing the stigma and the threat of competition with untrained practitioners.[2]

Physicians also had to establish their legitimacy in more substantive ways, that is, by demonstrating that their superior training enhanced their abilities to diagnose and cure disease. In some emergent specialties, such as neurology, physicians faced the additional challenge of convincing others that the phenomena in question were indeed medical disorders and that they stemmed from neurological causes. Neurologist George M. Beard likened the challenge facing his aspiring specialty to that of settling of the American West. In the territorial period, he wrote, anyone could occupy the land simply by staking out a claim and cultivating it. With the advance of immigration, squatter's rights gave way to formal ownership and the organization of territories into states. In parallel fashion, "astronomy, chemistry and physics, having already reached the organized stage, are now wholly in the possession of experts, who give their lives to the cultivation of their respective domains, while some of the younger sciences are yet in the territorial condition." The study of the brain, he said, is still "everyone's land; whoever is especially eminent for excellence in physics, in chemistry, in law or literature, in theology or business, or in any realm of human activity, save the study of the nervous system, is liable to be called upon by an inward voice, to be required by public opinion to enter in and take summary possession."[3]

Somnambulism and trance were at the heart of this contested territory. The spiritualist interpretation of these states as the gateway to the other world rejected both the pathological designation and the neurological explanation of these phenomena. In continuing to assert their claim to this territory, spiritualists provided the chief obstacle to the secularization of trance and the chief threat to the professional aspirations of neurologists.[4] Beard was not alone in his efforts to win this territory for medical science. As historians Brown and Shortt have argued, "a group of prominent Anglo-American medical men, whose major professional interest might conveniently be designated neuroscience, launched a polemical attack on spiritualism" during the 1870s and early 1880s. Among the leading figures, according to Shortt, were "the physiologist W. B. Carpenter, the neurologists William A. Hammond and George M. Beard, and the alienist Henry Maudsley."[5] Beard is, for our purposes, the most interesting of these figures. While the others write articles attacking Spiritualism, Beard provides the most sophisticated theory of trance. The monograph quoted above, which was specifically intended to bring "cerebral physiology and pathology out of the territorial stage and into the organized stage," outlined Beard's "new theory of trance" and applied it specifically to religious "delusions."[6] Perhaps owing to the pointedness of his attack and his ultimate prominence within the profession, Beard was the neurologist most frequently cited by those outside neurology from Madame Blavatsky to William James.[7]

According to Beard, a "tripod" of "trance, the involuntary life, and human testimony" supported religious delusions. Those who had mastered "the psychology of these three departments," a feat, he said, made possible by the new science of neurology, could explain not only "spiritism, ancient and modern, but, in good measure, all the great delusions of history." According to his friend and medical partner, A. D. Lockwood, Beard's animus toward things religious was a reaction to the religion of his childhood. The son of a Congregationalist clergyman, Beard was reared, in Lockwood's words, "in all the strictness and strait-laced orthodoxy of the times." Beard kept a diary during his adolescence, which his daughter allowed Lockwood to read after his partner's death. It revealed, he said, "how the youthful soul can be submerged in gloom and deprived, through a well-meant but hurtful theology." Although Beard gradually took on a "rational" approach to life, he was not, Lockwood said, "without scars" and "the pendulum which had swung so long in one direction [in his childhood] made an equal arc in the other" as an adult.[8]

The turning point for Beard was "the recent demonstration of the fact that it [trance] is a subjective, not, as the world had unfalteringly assumed, an objective state." This discovery, which brought trance out of the realm of delusion and into the realm of science, may have been central to his personal transformation as well. It was, Beard claimed, as radical a revolution in relation to knowledge of the brain as Copernican theory was for theories of the universe, and called into question all nonexpert testimony with respect to trance. Neurology, he said, must "push utterly aside" the common assumption that "the senses are worthy of trust" and rely exclusively on the expert testimony of neurologists. "The rejection of nonexpert human testimony is, and has ever been," he wrote, "the first step in the

6. Humorous depiction of experts attempting to explain Spiritualist phenomena. From Andrew Jackson Davis, *The Fountain* (1870).

development of a science; it is only by rejecting or ignoring all testimony save that of experts that any science is possible."[9]

What the experts knew, which ordinary people did not, was that such "popularly alleged phenomena of trance [as] clairvoyant, or second-sight power, or the existence of a second sense" did not exist. With regard to all such claims, Beard said, "I may say that there are not, and never have been, and never can be any such phenomena."[10] Beard rejected such claims as contrary to physiological observation and incompatible with evolutionary theory, and thus he attributed them to subjective human testimony rather than to trance proper.[11] He reconstituted trance, theoretically and in practice, so as to exclude any reference to "passing beyond the use of the external senses." In the hands of neurological "experts," trance became "a functional disease of the nervous system, in which the cerebral activity is concentrated in some limited region of the brain, with suspension of the activity of the rest of the brain, and consequent loss of volition."[12] In dividing up the figures of the clairvoyant somnambule and the trance medium, the neurologists claimed somnambulism and trance, while stripping them of their associations with clairvoyance, second sight, and thought reading. Clairvoyance and associated phenomena were henceforth relegated to the realm of the occult, where they were taken up by new metaphysical movements.

Beard discussed four varieties of trance: spontaneous, self-induced, emotional, and intellectual. "All genuine trance preachers and speakers," he wrote, "represent the self-induced variety." The spiritualists' descriptions of mediums "as 'fully developed,' or 'partially developed,' or as 'developing,' has," he said, "a basis in truth," since the aspiring medium "oftentimes needs practice to acquire the habit of readily, and at will, entering the trance." He made an analogy to a "chandelier of gas-burners," later picked up by William James, to differentiate between waking, trance, sleep, and death. "When all the burners of the chandelier are fully lighted, that is the normal waking state; when all of the burners are turned down low, but not turned out entirely, as usually is the case in public halls, before the opening of entertainments, that is ordinary sleep; if I turn out entirely all the burners except one, and that one, as often happens, flames all the more brightly from increased pressure, that is trance; if all the burners are turned out entirely and permanently, that is death."[13]

Beard was particularly interested in the alterations of will and memory associated with trance, both of which he understood as pathological. Although Beard compared trance to sleep throughout, one of the chief differences between sleep and trance lay in the way that persons responded to suggestion in the two states. Although sleepers could respond to suggestion, they did so neither "consciously [nor] coherently." To respond intelligently, sleepers had to wake up. In contrast, he said, the entranced person is "a living active personality, more active in certain directions than when in the normal state; and yet he is only a fraction of his normal self; consequently he is, or may be at the mercy of any external suggestion that is offered." Those who are entranced respond "consciously and consistently . . . without coming out of the trance." Strictly speaking, Beard concluded, "trance is not sleep at all; it is rather another form of waking life, over which the will has little or no influence."[14]

Willing, according to Beard, is an activity coordinated by all the faculties of the mind. When entranced, cerebral activity is concentrated in a limited region, thus, displacing the will. What Beard called "the involuntary life" takes over when the will is impaired and accounts for the "automatism of trance, . . . [its] first observed and most distinguishing feature." He compared the mind to a wagon wheel in which the "voluntary functions may represent the narrow hub, while the involuntary are represented by all the area between the hub and the periphery. . . . Now, in the state of trance, this little inner circle, of what we call volition, is encroached upon by the involuntary life, and in the deeper stages is entirely displaced by it."[15] Beard's use of the phrase "the involuntary life" marked a significant move beyond Sunderland's awkward references to "trance and correlative phenomena" and pointed toward a more fully developed idea of the subconscious mind. Trance, for Beard, was a mental state that altered the relationship between the voluntary and involuntary realms of the mind. In articulating a scientific theory of a trance, Beard stood on the boundary between the older mesmeric psychologies and the new scientific psychologies of the subconscious. His writings simultaneously signaled a high-water mark in relation to nineteenth-century theories of trance and laid the groundwork for the incorporation of trance into emergent theories of the subconscious.

Beard also offered a more comprehensive analysis of the modifications of memory associated with trance, particularly in relation to cases of "divided or double consciousness." Both Sunderland and Beard understood double consciousness as involving the alteration, in Sunderland's words, of "two distinct Individualities, so distinct, that when in one state they have no recollection of the other." While Sunderland was aware of such cases and noted that double consciousness is "common in states of Somnambulism and Trance," he did not attempt to integrate double consciousness into his theory of trance.[16] Beard reflected on two published cases, that of Miss Reynolds (published by Dr. J. R. Mitchell in 1860) and Felida X. (published originally in French by Dr. Azam and appearing in English in 1876). He used them to illustrate his contention that in even the deepest states of trance there is "probably always consciousness at the time, but it is not always or usually remembered consciousness." In contrast to sleep, however, he said that when a person reenters "the trance state . . . these impressions of the previous attack of trance, forgotten during the intervening normal state, [are brought] to consciousness, and thus the subject carries on an independent life, just as though there had been no intervening normal state."[17] Here, too, Beard stood on the boundary between the mesmeric psychology and the new psychology of the subconscious. Like his successors, he was fascinated by cases of double consciousness and sought to fully incorporate them into his theory of trance. Like his predecessors, however, he conceived of double consciousness solely in terms of the alteration of states of consciousness with an associated loss of memory between states. In the medical literature, there was no suggestion before the late 1880s that two distinct streams of consciousness might exist simultaneously within one body.[18] This was not the case, as we shall see, with the new religious movements who actively cultivated experiences of conscious clairvoyance.

TRANCE AND NEW RELIGIOUS MOVEMENTS

During the 1870s and 1880s, metaphysical and occult forms of religion emerged with varying relationships to Christianity, Spiritualism, and animal magnetism. The metaphysical movement that gave rise to Christian Science and, eventually, New Thought had its origins in the thought and practice of Phineas P. Quimby and four of his students, Mary Baker Eddy, Annetta and Julius Dresser, and Warren Felt Evans.[19] Two former Spiritualists, Helena Blavatsky and Henry Olcott, founded the Theosophical Society, the major new occult tradition of this period. Theosophy embraced its roots in Spiritualism and animal magnetism, claiming both as foundational to the occult science upon which the universalistic theosophical tradition was based. While Quimby was skeptical with respect to Spiritualist claims, his healing practices were derived from the mesmeric tradition. Mary Baker Eddy and her followers rejected Spiritualism and animal magnetism outright. Those associated with the rise of New Thought varied in their attitudes toward psychology. Although most looked back to Quimby, and all stressed the God or Christ within, some, following the lead of the Dressers, downplayed Quimby's psychological orientation, while others, following Evans's lead, enhanced it. In its attitudes toward psychology, New Thought occupied a middle ground between orthodox Christian Science, on the one hand, and Theosophy, on the other.

All three traditions rejected the Spiritualists' understanding of trance as the gateway to the spiritual realm and each found their understanding of religious experience mirrored in the life of Jesus. Significantly, however, all three, including Christian Science, promoted a more "developed" form of consciousness that retained certain features of trance and somnambulism while rejecting others. In rejecting animal magnetism, Christian Science adopted a theological attitude and strategy toward other religions similar to that of evangelical Protestants and Seventh-day Adventists. Theosophy and New Thought continued the work of integrating psychology with Christian theology, on the one hand, and with the comparative study of religion, on the other, begun by the Spiritualists.

Jesus as Clairvoyant

Phineas P. Quimby, like Sunderland and many others, learned of animal magnetism from Charles Poyen in 1838. From 1843 to 1847 he gave lecture-demonstrations on animal magnetism accompanied by a "clairvoyant somnambule," Lucius Burkmar. In an essay on "Spiritualism and Mesmerism" written in the early 1850s, Quimby describes a point during his travels with Burkmar, when, he said, "I . . . became a medium myself, but not like my subject. *I retained my own consciousness and at the same time took the feelings of my patient.*" As a conscious medium, he continued, he was able feel his patients' aches and pains and their state of mind, while remaining conscious himself.[20]

Although some have lifted up Quimby's emphasis on altering ideas (as opposed to manipulating fluids) as his central contribution to the history of psychology, the *way* that he altered ideas has received less attention.[21] The center of Quimby's healing practice, and his central *clinical* contribution to the mesmeric healing tradition, lay in his ability to operate from two states of consciousness simultaneously. Quimby described these two states as "natural" and "clairvoyant," indicating that "[e]veryone knows that the clairvoyant state is different from the natural state. . . . Persons in a clairvoyant state can talk, using the same organs as when awake, they also have every faculty which they possess in the waking state, independent of the natural body, and space and time may or may not be annihilated."

In mesmerized subjects (i.e., clairvoyant somnambules, such as Burkmar) and (trance) mediums, the clairvoyant state ordinarily displaced the natural state. When Quimby says that his approach to religious healing does not involve mesmerism, trance, or mediumship, he should not be read as rejecting psychological methods or avoiding altered states of consciousness altogether. Rather, his criticism was focused on what he took to be the central characteristic of these particular "states"—their displacement of ordinary consciousness and the accompanying loss of memory. The more ideal situation, he suggested, would be "if a man could retain his reason and natural senses, and *at the same time* be conscious of the other state[.] [H]e would be a man beside himself, thus making two living intelligences in one identity acting though one [organism]."[22]

Quimby entered this state by becoming "purely passive" and "rid[ding] himself of all beliefs and every theory of man" while in the presence of a patient. This openness allowed him to be affected by the thoughts and feelings of his patients. It was "the patient's [troubled] mind . . . [that] put[] him into a clairvoyant state" and allowed him to see his patient's "errors and opinions" directly. Maintaining his awareness of his own natural state, he described himself as being in "two states at once" or simultaneously "two persons" in one body.[23] By retaining these two identities simultaneously, Quimby was able to "see the error" from the higher clairvoyant state and "explain it to the natural senses."[24] Or, put another way, having "two living intelligences . . . acting through one [organism]" allowed "the clairvoyant man . . . [to] correct the errors of the man of the flesh and blood."[25] It was by correcting their "errors" that Quimby healed his patients. As he described the process, referring to himself in the third person: "Dr. Quimby, with his clairvoyant faculty, gets knowledge in regard to the phenomena, which does not come through his natural senses, and by explaining it to the patient, gives [another] direction to the mind, and the explanation is the science or cure."[26]

Quimby's experience of what we might call co-consciousness, developed in the context of his healing practice, gave him a means of understanding key Christian doctrines and provided the basis for his Christian understanding of the healing process. In his mature thought, the distinctions that informed his healing practice—natural and clairvoyant, matter and wisdom, error and science, opinion and truth—were extended to Jesus and Christ/God.[27] Thus, theologically, Quimby made a careful distinction between Jesus, the natural man with "a natural body of flesh and blood," and "Christ" or "God." Christ, he said, "was never intended to be applied to Jesus as a man, but to a Truth superior to the natural man."[28] In another context, he described God as "the embodiment of light or clairvoyance" and said that "[a]s Jesus became clairvoyant He became the son of God and a part of God. . . . Jesus attached His senses as a man to this light or Wisdom, and the rest of the world attached theirs to the thought of darkness or the natural man."[29]

For Quimby, Jesus' baptism in the Jordan, where God announced that Jesus was his beloved Son, marked a turning point in Jesus' development as a clairvoyant. With the reception of the "Holy Ghost or Truth," what had been a matter of "belief" became a matter of "science." There, Quimby wrote, "Jesus entered into his water or belief, and understood it, and when He came out of the water, the Heavens were opened to Him alone, and the Holy Ghost descended like a dove and lit on Jesus and a voice said to Him alone, 'This is my beloved Son (or Science), in whom I am well pleased.' " According to Quimby, "[t]his Science had no name till Peter gave it the name of Christ, as an answer to the question put to him by Jesus—'Whom do the people say that I, this power, am?' " Quimby emphasized that it was the power within Jesus, not Jesus the man, who was recognized as "the Christ, the living God (or Science)."[30]

The distinction between Jesus and Christ was crucial throughout. Thus, while the body of Jesus was crucified, it was Christ or Truth who was resurrected. According to Quimby, "Jesus never believed in the natural body rising . . . the resurrection from the dead was *a resurrection from an error to a truth*."[31] Jesus' awareness "that He, Jesus, could be in two places at same time and be outside of the body called Jesus" led him to anticipate the post-resurrection appearances of the Christ. "Christ or Truth," said Quimby, "had the power to assume any form it pleased."[32] Quimby's careful distinction between the two "persons"—Jesus and Christ—who inhabited the body of Jesus during Jesus' lifetime allowed Quimby to claim that "Jesus as a man knew nothing of Christ" and, in parallel fashion, that "neither does P. P. Quimby as a man know anything of this Wisdom or Truth." Quimby described himself and Jesus as "mediums"—"P. P. Q. is the medium of the Truth to correct the errors of the world, just as Jesus was the medium of God or Science to convince man of his errors and lead him to Christ, health, or Truth."[33]

Quimby used the story of the healing of the centurion's servant to illustrate how Jesus and Christ acted together in the healing process. He indicated that "when the centurion came to Jesus . . ., Jesus was not aware of the fact [that his servant was sick], but immediately became subject to His clairvoyant state, saw the servant and administered unto him."[34] Jesus, thus, healed as Quimby healed, by entering into a clairvoyant state. Quimby explained to his patients that when he took on their feelings, "*I am with you*, not myself as a man but this great truth which I call Christ or God." Moreover, he stressed that "this Christ or God in us is the same that is in Jesus, only in a greater degree in Him."[35] Thus, the Christ in Quimby engaged the Christ in his patients and both recapitulated the resurrection from error into truth. As he explained to Mrs. P., a patient: "I will now sit down by you again and listen to your groans, for I feel the pain of the bands that bind you across the chest. Now this that feels is not P. P. Quimby, but the Christ and that which complains is not Mrs. P. but the Christ in Mrs. P. struggling to roll the stone from the sepulchre of her tomb, to rise from the dead or error, into the living God or Wisdom."[36]

Jesus as Demonstrator

Mary Baker Eddy, who as Mary Patterson was a patient and student of Quimby in the early 1860s, modified and extended the dichotomies that marked Quimby's thought and sharpened the opposition between them to the point that Truth became accessible only through revelation. Although Eddy retained Quimby's distinctions between error and science, belief and truth, she more often juxtaposed matter and spirit, rather than matter and wisdom. Moreover, in time, she added the crucial distinction between "mortal mind" and "immortal Mind." This distinction allowed Eddy to fully differentiate spirit from matter and thus to conceptualize more fully the difference between her theology and Quimby's.

In contrast to Quimby, Eddy understood these distinctions as mutually exclusive. "Perfection," she said, "is not expressed through imperfection, therefore Spirit cannot pass through matter; there are no temporary sieves, even, that strain Truth through error."[37] The result, according to Eddy, is that we cannot refer to "Spirit *in* matter [or] Soul *in* body" because the "Soul of man [exists] outside of matter."[38] Eddy's understanding of Soul outside matter can be read as a radical idealization of Quimby's "clairvoyant state." Indeed, the goal of Christian Science as represented in the early editions of *Science and Health* can be understood as a permanent out-of-body experience, wherein the existence of "life outside matter" constitutes the basis for immortality.

The way Eddy radicalized Quimby's understanding of clairvoyance becomes more evident if we consider Eddy's distinction between the "personal sense" and the "spiritual sense."[39] There was an evident parallel between Eddy's personal and spiritual sense and the lower and higher senses that Quimby associated with the natural and clairvoyant states, but they viewed their respective lower senses very differently. Where there was value for Quimby in both the natural and clairvoyant states, and reason in his view to embody both states simultaneously, the personal and spiritual senses stood, for Eddy, in complete opposition. The "spiritual senses," she declared flatly, "are true, and the personal false."[40]

In the early editions of *Science and Health*, Eddy devoted a significant amount of attention to clairvoyance and its relationship to the personal and spiritual senses. In some contexts, she linked clairvoyance to mesmerism and mediumship and thus to the mind of man (or mortal mind). There it stood in opposition to science and Truth. Thus, she could state that "clairvoyance reaches only the fancied realities of mortal mind, whereas science admits none of these things, but reveals Truth, outside of mortality and error." In other contexts, however, she referred to "genuine clairvoyance" and indicated that "to admit mind sees, hears, feels, etc., without the agency of matter, is a step toward science." Indeed, she added that, from the perspective of Spirit, clairvoyance or the ability to see without the use of the eyes is the normal state of affairs. "We are accustomed," she said, "to think seeing without optic is second sight, but this is first sight; even our normal condition of being. He that formed the eye, did He not see? Hath not Spirit every faculty of Intelligence?"[41]

While Eddy unequivocally linked mesmerism and Spiritualism with the personal sense and, thus, considered them both illusory, she associated (false) clairvoyance with the personal sense and (true) with the spiritual sense. Thus, "the science of being enables us to read mind, foretell events, . . . and receive inspirations from God; but not from idle curiosity, or to work evil, or dip into the experience of the dead, or connect erring and mortal belief with Principle and its phenomena." In science, she said, "we read mind from the stand-point of Soul." Indeed, those sufficiently advanced in "the science of being . . . blend with the Truth of being [to become] . . . seers and prophets involuntarily." As such, they are not "controlled by 'spirits,' [or] persons, but by Spirit."[42]

Eddy's "spiritual sense" can be viewed as a refinement of Quimby's idea of clairvoyance as a "higher sense." Although Quimby rejected any connection with animal magnetism and cultivated a distinctive experience of two co-conscious "persons" in one body, his understanding of clairvoyance was nonetheless rooted in the empiricism of the mesmeric tradition, broadly defined. Most specifically, the mesmeric tradition associated the experience of the "person" or self leaving the body and entering into another with clairvoyance, visions, trance, and mediumship. The essence of wisdom, for Quimby, lay in the knowledge that a person in the clairvoyant state could be "beside itself" and "outside of matter," that is detached from its own body and able to enter into the mind of another so as to "feel [their] pains."[43] The spiritual ideal for Eddy was not a state of co-consciousness wherein the higher and lower, natural and clairvoyant, human and divine co-existed within one body. Rather the spiritual ideal for her was one of escape from the "imaginary self-hood" associated with the belief in the reality of matter, body, and the personal (physical) senses. In this state of "genuine clairvoyance" in which all is Spirit and Truth, matter and body have no reality. The essence of Christian spirituality, for Eddy, was "to be absent from the body and present with the Lord."[44]

In the first edition of *Science and Health*, Eddy described Jesus as the connecting link between science and personal sense, the one who "mapped out the path of the science of being" for us to follow. As a human being, he modeled the choice between belief in the illusionary reality of personal sense and Truth as revealed through the spiritual sense. Eddy described Jesus as embracing a rather ascetic lifestyle in which he "experienced few of the so-called pleasures of personal sense" and "through poverty of sense was enriched by Soul." In contrast to Jesus, "Christ the Soul of man never suffered." "To be Christ-like is," she said, "to break the fetters of personal sense . . ." and, thus, "to triumph over sickness, sin, and death, to open the prison door to the captive."[45] Humans, according to Eddy's reading of scripture, are thus faced with a choice between "two masters," the so-called reality of personal sense or the true reality of spiritual sense. "To those buried in the belief of Life in matter, and insisting that we see alone with eyes, and hear with ears, and feel through nerves, [Jesus] said, 'Having eyes ye see not, and ears ye hear not, that ye might understand and be converted and I might heal you.' " Whereas the belief of the unconverted in personal sense "shut out the communications of Soul, . . . Jesus adhered to one [master] only, [and] was guided by spiritual sense."[46] In insisting that it was impossible to serve two masters, Eddy asserted, in contrast to Quimby, the complete incompatibility of the physical and spiritual senses.

Although Eddy and Quimby's depictions of Jesus shared a number of common features, the crucial differences lay in the details. Where Quimby's Jesus *developed* his clairvoyant abilities and attached his higher senses to the Wisdom that is God, the true immaterial (and therefore genuinely clairvoyant) nature of Eddy's Jesus was *revealed* through his spiritual sense, not developed. Where Truth or Christ dwelt *in* Quimby's Jesus, Eddy's Jesus *demonstrated* Truth or Christ.[47] For Eddy, Jesus' life was a series of "demonstrations" of this "divine Principle." Jesus demonstrated "God" or "Truth" to his disciples by "casting out error, healing the sick, and raising the dead." His "highest, and most convincing" demonstration, however, came with his crucifixion. "The final triumph of Spirit over matter, of the divine over the human, Jesus reached in that supreme hour of mockery, desertion, and crucifixion, and it all aided his highest demonstration" and provided the ultimate "example of proof of divine science."[48] The purpose of healing in Christian Science was not simply or even primarily to heal, but to demonstrate the "divine Principle."[49]

These differences had implications for the way that each understood the relationship between psychology and religious experience. Healing for Eddy was not, as with Quimby, a matter of entering a mental state that was simultaneously natural and clairvoyant, but of focusing the attention in faith on God as divine Principle. "The physical healing of Christian Science," according to Eddy, "results now, as in Jesus' time, from the operation of divine Principle, before which sin and disease lose their reality in human consciousness."[50] How that operation was experienced subjectively is suggested by Eddy's description of her own experience of being healed not long after Quimby's death. Eddy viewed this experience as the moment in which the Truth of Christian Science was revealed. According to Albert Farlow, who interviewed Eddy later in her life, "it was not clear to Mrs. Eddy by what process she had been instantaneously healed, but she knew that her thought had turned away from all else in contemplation of God, His omnipotence and everpresence, His infinite love and power." Contemplation of God led to an "overwhelming consciousness of the divine presence" and it was this "consciousness of the divine presence [that] had destroyed her fear and consciousness of disease exactly as the light dispels the darkness." She learned in time that "similar thoughts in connection with the ills of her neighbors" resulted in healing as well and it was, she said, "in this manner that she discovered how to give a mental treatment."[51] This account suggests that Christian Science practitioners employed what might be described as a form of contemplative prayer as the basis of their "mental treatments." Through contemplation of the divine Principle, the unreal self-hood attached to the physical senses dropped away and with it the reality of sin and disease.

Quimby's belief that all people had the potential to access the supersensible realm by means of the "[Christ] principle . . . in every man" made his understanding of the supersensible realm compatible with a naturalistic psychology, despite his explicit rejection of animal magnetism.[52] Warren Felt Evans later built on this compatibility and grounded Quimby's thinking more explicitly in the mesmeric tradition. Eddy, by heightening the distinction between the material and the spiritual, and narrowing the scope of revelation to scripture as interpreted by *Science and Health*, rejected this route. By linking authentic religious experience to special revelation rather than natural psychological abilities, Eddy made Christian Science and the psychology of animal magnetism incompatible.

Quimby's rejection of special revelation was in keeping with both Spiritualism and the later New Thought tradition, while Eddy's insistence on revelation aligned Christian Science strategically with evangelical Protestantism as represented by Edwards and Wesley and with Seventh-day Adventism. In Christian Science, as in evangelical Protestantism and Seventh-day Adventism, naturalistic psychological explanations were used to account for counterfeit religious experience or false religion. Just as Edwards located the origins of "true religion" and "enthusiasm" in two diametrically opposed sources (the divine supernatural sense, on the one hand, and impressions on the imagination, on the other), so too Eddy grounded true and false religion respectively in the spiritual and personal (or physical) senses. This approach to true religion allowed Eddy, like Edwards, to freely embrace naturalistic psychological explanations of *false* religion, while at the same time guarding what she took to be true religion from the threat of explanatory reduction.

As was also the case with Edwards and Wesley, true and false religion could be distinguished logically on the basis of its origins and empirically on the basis of its "fruits." As with "true religion" and "enthusiasm," the difference between Truth and error was not always evident to those whose spiritual sense had not been awakened. Just as "formalists" were incapable of distinguishing between "true religion" and "enthusiasm," so too those operating from their personal sense were incapable of distinguishing Truth from error.[53] In the wake of rancorous controversies between herself and her students in the late 1880s, Eddy inserted a passage in *Science and Health* explaining that "the more closely error simulates Truth" the more potent and dangerous it becomes.[54] Eddy formulated the concept of Malicious Animal Magnetism during this latter period to identify the error or counterfeit that most closely simulated the Truth of Christian Science and thereby posed the greatest threat to it.

Jesus as Adept

The Theosophical Society, founded in 1875 by Helena Blavatsky and Henry Olcott, emerged out of Spiritualism and continued to view the mesmeric tradition as foundational to its worldview. As prolegomena to their new "Science of magic," however, Theosophists mounted a significant critique of Spiritualism. In the words of historian Stephen Prothero, "the theorizing of Blavatsky and Olcott amounted to nothing less than an attempt to effect a paradigm shift from Spiritualism to what would be called theosophy—from a tradition of mediums (predominantly female) who passively channeled spirits of the dead in the darkness to a tradition of adepts (predominantly male or, in Blavatsky's case, ostensibly androgynous) who worked in full light, cajoling 'elementary spirits' and actively manipulating occult forces in accordance with occult laws."[55]

The critique of mediums as too passive was at root a critique of the Spiritualist interest in (unconscious) trance states as a doorway to the other world. This sort of critique from within was not new in the 1870s. Beginning in the 1850s, many male mediums harbored an antipathy toward unconscious trance mediumship, viewing it as passive and, therefore, antithetical to manliness. John Shoebridge Williams "refused to be one of those 'sleeping, agitated, and as it were, tied mediums' who 'give themselves up . . . as machines yield themselves to the power that moves them.' Whereas 'the mesmerized person has no measure of control over what goes on while he is mesmerized,' the manly medium, he insisted, has 'fredom [sic] and rationality of its own.' " In keeping with his need to maintain some measure of control while mesmerized, Williams adopted a more conscious mediumistic style that he believed more fitting for men.[56] Similarly, La Roy Sunderland, writing in 1853, questioned whether "a human being, conscious of his true MANHOOD, [could] yield up his own *will*, his own soul and body, to be *possessed* and *controlled* by apocryphal spirits?" While encouraging "investigation," Sunderland admonished his readers "not [to] unman [themselves], . . . not [to] give away [their] own self-hood" by allowing themselves to be possessed.[57]

Paschal Beverly Randolph, who along with Blavatsky and Olcott played an important role in the transformation of Spiritualism into occultism, began his career as a clairvoyant physician and spiritualist trance speaker in the early 1850s. He renounced Spiritualism in 1858, partly owing to what he viewed as the deleterious effects of trance. Looking back on his eight years as a medium, Randolph said that "the moment I yielded to that seductive influence [of "the trance condition"], I ceased to be a man, and became a mere automoton. . . . As a trance-speaker . . . I had not the control of my own mind . . . one-twentieth of the time; and . . . I do not now believe that during the whole eight years I was sane for thirty-six consecutive hours, in consequence of the trance and susceptibility thereto."[58]

Randolph did, however, acknowledge a "genuine spiritual trance" which, he said, mediums could induce in themselves at will. He described it as "a dreamy sort of ecstasy or *conscious trance*, during which they are frequently insensible to physical pain, and possess the extraordinary power of mental concentration, being able to pursue the thread of an argument, trace a principle, and follow an idea almost infinitely beyond their waking capacity. It is this kind of trance that educates the person, and makes philosophers and orators; and not the ghost-induced state. This trance can easily be induced. . . . It is in short the highest state of mesmerism."[59] He also alluded to this state as "a kind of waking clairvoyance," an idea he developed more fully in two works that he published on the subject in the early 1860s.

The chief advantage of (waking) clairvoyance for Randolph, as for Quimby, was that where "a medium is a machine played on and worked by others, . . . the clairvoyant sees, knows, understands, learns and grows in personal and mental power day by day." In the words of his biographer, "clairvoyance [for Randolph] not only was an exceedingly sublime state of vision, but it was also a conscious phenomenon, rather than a result of trance."[60] In the early 1870s Blavatsky and Olcott, following Randolph, took up the charge that mediums passively channeled spirits rather than actively manipulating occult forces.[61] The early leaders of the occult movement—Randolph, Blavatsky, Olcott, and Emma Hardinge Britten— did not simply reject Spiritualism and the mesmeric tradition in the manner of Quimby and Eddy. Rather they understood Spiritualism as a necessary stage in a larger process of spiritual evolution and continued to view the mesmeric tradition as foundational to their worldview.[62]

The reform of Spiritualism initiated by Olcott and Blavatsky in the 1870s built on the tendency of the more learned Spiritualists, such as Peebles and Howitt, to view Spiritualism as a universal religion grounded in the wisdom of the ages. Olcott criticized the masses of Spiritualists, himself included, for "attending circles . . . year after year, gaping at fresh wonderings, . . . and never turning over old books, nor ransacking old libraries to see what our progenitors knew about this sort of thing."[63] Despite what he took to be the superiority of Occultism to Spiritualism, he said that "[t]here is sweet satisfaction in knowing that . . . both can better afford to enter into the field of controversy than either of their antagonists. The

Occultist can point to the irrefragable proof that every existing religion is the direct descendant of ancient theogonies, and the Spiritualist cite from historical records, the evidence that his phenomena are as old as the race itself." The book that Olcott "particularly recommend[ed]" to interested Spiritualists was Ennemoser's *History of Magic* translated by William Howitt, adding that "Mr. Howitt's own *History of the Supernatural* covers pretty nearly the same facts." As we have seen, the wide-ranging comparative perspective of both Ennemoser and Howitt was informed by a mesmeric understanding of psychological states. Following their lead, Olcott insisted that "[n]either Eastern Magic nor Western Spiritualism can be understood, until one has carefully studied the phenomena of Animal Magnetism, or Mesmerism."[64]

Aided by contacts established in India and Ceylon by Spiritualist James Peebles during his first world tour, Blavatsky and Olcott began an Asian correspondence in 1877 that led to the formation of a branch of the Theosophical Society in Bombay, the departure of Blavatsky and Olcott for India in 1878, and the inauguration of the Society's explicit interest in a theosophically informed approach to the religions (as opposed to the "magic") of the East.[65] In a lecture given in India in 1882, Olcott outlined what he took to be the "common foundation of all religions." The four general characteristics of the "rock upon which the world's theological superstructures are reared," he began, are the idea that there is a nonphysical part of human nature, that this nonphysical part continues after death, that "an Infinite Principle under[lies] all phenomena," and that a relationship exists "between this Infinite Principle and the non-physical part of man." According to Olcott, these insights are not accessible to the physical senses, but only to "psychical intuition."[66]

In the remainder of the lecture, Olcott built an intellectual bridge between the mesmeric tradition and Hindu philosophy using as his point of connection the Sanskrit notion of the *Māyāvirūpa* or the "human 'Double.' " The advantage of Hindu philosophy, he argued, is that, unlike the scientific "Materialism" and religious "Dualism" of the West, it made room for a "middle nature" between the "gross body" and the "divine and eternal principle." This middle nature or "Double" could be "separated from the living body at will, projected to a distance, and animated by the full consciousness of the man."[67] The Double is projected, Olcott said, by "an expenditure of energy" set in motion through the "concentration of the will." The power to do so, while either "natural or acquired," is in either case "an uncommon power, and can never be exercised at all times except by the true proficient in psychological science." Adepts are "gifted with [this] power" and thus are able "to get outside the illusion-breeding screen of the body and acquire an actual perception of the 'Divine' truth through the developed psychical senses."[68]

According to Olcott, those who do not possess these gifts must either wait to be reborn with greater abilities or immerse themselves in the "elementary stages leading up towards adeptship" in the hope of facilitating their development. The most important task at the elementary stage was the study of mesmerism. Such study, according to Olcott, provided proof that the mind could separate from the body, that thoughts could be transmitted from one mind to another, and that communication could occur at a distance.[69] Although no amount of study could turn individuals into Adepts if they did not possess the requisite gifts, the study of mesmerism could provide an empirical introduction to the kinds of capacities cultivated by Adepts.

Because both Blavatsky and Olcott were drawn to the traditions of the East rather than the West, esoteric Christianity *per se* was not their primary focus. Nonetheless, given that, in their view, theosophical wisdom "underlies every exoteric scripture and religion," they both criticized exoteric (or Church) Christianity and highlighted the esoteric truths that had been obscured by uninitiated Christians.[70] Not surprisingly, Theosophists understood Jesus as "an adept." As such, they equated him with other Greco-Roman figures noted for their magical powers and occult knowledge, such as Pythagoras and Appolonius. They described him, probably following Masonic teachings, as having a connection with the Essenes and as having been initiated into "the Jewish *Kabala*" and "the secret wisdom of Egypt."[71] According to Blavatsky, there was enough in the four gospels, especially in the parables, to reveal the essence of Jesus' esoteric teachings: "the unity of a spiritual God, whose temple is within each of us, and in whom we live as He lives in us—in spirit."[72]

Jesus, however, was misunderstood by his followers, very few of whom were themselves initiated. According to Blavatsky, "Paul was the only one of the apostles who . . . understood the secret ideas underlying the teachings of Jesus, though he had never met him." As an initiate, Paul understood the hidden meaning of the word Christ, "the abstract ideal of the personal divinity indwelling in man."[73] The esoteric spelling of Christ as "Chrestos" revealed this hidden meaning. The Chrestos was not unique to Christianity, but rather was equivalent to the "Atma-Buddhi-Manas" of Hinduism.[74] Thus, Blavatsky could describe both "the man Jesus as well as the man Christna [Krishna], . . . [as] united to their *Chrestos*."[75]

The Christ Within

The tradition that came to be known by the mid-1890s as "New Thought" had as its chief interpreters Julius and Annetta Dresser, both patients and students of Phineas Quimby, and their son, Horatio Dresser, editor of the *Quimby Manuscripts*, published in 1921. In a lecture titled "The True History of Mental Science" delivered in 1887, Julius Dresser challenged Mary Baker Eddy's claims to a new revelation and traced the history of the "Mental Science" movement, including Christian Science, back to the teachings of Phineas Quimby. In support of his claims, he quoted from "that able writer upon Mental Science, Dr. W. F. Evans," who claimed that "the late Dr. Quimby, of Portland . . . embraced this view of the nature of disease, and by a long succession of most remarkable cures . . . proved the truth of the theory [that by changing wrong beliefs, we can cure disease]."[76] This speech marked the beginning of a long and bitter controversy between "orthodox" Christian Science and the dissenting tradition that came to be called New Thought over the relationship between Eddy and Quimby. It also marked the creation of a history of mental science that, by incorporating Christian Science into its narrative, placed the dissenters on an equal footing with Eddy as mutual heirs of the Quimby tradition. Warren Felt Evans, also a student of Quimby and author of six books on mental healing (two of which were published before *Science and Health*), assumed a key place in this new history.[77]

Widely read and religiously peripatetic, Evans spent about twenty-five years as a Methodist minister, leaving the ministry in 1864 to join the Swedenborgian Church of the New Jerusalem. He consulted Phineas Quimby regarding his own health in 1863 or 1864 and, with Quimby's encouragement, began his own healing practice shortly thereafter. His books on religious healing, published during the twenty years prior to his death in 1889, synthesized elements from Methodism, Swedenborgianism, mesmerism, and esoteric Christianity.[78] Reading Quimby, Eddy, and Evans alongside one another, it is hard not to view Eddy and Evans as sibling rivals descended from the same parent. Where Eddy ultimately rejected the mesmeric tradition as a malicious inversion of Christian Science, Evans viewed the "influence or action of mind upon mind" as the foundation of religious healing. Well-read in the mesmeric tradition, Evans concluded that "there are a variety of phenomena, passing under the names of Mesmerism, Psychology, Biology, Animal Magnetism, Pathetism, Hypnotism, and even Psychometry, that are reducible to [this] one general principle."[79]

Where Quimby referred to a "higher sense," Eddy to a "spiritual sense," and Olcott to a "human double," Evans initially referred to the "spiritual senses" in the plural, later to the "sympathetic sense," and finally to the "faculty of Intuition." Evans understood the spiritual senses as "our ordinary senses acting independently of the bodily organs." Like the Theosophists, Evans viewed the mesmeric tradition as providing evidence that the senses could act independently of the body. Nonetheless, the full use of the spiritual senses, according to Evans, involved something "far higher and more spiritual" than the usual mesmeric phenomena of trance, somnambulism, or clairvoyance. Most notably, those who made full use of their spiritual senses did so, not in trance or a somnambulistic state, but "in perfect consciousness and wakefulness." The "inner being" of such persons, he wrote, arises "above the limitations of time and space, and the bondage to material things, and the spiritual man, the interior life, . . . attain[s] to freedom, such as it usually enjoys only after it has become divested of the external body."[80]

Everyone, Evans believed, has spiritual senses, and it was merely a matter of time, he hoped, before everyone would be "educated into the[ir] normal use."[81] Jesus, as might be expected, had full use of *his* spiritual senses and utilized them "in a degree never seen before." According to Evans, Jesus' "inner selfhood was not in bondage to material limitations," but rather was "subject to the laws that govern . . . the spiritual world." As such, Jesus "possessed the power of transferring his mental presence and spiritual force through any extent of spatial distance," the ability to read thoughts, disclose the future, and cure disease. Jesus utilized his spiritual senses more fully than others, yet he was not uniquely gifted in this regard. "[W]hat the divine nature did for him," Evans wrote, "it is willing to do for us, in a degree, and we may be glorified or spiritualized with him." This, he added, is "certainly the teaching of the New Testament."[82]

Evans explained Jesus' miracles in terms of the power of one mind to act upon another (independent of the body) in such a way as to induce mental changes. Both healing and religious conversion, according to Evans, partook of this power to introduce new mental states. The introduction of a new mental state was, properly speaking, "a new spiritual birth," which provided the patient or convert with "a better interior life."[83] This understanding informed Evans's view of the Protestant revival tradition, which he viewed as inducing effective, but not supernatural, changes in "men's souls." Thus, he wrote that in the popular revivals, "the united effort of the minister and of those in sympathy with him, [is] directed to the production or induction of a new mental state upon the 'anxious' or 'penitent.' " Although ministers generally succeeded "in effecting the desired result, the *conversion* or change of the soul," he noted that "they might do it much easier, if they were good magnetizers, and understood the laws that control the action of mind upon mind."[84] Nor was it just the effects of revivals that could be accounted for in this way. "All forms of religion," according to Evans, "effect such mental transformations, both the evangelical and the heretical. Mahometans, Shakers, Adventists, and even Mormons, 'do so with their enchantments.' "[85]

In his later writings, Evans explicitly identified with the occult or esoteric tradition and attempted to formulate a Christian Theosophy that drew from the world's religions, while maintaining the superiority of Christianity. In doing so, he spelled out more explicitly his understanding of the distinctive features of the inner life of Christianity as they related to his general theory of religion.[86] He began with the idea that spiritual knowledge in all traditions is imparted, "not by verbal discourse merely, but by the silent influence of mind upon mind." This form of education, for which the Hindu adepts were widely known, was, he acknowledged, "entirely unrecognized" in the West. Nonetheless, he claimed, it was "practised by Jesus, and belongs to Christianity." Most crucially, he argued that Christians can enter into "sympathetic (or psychometric) relations" with "the still living personality of Jesus" through "the Paraclete, or spirit of truth, which was promised, to teach us all things and guide us into all truth." According to Evans, the distinctive feature of Christianity, that which sets it "apart from all other religions," is the fact that "*he* [Jesus Christ] *can and does lodge himself, and incorporate and repeat himself, in his true disciples.*" Christians, therefore, he said, "no longer live a mere natural life, but a supernatural life, a life so little their own that Paul could affirm in truth: 'I am crucified with Christ: nevertheless I live; yet not I, but the Christ liveth in me.' "[87]

Writing in the mid-1880s, Evans described Jesus not as a "mere external and historic person, but an everywhere present saving principle" present to us as "the principle or faculty of Intuition," the heir to what Evans previously referred to as the spiritual or sympathetic sense. Drawing from the hermetic tradition, he claimed that the development of the intuition in man, as in the case of Jesus, is "symbolized by the dove coming upon him." Intuition, he wrote, is thus "the only faculty in man through which divine revelation comes, or ever has come. By means of it we gain access to an interior and permanent region of knowledge, where are stored up all the truth which were ever known or can be known,—the universal Christ, in whom are hid all the treasures of wisdom and knowledge."[88]

Julius Dresser gave his provocative lecture on the history of mental science just two years before Evans's death. Viewing Evans as the great interpreter of Quimby, the Dressers tended to read Quimby through Evans. Thus, while acknowledging the importance of animal magnetism as an empirical tradition on the development of Quimby's thought, both Julius and Horatio Dresser downplayed the importance of clairvoyance for Quimby. As Robert Peel points out in his biography of Mary Baker Eddy, Horatio Dresser "pointedly ignored Quimby's crucial conception of 'the Christ' as a clairvoyant power by which the healer was able to perceive a person's mental atmosphere or identity and feel his sickness; instead he wrote as though this pragmatic concept were roughly equivalent to Mrs. Eddy's theistic definition of Christ as 'the true idea voicing good, the divine message from God to men speaking to the human conscience.' "[89] At certain points in the text of the *Quimby Manuscripts*, Dresser even goes so far as to insert "intuitive" in brackets after "clairvoyant" to make sure that the reader understands exactly what Quimby meant![90] Thus, by the late 1880s, the emergent New Thought tradition, while finding its origins in the empiricism of animal magnetism rather than in the divine revelation of Christian Science, had begun to lose sight of the way that the psychology of animal magnetism informed the deeper structure of its thought. New Thought would rediscover psychology at the turn of the century, when it embraced without much difficulty the new notion of the subconscious.[91]

The new religious movements of this period—Christian Science, Theosophy, and New Thought—all wrestled in their own way with the problematic of religious experience formulated by Edwards. They all sought a way of grounding authentic religious experience or knowledge in a spiritual (i.e., nonphysical) sense in a way that did not contradict the naturalistic theories of mind of their day. Eddy, like Edwards, associated authentic religious experience with a new spiritual sense that was supernaturally awakened only in believers of a like persuasion. Spiritualists, Theosophists, and proponents of New Thought grounded religious experience in a naturally occuring spiritual sense, which informed all the world's religions and was potentially available to persons of all faiths. It is perhaps not coincidental that the founders and/or leading proponents of the universalistic new religions (e.g., Spiritualists Emma Hardinge Britten and James Peebles, Theosophists Helena Blavatsky and Henry Olcott, and New Thought proponent Warren Felt Evans) were all either well traveled or widely read, whereas those who relied on exclusivist revelations or visions (e.g., Ellen G. White and Mary Baker Eddy) were more limited in their experience.

PROTESTANTS AND TRANCE

Faith Healing

Following the interactions of mesmeric psychology and religion has taken us to a variety of new religious movements that most evangelical Protestants would have considered either marginal to the tradition or well beyond its pale. Mainline Protestants, still informed by the academic psychology of the moral philosophers, did not take seriously either the new religions or the mesmerically based psychology upon which they were based until after William James published his *Varieties of Religious Experience* in 1902. During the 1880s, Methodists did begin to use mesmerically derived psychology to think about contemporary phenomena within their own tradition. They were led in this effort by James Monroe Buckley, a self-educated psychologist of religion whose stature approached that of La Roy Sunderland.

Buckley, like Sunderland, was a Methodist minister who shared Sunderland's fascination with psychology and religious experience. Unlike Sunderland, however, Buckley remained within the church and, as editor of *The Christian Advocate* (New York), the denomination's most prestigious and widely circulated weekly, he wielded tremendous influence within the church. Moreover, where Sunderland was a radical with views on issues such as abolition, theological education, and psychology that set him well outside the Methodist mainstream, Buckley was above all else a churchman, conservative on some issues, such as women's ordination, and progressive, in a rationalistic sort of way, in terms of theology. Respectable and "formalistic," he was dedicated to imbuing the pages of the *Christian Advocate* with "a tone of genuine spirituality, free alike from cant and superstition."[92] During the 1880s and 1890s, Buckley utilized a mesmerically based psychology of religion to criticize what he took to be unfortunate developments within the holiness movement, while at the same time protecting what he took to be the essentials of the faith. In the process, he introduced Sunderland's work to a new generation of Methodists and began the process of rehabilitating Sunderland's reputation within the church.

Buckley's credentials in psychology were, like Sunderland's, the product of wide reading and careful observation. He saw his first "performances in 'animal magnetism' " in 1849 or 1850 and a few years later watched as his "devout" boarding-school roommate was "brought from a [revival] meeting in a 'trance' and placed upon the bed." In 1856, while in college, he witnessed his first spiritualist "trance medium" and "inspirational speaker" and visited the Oneida Community, where healings were taking place. In 1857, he said, "I found certain 'Millerites' or 'Adventists' in the interior of Connecticut who claimed power to heal diseases by prayer and without medicine, and—if they could attain sufficient faith—to raise the dead." "Trances," he added, "were also common among the Millerites at their camp-meetings, as they had been among the early Methodists, Congregationalists in the time of Jonathan Edwards, and certain Presbyterians and Baptists in the early part of this century in the South and the West."[93]

Buckley's first appointment, probably in the mid-1850s, was to a Methodist church where, he said, "one third of the leading male and many of the female members of the Church . . . had become Spiritualists, [and] had formed a society, where mediums were common." This seems to have been the event that sparked his investigative curiosity. For some eight years thereafter, he said, "he gave most of his leisure to the investigation of the subject, and publicly and privately contended against it in the cities of New England, where he lived, and in the West. Whatever is new in the subject [he said] he reads, and no phenomena of importance have been presented down to the present time [1882] which he has not seen, either as original experiments or accurate reproductions."[94] Intrigued by the tales still told of Sunderland by his older colleagues in the ministry, as well as by their numerous shared interests, Buckley interviewed Sunderland not long before Sunderland's death. Buckley's lengthy obituary for Sunderland and his appreciative estimate of his psychological work, if not his theology, appeared in the *Christian Advocate* in 1885. A year later, Buckley's own investigations of religious phenomena, including Methodist faith healing, were serialized in *The Century Magazine* and appeared in book form under the title, *Faith-Healing, Christian Science and Kindred Phenomena* (1887).

Faith healing, long assumed by most mainline Protestants to have ended with the early church, reemerged as phenomena to be reckoned with during the 1880s. The three leading proponents of faith healing were Charles Cullis, William E. Boardman, and Albert B. Simpson, all of whom were associated with the holiness movement. After experiencing sanctification in the early 1860s, Cullis, a college-trained physician and an Episcopal layman, established a home in Boston for consumptives, most of whom were terminally ill. In time, a number of other "faith works" were associated with it, including children's homes and orphanages, a cancer home, a deaconess training program, a faith training college, and various rescue and foreign missions. Cullis also established a publishing house devoted primarily to holiness literature. In 1873, after visiting a faith cure home in Switzerland, Cullis initiated prayer for bodily healing as a part of the faith work in Boston. Bodily healing had little public visibility, however, until Cullis published his book, *Faith Cures* in 1879. William Boardman, a Presbyterian minister and author of several well-known books on holiness, established a close working relationship with Cullis in the 1870s and published his own work on healing, *The Great Physician*, in 1881. Testimonies to healing at his Palmer-style Tuesday meetings for holiness led Cullis to begin weekly prayer services for the sick in 1881 and establish a "Faith Cure House" in 1882.[95]

Faith healing also gained popularity in conjunction with annual "Faith Conventions" held to promote sanctification (or the second blessing) at Methodist camp-meeting grounds. Albert Simpson, also a Presbyterian minister, integrated healing into his New York City ministry in the wake of the Faith Convention held in 1881, and three years later he founded a faith cure home in conjunction with a number of New York ministers. The Convention held at Old Orchard Beach, Maine, the following year attracted widespread note in the Methodist periodicals. *Zion's Herald*, published by the New England annual conference, commented on "the great number of testimonies given of physical healing in answer to prayer." The rapid increase in such testimonies indicated, according to the editor, that the church was passing into a new era in which "the saints are taking Christ as a physician of both soul and body."[96] Buckley provided his readers with a more caustic assessment, commenting:

> On the one hand, we have no desire to say a word that could be construed into disparagement of the faith or zeal or Christian character of . . . Dr. Cullis. On the other hand, the spectacle of 600 invalids passing in procession before the Doctor, some tottering on crutches, some carried in invalid chairs, dwarfs, cripples, blind persons, each to be anointed with oil, and prayed over, for the purpose of being healed, does not seem to us altogether edifying.[97]

Despite such criticism, interest continued to grow throughout the 1880s. In addition to clergy incorporating healing into their ministries, numerous lay persons, many of them women, founded faith cure homes patterned on Cullis's work in Boston. The prayers of a faith healer named Mrs. Mix healed Carrie F. Judd (later known as Carrie Judd Montgomery) of a debilitating illness. Judd, a friend of both Cullis and Simpson, founded a faith cure home in Buffalo, New York, in 1882 and one of the earliest faith healing periodicals, *Triumphs of Faith*, soon thereafter.[98]

Two books critical of the Protestant faith healing movement were published in the mid-1880s, both by Methodist ministers. The first, *Faith-work, Christian Science, and Other Cures* (1885) by L. T. Townsend, a professor at Boston University, was long on advice and short on explanation. Townsend took a pragmatic approach to the contending healing traditions and advised Methodists to make use of both physicians and prayer. He observed that even the most "ignorant quack" could claim some successful cures and chalked such healings up to "credulity on part of the patient, and brazen impudence on part of the quack."[99] Buckley, while making much the same point, approached the subject in a far more scholarly and sophisticated way. First of all, he insisted, as William James would some fifteen years later, that "it is necessary to proceed *without regard to the question of religion*, in determining whether the facts can be accounted for upon natural principles." Second, through his comparisons, Buckley sought to determine whether there were common effects and limitations in every case, and thus presumably an underlying mechanism or common cause. In making comparisons, Buckley drew upon cases from textbooks in "mental physiology," experiments he had conducted, and claims made by various religious and occult groups.[100]

He found that "in comparison with the Mormons, Spiritualists, Mind-Curers, Roman Catholics, and Magnetizers, the Protestant Faith-Healers can accomplish as much, but no more." All, he said, were able, in most instances, to cure nervous diseases and often could effect cures of diseases such as dropsy, tumors, rheumatism, sciatica, gout, neuralgia, contraction of the joints and certain inflammatory condition. None was able to dispense with surgery in complex cases and none could "restore a [missing] limb, or eye, or finger, or even a tooth." He compared this with the New Testament, which he stressed, stated that Jesus "healed *all* manner of disease, and all manner of sickness," including, Buckley claimed, restoring the "maimed" and raising up the dead.[101]

In seeking an underlying explanation, he interviewed and allowed himself to be treated by any number of different kinds of healers. He was particularly interested in discovering how faith healers explained the cures of their competitors, averring that "when quacks fall to discrediting each other, principles may be discovered." Thus, a spiritualist healer named Dr. Newton explained to Buckley that the cures of another spiritualist healer, whom he considered an "unmitigated fraud," were due to "the faith of the people and the concentration of their minds upon his operations, with the expectation of being cured." When Buckley asked if this wasn't the way in which he, too, effected cures, Dr. Newton insisted that "the difference between a genuine healer and a quack . . . is as wide as the poles." Believing that Newton "had inadvertently [given] the whole explanation," Buckley let the matter drop, not wanting to "put an end to the conversation."[102]

Generally, then, Buckley argued that the "claims of Christian faith-healers to supernatural powers are discredited by three facts:

> (1) They exhibit no supremacy over pagans, spiritualists, magnetizers, mind-curers, etc.
> (2) They cannot parallel the mighty works that Christ produced, nor the works of the apostles. (3) All that they really accomplish can be paralleled without assuming any supernatural cause, and a formula can be constructed out of the elements of the human mind which will give us as high average results as their prayers or anointings. That formula in its lowest form is *concentrated attention.*"[103]

Buckley's own experiments over the years were designed to test this last claim. He described healing a person with a toothache and another with nausea and a headache by applying a silver dollar to the affected area. He also described treating a woman's arthritic hands by having her concentrate her attention on a pair of knitting needles. In the late 1860s, he conducted a series of experiments, much like Sunderland's, designed to show that the effects of animal magnetism were the results of subjective mental conditions. In one instance, he tested his theory at a meeting of a literary society in Stamford, Connecticut, where he asked eight persons to stand, holding hands with their eyes closed. In a few minutes, he said, "five passed more or less fully into the trance state." One of the witnesses recalled "the honest conviction with which a prominent lawyer believed himself sitting on a log looking into the muddy bottom of a stream of water [and] a young man whose trembling legs were made to bend under the enormous weight of an envelope placed over his head, when told it weighed a ton."[104]

Buckley's explanation of healing by means of concentration of the attention paralleled Beard's explanation of trance. Whereas Beard spent a great deal of time explaining the trance state and applying it to a relatively undifferentiated set of "delusions," Buckley spent little time theorizing about trance and correspondingly more time applying it to actual instances of healing among Mormons, Catholics, Protestants, Spiritualists, and magnetizers. In their careful attention to the religious phenomena they were interpreting, Buckley and Sunderland shared much.

They parted company, however, when it came to Christian revelation and biblical miracles. Where Sunderland naturalized all of Christianity, Buckley, like most mainline Protestants of the 1880s, sought to safeguard revelation and biblical miracles.[105]

In his two-part notice of Sunderland's death, Buckley paid glowing tribute to Sunderland as a psychologist, stating that there was "not one idea . . . the late Dr. G. M. Beard set forth on these subjects that this man had not declared fore Dr. Beard was out of the cradle."[106] Theologically, however, Buckley found Sunderland's course highly disturbing and, in his second installment, he "trace[d] his deplorable plunge, not only into infidelity, but into the depths of blasphemy."[107] In the end, Buckley said, "Mr. Sunderland concluded that . . . all conversion and all revelation might be a myth, and attempted to account for Christianity on natural principles." When Sunderland sought to explain conversion and revelation in terms of trance, "he made the mistake," according to Buckley, "of confounding the accidental with the fundamental." The fundamental elements in Christianity, according to Buckley were the "doctrines of God and Christ . . . and the *permanent* and *radical* effects on the *character* made by belief in and practice of them." There was no correlation, he said, between the transformation of character and trance.[108]

The idea that Christianity was fundamentally about the formation of character was characteristic of moderate and progressive evangelical Protestants of this era. While this formed and would continue to form the basis for significant Protestant opposition to a positive synthesis between theology and mesmeric psychology, readers continued to raise difficult issues with respect to conversion, biblical miracles, and revelation. Some readers pointed out that "if faith-healing can be demonstrated to be subjective, what is called conversion can be accounted for similarly." Buckley acknowledged that this was indeed the case, if what was meant by conversion was "the cataleptic condition [i.e., falling to the ground as if dead]." This sort of conversion, he acknowledged, "occurred in the time of Jonathan Edwards, [among] certain Presbyterians and Baptists in the early part of this century in the South and West, and the early Methodists, and is still common among colored people, Second Adventists, and the Salvation Army." He differentiated, as we might expect, between "the cataleptic condition" and true conversion. He added, in the fashion of Edwards, that conversion experiences might be "sufficiently intense to produce tears of sorrow or joy, trances, or even lunacy[,] but neither the lunacy, the trances, nor the tears are essential parts of the conversion." The latter, he attributed, in standard fashion to "emotional excitement, differing in individuals according to temperament and education."[109]

Readers also asked why the principles he applied to modern examples of healing did not apply to the miracles of Christ, why, specifically, he did not "sift the evidence in the same way, and explain the facts on the same grounds." His responded by saying that "the credibility of the record concerning Christ's works is a question which cannot be raised by Christians, whether they hold the superstitions of the faith-healers or not." He quoted Faraday's refusal "to apply those mental operations which I think good in respect of high things to the very highest." Although he said he did not quote Faraday to "shield [him]self . . . from the charge of inconsistency," he, like Faraday, seemed willing to bear that reproach. Buckley's attempt to safeguard biblical miracles and revelation by pointing out the limitations of the scientific method and the basic difference between nature and revelation was typical of Protestants during the 1880s, although, as we have seen, new religious movements had been comparing ancient and modern miracles since the 1850s.[110] It would be another decade before some liberal Protestants, too, would want to make that move.[111]

Advocates of faith healing, aware of competition from the new religious movements and of critics such as Buckley, attempted to distance themselves from them, albeit in relatively unsophisticated ways. W. H. Daniels, in his biography of Cullis, claims, for example, that "[t]he casting-out of devils from lunatics, and the salvation of [terminally ill] souls" lifted the work of faith healing "entirely out of the range of 'animal magnetism,' 'mesmerism,' 'electric phenomena,' 'Christian (?) science,' 'spiritualism,' and the like." Skeptics offered explanations, but Daniels was content to state that "the presence and work of the Holy Spirit upon the soul, in co-operation with the work of the Great Physician upon the body . . . affords an unerring proof that these cures are wrought by the supernatural."[112]

Carrie Judd criticized Christians who visited or investigated Spiritualist healers. She lamented the fact that persons "who would reject the thought of consulting a spiritualist on any other subject . . . would, nevertheless, think it no harm to take his advise medically, submitting to such counsel received by him while in a 'trance.' "[113] Referring (mistakenly) to Buckley, she was ashamed to read that "a prominent Methodist Episcopal minister in the East . . . had attended over a hundred Spiritualist seances!" She added, that if "the learned D.D. [had] spent one-half as much time in the little prayer-meetings of those who believe in Jesus' power to heal the body, we think he would have better understood their faith, and their so-called 'claims.' "[114]

Judd also reprinted numerous articles from other periodicals, most of them on Christian Science, which, of all the new religions, seemed to pose the greatest challenge to Protestant faith healers. Evangelicals could easily distinguish between faith cure and most other systems on the basis of their respective curative agents, but Christian Science was a more elusive target. Thus, the Rev. Hogg explained that faith cure relied upon prayer to a personal God, mind cure upon "the direct influence of a strong will over a weaker one," magnetic healing upon mesmeric force, and clairvoyant healing on "ghostly eyes that can search and scan the inside of a man." Christian Science, because of its vehemently antipsychological stance, could not be so readily secularized and written off. Defenders of faith healing were thus forced to tackle the theology of Christian Science head on, seeking in each case to establish its "unchristian" character.[115]

Whereas Protestant faith healers reacted defensively to Buckley's critique, Christian Scientists embraced it. A reviewer for the *Christian Science Journal* claimed that Buckley accurately described "the theory of a large majority of charlatans calling themselves mental healers," while making no mention of the (true) teachings of Christian Science. The reviewer concluded that although Christian Scientists "may not have looked for an ally from this quarter . . . Dr. Buckley *is* an ally, though an unconscious one." Because their dualistic theology actively demonized animal magnetism, Christian Scientists could easily appropriate the latest in psychological thinking as a means of criticizing others, while deflecting criticism aimed at themselves.[116]

Methodist Camp and Tabernacle Meetings

Faith healing, the most sensational new development within the holiness tradition during the early 1880s, drew its most prominent advocates from the Reformed side of the movement. Whereas the holiness movement came together around an experience of sanctification following conversion, often referred to as the "second blessing," the Reformed and Methodist sides of the tradition retained somewhat different emphases. The Reformed side, often designated as the "Higher Life movement," evinced interest in healing, biblical prophesy, and eschatological speculation; the Methodist or Wesleyan side of the movement remained preoccupied with the promotion of the holiness experience itself.[117] Leaders of the Higher Life movement organized and participated in revivals, but the Methodist experience of holiness remained intimately and distinctively bound up with the camp-meeting tradition. In the latter decades of the century, camp meetings remained largely outside the public eye and were relatively isolated from debates over psychology and religious experience. Within this sheltered space, the Wesleyan holiness movement elaborated on the camp-meeting tradition and laid the groundwork for the emergence of Pentecostalism. Debates about these developments within the tradition were cast, for the most part, not in the language of popular psychology, but in the idiom of "fanaticism" vs. "old-time Methodism."

The connection between the camp meeting and the experience of holiness was revitalized in 1867 with the formation of the "National Camp Meeting Association for the Promotion of Holiness" (NCMA) Founded by a group of Methodist ministers with the support of several Methodist bishops, the Association had as its goal to hold one or more national camp meetings a year that focused specifically on holiness. The meetings were deliberately scheduled early in the camp-meeting "season" so as to maximize their influence on, while avoiding direct competition with, the regular camp meetings.[118] Given the centrality of the doctrine of holiness within the Methodist tradition, the organizers sought less to diffuse "a dogmatic idea" than to promote "a profound religious experience."[119] Recognizing that their critics within the church might brand them as "schismatic, fanatical, or disloyal" despite their years of service to the denomination, the organizers of the NCMA sought diligently to protect the holiness movement from the perils of fanaticism. Two years after the first of the national camp meetings, John Inskip was relieved to report that "in the main," they had been "remarkably successful." In fact, he said, "our meeting has been much less disturbed in the way intimated than ordinary camp-meetings frequently are."[120]

Methodists had been sensitized to the potential links between holiness, camp meetings, and schism during the 1850s, when the Genesee Conference was caught up in controversies that led to the formation of the Free Methodist Church in

1860. B. T. Roberts and his followers (nicknamed the "Nazarites") took distinctive stands on a number of issues, but the heart of their disagreement with the more liberal, urban Methodists within their conference had to do with religious experience. The Bergen camp meeting, as Gregory Van Dussen has argued, provides a window on this aspect of the controversy.[121] According to B. T. Roberts, the liberals considered the Bergen camp meeting a "hot bed of fanaticism" and "the most objectionable" of all the Nazarite meetings. Many who attended the camp meeting, however, were reminded of "the early days of Methodism in this country" and declared that it was not fanaticism at all, but rather, "old-fashioned Methodism."[122]

What constituted "old-fashioned Methodism" was not explicitly discussed, but, as Kathryn Long has pointed out, the phrase carried different meanings for different factions within the church. When Phoebe Palmer and her supporters referred to "pure, primitive, Wesleyan Methodism," they had in mind the Methodism of John Wesley. When B. T. Roberts and his followers referred to "old-fashioned Methodism," they were thinking of early American Methodism or, in Long's words, "a church of the poor, of plain people, where the 'mighty impulses' of God's Spirit were expressed through 'strong emotion' and preaching in 'thunder tones.' "[123] This Methodism was embedded in the bodily memories of the older generation and brought vividly to mind when older Methodists happened upon an "old-fashioned" camp meeting. It also took form, it turns out, in the written history of G. W. Henry, a Methodist (local) preacher, whose *Shouting in All Ages of the Church* was first published (by the author) in Oneida, New York, in 1859, just prior to the expulsion of the Nazarites.

The timing of the book's publication was probably not coincidental. Henry was not only sanctified, he likened his experience to that of Benjamin Abbott, whom he (reasonably enough) lifted up as an exemplary shouter.[124] Henry attended the Bergen camp meetings in the late 1850s, while he and another local pastor were serving at Third Methodist Episcopal Church in Syracuse. Third Church broke from First M. E. over the issue of worship and, as Henry put it, "The bees that swarmed were noisy. Incessantly they praised God. They sang, they shouted, screamed, and leaped for joy." Tensions remained high between First and Third Churches, and the bishop, perhaps unwittingly, appointed an unsympathetic preacher, who soon departed. Henry indicated that some time after he and Brother Davis stepped in, "the officers of the church, together with their accusers [from First Church], had an audience before Bishops Janes, Ames, and Baker," all known for their sympathy toward the holiness movement. "As the accusers made known their grievances," according to Henry, "Bishop Ames would say,—'Amen! Brethren, this is the old way. When I was a circuit preacher, we used to dismiss the congregation for those who wished to retire as soon as preaching was over, then we could remain to sing and pray if any soul wanted salvation.' " The bishops decided that Third Church had been "persecuted" and appointed a more congenial preacher.[125]

Henry wrote his *History of Shouting* to defend "the old way" in what he described as "a kind of family quarrel" over "shouting" within the Methodist Church. The scriptural part of his history elaborated on the oral narrative developed by "shouting Methodists" in the late-eighteenth and early-nineteenth centuries. Many chapters were devoted to Moses, the exodus, the entry into Canaan, and David dancing before the ark as it was brought into Jerusalem. The narrative resumed with a chapter on rebuilding the temple and from there passed on to the birth of Christ, selected miracle stories, Jesus' entry into Jerusalem, the passion and resurrection, and finally, Pentecost, which Henry presented as "a model revival of religion." The Second Temple and Pentecost were typologically linked, as they were for the earlier shouters. At Pentecost, according to Henry, the "foundation of a spiritual temple" was laid, built from "the souls of the redeemed." As at the laying of the foundation of the Second Temple, he said, "we will . . . take the liberty to shout and sing hosanna at the laying of the foundation of this most glorious of all temples, and ask no man's pardon."[126]

The last half the book was devoted to the history of shouting from the time of Wesley down to his own day. The key figures were Wesley, Edwards, Christmas Evans (of Welch jumper fame), and the American Methodist itinerants Benjamin Abbott, Peter Cartwright, and J. B. Finley. Henry's reading of Wesley and Edwards was not the "respectable" reading of the better-educated theologians in either the Methodist or Reformed traditions. While they emphasized Wesley's apologetic writings, Henry mined the rich resources of Wesley's journals.[127] He was sorely tempted to throw in all of Edwards, whom he declared "much ahead of us and some of our Methodist friends," but he contented himself with several chapters' worth of extracts of the sort that the New England theologians sought to downplay.[128] The three American itinerants to whom he devoted a total of six chapters— Abbott, Cartwright, and Finley—represented the lens through which he read the tradition and constructed his history. Abbott we have discussed at length. Of the three, Cartwright is probably the best known to modern Methodists, as his well-written and engaging journal is often used to illustrate "old-fashioned Methodism." Extracts from the autobiography of J. B. Finley, a Cane Ridge convert who gave extensive descriptions of early camp meetings, provided the link between the history of shouting and the camp-meeting tradition. Henry placed Finley's description of the great camp meeting at Cane Ridge "as a sort of cap-stone . . . to [his] noisy book."[129]

Henry's history of shouting provides a window into the sensibilities of the Nazarites and the more radical wing of the developing holiness movement. In light of it, we should not be surprised to learn that many of B. T. Roberts's followers believed that God was present at the Bergen camp meetings. As they put it: " 'God is here. There is power here; there appears to be a stream of holy fire and power encircling this camp-ground.' "[130] Nor should we be surprised to learn that other, less sympathetic observers viewed the camp meetings as filled with "the wildest extravagances." "Men and women pray[ing] at the top of their voices . . . persons [falling] to the ground . . . [and hours] sometimes elaps[ing] before they awoke to consciousness."[131] While Henry described the late 1850s as a time of great trial for shouting Methodists, the quarrel within the Methodist family did not end with the departure of the Free Methodists. Indeed, the quarrel continued into the 1890s, by which time most of the more ardent holiness leaders concluded that their efforts to reform the church from within had failed, and they departed to form independent holiness denominations.

The primary effect of the late-nineteenth-century holiness movement was not the reform of the church, as the leadership hoped, but the creation of an ever-widening gulf between what we might call the religion of the church and the religion of the camp meeting. The religion of the church was grounded in Sunday worship and the various activities of the local congregation. During the last decades of the century, Methodist churches became more ornate. Worship, particularly in the cities, became more liturgical (that is, more "formal"), and traditional class meetings were gradually replaced with mission societies and service groups. At the same time, the leadership of the holiness movement encouraged the formation of regional, state, and local holiness associations modeled on the NCMA. The associations maintained holiness evangelists, who made the rounds of camp meetings and encouraged the formation of "holiness bands," modeled on Phoebe Palmer's Tuesday meetings. Holiness leaders insisted that the camp meeting was no substitute for the church; nevertheless, they surrounded the camp meeting, which had never been a formal part of the Methodist church, with an array of associated structures. In so doing, they heightened rather than bridged the gulf between the local church and the camp meeting and unwittingly encouraged the formation of independent holiness denominations.[132]

Like the organizers of the NCMA, scholars usually interpret the late-nineteenth-century holiness movement as a reaction against the growing worldliness of late-nineteenth-century Methodism. Organizers stressed the "sad declension in spirituality in the churches . . . [and] the growing opposition to the subject of entire sanctification as a distinct experience." They viewed the "National Camp-meetings . . . mainly [as] a revival of the spirit of the camp-meetings of early times," indicating that they were not, "and were never intended to be, confined exclusively to the sanctification of believers." While the NCMA did revive the tradition associated with the earlier camp meetings, they extended and developed it as well. There was, in other words, an internal logic to the development of the camp-meeting tradition that contributed to the desire for independent denominations.[133]

The most revealing development was the emergence of the tabernacle meeting. In 1887, the NCMA reported that it had held "sixty-seven national camp meetings and eleven Tabernacle meetings . . . distributed through sixteen states of the Union, extending to both shores of the Continent, and to the far-off East."[134] Whereas the national camp meetings were held near small towns in the east and midwest, the first tabernacle meetings were held in western cities, such as Sacramento, Santa Clara, San Francisco, and Salt Lake. A decade later, tabernacle meetings were held in England and India as part of an "Around-the-world evangelistic tour with the tabernacle."[135] Although John Inskip led virtually all the camp and tabernacle meetings sponsored by the NCMA up until his death in 1883, his biographers, writing in 1885, devoted considerably more attention to the new urban tabernacle meetings than to the more traditional camp meetings.

Reformed evangelists had been holding urban revivals for years on the model developed by Charles G. Finney, but neither they nor the Methodists held "tabernacle" meetings until the 1870s. The tabernacle filled a practical need for a large urban meeting space without specific denominational ties, but the decision to call these spaces (whether buildings or tents) tabernacles was a significant one.[136] Beginning with William Rhind's book *The Tabernacle in the Wilderness* (1842) and continuing into the 1890s, a spate of books expounded on the ark of the covenant, the tabernacle in the wilderness, and the tabernacle in the temple as types of Christ and the church. These books were replete with pictures of the Israelites encamped in the wilderness and the interior of the temple and its furnishings. In them the reader could discover the layout of the encampment, including the location of the tabernacle and the tents of the various Israelite tribes, and the meaning and significance of every aspect of the tabernacle and temple. Books with titles such as *The Jewish Tabernacle and Its Furniture in their Typical Teachings* (1874) elaborated on the ark, the mercy seat, the cherubim, the shewbread, the golden candlesticks, the priests, the altars, and the different offerings and feast days as types or shadows of Christ.[137] Following the typology laid out in Hebrews, they depicted Christ as the "high priest" of "a greater and more perfect tabernacle," who redeemed humankind not with the "blood of goats and calves, but by his own blood" (Heb. 9:11–12).

Even as the Letter to the Hebrews encouraged the reader to focus on Christ as priest of the new tabernacle, much of the tabernacle literature was more interested in the tabernacle as dwelling place of God and, by extension, *Jesus* as the new tabernacle. This typological line of thinking was spelled out most fully in *The Shekinah; or, The Presence and Manifestation of Jehovah* (1857), written by the British Methodist William Cooke. Although the word Shekinah does not appear in the Bible, Cooke explained that it was derived from the Hebrew root *shakan*, to dwell, and was used by early Jewish writers to "express the fact that Jehovah dwells with his people." As a noun (*mishkan*), he explained, "it indicates the *place*—the tabernacle or temple—in which Jehovah condescended to reveal his glory."[138]

According to Cooke, "the most usual symbol of his [Jehovah's] presence in ancient times was a fiery or luminous cloud, which the Jews called *The Shekinah*, and which, during the period of their economy, dwelt between the cherubim in the Holy of Holies." In the gospel of John, the apostle took up "the ancient symbol of the tabernacle and its glory," according to Cooke, and "applied them to him [Jesus] as their living antitype and substitute, declaring that 'the Word was made flesh and dwelt among us, and we beheld his glory.' " The Feast of Pentecost, the day on which the Spirit descended on the disciples, was prefigured by "the display of Jehovah's presence at Sinai" (Ex. 19: 16–20). Just as the atonement of Christ was prefigured by the Passover, so the descent of the Spirit was prefigured by descent of "the Shekinah . . . on that mountain [Mt. Sinai] in the sight of all Israel." Just as the Shekinah dwelt in the temple in Jerusalem, so too with the descent of the Holy Spirit, the Shekinah was enshrined in the temple of the church and in the person of each disciple.[139]

The Shekinah theology served to highlight the biblical references to the physical and natural manifestations of the presence of God. God's appearance in the burn-

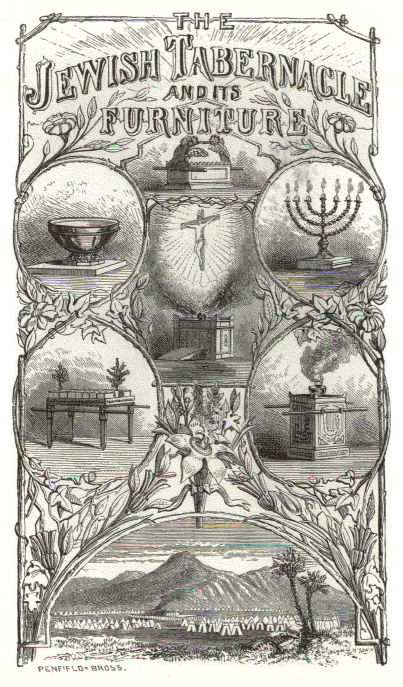

7. Title page from a book on Old Testament typology, showing the Israelites encamped in the wilderness around the tabernacle (lower) and the Shekinah or presence of God, with Christ superimposed, in the Holy of Holies in the Temple (center). From *The Jewish Temple and Its Furniture* (1874)

ing bush and in the pillar of cloud and fire were hallmarks of this tradition. When God displayed his presence at Sinai in the sight of all the people, "Mount Sinai was wrapped in smoke, because the Lord had descended upon it in fire; . . . while the whole mountain shook violently" (Ex. 19:18). When Moses completed the construction of the tabernacle, "the cloud covered the tent of meeting, and the glory of the Lord filled the tabernacle." In the journey to the promised land, the Israelites were led by the cloud on the tabernacle by day and the fire in the cloud by night (Ex. 40:34–37). When the ark was brought into the temple, "the house of the Lord was filled with a cloud, so that the priests could not stand to minister . . . for the glory of the Lord filled the house." At the dedication of the Temple, "fire came down from heaven and consumed the burnt offering and the sacrifices" and "the glory of the Lord" again filled the temple (2 Chr. 5: 13–14, 7:1). Cooke stressed that similar manifestations occurred when the Spirit descended at Pentecost. The "descent of fire" at Pentecost, he said, "proclaims the Holy Spirit to be the God that answereth by fire, the true Shekinah now come down to dwell with his church and fill it with glory."[140]

While the books on the tabernacle made much of the physical and natural manifestations of God in the Old Testament, they viewed them as ending with manifestation of God's presence in Christ. Thus, as William Brown explained:

> The Christian pilgrim [unlike the Israelites] is favoured with no such visible manifestation of the Deity as he travels through the wilderness of Canaan. He must hold his way without ever seeing with bodily eye 'the glory,' and without ever hearing the audible voice of Him who spake in the cloudy pillar. . . . The Hebrews, in the march to the Holy Land, were a type of the Christian in his journey through this world to heaven. Jesus is the glorious shekinah, that walks before him all the way to the better land.[141]

Even Cooke, who claimed with the holiness movement that "the promises" of the Father with respect to the Holy Spirit are "as fresh now as when they were first uttered," acknowledged that "the miraculous gifts of the Spirit may not be continued."[142]

The Shekinah theology seamlessly blended the high points of the shout tradition with the altar theology of Phoebe Palmer, while overcoming some of the exegetical leaps noted by the shouters' critics. In the tabernacle as type, the shouters' emphasis on shouting "glory" in the presence of God came together with Palmer's emphasis on consecrating oneself at the altar and the promise of the Holy Spirit. Although the Shekinah was not explicitly mentioned, these themes were all evident at the first tabernacle meeting sponsored by the NCMA. Here, though, as with the shouters, typological thinking was extended beyond scripture, such that the tabernacle of the Israelites was visibly present in Sacramento. According to Inskip's biographers, "the whiteness of the great tent, with a capacity to hold four thousand persons [erected in the center of Sacramento], was a picture never to be forgotten. But beyond its symmetry and beauty, it had a special significance: though there was no visible pillar of cloud or fire resting upon it, an *invisible* presence which once could feel, was there, and pervaded the place."[143]

The thirteenth day of the meeting particularly stood out. McDonald and Searles noted that there was always "*one day*, sometimes earlier, sometimes later, during the progress of the[ir] meeting[s], [which] is signalized by a special baptism of the Holy Spirit." The thirteenth day in Sacramento was that "one day."

> The prevailing spirit was that of expectancy, or waiting. The powers of the heavenly world seemed to settle down upon the people, and the ministers never seemed so inspired and filled with love and the Spirit of Jesus, who seemed almost to be visibly present. . . . A wonderful power came upon all. Many were stricken down under the mighty shock. Many felt themselves beginning to go down as when metal begins to melt, and seemed forced to lie prostrate upon the ground. There was an indescribable power that went surging through the soul, until life seemed suspended on a single thread. It would have been easy then to have taken another step and passed over the narrow stream that separated this from the heavenly land.

To this point, the account sounded much like those of earlier camp meetings. It emphasized the nearness of the heavenly world, the power that came upon the people, and the people falling and lying prostrate on the ground. While the people were struck down much as they had been in the past, they rose up in a new way. Thus, the narrative continued:

> Then, also, a strange thing occurred to some. It was not a light, nothing of a cloud-form; but as it were, a haze of golden glory encircled the heads of the bowed worshippers— a symbol of the Holy Spirit; for then that company knew that they were baptized with the Holy Ghost and fire. The preachers seemed transfigured. All were melted into tears and sobs, and murmurs of praise and glory. Truly the day of Pentecost has finally come,—and the scene of the upper chamber was repeated, and all were filled with the Spirit.[144]

Here we have a physical manifestation of the presence of God in the "haze of golden glory [that] encircled the heads of the . . . worshippers." It was both a symbol of the Holy Spirit and a sign that they had been "baptized with the Holy Ghost and fire." In connecting the "haze of golden glory" that was not "a cloud-form" with the day of Pentecost, this narrative, like the earlier shout tradition, made a typological connection between Pentecost and the Jewish Temple. Where the shouters saw Pentecost prefigured in the shouts that went up when the *Second* Temple was dedicated, the later holiness movement saw Pentecost prefigured in the "fire that came down from heaven" and in "the glory of the Lord that filled the house" when the *First* Temple was dedicated.

The defining feature of the Methodist camp-meeting tradition was its insistence on the presence of God in the camp and in the individual. In his study of the late-nineteenth-century Methodist camp meetings, historian Steven Cooley emphasizes that the camp was a place where God was understood to be present. Moreover, the images that Cooley identifies as most deeply rooted in the later camp meetings—those of the camp as Canaan, Jerusalem, Temple, and Heaven—were those inherited from the old-time Methodist camp meetings.[145] The newer developments were apparent in the interlinked images of fire, altar sacrifice, and Pentecost.[146] Leaders of the NCMA did not simply invoke the "power of the Spirit," but called for a "baptism of fire" and "a fresh endowment of 'power from on high.' " Fire, as Cooley points out, was a symbol of God's holiness in and of itself, since by fire, God purged sin and consecrated sacrifices. Phoebe Palmer's altar theology built on Wesleyan hymns that associated the refining fire with Old Testament sacrifice and the baptism of the Holy Ghost and fire. At holiness camp meetings, many, according to Cooley, "composed Palmer's scene of the altar, laid themselves on this altar as a living sacrifice, and waited for the fire of heaven to fall, consume, and purify."[147]

As the account of the tabernacle meeting in Sacramento indicates, the most striking shift in emphasis lay in the reworking of the image of Pentecost. Whereas the early camp-meeting tradition associated Pentecost with shouting, the later Methodist-Holiness movement, influenced by Phoebe Palmer, came to view Pentecost in relation to the baptism of the Holy Spirit.[148] This was not, however, the baptism of the Spirit evidenced by speaking in tongues promoted by the later Pentecostal movement, but a baptism of the Spirit linked to entire sanctification. The National Holiness Association at first made no explicit connection between Pentecost and sanctification, but by 1885 the movement, in Cooley's words, "formally associated justification with the work of Christ on Calvary and sanctification with the work of the Holy Ghost at Pentecost."[149] The association between Pentecost and entire sanctification was an enduring one within the holiness tradition and the primary source of conflict between holiness and pentecostal groups at the turn of the century.

Although holiness leaders were determined to avoid "fanaticism," Cooley's analysis of the camp-meeting handbooks of the 1860s and 1870s suggests that for several decades holiness leaders successfully legitimated both the silent meditation associated with Palmer's Tuesday night meetings and the noisy shouting associated with the old-fashioned camp meeting. At the NCMA-sponsored meeting at Mannheim in 1868, the closing speaker told the newly sanctified "not [to] take [their] particular experience as the standard for others." Some, he said, meditate quietly, others sit and sing, while still others "may 'cry out and shout' at the revealings of the Divine presence." He encouraged them to accept these differences because they were the result, in part, of differences in education and "natural temperament."[150] Shouting remained a legitimate part of the camp-meeting experience, but the loss of consciousness was frowned upon. A participant at the camp meeting at Round Lake observed that while at times the "emotion became so uncontrollable as to make a pentecostal shout[,]" still no one "went wild," only one person "lost sense or consciousness," and there was "no case of trance."[151] Even though trance was discouraged at holiness camp meetings, it did not disappear. A little over a decade later, holiness evangelist Maria Woodworth brought "old-fashioned Methodism" into public view and was promptly dubbed "the trance evangelist" by the press.

Trance Evangelism

Maria B. Woodworth was a focal point for competing interpretations of the experiences associated with the old-time Methodist camp meeting. Although not a Methodist, Woodworth identified with the Methodist tradition and was characterized by sympathetic Methodists as promoting "old-fashioned Methodism."[152] The controversies surrounding her ministry might have stayed within the church community had the press not become involved. Because she was holding public revival meetings and undoubtedly relied upon the publicity to generate crowds, her meetings were discussed at length in the papers, whereas camp-meetings generally were not. It was in this context of itinerant holiness revival meetings that the revival tradition, in its old-time Methodist form, was opened for public scrutiny and subject to comparative and medical analysis under the heading of "trance evangelism."

When people referred to Woodworth as a "trance evangelist," they had both her behavior and that of her followers in mind. Prior to accepting the call to preach, Woodworth experienced visions and at least one out-of-body experience in which she "float[ed] away" from her body and was set down in heaven. When she finally yielded to the call to preach, "[t]he glory of God came upon [her] like a cloud, and [she] seemed to be carried away hundreds of miles and set down in a field of wheat, where the sheaves were falling all around [her]." This sense of leaving her body often recurred while she was preaching, typically in conjunction with pleading with sinners to come to Jesus by telling them of God's love and "the beautiful home in heaven" that God had prepared for them. Often she would find herself "lost in the love and glory of Christ" and at such times, she said, "I feel as though the congregation was left behind, and I was floating upward in a cloud of glory."[153] Although from the start "the power" came upon her when she preached, congregations initially responded with more subdued weeping and "death-like solemnity." It was not long, however, before the power of God began to manifest itself in a noisier fashion. At a Methodist church in Ohio in 1882, "all that were present came to the altar and made a full consecration and prayer for a baptism of the Holy Spirit and fire." It came that night, as "[f]ifteen came to the altar screaming for mercy [and] [m]en and women fell and lay like dead."[154]

This power—manifest in healings, visions, and people falling as if dead—lay at the center of the controversies that surrounded Woodworth revivals. The controversy reached unprecedented heights in St. Louis when two "regular" physicians, described by one paper as "authorities on insanity and neurology," accused her of hypnotizing her followers and attempted to have her declared legally insane. Reading of the controversy in the papers, a "mesmerist" decided to investigate the charges "to satisfy his own mind if those persons who are overpowered or placed in a trance were really under the influence of mesmerism or hypnotism, as [he initially] . . . believed they were." After examining many who were, as they called it, "under the 'power,' " he found no "signs of either mesmerism or

PROSTRATED ON THE PLATFORM.

8. Holiness evangelist Maria Woodworth leading a revival meeting in St. Louis. From "Strange Scenes," *St. Louis Post-Dispatch*, August 21, 1890.

hypnotism" and testified to this effect at Woodworth's trial. The judge averred that the prosecution might have had a case had they claimed she was a nuisance, but finding no evidence that she was insane, he dismissed the case.[155]

The trial and the attendant publicity surfaced three significant perspectives on the "power"—neurological, mesmeric, and holiness—and whetted the public's appetite for more. Before the trial was concluded the pastors of First Methodist, Glasgow Avenue Presbyterian, and Immaculate Conception (Roman Catholic) Churches called for an inquiry into the power used by the evangelist. A few weeks later, the *Post-Dispatch* reported that "the much-vexed question of faith healing [might be] finally settled in St. Louis." Woodworth indicated her willingness to stay on through the winter, "chiefly because she wants the question as to her methods finally settled."[156] Although it is not clear if there was any formal inquiry into the nature of the "power," the *Post-Dispatch* and the *Globe-Democrat* published three lengthy articles that looked at the phenomena from the perspectives of medicine, animal magnetism, and comparative religion.

In an article entitled, "Religion of Hysteria," the *Post-Dispatch* published a medical explanation of "Mrs. Woodworth's Miracles" by a Dr. Chartier that soon appeared in a medical journal. The *Post-Dispatch* introduced the article with the observation that the medical profession was divided into "two sects," one of which "believes that all the cases of trance are purely hysterical; the other that some are hysterical while others are hypnotic." Dr. Chartier, who was of the former persuasion, described Woodworth's meetings as revivals only insofar as "the hysterical and hypochondriac propensities of a certain category of neurasthenic subjects are revived under the pretence of religion." He closed his article by urging physicians to "insist upon the danger that lurks in such 'meetings,' in the fact that they develop hysteria and other latent neuroses by contagion, not seldom driving the subjects already affected to insanity and paralysis."[157]

A week later, the *Post-Dispatch* printed a lengthy article on "magnetic phenomena" based on the research of one of its reporters. This lavishly illustrated piece opened with a discussion of Anton Mesmer, his theory of magnetic fluids, and his method of healing. It indicated that recent attempts to explain these "remarkable phenomena . . . on scientific principles" concluded that both "people and animals can be put into a sort of comatose state, in which they lose all personal will power, so that they are not able to move a limb." This condition, which scientists referred to as "the cataleptic state," could, according to the reporter, "be carried so far that the mental functions are temporarily suspended, delusions of sight, smell and taste take place, and the most remarkable abnormalities of the activity of the brain are produced." Most of the rest of the article was devoted to a discussion of the results of experiments on various animals, including chickens, sparrows, pigeons, frogs, and crabs. The article did not mention Woodworth in the text itself, but her picture appeared at the top of the first column and was juxtaposed with pictures of Mesmer magnetizing a woman, a physiologist experimenting on three men, and five pictures of hypnotized animals, the largest of which showed four "hypnotized crabs" in distinctly uncrab-like postures.[158]

The text indicated that the sketches of the animals were made from "instantaneous photographs" and described how the experiments were performed.

> The hypnotized chicken, for instance, was placed upon the table, held fast with one hand and gently stroked with the other. In a short time it succumbed to the influence and was then placed into the position in which it was photographed [balanced on its chest with one leg folded up and the other extended into the air]. The hypnotizer yelled at the sleeping animal, and after ten or twelve minutes of complete rigidity it flew away with a merry cackle.

Having described animals who "succumbed to the influence" and became completely rigid, the article concluded with the statement that "physiological researches have torn the veil of mysticism and farce from the various tricks with which these touring fakirs regaled the public by demonstrating that the whole thing consists of a temporary disturbance of the functions of the nervous system and the ganglious membrane."[159]

The article in the *Globe-Democrat* was the most sympathetic, making the case that "the religious trance is an old as religion itself" and indicating that "persons of peculiar temperaments and intense religious feeling have frequently been subject to the strange state which may be seen nightly at Mrs. Woodworth's tent." The essay provided an extended discussion of trances in India, the "dancing dervishes" of Islam, the "dancing mania" in thirteenth-century Europe, the Camisards [or "French prophets"], the Jansenists, the Puritans, the Wesleyan revival, the Kentucky "manifestations," the "jerks" in Ireland, various "isolated cases" (e.g., Mohammed, Joan of Arc, St. Anthony, Martin Luther, St. Teresa), and examples of "faith-cures and miracles" to support its contention that "the phenomenon [the

9. A St. Louis newspaper comparing the effect of holiness evangelist Maria Woodworth (upper left) on her followers with the states induced in humans and animals by means of animal magnetism and hypnosis. "Magnetic Phenomena," *St. Louis Post-Dispatch*, September 21, 1890.

trance condition] has been common in religious history." Nor, the paper was quick to point out, "have the terrible consequences predicted by wiseacre doctors resulted from even the most widespread epidemics of this character." While asserting that "all the learned talk about its danger to public health and safety may be dismissed as idle words," the *Globe-Democrat* nonetheless held that "there was no especial mystery about it." Recapitulating the views of respectable Protestants and academic psychologists, the paper described the trances as "a condition associated with intense religious excitement, and so frequently present in great religious gatherings as to excite little attention save among those to whom the history of such meetings is a novelty." At bottom, such phenomena, "still frequently . . . seen in quarters of this country where education has not trained the people to self-control," were associated with ignorance, but not insanity.[160]

James Monroe Buckley visited the "Woodworth Temple" in St. Louis a few months after the trial. He published an editorial letter on "The 'Trance Evangelist' " in the *Christian Advocate* in which he advanced an explanation in keeping with his earlier work and not unlike that offered by the *Globe-Democrat*. He had "no doubt," he wrote, that the "trances" at Woodworth's revivals were "of the same nature as those which happened in early Methodism, and occur still among the colored people and among Baptists and Methodists in some parts of the world, Adventists, and other sects holding camp-meetings, and are precisely of the same nature as the jerks which occurred in the early part of the century." He chalked them up to "continuous and contagious excitement," adding that they take "their peculiar accidental type from the prevalent fashion." Following Tylor and others, he saw them as "survival[s] of a state to which increasing knowledge and self-control must put an end." While conceding that such phenomena might "occur to those who are under the influence of that SPIRIT," he viewed self-control as the higher virtue, claiming that "the Bible teaches that we should never lose our self-control under the influence of any religious emotion whatsoever."[161]

In these debates over the nature of the power, physicians, especially neurologists, and holiness advocates held diametrically opposed views, the former viewing the trance phenomena as pathological and the latter as the Spirit of God. The accounts in the St. Louis papers and the Methodist *Christian Advocate* suggest that there was a significant middle ground between these two extremes. This position was secularizing in its approach to the trance phenomena, while at the same time often sarcastically critical of the pathological explanations of the physicians. It was rooted in a knowledge of the popular psychology and popular religion of the nineteenth century, which while viewing "trance" as abnormal, in the sense of being unusual, did not view it as inherently pathological. This awareness allowed the *Post-Dispatch* to proclaim that "all the learned talk of hypnotism is stuff and non-sense—mere quackery," while the *Globe-Democrat* could assert that "all the learned talk about its [religious trance's] danger to public health and safety may be dismissed as idle words."[162]

The papers also revealed the variety of views held by those who attended Woodworth's meetings. The reporter for the *Post-Dispatch* described himself as "thoroughly mystified" by the Woodworth revival he attended. Those he interviewed offered a range of perspectives. The State Evangelist for the Y.M.C.A., who had just come to observe, said he had not seen anything like it and that it was beyond his comprehension. "It must be," he said, "that the people who go into that state are led into it by their imagination and the force of will stronger than their own." A "colored pastor" from North St. Louis said "that he had seen such things in his church but they were indulged in only by the more ignorant." A practicing physician, whose little girl had fallen into trance, when asked whether he thought "it [was] injurious to [his] daughter to go into such a state," replied: "No, I do not. She feels better afterwards and likes to see the beautiful things. She seems stronger afterwards even. I do not think it has a debilitating effect." The reporter closed with a description of the butcher's daughter lying in trance on a bench. "Her face wore a beatific smile and she seemed more like an ethereal spirit in the uncertain flickering of the electric light than like a human being."[163]

These journalists, whether writing for secular or denominational papers, demonstrated an ability to comprehend the viewpoint of Woodworth and her followers, while nonetheless presenting a range of explanations of her revivals. Whether this was the result of their own sympathies, the necessity of conducting interviews, the demands of a mass-circulation, or a sense of professional standards, the journalists demonstrated an ability to engage critically, while representing a point of view not their own. In an editorial published during Woodworth's trial, the *Post-Dispatch* provided a remarkable example of detached, yet sympathetic analysis.

> The manifestation of what Mrs. Woodworth calls the power of the Spirit is not a new thing. It is an important element in the religious belief and practice of a large section of the church militant. It accompanies to a greater or lesser extent all the efforts of the so-called revivalists and evangelists. . . . The singing of monotonous songs, the repeated exhortations, the excitement of a throng wrought up to an intense devotional phrensy are depended upon for results of which trances, vision-seeing and strange nervous involuntary action are common examples. They are regarded by those who engage in such devotional exercises as evidence of divine power directly and actively exerted, and any attack upon them is resented as attacks upon religion. The charge that such phenomena are due to mental excitement or mesmerism, and its influence upon the nervous system[,] is laid to skepticism.[164]

The controversy surrounding Woodworth's revivals in St. Louis suggests that "non-experts" did not cede the subject of trance to the "experts," much as the neurologists wanted them to. Many voices found their way into the pages of the St. Louis newspapers, including those of neurologists, mesmerists, ministers, and people who attended Woodworth's revivals. Those who attended the revivals no less than those who observed from a distance contested the revivals' meaning and the newspapers allowed these different views to surface in their coverage. The dominant view, propounded by reporters and respectable Protestants, drew on a widespread familiarity with popular religion and popular psychology to argue that such phenomena were common in the history of religion and could be explained in terms of trance and mental excitement. The newspaper coverage, however, revealed considerable familiarity not only with the popular psychology of animal magnetism and trance, but also with the latest views of neurologists on hypnotism and hysteria. The papers, moreover, evinced skepticism regarding the experts' warnings about the revivals' threat to the health of individuals and the community. In marked contrast to the "experts," the newspaper reporters and editorialists attempted to convey the point of view of believers, even though they did not share them.

If the dominant tendency was to poke fun at the fears of the experts and support the right of Woodworth and her followers to their religious interpretation, most commentators nonetheless used popular psychology to explain the revival phenomena in secular terms. Although the newspapers downplayed the pathological, they still set scientific explanation and religious experience in opposition to one another. The Spiritualists' understanding of trance as the doorway to the other world—and thus their contention that scientific explanation and religious experience were compatible—was notably absent from the conversation. Nor were the new religious movements—Christian Science, Theosophy, and New Thought—visibly represented. As we will see in Part III, Christian Science and New Thought took a more prominent role in public discussions in the next twenty years as the mediating position between science and religion advocated by Spiritualists, Theosophists, and New Thought gained new respectability.

HYSTERICS AND TRANCE MEDIUMS

Two major research efforts initiated during the 1880s set the stage for the developments in Part III—those of neurologist Jean Martin Charcot at the Salpêtrière Hospital in Paris and those of the SPR in England. The former was known for research on hysteria, the latter for research on Spiritualism and psychical phenomena. Whereas the focus of the one was on medical pathology and the other on apparently normal religious and "occult" phenomena, both mediated the shift from the language of animal magnetism to the new clinical discourse of hypnosis and the subconscious.

During the late 1870s, Charcot began taking more of an interest in the cases of hysteria on his service. He approached hysteria as he had other neuropathological diseases, seeking to develop a model for organizing its symptoms. He gained international attention for his use of hypnosis as a means of experimentally replicating the symptoms of hysteria and, in the process, legitimated hypnosis as a tool for medical research. Charcot's approach to hysteria was almost entirely neurological. He assumed that in most cases there was an underlying organic lesion. Moreover, he assumed a close relationship between hysteria and hypnosis, basically maintaining that hypnosis was a manifestation of hysteria. During the 1880s and 1890s, Charcot's understanding of hypnosis was challenged by Hippolyte Bernheim, professor of medicine at Nancy, based on his clinical work and that of A. A. Liébeault. Highlighting the role of suggestion in hypnosis, they claimed that virtually all hypnotic phenomena up to and including somnambulism could be induced in mentally normal individuals. Late in his career, Charcot began considering psychogenic explanations for hysteria, largely as a consequence of collaboration with Pierre Janet, the most psychologically minded of his students. Despite his basically nonpsychological approach, Charcot, according to historian Christopher Goetz, had "an avant-garde image among the younger generation of medical men and philosophers [such as Janet] who aspired to a 'new psychology' founded upon objective physiological data and methods."[165]

Charcot and especially some of his associates epitomized the materialistic approach to religion. In collaboration with his associates Bourneville and Richter, Charcot published volumes that retrospectively diagnosed instances of possession and ecstasy as cases of hysteria. Many of their patients, moreover, were young women who had been brought up in convent schools and had been through periods of intense religious involvement. Their experiences, both past and present, were diagnosed as manifestations of hysteria. Although Charcot valued the demystifying role that hysteria could play with regard to miracles, visions, and ecstatic experiences, his associates were responsible for generating the cruder and more blatantly anticlerical attacks associated with Charcot's name.[166] Late in life, Charcot wrote a little-known essay on faith healing that was uncharacteristically moderate in tone. In it, he acknowledged that some of the cures at Lourdes were well attested. He even admitted that he had sent some of his own patients, "intractable cases of nervous illness, from the Salpêtrière to Lourdes for treatment."[167]

Much of the secondary literature on the SPR emphasizes the connection between its aims and those of the Spiritualist movement, thus suggesting little common ground between the SPR and the research at the Salpêtrière. While admittedly many of its founders hoped that the new Society might be able to place the question of life after death on a firmer scientific footing, the aims of the SPR were actually much broader. Their stated objective was to investigate, in an organized and systematic way, "that large group of debatable phenomena designated by such terms as mesmeric, psychical, and Spiritualistic." In addition to phenomena associated with Spiritualism, research committees were established to investigate possible influences of one mind upon another; apparitions at the moment of death and haunted houses; and hypnotism, clairvoyance, and the "forms of so-called mesmeric trance." During the 1880s, the SPR investigated claims put forth by Theosophists, as well as Spiritualists. The Society also conducted a massive "census of hallucinations" to determine the incidence of visionary experiences in the normal population and test Charcot's assumption that all such phenomena were manifestations of hypnosis and hysteria. The *Proceedings* devoted many pages to reviews of literature in neurology and psychology and were largely responsible for bringing the new French experimental research on hypnosis and hysteria to the attention of an English-speaking audience.[168]

In contrast to the neurologists, both in the U.S. and Europe, the psychical researchers, most of whom had distinguished academic credentials, refused to assume a materialist stance *a priori*. With their focus on mesmeric, psychical, and Spiritualistic phenomena among presumptively normal persons in the general population, rather than hysterics in hospital wards, they formed a tenuous bridge between popular religion, neurology, and the new frontiers of experimental psychology. Those associated with the Society knew how tenuous the bridge was, and no one worked harder to secure its footings than William James. In "The Hidden Self," an essay published in *Scribner's Magazine* in 1890, James acknowledged that few things had "been treated with a more contemptuous scientific disregard than the mass of phenomena generally called *mystical*." Yet, he said, no matter where you look in the records of the past, "you find things recorded under the name of divinations, inspirations, demoniacal possessions, apparitions, trances, ecstasies, miraculous healings and productions of disease, and occult powers possessed by peculiar individuals over persons and things in their neighborhood." While most assume that "mediumship originated in Rochester, N.Y., and animal magnetism with Mesmer, . . . there was never a time," he said, "when these things were not reported as abundantly as now."[169]

James's aim was not to defend mysticism at the expense of science, but to mediate between them. In head-to-head debates between "Mystics and Scientifics," he claimed that "the Mystics . . . have usually proved to be right about the *facts*, while the Scientifics had the better of it in respect to the theories."[170] James's overarching agenda was comparative. Rather than pit the research of the French on hysterics against the SPR's research on mediums, James called for "*[a] comparative study of trances and sub-conscious states*."[171] James's attempt to mediate between the "Mystics and Scientifics" was entirely in keeping with the spirit of the SPR. As a quintessential mediating body, the SPR, like the early Spiritualists, attempted to bridge the worlds of science and religion. They did so, however, not in an era of popular religion and popular psychology, but at a time in which medicine, psychology, and theology were bent on establishing their credentials as modern professions. It was, in other words, a very different playing field. Nonetheless, over the course of the next two decades, the SPR played a crucial role in both formulating and disseminating the new concept of the subconscious. In their hands, the subconscious itself became a mediating concept.

PART THREE

Religion and the Subconscious, 1886–1910

10. Binet's "Graphic Method" for demonstrating the presence of a (co-conscious) secondary personality. Each pair of lines represents the simultaneous actions of the sensible and insensible arms of "an hysterical patient, hemi-anæsthetical on the left side." The simultaneous, yet distinctively different, action of the two arms was thought to demonstrate the presence of a co-conscious secondary personality. From Alfred Binet, *On Double Consciousness* (1889), 46–51.

WHEN PIERRE Janet received his *doctorat ès-lettres* from the Sorbonne in 1889, he was already well known in philosophical and psychological circles. Although his training was in the traditional field of philosophical psychology, his main thesis, based on his study of the "hysterical somnambule" Léonie, reflected his interest in the emerging field of experimental psychology. His preliminary report on Léonie in 1885 drew a series of distinguished visitors to the hospital at Le Havre, where she was a patient, including notables from the world of French neurology and Frederic Myers, A. T. Myers, and Henry Sidgwick from the Society for Psychical Research (SPR) in London. The results of Janet's experiments were published serially in the *Revue philosophique* between 1886 and 1889 and provided the basis for his thesis, *L'Automatisme psychologique*, published in 1889. Because of his interest in psychopathology, Janet then pursued a medical degree, spending much of his time examining patients in Charcot's neurology wards at the Salpêtrière.[1]

Janet's study of Léonie represents both a continuation of the older psychology of animal magnetism in the new and more respectable guise of hypnosis and the beginning of a new experimental psychology of the subconscious. Apparently unaware of the connection between hypnotism and mesmerism until he discovered that Léonie had been magnetized in the past, Janet began reading the writings of the animal magnetizers. There he found, as Ellenberger reports, that "everything taught by Charcot and Bernheim as amazing novelties has already been known to these obscure men."[2] Janet acknowledged this debt publicly in *L'Automatisme psychologique*, reminding his readers that "[e]xperimental psychology . . . began by being animal magnetism and spiritism" and admonishing them "not [to] forget this fact, nor laugh at our ancestors."[3] What set this new psychology off from the old was Janet's discovery that Léonie manifested simultaneously *co-existent* states of consciousness, which he referred to as "*secondary* selves."

The idea of the secondary self, as opposed to *alternating* (i.e., noncoexistent) personalities, which as we have seen were widely discussed in the era of animal magnetism, undergirded what Alan Gauld has referred to as the "golden age of the subconscious."[4] In an article on Léonie published in 1886, Janet provided the first widely acknowledged experimental evidence for such secondary selves.[5] William James referred to Janet's discovery in the *Varieties of Religious Experience* as "the most important step forward that has occurred in psychology since I have been a student of that science."[6] This basic discovery, which James attributed to Janet in the *Varieties* and, in other contexts, to Janet, Edmund Gurney, and Alfred Binet, marks the beginning of the golden age of the subconscious.[7] For the purposes of this narrative, it signals the decisive conceptual shift that informed the interaction between psychology and religion between 1886 and 1910.[8]

Janet's work had an important influence not only on French clinical research but also on an international group of researchers in England, the United States, and Switzerland who shared his interest in the experimental psychology of the subconscious.[9] Among the leading figures in this well-connected circle were, in addition to Pierre Janet and William James, the French psychologist Alfred Binet, the Swiss psychologist Théodore Flournoy, the British psychical researchers Frederic Myers and Edmund Gurney, and the American neurologist Morton Prince. Alan Gauld referred to this group collectively as the "Franglo-American school" and Eugene Taylor as the "French-Swiss-English-and-American psycho-therapeutic alliance."[10] In keeping with the French tradition of clinical research, these researchers had a particular interest in experimental case studies. Along with Léonie, the best known were the spiritualist mediums, Hélène Smith and Mrs. Piper, studied respectively by Théodore Flournoy and William James, and Miss Beauchamp, whose multiple personalities were studied by Morton Prince.[11]

Janet had a particularly strong following in the United States between 1896 and 1910. He made six extended trips to the United States, received several honorary degrees from American universities, and had close scientific friendships with a number of eminent psychologists and psychiatrists, including James, Prince, and others.[12] Most of the Americans who concerned themselves with the French clinical research were, like James, physicians associated with Harvard or working in the Boston area. This group, often referred to as the Boston school of psychotherapy, included in addition to James, Henry Pickering Bowditch, Richard Cabot, Morton Prince, James Jackson Putnam, and Boris Sidis. As physicians concerned with psychopathology, Prince, Putnam, and Sidis continued the French researchers' interest in multiple personality. Although most of the Boston group was involved to some degree with the American branch of the SPR, James was the only one with strong ties to both the SPR and the new academic psychology. None of the key British figures associated with the SPR—Henry Sidgwick, Edmund Gurney, Frank Podmore, or Frederic Myers—were physicians or academic psychologists; most had degrees in the humanities.[13]

Both in the emergence and in the later demise of the idea of the subconscious, there were two levels of potentially serious disagreement. The first level was between those who embraced the concept of the subconscious and those who rejected it. The second was between different conceptions of the subconscious. Those who rejected the idea of the subconscious altogether held that seemingly intelligent action could proceed physiologically without ever becoming conscious, while those who accepted the idea held that intelligent action was always linked to consciousness. Those who held the former view explained unremembered actions in terms of the theory of unconscious cerebration. Those who held the latter view explained unremembered actions in terms of memories that were either split-off from the primary center of consciousness or so fleeting as to be forgotten. Janet, Binet, Gurney, Myers, and James all rejected the theory of unconscious cerebration as inadequate in light of the experimental evidence of coexistent states of consciousness reported by Janet and later supplemented by the findings of Gurney and Binet. The theory of the subconscious, informed by the new research on secondary selves, was premised on the notion that consciousness was divisible. Janet referred to this as the *désagregation* of consciousness; James to the splitting off or dissociation of portions of consciousness.[14] The subconscious, in other words, presupposed a dissociative model of consciousness.

Those who accepted the dissociative model of consciousness assumed that selves were constituted by "chains of memory." While memories were "associated" within a chain, they were "dissociated" between chains. Through hypnosis, researchers engaged (and created) chains of memory that were dissociated from the chain of memory that constituted the person's usual sense of self.[15] This new model of the mind marked a distinct advance over the older theories of trance. La Roy Sunderland believed that the induction of particular mental states depended on associations between the state and the process believed to induce it. These associations were bodily memories or, as he said, habits. The new theory, in effect, postulated that chains of bodily memories, if sufficiently extensive and elaborate, could in turn constitute distinct selves or personalities. These dissociated memory chains, which could be tapped and extended by means of hypnosis and automatic writing, offered a theoretical model whereby two "selves" could coexist in one body. During this period, researchers elaborated on this basic dissociative model to explain phenomena, such as the growth and development of alleged discarnate spirits and the emergence of co-consciousness between alter personalities, that were well beyond the reach of Sunderland's theory.

Those who accepted the dissociative model disagreed about the conditions under which the splitting of consciousness could occur. Janet, who viewed all manifestations of a secondary self as symptomatic of hysteria and, thus, as inherently pathological, stood apart from Binet, Gurney, Myers, and James, all of whom believed that secondary centers of consciousness could exist in healthy persons. In this regard, Janet continued to reflect the views of his mentor, the neurologist Jean-Martin Charcot, while the views of the others reflected Charcot's rivals at Nancy as well as their own experimental work with healthy subjects.[16] Those who accepted the evidence for the dissociation or splitting of consciousness did not agree, in other words, as to what it entailed theoretically. The basic question was whether "all the phenomena of hypnotism, double consciousness, &c.," as Myers put it, could be explained "as mere morbid disaggregations of the empirical personality."[17] Was the healthy mind unified and the diseased or defective mind divided, as Janet maintained? Or was the mind, as Myers was to conclude, naturally "multiplex"? It was on this level, the level of theory, that James, generally speaking, allied himself with Myers rather than Janet.

Where Charcot and Janet viewed hypnosis as an abnormal state allied to hysteria, Myers viewed hypnotism as one of many ways of evoking the development of secondary personalities. Writing in 1889, he theorized that "each of us contain the potentialities of many different arrangements of the elements of our personality, each arrangement being distinguishable from the rest by differences in the chain of memories which pertains to it." The "normal or primary self . . . with which we habitually identify ourselves" consisted, according to Myers, of that part of the self selected (in the evolutionary sense) for its fitness in dealing with our "ordinary physical needs." Myers did not view it as "necessarily superior in any other respect to the latent personalities which lie along side it." Moreover, he said, "we can at present assign no limit . . . [to] the fresh combinations of our personal elements that may be evoked by accident or design." A variety of normal and pathological phenomena, according to Myers, might evoke such fresh combinations. Thus, he said, "dreams, with natural somnambulism, automatic writing, with so-called mediumistic trance, as well as certain intoxications, epilepsies, hysterias, and recurrent insanities, afford examples of the development of what I have called secondary mnemonic chains,—fresh personalities, more or less complete, alongside the normal state." Hypnotism, in this view, was simply a name "given to a group of empirical methods of inducing these fresh personalities,—of shifting the centres of maximum energy, and starting a new mnemonic chain."[18]

The concept of automatism provided Myers with the crucial link between the SPR's experiments on automatic writing and Janet's research on hysteria. Working by analogy, Myers argued in 1889 that "automatic writing is but one among a whole series of kindred automatisms which have been intermittently noted, divergently interpreted, since history began." James later referred to this as a "great simplification" that in one stroke placed "hallucinations and active impulses under a common head, as *sensory* and *motor automatisms*."[19] The common feature of automatisms in Myers's view lay in the fact that they were "*message-bearing* or *nunciative*." He did not mean by this that all such messages came from sources outside the mind of the automatist, although he wanted to leave open the possibility that they might in "some few cases." Rather, he assumed that most messages were communicated from one stratum of the personality to another. "Originating in some deeper zone of a man's being," he said, "they float up into superficial consciousness as deeds, visions, words, ready-made and full-blown, without any accompanying perception of the elaborate process which has made them what they are."[20] Automatisms took their place in Myers's fully developed theory of the self as the primary means of communication between the subliminal and supraliminal levels of consciousness. As such, they would play a central role in the psychological theory of religion articulated by James in his *Varieties of Religious Experience*.

Myers also developed his theory through a close reading of Janet's publications on Léonie. Although much of his commentary was highly enthusiastic, his critique focused on Janet's contention that Léonie's experiences were simply and completely pathological. Myers thought he saw evidence in Janet's discussions of Léonie to suggest that ecstasy was more than just a phase in a "hysterical attack." While he admitted that ecstasy did appear "along with other instabilities in the course of hysteria," he was inclined to the view that "ecstasy is to hysteria somewhat as genius is to insanity." Distinguishing between hypnosis and hysteria, Myers suggested that both genius and ecstasy had a positive relation to "hypnotic trance, with its liberation from petty preoccupations, its concentration in favourite channels."[21] To suggest a link between genius, ecstasy, and hypnotic trance was not, in Myers view, to equate ecstasy with hysteria.

In Léonie, or more precisely her secondary personality, Léonore, Myers thought he saw evidence to support this understanding. As Léonore, Léonie passed into what both Janet and Myers agreed was "plainly a state of so-called ecstasy." In it,

Myers wrote, "[s]he grows pale, she ceases to speak or to hear, her eyes, though still shut, are turned heavenward, her mouth smiles, and her face takes an expression of beatitude." But her state differed from that commonly seen in "hysterical attacks" not only because Léonore remembered it but because it brought with it "the most complex of all the chains of memory." This, Myers thought, confirmed a thesis he had already "hinted at," namely, "that the state of ecstasy, although generally associated with hysteria, . . . must not therefore be assumed to be *in itself* a morbid or degenerative condition, but that the possibility of entering it may be purchased by a perilous degree of nervous instability."[22] The idea that "a perilous degree of nervous instability" might provide entryway into ecstasy, and religious experience more generally, also appeared in the *Varieties*.

Myers unfolded his own fully developed alternative to Janet's theory of pathological *désagrégation* in a series entitled "The Subliminal Consciousness," published in the *Proceedings* between 1892 and 1894. Many of the central ideas had already appeared in his earlier articles on automatic writing and in his reviews of the French research. His explicit aim in these essays was to construct an alternative to the explanations of the French schools at Paris (hysteria) and Nancy (suggestion) by bringing together the research on hypnotic trance, automatic writing, alternations of personality, telepathy, and clairvoyance.[23] He summarized his alternative theory in a much-quoted paragraph:

> I suggest, then, that the stream of consciousness in which we habitually live is not the only consciousness which exists in connection with our organism. Our habitual or empirical consciousness may consist of a mere selection from a multitude of thoughts and sensations, of which some at least are equally conscious with those that we empirically know. I accord no primacy to my ordinary waking self, except that among my potential selves this one has shown itself the fittest to meet the needs of common life. I hold that it has established no further claim, and that it is perfectly possible that other thoughts, feelings, and memories, either isolated or in continuous connection, may now be actively conscious, as we say, 'within me,'—in some kind of co-ordination with my organism, and forming some part of my total individuality.[24]

Myers used the word "subliminal" to refer to all the "psychical action" occurring "below the threshold of our habitual consciousness." To call it " 'unconscious,' or even 'subconscious,' " he said, "would be directly misleading; and to speak (as is sometimes convenient) of the *secondary* self may give the impression either that there cannot be more than two, or that the *supraliminal* self, the self above the threshold,—the *empirical* self, the self of common experience—is in some way superior to other possible selves."[25]

Myers's primary contribution to the experimental psychology of the subconscious was not, in James's view, as an experimental researcher but as a theorist. His theory of the subliminal consciousness, as James noted, provided the chief alternative to Janet's theory of pathological mental *désagrégation*.[26] Although James was convinced that secondary centers of consciousness could exist in healthy persons through his observations of Mrs. Piper and his participation in the census of hallucinations conducted by the American branch of the SPR, Myers developed a theory to account for this evidence. In James's words, Myers made "the first attempt in our language, and the first thoroughly *inductive* attempt in any language, to consider the phenomena of hallucination, hypnotism, automatism, double personality, and mediumship as connected parts of one whole subject. No one seems to me to have grasped the problem in a way both so broad and so sober as he has done."[27]

Myers's theory of the subliminal self provided a new psychological framework for understanding a wide range of phenomena, including many religious phenomena, without reducing them to epiphenomena of psychopathology or necessarily ruling out influences beyond the self. When Myers began formulating his theory, he recognized that his explanation of the "trance of the automatist" was "by no means identical" with that of the Spiritualists, "who say that the writing medium is 'mesmerized by the controlling Spirit.'" He added, however, that "in putting forward this new explanation, which refers the trance to a mere change of cerebral equilibrium—a mere shifting of the psychical centre of energy within the personality of the automatist himself,—I do not mean to deny the possibility that some influence external to the writer's may at times be operative."[28] By placing the pathological, the normal, and the potentially supranormal within a common frame of reference, Myers created a theoretical space (the subliminal) through which influences beyond the individual, should they exist, might be expected to manifest themselves. In explaining spirit possession as a "shifting of the psychical center of energy *within the personality of the automatist himself*" without ruling out "the possibility that *some influence external* to the [automatist] may at times be operative," Myers modeled the open-ended approach to explanation that James later adopted in the *Varieties*.

In 1899, Théodore Flournoy published his book-length study of the spiritualist medium Hélène Smith, a detailed examination of the mythopoetic functions of the subliminal imagination and the first major attempt to account for spirit possession in strictly psychogenic terms. It was, in effect, the first major study of the growth and development of a religious "other," in this case an alleged discarnate spirit, from a psychological point of view. As Myers commented in his review, "the book . . . is indeed, for the most part, critically destructive in its treatment of the quasi-supernormal phenomena with which it deals." But, he added with obvious enthusiasm, "what a mass of conceptions a competent psychologist now takes for granted in this realm, which the official science of twenty years ago would scarcely stomach hinting at!"[29] James read the book "with loud exclamations of joy" and wrote his friend declaring that he thought "[his] volume had probably made the decisive step in converting psychical research into a respectable science."[30] More recently, Henri Ellenberger described it as a classic on a par with Freud's *Interpretation of Dreams*. Noting the importance of the mythopoetic aspect of the unconscious, Ellenberger lamented the fact that "with the exception of a few brilliant studies such as that by Flournoy about his medium Helen Smith, this mythopoetic function has not received the attention it deserves."[31]

Flournoy's volume was followed by the publication of James's Gifford Lectures, *The Varieties of Religious Experience*, in 1902 and Myers's posthumously published two-volume work, *Human Personality and Its Survival of Bodily Death* in 1903. These volumes, all of which were widely reviewed, brought "subliminal psychology" to the attention of both academic psychologists and the general public.[32] In the academic world, James's *Varieties* gave instant credibility to fledgling efforts in the psychology of religion and inspired the creation of a new subdiscipline bridging psychology and religion.

The last major contribution of this group of researchers was Morton Prince's *Dissociation of a Personality* (1905), an in-depth study of the multiple personalities of Clara Norton Fowler, a.k.a. "Miss Beauchamp." Each of Miss Beauchamp's personalities was defined by a distinct chain of memories and the relationship between the memories of the various personalities was complex. B II shared memories with B I who was amnesic for B II. Prince described B III, also known as Sally, as "co-conscious" with the others. While B I and B II were unaware of her, she was "aware of, or could tune into, what was going on in the minds of B I and B II, and thus had access to their past histories even if she did not exactly share their memories. She mentally intruded upon B I, forcing visions upon her and causing her to tell lies and perform socially unacceptable actions."[33] Although Prince interpreted her case in strictly psychological terms, the study sparked considerable discussion in religious circles. Some believed that "Sally" was a discarnate spirit who had lodged herself in Miss Beauchamp. James found in Sally's co-conscious relationship with Miss Beauchamp's other selves a model for how God might relate to humans.

By 1910 interest in the subconscious had begun to wane in elite circles. While Janet lectured in the United States in 1904 and 1906, Sigmund Freud was the center of attention at Clark University in 1909. Where some physicians initially supported the Emmanuel movement, a healing movement led by mainline Protestant clergy that drew on the psychology of the subconscious, they were largely united in their opposition after 1908. Where academic psychologists responded favorably to Flournoy's book in 1900, widespread discussion of the idea of the subconscious in psychology journals between 1903 and 1909 led to a resurgence of interest in "unconscious cerebration." As the new departments of psychology matured, they looked not to the hospital-affiliated clinics of France, but to the university-affiliated laboratories of Germany for inspiration. They identified experimental psychology with Wilhelm Wundt, not with Charcot or Janet and, in the words of historian Nathan Hale, "[t]o psychologists who prided themselves on their scientific Wundtian heritage the subconscious of the Boston school of psychotherapy, and of Josiah Royce and William James, represented a regression to the 'occultism' of the Middle Ages."[34]

In 1907, Hugo Münsterberg, James's colleague at Harvard, associated "the three dominant theories of the subconscious"—subliminal consciousness, pathological dissociation, and unconscious cerebration—with laymen, physicians, and psychologists, respectively.[35] The way in which Münsterberg mapped the field had the largely intended effect of dividing the proponents of the "experimental psychology of the subconscious" into different camps. Janet and Prince became physicians (which they were), despite the fact that Janet's appointment was in psychology; Myers became a layman; and Flournoy and James were left in academic limbo. In adopting a *physiological* interpretation of the subconscious and relegating the *psychological* interpretation of the subconscious to physicians and laymen, Münsterberg accurately depicted the direction that most academic psychologists would take. Although Jungian psychology retained many of the features of the pre-Freudian subconscious, Jung's thought was marginalized by a Freudian emphasis on repression rather than dissociation. Across the spectrum, the proponents of the subconscious were marginalized within disciplines they helped to found. James and Flournoy were largely written out of the history of experimental psychology, Janet out of psychiatry, and Jung out of psychoanalysis, while Myers and psychical research never really gained a foothold in the academy.

In Part III, I explore the efforts of the mediators, armed with an open-ended concept of the subconscious, to secure a foothold in academic psychology and mainline Protestantism. Chapter Seven focuses on the flowering of the psychology of religion in the academy and Chapter Eight on movements of spiritual renewal within turn-of-the-century Protestantism. Within the academic psychology of religion, I focus on two figures—William James and George Albert Coe—whose psychologies of religion, while working with many of the same "pieces," arranged them in sharply opposed configurations based on different understandings of the subconscious and of religion. In the final chapter, I contrast three renewal movements within turn-of-the-century Protestantism—the Emmanuel healing movement, Pentecostalism, and the religious education movement. While the mediating tradition flowered briefly within both the academy and the church during the first decade of the twentieth century, it was rapidly rebuffed by academics hostile to a religious interpretation of involuntary experiences within the universities and the theological schools. Nonetheless, religious interpretations of involuntary experiences remained very much in evidence at the popular level.

CHAPTER SEVEN

The Psychology of Religion

THE "NEW PSYCHOLOGY" emerged during the 1890s amidst a complex reshuffling of academic disciplines and medical specialties in Europe and the United States. The story of its emergence, as recounted in psychology textbooks, typically begins in Germany with Wilhelm Wūndt and the founding of a laboratory for experimental psychological research in Leipzig in 1879. In his *History of Experimental Psychology* (1929), Edwin Boring credited James with recognizing "the significance of the new experimental physiological psychology" emanating from Germany. He gave G. Stanley Hall, who studied with Wūndt, credit for pioneering everything new, from the psychological laboratory to educational psychology to the psychology of religion. During the 1890s, numerous professors, many of them students of Hall's at either Johns Hopkins or Clark University, were appointed to positions in psychology. The establishment of psychological laboratories, especially at the major universities, accompanied the appointment of faculty in the new discipline. Hall founded the *American Journal of Psychology* in 1887, initiated the formation of the American Psychological Association in 1892, and founded the *American Journal of Religious Psychology and Education* in 1904.[1]

The "New Psychology," in this reading of history, was part of the transformation of American higher education at the turn of the century. Prior to 1890, clergymen professors taught "mental and moral philosophy" as the capstone of the traditional liberal arts curriculum; after 1890, nonclergy taught "psychology" as part of the social science curriculum in the new secular university. Two features made psychology "new" in this telling of the tale: (1) its divorce from philosophy and, more broadly, from an academic curriculum in which all disciplines, including philosophy, were the handmaidens of theology; and (2) its embrace of the "laboratory," emblem of the experimental sciences and sign of its new status as a university discipline.

Wūndt and Hall played an equally prominent role in most accounts of the emergence of the subfield of the psychology of religion. In his textbook for theological students, W. B. Selbie credited Wūndt with opening the first psychological laboratory and giving "a great impetus to the application of psychology to the study of religion by his own contributions to the psychology of early mythological and religious ideas." But, he went on to say, "it is the Americans who are the real pioneers in the psychology of religion proper." He described Stanley Hall as the first to write on the psychology of religion (1891) and as the founder of a school that focused particular attention on adolescence, especially in relation to "education both religious and general." Hall was followed, according to Selbie, by "a brilliant succession of writers," including James H. Leuba, Edwin Starbuck, Edward Scribner Ames, George A. Coe, George M. Stratton, William James, and

James Bissett Pratt. The "salient characteristic of this American school," he wrote, "is a careful study of the phenomena of religious experience derived mainly from biographies, introspection, and a systematic use of the questionnaire." The Americans, he added, are inclined to "emphasize the abnormal" and "obscure the line of demarkation (sic) between psychology and philosophy." Although he credited James's *Varieties of Religious Experience* with giving "a fresh stimulus to the study of the psychology of religion in Germany," he found some truth in Wundt's statement that the "*Varieties of Religious Experience* is not psychology at all, but rather an extract from a pragmatic philosophy of religion."[2]

In the most recent and most historically oriented of contemporary textbook introductions to the psychology of religion, David M. Wulff surveys the three main traditions in the modern psychology of religion—the Anglo-American, German, and French—and indicates that "it was in the United States that the psychology of religion first gained momentum." He notes the connections between it and the spirit of reform permeating both the social sciences and liberal Protestantism at the turn of the century. He cites George Coe, the Clark school (Stanley Hall and his students Edwin Starbuck and James Leuba), and William James and his student James Pratt as the leading figures. Wulff lifts up Starbuck's work as most characteristic of the Clark school, noting its focus on religious development and conversion, both interests of Hall's, and Starbuck's "commitment to gathering facts in the largest number possible and then to quantifying them in order to reveal general trends." This, he says, was "the distinguishing feature of both the Clark school and, to this day, of American psychology of religion."[3] While recognizing that James drew upon Starbuck's questionnaires for the *Varieties*, Wulff notes that James selected out "relatively rare" and more extreme cases. He acknowledges that despite "widespread criticism—principally for the pathological extremity of its cases—the *Varieties* rapidly became known worldwide as the leading contribution to the field." Wulff concludes, however, that the influence of the *Varieties* was "largely general . . . for in it *James elaborated neither a specific theory nor a particular method*, beyond the judicious use of personal documents. He provided instead the first clear example—albeit perhaps an imperfect one—of the descriptive approach to religious phenomena."[4]

The flowering of the psychology of religion movement makes little theoretical or methodological sense when viewed in relation to the triumph of German laboratory science in psychology departments across America. Boring, however, provided the basis for an alternative reading when he noted that James not only baptized the German experimentalism, but also Americanized the new psychology by "emphasizing the functional meaning of the mind." To all appearances America was duplicating German laboratory psychology, but Boring indicated that under the surface and quite unrecognized at first, a distinctively American functional psychology began to emerge. It flowered, according to Boring, at the University of Chicago under the influence of John Dewey, "where philosophers and psychologists were working together."[5] In contrast to the psychologists with a German orientation, Dewey, James, and most of the early American psychologists of religion taught not in freestanding psychology departments, but in philosophy departments that included philosophy, psychology, and sometimes education.[6] Methodologically, turn-of-the-century psychology of religion comes into focus only if situated in relation to this distinctively American functional psychology, broadly interpreted to include James, Dewey, and other lesser known figures, all of whom were linked by an outlook that was simultaneously empirical, functionalist, evolutionary, and pragmatic.[7]

Boring, as Eugene Taylor notes, left a great deal of the history of psychology out of his influential textbook. Among other things, he did not mention the contributions of the French clinical tradition of experimental psychology or of the impact of theories of the subconscious on developments in the United States. Nor, as Taylor points out, did he give any clues as to "why experimental psychology was equated with psychical research in the minds of the American public between 1880 and 1910." The psychology that Boring describes as distinctively American was not, as Taylor has cogently argued, simply a home-grown product, but must be viewed in relation to the French clinical tradition in experimental psychology and the British Society for Psychical Research (SPR). Theoretically, the emergence of the psychology of religion makes little sense unless viewed in relation to the experimental psychology of the subconscious.[8]

In short, I argue, contrary to Wulff, that James in fact had both a particular method and a specific theory and that the former cannot be understood apart from James's pragmatic functionalism or the latter apart from the experimental psychology of the subconscious. Indeed, I suggest that the psychology of the subconscious provided the theoretical underpinnings for most of the significant contributions to the psychology of religion during its most fertile period, although the contributors differed both in their understanding of the theory and its implications for religion. This approach foregrounds what I take to be the psychology of religion's most significant contribution to the study of religion, that is, the application of a dissociative model of consciousness to a wide range of religious phenomena, including possession, conversion, the bodily phenomena of revivals, visions, and mysticism. The dissociative psychology of religion of this era stands in evident continuity with the earlier mesmeric psychology of religion, both theoretically and with respect to the range of ways in which psychological explanation and religious faith were conjoined.

Within the academic psychology of religion, I focus on two figures—William James and George Albert Coe—who, while working with many of the same intellectual components, arranged them in sharply opposed configurations based on different understandings of the subconscious and of religion. Both their psychologies of religion provided implicit rereadings of the traditional Methodist understanding of religious experience. James explained it and religious experience in general as the result of incursions of the subliminal self into consciousness, whereas Coe cast it as an evolutionary precursor to a modernist understanding of Christianity. In keeping with the romantic tradition, James attempted to integrate religion, specifically religious experience, with an empirical approach to psychology. Although more theoretically sophisticated and academically respectable than the psychologies associated with the universalistic new religions—Spiritualism,

Theosophy, and New Thought—James's psychology of religion can be located in the same genre.[9] Coe, like many rationalists before him, used the psychology of the subconscious to explain primitive (i.e., false) religion, while rooting his modernist theology in the psychology of consciousness.

EXPLAINING CONVERSION

Viewed from the perspective of the subconscious, two widely noted characteristics of the early-twentieth-century psychologists of religion still stand out: their notable interest in the psychology of conversion and their ties to liberal Protestantism. These common features, however, obscure important underlying differences. Indeed, the nature of their ties to liberal Protestantism might be examined as one context for understanding the differences between their psychologies of religion. Here I focus particularly on James and Coe, not because they represent the others, but because, through their lives and their writings, they exemplified two common strategies that liberal Protestants and former Protestants used to distance themselves from their evangelical heritage at the turn of the century.

Neither had a traditional Christian conversion experience. Coe (to borrow James's language) was a classic healthy-minded, once-born soul, who discounted the need for a distinct experience of conversion; James, although not exactly "twice-born," clearly placed himself among the "sick souls" of the world. He saw transformative value in the traditional Protestant conversion experience and abstracted from it to create a generic, universal understanding of the process. In formulating their understanding of conversion, both James and Coe drew upon a dissociative model of consciousness and both built upon the work of Edwin Starbuck.

Edwin Starbuck

Historians usually describe Starbuck as Hall's student, since he earned his Ph.D. under Hall at Clark. In terms of his formation as a psychologist of religion and in terms of his life-long orientation toward the psychology of religion, however, Starbuck might better be understood as a student of William James. A more accurate understanding of Starbuck's relationship to his teachers—James, Hall, and Münsterberg—illuminates both the rivalries among the leading figures in psychology and the role that James and the subconscious played in the development of the psychology of religion beginning in the early 1890s.

Starbuck's graduate career began at Harvard in 1893, when he enrolled as a student in the philosophy department. He chose Harvard because its courses in religion seemed the "most dispassionate" and because of the "great constellation of outstanding men in philosophy and psychology." James had begun teaching the "new psychology" in the philosophy department in 1874, while still holding an appointment in physiology. His graduate course, "The Relations between Physiology and Psychology," marked the first shift away from a strictly philosophical approach to the study of psychology. James was allowed to teach his first purely philosophical course in 1879, and his appointment was formally changed from physiology to philosophy in 1880. During the 1890s, faculty taught courses in philosophy, sociology, experimental laboratory psychology, and comparative religions under the auspices of the philosophy department. Münsterberg took over the teaching of experimental laboratory psychology from James when he was appointed in 1892, freeing James to teach courses in philosophy, philosophical psychology, and psychopathology. James offered a course in the psychology of religion only once, in 1902.[10]

Starbuck took three psychology courses at Harvard, two with Münsterberg and one with James. As there were no courses in the psychology of religion at that time, he pursued what was to become his central interest outside of his course work. "The central guiding principle was that the study must deal *primarily with the first-hand religious experience of individuals*, not so much with their *theories* about religion as with their actual *experiences*" (emphasis in original). In order to get at first-hand experience, Starbuck developed a series of questionnaires on conversion, the breaking of habits, and religious development, which he began circulating in 1893. James took an interest in his work and, given the controversial nature of the research, signed a copy of the questionnaire to indicate that it was being circulated with his approval. Münsterberg, according to Starbuck, was "moderately impatient" with the whole idea of the psychology of religion. Although Starbuck found him helpful in relation to his laboratory research, "when it came to seeking some suggestions about the study of religion he was antagonistic and finally explosive. He declared that his problems were those of psychology, while mine belonged to theology, and that they had nothing to do with each other."[11]

When it became clear that he could not complete a doctorate in the psychology of religion at Harvard owing to the lack of courses, Starbuck transferred to Clark. Although he did so specifically to continue his research in the psychology of religion, he reported that Hall "made vigorous and persistent efforts to draft me off into some other area of interest," saying "that orange I had sucked dry." At the same time, Starbuck said, Hall was "assembling periodically a half-dozen students . . . picturing the possibilities of the application of psychology to religion and saying that the next ten years at Clark University might well be devoted to studies in that field." He also indicated that on his first visit to Clark, he learned that "a Clark student had issued without acknowledgement a syllabus which was almost a reproduction of [his] original one on conversion." He learned, too, that Hall himself "had prepared a revision of [Starbuck's] . . . four-page questionnaire [on religious development] which he was about to issue."[12] Although Starbuck expressed his appreciation for Hall in a number of instances, he described him as "hungry . . . for prestiges and priorities." According to Starbuck, "[h]e never ceased to claim precedence in the psychology of religion or imply it in writing."[13]

Although Hall made a number of dubious claims, he is rightfully known for his work on adolescence, and research on the links between adolescence and conversion were central to the work of Hall and his students at Clark. Hall claimed priority in the psychology of religion based on an 1881 lecture series, which, in his words, "attempt[ed] to demonstrate that adolescence was the age of religious impressibility in general, and of conversion in particular."[14] Starbuck's work on conversion, as Hall probably recognized, was only partially encompassed under this rubric, however. In discouraging Starbuck from continuing the research he had begun at Harvard, Hall probably sought to bring Starbuck more fully into his orbit and to undercut the influence of William James. James's interests in psychopathology and psychical research, already apparent in the 1890s, foreshadowed an entirely different starting point for the psychological study of religion.

The theoretical and methodological ties between James and Starbuck were readily acknowledged by both. First, both agreed that "the [psychological] study [of religion] must deal *primarily with the first-hand religious experience of individuals*, not so much with their *theories* about religion as with their actual *experiences*" (emphasis in original). Starbuck did not indicate whether this was his idea or James's (or one presupposed by a number of faculty in the department), but it certainly sounds like the approach James would have promoted. Second, James not only supported Starbuck's use of questionnaires as a research tool, Starbuck shared his questionnaires with James and James drew upon them in writing the *Varieties*. James wrote a preface for Starbuck's *Psychology of Religion* (1900), in which he acknowledged that his reading of Starbuck's manuscript and "a large proportion of his raw material" had allayed his skepticism regarding the use of questionnaires and amply justified Starbuck's own confidence in his methods. Third, Starbuck described three sets of "consistencies" that he saw emerging from his questionnaire data before he left Harvard for Clark: "the piling up of age frequencies near pubescence; likeness of the phenomena of conversion and those attending the breaking of habits; the signs of the dissociation of personality and its recentering, not unlike the split-personality experiences described by James, Prince, and Janet."[15] In his *Psychology of Religion*, Starbuck used "subliminal" and "subconscious" interchangeably and drew on James's *Principles of Psychology* to argue that "*spontaneous awakenings* [i.e., conversions] *are . . . the fructification of that which has been ripening within the subliminal consciousness*" (PR, 107–8).

George Coe

The son of a Methodist minister, George Coe spent his childhood in parsonages in the small towns of upstate New York and attended the University of Rochester. He then pursued his graduate studies at Boston University, initially intending to follow his father into the ministry, only to be told by three different professors during his first year that he was " 'cut out for' a professor, specifically a professor of systematic theology." During his four years of study in Boston, he gradually turned from theology to philosophy, rejecting what he viewed as the apologetic presuppositions of theology for science and historical criticism. Toward the end, he worked most closely with the Methodist philosopher Borden Parker Bowne, concluding in the end that Bowne's philosophy was "in reality theological apologetics" as well. Through further study in Germany and unnamed contacts in the

U.S., Coe pondered the challenge that Herbert Spencer's theory of social evolution posed for the religious understanding of human nature, a challenge that preoccupied Bowne (and James). Coe ultimately parted company with Bowne over the issue of empirical research. Bowne, in Coe's words, "treated as superfluous or worse the endeavours, then beginning, to develop a scientific psychology." Soon after Coe was hired to teach philosophy at Northwestern in 1891, he introduced a course in "physiological psychology" and established a psychological laboratory.[16]

Coe, like Starbuck, published an important empirical study of conversion in the late 1890s, which was shortly thereafter incorporated into a book-length study. Coe's article, an empirical study of the conversion experiences of 74 predominantly Methodist college students (50 male and 24 female), appeared in 1899, two years after Starbuck's. Their books—Starbuck's *Psychology of Religion* and Coe's *The Spiritual Life*—both appeared in 1900 and were frequently reviewed together as the leading examples of the new psychology of religion. Coe built explicitly on Starbuck's work, using questionnaires not only to elicit information about conversion but also about the student's personality. The questionnaires were supplemented with personal interviews, observation by Coe and others, interviews with friends and acquaintances of the students, and, "in order to get at the facts of suggestibility, hypnotic experiments . . . upon all the important cases that were accessible."[17] Over half the students in Coe's sample had had a dramatic conversion experience and more than a quarter experienced "mental and motor automatisms," i.e., the striking dreams, visions, or involuntary bodily movements associated with old-time Methodism. When the study appeared as a chapter in *The Spiritual Life*, Coe added that he had found "the same general results in an examination of scores of cases of seeking for the experience commonly called 'entire sanctification' " (*SL*, 105).

In the book, Coe also explained the "striking psychic manifestations which reach their climax among us in emotional revivals, camp meetings, and negro services," describing them as "essentially hypnotic and hallucinatory." Variously referred to in Methodist circles as "trances, visions, [and] the 'Power [of the Spirit]'," such experiences were common, he indicated, albeit in different forms, throughout the history of religion. He gave a number of examples, adding that "all these and a multitude of similar phenomena were produced by processes easily recognized by any modern psychologist as automatic and suggestive" (*SL*, 141). These were not new explanations, as we have seen, and although they located him within a tradition of psychological interpretation that went back to the animal magnetizers, they were not what set his book apart.

Coe's concern was less with those who had had traditional conversion experiences than those who expected to have such experiences and did not. As he put it, "why is it that of two persons who have had the same bringing up, and who seek conversion [or sanctification] with equal earnestness, one is ushered into the new life with shoutings and blowing of trumpets, as it were, while the other, however earnestly he may seek such experiences, never attains them at all[?]" (*SL*, 104). This was, of course, Coe's own question. Coe grew up with a traditional Methodist understanding of the importance of religious experience. When he was young, he said, Methodists "laid great store by 'testimony' to a 'personal experience' of 'conversion' and 'witness of the Spirit' or 'assurance' that one had been pardoned and 'accepted' of God." Like many of his modernist peers, he never had a conversion experience.[18] This absence provoked considerable distress and he turned without success to his father's library in search of answers. While an undergraduate at the University of Rochester, he finally "cut the knot by a rational and ethical act." Convinced, like Phoebe Palmer, that it was his duty to "commit [himself] to the Christian way of life" by an act of will, whether or not he received the "internal 'witness' or 'assurance,' " he did so. Although he never received the "internal witness," this act brought an end to his emotional turmoil. It also, in his words, "started a habit of looking for the core of religious experience in the ethical will; moreover, it led on towards endeavours to explain the experiences that some had while I did not have them."[19]

Coe's distinctive contribution and the "chief interest of the volume," as Starbuck noted in his review, was its focus on "temperament, both as a factor in the variety of religious experiences and in the determination of the peculiar types of religious expression."[20] Actually, Coe argued that there were "three sets of factors [that] favor the attainment of a striking religious transformation—the temperament factor, the factor of expectation, and the tendency to automatism and passive suggestibility" (SL, 504). Coe used two different schemas for describing temperament: division according to the predominant faculty (i.e., sensibility [emotion], intellect, and will) and division according to the promptness and intensity of mental processes (i.e., rapid-strong [choleric], rapid-weak [sanguine], slow-strong [melancholic], and slow-weak [phlegmatic]). He found that those for whom emotion was the predominant faculty and those whose mental processes were melancholic or sanguine were likely to have dramatic conversion experiences. Those for whom intellect was the predominant faculty and those whose mental processes were choleric (i.e., oriented toward practical action) were not. Those least likely to experience a sudden conversion, in other words, were intellectuals with an orientation toward practical action, that is, people like Coe himself.

Although this was the first empirical study that attempted to demonstrate a correlation between temperament and religious experience, temperamental differences had not gone unnoticed even in holiness circles. Coe quoted a Methodist minister who told him that there were "two distinct classes of members" in his church, "a group of substantial persons of high character and agreeable conduct, who support the enterprises of the church with their money, but are rarely or never seen at prayer meeting . . . [and] a class of members who can be relied upon to be present at the prayer meeting, who would rush to the altar to pray with a sinner, and who, if he should rise shouting, would scarcely know whether they were in the body or out of the body" (SL, 216). Coe commented that, without being aware of it, the minister had made a clear distinction between two temperamental groups. "On the one side he ranged the members of his flock who manifest either the melancholic or the sanguine characteristics in excess, and confessed that the spiritual exercises of his church appealed almost exclusively to them. On the other side he ranged the more choleric and more balanced characters, against whom, it appears, there lies a suspicion of defective spirituality" (*SL*, 216–17). This temperamental difference, Coe claimed, was what "distinguishes holiness movements from the ordinary life of the churches. A holiness band or sect that separates itself from the general life of the church is organized and held together chiefly by temperamental affinities. . . . It is no more possible for the generality of Christians to attain the ecstasy or maintain the exalted serenity often proclaimed as their privilege than it is for them all to feel drawn toward the life of monks, nuns, and hermits" (*SL*, 217).

Coe articulated a conclusion that was to become a commonplace in the psychology of religion. In everyday language, it would find a place in (usually disparaging) references to "emotional religion" and "emotional" experiences, where what was coded as "emotional" was the traditional sort of Methodist conversion experience. Coe's use of the term "emotional" was evaluative rather than descriptive. As he acknowledged, he used the word not to refer to the emotional coloring that accompanied all aspects of life, but to refer to what he took to be "feeling for its own sake." Thus, he says, "when we speak of emotional temperament, emotional novels, emotional religious meetings, and the like, what we really have in mind is not merely the abundance of emotion, but also the quality." In analyzing the hymns and prayer-meeting songs associated with Methodism, he was concerned to identify those that promoted "introspection, subjectivity, [and] self-consciousness," on the one hand, and those that promoted "practical activities and interests and facts," on the other (*SL*, 219–21). When he described traditional Methodism as "emotional," he targeted its alleged one-sided emphasis on subjective experience. Coe's research thus recast the traditional Methodist understanding of religious experience, such that signs of "the power of God" or "the witness of the Holy Spirit" became mere manifestations of a particular temperament.

William James

James devoted seven of the *Varieties*' twenty lectures to the subject of conversion. In Lectures 4–7, he introduced the distinction between the religion of the "healthy-minded" and "sick-souls," the former undergoing the gradual conversion associated with the "once-born" and the latter the sudden conversion of the "twice-born." He then elaborated on the process of sudden conversion in his lectures on "The Divided Self, and the Process of Unification" and "Conversion." In the lecture on Conversion, he referred extensively to the work of Starbuck and Coe, building on Starbuck's discussion of the subliminal and Coe's correlations between sudden conversion, suggestibility, and automatisms (195–96). Like Coe, James associated sudden conversion experiences particularly, but not exclusively, with Methodism. He thought that most Protestants set little store by "instantaneous conversion," allowing "ordinary religious duties . . . to suffice for his salvation." For Methodists, he said, this was not enough. For them, there must be an "acute crisis of self-despair and surrender followed by relief." Without this, "salvation is only offered, not effectively received, and Christ's sacrifice in so far forth is incomplete" (186).

Although James acknowledged Coe's findings on temperament, he nonetheless found psychological value in sudden conversion experiences that Coe did not. In emphasizing sudden conversion, "Methodism," he stated, "surely here follows, if not the healthier-minded, yet on the whole the profounder instinct. The individual models which it has set up as typical and worthy of imitation are not only the more interesting dramatically, but psychologically they have been the more complete" (186). James even went so far as to lift up Borden Parker Bowne, the well-known liberal Methodist philosopher under whom Coe had studied, to illustrate the "shallowing effects" of the intellect on religion. In a line quoted enthusiastically by holiness theologians, James encouraged his readers to "[s]ee how the ancient spirit of Methodism evaporates under those wonderfully able rationalistic booklets of a philosopher like Professor Bowne."[21]

In an exchange of letters written while he was writing the *Varieties*, James chided Bowne saying, "I myself have enough of old Lutheran sentiment in my bones to believe that you are too unsympathetic with the mystical needs of man in making as light as you do of the theological symbols in which they have clothed themselves. It seems to me that extravagance of some sort is essential to the *direct* religious life."[22] In his manuscript notes, he came back to Bowne as he struggled to clarify his aim in writing the *Varieties*. "Bowne's attitude," he noted, "is sensible and prosaic. The more original religious life is always lyric . . . and its essence is . . . to feel an invisible order . . . [wherein] the common sense values really vanish." There is, he concluded, "[a] genuine antagonism between commonsense religion like Bowne's and that of the more extravagant prophets of whatever kind. Each is foolish to the other, for each lives in the light of a different world."[23] The religion that interested James, as Ralph Barton Perry observed, "was closer to the simple piety of the evangelical sects than to that of modern religious liberalism."[24]

From James's perspective, Coe was clearly a healthy-minded, once-born soul, who, like his former teacher, had distanced himself in a sensible and prosaic way from the religion of his childhood and not, like James, a one-time "sick soul" with a vicarious attraction to old-time Methodism. James, of course, was not and never had been a Methodist. His family, at least on his father's side, were Scots-Irish Presbyterians. James's father, whose enormous influence on his son has been analyzed at length, dropped out of Princeton Theological Seminary and had a dramatic and ostensibly sudden conversion to Swedenborgianism in 1844. Although James rejected his father's Swedenborgianism, most James scholars agree that William's struggle to find his vocation during the 1870s and 1880s involved a complex process of accommodation to and differentiation from his father. Intellectually, as Mark Schwehn has argued, that involved developing a view of consciousness that, counter to the materialistic science of his day, had a legitimate place for religious experiences such as his father's. James's more or less playful identification with Methodism may well have been a stand-in for what surely would have been a far more problematic identification with his father's Swedenborgianism.[25]

In a letter to James Leuba, written in 1904, James claimed that he had "no living sense of commerce with a God" and envied those who did. "The Divine," he said, "is limited to impersonal and abstract concepts which, as ideals, interest and determine me, but do so but faintly in comparison with what a feeling of God might effect, if I had one." At most, he was willing to describe himself as having a "mystical germ" of experience, the embryonic form but not the fully realized thing. The key to his disclaimer lies, I think, in his sense of his own experience as "impersonal and abstract" and thus as a faint version of what he took to be the real "feeling of God." This sense of distance was rooted, I suspect, in his own ambivalence toward Christianity (and his father's Swedenborgianism). As he said to Leuba: "I have grown so out of Christianity that entanglement therewith on the part of a mystical utterance has to be *abstracted from and overcome* before I can listen."[26] This sense that the mystical utterance had to be abstracted and disentangled from the tradition before it could "speak" to him points to the strategic alternative represented by the *Varieties*. Whereas Coe distanced himself from the traditional Methodist understanding of conversion altogether, James sought to abstract what he took to be its mystical core in order that it might continue to engage him.

MAKING RELIGIOUS EXPERIENCE

The *Varieties* as a whole has been read in any number of ways. Here I interpret it as the quintessential theoretical expression of the mediating tradition between psychology and religion. With the publication of the *Varieties*, William James constituted "religious experience" in a technical sense as an object of study, defining it as a generic "something" that informed "religion-in-general" apart from any tradition in particular.[27] He did so empirically, abstracting that which he identified as religious experience from the particular contexts in which it had been embedded and linking these diverse experiences together theoretically by means of the experimental psychology of the subconscious. To do this, James drew on first-person accounts from a variety of traditions, although the majority of his selections were from Protestant evangelicals. James's efforts can be located in relation to the philosophy of religion, particularly the phenomenology of religion; Protestant supernaturalism; and secular scientific (positivist) understandings of religion.

Ernst Troeltsch, who described James as having made "the first thorough-going contribution from America to the philosophy of religion," pointed out that James had much in common with his European counterparts. Both were committed, Troeltsch said, to "a true *philosophy* of religion, that is to say not a one sided sectarian or theological treatment of the subject." Contrasting the philosophy of religion with "the theology of the churches," he said that the former sets out "from the whole wide field of religious phenomena," whereas the latter begins "from a given theological norm." The goal of the theologian is set by "outside authority or dogma," but the philosopher of religion "compares and appraises the phenomena with entire freedom, according to a standard which the philosopher himself has first to discover and justify." Although the philosopher of religion, according to Troeltsch, did not assume the "supernaturalism of the church," he was quick to point out, in light of James's professed "piecemeal supernaturalism," that his was not the supernaturalism of the churches. "Supernaturalism is for him . . . no exclusive attribute of Christianity, but pertains to every religion, and simply means the repudiation of rationalism and monism with their faith in law."[28]

The chief difference between James and the Europeans, according to Troeltsch, lay in the latter's commitment to Platonic or Neoplatonic rationalism and the former's commitment to an anti-Platonic radical empiricism. Both, he said, understood religion in relation to consciousness, but they understood consciousness in very different ways. The Europeans, according to Troeltsch, presupposed an "*a priori* unity of consciousness" and a "connection between contingent individual consciousness and consciousness in general." They understood that which approximated this universal consciousness in the individual as the "essence of religion." James began with a psychological understanding of consciousness as "a stream of psychophysical occurrences, not to be limited and not to be resolved, a bundle of continuous experience in constant motion, which, starting from some physical stimulus, pass on through mental activity, and are discharged in action." In this conception, consciousness was not necessarily unified and there was no essence of religion.[29] This meant, Troeltsch said, that "James is more than the religious psychologist who has added a new field to the philosophy of religion. He is, by the very act of making the philosophy of religion into a psychology of religion, the representative of an altogether opposite type of the philosophy of religion." Starting from the premise of a unitary essence, the European philosophy of religion, according to Troeltsch, "seeks to comprehend the historical stages of evolution as teleological, James knows the varieties only as psychological variations, in every case dependent on general psychical condition and nervous constitution."[30]

While James, like other philosophers of religion, was oriented toward the "whole wide field of religious phenomena," his primary concern was not with the comparative study of religion, but with the relationship between religion and science and, more narrowly, religion and psychology. James viewed the *Varieties* as a contribution to the "Science of Religion," but he rejected what he described as "the sectarian scientist's attitude," rooted, he believed, in their secularized Platonism.[31] Although James, like they, sought to explain the origins of religion, he resisted, like most of the philosophers of religion of his day, the social scientists' efforts to do so in strictly secular terms. Thus, while James was, among other things, a psychologist and described his approach to the varieties of religious experience as psychological, he is not easily classed with either his contemporary social scientists or philosophers of religion, although he shared some characteristics with both. In his effort to mediate between religion and psychology, James shared much with new religious movements, such as Spiritualism, Theosophy, and, especially New Thought. His metaphysically informed efforts at mediation were vastly more sophisticated than theirs, however, and brought a new legitimacy and prestige to these popular movements. While the explicitness of James's metaphysical commitments was unusual in a social scientist (and led many to claim that he was *really* a philosopher), it was the nature rather than the fact of such commitments, as Troeltsch clearly recognized, that set the *Varieties* apart from other scientific studies of religion. These metaphysical presuppositions informed his most important innovations in theory and method in the study of religion: his comparative method, his psychological theory of religious experience, and his distinction between the "science of religion" and "living religion."

This reading of the *Varieties* proceeds in a more or less linear fashion attending most closely to the preliminary material concerning his approach and method in lectures 1–3, the theoretical material in lectures 8–10, 19–20, and the discussion of living religion in lectures 20–21.

Method in the Science of Religion

James made it clear at the outset that his subjects would be persons of the sort that have filled the pages of this book. He was interested, he said, in first-hand experience, that is, in "the original experiences which were the pattern-setters" for the "ordinary religious believer." He was interested, in other words, in " 'geniuses' in the religious line," persons who, like other geniuses, have "often shown symptoms of nervous instability." Perhaps more than other kinds of genius, he said, "religious leaders have been subject to abnormal psychical visitations." He described them as "creatures of exalted emotional sensibility," often subject to "melancholy" and liable to "obsessions and fixed ideas" and other evidences of "a discordant inner life." "Frequently they have fallen into trances, heard voices, seen visions, and presented all sorts of peculiarities which are ordinarily classed as pathological." He cited George Fox, who was for many the quintessential enthusiast, as an exemplar of the type of religious figure he had in mind (15–16). He did so, however, knowing that Fox was well-tarred with the brush of enthusiasm and, indeed, he acknowledged toward the end of his lectures, that "if any of you are enemies of what our ancestors used to brand as enthusiasm, and are, nevertheless, still listening to me now, you have probably felt my selection to have been sometimes almost perverse, and have wished I might have stuck to soberer examples" (383).

James structured the *Varieties* around two questions relating to this sort of religious experience, one of "fact" and one of "value." The first was a question about "the religious propensities" and the second, a question about their "philosophic significance." The first asked about the nature and origins of such experiences; the second asked about their meaning and significance. The first was a historical question; the second was a question of value. The latter depended, according to James, on "some sort of general theory as to what the peculiarities in a thing should be which give it value." He stressed that the answer to one question could not "be deduced immediately from the other" (13–14). On the basis of this distinction, James made three significant methodological moves: (1) he rejected a quest for origins in which origins were equated with meaning or significance, i.e. value; (2) he maintained that the value of a thing should be assessed in light of the thing's distinctive function; and (3) he adopted a comparative methodology in order to (a) lay bare the causes in which a thing originates and (b) establish the thing's unique function (on the basis of which it could then be judged).

James devoted much of his first lecture (10–21) to a long digression designed to assure his audience that "explaining [the] origin [of the soul's secrets] would [not] simultaneously explain away their significance" (17). In what Mark Micale has described as "the most thoroughgoing critique of the practice of rediagnosing religious phenomena in neuropathological terms,"[32] James argued that the "medical materialists," like religious dogmatists, took origins as their sole criterion of truth. Where medical materials located the origins of religious phenomena in pathology (epilepsy, hysteria, hereditary degeneration, etc.), religious dogmatists located it in such things as immediate intuition, pontifical authority, supernatural revelation, direct possession, and automatic utterance. "The medical materialists are therefore only so many belated dogmatists, neatly turning the tables on their predecessors by using the criterion of origin in a destructive instead of an accreditive way. They are effective with their talk of pathological origins only so long as supernatural origin is pleaded by the other side, and nothing but the argument from origin is under discussion" (24).[33]

James's little-noted discussion of his comparative method framed his excursus on medical materialism. The primary locus of comparison for James was between religious and nonreligious phenomena, including psychopathological ones. In pursing the nature of the religious propensities in terms of their "history and natural antecedents," he said, "we cannot possibly ignore [the] pathological aspects of the subject. We must describe and name them just as if they occurred in non-religious men." To describe and name is, in effect, to classify, and doing so, as he acknowledged, requires comparison. "The first thing the intellect does with an object is to class it along with something else. . . . The next thing the intellect does is lay bare the causes in which the thing originates" (17). Mention of this second step then precipitated his excursus on medical materialism and his extended attack on the fallacy of equating the explanation of origins with the "explaining away" of significance.

When he surfaced many pages later, he took up the question of why, if the religious life was to be judged by its results and not its origins, he must "threaten [his listeners] . . . at all with so much existential study of its conditions?" In short, he asked rhetorically, "why not simply leave the pathological questions out?" He gave two answers: "First, I say, irrepressible curiosity imperiously leads one on; and I say, secondly, that it always leads to a better understanding of a thing's significance to consider its exaggerations and perversions, its equivalents and substitutes and nearest relatives elsewhere." His point was not to equate the object of study and its comparates or "to swamp the thing in the wholesale condemnation" associated with the "inferior" things to which it is compared, but rather to contrast them, so that "we may . . . ascertain the more precisely in what its [the object of study's] merits consist" (26). Comparison thus not only laid bare the "causes in which the thing originates," it also provided the basis for "understanding a thing's significance." Comparison, in short, provided a means of answering the first question and at least laid the groundwork for answering the second.

He illustrated his point with respect to religious phenomena by pointing out that melancholy, happiness, and the trancelike states associated with religion were "special cases of kinds of human experience of much wider scope." Whatever else they might be by virtue of being religious, he said, "religious melancholy . . . is at any rate melancholy. Religious happiness is happiness. Religious trance is trance." Are we not, he asked, more "likely to ascertain the distinctive significance of religious melancholy and happiness, or of religious trances, . . . by comparing them as conscientiously as we can with other varieties of melancholy, happiness, or trance, than by refusing to consider their place in any more general series, and treating them as if they were outside of nature altogether?" (28). This, at any rate, was the supposition he hoped his lectures would confirm. Indeed, he concluded his first lecture with the statement that "the only novelty" he could imagine his lectures to possess lay in the breadth of the phenomena "morbid or healthy" to which he would compare the "religious phenomena . . . in order to understand them better" (29).

In his second lecture, James circumscribed his topic by offering a definition of religion and then formulated a preliminary answer to the second of his two questions. He began by rejecting an essentialist definition of religion, arguing that there was no "simple abstract 'religious emotion' . . . present in every religious experience without exception" (31). There was, in other words, no one elementary religious emotion (or, he suspected, any one object or act), only a common storehouse of emotions (or objects or acts) upon which to draw. In the absence of such an essence, and in keeping with his interest in examining "first-hand" religion, he stipulated a definition that privileged "*the feelings, acts, and experiences of individual men in their solitude . . . in relation to whatever they may consider divine*" and discounted "second-hand" religion, i.e., institutions, ecclesiastical organizations, and systematic theology (31–32, 34, emphasis in original). He understood the divine, practically speaking, as extreme and unmistakable instances of a solemn, serious, and tender attitude toward what a person holds to be the primal truth (34–40).

Next he turned to the meaning and significance of this attitude, which for James, had to do with its function, i.e., what it did. He sought the function of a religious attitude or experience much as he would seek the function of a bodily organ, that is, by asking "after its most peculiar and characteristic sort of performance." James insisted that we must judge religious experiences by the "element or quality in them which we can meet nowhere else" (44). He argued that the "state of mind, known to religious men, but to no others" is one "in which the will to assert ourselves and hold our own has been displaced by a willingness to close our mouths and be as nothing in the floods and waterspouts of God." In such states of mind, "[t]he time for tension in our soul is over, and that of happy relaxation, of calm deep breathing, of an eternal present, with no discordant future to be anxious about, has arrived" (46). He claimed that this sort of happiness was found "nowhere but in religion" (47).

Religions, he argued, encourage this attitude. In the religious life, he said, "surrender and sacrifice are positively espoused: even unnecessary givings-up are added in order that the happiness may increase." This paradoxical combination of sacrifice/surrender and happiness allowed James to pinpoint what he took to be the distinctive function of religion:

Religion thus makes easy and felicitous what in any case is necessary; and if it be the only agency that can accomplish this result, its vital importance as a human faculty stands vindicated beyond dispute. It becomes an essential organ of our life, performing a function which no other portion of our nature can so successfully fulfill. . . . Of the farther office of religion as a metaphysical revelation I will say nothing now. (49, emphasis in original)

Here he hinted at two answers to his question regarding the *significance* of religious propensities, to wit: "Religion makes easy and felicitous what in any case is necessary" and "Religion gives access to metaphysical revelation."

In the second lecture, James moved from defining religion as the the inner experience of believers in relation to what they took as primal truth to a consideration of the significance of that relationship, considered functionally. In other words, given a stipulated relationship, James then asked *what* it accomplished. In lecture three, James asked *how* this relationship accomplished this distinctive function. He did so by lifting up what he took to be another central characteristic of the religious life, specifically, "the belief that there is an unseen order, and that our supreme good lies in harmoniously adjusting ourselves thereto." He described "this belief and this adjustment . . . [as] the religious attitude in the soul."

Such an attitude, he said, entailed certain "psychological peculiarities" (51), to wit, a sense of the "real presence" of that which the believer considers divine. Psychologically speaking, he said, "it is as if there were in the human consciousness a *sense of reality, a feeling of objective presence, a perception* of what we may call '*something there*,' more deep and more general than any of the special and particular 'senses' by which the current psychology supposes existent realities to be originally revealed" (55, emphasis in original). Many religious persons, in other words, "possess the objects of their belief, not in the form of mere conceptions which their intellect accepts as true, but rather in the form of quasi-sensible realities directly apprehended." They have "a sense of the real presence of these objects" (59).

The relationship of believers with what they took to be primal truth was not an intellectual one, but rather a direct engagement with something that seemed real, i.e., seemed to be objectively present. Intellectual reflection, James contended, followed from such "inarticulate feelings of reality," but the "inarticulate feelings" were foundational. In the religious realm, he claimed "the subconscious and non-rational . . . thus hold primacy" (67–68). Here James prefigured his answer to his question regarding the *origins* of the religious propensities. For it was the experienced quality of the relationship as a direct engagement, rooted in the subconscious and nonrational, that accounted, in James's view, for *how* religion was able to accomplish what it did.

In his approach to a psychological science of religion, James shared much in common with other social scientists of his era. If we compare, for example, James's *Varieties* and Durkheim's *Elementary Forms*, we can see that both were constructed in relation to three interconnected attributes of religion: definition, origin, and function. Both James and Durkheim were interested in the origin and function of religion. Both presupposed that, behind the diversity of forms that it assumed, religion (to quote Durkheim) "universally fulfil[s] the same functions." They identified, of course, different origins and functions. Where Durkheim located the origins or causes of religion in "collective realities" (i.e. society), James located them (as a psychologist) in individual realities (i.e., the subconscious). Where Durkheim understood the function of religion in relation to the unification of society (i.e., the obligations of the individual to the group), James understood the function of religion in relation to the transformation of the self (i.e. the harmonious adjustment of the individual to an experienced, yet unseen, order). In each case, their conclusions followed (circularly) from an appropriately chosen definition of religion. Thus, where James defined religion in terms of the individual's relationship to what s/he considered divine, Durkheim defined religion in terms of "a unified system of beliefs and practices relative to sacred things . . . which unite into one single moral community called a church all those who adhere to them."[34] James defined religion in terms of the individual and discovered its origin and function in the individual. Durkheim defined religion in terms of the social (i.e., the moral community called a church) and found its origin and function in society.[35]

They differ most significantly in terms of method, and this, I think, is where James's contributions to the study of religion have been overlooked. To discover the origin of religion Durkheim turned to what he took to be its simplest and most primitive form. In doing so, he set up a tacit comparison between "civilized" and "primitive" religion, in which he sought to discover the origin and function of religion in the presumed simplicity of the primitive. James, by way of contrast, set up and defended an explicit comparison between religious and nonreligious forms of experience, in which origins and functional significance were linked, but not equated. Thus, for James religious and nonreligious experiences, including pathological ones, had their proximate or mundane origins in the subconscious. Nonetheless, these experiences served different functions and thereby had different value for human life.

Their differences in method were connected to different views of psychopathology, evolutionary theory, and ultimately metaphysics. Where James was able to make fruitful comparisons between religion and psychopathology, Durkheim was not. In fact, Durkheim's argument was premised on the rejection of psychopathology as an explanation of the origins of religion. Thus, when he sought to identify the most elementary form of religion from among what he took to be the three basic contenders, he rejected animism and naturism because, in his view, they necessitated regarding "religion as the product of a delirious imagination," in short, as products of psychopathology. Because he equated origin and function, Durkheim identified what he took to be pathologically rooted phenomena (animism and naturism) as secondary elaborations on something more fundamental and primitive, i.e. totemism, which, according to Durkheim, was social rather than psychological in its origins.[36]

James, by way of contrast, not only lifted up George Fox as an exemplar of the sort of religious experience he wanted to consider, he acknowledged at the outset that, "from the point of view of his nervous constitution, Fox was a psychopath or *détraqué* of the deepest dye" (7). Contrary to today's usage, James did not mean to suggest that Fox was amoral or antisocial. Rather James used "psychopath" or "psychopathic temperament" to refer to a mind that was to some degree "unbalanced" or "unintegrated." In his Lowell Lecture on degeneration, he defined the "neurotic constitution" and the "psychopathic temperament" as " 'a mind discordant with itself that doesn't keep together,' subject to 'impulses and obsessive ideas.' "[37] From the *Varieties*, we learn that James thought that religious biographies often depicted persons with psychopathic temperaments accompanied by automatisms, such as the sense of being the instrument of a higher power (inspiration), sudden perceptions or convictions of new truth, and/or obsessive impulses to action (142, 376–81).

James's ability to make fruitful comparisons between religious and pathological experiences was rooted, as we have seen, in his insistence on the distinction between function and origin. This distinction, indeed his whole methodology, was rooted in his understanding of evolution. Although as an adolescent he was initially attracted to the evolutionary theory of Herbert Spencer, James later forcefully rejected Spencer for Darwin and extended a Darwinian understanding of evolution to the realm of consciousness and ideas. As James read him, Spencer, like the medical materialists, equated origin with function in a circular fashion, such that the environment caused adaptations whose function was the adaptation of the organism to its environment. Darwin, in what James viewed as his crucial theoretical move, separated causal origin from function. In Darwin's theory, variations arose *spontaneously* by means of causal mechanisms (e.g., random genetic mutations) that were independent of their outward relations. The variations best fitted to the outward environment (i.e., most functional) were then selected for survival.[38]

James extended Darwin's logic to argue, contra Spencer (and Lamarck), that "the novel ideas produced by men of genius . . . were not due to direct adaptations, to immediate environmental coercion." Rather, James contended, "new modes of thought and conceptual innovations sprang up in the mind as spontaneous mental variations" and were only accepted if they continued to meet the test of survival. Both Spencer and James held to theories of social evolution, but in James's theory geniuses or "great men" played a pivotal role. The ideas of geniuses were in effect spontaneous variations in the social organism, which if adapted to the needs of their environment would be selected for survival and provide the basis for new developments.[39] James's critique of Spencer and his critique of medical materialism, thus, were intimately connected. Both Spencerian evolution and medical materialism equated origins and function. In the former case, this meant that consciousness had no role in the process of social evolution, and in the latter, that genius was equated with insanity and ecstasy with hysteria.

Darwin, so understood, provided the basis for James's attack on medical materialism, his comparative methodology, and his focus on religious geniuses. Myers and the work of the SPR provided the basis for an alternative understanding of the subconscious as a potential source of spontaneous variations that might further the development of the individual and the social evolution of the whole. As we have seen, Pierre Janet viewed the healthy mind as unified and the dissociation of consciousness as inherently pathological and thus always devolutionary. Myers, by way of contrast, viewed the mind as multiplex. His understanding of the relationship between evolution and consciousness was consequently more complex. As summarized by James:

> The cornerstone of his [Myers's] conception was the fact that consciousness has no essential unity. . . . Myers therefore makes the suggestion that the whole system of consciousness studied by the classic psychology is only an extract from a larger total, being a part told-off, as it were, to do service in the adjustments of our physical organism to the world of nature. This extract, aggregated and personified for this particular purpose, has, like all evolving things, a variety of peculiarities. Having evolved, it may also dissolve, and in dreams, hysteria, and divers forms of degeneration it seems to do so. This is a retrograde process of separation in a consciousness of which the unity was once effected. But again the consciousness may follow the opposite course and integrate still farther, or evolve by growing into yet untried directions.[40]

Consciousness in this view "aggregates and dissipates" and in doing so may evolve or degenerate. Dissociation, although generally linked with degeneration, may simply prefigure a reaggregation of the personality and growth in new and untried directions. James thought that "Myers's general evolutionary conception . . . [was] a hypothesis of first-rate philosophic importance," and we find it presupposed in the *Varieties*.[41] Its most startling feature, and one in keeping with James's metaphysical view of the universe as "unfinished, growing in all sorts of places where thinking beings are at work," was its indeterminacy and open-endedness.[42]

The Darwinian model of social evolution that James brought to thinking about religious experience, thus, presupposed (1) the importance of religious geniuses who would (2) produce spontaneous mental variations that would (3) be tested in the environment such that the fittest would survive. In James's psychological theory of religion, the subconscious was the well from which these new variations sprung. By interpreting the subconscious in terms of Myers's theory of the subliminal, James replicated on the level of theory that which he presupposed in terms of method, i.e. the idea that origins and functional value could not be equated. The subconscious, as understood by Myers, provided a conceptual place from which both psychopathology and religious genius might emerge, while saying nothing, as James repeated over and over again, about value.

Indeed, for James the real beauty of Myers's understanding of the subconscious was that it ultimately said very little about origins. In adopting Myers's conception, James left open the question of where the subconscious ended, whether in the personal self or beyond it, and thus placed *ultimate* questions about origins outside the purview of the science of religions. This maneuver allowed him to engage the question of origins in a proximate sense as a scientist of religion while deferring consideration of its origin in the ultimate sense. Given the ambiguity of subconscious origins, James emphasized that all that emerged from (or through) the subconscious had to be tested in terms of "the way in which it works on the whole." This James said was his "empiricist criterion; and this criterion the stoutest insisters on supernatural origin have also been forced to use in the end." When he alluded to Jonathan Edwards's principle of discernment, saying "by their fruits ye shall know them, not by their roots," we should hear it as simply another way of stating his claims about functions and origins (24–25).

A Psychological Theory of Religion

In his concluding lecture, James provided a concise statement of the function of religion, a statement that Henry Samuel Levinson has referred to as James's theory of religion.[43] Religion, James there stated, consists in an uneasiness, i.e., "a sense that there is *something wrong about us* as we naturally stand," and its solution, i.e., "a sense that *we are saved from the wrongness* by making proper connection with the higher powers" (400). It would more accurate, in my view, to say that this is a statement of the *first half* of James's theory of religion. As a theoretical statement of what religion *does*, that is its function, it provides (at least) a partial answer to the question of value that he posed at the outset.

In the paragraph that follows, he elaborated on what religion does from the standpoint of the religious individual. The individual, "so far as he suffers from his wrongness and criticizes it," experiences within himself a division between the "wrong part" and something higher. At the moment of salvation, the individual "*becomes conscious that this higher part [of himself] is conterminous with and continuous with a MORE of the same quality, which is operative in the universe outside of him, and which he can keep in working touch with, and in a fashion get on board of and save himself when all his lower being has gone to pieces in the wreck*" (400, emphasis in original).

The second half of James's theory of religion consisted in an explanation of *how* religion performed its function, that is, an explanation of its (proximate) origins and, thus, an answer to the first of his two questions. Specifically, James sought to explain, theoretically, the "more" referred to in the previous paragraph. In keeping with others we have examined who sought to mediate between science and religion, James wanted to account for *how* religion does this in a way that would allow both psychologists and religious believers to acknowledge such experiences as in some sense real. According to James, "the *subconscious self* is nowadays a well accredited psychological entity; and I believe that in it we have exactly the mediating term required" (402). For James, the subconscious, which he also referred to as "consciousness beyond the margin" or the "subliminal," was both a mediating term and a proximate, if not ultimate, explanation of the origins of religion. The subconscious thus played the role in his theory that animal magnetism, trance, or conscious clairvoyance/suggestion played in earlier theories. James developed his argument for the subconscious self as mediating term in relation to three religious phenomena: conversion, mysticism, and prayer. I will consider each in turn.

CONVERSION

Taken most generally, James understood conversion psychologically in terms of a field theory of consciousness. In the field theory, the "mental field," rather than the "idea," is the basic unit of mental life. Mental fields succeed one another and in so doing constitute a stream of consciousness. Each field has a center or focus and a margin. Objects of attention are clustered at the center and as the attention shifts elsewhere they fade to the margin. The margin of the field is indeterminate and "our whole past store of memories floats beyond this margin, ready at a touch to come in; and the entire mass of residual powers, impulses, and knowledges that constitute our empirical self stretches continuously beyond it" (188–89). In terms of field theory, "To say that a man is 'converted' means, in these terms, that religious ideas, previously peripheral in his consciousness, now take a central place, and that religious aims form the habitual centre of his energy" (162).

The field theory, however, was not enough for James. Immediately, he criticized it on two counts. First, "ordinary psychology" assumed that "all the consciousness a person now has . . . is there in the 'field' of the moment." Second, it assumed that "what is absolutely extra-marginal" does not exist and "cannot be a fact of consciousness at all" (190). Thereupon followed his reference to the discovery of 1886, which demonstrated "that, in certain subjects at least, there is not only the consciousness of the ordinary field, with its usual centre and margin, but an addition thereto . . . which are extra-marginal and outside of the primary consciousness altogether." This discovery of "a consciousness existing beyond the field, or subliminally as Mr. Myers terms it, casts light on many phenomena of religious biography" (190).[44]

In retrospect anyway, the shift from field theory, with its center and margin, to consciousness *beyond* the margin proved to be the crucial divide across which even the most sympathetic psychologists and psychologists of religion had difficulty following James. Knowing that, it behooves us to pause to consider exactly why James himself considered this move so crucial. According to James, "[t]he most important consequence of having a strongly developed ultra-marginal life . . . is that one's ordinary fields of consciousness are liable to incursions from it of which the subject does not guess the source." Myers, noted James, refers to these incursions from "the subliminal parts of the mind" as automatisms, whether sensory or motor, emotional or intellectual (191). James, in short, moved to a theory of consciousness beyond the margins because it did a better job of explaining automatisms and the phenomena associated with them, i.e. religious genius, the psychopathic temperament, and, as he suggested in this lecture, instantaneous conversions (the "type by self surrender").

Again, since so many who succeeded James marginalized automatisms as either psychopathological or primitive or both, we need to focus on why James did not. The reasons, in my view, are simultaneously methodological, empirical, personal, and metaphysical. Methodologically, James believed, as we have seen, that extreme examples give the clearest evidence of a thing's distinctive function. Empirically, James thought that the psychopathic temperament shed light on what he took to be the "normal evolution of character." To some degree for all and "to the greatest possible degree if we are decidedly psychopathic, . . . the normal evolution of character chiefly consists in the straightening out and unifying of the inner self" (142). Instantaneous conversions, i.e., those involving self-surrender, were but one instance of this larger psychological process. Such conversions were, in his view, central to the development of religion in the West. Indeed, he claimed that the "whole development of Christianity in inwardness has consisted in little more than the greater and greater emphasis attached to this crisis of self-surrender." He traced this line of development running from Catholicism to Lutheranism to Calvinism to Wesleyanism and then, beyond technical Christianity altogether, into "transcendental idealism, whether or not of the mind-cure type" (173).

We know also that James inserted his own experience into his lecture on the sick soul as a further example of the sort of psychopathic temperament exemplified by John Bunyan. In light of his own personal experience, he undoubtedly had a stake in finding value in, rather than simply writing off, the more extreme forms of experience. Beyond his half-serious defense of traditional Methodism, we know that he struggled mightily to differentiate himself from his father, while at the same time honoring the legitimacy of his father's religious commitments. While some scholars have denied any connection between James and his father's Swedenborgianism, Eugene Taylor has suggested that the *Varieties* can be read as "describing the process of religious transformation that Swedenborg experienced from the standpoint of a psychology of religion."[45] While it contains remarkably few direct references to Swedenborg or Swedenborgians, there are several passages that bear out Taylor's suggestion. The passage just quoted, for example, referring to the importance of a crisis of self-surrender in "transcendental idealism," could well be construed as a reference to Swedenborg, locating him at the apex of a line of development that began within Christianity. James's comment that "Swedenborg's case is of course the palmary one of *audita et visa*, serving as a basis of religious revelation" (379, n. 27) is more definitive. Were James to dismiss automatisms, i.e. voices and visions, he would have had to write off Swedenborg's revelations as well. Pointing to more subtle lines of influence, Paul Croce roots James's mediating impulse in his father's Swedenborgianism. He adds that "the tug from his spiritual heritage was not just a lure to mediate, but it also provided him with an outline of how to do so in a specific way," that is, through "a spirituality that was set in nature and . . . empirical in character."[46] This was an orientation that James shared, not just with his father, but with the popular mediating tradition more generally.

Metaphysically, we know that James was moving toward a philosophically defensible, pluralistic, panpsychic, radical empiricism that came to full fruition in *A Pluralistic Universe* (1907). Given the direction he was headed and given that many of the key points of his more fully realized metaphysic were already in place when he was writing the *Varieties*, it is hard to avoid a sense that James's metaphysical preferences were playing a role in his choices as well.[47] This seems most evident in his rather muddled discussion of the competing explanations of incursions from beyond the margins. Thus, on the one hand, he indicated that new research had made Carpenter's older, purely physiological concept of "unconscious cerebration . . . almost certainly a misnomer, . . . better replaced by the vaguer term 'subconscious' or 'subliminal' " (170). A bit further on, he indicated that "psychology, defining these forces as 'subconscious,' and speaking of their effects as due to 'incubation,' or 'cerebration,' implied that they do not transcend the individual's personality" (174). Finally, in a note, he candidly confessed "that there are occasional bursts into consciousness of results of which it is not to easy to demonstrate any prolonged subconscious incubation." These "bursts," he said, "would have to be ascribed either to a merely physiological nerve storm, a 'discharging lesion' like that of epilepsy; or, in case it was useful and rational, . . . to some more mystical or theological hypothesis" (192, n. 4). Although he made this last remark to warn his readers that "subconscious incubation" would not be sufficient to account for all the facts, he pointed beyond its insufficiency to two explanatory alternatives: a physiological nerve storm or a more mystical hypothesis. That James did not simply retreat, as would virtually all his psychological colleagues, back to the physiological explanation suggests the role that his metaphysical choices played alongside, and indeed interwoven with, his empirical observations and personal commitments. His decision to stick "as far as possible to the more 'scientific' view" and to defer for the time being "the question of its absolute sufficiency" reflected his interest in building a case for the "subconscious" as a mediating term amenable to both secular psychologists and religious believers.

MYSTICISM

James's understanding of mysticism was conceptually parallel to his understanding of the subconscious, although the tendency to focus on the famous four marks of mysticism (ineffability, noetic quality, transiency, and passivity) has obscured this parallelism. Few who cite James as an authority on mysticism note that midway through the lecture, he admitted that "in characterizing mystic states as pantheistic, optimistic, etc., I am afraid I have over-simplified the truth." He did so he said in order to "keep closer to the classic mystical tradition." But, he confessed, "classic religious mysticism . . . is only a 'privileged case.' " It is, he said, "an *extract*, . . . carved out from a much larger mass . . . and kept true to type by the selection of the fittest specimens and their preservation in 'schools' " (336; emphasis in original). Not only was religious mysticism taken as a whole "much less unanimous" than he had allowed, *religious* mysticism was only half the story. "The other half [of mysticism] has no accumulated traditions except those which the text-books on insanity supply." From the point of view of "their psychological mechanism," he said, it was evident that "the classic mysticism and these lower mysticisms spring from the same mental level, from that great subliminal or transmarginal region of which so little is really known" (336–38).

Here James made explicit the role of the subconscious in his evolutionary psychology of religion. The subconscious was the source of a great variety of mystical productions (a veritable hodge-podge of the religious, the psychopathological, and much else besides) from which the "fittest specimens" were selected and preserved in "schools" by means of "traditions." The value of the mystical variations was determined, in other words, by the schools in keeping with their traditions. In doing so, they were able to ensure that mystical experience within their tradition stayed "true to type." Thus when we read James's statement that "personal religious experience has its root and centre in mystical states of consciousness," we should not assume that "its root and centre" was anything other than the subconscious (ambiguously construed). Also, when he added that "for us . . . such states of consciousness ought to form the vital chapter from which the other chapters get their light," we should not assume that this light was, for James, unambiguously positive (301). Indeed, if we consider the whole of mysticism as he presented it, we are thrown back, as he repeatedly insisted, on the equivocal origins of mysticism (and religious experience) and the ever-present need not only for discernment, but perhaps even for *schools* and *traditions* of discernment. His mention here of schools and traditions will prove instructive when we turn from James's theory of origins to his discussion of "living religion" and consider the role of living traditions in assessing the value of experiences for life.

PRAYER

In its widest sense, prayer, for James, signified "every kind of inward communion or conversation with the power recognized as divine." As such, and in keeping with his stipulated definition of religion, it was, he said, "the very soul and essence of religion" (365). Studied as an "inner fact, . . . apart from ecclesiastical or theological considerations," religion, he said, "has shown itself to consist everywhere, and at all its stages, in the consciousness which individuals have of an intercourse between themselves and higher powers with which they feel themselves to be related." If prayer in this sense was not effective, if nothing was really transacted, if the world was "in no whit different for its having taken place," then, James said, prayer as a "sense that *something is transacting*" was "illusory" and religion "rooted in delusion." In his discussion of prayer the question of authenticity, thus, was central (367). He quoted Myers to the effect that "in prayer, spiritual energy, which otherwise would slumber, does become active, and spiritual work of some kind is effected really [whether its immediate effects are subjective or objective]" (376, 367–77). Here we have intimations of the role that the subconscious played, for James, in establishing the truth of religious experience.

THE SUBCONSCIOUS

At the end of his penultimate lecture, James provided a summary answer to his question about origins. Looking back over the ground he had covered, to the phenomena of inspiration, religious mysticism, the striking and sudden unifications of the self in conversion, and the extravagant obsessions associated with saintliness, he said, "we cannot, I think, avoid the conclusion that in religion we have a department of human nature with unusually close relations to the transmarginal or subliminal region." The transmarginal or subliminal was, for

James, the source of a whole variety of phenomena, including our dreams, mystical experiences, sensory and motor automatisms, hypnotic and hypnoid phenomena, delusions and hysteria, and super-normal cognitions. "It is also the fountainhead of much that feeds our religion. In persons deep in the religious life, as we have not abundantly seen,—and this is my conclusion,—the door to this region is unusually wide open" (380–81).

Having arrived at this conclusion, James began his last lecture by summarizing the characteristics of the religious life (382–84). This summing up concluded with his statement of the "common nucleus" of all religions, quoted above. It was interrupted by a long excursus (383–397) on the distinction between the "science of religion" and "living religion," which I take up in the next section.[48] Having established what he took to be the common nucleus of religion (400), he then asked about "the objective 'truth' of its content" (401). This critical assessment, he had already suggested, was the final task that a science of religion must perform, "in the light of other sciences and in that of general philosophy" (386).

It was at this point in the discussion that he introduced the "subconscious self" as "the mediating term required" to fulfil the duty of "the science of religions . . . to keep religion in connection with the rest of science" (402). He then proposed his famous hypothesis:

> Whatever it may be on its *farther* side, the 'more' with which in religious experience we feel ourselves connected is on its *hither* side the subconscious continuation of our conscious life. Starting thus with a recognized psychological fact [the subconscious defined in terms of Myers's subliminal consciousness (402–3)] as our basis, we seem to preserve a contact with 'science' which the ordinary theologian lacks. At the same time the theologian's contention that the religious man is moved by an external power is vindicated, for it is one of the peculiarities of invasions from the subconscious region to take on objective appearances, and to suggest to the Subject an external control. In the religious life the control is felt as 'higher'; but since on our hypothesis it is primarily the higher faculties of our own hidden mind which are controlling, the sense of union with the power beyond us is a sense of something, not merely apparently, but literally true. This doorway into the subject seems to me the best one for a science of religions, for it mediates between a number of different points of view (403–4).

The subconscious not only mediated between science and religion, it also provided the common ground wherein those with different theological and philosophical "over-beliefs" could come together. James's notion of "over-beliefs" rested on his functionalist understanding of religion, that is, on the idea that beneath its diversity of forms religion filled a common, albeit stipulated and thus provisional, function that both the scientist and the believer could recognize. The task of the science of religion was to identify the common feature or features empirically and explain their origin and function. Beliefs, theological or metaphysical, that fell outside this nucleus counted in James's view as "over-beliefs." The subconscious, thus, marked the boundary (or doorway) between a science of religion and over-beliefs about religion. James stressed, however, that "it is only a doorway, and difficulties present themselves as soon as we step through it." For here, as he said, "the over-beliefs begin" (404). If we ask where the subconscious ends, whether in the personal self or beyond it, we are, according to James, in the realm of over-beliefs. If we conceptualize the "more" in theological terms as God or gods or in metaphysical terms as monist, dualist, or pluralist, we are in the realm of over-beliefs. The subconscious thus served not only as a mediating term between science and religion, but also as a mediating term between divergent theological and metaphysical views. Use of the term, with its deliberate ambiguities, allowed James to argue, as a scientist of religion, that religious experience had a "positive content . . . which . . . is *literally and objectively true as far as it goes*" (405).

James, thus, constituted religious experience both in terms of its common function (saving the individual from a designated wrongness via a felt connection to a higher power) *and* its origins in the subconscious or consciousness beyond the margins. James defined religion by abstracting what he took to be common features from the particular traditions. He did so not only as a means of mediating between religions but also as a means of mediating between religion and the secular social sciences. Like the more secular social scientists, James sought to explain the origins and function of religion. Because he, like the phenomenologists, resisted the tendency to secularize religion, he sought a way to explain the origins of religion without explaining religion away. He proposed the subconscious as the mediating term that could keep "religion in connection with the rest of science." As such, its job was to mediate between a variety of explanations of the origins of religion—natural and supernatural, as well as secular and religious—and, in doing so, to establish the truth of religion in a limited sense ("as far as it goes"). When discussing the subconscious as a scientist of religion, James bracketed or suspended his own "over-beliefs" in order to constitute a theoretically grounded concept of religious experience that, he hoped, would appeal to both secular scientists and religious believers.

The image James most often used to depict the "more" in the *Varieties*—that of "a larger power which is friendly to [us] and [our] ideals"—did not, in his view, necessarily transgress the requirements of the science of religion. While meeting the practical needs of religion, such a belief required metaphysically only that "the power should be both other and larger than our conscious selves" (413). The image of a higher power thus fully exploited the ambiguities inherent in the idea of the subconscious. In saying that the power must be understood only as "both other and larger than our conscious selves," he positioned it on the boundary between religious and secular, natural and supernatural conceptions of religious experience. A higher power could be no more than an upwelling *from* the personal subconscious (i.e., naturalistically religious or secular in origin) or it could be an upwelling *through* the personal subconscious (i.e., supernaturally or naturally religious in origin). Where one stood on these metaphysical questions was, for James, a matter of over-belief. Only in the conclusion and postscript, did James explicitly address his own over-beliefs regarding the subconscious and the more.

Living Religion

This analysis has so far left unaddressed the question of how far a science of religion could go, in James's view, toward answering his second question, i.e., the question of the importance, meaning, or significance of religion. Clearly, in James's view, the science of religion had a role to play in answering this question. As we have seen, James stated that comparison provides the basis for "a better understanding a thing's significance" (26) and allows us to establish a thing's unique function or essence which is "the thing by which we finally must judge them" (44). Although comparison was, in James's view, necessary, neither passage suggested that it was *sufficient* for determining the value of a thing. Ultimately, James insisted "we are thrown back upon the general principles by which empirical philosophy has always contended that we must be guided in our search for truth," to wit: "*immediate luminousness*, in short, *philosophical reasonableness* and *moral helpfulness* are the only available criteria" (23). In order to understand the limits of the scientific understanding of the value of religion, we need to understand James's distinction between the science of religion and living religion. A science of religion could recognize the theoretical value of religion, but only in the context of living religion could individuals actually judge religion's value for life and test the way it "worked upon the whole."

James discussed the distinction between the science of religion and living religion in Lecture 20 in an excursus defending the validity of the "religious man's experience" as legitimate evidence of "experimental converse with the divine" (383–84). He structured his defense around two "vexing questions" that he used to argue for the value of diversity and particularity. The first had to do with whether the existence of a diversity of religious dispositions, beliefs, and practices in the world was regrettable. James answered with an emphatic "no," insisting that the elimination of such diversity was neither practical nor desirable and that we must recognize that "we live in partial systems, and that parts are not interchangeable in the spiritual life." His hypothetical questioner then asked if "this one-sidedness [would not] be cured if we should all espouse the science of religions as our own religion?" The answer to this question was "no" as well, setting up James's reflections on the relationship between "the theoretic and the active life" (384–85).

James's distinction between the theoretical and the active life was premised on the idea that "knowledge about a thing is not the thing itself." The scientist might "understand everything about the causes and elements of religion, and might even decide which elements were qualified, by their general harmony with other branches of knowledge to be considered true," and still find it hard "to be personally devout" (385). "Knowledge about life," he insisted, is not the same as the "effective occupation of a place in life, with its dynamic currents passing through your being" (386).

The chief characteristic of living religion, and what made it so problematic for scientists, was that it revolved, according to James, around the individual's interest "in his private destiny." The one fundamental fact of religious thought, he said, is that "it is carried on in terms of personality" (387). Science, however, repudiated the personal point of view, maintaining, according to James, that "[t]he less we mix the private with the cosmic, the more we dwell in universal and impersonal terms, the truer heirs of Science we become." James believed that the impersonality of the scientific attitude was shallow. "The reason is that, so long as we deal with the cosmic and the general, we deal only with the symbols of reality, but as soon as we deal with private and personal phenomena as such, we deal with realities in the completest sense of the term" (393). The science of religion dealt with the cosmic and the general, living religion included the private and personal. The former dealt with symbols of reality, the latter with reality itself.

James's understanding of "reality in the completest sense of the term" was grounded in his metaphysical understanding of experience.[49] Experience, like the subconscious, functioned as a mediating category for James. A "full fact" of experience, he said, consisted of "[a] conscious field *plus* its object as felt or thought of *plus* an attitude towards the object *plus* the sense of self to whom the attitude belongs." He added that "such a concrete bit of personal experience may be a small bit, [but] it is a solid bit as long as it lasts; not hollow, not a mere abstract element of experience, such as the 'object' is when taken all alone. It is a *full* fact, even though it be an insignificant fact; it is of the *kind* to which all realities whatsoever must belong; the motor currents of the world run through the like of it; it is on the line connecting real events with real events" (393). He graphically illustrated this distinction by pointing out that a meal composed of "one real raisin . . . instead of the word 'raisin' . . . might be an inadequate meal, but it would at least be a commencement of reality" (394). It is only at the level of the individual, James argued, that this reality commences. There, he said, "we [can] catch real fact in the making, and directly perceive how events happen, and how work is actually done." By comparison, "the world of generalized objects which the intellect contemplates is without solidity and life" (395).

The distinction between living religion and the science of religion paralleled and was premised upon the distinction between the full fact of experience and generalized objects abstracted from experience. Living religion, like the former, consisted of an object as felt or thought ("the More with which we feel ourselves connected") *plus* an attitude toward the object (an "over-belief" about "the More" as it relates to "me"). The science of religion, in so far as it was, in James's view, premised on an abstraction from experience (the universal idea of the More independent of a felt relationship to "me"), was "hollow," i.e., merely theoretical. When we pass from the realm of theory into a *felt connection* with a higher power, we pass, James thought, from the realm of theory into the realm of living religion. This felt connection was a full fact of existence consisting of an object as felt or thought *plus* an attitude toward the object. As such, it was inescapably particular, and personal. Living religion or, as I have called it, religion in practice was embodied; it occupied, as James said, a particular "place in life." Over-beliefs, as the theoretical manifestation of the particular and the personal, reflected the "the varied world of concrete religious constructions" (397). Over-beliefs, James said, are "essential to that individual's religion," which means, he added, that they "are absolutely indispensable" (405).

James's distinction between the science of religion and living religion suggests that he could have answered the question of value either at the level of theory or at the level of lived religion. Theoretically, we know that James would have us finally judge a thing in light of its unique function. Functionally, we know that for James religion moves us from "an uneasiness" to "its solution," i.e., to "a sense that we are saved from the wrongness by making proper connection with the higher powers." This suggests that at the level of the science of religion, he would have us judge religions on the basis of how well they actually accomplished what they set out to do. He would have us judge them, I would infer, in terms of how effectively a religion saves its practitioners from "wrongness," as they understand it.

What this might entail in academic (as opposed to religious) practice becomes apparent if we think about James's relation to the mental healing movements, i.e., Christian Science and New Thought. In March 1898, in one of his few overtly political acts, James testified against a medical licensing bill that would have barred uncredentialed healers from practicing without a license in Massachusetts. James argued against the bill because "there can be no doubt that if the proposed law were really enforced it would stamp out and arrest the acquisition of that whole branch of medical experience" that was emerging from the mental healing movement. In the area of mental healing, where the state of expert knowledge was so imperfect, "it is enough," James said, "for you as legislators to ascertain that a large number of our citizens, persons as intelligent and well educated as yourself or I, persons whose numbers seem daily to increase, are convinced that they do achieve them [the successes that are claimed]."[50] James argued, in short, that these movements should be evaluated in terms of their actual ability to heal as evidenced by *the testimony of those who claimed they had been cured*. James argued not from first-hand knowledge, although he may have had some, but rather on the wider scientific grounds of "logic and experiment" (23). If expert knowledge was manifestly imperfect, logic suggested that the experiments with mental healing should be allowed to continue.

Within the realm of living religion, James located judgments made by practitioners within a world of concrete religious constructions. At this level, questions of value would be decided, at the more conservative end of the spectrum, by "schools" on the basis of "traditions" that included within them criteria for ensuring that their tradition stayed true to type. At the more innovative end of the spectrum, questions of value would be decided in a more open-ended evolutionary marketplace, that is, based on whether people identified with any given "uneasiness" and found themselves "saved" from it in the actual practice of the religion. It is on the level of living religion that he would have held that judgments should be "based on our own immediate feeling primarily; and secondarily on what we can ascertain of their experiential relations to our moral needs and to the rest of what we hold true" (23).

These were the criteria that James brought to his own over-beliefs. Subjectively and objectively James found value in the over-belief "that the world of our present consciousness is only one out of many worlds of consciousness that exist." "Those other worlds," he said, "must contain experiences which have a meaning for our life also; and . . . although in the main their experiences and those of this world keep discrete, yet the two become continuous at certain points, and higher energies filter in." He said that he could, of course, put himself into "the sectarian scientist's attitude, and imagine vividly that the world of sensations and of scientific laws and objects may be all," but he found that "by being faithful" to this over-belief, he seemed "to keep more sane and true." Not only was he subjectively happier, but, he said, viewed objectively, "the total expression of human experience . . . invincibly [urged him] beyond the narrow 'scientific' bounds" (408).

In his private correspondence and in later writings, James drew on Fechner's image of "the mother-sea" to depict the relationship between this world and those other worlds. In an essay on psychical research published toward the end of his life, he wrote:

> Out of my experience, such as it is (and it is limited enough) one fixed conclusion dogmatically emerges, and it is this, that we with our lives are like islands in the sea, or trees in the forest. The maple and pine may whisper to each other with their leaves, and Conanicut and Newport hear each other's fog-horns. But the trees also commingle their roots in the darkness underground, and the islands also hang together through the ocean's bottom. Just so there is a continuum of cosmic consciousness, against which our individuality builds but accidental fences, and into which our several minds plunge as into a mother-sea or reservoir. Our 'normal' consciousness is circumscribed for adaptation to our external earthly environment, but the fence is weak in spots, and fitful influences from beyond leak in, showing the otherwise unverifiable common connexion.[51]

In *A Pluralistic Universe*, James brought the analogy of dissociation and co-consciousness to this Fechnerian image of the "mother-sea" or "world-soul." The analogy was initially proposed by F.C.S. Schiller, following the publication of Morton Prince's *Dissociation of a Personality* (1905), in a (presumably) tongue-in-check essay, titled "Idealism and the Dissociation of a Personality." There Schiller suggested that concepts borrowed from empirical psychology, specifically the dissociation of personality, might offer a cure for the philosophical ills facing idealist monism. James took the idea of thinking of "the absolute as morbidly dissociated, or even as downright mad" with considerable seriousness, suggesting the "the path that Mr. Schiller and [Mr. Gore] have struck into is likely to prove a most important lead."[52] In *A Pluralistic Universe*, James indicated that "the evidence [of ordinary psychology, psychopathology, psychical research, and religious experience] . . . sweep[s] us very strongly toward the belief in some form of superhuman life with which we may, unknown to ourselves be co-conscious. . . . The outlines of the superhuman consciousness thus made probable must remain, however, very vague, and the number of functionally distinct 'selves' it comports and carries has to be left entirely problematic" (*PU*, 140).

Much to the consternation of James's colleagues in psychology and the psychology of religion these images were widely popularized during the early twentieth century. The widespread dissemination of supposedly scientific images had an impact on the response of James's colleagues to his work. James recognized the problem but, in keeping with his evolutionary views, was not troubled by it.

> It is true that superstitions and wild-growing over-beliefs of all sorts will undoubtedly begin to abound if the notion of higher consciousness enveloping ours, of fechnerian earth-souls and the like, grows orthodox and fashionable; still more will they superabound if science ever puts her approving stamp on the phenomena of which Frederic Myers so earnestly advocated the scientific recognition, the phenomena of psychic research so called—and I myself firmly believe that most of these phenomena are rooted in reality. (*PU*, 142)

The religious "gems," James maintained, must be extricated from this mass of "superstitions and wild-growing over-beliefs" through a "competition for survival." To short-circuit this evolutionary process would simply reproduce "the hollow unreal god of scholastic theology, or the unintelligible pantheistic monster, instead of *the more living divine reality* with which it appears certain that empirical methods tend to connect men in imagination" (*PU*, 143, emphasis added).

EXPLAINING THE SUBCONSCIOUS

Psychologists on the Subconscious

In early 1903, James wrote Theodore Flournoy that "the book has sold extraordinarily well in English, for a book that costs over three dollars. The tenth thousand is already being printed; I get enthusiastic letters from strangers; and the reviewers, although, *without* a single *exception*, they all use the word 'unsatisfactory,' having eased their conscience by that term, they proceed to handle me with sympathy and praise." James had anticipated this response believing "it will doubtless be a popular book,—too biological for the religious, too religious for the biologists."[53] The academic psychologists reacted as James had predicted. Virtually all rejected Myers's theory of the subliminal mind outright. A few were open to a psychological interpretation of dissociation, but typically associated dissociation with psychopathology. Most, however, rejected a psychological interpretation of dissociation altogether, preferring instead to resuscitate Carpenter's physiologically based theory of unconscious cerebration. In doing so, they eliminated the idea of co-consciousness and rejected the theoretical foundations of the subconscious developed by Janet.

Two points seem evident in these discussions. First, the impetus to discuss the subconscious arose outside the German laboratory tradition. The discussion was a response to the publications of James and other more clinically oriented experimental psychologists of the subconscious and did not reflect an inherent interest in the subject on the part of psychologists trained in the German laboratory tradition. Second, the critics' repeated references to popular religion suggest that the "subconscious" played much the same role in the emergence of psychology as an academic discipline as "trance" and "somnambulism" played in the emergence of neurology as a medical subspecialty thirty years earlier. In the struggle for interpretive control of the "subconscious," both the content and the style of the *Varieties* posed a threat. Substantively, the theory of the subliminal mind gave experimental legitimacy both to psychical research and the findings of those experienced in the ways of religion. Stylistically, its very readability made it accessible to persons outside the field of psychology. The psychologists' uncompromising rejection of a psychological theory of the subconscious effectively redrew the boundaries between the science of psychology, on the one hand, and psychical research and popular religion, on the other.

In 1903, Joseph Jastrow, professor of psychology at the University of Wisconsin, acknowledged that "it is quite out of the question any longer to refer to these facts [regarding the subconscious] in a footnote, or to treat the issues involved as merely subsidiary; on the contrary, there is hardly a chapter in psychology that can be considered to be adequately portrayed or even truthfully sketched, that fails to incorporate the significant aspects of its subject derived from the study of the subconscious forms of the processes involved." Nonetheless, most academic psychologists, according to Irving King of the Pratt Institute, were "somewhat chary of the subconscious" and viewed "a good deal that passes under that category . . . [with] suspicion." "Certain phenomena," he went on to say, "are discounted, because to accept them seems to lead to dangerous consequences." In a veiled attack on Myers, King indicated that it was "the utterly unscientific and in the highest degree fanciful theories of a subconscious mind with extraordinary powers, an apparent recrudescence of the savage notion of the soul, which have of late years been advanced by certain pseudo-psychologists," that posed the greatest threat.[54] Jastrow acknowledged similar fears, indicating that "the very latitude of this theory [of the subliminal self] makes it hospitable to a wide range of considerations,—many of them supported by questionable data and strained interpretations,—and renders it liable to affiliation with 'occult' conceptions of every shade and grade of extravagance." Finally, Jastrow joined King (like Tylor and Beard before them) in ridiculing the theory of the subliminal mind for making a mockery of evolution, such that the "endowments and achievements [wrought by evolution were] outdone by a confined and untutored 'double,' that this same mind has all the while unwittingly nurtured."[55]

Countering the theories of Janet and Myers, King offered a physiological interpretation, proposing that "we . . . conceive of the subconscious, not as dim consciousness, nor as something psychic, and yet not self-conscious; but rather as a physical mass of neural dispositions, tensions, and actual processes which are in some degree, perhaps, organized; the remnants of habits, experiences, both those which have lapsed from consciousness and those which have never penetrated to the central plexus." Arguing "that what is not in self-consciousness is a physical tension or process," he was able to claim that "dissociated ideas are not psychical affairs at all." Also in 1906, A. H. Pierce, professor of psychology at Smith College, resuscitated Carpenter's theory of unconscious cerebration. He acknowledged that the " 'subconscious,' with its included meanings of 'split-off' or of 'subliminal' consciousness, has seemed to many to do a masterly service in clearing up the facts which Carpenter and his followers attributed to unconscious cerebration." But, he went on to say, "those of us who find ourselves unable to accept that doctrine of subconsciousness which makes of it a detached, split-off companion of our normal consciousness are the ones, naturally, who feel an interest in discussing the status of unconscious cerebration."[56]

A year later, Morton Prince, professor of neurology at Tufts Medical School, published a "Symposium on the Subconscious" in his newly founded *Journal of Abnormal Psychology*. He invited four professors of psychology—Münsterberg from Harvard, Jastrow from Wisconsin, and Thèodore Ribot and Pierre Janet of the Collège de France—to give their views alongside his own. A. H. Pierce, in a review, professed himself quite satisfied with the outcome. First of all, he noted, "the mystic, wonder-working, 'subliminal' view is disavowed by all of the writers, sometimes quite summarily." This meant, he said, that "the basal question . . . reduced . . . to its lowest terms . . . is simply and solely this: Do certain observed phenomena, notably the automatic behaviors of hysterics and other abnormal subjects, require us to postulate a dissociated consciousness for their explanation, or are they to be understood as manifestations of a disordered cerebral mechanism which now functions without concomitant psychical states? Here, then, is the fundamental alternative: Is the interpretation to be psychological or physiological?" Pierce, who thought only one author (Prince) "unqualifiedly support[ed] the psychological [interpretation]," assigned the "honors of the [the] symposium . . . to those who prefer the physiological interpretation."[57] Morton Prince took Pierce to task for his misreading of Janet, pointing out that "the whole basis, the very foundation of Janet's doctrine of hysteria is dissociated ideas, not physiological processes; and if one thinks that this investigator has recanted, one has only to take the trouble to read his latest book, 'Lectures on the Major Symptoms of Hysteria' (1907), where his theories are restated."[58]

In his contribution, Münsterberg, as indicated earlier, recast the discussion by identifying three dominant theories (subliminal consciousness, pathological dissociation, and unconscious cerebration) and their primary backers (laymen, physicians, and psychologists). Morton Prince gave this typology further weight by building upon it in his introduction and conclusion to the symposium.[59] According to Münsterberg, "the popular mind clings" to a theory of subliminal consciousness because "it is on this basis easy to bring the subconscious selves into telepathic connection or to link them with mystical agencies." He noted by way of contrast, that "the physiological explanation [unconscious cerebration] gives small foothold for that mystical expansion of the theory which seemed so easily reached from the subconscious mental life." Indeed, he added that "it is not the least merit of the physiological explanation that it obstructs the path of pseudo-philosophy."[60] With this analysis, as noted in the introduction, Münsterberg in effect cast James, his senior colleague in psychology at Harvard, in among the mystically inclined psychological "laity."

The Subconscious and the Primitive

The young psychologists of religion that followed on the heels of James and Hall were, like James, more interested in demonstrating the viability of religion in a modern scientific age than in policing the boundaries of psychology as an academic discipline. They were uneasy, however, with James's virtual identification of (authentic) religious experience with both popular religion and psychopathology in the *Varieties*, and shared his critics' view that the theory of the subliminal mind somehow ran contrary to accepted ideas of evolution. In light of the anxieties of the academic psychologists and the uneasiness of the younger psychologists of religion, the publication of Frederick Morgan Davenport's *Primitive Traits in Religious Revivals* (1905) was a major event. *Primitive Traits*, subtitled *A Study in Mental and Social Evolution*, originated as Davenport's doctoral dissertation in political science at Columbia. Although Davenport, who was appointed to a position in sociology at Hamilton College, did not identify professionally as a psychologist of religion, the effects of his work can be seen in virtually all the later synoptic works in the psychology of religion. Davenport's work can be read as a counter to, even an inversion of, James's *Varieties*, analogous to Tylor's evolutionary inversion of modern spiritualism.

Davenport took only one direct shot at James, and that toward the end of his book, where he took "straightforward issue with those who still hold that the subconscious, the imperfectly rational, the mystically emotional, in spite of all its vagaries, is, par excellence, the channel of the inflow of divine life." Recognizing that he was "running counter to the philosophic 'perhaps' of that distinguished psychologist, Professor William James," he, nonetheless forthrightly declared that "I, for one, cannot believe that the feet of the supernatural deliberately chose to tread the slime of the subliminal, the lower mystical marsh lands of the human spirit, while avoiding the sunlit hills of full rational consciousness. It is far easier to believe that the influence of the divine is increasingly evident in the whole process of mental evolution."[61] Although these statements come toward the end, his rereading of James is evident from the start.

The heart of his rereading lies in his tentative association of the susceptibility to incursions from the subliminal mind with the primitive. In his chapter on "The Mind of Primitive Man," he indicates that "the primitive type . . . is a physically active, highly emotional type, with feeble reasoning powers,—child of conjecture and imagination." To the central characteristic of a vivid imagination, Davenport brings "a group of primitive characteristics, the chief of which is nervous instability, with its inevitable accompaniments of remarkable imitativeness and suggestibility and great lack of inhibitive control." He refers to this "peculiar condition," which includes the ability to enter "hypnotic trance with little difficulty," as "*normal* nervous instability, for there seems to be no evidence of any large amount of nervous disease or insanity among primitive men." He ties this all together with "the suggestion that a correlation which others have contended for between nervous instability and a large subliminal field of consciousness [citing James, *Varieties*, 251] may find further confirmation in an investigation of the mind of primitive man." "Among primitive people," he said, "the appearance of the sensory and motor automatisms—active convulsion as well as hallucination and vision . . ., as well as the so-called demonic states—. . . seems usually to be marked by a considerable fading of the field of normal rational consciousness, and very frequently by the emergence into view of that mysterious and active double personality which has so puzzled psychologists."[62]

Davenport linked the idea of the normal nervous instability of primitive man with two bodies of literature, the French social psychology of the crowd and the anthropological literature on "northern Siberian tribes and North American Indians." Davenport drew on Gustave Le Bon's *The Crowd* to show that "the mind of the crowd is strangely like that of primitive man." In the context of a crowd, he wrote: "Reason is in abeyance. The cool, rational speaker has little chance beside the skilful, emotional orator. The crowd thinks in images, and speech must take this form to be accessible to it." The connection between the normal nervous instability of the primitive mind, the sensory and motor automatisms associated with the subconscious, and the suggestibility of the crowd formed the theoretical basis that allowed him to identify the "primitive traits [in religious revivals] which need elimination or modification in the interest of religious and social progress." While the connection between the primitive mind and crowd psychology was well-developed, the connection to the anthropological literature was made only in passing.[63] It pointed, however, to a rich vein of associations that would be mined by later psychologists of religion as they attempted to connect the "primitive" features of revivals with other forms of so-called primitive religion.

In the chapters of his book, Davenport recapitulated much that had been included in earlier histories of enthusiasm, animal magnetism, the supernatural, and shouting. He opened with a chapter on a new subject—the Ghost Dance religion of the 1890s—but followed it with chapters on such familiar topics as the "Religion of the American Negro," the Kentucky revivals, the Ulster revival of 1859, Jonathan Edwards and the New England awakening, Wesley and the English awakening, and the evangelists Nettleton, Finney, and Moody. Throughout he used the concept of the primitive to "segregate out," in his words, "the primitive and baser elements in the revival," whether they were found in such presumptively "primitive" contexts as the Native American ghost dance and "Negro religion" or as "survivals" in the revivals of the white middle-class. The synoptic psychologies of religion that followed all included a chapter on either conversion or revivals that referenced not only Starbuck but also Davenport and crowd psychology. More important, subsequent psychologies of religion, in contrast to the *Varieties*, all followed Davenport in adopting a unilinear or stage theory of religious evolution, as opposed to the open-ended view espoused by James.

The Psychologists of Religion

James Bissett Pratt, a student of William James; Edward Scribner Ames, a student of James, John Dewey, and psychologist James Angell; and George Coe, whom we have already met, authored the three most important general psychologies of religion published prior to World War I.[64] Their general works, supplemented by articles written by them and their colleagues Edwin Starbuck and James Leuba, can be read as an extended conversation about and response to the *Varieties*. Like James, each relied upon the concept of the subconscious, although they disagreed about how it should be interpreted and about its relationship to authentic religious experience. Each adopted an evolutionary perspective on religion that allowed them to reposition what they took to be the highest form of religious experience relative to the first-hand experience singled out by James and to distance "higher" forms of religious experience from both psychopathology and popular religion. They carried on a conversation among themselves over the relationship between reason and emotion, on the one hand, and self and society, on the other, in the psychology of religion, each seeking to correct what they viewed as flaws in their predecessors.

SUBCONSCIOUS AS FEELING: PRATT

Edwin Starbuck, who was, as of 1906, professor of philosophy and psychology at the University of Iowa, and James Bissett Pratt, professor of philosophy at Williams College, were James's most whole-hearted supporters among the psychologists of religion; but even so, their support was qualified in significant ways. In general, they placed greater emphasis on what they took to be ordinary (i.e., to James's way of thinking, "second-hand") experience, rather than on the exceptional (i.e., "first-hand") experiences that so intrigued James. They understood the subconscious, in this ordinary sense, as the margin or fringe of consciousness from whence come spontaneous intuitions connected with instinct or feeling. They both, Pratt more so than Starbuck, rejected the idea of split-off co-conscious states and automatisms as attributes of the normal subconscious and downplayed their significance in relation to the normal experience of conversion (Starbuck) or higher forms of religion (Pratt).[65]

Pratt understood the subconscious as "a continuation of the field of vital feeling." He explicitly rejected "Myers' hypothesis of a secondary personality" as "unsupported by the facts." In his later work, he similarly rejected "co-consciousness" as a defining feature of the subconscious, because "the co-conscious, so far as the evidence goes, is either non-existent or practically negligible in normal persons." Taken, however, in a broader sense to include "the physiological, the fringe, and the co-consciousness in those who possess it," he said, "we cannot fail to be impressed with the enormous influence exerted by [it] upon our lives." Crediting the work of Starbuck and James, he added that "[i]t is plain . . . how important an influence the subconscious in this broader sense exerts upon each man's religion." Although unwilling to conclude that James's "religious geniuses . . . are *mere* 'psychopaths,' " he emphasized that "the highest type of man in the religious life as well as elsewhere is the unified and rational self." For our ideals, he stated, we should look "not so much to Ezekiel as to Amos, not so much to Fox as to Luther, not so much to Paul as to Jesus."[66]

To Pratt's way of thinking, a unified and rational self was informed by feeling. In his *Psychology of Religious Belief* (1907) he described three types of religious belief that progressively give way one to the next in all religions, however "primitive" or "civilized." Thus, he wrote, "everywhere we find the primitive basis of belief ["Religion of Primitive Credulity"] giving way before the advance of thought ["Religion of Thought"], thought bringing forth its twin offspring, theology and doubt, and turning at every crisis for strength and sure support to religious feeling and the instinctive demands which the human organism makes of the cosmos ["Religion of Feeling"]."

The religion of feeling manifested itself in two forms, one involving psychopathology and in many cases co-consciousness, and the other normal infusions of feeling from the fringes of consciousness. The former involved "a passionate, abnormal flinging away of all self-control." It was, Pratt said, "very susceptible of cultivation, and elaborate methods are concocted and pursued to bring it about." It was mostly commonly found among "uncivilized people or among the less cultured members of civilized communities." The latter type of feeling, we should not be shocked to learn, was "calm and quiet in its expression and usually spontaneous in its origin." Unlike the first type, it did not come on crowds, but "most often in solitude" and, of course, never went to "the fantastic and abnormal extremes of the first type." A high level of culture was a prerequisite for its appearance and, thus, he said, "one must look for it, not among the ecstatic dancers and medicine-men of the uncivilized, but among the Indian mystics, the Hebrew prophets, and the great religious leaders the world over."[67]

Pratt had this latter form of religious feeling in mind when, borrowing a phrase from James, he referred to the "mystic germ" that in his view informed "the great majority of . . . the religious class." This "mystic germ" was like an underground stream that flowed "underneath the externals of creed and cult, deep down in the hidden recesses of the conscious life." As such, it could not "be utterly abolished or destroyed by anything that science or criticism can do."[68]

SUBCONSCIOUS AS HABIT: AMES

Edward Scribner Ames, a professor in the philosophy department at the University of Chicago, criticized both Starbuck and Pratt for their overemphasis on feeling in religious experience and offered a reading of the *Varieties* in keeping with John Dewey's naturalistic understanding of William James. Ames credited Starbuck and Pratt with "extend[ing] the position of Professor James to the point of making feeling an independent source of experience in relation to extra-mundane realities." He noted that James had "been *interpreted* to stand for a kind of mysticism," but implied that it was Starbuck and Pratt's "extension" of James that made his views unacceptable to "many psychologists." Ames, like Dewey, lifted up not the mystical James but the James who made it clear that "the real problems of the philosophy of religion arise in the field of psychology, and are to be understood, if not solved, by the methods of that science."[69]

Drawing on the functional psychology of his teacher and colleague James Angell, Ames recast the psychology of religious experience by defining the subconscious in terms of the psychology of habit. Ames thought that Starbuck and Pratt were right when they argued that theological ideas were only the tip of the iceberg when it came to religious experience, but he disagreed with their assertion that the "non-intellectual factors of religion are chiefly the feelings." He argued that "[b]oth intellectual and affective elements in religious experience are secondary to and conditioned upon instinctive activity,—habit, custom, imitation,—and the interplay of various types of such activities." He used revivals to illustrate his point, conceding that "the method of awakening the crowd is certainly not that of reasoning, argumentation, analysis, and systematic thinking." But neither, he added, was it "that of transferring or eliciting feeling without an intermediate process." The mediating process, he argued, is the "awakening of instinctive, deep-seated impulses" by means of "suggestive, dynamic *representations* of the attitudes and experiences with which the crowd is to be inoculated. . . . The extreme emotionalism of the modern religious revival is caused by fascinating the attention with certain dynamic *images* which necessarily result in tensions and reactions of a violent nature."[70]

Ames, informed by wide-ranging reading in anthropology, turned to what he took to be the most primitive, i.e., simplest, forms of religion to differentiate the permanent from the accidental with respect to religion and thus to "gain a perspective in which the developed, historical religions might be interpreted." Religion, he concluded, "in its first form is a reflection of the most important group interests through social symbols and ceremonials based upon activities incident to such interests." Defining religion in terms of *group* rather than individual consciousness led Ames to emphasize ceremonial rather than prayer as the center of religious experience. For Ames, "ceremonials," rooted in custom and taboo and understood in relation to the psychology of habit, were "the most important factor in primitive religion." Prayer, which was the center of religious experience for James, "occupied a secondary and relatively subordinate place in primitive religion," according to Ames.[71]

Quoting James on the importance of the subconscious (specifically the passage about the 1886 discovery), Ames indicated that "the nature of this subconscious or subliminal reality is perhaps best described as a marginal field extending out from the focus of attention and full consciousness." He understood the content of the subconscious not in relation to feeling or intuition, as with Starbuck and Pratt, but in relation to "attention and habit." Specifically, he stated, "in the phenomena of habit it may almost be said that one sees the subconscious in the process of formation." Ames noted that "investigations of the more extreme phenomena of subconsciousness—dreams, somnambulism, hypnotism, lapses of personality, and the like—have revealed fundamental similarities with the commoner phenomena, such as the variations of attention, habit-formation, absent-mindedness, and association of ideas." He gave James credit for setting forth "the doctrine of different selves and of the centre and fringe of consciousness . . . brilliantly" and, in so doing, providing "a bridge of considerable scientific stability over the chasm which . . . seems to separate the waking self of conscious life and the mysterious subconscious self."[72]

Ames's praise of James should not allow us to lose sight of the magnitude of Ames's rereading of the *Varieties* and of the subconscious. James focused on the experience of the individual and defended prayer and mysticism, the traditional foci of the Christian spiritual life, as the authentic and viable center of religious experience. Starbuck and Pratt left their focus on the individual, while interpreting the subconscious in terms of feeling and intuition. Ames turned his focus to the group, identifying "religious consciousness . . . with the core of social consciousness," while interpreting the subconscious in terms of attention and habit. All were concerned with the viability of religion in the modern age. Its viability rested, for Starbuck and Pratt, on nonrational intuitions that could not be destroyed by science or criticism. Religion's viability rested, for Ames, on its ability to generate habits—"the inner soul of conscience, of duty, of patriotism, of social righteousness"—appropriate to "a democratic and scientific age."[73]

THE MYSTICAL INFERENCE

George Coe and James H. Leuba, unlike Starbuck, Pratt, and Ames, challenged James's mysticism. Their chief complaint was similar. The problem, in Leuba's words, was that James did not adequately distinguish between "what is immediately presented to consciousness and the interpretation of it furnished by the intellect" and, in Coe's words, that James accepted "as immediate intuition what is palpably an interpretation." Both presupposed James's distinction between "experience" and "over-belief," but argued that James had incorrectly located the boundary between them. Both believed that the qualities that James associated with mysticism—ineffability, noetic quality, transiency, and passivity—could be accounted for by the physiological sensations accompanying the trance state. Coe arrived at this conclusion by experimenting on himself. Through self-hypnosis, he induced a "mild trance" with three main marks: the modification of bodily sensations (a sense of separation from his body), a change in "self-feeling" (a blurring of the sense of self and object), and the experience of an agreeable feeling tone. In a letter to his former student Anton T. Boisen, Coe described this experiment as "reproduc[ing] the process (though not the content) of a mystical revelation."[74]

For both Leuba and Coe, the physiological conditions that informed mystical experience were those associated with trance, and both assumed that trance, taken to its limits, resulted in the complete loss of consciousness. Thus, Coe's central criticism of James's theory was that the experience of something "more" that James associated with an influx from the subconscious was simply an artifact of the "formal condition of trance." Specifically, according to Coe, "[t]he claim to having experienced enlargement, absorption, ineffable illumination [is] . . . entirely intelligible. The experience does tend to be ineffable, certainly, but not because of an unusual fulness of mental content; rather because of an unusual emptiness."[75]

Leuba, in a detailed analysis of a number of the more famous Christian mystics, expands on this point.

In itself the *completed* mystical trance is nothing (since in it the loss of consciousness is absolute). . . . The entranced soul described by our Mystics as naked, absolutely empty, etc., is to them, nevertheless, not the equivalent of non-existence. . . . When, self-consciousness having returned, the soul thinks of the preceding moments it becomes aware of a break in its life, of a void, of a nothing. This nothing is transformed into an existent something by the very fact that it has come to enjoy that particular kind of reality which the mind gives to all its objects. Only—and here is the error of our Mystics—this nothing-thought-of is by no means the same as the absence of consciousness constituting the void.

In the case of love mysticism, he stated, the mystics "assimilate God with the most blessed experience with which they are acquainted; they make Him in the image of the divine moments which precede and follow the loss of consciousness in ecstasy."[76]

The point was not, for either Leuba or Coe, that the mystic revelation had a physiological basis. Both recognized that a direct intuition of God, should such ever occur, could not happen apart from physiological processes. Their point was simply that the mystics' intuitions were interpretations and, thus, in Coe's words, that "the mystic acquires his religious convictions precisely as his non-mystical neighbor does, namely, through tradition and instruction, auto-suggestions grown habitual, and reflective analysis. The mystic brings his theological beliefs to the mystical experience; he does not derive them from it."[77]

SUBCONSCIOUS AS AUTOMATIC: COE

Whereas Coe tended toward a more physiological understanding of the subconscious than James, he, like James, associated the subconscious with automatisms. Like Davenport, and in contrast to the other psychologists of religion discussed here, Coe did not view the subconscious as central to authentic religious experience. Even if there was such a thing as co-consciousness, and Coe thought it was unlikely, Coe rejected the idea that something beyond the self could be accessed through the subconscious. Coe, like Ames, embraced the functionalist approach to psychology articulated by Ames's mentor and colleague James Angell and assessed religion in relation to its social value. Although Ames was probably the psychologist of religion that Coe admired the most, his fundamental disagreement with Ames regarding the role of human agency (or desire) in cultural evolution led to a fundamentally different rereading of the *Varieties*. Although Coe stood firmly on the side of the rational rather than the nonrational when defining the highest in religion, he more than any of the others sought a mediating position between the individual and the social.

Coe's various commitments positioned him in complicated ways in relation to the other psychologists of religion. Coe countered Starbuck's and Pratt's attempts to dissociate mysticism from automatisms and reasserted the link between automatisms, mysticism, and the subconscious laid down in the *Varieties*, but he did so only to sever the connection James had made between mysticism and religion. Coe criticized Ames for eliminating the role of human agency in the evolutionary process and, like James, upheld the importance of religious leadership in the evolution of culture. But rather than associating religious leadership solely with automatisms, Coe introduced a three-stage evolutionary typology that located reliance on automatisms at the bottom of the evolutionary ladder. The differences between James and Coe reflected divergent understandings of the subconscious, evolutionary theory, and definitions of religion. Their contrasting definitions of religion in turn reflected distinct intellectual commitments and life experiences.

Coe, who was familiar with the debates among the academic psychologists, had serious doubts about the idea of a "detached subconscious," that is to say, co-consciousness. He thought it likely that "between consciousness on the one hand, and brain process on the other, there is probably no third something, but the whole of what is included under such terms as 'secondary personality' is probably a phase of one or both of them." In saying this, Coe was not rejecting the idea of dissociation. Rather, he was inclined to understand secondary personalities as signs of mental processes that went on so far away from the center of attention that they never found "a place in the main chain of memory." Coe did not wrestle with the evidence for secondary chains of memory that so intrigued Janet, Myers, and James, and he may not have been familiar with that literature. Even if there were a detached subconscious, he argued, there was in his view little likelihood that it would reveal "a second or larger world."[78]

Coe's theoretical understanding of automatic phenomena probably went back to his reading of Havelock Ellis. Ellis's *Man and Woman* (1895), which Coe cited in *The Spiritual Life*, included a chapter, little noticed by later historians, on hypnotic phenomena. In a remarkable survey of the medical, anthropological, and religious literature, Ellis linked hypnotic and religious phenomena and placed the whole at the primitive end of the evolutionary continuum. Ellis concluded, as Davenport did later, that it was "natural that we should find hypnotic phenomena most highly developed among primitive races." He went beyond Davenport, however, to make an explicit connection between hypnotic phenomena and "shamanism," indicating that "the *shaman*, who is nearly everywhere the priest or priestess of savage races, presents the perfected type of hypnotic phenomena devoted to religious service and carried to the highest point of development."[79]

Shamanism, like enthusiasm, was a conceptual invention of the Enlightenment. It was widely adopted beginning in the eighteenth century as a generic term that linked what were taken to be common features of the northern Siberian tribes and the Native American Indians, e.g., their nervous instability, suggestibility, and susceptibility to hypnosis. It edged out competing terms, such as "the juggler" (defined as a diviner, magician, or enchanter) and the "medicine man."[80] Shamanism provided Coe with a means of reconceptualizing the psychology of religion. His reconceptualization took place in two steps. First, in a 1909 essay, he identified shamanism (i.e., "automatic experiences interpreted as possession") as the "primitive root" of all mysticism. Second, in *The Psychology of Religion* (1916), he located the shaman at the primitive end of a three-stage evolutionary typology of religious leadership, which ran from the shaman to the priest to the prophet. The marginalization of mysticism allowed Coe to argue that it was a mistake to identify religion with mysticism and, at the same time, lift up a definition of religion more in keeping with his own commitments and experience.

In his 1909 essay, Coe included under the heading of mysticism, religious ecstasy, inspirations of various sorts, and those "automatic experiences interpreted as 'possession,' and cultivated by the 'medicine man,' the shaman, or the 'witch doctor.' " Among the "inspirations," some of which he considered religious and some not, he included revivalism, the holiness movement, divine healing, spirit-communication, telepathy, clairvoyance, and premonitions. He laid out this whole set of phenomena in a chart with columns describing the experience, the associated practice, and their source or content.[81]

In Coe's commentary on his chart, he spelled out the dichotomies that informed his understanding of the relationship between religion and the subconscious. Specifically, he contrasted the scientific with the mystical, the former involving self-control and the latter the surrender of self control, with the result that "the mystical consciousness can not be analytical or critical." This contrast between self-control and automatic control carried over, he said, into the realm of values and purposes, where he distinguished between "values analyzed, approved, worked for in the full light of the individual consciousness" and "values hit upon more or less fitfully in conditions of automatic control." Coe believed that the actual values associated with automatic control were not, as many had been led to believe, instinctual ones, but rather "the habitual, the commonplace, [and] the socially expected."[82]

Coe's chief complaint against mysticism was that it was socially conservative. Thus, ironically, one of the basic disagreements between Coe and James was rooted in their assessment of the "fruits" of mysticism. Where James judged religious experiences of this sort in terms of their ability to unify a divided self, Coe judged them in terms of their ability to promote social change. Both were looking for religious experience to foster innovation, albeit of somewhat different sorts. James's and Coe's conclusions in this regard were only marginally empirical. Just as James's championing of visionary experience may have been tied in part to his father's Swedenborgianism, so too Coe's confidence that mysticism reinforced the commonplace and socially expected was undoubtedly informed at least in part by his conventional Methodist upbringing and his association of mysticism with the holiness tradition. At any rate for Coe and many other progressives coming out of conventional Protestant backgrounds, it was clear that "ethically progressive religion [must] break with the authority claimed for automatic inspirations" and foster an individualism essentially opposed to "automatic control."[83]

Coe structured his *Psychology of Religion* (1916) around three interconnected evolutionary typologies having to do with religious leadership, groups, and individual attitudes. The movement from the lowest to the highest stage was a movement from automatic control to self-control within the group as well as the individual. Thus, individuals progressed from impulsive to regulated to self-emancipating, while groups progressed from the religious crowd to the sacerdotal group to the deliberative group. At the most primitive level, in other words, the automatic experiences of the shaman were associated with the impulsive attitude and the religious crowd. At the intermediate level, the ritual, scripture, and doc-

A Survey of the Mystical

The Experience	Supposed Source or Content	The Deliberate Practise
The supreme mystical state (religious): Either Ecstasy or Permanent Automatism Supposed form: Complete absorption or loss of personality. Supposed content: Either zero or infinity. But these are only limiting notions.	God Tendency toward pantheistic conception	*The attempt to realize God as the all:* Yoga The Christian "Via Negativa" Christian Science and New Thought The method: Narrowing of attention and auto-suggestion.
Incomplete mystical states (religious): Inspirations The experience of the seer; Sense of guidance or of illumination;[6] Assurance or the witness of the spirit; Sense of divine communion; "Sense of presence"; "Anesthetic revelation"; "Cosmic consciousness." The form: Partial abeyance of self-control in mental functions. Occasionally, loss of muscular control also. The content: Somewhat specific ideas which commonly seem to be self-evidently or infallibly true.	God or Gods Generally conceived as transcendent	*Attempts to realize the God on special occasions or for special ends:* Oracles and Other Methods of Penetrating the Unknown Some Forms of Revivalism Holiness Movements and Allied Practises Divine Healing Transubstantiation The method: Surrender or quiescence of will, suggestion (largely social).
Incomplete mystical states other than religious: "Psychic Phenomena" This term includes supposed spirit-communication, telepathy, clairvoyance, premonition, etc.	A Spirit, A Living Man, or The Nature of Things	*Attempts to take advantage of supposed occult connections:* Mediumship in its Various Forms
The primitive root of the whole: Automatic Experiences Interpreted as Possession	Spirits	*Attempts to control spirits:* Certain Parts of Magic Shamanism

11. Coe's "Survey of the Mystical," depicting automatic experiences interpreted as possession (i.e., shamanism) as the primitive root of all mysticism. From George A. Coe, "The Mystical as a Psychological Concept," *Journal of Philosophy, Psychology, and Scientific Methods* 6, no. 8 (April 15, 1909):199.

trine of the priest were associated with the regulated attitude and the sacerdotal group. Finally, at the highest level, the "ethical communion with the divine" that characterized prophetic leadership was associated with the self-emancipating attitude and the deliberative group.[84]

In an illuminating chapter on the "Mental Traits of Religious Leaders," Coe walked a fine line between acknowledging the prevalence of automatisms among historically important religious leaders (by denying that automatisms were a sign of neurosis as long as they did not interfere with the person's functioning) and minimizing the importance of automatisms in figures he considered "prophetic" (188–89). "Neither Jesus nor the Buddha," he argued, "were made weak or inefficient by automatisms that he may have experienced; neither trafficked in them after the manner of the shaman; neither relied upon them as the basis of his certainty of the principles that he taught, but each rested the authority of his teachings either upon analysis of life or else upon the practical self-evidence of basal ethical ideals." Though both Jesus and the Buddha were "dissenter[s] from the existing social-religious order, each dissented, especially Jesus, in the interest of a wider and deeper sociality" (189).

In Coe's depiction of Jesus' interest in "a wider and deeper sociality," we get a hint of Coe's primary ethical commitment, to what he referred to as "the self-and-*socius* consciousness that makes us persons" (320). The self for Coe was not an isolated individual self, but always a person communicating with others. The centerpiece of cultural evolution was the self coming to consciousness in relation to others. Because self and society came to consciousness in tandem, the two could neither be separated nor prioritized. This coming to consciousness moved in certain preferred directions, i.e., toward greater consciousness, toward consciousness of more objects, toward greater control of those objects (including greater self-control), toward greater unification of objects (including greater unification of the self), toward expanded interaction or social communication, and finally toward greater contemplation or aesthetic appreciation (40).

Religion did not have a place in this list, Coe indicated, because it offered no particular value of its own. Religion rather was "a movement of reinforcement, unification, and revaluation of values as a whole, particularly in social terms" (41). In contrast to Ames, who equated religious consciousness with social consciousness (i.e., social values), Coe understood religion as the "movement within values" or the "revaluation of values," that is the dynamic process whereby "life [both individually and socially] organiz[es] and complet[es] itself, or seek[s] a destiny, as against the discrete values of impulsive or unreflective existence" (70–72). The evolution of religion, in other words, was linked to the self coming to consciousness in relation to others, where consciousness was associated with the unification and control of the self as manifest through deliberate, reflective action.[85]

In reemphasizing human agency in the process of evolution, Coe took the work of Ames back in the direction of James and the *Varieties*. Coe, like James, emphasized the unification of the self, but he emphasized that the self did so in relation to others. Where both James and Ames stressed the role of the subconscious in evolutionary development, Coe made coming to consciousness through deliberate, reflective action the central sign of evolutionary progress. Coe mediated between James and Ames with respect to mysticism and prayer. Where James understood both mysticism and prayer as central to religious experience and Ames rejected both in favor of collective ritual, Coe made prayer central, while downplaying mysticism.

For Coe, the relationship between human beings and God, like the relationship between humans, was by nature reciprocal. As such, it involved both "the recognition of the other as present" and the appreciation of "differences within a unity." Christian prayer at its best was a means of cultivating this reciprocity. The classical Christian understanding of mystical union, which Coe believed Christianity had borrowed from India by way of neo-Platonism, was problematic precisely because it involved the "extinction of reciprocity" through the absorption of the individual into the one (283–84). Despite his critical approach to mysticism, some of his closest acquaintances saw something of the mystic in Coe himself. One of his former students claimed that "when he talked about fellowship with God I felt the glow of his radiance, and he seemed transfigured." Although "fellowship with God meant something very precious to him, . . . he was quite helpless in transmitting what that was, so that a disciple could understand it and feel the same way."[86]

There is poignant evidence to suggest that it was the reciprocity of conjugal love that was for Coe the means of "initiation into the ultimate reality." Coe's wife, the professional musician Sadie Knowland Coe, died suddenly in 1905 after seventeen years of what appears to have been an unusually happy and egalitarian marriage. In 1922, Douglas Clyde Macintosh, newly appointed professor of theology at Yale Divinity School, wrote Coe seeking any wisdom he might have to offer in the wake of *his* wife's sudden death. Coe wrote him of the "positive meaning in tragedy" that he had discovered in "Tagore's treatment of conjugal affection," adding that he knew of "no westerner who has grasped quite as firmly the metaphysical problem that it involves, and this includes, of course, an interpretation of death and separation."

Recognizing that Macintosh might wonder how, "with [his] critical attitude toward mysticism, [he could] be so warm toward Tagore," Coe noted that "the core of certainty is not any alleged intuition *sui generis* that bursts through from some other realm, but the state of mind one is in who resolutely and idealistically *lives through ordinary experiences*." Tagore, he said, was "most clear on this point."

> When death brings separation, there is no flight to a substitute or solace. Nevertheless conjugal affection here is treated as initiation into the ultimate reality. Hence it seems to me that Tagore finds the larger truth mediated by the way that one voluntarily takes the marital relation. The way into this larger reality is the revaluation of values.[87]

This letter suggests that Coe's inability to convey the source of his own relational mysticism to his students was due not to the ineffability or the incoherence of his experience, but rather simply to its intensity and intimacy.

CONCLUSION

At a conference on the psychology of religion held in 1938, Anton T. Boisen, a student of George Coe, presented a paper on "The Present Status of William James's Psychology of Religion." Boisen, whose interests in psychopathology and mysticism mirrored those of William James in many ways, noted that "there was general agreement among the distinguished psychologists present that the movement which had been launched so enthusiastically at the turn of the century and had reached so brilliant a climax in William James's *Varieties of Religious Experience* had spent its force." Although most scholars agree that the empirically based psychology-of-religion movement lost its momentum within a decade or two, few, in my view, have accounted for its decline as cogently as Boisen. Boisen pointed to two broad factors: the breakdown of the international movement of which the American psychology of religion was a part, and the retreat from psychopathology on the part of the younger generation of psychologists of religion.

With respect to the first: Boisen was not only aware that the psychology of religion was an international movement, a fact that scholars have only recently been rediscovering, but he also recognized the role of both the transformation of higher education and the First World War in destroying these international ties. Thus, he described William James not only as "a pioneer and explorer," but also as "a representative of the old order when philosophy and psychology dwelt together and the scientist was also a scholar who was at home in other departments of human knowledge." He was, Boisen pointed out, "a splendid incarnation of the old cosmopolitan culture, a man grounded in the study of Latin and Greek—without which he could not have graduated from college—and thoroughly at home in the language and literature of Germany and France." The next generation of psychologists of religion, most of whom held positions in departments where philosophy and psychology still mingled, shared this broad training with James. Unlike James, however, they "fronted more the coming age," as Boisen put it, and were all succeeded by specialists, "men trained in the time when philosophy and psychology had been divorced and psychology was bent on establishing itself as a respectable 'brass-instrument science.'" Few of these specialists had the training or inclination to study religion and few in religion continued to make use of scientific method. The First World War, which brought the German and French empirical work in the psychology of religion to a halt and fostered a turn toward neo-orthodox theology, simply reinforced a process of fragmentation that was already well underway in the new universities.[88]

With respect to the second factor, Boisen argued that James's interest in psychopathology permeated the *Varieties* and provided the basis for some of its most brilliant insights. He accurately noted that James's "younger associates in this century did not share this interest. Some," he said, "were crusading against the excesses of nineteenth-century revivalism [as in the case of Coe] and all were critical of his interest in the pathological and his tenderness for the mystical."[89] By adopting a stage-theory of evolution, in which they identified automatisms with the mental instability of primitives, the younger generation of psychologists of religion beat a hasty retreat from the "religious psychopath" who played such a prominent role in the *Varieties*. Although their understanding of religion at its highest and most civilized differed, Pratt, Ames, and Coe all agreed that it was not characterized by automatisms. The retreat from psychopathology, according to Boisen, diverted the impetus that originally informed the psychology of religion into religious education on the one hand and the philosophy of religion on the other.[90]

There were, however, several interrelated points that Boisen overlooked. Boisen's comments suggest that he associated "experimental psychology" solely with the German laboratory tradition and was unaware of the French clinical tradition in experimental psychology that informed William James. Nor is there anything to suggest an awareness of the contributions of the SPR and their sense that they too were contributing to an experimental psychology of the subconscious. When Boisen made reference to psychopathology, he didn't have the same thing in mind as when James referred to the "psychopathic temperament." For Boisen, who was himself hospitalized on several occasions, schizophrenia, not hysteria or neurasthenia, was the archetypal mental illness. Although the concept of psychopathology remained a constant, its meaning changed over the intervening decades, such that the dissociative psychology of the subconscious completely disappeared from view. Not only had Janet been eclipsed, but also the more controversial work of the SPR. The history of animal magnetism that preceded both had receded from sight as well.

If we expand our horizon to take in Myers, Flournoy, Buckley, Beard, and Sunderland, we can see not only the psychology of religion's retreat from psychopathology, but also its retreat from psychical research and the comparative study of dissociation, trance, and somnambulism in presumptively normal persons. The fits, trances, and visions that nineteenth-century theorists associated with animal magnetism, somnambulism, and trance were more commonly understood by critics as delusions than as insanity. At the turn of the century, most scientists linked such phenomena, now conceptualized as "sensory and motor automatisms," with the mental weakness of the hysteric or the primitive. Although the SPR made a valiant effort to challenge such views, it never achieved the legitimacy it sought in the academic world. It was not until the 1960s that the academic study of trance and dissociation was taken up again by anthropologists and humanistic psychologists under the rubric of "altered states of consciousness." On a popular level, however, both the findings of the SPR and their idea of the subconscious were received enthusiastically by some both inside and outside the Protestant churches.

CHAPTER EIGHT

Varieties of Protestant Religious Experience

WHEN THE "power" manifest at Maria Woodworth's revivals was discussed in the St. Louis papers in 1890, explanations were offered by neurologists, mesmerists, reporters, and "respectable" Protestants, as well as by Woodworth-Etter and her supporters. The neurologists were the ostensible scientific experts, but their learned talk about hysteria, hypnotism, and the threat Woodworth's revivals posed to public safety was derided in the papers. The reporters and leading Protestant commentators, such as James Monroe Buckley, drew on their knowledge of popular psychology and religion to argue that manifestations of this power were common in the history of religion and could be explained in terms of trance and mental excitement. In 1890, nonexperts—journalists, church leaders, and church people—were broadly familiar with matters of mesmerism, trance, and religion, but their knowledge had been taken up in relatively limited ways by academics and professionals.

Whereas Protestants in 1890 used mesmerism and trance to explain forms of Protestantism they wanted to discredit, they rarely used mesmerism or trance to explain phenomena they took to be authentic. In contrast to the Spiritualists and the intellectual heirs of Phineas Quimby, they did not use psychology to interpret people or events depicted in the New Testament, such as Jesus' miracles, the resurrection, Paul's conversion, or the experience of the disciples at Pentecost. By 1910, all this had changed. Much of the credit for this change can be attributed, directly and indirectly, to the Society for Psychical Research (SPR) and its prominent supporters, such as William James. Between 1890 and 1910, the SPR. provided some Protestants with a seemingly scientific and academically respectable bridge between science and religion.[1] This view did not displace the others, however. It simply made the picture more complex.

In contrast to earlier periods, Protestants at the turn of the century explained involuntary experiences in three ways rather than just the usual two—as natural and false, as natural and true, and as supernatural and true. Protestants enlisted the concept of the subconscious in each of these three explanations. In order to do so, however, they had to define the subconscious in different ways. Those who understood involuntary experiences as natural and false equated the subconscious, following Coe, with the primitive and unscientific. Those who understood involuntary experiences as natural and true equated the subconscious, following James and Myers, with the mystical and the scientific. As long as there were only two options, supernatural and psychological explanations of involuntary experiences stood in opposition to one another. The popularization of the mediating position gave Protestants the option of arguing that God and Satan acted through the subconscious to create both real and counterfeit experiences.

In this chapter, I focus on three developments within turn-of-the-century Protestantism, each of which was associated with a different approach to involuntary experiences: the churching of New Thought, the rise of Pentecostalism, and the modernization of religious education. I use the first phrase to describe the Protestant appropriation of the Jamesian subconscious in ways that, deliberately or not, recapitulated a variety of themes originally introduced by Quimby and his heirs in the New Thought movement. The Emmanuel Movement, a church-based healing movement that sought to recover the spirit and power of the religion of Jesus, spearheaded this effort. Led by two Episcopal priests, Elwood Worcester and Samuel McComb, the movement mediated between science and religion, combined the psychology of the subconscious and modern biblical criticism, and promoted a naturalistic version of Jesus' healing ministry within the mainline churches. Parallels with New Thought were also evident in the writings of Protestant scholars who utilized the Jamesian subconscious as a means of interpreting mystical experience in general and the incarnation of Christ in particular.

While the Emmanuel Movement shared the universalizing tendencies of New Thought, Pentecostalism was exclusivist in orientation. Two prominent early Pentecostals—Charles F. Parham, the leader of the Apostolic Faith Movement, and William J. Seymour, the leader of the Azusa Street revival in Los Angeles—recapitulated the attitudes of Jonathan Edwards and John Wesley toward involuntary experiences.[2] Parham, like Edwards, was preoccupied with the problem of counterfeits. He not only used secularizing forms of psychology to discredit the "fanaticism" of others within the movement but also used the subconscious to explain the action of the Holy Spirit in true believers. Seymour, like Wesley, was not particularly concerned with counterfeits. He drew upon the Bible to defend involuntary experiences and reworked the typologies of the camp-meeting tradition to provide a theological framework for a richly embodied experience of the Holy Spirit.

The religious education movement was a modernist effort to reformulate theological education and parish ministry around a vision of ministry as education. It was, in the traditional Protestant sense, "formalistic" or anti-experiential. Here, as in other rationalistic forms of Christianity, involuntary experience had no real place and the psychology of involuntary experience was used to discredit what was for modernists "false religion." In the modernist Sunday School curriculum, the psychology of the subconscious played a shadow role, delegitimating the evangelical emphasis on conversion, downplaying or erasing what for the Emmanuel and Pentecostal movements were the high points of the biblical narrative.

Although the mediating tradition flowered briefly within both the academy and the church during the first decade of the twentieth century, it was rapidly rebuffed by academics hostile to a religious interpretation of involuntary experience within the universities and the theological schools. By 1920, the rationalistic, developmental psychology championed by George Coe was firmly ensconced in the new departments of religious education in the university-related divinity schools and the more liberal Methodist and Baptist theological seminaries. Nonetheless, religious interpretations of involuntary experiences remained very much in evidence at the popular level. The universalizing mysticism of William James lived on among ordinary Protestants in the form of Christian–New Thought hybrids. Conversion experiences of the kind studied by Starbuck and Coe, while rapidly disappearing in the more liberal Protestant churches, found a home in the new independent denominations.

Many turn-of-the-century Protestants eventually aligned themselves, at least tacitly, with one of the two competing views of the subconscious—the subconscious as subliminal (James and Myers) or the subconscious as primitive (Davenport and Coe)—but few made such distinctions at first. During the 1890s, ordinary Protestants, insofar as they were aware of the idea of the subconscious at all, associated it with the SPR and the vaguely differentiated proponents of mental healing or mind cure. Thomson Jay Hudson, a journalist, civil servant, and self-taught psychologist, who died in 1903, was largely responsible for popularizing the related concept of the "subjective mind" during that decade. He published his first book, *The Law of Psychic Phenomena*, in 1893, followed by a series of others with titles such as *A Scientific Demonstration of the Future Life* (1901), *The Law of Mental Medicine* (1903), and posthumously, *The Evolution of the Soul* (1904). They were based, he said, on "the facts of experimental psychology as developed by thirty years of my own experimentation, and of that of the Society for Psychical Research beginning in 1882." All contained a potent popular blend of psychical research, psychology, evolutionary theory, mental healing, and liberal Christianity.[3]

Hudson's central hypothesis was that "man is endowed with two minds," one subjective and the other objective. The former was understood as incapable of inductive reasoning and "constantly amenable to control by suggestion." It also possessed "the power of transmitting intelligence to other subjective minds . . . [by means of] telepathy." Telepathy, according to Hudson, had no normal functions in this life. Its purpose, rather, was to facilitate communication between discarnate subjective minds (i.e., souls) after death. According to Hudson, "the facts of psychic science fully and completely sustain the religious philosophy of Jesus of Nazareth, demonstrate his perfect mastery of the science of the soul, and confirm every essential doctrine of the Christian religion."[4] The leaders of the SPR were decidedly ambivalent with respect to the efforts of their erstwhile promoter. Even considered "as a purely popular, unscientific handbook," the Society's reviewer could only muster faint praise for *The Law of Psychic Phenomena*, a book that promoted the Society's efforts while violating most of its standards for scientific research.[5]

In 1902, following the publication of Starbuck's *Psychology of Religion*, Coe's *Spiritual Life*, and James's *Varieties*, a Chicago newspaper reported that "the interest excited by the suggestive but often unscientific books of such a writer as [Thomson Jay] Hudson, and the attention given to the researches of James, Starbuck, and Coe, show that the Christian world is prepared to consider the psychological side of religion and the spiritual life." George Coe received letters from clergy struggling to sort out the popular from the scientific. The Reverend E. R. Lathrop wrote in 1902 to ask George Coe's opinion of "the theory of Prof. Thos. Jay Hudson in his book 'The Law of Psychic Phenomena.' . . . Is this theory accepted by our professors of intellectual philosophy? Of course a country parson is not competent to sit in judgment upon such occult themes. Let us have the judgment of an expert." Reverend William Marsh, a Methodist minister in Utica, New York, wrote at Borden Parker Bowne's suggestion to get Coe's advise on a paper he was writing for his minister's association. Marsh indicated that he had read an eclectic mix of books in preparation for his talk on "Dual Mental Organization," including "Dr Hudson's books 'Psychic Phenomena' and 'The Divine Pedigree of Man,' also a book by [Boris] Sidis [a student of James at Harvard] on 'The Psychology of Suggestion.'" He added that he had also read "the mental scientists such as Wood, Trine, &c.," that is, New Thought writers, Ralph Waldo Trine, author of the best-selling book *In Tune with the Infinite*, and Henry Wood, author of *The New Thought Simplified*. Marsh asked Coe for his suggestions onwhat else to read, indicating that "Dr Bowne did not seem to think Hudson was an *authority*, although he did not say just that. What is your own estimate of his theory of the dual organization of mind? It is a subject of intense interest."[6]

As these ministers' letters suggest, turn-of-the-century Protestants interested in psychology were reading an eclectic mix of books including the strictly academic writings of Boris Sidis, the relatively academic works of Starbuck, James, and Coe, and the manifestly popular writings of Hudson and New Thought writers, such as Trine and Wood. As of 1902, the writings of Coe and James were regularly included on lists of new books recommended for Christian ministers, students, and workers.[7] Although both were recommended to and read by the clergy, James and Coe directly and indirectly promoted very different aims. Primarily through his writings, William James promoted and legitimated the flowering of interest in the subconscious as a scientific and mystical concept, whereas Coe, both in his publications and his teaching, opposed such a view, referring to it disparagingly as "psychic theology." In time, very different segments within turn-of-the-century Protestantism took up their opposing views of the subconscious.

THE CHURCHING OF NEW THOUGHT

The flowering of the Jamesian subconscious among mainline Protestants was accompanied by the Protestant appropriation of a variety of themes originally introduced by Quimby and his heirs in the New Thought movement. In 1900, Christian Science stood as a challenge to the multitude of small non-Christian Science mind-cure groups and the mainline Protestant churches. It was unified, practically oriented to real human needs, and growing rapidly. Horatio W. Dresser, son of mind-cure pioneers Julius and Annetta Dresser and a former student of James's at Harvard, and Elwood Worcester, a psychologically trained parish priest at Emmanuel (Episcopal) Church in Boston, both drew upon the psychology of the subconscious to mount a response to Christian Science. Dresser used the psychology of the subconscious to reinterpret the writings of Phineas Quimby and provide a unified theoretical foundation for the dissenting mind-cure groups under the banner of New Thought. Worcester used the psychology of the subconscious to link modern science and modern biblical scholarship and provide an "orthodox" foundation for a healing movement within the mainline Protestant churches.

Worcester and the leaders of the Emmanuel Movement took pains to distinguish themselves from their American competitors. They stressed that the Emmanuel Movement promoted "psychotherapy" not "mind-cure" and located their antecedents in the French experimental psychology of the subconscious and not in Christian Science or the Holiness-based "faith-cure" movements. Although much, in fact, did distinguish the Emmanuel Movement from Christian Science and the faith-cure movement, there was much less—apart from institutional affiliation—that separated the Emmanuel Movement from New Thought, especially in the updated version presented by Dresser. Similarly, William Sanday, a very prominent and relatively conservative Anglican New Testament scholar would not have viewed himself as contributing to the churching of New Thought. Nonetheless, his use of a Jamesian psychology of the subconscious to develop a new biblically based Christology brought ways of thinking about mysticism and the incarnation that had long been popular in the New Thought tradition into the mainstream of Protestant theological scholarship.

Horatio W. Dresser

In 1906, when Dresser published *Health and the Inner Life*, various terms were still used to designate the movement that came to be known as "New Thought." While accepting "New Thought" as the latest and most popular of designation for the "more rational" side of the movement, he referred to the movement as a whole, including Christian Science, as the "mind-cure" or "mental-healing" movement.[8] Although Christian Science was unified, Dresser described the "more rational" side of the movement as highly fragmented. "Little 'centres of truth,' independent churches, and metaphysical clubs have been established here and there throughout the English-speaking world" (8). This fragmentation led many to place a disproportionate emphasis on the teachings of Christian Science when referring to the mind-cure movement and obscured what Dresser took to be the underlying commonalities uniting the more rational groups. The remedy, Dresser thought, was a return to the origins of the movement, that is to methods and teachings of Phineas Quimby, in order to explain "the peculiar connection of health with religion that constitutes the strangeness of the phenomenon [of mental cure]" (13).

Dresser emphasized that Quimby viewed man as possessing "a dual nature," whose two sides he variously designated as science and ignorance, wisdom and opinions, mind and matter, the real man and the natural man, Christ and Jesus. Quimby's claim that disease was the result of mental error was confusing, according to Dresser, to many who "were not conscious of having thought themselves into disease" (66–71). According to Dresser,

> The mystery in regard to the connection between mind and matter begins to be cleared up when one discovers that mental activity is not limited to the highly conscious life, but is intimately connected with the vast realm of subconscious life. In this deeper, more

or less hidden part of our nature there is undoubtedly a close relation with the region which the investigators of the Society for Psychical Research denominate the 'subliminal.' (72–73)

Thus, when Quimby spoke of disease "as an 'error,' as due to 'false reasoning,' " he was referring, according to Dresser, to an "entire subconscious train of sequences" and not simply to conscious "errors" (76).

Dresser also noted that "telepathic and similar psychic experiences" were rooted in the subconscious (72–73) and interpreted Quimby's clairvoyant abilities and his use of such abilities in the healing process in light of the contemporary findings of "psychic science." Thus, according to Dresser, "at the present time many students of psychic science are reaching this same conclusion, in part, which Mr. Quimby reached so long ago; namely, that the facts of clairaudience, clairvoyance, telepathy, and the ability to heal mentally at a distance prove the existence of a part of us which can live and act independently of matter" (89).

Dresser emphasized that from the start the mind-cure movement had been both religious and scientific. "The science," he said, "is the religion. The power to heal disease, either in oneself or in another, is the ultimate practical test of the 'the truth' in question" (227). The movement's central religious contention was that "to be set free by spiritual truth is to see that life springs from a single Source, that it becomes one and harmonious for us when we enter into adjustment with the guidances of omnipresent Wisdom. The clue to this adjustment is the Christ spirit, the ideal which the life of Jesus exemplified" (232). In noting the movement's relation to science, Dresser indicated that the term had often been used loosely within the movement. He stated that "Hudson's *Law of Psychic Phenomena* came nearer the scientific ideal, but was equally disappointing in the end." He concluded that the "psychological reconstruction [of the mental healing movement] can best be accomplished by reference to the psychology of Professor William James, culminating in his *Varieties of Religious Experience*." In his insistence that "actual 'work' is accomplished" by religion, James provided "the connecting link between general religious experience and the specific application to health for which Quimby, Evans, and their followers have stood." By providing "the spiritual-healing people," as Dresser called them, with respectable scientific underpinnings, James made it possible for them "to take their place in an intelligible psychological and religious system" (247–48).

If James's *Varieties* allowed the "spiritual-healing people" to find an intelligible and increasingly respectable place in the world, the movement's unremitting emphasis on "mak[ing] Christianity practical" posed a sharp challenge to the churches. In an aside to his more churchly readers, Dresser commented that if, as a result of the movement's emphasis on practical Christianity, "people have lost interest in the churches and have turned to mind-cure books for spiritual satisfaction, there is but one course to pursue—to be as concretely practical as the mind-cure people" (228–29). Wittingly or not, this was the challenge that the Emmanuel Movement arose to address.

Elwood Worcester and Samuel McComb

In his accounts of beginnings of the Emmanuel Movement, Elwood Worcester returned repeatedly to the church's loss of spiritual power and the challenge that Christian Science posed to the churches. In a speech to the Episcopal Club of Massachusetts in 1907, Worcester confessed that "a good many of us feel that in some way something has evaporated out of the gospel of Christ, and the Christian religion." Many ministers, he said, "have the sad feeling . . . that it is getting harder and harder for them year by year to do the work of the ministry and to produce the spiritual effect on their people that they long so much to do."[9] In the introduction to *Religion and Medicine*, Worcester observed that the real spiritual movement of the day was taking place outside the churches. "There," he said, one finds "a marked tendency to dispense with the tedious processes of criticism and dogma and to return to the Christ of the Gospels and to accept His words in a more literal sense." Two characteristics of the movement stood out: its "renewed belief in prayer" and its "confident expectation that religious and spiritual states can affect health."[10]

Rather than simply ridiculing Christian Science, Worcester urged his readers to look "beneath the vulgar and repulsive exterior of Christian Science . . . to find a truth in it, a gift for men, a spiritual power answering to men's needs which the churches at present do not possess."[11] That truth, Worcester argued, could be found and more fully realized within the context of orthodox Christianity and orthodox science. "It is not necessary to go outside of orthodoxy, it is not necessary to desert true science," he maintained, "to lay hold of this wonderful healing power that has been discovered within the mind." Alluding to the "fine body of literature growing today on the power residing in the soul," he set forth the aim of the new work inaugurated at Emmanuel Church as one of laying "hold of these newly defined psychical powers through the means within our grasp, religious faith and exact science."[12] Or as he elaborated in his lecture on "Mental Healing," "we have based the work that we have been doing fairly and squarely upon the combination of two good principles, and those are,—the religion of Christ which is contained in the New Testament and substantiated by modern scholarship, and the best scientific help we have been able to obtain, and by that I mean medical assistance and also the sound psychology of our day."[13]

The Emmanuel Movement began at Emmanuel [Episcopal] Church in Boston in 1906 under the leadership of Worcester and his associate, Samuel McComb. It spread rapidly to Protestant churches across the country by means of newspaper publicity, articles in popular magazines, and how-to books written by clergy. The movement reached its peak around 1908, at which point many of the physicians associated with the movement, discomfited by its rapid growth, withdrew their support. During its heyday, two distinctive features set it apart from the mind-cure movement: the formal involvement of physicians as well as clergy and its association with traditional Protestant churches.[14]

Like the mind-cure movements, however, the Emmanuel Movement sought to mediate between science and religion. Although both Worcester and McComb were better trained and more scholarly than most mind-cure leaders, they, like Quimby, Evans, and Dresser, brought together a psychology with debts to Mesmer and a relatively literal reading of the New Testament. The Emmanuel Movement weekly classes, like Phoebe Palmer's Tuesday night meetings for the promotion of holiness and the Spiritualists' public Sunday evening services, were open to persons of various religious affiliations and scheduled so as not to compete with Sunday morning worship in the churches. Finally, the Emmanuel Movement shared with the Spiritualists an enthusiasm for promoting biblical miracles, interpreted naturalistically, in the modern world.

THE PSYCHOLOGY OF THE SUBCONSCIOUS

The "exact science" to which Worcester referred was physiological psychology, specifically the experimental psychology of the subconscious, and the "medical assistance" he obtained was from physicians, some of them neurologists, associated with what Hale has called the "Boston school of psychotherapy." The leading physicians associated with the movement in its early stages were James J. Putnam, professor of neurology at Harvard, and Richard Cabot, an internist at Massachusetts General Hospital. Isador Coriat, a former student of Morton Prince at Tufts, joined Worcester and, Worcester's assistant in the work, Samuel McComb, as their long-standing medical consultant. The physicians accepted the reality of the subconscious, but they did not interpret it in religious terms.[15]

Both Worcester and McComb were well educated and had pursued advanced work in psychology in Germany. Nonetheless, both followed James and Myers in interpreting the subconscious in terms of the subliminal mind. Worcester, after graduating from Columbia and obtaining a ministerial degree from General Theological Seminary in New York, studied under Wilhelm Wündt at Leipzig. Worcester initially planned to write his dissertation under Wündt, but upon discovering that this would entail an extra year of laboratory work, he decided to write on the religious philosophy of John Locke. Although Worcester's study with Wündt is often mentioned, he was more deeply influenced by Wündt's teacher Gustav Fechner, a connection Worcester shared with William James and which James, as we have seen, highlighted in A Pluralistic Universe. Worcester found it hard to write of his relationship with Fechner, because "his soul entered so deeply into my soul, his thought has so accompanied me through life, that I can no longer distinguish the transcendent quality of his mind from the man of flesh and blood."[16]

Although Worcester lifted up Fechner, Wündt, and James as the chief influences on his psychological views, he shared with Fechner and James an openness to spiritual phenomena and an interest in psychical research. The earliest experience of this sort that Worcester described took place when he was a young man in despair about his prospects due to the collapse of his family's fortunes. He reported that he saw a strange light "accompanied by an audible voice and . . . plainly heard these words, 'Be faithful to me and I will be faithful to you.' " He indicated that his father had a great curiosity with regard to psychic phenomena and that his father-in-law, an Episcopal bishop, had "an even keener interest" and encouraged the priests in his care to keep a record of any unusual psychic experiences. Although most of his teachers were hostile to the subject, he noted that Fechner was an exception. Fechner not only had an interest in Augustine's stories of "prophetic dreams and apparitions," he also "attended 'sittings' given by D. D. Home and other mediums."[17] Worcester's references to Wündt, thus, did not mean that he was aligned psychologically with the German laboratory tradition. Rather, his sympathies lay with the kind of psychological research promoted by Fechner, James, and Myers, a psychology interested in and open to the findings of psychical research.

The Emmanuel Movement was inaugurated in November 1906 through a series of four lectures, two by physicians and two by ministers. In his lecture, McComb echoed James in claiming that "the greatest psychological discovery of modern times . . . was the subconscious mind." He lifted up Paul Dubois's *Psychic Treatment of Nervous Diseases* and Joseph Jastrow's *The Subconscious* "as text books for the movement." But he sounded less like Jastrow and more like Myers and James when he described "the subconscious . . . [as being] in closest relation with the religious life, and the uprush from its works [as acting] so marvelously upon life that in common affairs we behold its performances as miracles."[18]

In a series of lectures given to clergy eighteen months later, McComb located the Emmanuel Movement within the larger "history of mind cure." Locating the origins of "modern scientific psychotherapy . . . in the 'animal magnetism' of Mesmer," he traced the development of psychotherapy in Europe, mentioning such figures as the English physicians James Braid and Hack Tuke and the French neurologists and psychologists, Bernheim, Charcot, Janet, and Binet. He described the Americans—Morton Prince, Boris Sidis, and Isador Coriat—as "among the greatest living experts in psychotherapy." Significantly, his history of "mind cure" did not end with the history of psychotherapy. According to the *Boston Herald*, McComb "also alluded to the work of Dr. Quimby" and his influence on Mary Baker Eddy and Christian Science. He concluded that the Emmanuel Church clinic will "have made no small contribution" if it does nothing else than "bridge over the chasm" that has too long divided the religious and scientific healing movements.[19] The bridge between them was the subconscious, specifically the subliminal self of Myers and James, the subject of his next lecture. There McComb identified himself "with James, Myers, Coriat and the others who consider the subconscious to be a normal and highly influential factor in personality" and went into some detail about Myers's understanding of the subliminal self.[20]

Worcester's chapter on suggestion and the subconscious mind on *Religion and Medicine* (1908) combined elements from James, Myers, and Thomas Hudson's *Law of Psychic Phenomena*. Like James, Worcester concluded that Janet's view of the subconscious was too narrowly conceived. "A power which quickens our intellectual processes, which heightens our will power, cannot be regarded as pathological," he argued. He concluded that "the subconscious mind is a normal part of our spiritual nature . . . and in closer contact with the Universal Spirit than reason" (*RM*, 42). Like Hudson, Worcester emphasized the role of suggestion in healing and the role of faith in making suggestions efficacious. Although he and

McComb sought to "awaken faith," Worcester stressed that they did not "desire blind or fanatical faith." Differentiating their work from that of other religious healers, he said, "we lay absolutely no claim to personal power, we explain as fully as possible the nature of the means we employ, and call attention to the limitations of such methods, and accept as patients only persons suffering from functional disorders" (RM, 54). Suggestion, according to Worcester, rested on the mental capacity for dissociation, that is on "the concentration of the mind on some things to the exclusion of others." The successful use of suggestion depended upon "a certain degree of dissociation in which the command or assurance [given by the therapist] dominates our mind to the exclusion of other thoughts." While some healers used hypnosis to "deepen the dissociation" and addressed suggestions "directly to the subconscious," Worcester believed hypnotism was not necessary for the treatment of "the ordinary neuroses" (RM, 44, 59, 65).

They followed Hudson's lead when they emphasized the role of suggestion in healing, but they went beyond him when they entered into therapeutic dialogues with their patients while they were in a "calm, passive, and relaxed condition." The aim of the dialogue, according to McComb, was to "rouse the energies of the conscious mind, to convince it of the unsubstantial character of the miseries that obsess it." In these dialogues, he said, "an effort is made to dig out of the mind the concealed cause of its wretchedness, to analyze the cause, to hold it up, so to say, in the clear light of consciousness, and so divest it of all its malign power."[21]

Religion and Medicine received mixed reviews. The most scathing critique came, rather predictably, from an academic psychologist. Lightner Witmer, a psychologist at the University of Pennsylvania, criticized Worcester for citing Hudson and Bramwell as authorities and for weaving the views of "the pseudo-psychologist Frederic W. H. Myers . . . into the warp and woof of [his] theory." Although he knew that Worcester had studied with Wundt, Witmer insisted, rightly enough, that "the psychology of the Emmanuel Movement is not the psychology of Wundt, nor indeed of any psychological laboratory. It is the psychology of Hudson, Bramwell, and Myers." Moreover, he stated, "the driving force that has brought conviction to Worcester and his associates is Professor William James."[22] Witmer then proceeded to attack James's authority as a psychologist. After surveying James's association with the Society for Psychical Research and his contributions to "modern experimental psychology," Witmer concluded that there was "little warrant in fact for considering James a psychologist, in the meaning which must be given to this term since G. Stanley Hall brought 'psychology' from Germany and established the first laboratory of the science at Johns Hopkins University."[23]

In *The Christian Religion as a Healing Power*, published eighteen months after *Religion and Medicine*, Worcester and McComb both qualified their discussion of the subconscious. Worcester acknowledged that "the doctrine of the subconscious is a mere theory, denied by some respectable psychologists; yet, if we regard it only as a symbol, it stands for experiences of great importance" (12). McComb insisted that "the fact of the subconscious . . . can hardly be disputed," while emphasizing that "the Emmanuel work does not depend upon any [particular] theory, whether physiological or psychological, of the subconscious" (99).

THE RELIGION OF CHRIST

Worcester and McComb, like others who approached religion experientially, focused on the "signs and wonders" or "miraculous" aspects of Jesus' ministry. They did not, however, interpret these accounts as miraculous in the traditional, supernatural sense of the term, but, like others in the mediating tradition, as simultaneously natural and religious. This emphasis can be read, as Bruce Mullin has done, in relation to the turn-of-the-century quest for "evidences" of the truth of Christianity and the erosion of the orthodox Protestant contention that miracles ended with the early church. For our purposes, however, it is more important to note the connection between "signs and wonders" and experience. If we construe the signs-and-wonders tradition broadly to include not only the miracle stories, but also Paul's conversion and out-of-body experiences, Peter's visions, and the descent of the Holy Spirit at Pentecost, it becomes clear that we are not only talking about "evidences" of Christianity, but also about the manifestation of the power or presence of God in the lives of human beings. Worcester and McComb, like the Spiritualist and the Holiness/Pentecostal traditions, read the Bible as testimonies of experience.

When Worcester read the New Testament and early church history, he recognized, he said, "that something valuable had been lost from the Christian religion, and that Christianity had not always been so unsuccessful in its appeal to human nature as it is now." What had been lost, he maintained, was "a religion of the Spirit and of Power." It was the desire to overcome this loss that led Worcester to focus on "the healing ministry of Jesus." There, he said, "we come most directly into contact with his personality, his compassion, his understanding of his mission. It is customary for rationalists and unbelievers generally to make light of this portion of the Saviour's life."[24]

In contrast to the evangelical depiction of Jesus as preacher, Worcester and McComb lifted up Jesus the physician, arguing that "our Lord's healing message [was] . . . part of His permanent message to humanity."[25] In *Religion and Medicine*, they provided a detailed analysis of the healing of the paralytic, arguing that the "secret of Christ's healing power . . . [was] His sense of filial dependence upon God expressed in faith and prayer." They argued that Jesus recognized "the moral causes" which often lie behind "physical disease" and that "Christ's healing power required as a psychological medium and spiritual condition faith on the part of the healed or of his friends or of both." In the relationship between "Paul the Theologian" and "Luke the Physician," they found religious precedent for clergy and physicians "join[ing] hands for the alleviation of human suffering."[26]

Worcester and McComb's central premise, like that of others who used the Bible as a guide to experiencing religion, was that what they were able to do then, we should be able to do now. Thus, Worcester argued, "if these miracles [the miracles of Christ] were the outcome of faith we ought to be able to do something of the same kind today." Worcester anticipated that the discoveries of modern psychology would result in a book on "the miracles of Christ that will revolutionize the thoughts of the world upon that subject." Although such discoveries clearly provided evidence of the truth of Christianity, Worcester stressed that a new understanding of Christ's miracles would lead to "a deeper, a more spiritual life, a greater likeness to the Master and a greater knowledge of his benevolent purposes for men."[27]

In contrast to the camp-meeting tradition, Worcester and McComb turned to the latest in biblical scholarship to defend their interpretation of Jesus while at the same time acknowledging that "a return to the first century . . . was impossible." Their aim, as Worcester described it, was "to introduce a new conception into the life of the Church which would aim at combining the disposition and power of Jesus and *a sense of the reality of the Spiritual world* with the views and practices of modern science." Like others in the mediating tradition, Worcester rejected the traditional conception of miracles, as an "overturning or suspension of universal laws." Nonetheless, "in the linguistic sense of marvels unheard of in the past, attainable by a combination or application at a given point of energies long in existence, [miracles] must be admitted by everyone who has kept pace with discovery in our modern civilization." Significantly, with the adoption of a mediating position between psychology and religion, Worcester, though long considered "a rationalist" by his fellow clergy, came to be regarded by many within his church "as a fanatic."[28]

THE UNIVERSALIZING TENDENCY

The universalizing tendencies within the Emmanuel Movement, although never systematically developed, were nonetheless pervasive. They were most apparent in the thought of Worcester and McComb and in the openness of the movement to persons of any or no religious persuasion. These universalizing tendencies reflected Worcester's and McComb's understanding of the subconscious as a doorway to the Universal Spirit, their (nonexclusive) understanding of Jesus and the disciples as a psychological healers, and their belief that the naturalistic "miracles" of the New Testament were replicable in the present. Both their writings and their inclusive practice witnessed to their view that such healing power was limited neither to Jesus and the early church nor to modern Christians.

Worcester began studying the religions of the world when he was a professor at Lehigh University and continued after accepting a call to a church in Philadelphia in 1896. The result was a series of lectures that he delivered at the university and used as a study series in his Philadelphia parish. The lectures, which he described as "the best piece of historical and critical work" he had ever done, "contained innumerable gems of thought from the Vedic Hymns, the Upanishads, Zoroaster's Gathas, priceless sayings of Buddha, of Confucius and others Chinese philosophers, and many witty words of Mohammed."[29]

It was probably this period of study that led to what he described as "the second religious experience of [his] life," his encounter with "the second religious personality that has blessed this world—Gautama Buddha." Of this experience he said only that "in Buddha I found the two supreme virtues which I had found in

Christ—absolute trust in the spiritual, and a Saviour's pity for the sorrows of the world. From these two creators I learned the power and the simplicity of spiritual religion." Two things stand out in this short passage. First, he mentioned this experience in relation to the two lines of thought—"the critical study of the New Testament and the study of physiological psychology"—that informed the health work at Emmanuel. Second, he seemingly subsumed his study of Buddhism and his experience of the personality of the Buddha under his study of the New Testament and his experience of the personality of Christ. Nonetheless, he did not *subordinate* the Buddha to Christ, but *equated* them, while at the same time emphasizing that it was "from these *two creators* [that he] learned the power and the simplicity of spiritual religion."[30] This tendency to equate the world's religions, as we have seen, was characteristic of many within the mediating tradition.

If we turn to a longer account of McComb's lecture on the history of mind cure, we find that it was not simply a history of modern psychotherapy beginning with Mesmer, but a universal history of mental healing in the manner of the histories of animal magnetism and spiritualism. Mental healing began, he declared in "the ancient union of the functions of priest and physician." He then provided a survey of the ancient and medieval world, mentioning Egypt, Greece, Rome, healing accounts in the Old Testament, and healings associated with famous medieval figures, such as Francis of Assisi and Bernard of Clairvaux. Mesmer, in McComb's account, was not simply the father of modern psychotherapy, but also "an ardent student of the mediaeval mystics and caught his inspiration from them."[31]

Worcester downplayed the impact of the Buddha on his spirituality as well as his and McComb's growing interest in psychical research. Nonetheless, the emphasis on mental healing in all times and places was enough to surface the charge, also leveled against Spiritualists and psychical researchers, that the Emmanuel Movement was promoting a resurgence of primitive thinking. The most feverish attack came from Dr. Dercum, a neurologist in Philadelphia who equated the Emmanuel Movement with hypnotism, hypnotism with hysteria, and hysteria with the primitive. Inverting McComb's history, Dercum stated:

> Every now and then in the history of the world there is a recrudescence of mystic medicine. At times it assumes forms which are pseudo-scientific, at others pseudo-religious. . . . Since time immemorial superstition and magic have played a role in the treatment of disease. Four thousand years ago, in Egypt, religious and mystic rites were practices with the sick. . . . The Hebrews of ancient times cured by the laying on of hands and the Lybians stretched their bodies on the bodies of the sick. Shall we speak of the Pythonism of the Greeks, or of those still existent practices in which hysteria plays the dominant role, such as are found among the various savage tribes of the world? Or of the rites of Shamanism or of the Indian 'medicine man?'

In sum, reported the *North American*, "Dr. Dercum characterizes the Emmanuel movement as being one with the ever-recurrent forms of mystic medicine—a disposition that places Dr. Worcester on a plane with the Indian 'medicine man.' "[32]

THE WEEKLY MEETINGS

The heart of the health work at Emmanuel Church lay in the weekly meetings, sometimes referred to as "mental health classes." These meetings involved both individual meetings with a physician and/or minister, a religious service, and a social meeting. For two years the weekly meeting was conducted as a "clinic" with both physicians and clergy present. During this period, the physicians interviewed the patients in order to identify those with "functional" as opposed to "organic" illnesses. Those with functional illnesses then met with one of the ministers for treatment. After two years, the clinic as such was discontinued in response to criticism from the medical profession and patients were accepted for treatment only when referred by their physician. Although a patient might have met with the minister for therapy only a few times, they typically returned on a regular basis to participate in the service and social meeting.[33] Worcester attached religious significance to all three aspects of the weekly meeting—the individual therapy, the service, and the social gathering—and viewed each as having the power to effect healing.

Worcester used suggestion to treat patients in the individual sessions. He began by making the patient "calm and quiet" and explaining to them how to achieve this condition on their own at home. He placed his patients in a comfortable chair, instructed them to relax, and then, standing behind them, stroked their heads to sooth and distract them. He instructed his patients not to let their thoughts run on unchecked but to "lazily follow [his] words," and when he made a useful suggestion to repeat it to themselves. Worcester first gave suggestions intended to relax the patient and then suggestions intended to heal. He made "the suggestions as positively and simply as possible," often repeating them more than once. The entire treatment usually lasted from fifteen minutes to an hour, depending on the case.[34]

Worcester stated that he "personally attach[ed] a religious importance to this state of mind." In this state, he said, "when our minds are in a state of peace and our hearts open and receptive to all good influence, I believe that the Spirit of God enters into us and a power not our own takes possession of us." Jesus, he believed attached great importance to "calm and peace, . . . warn[ing] men against injurious agitation and passion, against anger, fear, and anxious care, and the importance which He attached to calm and peace." Referring to the universe as "a great storehouse of invisible energy" and sounding a lot like William James, he asked, if "the whole moral and religious life [did not] testify to the existence of unseen spiritual powers which are friendly to us." This was, he said, "unquestionably the belief of Christ."[35]

The religious services included the singing of familiar hymns, the reading of prayer requests solicited before the start of the service, the reading of a scripture lesson (usually "the words of Jesus in a new translation"), a short practical address on "matters pertaining to right thought and the conduct of life," and an invitation to stay for the social meeting that followed. A reporter for the *New York Evening Post* described the religious services as "mildly reminiscent of the old-fashioned

12. The Reverend Dr. Samuel McComb, Episcopal priest and cofounder of the Emmanuel Movement, speaking with a patient. Courtesy of the Francis A. Countway Library of Medicine, Boston, Massachusetts.

prayer-meeting at its best."[36] McComb thought such fervent "prayer meetings" had rarely been seen "in New England except in connection with special evangelistic or revival efforts."[37] A prominent New York lawyer exclaimed to Worcester after one of the meetings, "I thought the mid-week prayer meeting was about as dead as the dodo bird but there must have been a thousand people here tonight." Worcester added that "during the summer these meetings are discontinued and the people, of course, are aware of the fact; yet they come and gather round the door of the church, and sometimes conduct a simple service for themselves on the church steps." When he asked why they had come, one of the women said, "We know there is no service, but we like just to come and look at the church and to think of all the good times we have had here."[38]

Worcester thought that suggestion was at work not only in the individual sessions, but in the religious services as well, creating what he referred to as a "mass impression." It should not, he insisted, "be confounded with a lawless and ungovernable mob spirit of strong excitement. Here there is no excitement, no fanaticism, no sensationalism, but earnest faith tempered by sober thought." The "mass impression" evoked in the religious services was grounded in prayer and led to what Worcester described as "possession." Thus, he said, "when the human spirit is calm and impressionable and open to all good influence, I belief that a higher Spirit, the Spirit of all goodness enters into us, takes possession of us and leads us in better ways."[39] Basic ground rules ensured that a similar spirit pervaded the social meeting. People were told they could talk of anything "except sickness." A simple supper was served accompanied by music. "This of course enhances the social spirit," Worcester said, "but to me it means more: I attach an almost religious significance to eating and drinking with those I love. Twice a week in Emmanuel Church, on Wednesdays and Sundays, a table is spread where we eat together and at which everyone is welcome for what he is, not for what he has."[40]

If the meetings were, as the *Evening Post* reporter said, "reminiscent of the old-fashioned prayer meeting," they were prayer meetings of a distinctively nonsectarian sort. According to the *New York Times*, "Episcopalian and Methodist, Roman Catholic and Jew, men and women of every Church and of no church, meet together, drawn by the ties of common suffering, to voice their common hopes and desires in prayer and hymn, to hear words that may inspire and comfort."[41] The *Church Times* reported: "the Sunday night neurasthenic meetings, as they were popularly known, soon overflowed with outsiders. They came from every quarter of the town, and every creed was represented. There were Hebrews and even Catholics present. The new thought adherents swarmed like bees to honey, and strange little dowdy figures shrunk here and there in corners, suggesting evangelicalism gone astray to a ritualistic temple."[42] Worcester and McComb encouraged all attendees to "hold to his or her faith," welcoming them as members of Emmanuel Church only if they had no other religious home. Those who adopted the Emmanuel format elsewhere did the same. Lyman Powell, a Congregationalist minister, said he "discouraged every disposition on the part of my patients from other folds than mine to attend the services of my church [and] . . . in most cases exacted a pledge from them of renewed zeal and faithfulness to their own denomination."[43]

Christian Scientists, as we might expect, insisted on the distinction between Christian Science and the psychotherapy of the Emmanuel Movement, whereas New Thought leaders viewed the Emmanuel Movement as legitimating and extending their own views. In response to a talk given by Dr. Cabot to the Men's Club of a Boston church, J. V. Dittemore spoke for the Christian Scientists, noting that they rejected the idea "that Jesus used in his practice either suggestion or auto-suggestion, nor," he added, "will they believe that he was a hypnotist."

To assume that Jesus' power to heal was limited to "a man-selected list of so-called nervous diseases," he continued, was "directly contrary to Bible teaching and to the history of the healing of primitive Christianity, not only in the time of Jesus, but during the first three centuries of the Christian era."[44] Mrs. Norris, a New Thought leader from North Dakota, by way of contrast, "welcome[d] the Emmanuel movement . . . because it has made us respectable, instead of being classed with the cranks, for the ministers and doctors are coming over to our general idea.' "[45]

In a retrospective on the Emmanuel Movement, occasioned by McComb's departure to become the Canon of the Episcopal Cathedral in Baltimore in 1915, Hartt described the movement's spectacular beginnings. It was, he said, "something of a sensation and very much of a fight."

> Crowds thronged the public clinics. Newspapers blazoned the novel adventure far and wide. Enthusiasts, cranks, and irresponsible amateurs stole its principles, or claimed to, and it was a slow town that had not its 'Emmanuel movement copied straight from Boston' after somebody's seven days' sojourn here. . . . Meanwhile, unnumbered whoops of ridicule, denunciation and abuse went up from the critical or unbelieving. A local paragrapher dubbed the movement 'a mission to the fidgety.' Neurologists by the score condemned it. A medical journal poked fun at Dr. Worcester's 'healing words.' And while a part of the clergy accepted Emmanuelism as 'applied Christianity' or as 'a way to head off Christian Science by performing the same cures without recourse to Mrs. Eddy's philosophy,' there were ministers who saw in it a rising menace. . . . As for the laity (in both senses, medical and ecclesiastical), they inclined more or less to the opinion that a shoemaker should stick to his last. All in all it was a glorious row—wild sport for all the participants and a circus to the onlooker, while a whacking opportunity for editors and publishers.[46]

Worcester wrote in his autobiography that they could have handled the situation they had created "easily enough" in the first years of the movement, "if it had not been for the newspapers, which, in some uncanny way, sensed from the beginning the uniqueness of our undertaking and gave undue prominence to it in their columns." Worcester only added fuel to the fire when he agreed in 1908 to write a series of eight articles for *The Ladies' Home Journal*. "I stipulated that with each article should appear a notice that I could not answer personal letters in regard to it. Nevertheless during the ensuing year, I received about five thousand such letters to most of which I replied. These articles, more than anything else, brought our work before the whole country."[47]

The enthusiastic response generated by the widespread publicity alarmed the physicians allied with the movement. In December 1908, the lead article on the front page of the Boston *Sunday Herald* proclaimed the "Emmanuel Movement Deplored by Eminent Physicians of Boston" and that "Specialists in Nervous Diseases" were of the opinion that "the Movement Has 'Bolted.' " The stated issue was training. Physicians and psychologists across the country concurred, according to the *Herald*, that the "attempted treatment of nervous diseases through suggestion by those [clergy and laymen] who, the doctors say, are totally unfit by training or experience to diagnose between delicate organic diseases and psychic disturbances" was a major problem. Given that such diagnoses were, in theory anyway, performed by physicians, not by clergy, both historians and contemporary observers have sought to locate the hostility of the physicians more generally in issues of professional status. The *Herald* thus attributed the antagonism in part to "the ready assumption on the part of many clergymen that they could cure diseases which have baffled the best medical authorities in the world."[48] According to medical historian Sanford Gifford, "the universal point of attack, underlying all shades of opinion, was the simple issue of professional status: nonphysicians were treating patients with medical illnesses, even if these illnesses were functional and not organic."[49]

By 1908, both James Putnam and Richard Cabot had backed away from the movement, albeit for somewhat different reasons, and in 1909, the public clinics at the church were suspended. Physicians were no longer present at the weekly meetings to screen for functional disorders and patients thereafter were accepted only when referred by their physicians.[50] This new approach quieted the firestorm of criticism and allowed the movement to go on largely unattended by publicity. In 1915, Hartt indicated that, while the work had proceeded apace, "the average Bostonian has pretty much forgotten that the Emmanuel movement exists, while physicians and clergymen are coming to regard it as uninteresting, almost, since so hopelessly legitimate."[51]

The Emmanuel Movement was, for the most part, a popular movement. Although courses in "psycho-religious therapeutics" were offered at a few theological schools in New England (Yale, Hartford, and Tufts) before 1910, courses in "psycho-therapeutics" were not widely or regularly offered in theological schools until several decades later, when they appeared in conjunction with the emergence of pastoral counseling.[52] Widely seen as an alternative to Christian Science, the applied Christianity of the Emmanuel Movement was not as easily distinguished from New Thought. Thus, the publicity accorded the Emmanuel Movement served indirectly to promote and legitimate New Thought. At the same time, the eager response to the Emmanuel Movement fed off interest already aroused by such New Thought best-sellers as Ralph Waldo Trine's *In Tune with the Infinite*, Annie Payson Call's *Power Through Repose*, Horatio Dresser's *Power of Silence*, and Charles Brodie Patterson's *The Will to Be Well*.[53] In 1908, New Thought writer, Elizabeth Towne, estimated that "there are perhaps a million or more people in the churches who are just taking up New Thought under the guise of the Emmanuel Movement." Millions more, both in the church and out, she said, are "catching the spirit of New Thought and are practicing it more or less in their daily life without acknowledging the name."[54]

WILLIAM SANDAY

If the subconscious was popularized at the parish level by means of its associations with mental healing, psychotherapeutics, and applied Christianity, it broke into the theological schools by virtue of Protestant intellectuals' new-found fascination with mysticism. As in the case of the Emmanuel Movement, biblical interpretation was a central focus. But where the Emmanuel Movement turned to the Jamesian subconscious as a foundation for healing, a few scholars of repute employed it to explain the "mystical" experiences of Paul and Jesus without explaining them away. In doing so, they took up theories that had been proposed decades earlier by advocates of the new religions.

The most notable figure to make this sort of argument was William Sanday, Lady Margaret Professor at Oxford. Sanday, a highly respected New Testament scholar, was known for his cautious conservatism in matters of biblical interpretation. By about 1910, however, he came around to the modernist view that there were no grounds for granting the miracles of the New Testament special status. Committed to preserving the lineaments of orthodoxy while remaining within the parameters of acceptable science, Sanday looked to James's psychology to undergird his Christology.[55]

Sanday laid the foundations for his Christology in two steps. He dealt first with the general question of "divine indwelling" in light of the new literature on the psychology of mysticism and, second, with the more specific question of the incarnation or divine indwelling in Christ. Sanday opened his discussion of the "presuppositions of a modern Christology" by attending to the new psychology of the subconscious. He quoted the passage from the *Varieties* on "the most important step forward in psychology" and indicated that "for us in England the recognition of this wider field of psychology is chiefly associated with the late F.W.H. Myers and the Society of Psychical Research." He then provided a long quote from Myers on the subliminal self and advanced his belief that the "subliminal consciousness . . . is destined to be of much importance and (I would even hope) of much value in the future of theology as well as psychology." He indicated that he had read Jastrow's *Subconscious*, but found it lacking in "scientific precision." The book, he said, "that has been to me most really helpful is Prof. William James's *Varieties of Religious Experience*."[56]

In his discussion of mysticism, Sanday took two passages from Galatians as typical: "One is that great text in Galatians (ii. 20): 'I have been crucified with Christ; yet I live; and yet no longer I, but Christ liveth in me.' And the other is in the same Epistle (iv. 19): 'My little children, of whom I am again in travail until Christ be formed in you.' " He argued that "normal" Christian mysticism, as compared with "abnormal or eccentric" consisted in "the doctrine, or rather the experience of the Holy Ghost. It is the realization of human personality as characterized by, and consummated in, the indwelling reality of the Spirit of Christ, which is God." Here we see the evangelical Protestant emphasis on the experience of the indwelling of the Spirit (Edwards) and the witness of the Spirit (Wesley) depicted not as "experimental religion" or "true Christian experience" but as "normal Christian mysticism," an ecumenical move that both Edwards and Wesley would have found disquieting.[57]

Then, in a marked break with the evangelical tradition's emphasis on the indwelling of the Spirit as a supernatural event, Sanday argued that "the deepest truth of mysticism, and of the states of which we have been speaking as mystical, belongs not so much to the upper region of consciousness . . . as to the lower region of the unconscious." Even more pointedly, he argued, that it would be "a clear gain if we firmly grasp the fact that the work of the Holy Spirit, the true and proper work, the active divine influence brought to bear upon the soul, does belong to this lower sphere. It is subliminal, not supraliminal." Concluding that "the proper seat or *locus* of all divine indwelling, or divine action upon the human soul, is the subliminal consciousness," he moved on to make a similar case for Christ, to wit: "that the same, or the corresponding, subliminal consciousness is the proper seat or *locus* of the Deity of the incarnate Christ."[58]

Noting the "difficulties . . . involved in the attempt to draw as it were a vertical line between the human nature and the divine nature of Christ," Sanday suggested that these difficulties "disappear, if, instead of drawing a vertical line, we rather draw a horizontal line between the upper human medium, which is the proper and natural field of all active expression, and those lower deep which are [the] . . . natural home of whatever is divine." This line, he said, is "inevitably drawn in the region of the subconscious." The net result was a Christology not unlike that of Phineas Quimby in which "that which was divine in Christ was not nakedly exposed to the public gaze; neither was it so entirely withdrawn from outward view as to be wholly sunk and submerged in the darkness of the unconscious." In this conception, the divinity was understood as coming to expression through "the narrow neck" of human consciousness, while the human was understood as, "in its deepest roots, directly continuous with the life of God Himself."

Scholars roundly criticized Sanday, as they had Worcester, for depicting Myers and James as experts. This time, however, it was their philosophical credentials that were called into question. In response to one reviewer, Sanday conceded that he did not consider "Myers . . . a philosopher in the strict sense at all," but James, he said, "would count for rather more than this." One of Sanday's reviewers, finding the idea of "subliminal consciousness" contradictory, clearly had no knowledge of the concept of dissociation on which it was based. Others confronted him with the evolutionary argument, accusing him of viewing conscious processes as "inferior to the sub- and unconscious." Sanday, clearly taken aback by the vehemence of the criticism, modified his theory somewhat but did not entirely repudiate it.[59]

In his essay on "Religion and the Subconscious," Coe sarcastically announced "that the path between God and the human" had been found in the subconscious. Deploring the rise of "psychic theology," Coe argued that church leaders such as Worcester and Sanday had associated "the highest inspirations of the Christian religion . . . with the performances of the modern 'psychic.' " To see the "full significance" of this new development, he pointed out that "the mind-reader, fortune-teller, or diviner, however modern, is the historical and psychological descendent of the shaman and the medicine man." Although twenty-five years previously no Protestant clergyman would have found "anything but delusion and moral decay" in spiritualism, "today," he said, "various prominent ecclesiastics not only lean toward the notion of spirit communication, but also look to this source for support for the Christian belief in spiritual realities."[60] Coe's remarks, while critical, reflected the willingness of some mainstream Protestants to deal with the challenges posed by the new religious movements by incorporating their approaches to psychology, biblical exegesis, and religious experience into the church. Maintaining their exclusivist theological stance, some Pentecostals also found lessons in the new religious movements.

PENTECOSTAL REVIVALS

Like Elwood Worcester, Charles F. Parham, the leader of the Apostolic Faith Movement and one of the founders of Pentecostalism, was aware of the threat that the new religions posed to a church lacking spiritual power. Parham's first book, a collection of sermons titled *A Voice Crying in the Wilderness* (1902), was published a year after he and his Bible school students in Topeka, Kansas, experienced the "power of Pentecost" as evidenced by speaking in tongues. In one of his sermons, he told the story of "[a] very pious man, [a] member of the Baptist church, Marshaltown, Iowa, [who] received the Baptism of the Holy Spirit. His church not honoring the presence and power of the Holy Ghost in their midst, he was gathered in by the Spiritualists who persuaded him that his Pentecostal power was but a manifestation of their nefarious mediumship." Parham had no idea how many such cases there were in the world, but, he said, "we do know that the narrowness of modern church Christianity, by refusing to believe and receive true Bible doctrines has driven many thousands into Spiritualism, Theosophy, Christian Science and infidelity."[61]

Parham, in keeping with the exclusivist stance of evangelical Protestantism, rejected these new religions as false. In labeling them "counterfeits," however, he mirrored Worcester's sense that they nonetheless pointed to something real that "church Christianity" did not possess. Although Parham had studied the claims of the healers—"Medical, Mental, and Christians Sciences, hypnotism, etc."—he was more preoccupied with Spiritualism. Convinced that "wherever the counterfeit exists, the real must also," Parham had long viewed the Spiritualists as having the counterfeit version of what he thought Christianity needed most. In fact, Parham indicated he had "prayed for this present truth [i.e., the Pentecostal truth] given in this book" for years specifically to "confound those workers of magic." While "99 per cent" of Spiritualism was, in his view, "slight [sic] of hand," some instances of mediumistic possession and "speaking under the control of evil spirits" manifested a genuine, albeit anti-Christian power. In 1901, "when the power of Pentecost came," he said, "we found the real," that is the real Christian version of which Spiritualism was the counterfeit.[62]

If Charles Parham, preoccupied with counterfeits, was (loosely speaking) the Jonathan Edwards of Pentecostalism, then William J. Seymour was Pentecostalism's John Wesley. Seymour had been a student at Parham's Bible School for a short while in the early 1900s. By 1906, he was a recognized minister in Parham's Apostolic Faith Movement and the founder of the Azusa Street Mission in Los Angeles, the fastest growing and most publicized of the Pentecostal revivals. Although the "Pentecostal fire" fell on Los Angeles in April 1906, Parham did not visit until the following October. Seymour played up Parham's long-awaited visit in his monthly newspaper, *The Apostolic Faith*. Many came to view Azusa Street as the birthplace of Pentecostalism, but Seymour explained that the Pentecostal work had begun "five years ago . . . when a company of people under the leadership of Charles Parham, . . . tarried for Pentecost in Topeka, Kan[sas]."[63]

Unknown to Seymour, Parham began distancing himself from the revival in Los Angeles in the weeks prior to his visit. In response to newspaper coverage depicting the Azusa meetings as wild and fanatical, Parham told the *Topeka Daily State Journal* that his was "a dignified movement, directed by the Almighty power, [that] . . . has no connection with the sensational Holy Rollers." Although he conceded that his meetings "were no dull affairs," he stressed that "when any of that class [Holy Rollers] come to our meeting and begin throwing fits, we quietly have the attendants take them out."[64] When Parham arrived in Los Angeles his fears were not assuaged. In "A Note of Warning" published on December 1, 1906, he wrote that at Azusa Street he found "found hypnotic influences, familiar-spirit influences, spiritualistic influences, mesmeric influences, and all kinds of spells, spasms, falling in trances, etc. All of these things are foreign to and unknown in this movement outside of Los Angeles, except in the places visited by the workers sent out from this city." He acknowledged that "people sometimes fall under the power of God, and that there are times that God thus deals with his creatures that resist Him; but these cases are exceptional and not general." The regularity with which people were "falling under the power in Los Angeles" signaled, according to Parham, that it was "to a large degree, . . . produced through a hypnotic, mesmeric, magnetic current[,]" rather than by the power of God.[65]

The faithful at Azusa Street were not particularly happy with Parham either. "After preaching two or three times," Parham said, "I was informed by two of the elders, one who was a hypnotist (I had seen him lay his hands on many who came through chattering, jabbering and sputtering, speaking in no language at all) that I was not wanted in that place." Parham began holding his own meetings at the W.C.T.U. Building. There, he reported that "between two and three hundred who had been possessed of awful fits and spasms and controls in the Azusa Street work were delivered, and received the real Pentecost teachings and many spoke with other tongues." In the December issue of *The Apostolic Faith*, the Azusa leadership acknowledged that they had been overly "hasty" in their positive statements about Parham and indicated that "he [was] not the leader of this movement of Azusa Mission." Instead, they declared, "the Lord was the founder" and "Bro. Seymour . . . a humble pastor of the flock over which the Holy Ghost [had] made him overseer."[66]

There is evidence that other Pentecostal leaders regretted Parham's condemnation of Azusa Street and would have discouraged it had they been consulted. W. Faye Carothers, one of Parham's leading supporters, viewed Parham as overly quick to denounce "fanaticism" and would have been more willing than Parham to tolerate diversity in order to maintain the unity of the movement. Scholarly analyses of the incident have emphasized the underlying issues of authority and race at work in the conflict. Seymour's mission was attracting people from all over the country, threatening to upstage Parham's efforts, at a point when he was struggling to consolidate his leadership and hold together an increasingly fissiparous movement. Seymour was black, as were others in positions of leadership at Azusa, and the meetings were multi-ethnic in composition. Contemporary reports indicate that blacks and whites were present in about equal numbers, along with Hispanics and others. Parham, who was white, was unaccustomed to and uncomfortable with racially mixed meetings. In the wake of the sexual scandal (allegations of sodomy) that broke around Parham in early 1907, Parham's rhetoric became harsher and his retrospective denunciations of the Azusa Street revivals took on more sharply racist overtones.[67] Although issues of race and authority were important, the overt focus of the conflict was over experience in the context of worship. Parham viewed much of what he witnessed at Azusa Street as counterfeit and discredited their experience in psychological terms.

Two points stand out in Parham's critique of Azusa, both more Edwardsean than Wesleyan in their attitude toward bodily manifestations. First, he was concerned that people were having "spells, spasms, falling in trances" and "falling under the power" on a regular basis. People did such things in Parham's revivals as well, but he said such experiences were "exceptional and not general" in his meetings. At his meetings, people were not "possessed of awful fits and spasms and controls." When they were, Parham had them removed. In other words, apart from speaking in tongues, Parham, like Edwards and numerous others, discouraged physical manifestations at his meetings. Second, Parham had a narrow definition of authentic tongues. As historian James Goff points out, Parham believed that the authentic "Bible evidence" was always speech in a human language unknown to the speaker, i.e., xenoglossic tongues.[68] Authentic tongues speech, like Edwards's new spiritual sense, was strictly supernatural. Parham, like Edwards and in contrast to Wesley, was not inclined to blur the distinction between primary and secondary causation. At Azusa Street, he saw a great deal of "chattering, jabbering, and sputtering" that seemed to correspond to no known tongue.

When it came to visible manifestations of the Spirit, Parham argued that xenoglossic tongues speech was the crucial evidence. Writing in 1902, he noted that all Christians know "we are to be the recipients of the Holy Spirit, but each have their private interpretations as to His visible manifestations; some claim shouting, leaping, jumping, and falling in trances, while others put stress upon inspiration, unction and divine revelation." Based on "a careful study of Acts 1:9," he knew that the authentic manifestation was xenoglossia, which alone provided the disciples with "the power to make them witnesses" to all nations. Whether or not tongues were genuinely xenoglossic was a matter for further discernment. It helped if someone could identify the language being spoken, but Parham was convinced that one could recognize true xenoglossic tongues by the way they were produced as well. Thus, he said, "the Holy Ghost does nothing that is unnatural or unseemingly [sic], and any strained exertion of body, mind, or voice is not the work of the Holy Spirit, but of some familiar spirit, or other influence brought to bear upon the subject."[69]

Parham, in keeping with the attitude of the Reformed revival tradition and more "respectable" sorts of Methodists, thought that all but the purely supernatural (i.e., in this case, authentic tongues) could and should be discouraged. Having been exposed to the popular medical and mind-cure literature, he explained what he took to be false religion in psychological terms. He explained the bodily manifestations he saw at Azusa in terms of "a hypnotic, mesmeric, magnetic current." He explained the "false" tongues in terms of excessive laying on of hands and coaching seekers by "the suggestion of certain words and sounds, the working of the chin, and the massage of the throat."

What is perhaps most surprising about Parham, however, is that he explained the authentic supernatural operation of the Holy Spirit in terms of the *subconscious* and concepts borrowed from New Thought. In a second collection of sermons, published in 1911, he wrote:

> The anointing of the Holy Spirit is given to illuminate His Word, to open the Scriptures, and to place the spiritual man in direct communication with the mind of God; man will be in instant communication with the mind and will of God, and not only so, but to directly connect this mind with your spirit. This is occultic in the sense that the mind of the spirit in you becomes the receptacle for the thought waves of wisdom that have been let loose by the minds of the church of the past ages, until the wisdom of the ages, floating ever upon the waves of ether, are at your command to draw from. This is a profound, though little understood truth. But let us get this one simple thought: Let us realize that it is not this poor, spongy brain that has absorbed a little modern wisdom—the thought of other people—but let us know that *it is possible for God to speak through the subconscious mind by His Holy Spirit's power*, until, trained and in touch with the power of Divinity, beautified and enhanced in spirituality, it is tuned to catch the deeper thoughts of God and of the ages and transmit them to others.[70]

Here, in an exclusivist tradition where we would least expect it, we find the appropriation of a rich mix of concepts borrowed from psychical research (the subconscious) and New Thought (mind, wisdom) to explain the means whereby the "spiritual man" enters into "direct communication with the mind of God." God, Parham said, speaks through "the subconscious mind by His Holy Spirit's power," training the mind until it is "tuned to catch the deeper thoughts of God . . . and transmit them to others." Given Parham's exclusivist commitments, we should not take this to mean that Parham was allying himself with New Thought. Rather in keeping with his dictum that "wherever the counterfeit exists the real must also," Parham viewed authentically Spirit-baptized Pentecostals as the ones who were *really* "in tune with the Infinite," to borrow Ralph Waldo Trine's phrase, via their subconscious minds. All the rest were but counterfeits.

While Parham was busy borrowing concepts from the "counterfeits" outside the Pentecostal movement and attempting to distinguish between the authentic and inauthentic within Pentecostalism, Seymour and others associated with the Azusa Street Mission were shaping and interpreting their experience in relation to older traditions. In the pages of *The Apostolic Faith*, the monthly newspaper of the Azusa Street revival, and Frank Bartleman's account of *How Pentecost Came to*

Los Angeles, we can see the shape that this new experience took at one influential center at the height of the Pentecostal revival. Seymour and Bartleman, in contrast to Parham, viewed a much wider range of experiences as authentic. In their writings, they interpreted bodily experiences condemned by Parham in terms of "divine trance" and the typologies of the tabernacle tradition.[71]

Many who were drawn to Azusa Street arrived by way of radical Holiness groups with Methodist roots. In Wesleyan Holiness circles, it was understood that the disciples were sanctified at Pentecost and, thus, that sanctification and the baptism of the Holy Spirit were one and the same. Pentecostals, however, believed that the disciples were sanctified *before* Pentecost and that the baptism of the Holy Spirit was a distinct experience in its own right. This understanding was drawn from the Reformed tradition and, in particular from the Keswick movement.[72] Pentecostals at Azusa Street, while embracing Keswick exegesis on this point, evidenced more continuity with the Methodist-dominated camp-meeting tradition than is usually apparent in secondary accounts of early Pentecostalism. The camp-meeting tradition, well maintained among the more radical Holiness groups, both black and white, provided the Pentecostals at Azusa Street with precedents for sacralizing their bodily experience in the ways that Parham found so offensive.

The testimony of William H. Durham, a Holiness evangelist from Chicago, provides a glimpse of what it was like to move from the Wesleyan Holiness tradition into Pentecostalism. In order to make the transition, Durham had to reassess his understanding of the baptism of the Holy Spirit. As a good Wesleyan, Durham had repented of his sins and experienced the joy of salvation long before he was drawn to Azusa Street. Moreover, in traditional Methodist fashion, he had also "grasped by faith the truth of sanctification" and the Spirit had "witnessed to [his] heart that the work was done." In 1902, he had received a call to the ministry. Throughout all those years, he reported, "the Spirit has been with me in a wonderful way. Sometimes I would be overcome by His power. In brief, I honestly believed I was baptized with the Holy Ghost, and testified to it." Longing in his heart for something more, he broke with the Wesleyan understanding of sanctification as the baptism of the Holy Spirit. His "heart hunger" drew him to Los Angeles where he spent almost a month at the meetings of the Azusa Street mission "seeking [his] Pentecost."[73]

Two things stand out in his testimony as strikingly different from anything that we have seen in the Methodist camp-meeting tradition: Holy Ghost singing and "possession" of the body by the Holy Ghost. Both were linked to speaking in tongues. The singing struck Durham forcibly at his first meeting at Azusa Street and immediately turned him into "an earnest seeker." Although he had attended "many large holiness camp meetings and conventions," he said he had never before felt "the power and glory that I felt in Azusa Street Mission." The power and glory was conveyed through "the most ravishing and unearthly music that ever fell on mortal ears." "When about twenty persons joined in singing the 'Heavenly Chorus,'" he said he knew "it came direct from heaven."[74]

Although the singing turned him into a seeker, nothing else of note apparently happened for the next two weeks. Then one Tuesday afternoon, having become "much disheartened, suddenly the power of God descended upon me, and I went down under it." He lay for two hours "under His mighty power," but knew he had not yet received the baptism. The same thing happened again on Thursday night. On Friday evening, the power again came over him and he "jerked and quaked under it for about three hours." That night, Durham reported, "He worked my whole body, one section at a time, first my arms, then my limbs, then my body, then my head, then my face, then my chin, and finally at 1 a. m. Saturday, Mar. 2, after being under the power three hours, He finished the work on my vocal organs, and spoke through me in unknown tongues." This experience left him with a conscious sense of having been possessed. As he put it: "I was conscious that a living Person had come into me, and that He possessed even my physical being, in a literal sense, in so much that He could at His will take hold of my vocal organs, and speak any language He chose through me."[75] Only those who had received the baptism with the Holy Spirit were able to sing in tongues or, to put it in Pentecostal terms, the Spirit only sang through those who had been baptized in the Spirit.

The Spirit and the Body

In the brief, formulaic descriptions of the Pentecostal experience recorded in *The Apostolic Faith*, we can hear idioms and cadences that run back through the Methodist camp-meeting tradition to the pages of Wesley's journals. At Azusa Street, "there is such a power in the preaching of the Word in the Spirit that people are shaken on the benches. Coming to the altar, many fall prostrate under the power of God, and often come out speaking in tongues. Sometimes the power falls on people and they are wrought upon by the Spirit during testimony or preaching and receive Bible experiences [i.e., the gift of tongues]." At the meetings at Eighth and Maple, a missionary spin-off from Azusa Street, Frank Bartleman indicated that manifestations of the "slaying power" were common. He describes "[a] young lady, [who] . . . came under the power of the Spirit, and lay for half an hour with beaming face lost to all about her, beholding visions unutterable. Soon she began to say, 'Glory! Glory to Jesus!' and spoke fluently in a strange tongue." In Homestead, Pennsylvania, "Rev. J. T. Body lay for hours under the power, then began to speak clearly and fluently in a new tongue." In Portland, Oregon, "the power fell before the meeting was half through and two received Pentecost; at night, two more. . . . The slain of the Lord lay so you can't move about the altar." In Zion City, Illinois, "the Holy Ghost fell, as they were praying for Him to come and manifest Himself. First one began to drop and then another until the floor was covered. The first to speak in unknown tongues was a young man who spoke in Chinese, Italian, and Zulu, which were identified. Then it was not long till the flood of joy began and all over the room they were praising and glorifying God in different tongues. Some were justified and sanctified. About twenty came through speaking in tongues."[76]

In the Azusa Street revivals, the Methodist practice of inscribing salient features of the Christian mythos on the body was reshaped by the Pentecostal insistence on the baptism of the Spirit, evidenced by tongues, as an experience distinct from sanctification. Whereas the idea of tongues as the initial evidence of the baptism was distinctively Pentecostal, the distinction between sanctification and the baptism of the Spirit was derived from the Keswick movement within the Reformed tradition. In the Keswick understanding, sanctification, premised on the full consecration of the self to God, was the prerequisite for the Spirit-filled life. Keswick teachings emphasized that self-centeredness was the essence of sin. Consecration of the self to God signaled the individual's willingness to turn the control of the self over to God. In the words of Andrew Murray, those who sought the full blessing of Pentecost had to recognize that "two diverse things cannot at once and the same time occupy the very same place. Your own life and the life of God cannot fill the heart at the same time. Your life hinders the entrance of the life of God. When your own life is cast out, the life of God will fill you. So long as *I myself* am still something, *Jesus himself* cannot be everything. My life must be expelled; then the Spirit of Jesus will flow in." In sum, according to Keswick scholar Steven Barabas, "consecration sweeps away all barriers between the believer and God and clears the ground for the Spirit's control of the personality."[77]

Keswick leaders made it clear, however, that turning over control of the self to God did not mean "becom[ing] automatons." Consecration was a matter of disposition, i.e., of "yielding" and "obedience," and not necessarily a matter of great emotion.[78] Pentecostals, to differing degrees, rejected such subtleties. Possession swept away all barriers between the believer and God and allowed the Spirit to take control of the person. The baptism of the Holy Spirit, evidenced by speaking or singing in tongues, stood as the sign that the Spirit, not the self, was in control. The baptism of the Spirit was understood as "an enduement of power" that equipped the Christian for "life and service," both of which were impossible if the Spirit was not in control.

Testimonies from Azusa Street and spin-off revivals suggest that not everyone experienced the possession of the Spirit in as full-bodied a fashion as William Durham. Frank Bartleman's experience represents the opposite end of the spectrum and illustrates the sort of experience that Parham expected. As Bartleman testified, "the Spirit manifested Himself through me in 'tongues' [while] . . . I was softly walking the floor, praising God in my spirit." At first, he heard (in his soul, not with his "natural ears") "a rich voice speaking in a language I did not know." Shortly thereafter, he found himself, seeming "without volition . . . , enunciating the same sounds. . . . My mind, the last fortress of man to yield, was taken possession by the Spirit."[79]

While this was still an account of "possession . . . by the Spirit," Bartleman did not fall to the floor and remain there for hours while the Spirit took possession of his body bit by bit. There was, he said, "no strain or contortions." There was "[n]o struggle in an effort to get the 'baptism.' . . . There was no swelling of the throat, no 'operation' to be performed on my vocal organs. I had not the slightest difficulty speaking in 'tongues.' " Perhaps just as significant, "there was no shouting crowd around me, to confuse or excite me. No one was suggesting 'tongues' to me at the time, either by argument or imitation." Drawing an analogy to child-birth, he said, "I do not believe in dragging the child forth, spiritually speaking, with instruments. A pack of jackals over their prey could hardly act more fiercely than we have witnessed in some cases. In natural child birth it is generally best to let the mother alone as far as possible."[80]

Charles H. Mason, founder of the Church of God in Christ, provided an account in which the spirit took control of more than just Mason's tongue, but he never fell to the floor either. He experienced the baptism at Azusa Street, he said, after "[he] surrendered perfectly to Him and consented to Him" as a bride to her hus-band. Immediately thereafter, he said, "I began singing a song in unknown tongues, and it was the sweetest thing to have Him sing that song through me. He had complete charge of me. I let him have my mouth and everything. After that it seemed I was standing at the cross and heard Him as he groaned, the dying groans of Jesus, and I groaned. It was not my voice but the voice of the Beloved that I heard in me." The Holy Ghost then sang through Mason again in "unknown tongues" and in a while he began "preaching in tongues." Throughout, Mason remained "passive in His hands," allowing the Spirit not only to control his mouth but to his entire body, such that "the gestures of my hands and movements of my body were His."[81]

Levi R. Lupton, a Holiness Bible school teacher from Alliance, Ohio, who re-mained "on the floor . . . for nine hours," gained new insight into the meaning of "consecrating [his] body" from his experience. Actually, he began by *asking* God to consecrate his body, to possess it "member by member" and "use it as never before." God, he said, "took [him] at his word and really took possession."

> I then became perfectly helpless and for a season my entire body become cold, and I was unable to move even to the extent that I could not wind an eye for a short time. Yet, I was perfectly conscious and restful in my soul and mind. After some three hours the power of God left my body except in my shoulders and arms, which remained stiff during the entire time I was upon the floor. After some four hours had passed, I began to speak in other tongues.

This experience taught Lupton, according to his own testimony, "what it meant to be clay in the hands of the potter." He maintained that others would never know what that meant "experimentally, until they as absolutely submit themselves to God for the same purpose."[82]

The Azusa leadership defended "falling under the power," and, thus, the more full-bodied experiences of possession by the Spirit, as a form of "divine trance." Five months after Parham's visit, *The Apostolic Faith* reprinted a short article titled "In Divine Trance" from a sister publication. "We know," it began, "that some look with disfavor upon falling under the power, and many regard with suspicion visions and revelations. But how can any, who really believe in the Bible, doubt the genuineness of that which fully bears the marks of being of God, and which is also in fulfillment of the prophecies and promises of His Word?" The original article cited a number of biblical passages in defense of "divine trance." The editor of the Azusa paper added a few more, including Paul falling "under the power of God" at his conversion and Paul's statement that he didn't know if he was in or out of his body when he was "caught up to the third heaven." Quoting the passage from the Book of Revelation where John said, upon seeing Jesus, "I fell at His feet as dead," the article concluded, so too have "many in this mission . . . seen a vision of Jesus and have fallen at His feet as dead."[83]

Where the Keswick movement understood full consecration as a mental act, Pentecostals understood it as an act of bodily possession. In some cases, such as Bartleman's, only the speech organs were possessed. In other cases, people testified that God took control of their whole body, whether standing or prostrate on the floor. Participants in the Azusa Street and related revivals accepted the entire range of experiences as legitimate. Azusa Street participants probably would have said Durham and Lupton were in a divine trance. They might have said that about Mason, too. Wherever the line was drawn between trance and not-trance, Parham did not want to see people crossing it. As he later put it, he wanted "holy enthusiasm and intensity without hysteria," insisting that "Christianity places us in *a normal state* with all our faculties consecrated to decency, order and service for God."[84]

Although Azusa participants acknowledged that there were counterfeit versions of their own experiences, they were less eager to look for them within their own ranks than was Parham. An article on counterfeits in *The Apostolic Faith* suggests that Azusa leaders did, however, view the new religions as counterfeits and their followers as demon-possessed. When the demon-possessed showed up at their revivals, Azusa Street Pentecostals, like Wesley before them, attempted to cast the demons out. Thus, the paper reported: "Spiritualists have come to our meetings and had the demons cast out of them and have been saved and sanctified. Christian Scientists have come to the meetings and had the Christian Science demons cast out of them and have accepted the blood."[85]

While Pentecostals undoubtedly converted some Spiritualists, Spiritualist J. M. Peebles, by then in his nineties, was fully aware of the challenge Spiritualism posed to exclusivist Christians. Noting evangelist Dwight Moody's growing interest in the baptism of the Holy Spirit, Peebles wrote him a tongue-in-cheek letter that was published in the San Diego *Daily Vidette* in 1899. Humorously playing up the similarities between Spiritualism and Moody's proto-Pentecostalism in a way designed to leave Moody squirming, Peebles wrote:

> You and I are both evangelists . . . Yes, my brother, with you I want to see a revival of religion, a return of pentecostal times, a return of that Christianity which gladdened and glorified the first three centuries after Christ. . . . Contemplating a fourth journey around the world, Brother Moody, I have thought since hearing the many good things that you have publicly said in the pulpit, that, if we could make up a sort of pentecostal combination, you to preach (and, I hope, be entranced, having the gift of tongues), I to interpret the tongues and heal the sick, Mrs. Freitag to give ballot tests, clairvoyant tests, clairaudient tests, and other spiritual manifestations, with Professor Towner to sing—what a power, what a mighty power, under the good providence of God, we should be evangelizing the world.[86]

While Pentecostals and evangelicals, such as Moody, could only view Spiritualism as a demonic counterfeit, universalists, such as Peebles, viewed the growing Christian interest in Pentecost as further confirmation of their own views. In teasing Moody about their similarities, Peebles intentionally, albeit silently, pointed to their differences.

The Spirit and Worship

In the descriptions of Pentecostal worship at Azusa Street and Eighth and Maple, the biblical imagery and exegetical framework of the Wesleyan camp-meeting tradition was still prominently on display. Other pan-Pentecostal motifs, more commonly noted in the literature were evident as well, but we miss the heart of worship at Azusa if we lose sight of the primal Methodist desire to shout "glory" in the presence of God. To get at the Methodist contribution, it is important to distinguish between the theological *content* of worship and theological reflections on its *form*. Although Methodist themes were less prominent in the content of worship, the camp-meeting tradition provided a theology *of* worship.

The theology of worship at Azusa Street built on the tabernacle typology embodied in the camp-meeting tradition. Referring to Azusa Street, Bartleman wrote that when the "Spirit would fall upon the congregation . . . God was in His holy temple. . . . The shekinah glory rested there. In fact some claim to have seen the glory by night over the building. I do not doubt it."[87] He used similar language to describe the meetings at Eighth and Maple, where he said, the atmosphere was such that "like the priests in the Tabernacle of old we could not minister for the glory." The "divine 'weight of glory' " rested so heavily upon them at times that they could only "lie on [their] faces." For much of the service, "all would be on their faces on the floor[.]" During such times, Bartleman lay on a platform in the church "while God ran the meetings."[88]

The tabernacle or Shekinah theology was inherited from the camp-meeting tradition, but Azusa Street participants reread the tradition in light of their Pentecostal understanding of the baptism of the Spirit. In keeping with their overall contention that their Holiness kin had mistakenly conflated sanctification with the baptism of the Holy Spirit, Azusa Street exegetes provided their fellow Wesleyans with evidence that the Old Testament as well as the New differentiated between them. They did so based on a rereading of the Old Testament types to show that they prefigured the distinction between sanctification and the baptism of the Spirit.[89]

The rereading of the tabernacle tradition does not have to be inferred or lifted from between the lines of discussions of other topics. It was explicitly developed in a series of five articles devoted strictly to this subject published between October 1906 and September 1907. The surprising prominence of this topic in the pages of *The Apostolic Faith* reflected the fact that Wesleyan Holiness advocates, as we have seen, thought about manifestations of God's presence in terms of the tabernacle typology. For those steeped in that tradition to find Pentecostal claims plausible, Pentecostals had to demonstrate that the distinction between sanctification and baptism in the Holy Spirit was not only evident in the New Testament but *prefigured typologically* in the Old Testament as well.

Although four of these articles were unsigned, Seymour acknowledged his authorship of the first. In a brief article titled, "The Way into the Holiest," Seymour recapitulated the journey of faith from a Pentecostal perspective. The image of the altar was at the center of the journey from justification through sanctification to baptism in the Spirit. After "Jesus, the Lamb without blemish," had purged and cleansed the soul, making it "whole, sanctified, and holy," the soul was ready for the baptism of the Holy Ghost. The baptism, Seymour said, was "a free gift upon the sanctified, cleansed heart." The fire burned continually in the heart, because God was "on the altar continually." God, he said, "stays there and the great Shekina of glory is continually burning and filling with heavenly light."[90]

The subsequent articles spelled out the way in which the baptism of the Holy Ghost was prefigured in more detail. In "The Baptism with the Holy Ghost Foreshadowed," we learn that "the Lord Jesus is the true tabernacle that God pitched and not man. The tabernacle in the wilderness was made after the pattern of the heavenly tabernacle which God showed Moses in the holy mount. We now have the true pattern which is the Lord Jesus Christ." Having made that connection, the article then explained how the three distinct experiences of the Christian—justification or conversion, sanctification, and the baptism of the Holy Ghost—were prefigured in the tabernacle's two altars and the Holy of Holies. Thus the "brazen altar, where whole burnt offerings are made" and upon which the Lamb of God was sacrificed, prefigured conversion. The "golden altar," at which believer's "consecrated [themselves] as living sacrifices," prefigured sanctification. Only the sanctified could enter the Holy of Holies.

> There [in the Holy of Holies] is the ark of the covenant overshadowed by the wings of the cherubim, and over the ark the great Shekina glory, a pillar of fire by night and pillar of cloud by day, presents the baptism with the Holy Spirit. There is no altar in the Holy of Holies for our consecration is all made in the Holy Place when we are sanctified. . . . Here the great Shekina glory rests upon us day and night, and we are filled and thrilled with the power of the Holy Spirit.[91]

In an article on Solomon's dedication of the temple as a "Type of Pentecost," the author emphasized the fact that all the priests who entered the Holy of Holies were already sanctified. "This," said the author, "is typical of Christ's people being sanctified before they receive the baptism of the Holy Ghost." Moreover, we learn that there were "120 priests" present at the dedication of the temple, "typical of the 120 disciples that were santified and in the upper room waiting for Jesus to baptize them with the Holy Ghost and fire."[92] The final article, "Salvation According to the True Temple," offered more precise interpretations of such temple furnishings such as the white linen, the shewbread, and the golden candlesticks. More significantly, however, it continually brought the reader back to the implications of the typology for their own spiritual life.

The article explained that "the only way men and women can be preserved is by living on the altar," such that "the holy incense of praise and prayer is always

13. The Shekinah, or Presence of God, above the Mercy-Seat in the Holy of Holies. From *The Jewish Temple and Its Furniture* (1874).

ascending from your heart to God." Thus prepared, the believer entered the Holy of Holies. The ark of the covenant, they were told, not only represented the Lord Jesus, but "the Lord Jesus Christ perfected in you." Above the ark was "the great Shekina glory," the manifestation of the divine presence. Its supernatural character was evident in the fact that it lit up the Holy of Holies, despite the fact that "the Holy of Holies did not have any light from the sun, neither did it have any candle." When a person was baptized with the Holy Ghost, "they [were] filled with continual light."[93] The light of the Holy Ghost that filled the baptized was the Shekina glory. As another article explained, "Every man or woman that gets sanctified gets the witness of the Spirit. But when you enter into the Holy of Holies, you get the great Shekina glory upon you and the cloven tongues of fire, and speak as the Spirit gives utterance, and the pillar of fire guides you every day of your life."[94]

For those imbued with the theology of the tabernacle, the baptism of the Holy Ghost was not simply a matter of speaking in tongues. As was the case with the camp meeting tradition more generally, Pentecostals in Los Angeles extended their typological exegesis beyond scripture, such that the tabernacle of the Israelites was visibly present at the Seymour's revivals at Azusa Street and Bartleman's at Eighth and Maple. Typological exegesis gave rise not only to the expectation that they would "speak as the Spirit [gave them] utterance," but that the very presence of God—"the great Shekina glory"—would be manifest in and through their bodies. That they might regularly respond to that presence with their whole bodies would only seem natural to those who had been spiritually formed in the camp meeting tradition.

Although typological exegesis was taken for granted by nineteenth-century evangelical Protestants, the more mainstream exegetical works in this genre frequently warned against "excesses" of the sort committed by Origin and many medieval Catholic exegetes. During the 1890s, some exegetes began warning of the danger of "modern rationalism" as well. Francis R. Beattie, professor of systematic theology at Louisville Presbyterian Seminary, for example, pointed out that "radical higher criticism" seemed oblivious to "the nature and value of the study of the types of Scripture." This, he thought, was another dangerous extreme, which "sound exegesis must also firmly condemn." Beattie noted the important role that types played in showing "the unity and harmony of the several parts of the Sacred Scriptures" and revealing "that one divine mind must have presided over the production of both Testaments." This, he said, is "a matter of the highest value at the present day," because it tended to confirm "the divine origin and inspiration of the Scriptures . . . against modern naturalistic views."[95]

Typology not only had apologetic value, according to Beattie, it also tended "to conserve and foster evangelical views of Scripture truth." Indeed he suggested a link between typological exegesis and authentic religious experience. He lifted up Augustine, the Reformers, and especially the Pietists, who, he said, "cultivated the study of typology diligently in connection with their deep and devout religious life and activity." Similarly, he said, "we observe, side by side with the revival of religion which occurred in many quarters about the beginning of this century, a renewed interested in the study of typology." From this, he concluded, "it seems quite evident . . . that the right study of the types of Sacred Scriptures conduces to evangelical views of the doctrines of grace, and proves eminently helpful to a genuine and spiritual religious experience."[96]

Beattie's observations highlight the particularly close relationship between typological exegesis, revivalism, and religious experience. Nonetheless, we should not miss his larger point. Protestant orthodoxy, and we might add Catholic orthodoxy as well, presupposed typological exegesis. Traditional tenets of Christianity, such as the unity and harmony of the Christian scriptures (i.e., the Old and New Testaments) as well as their divine origin and inspiration, were presupposed and legitimated by typological exegesis. The Enlightenment challenged the premises that informed typological exegesis and substituted historical critical methods in their stead. While the Spiritualists and other new religious movements rejected typological exegesis along with creeds in order to free themselves from the strictures of orthodoxy, the new scientific methods did not work their way into Protestant seminary curricula until the turn of the century. As they did, the modernist impulse unraveled the evangelical synthesis that informed traditional understandings of religious experience.

THE MODERNIZATION OF RELIGIOUS EDUCATION

Looking back, in 1935, on the rural Midwestern Protestant churches he had studied in the early teens, Anton Boisen observed that everyone's goal then was to save souls. In those days, he said, "even large and influential bodies, like the Methodists, taught their people to expect a period of 'conviction of sin' followed by a more or less clear-cut 'baptism of the Holy Spirit.' " He recalled that in 1900, in the Midwestern college town where he had grown up, "some of the older people [in the Methodist church] still shouted their 'Amens' whenever the spirit moved them without regard to the susceptibilities of the sophisticated." Sometimes, he added, "some of us who belonged to the more sedate communions went . . . to the Methodist church to see the fun. But all of us believed more or less in revivals; and when Wilbur Chapman came to town, we all participated in his evangelistic services."[97]

Now, in the thirties, he said, things were different. In his hometown, "the Methodists today worship in a large and costly church. The older people with their 'Amens' have long since passed away. There is now a stately service which appeals to college people. No longer do they labor to produce conversion experiences." Indeed, he added, "the conversion experience has pretty much dropped out of the picture, so far as the liberal Protestant churches are concerned. The evangelists who forty years ago were so very plentiful are no longer much in evidence, and an inquiry among a group of prominent liberal ministers revealed among [new members] . . . not a single case of a sudden transformation of character such as Starbuck had described."[98]

Although the decline in conversion experiences was undoubtedly causally overdetermined, a complex and interconnected set of changes within the more liberal

Protestant theological schools played a crucial part in this transformation. On the one hand, the introduction of new methods of historical critical biblical exegesis deconstructed the typological exegesis that had undergirded traditional forms of evangelical religious experience; on the other, the new field of religious education provided a new model of ministry that focused on education rather than conversion. In the new graded Sunday School curricula promoted by George Coe and the Religious Education Association, the new approach to exegesis and ministry were fully integrated. The churches that became "liberal" in the early twentieth century, in other words, did not simply drift away from an emphasis on the conversion experience. Leading modernists actively promoted a new outlook that replaced evangelism with education within the liberalizing sectors of Protestantism.

Seminary Curricula

A study of over a hundred Protestant theological schools in the U.S. and Canada commissioned in the early 1920s by the Council of Church Boards of Education described departments of religious education as "new and extremely plastic elements in theological seminaries." The report indicated that the Lutherans and Episcopalians had the least interest in this new work; the Presbyterians and other Reformed churches only a little more. By far the greatest interest was found among "the Baptist and Methodist communions and in the very large institutions." The study mentioned, in particular, Garrett (Methodist), Chandler (Methodist), Yale Divinity (Congregationalist), Boston University School of Theology (Methodist), Southwestern Baptist, the Divinity School of the University of Chicago (Baptist), Chicago Theological Seminary (Congregational), Union Theological in Virginia, and Union Theological in New York (independent).[99] The traditions with the least interest in religious education were those with a strong liturgical or confessional orientation, i.e., the Episcopalians, Lutherans, and Presbyterians. The traditions with the greatest interest were simultaneously those with the most pronounced historical commitment to revivalism and the conversion experience (i.e., the Methodists and the Baptists) and those with the most marked reputation for theological modernism (e.g., Union in New York and the University of Chicago Divinity School).[100]

The psychology of religion entered the theological curriculum along with courses in religious education. Such courses were seen as foundational to religious education and were normally offered by religious education faculty and listed under that department.[101] According to the Kelly report, courses in the psychology of religion were offered in "twenty-six seminaries, or in one-quarter of all the seminaries whose catalogues were examined. The courses range[d] from one-hour courses . . . to ten hours given at Union Theological Seminary, New York City." Kelly noted that "the distribution of these courses among denominations is approximately the same as that of departments of religious education; Methodist and Baptist seminaries, or those whose denominational origin has some kinship to these denominations, and independent institutions are pioneers in these investigations."[102] The Methodist schools were singled out as placing an "[u]nusual emphasis . . . upon religious education and psychology of religion."[103]

The report helps us to understand the significance of Coe's work at Union and the role that he played in the transformation of theological education in the early twentieth century. Of the early psychologists of religion, he was the only who taught in a theological school, although Edward Ames, whose appointment was in the department of philosophy, had close associations with the Divinity School at the University of Chicago. The fact that Coe was a Methodist and accepted an appointment at Union (over a position at the University of Chicago) in order to pursue his interests in the psychology of religion and religious education positioned him at the center of this transformation. The fact that he was a founder of the Religious Education Association (along with William Rainey Harper of the University of Chicago) and wrote the first widely used textbooks in both the psychology of religion and religious education suggests the scope of his influence beyond Union.[104]

Ames spelled out the underlying connection between the psychology of religion and religious education within the context of Protestant theological education. As he reminded his readers, the psychology of religion was in its origins nothing if not practically oriented. The earliest work in the field, he reminded his readers, dealt "almost exclusively with conversion" because that was where "the whole task of Protestant Christianity has been felt to focus." The stakes for evangelical Protestantism were enormous, since, as Ames emphasized, "the question of methods in religious work turns upon the psychology of religious experience." Setting up revivalism and religious education as opposing methods, he added, "[t]he relative value of revivalism, and of religious education, *depends upon the comparative significance of the different types of conversion and upon the means by which they are occasioned.*"[105] The psychology of religious experience, as understood by Coe, was not simply an adjunct to religious education. Rather in delegitimating the traditional Methodist and Baptist emphasis on conversion, the psychology of religion laid the foundation and created the need for the new modernist emphasis on religious education.

Neither Ames nor Coe understood religious education as simply one aspect of the theological curriculum but rather as its new center.[106] Education, as opposed to evangelism, was the new paradigm for ministry. The psychology of religion, thus, was foundational not only to religious education but also to the theological curriculum as a whole. According to Ames, "[t]he psychology of religious experience becomes the conditioning science for the various branches of theology, or rather, it is the science which in its developed forms becomes theology or the philosophy of religion." Nor was it simply preparation for theology, since, as Ames said, "in its most elementary inquiries, it is already dealing with essentials of theology and the philosophy of religion."[107]

The psychology of religion that informed theological education in the early twentieth century was that of Coe rather than James. As Arthur McGiffert, president of Union and past-president of the Religious Education Association, wrote in 1919, "Religious education in a democracy should not be such as to encourage the delusive belief in supernatural agencies and dependence upon them, but it should be such as to convince everybody that things can be controlled and moulded by the power of man."[108] Sheldon Smith cited the psychology of religion as one of three factors that nourished the turn to "anthropo-centrism" during this period. The psychology of religion was "so captivating during the first quarter of the twentieth century that it almost eclipsed theology as an academic discipline in some divinity schools." Further emphasizing the correlation between the psychology of religion and the attack on supernaturalism, Smith noted that "this whole emphasis upon the religious consciousness was anathema to most post-liberals, and they recoiled from 'psychologism' as a mortal enemy of theocentric religion."[109]

Modernism in the Parish

If the psychology of the subconscious worked its way into the Protestant parish from the religious margins, the modernist religious impulse worked its way down from the top. This is not to say, however, that there were no clergy or laity who hungered for this new approach. Responses to Coe's first book on the psychology of religion, indicate that his work spoke to a definite desire on the part of the more progressive Methodist clergy for a modern scientifically justifiable way to move away from their experientially oriented evangelical heritage.

One of the most interesting and detailed accounts of a successful attempt to popularize Coe's understanding of religious experience at the congregational level came from Clarence Abel, the pastor of Trinity Methodist Episcopal Church in Chicago. Abel wrote Coe in 1903 to inform him of the surprising results of his "efforts to make practical evangelistic application of the more scientific conception of religious experience" at the church of a colleague in rural Rock Falls, Illinois. Abel was surprised that "the people out there in the country welcomed eagerly the departure from the old line revival methods and before the two weeks were over," he said, "we had full houses and many evidences of a profound impression created for good." He was so encouraged by their response that he decided to attempt the same thing at his own church in Chicago. "I am convinced," he said to Coe, "that there is a surprisingly ready field for what for lack of better phraseology I call 'Scientific Evangelism.' My whole impulse in the direction of the various things that now occupy my mind and energies dates from the inspiration and illumination of your teachings."[110]

In a letter to written to Abel afterward, the pastor of the rural church, the Reverend Dingle, described his congregation as "captivated mind and heart by [Abel's] presentation of the Christian life and religious experience from the modern scientific viewpoint." No longer, he said, will they "interpret their Christian experience as a thing of caprice, nor will God be to them the far away God of transcendency, but he will be the ever-present Helper and Companion." Dingle, moreover, was gratified both by the level of interest and by the fact that the interest was not confined to any one segment of the congregation. "From the most cultured people we have to the uncultured, and from the ripest saint to the novice in religious things it was equally instructive and inspiring. It augurs well, I think, for the future of the church that 'the common people listen gladly' to a rational interpretation of the principles and claims of Christianity."[111]

The usual vehicle for promoting the new, scientific approach to religious experience at the grassroots level was the modernist Sunday School curriculum, which did so indirectly. The psychology emphasized in descriptions of such curricula was the developmental psychology associated with progressive education, both secular and religious, rather than the psychology of the subconscious that informed the modernist critique of evangelical religious experience. The two key concepts that informed the progressive view of education were a developmental conception of the self and the idea of society as a social organism. As we have already seen, Coe viewed the person, not as an isolated individual, but as a "self-in-socius." The centerpiece of cultural evolution, for Coe, was that of the self coming to consciousness in relation to others.[112]

Coe and others designed and promoted the modernist "completely-graded" Sunday School curriculum as a means of facilitating this process. The only place where psychology was explicitly taught was in the normal school curriculum where Sunday School teachers in training studied the "principles of psychology and religious education." The primary emphasis was not on the psychology of religion, but on the general principles of psychology and the psychology of child development. It was this psychology that explicitly informed the curriculum itself and was spelled out, for the benefit of the Sunday School teachers, in the teacher's guides for each year's curriculum.[113]

For our purposes, the curriculum for the Intermediate Department, ages thirteen to sixteen, is the most crucial, because it was during those years that the curriculum designers sought "to bring the adolescent into vital relations with Christ and the Church." Specifically, during their last year in the Intermediate Department, it was expected "that every pupil who has not already awakened to a personal religious life shall make a definite decision for Christ [and that] . . . every pupil shall be a church member before the end of the year." This, in other words, was what replaced the traditional conversion experience in the modernist understanding of Christian development. The course of study designed to effect these changes in the sixteen-year-olds was "The Life of Jesus."[114]

Where evangelicalism offered sermons, certainty, and a typological exegesis of scripture informed by orthodox doctrinal formulations, the modernist curriculum for sixteen-year-olds offered discussions of controversial topics, scholarly uncertainty, and historical critical exegesis cut loose from orthodox doctrine. The teacher's manual stressed that "the teacher has no right and probably has not sufficient wisdom to impose his own opinion upon his pupils." Calling upon the methods of the progressive high school, teachers were told they were to "discover in the laboratory of the world's thought and experience, together with your class, who Jesus Christ was." When it came to controversial subjects, such as miracles, the teacher was "to be both honestly frank and completely tolerant." Teachers should acknowledge to their students that Christian thinkers were not all in agreement regarding the miracle stories. The yearlong curriculum covering the life of Jesus was based on the latest in historical critical scholarship. It relied primarily on the gospel of Mark and the older elements from the other synoptic gospels. As the teacher's guide explained, "the endeavor of this course is to reconstruct the historical life with its main movements, as far as the biblical and archaeological material enables us to do so."[115]

Two things were expected to draw the sixteen-year-olds into a commitment to Christ and the church: the innate appeal of the life of Jesus and the " 'gang' instinct" characteristic of sixteen-year-olds. The curriculum was written so as "to portray Jesus over against the shadow of His contemporaries and enemies, in such a fashion that the pupils will instinctively and passionately take sides with Him." The teacher was to trust that this "portrait of the Master" taken "as a dramatic whole . . . will conquer affection by its own winsomeness." The teacher was to ensure that this happened by forming the students into two social clubs, one for the boys and one for the girls. Given such an outlet for their gang instinct, "the teacher will be surprised to find how inevitably these decisions [for religious committal and church membership] are taken by almost this entire group in concert."[116]

The central theme of the curriculum was that of Jesus as teacher and proclaimer of the Kingdom of God. The Kingdom of God was linked to the transformation of society. The lesson on the parables stated that "Jesus was not a revolutionist, in the sense that He ever consented to lead a bloody revolution. But He was a revolutionist, in the sense that He sowed the idea of the triumph of God's Kingdom in the hearts of men, and this idea has ever since been transforming the world." Passages that the Emmanuel Movement and Pentecostalism viewed as central were downplayed. The curriculum encouraged thoughtful discussion of the miracle stories and offered naturalistic explanations of the healing accounts, which would have pleased the Emmanuelists and upset the Pentecostals. Both would have been offended, however, by the way the curriculum ultimately trivialized the miracles, depicting the early Christians as succumbing to the "common tendency to overemphasize mere marvels."

Pentecost did not actually appear as part of the life of Jesus or elsewhere in the graded curriculum. The promise of the Comforter was mentioned. In a chapter on "Jesus' Attitude in the Face of Death," the students were told that "Jesus expected that He would soon manifest Himself to His friends in their daily life [in some spiritual way]. This Comforter, this 'Spirit of Christ' as Paul calls it, is to continue the Messianic work." Specifically, the lesson stated, "the promise is that His presence shall be a help in doing their daily duties and in setting up there the Kingdom of Heaven."[117] Young Protestant modernists were expected to find evidence of God's presence in the moral worth of individuals, in the everyday routine of daily duties, and in progressive efforts to realize the Kingdom of Heaven on earth. God's presence was not to be sought in unusual experiences or unexpected or extraordinary events.

Although this narrative closes when Protestant modernism was at the height of its influence in the theological schools and in Protestant church life more generally, this is not a story of secularization and modernization. All three of the varieties of Protestant religious experience depicted here lived on and indeed are still viable options within Protestantism today. The Christian–New Thought hybrids have flourished not only in the pews, but also in the spirituality of Alcoholics Anonymous (AA) and its later offspring. AA drew explicitly on William James for its conception of "spiritual experience" and reflects his pragmatic spirit. The conclusion of the *Varieties*, moreover, echoes quite explicitly in AA's references to a "Higher Power." Pentecostalism, too, has not simply flourished in the twentieth century, it has become a worldwide phenomenon and the fastest growing segment of the international church. Moreover, as the charismatic movement, it has been making significant inroads into mainstream, middle-class Protestant churches since the early 1970s. Indeed, Protestant modernism, at its peak as this book ends, is perhaps the most beleaguered of the three varieties today. Challenged in the 1930s by neo-Orthodoxy, in the 1950s by the liturgical movement, and in the 1960s by the Second Vatican Council, mainline Protestants, including the Methodists, have shown an increasingly strong interest in liturgically based spiritualities. One of the few links between the new mainline Protestant forms of spirituality and the old Protestant modernism is that both view themselves as "not-evangelical."

I WANT to explore what this swath of history from Wesley to James, framed as it has been around the topic of experiencing religion and explaining experience, suggests about involuntary experiences. In the first part, I consider what we can learn methodologically from a historical approach to involuntary experiences. I focus on three topics: the implications of the threefold historical typology that has structured the book for how we think about the field of religious studies; the implications of the constructedness of the category of religious experience for the study of experience; and the claim that experience cannot be separated from the communities of discourse and practice that give rise to it without becoming something else. In the second part, I consider what this particular swath of history has to offer when approached in terms of the interplay between theory and practice. I lift up what it can contribute to a naturalistic theory of involuntary acts, to the study of religion in practice, and to our understanding of the interplay between theory and practice.

CONTRIBUTION TO THE STUDY OF RELIGION

A Threefold Typology

In the Anglo-American world, and probably in the West more generally, two sets of dichotomies have been the locus of much contestation—the dichotomy between the natural and the supernatural and the dichotomy between the secular and the religious. These four terms give rise to at least three logically consistent ways to characterize experience—as secular and not religious, as supernatural and not natural, and as natural and religious. These are the three ways of characterizing experience that we have been following throughout this book. Because many subjects of this book have been inclined to speak of true and false religion, I have also characterized these three ways of constituting involuntary experiences as natural and false, supernatural and true, and natural and true. I have referred to the third way as the mediating tradition.

At the outset of this narrative, Protestants attempted to discredit forms of Protestantism they deemed false by comparing them to non-Protestant phenomena and explaining them in naturalistic or secularizing terms. This desire led to the expansion of the idea of "false religion" beyond Protestantism and the development of more comprehensive explanatory theories. Midway through the book, mediators emerged to claim that what had been deemed "false religion" was in fact "true religion." For the mediators, "true religion" *was* "religion-in-general" and authentic religious experience and naturalistic explanations of religion were not incompatible. As the quintessential theorist of the mediating tradition, William James was responsible for constituting "religious experience" as an object of study in the modern sense, defining it as a generic "something" that informs "religion-in-general" apart from any tradition in particular.

For more than a century and a half, Protestants viewed "enthusiasm" as the epitome of false religious experience. Protestants and ex-Protestants, such as Chauncy, Edwards, and Hume, compared instances of enthusiasm in order to explain such experiences in naturalistic or secularizing terms. Beginning in the late eighteenth century, European thinkers incorporated the older histories of enthusiasm into histories of mesmeric phenomena. The mesmeric histories, although still histories of false religion, ranged widely across time, culture, and religious traditions for their examples. During the 1840s, Americans with an interest in mesmerism, such as La Roy Sunderland, were responsible for disseminating magnetic interpretations of revival phenomena and giving American examples of magnetic phenomena a prominence they did not have in the European-authored histories of magnetism.

The German Romantics, most notably Jung-Stilling and Justinus Kerner, forged links between animal magnetism and true religion that were taken up by American Spiritualists during the mid-nineteenth century. As an influential grassroots movement, Spiritualism popularized a new understanding of religion, linked not to an exclusive supernatural revelation, but to a universal faith in spirit communication through "mediums," which, in their view, characterized all religions. Rather than viewing universality (and hence comparability) as a degrading lack of uniqueness, Spiritualists gradually came to view universality as persuasive testimony to the truth of their religious claims. Theosophists shared this outlook, viewing Theosophy as a universal religion grounded, not in spirit communication, but in the occult wisdom available to adepts in all ages. Such universalizing tendencies were also apparent in New Thought, which embraced the universal action of mind upon mind as the foundation of all religion, and in the Emmanuel Movement, which understood the subconscious as the universal source of spiritual power. William James's psychological theory of religion offered a sophisticated philosophically informed universalistic understanding of (true) religion accessed through the subconscious. Edwin Starbuck, James Bissett Pratt, and Edward Ames also linked (true) religion with the subconscious, albeit with significant qualifications.

The mediating tradition was concerned with religion-in-general, although individuals and movements disagreed over how it was to be understood and how it was to be accessed. Mediators variously associated religion-in-general with spirits (Spiritualists), occult wisdom (Theosophy), and spiritual healing (New Thought, Emmanuel) and accessed it by means of mediums (Spiritualists), the psychical intuition of adepts (Theosophy), the influence of mind upon mind (New Thought), and the subconscious (Emmanuel). The mediators believed that the way in which they accessed religion was scientific rather than simply a matter of faith and that the character of their methods legitimated the religious reality of that which they discovered as a result of their method. The mediators constituted religion-in-general based on comparison and argued that religious reality as they experienced it was the common denominator of religion-in-general. Although opposed to secularizing explanations of religion, they were open to naturalistic explanations that did not, in their view, explain away religion.

The mediating tradition was constructed in response to scientific attempts to secularize religious experience, on the one hand, and orthodox attempts to constitute religious experience supernaturally, on the other. From the mid-nineteenth century on, all three ways of constituting experience vied with one another. The *secularizers* used comparison to explain (away) forms of religious experience that they deemed false. In the 1880s, neurologists, such as Beard and Hammond, attacked the Spiritualists' understanding of trance, and in the 1900s academic psychologists, such as Münsterberg, King, and Jastrow, attacked the psychical researchers' understanding of the subconscious. Their aim in both cases was to reconstitute theories of involuntary experience (i.e., trance and the subconscious) in purely secular terms so as to secure the concepts for their emergent scientific disciplines and eliminate any associations between their science and popular religion.

Protestants continued to appropriate secularizing explanations as a means of discrediting what they took to be false claims to religious experience. Like Charles Chauncy in the colonial period, James Monroe Buckley, Frederick Davenport, and George Coe applied the secularizing explanations of their era to revival phenomena they deemed false, while rooting their conception of true religion in conscious, rationalistic processes. In contrast to more experientially oriented Protestants, such as Edwards and Wesley, rationalistic Protestants viewed involuntary experiences in secular terms and thus minimized the role of religious experience within Protestantism. Edwards, Wesley, and their heirs within evangelical Protestantism had a more complicated understanding of involuntary phenomena. Whereas Edwards in particular made extensive use of naturalistic explanations, both he and Wesley left room for supernaturalistic interpretations of involuntary phenomena.

Supernaturalists, who could be secularizers when it came to false religion, understood true religion as particular, exclusivist, and revealed. They resisted the identification of true religion with religion-in-general. Respectable Protestant evangelicals, including respectable Methodists, generally looked askance on outward manifestations of inward experiences. Although they, in the tradition of Jonathan Edwards, conceded a great deal to naturalistic explanation, upstart populist movements within Protestantism, particularly those with Methodist roots, often did not. Many within the early Methodist, Adventist, Holiness, and Pentecostal movements followed John Wesley's lead and *resisted* naturalistic and secularizing explanations of involuntary experiences. When they could not avoid comparing their experiences with those of others, they typically preserved the supernatural integrity of their own experiences by explaining the experiences of others as satanic counterfeits rather than as naturalistic phenomena. Thus, Seventh-day Adventists demonized mesmerism, Christian Scientists demonized Malicious Animal Magnetism, and Pentecostals demonized Spiritualists and Theosophists.

There are many ways of describing the various approaches to the study of religion; one of the more common distinguishes between theological, phenomenological, and social scientific approaches. Some scholars reduce these three types to two. Samuel Preus distinguishes between "theology" and the "study of religion," describing the former as "religious" and the latter as "naturalistic." Robert A. Segal distinguishes between "religionists," who defend the "religiosity of religion," and "social scientists," who do not.[1] While the twofold typology obscures important distinctions, the threefold distinction between theological, phenomenological, and social scientific corresponds in part to the threefold historical typology depicted in the book. Insofar as theological and social scientific mean, respectively, a commitment to supernatural and to secular explanations, we can find direct lines of continuity between the subjects of this book and the contemporary study of religion. Those I have described as mediators, however, should not be equated with phenomenologists. Mediators were primarily concerned with mediating between science and religion; phenomenologists were primarily concerned with the comparative study of religion.

The threefold typology, based on the three chains of interpretation outlined in the book, illuminates a strand that has often been overlooked yet which was important in the Anglo-American context at popular and academic levels. Recognizing the ways that controversies within the academy have been shaped by Western distinctions between the secular/religious and natural/supernatural may allow us to move beyond them or use them more self-critically. More specifically, the chains of interpretation outlined here allow us to locate the construction of the modern idea of religious experience as a generic "something" that informs "religion-in-general" apart from any tradition in particular as a response both to the Protestant supernaturalist and secular scientific understandings of religious experience.

The Category of Religious Experience

"Religious experience" meant something very different in 1750 and in 1900 in the Anglo-American context. Within late-eighteenth- and nineteenth-century evangelicalism, "religious experience" meant religious experience as understood in a particular tradition. The phrase "religious experience" often appeared in the titles of religious autobiographies. There were, for example, numerous accounts of the "life and religious experience" or the "religious experience and spiritual trials" of individuals, both ministers and lay people. Almost all such accounts were by Protestant authors and a disproportionate number of the Protestants were Methodist.[2] In this usage, religious experience was presumptively authentic and particular. With the publication of the *Varieties*, William James theoretically constituted "religious experience" as an object of study, defining it as a generic "something" that informed "religion-in-general" apart from any tradition in particular. He did so by abstracting that which he identified as religious experience (some of which had been identified as such in its original context) from the theological contexts in which it had been embedded and linking these diverse experiences together by means of psychology.

In the historical context we have examined, the concepts of "enthusiasm," the "mesmeric state," and "the subconscious" were parallel constructs. Each abstracted particular experiences from the contexts in which they had been embedded and linked them together by means of a psychological or proto-psychological theory. Indeed, as we have seen, the experimental psychology of the subconscious underlying the *Varieties* was continuous with the early psychology of animal magnetism. Whereas anti-enthusiastic theories attempted to explain *false* religion, James, in keeping with the mediating tradition more generally, attempted to explain what he took to characterize religion-in-general, without at the same time intending to explain it away. Although James's approach, unlike that of the anti-enthusiasts, was sympathetic to religion-in-general and seemingly sympathetic to traditional supernaturalism, it too dramatically reconstituted the experience of Protestant supernaturalists. The concept of religious experience as a generic something (i.e., in his case, a movement from an uneasiness to its solution) that informs religion-in-general reconstituted traditional Protestant supernaturalism just as radically as did the concept of enthusiasm or the concept of a mesmeric state.

One of the ironies revealed by this study is that each of the major discursive categories used to think theoretically about involuntary experience—enthusiasm, mesmeric states, and the subconscious—carried assumptions about religion. Defined as "false inspiration," enthusiasm was an outright theological concept, freighted with assumptions about true and false religion. Mesmeric states and the subconscious, which emerged as more or less scientific terms, were freighted with conceptions about the natural and supernatural, science and religion, and, in the case of the latter, the normal and the psychopathological. The freighted character of both the theological and scientific concepts points to the ways in which each of these concepts was embedded in its own traditions of discourse and practice. Theorizing about religion is often explicitly connected to the practice of religion in the context of theological schools, but we tend to assume that such theorizing is more objective or dispassionate in secular universities where it is formally disconnected from the practice of religion within particular traditions. Although the two situations may be different, we should not be lulled into thinking the latter situation is less complex or less likely to impose its presuppositions on particular forms of religion in practice.

This book was structured so that we might examine the interplay between theory and practice both from the perspective of those constructing the concepts and from the perspective of those whose experiences were being reconstituted in terms of the new construct. In doing so, I wanted to make several points. First, that it matters what we call things. As scholars, we are involved in constituting the "objects" we study whether we are insiders or outsiders to the traditions we are studying. Second, we constitute the objects of our study by means of comparison whether we make these comparisons explicit or not. Third, since we cannot write ourselves out of this process, it is important that we take responsibility for the comparisons we construct. James was quite conscious of this process, although most who employ the modern concept of "religious experience" are less so.

Comparison, Colonization, and Transformation

The danger of not being aware lies in the power of such concepts to reconstitute and in the process to *subsume* the experience of others into what becomes, in effect, a reified colonizing discourse.[3] When we acknowledge our concepts as constructs and acknowledge the comparisons that inform them, they lose much of their power to colonize. If, following Marilyn Waldman, we stipulate our comparative "catchments" tentatively and heuristically, our comparative questions create sites for dialogue. In such a context, our experiences, our ideas about experience, and our engagement with the experiences of others all take their place in the flow of experience, as it is constituted and reconstituted, over time. I think we must acknowledge that this last process is inevitable. By approaching the experiencing and explaining of religion historically, I have tried to make the larger point that the experience of religion cannot be separated from the communities of discourse and practice that gave rise to it *without becoming something else.*

This point appears to be contradicted by La Roy Sunderland's and Mrs. M'Reading's claim that her experience of being "caught up to Paradise" in the context of a religious service preached by Sunderland in 1824 was "just the same" as her experience while "entranced" in 1839. The mesmeric tradition presumed that a common mental state (*an* experience as it were)—whether designated as mesmeric, magnetic, somnambulistic, trance, or hypnotic—informed the whole gamut of what I have called involuntary experiences. While mesmeric *discourse* postulated a common mental state, I want to suggest that mesmeric *practice*, rather than evoking some common mental state, instead evoked bodily knowledges, including personal and cultural memories, and recast them in new forms that were secular or naturalistic. In claiming that the new forms were in fact "the same as" the traditional religious forms, mesmerists rewrote the past, discrediting traditional religious practices and limiting their ability to reproduce themselves other than as a circumscribed counter-culture.

What makes Sunderland's story intriguing is that it actually contains traces of the past, of the prior narrative, that he and Mrs. M'Reading were intent on rereading. Sunderland referred to Mrs. M'Reading as his convert. Referring to her experience when Sunderland preached in her church in 1824, Mrs. M'Reading said, "I was then [in 1824] 'caught up to Paradise,' as St. Paul was, and . . . I saw Jesus and all the angels so happy." Although she does not say so explicitly, this was probably a description of her conversion experience. Sunderland describes himself or Mrs. M'Reading as inducing such experiences by means of pheno-magnetic practices, but I do not think the second experience could have happened the way it did without the first. While entranced, Mrs. M'Reading did not enter a generic mental state; rather, the new situation evoked bodily memories such that she (in some sense) returned to a heaven that she had first experienced in the context of a Methodist preaching service. Without those bodily memories formed in that very particular context, Mrs. M'Reading would not have had *that* experience.

Although the new story described the two experiences as identical and implied that the experience she had originally understood to be religious could be elicited by secular means, I suspect that this was only so in a very limited sense. Sunderland's stories were not intended to demonstrate his power to *produce* religious experiences, but rather to demonstrate his ability to elicit or replicate experiences through secular means that were in his view falsely deemed religious. In eliciting the "same" religious experience in what was in effect a "sterile" environment, Sunderland produced a counternarrative that discredited the tradition and undercut its ability to reproduce itself.

As in the case of "flashbacks" linked to trauma, "the same" experience occurred because a bodily memory was recalled or evoked. Nonetheless, once evoked by a mesmerist rather than a preacher the experience took on a different meaning. It was no longer an experience of conversion or sanctification or a visionary journey to heaven but a mental product of a mesmeric state induced by the mesmerist. While the bodily memory or "experience" was evoked in a new context, the inner form and content of that experience content was still derived from the older tradition. The new context in which the bodily memory or experience was evoked negated the older tradition by reconstituting the experience as mesmeric rather than visionary. The situation was parallel to what occurs when therapists evoke or work with flashbacks (i.e., the intense bodily memories) of victims of post-traumatic stress. The flashbacks in such cases are not literally "the same as" the original trauma, although this is not always apparent to the patient. Working with the flashback in the therapeutic context reconstitutes the flashback as a flashback and begins to make the bodily memory of the traumatic experience more manageable.

CONTRIBUTION TO A NATURALISTIC THEORY OF INVOLUNTARY ACTS

Sunderland might have agreed with the argument I just made, given that his associationist understanding of trance provides one possible way of explaining why experiences cannot be abstracted from the discourses and practices that constitute them without creating a new experience. If trance, as he argued, cannot exist in practice without "associations," then severing the relationship between a "mental state" and its "associations," whether in theory or in practice, destroys the original experience and reconstitutes it as something else. The associations serve to cue the experience. Thus, he wrote: "Some will sink into a state of trance, by merely sitting in the chair where they have been entranced before; and the sight of any place where the mind has been peculiarly impressed, revives the same feelings, and we live over again the scenes which, otherwise, had remained entirely obliterated from recollection."[4] What Sunderland referred to as peculiar impressions on the mind are analogous to what I, following Connerton, have been referring to as bodily memories.[5] The cue (e.g., the place where the original experience occurred) revives the bodily memory (i.e., the peculiar impressions on the mind, including the associated feelings) such that, in Sunderland's words, "we live over again the scenes which, otherwise, had remained entirely obliterated from recollection" (as, for example, with flashbacks). In the story about Mrs. M'Reading,

Sunderland's presence may have served as the associative cue that evoked her bodily memory of her earlier experience.

When Mrs. M'Reading lived over the experience of being "caught up to Paradise" in the mesmeric context, her experience was reconstituted as a mesmeric experiment rather than a heavenly journey. This new explanation of her experience probably replaced the older one and, thus, brought her visionary career to an end. If we bring Frederick Myers's notion of "chains of memory" to bear on this situation, we might envision some alternative scenarios. Had Mrs. M'Reading's bodily memory of being "caught up to Paradise" been evoked in the context of a Methodist or Millerite camp meeting, the outcome would probably have been very different. Rather than ending her visionary career, further experiences in that context would likely have extended or elaborated the "chain of memory" that she associated with Paradise. Although she only saw Jesus the first time she journeyed to heaven, they might have spoken the second time or he might have gazed at her intently (as he did Ellen Harmon). Had Mrs. M'Reading's experience been evoked in the context of a Spiritualist gathering some ten years later, she might not have assumed that animal magnetism and heavenly journeys were incompatible and her journey might have been taken as a sign of mediumistic abilities worthy of further development.

We can, in other words, imagine Mrs. M'Reading developing in a number of different directions. Had the bodily memory not been evoked at all, she might simply have remained a Methodist with a dramatic conversion experience. Evoked in a mesmeric context, she became a woman who was easily entranced, a good mesmeric "subject." Evoked in a Methodist or Millerite camp meeting, she might have become a visionary. Evoked a decade later in a Spiritualist circle, she might have become a medium. As a mesmeric subject, a visionary, or a medium, Mrs. M'Reading would have elaborated her bodily memories of the first experience, albeit in different ways. As a mesmeric subject, she reconstituted her memories as a secular experience. As a visionary, she might have elaborated them as a supernatural experience of a particular sort, (say) Millerite or Methodist. As a medium, she might have reconstituted them as both a natural and a religious experience of communicating with spirits. From the perspective of Myers's theory of secondary selves, Mrs. M'Reading would have been developing a secondary self through the elaboration of a chain of memories had she pursued any of these three courses. As a mesmeric subject, a Millerite visionary, or a Spiritualist medium, however, she would have held in each case a very different chain of memories.

Throughout the book, various figures compared natural or secularized experiences with religious ones. In making these comparisons, some looked more to psychopathology and others more to everyday phenomena. Chauncy, James, Myers, and Frederick Davenport looked to psychopathological phenomena (catalepsy, fits, hysteria, hallucinations, and neurosis) for comparison and, as a result, associated religious phenomena, such as falling to the ground, visions, and ecstasy with mental weakness or nervous instability. Others, such as Edwards and Sunderland, looked to more ordinary experiences and, as a consequence, explained the same religious phenomena in terms of impressions on the imagination, sympathy, habit, custom, and suggestion. If we were to put the six on a continuum from most pathologically oriented to least, Chauncy would come first, then Davenport, then Myers and James, followed by Sunderland, and then Edwards.

This rather odd line-up reflects their understanding of the place of reason and emotion in religious experience relative to the dominant cultural views of their time. Thus, Charles Chauncy and Frederick Davenport were the most rationalistically oriented. Not only did they interpret involuntary phenomena as indications of mental weakness or nervous instability, they viewed such weakness as characterizing women (Chauncy) and primitives (Davenport). Both Chauncy's and Davenport's views were widely held in their respective eras (early-eighteenth and early-twentieth centuries). Edwards and Sunderland were both influenced by the tradition of British moral philosophy that placed greater value on the affections and emphasized the role of habit, imagination, and sympathy in the formation of beliefs. This latter tradition dominated bourgeois Anglo-American Protestantism during most of the nineteenth century. Rationalistic Protestants, such as Frederick Davenport and George Coe were part of an early-twentieth-century backlash against what they took to be an overly emotional and "feminized" Protestantism. For James and Myers to concede that religious experience might be "purchased by a perilous degree of nervous instability" was simply to take their harshest challengers seriously in an era in which sympathy and sentiment were increasingly viewed as "feminine" and irrational.[6]

We can see something of what was and is at stake in these different explanations if we return to Chauncy's memorable description of "the *Speaker* [who] delivers himself, with the *greatest Vehemence* both of *Voice* and *Gesture*, and in the most *frightful Language* his Genius will allow . . . [having] its intended Effect upon *one* or *two weak Women*, [such that] the Shrieks catch from one to another, till a great Part of the Congregation is affected." Chauncy juxtaposed the "weak Women" who set off the congregation with an onlooker who was "in possession of himself, and capable of Observation."[7] To be strong was to be self-possessed and, as such, capable of engaging in reasoned, i.e., objective and detached, observation and explanation. In contrast to the weak women, the strong person was unaffected by the voice, gesture, and frightful language of the preacher. Chauncy's understanding points to a set of dichotomies that pervaded the Enlightenment view of involuntary experiences: strong/weak, self-possessed/possessed by another, rational/emotional, objective/subjective, and dispassionate/sympathetic. Since under Anglo-American law women, slaves, and colonized peoples were legally possessed by others, it is not surprising that many Enlightened thinkers associated their natures with weakness and the lack of self-possession. In a similar vein, Elizabeth Reis has argued that the Puritan understanding of the weakness of women's bodies rendered them more susceptible to possession by either Satan or Christ.[8]

Although it would be an exaggeration to say that Edwards and Sunderland never invoked gender or racial differences, their desire to explain involuntary phenomena primarily in terms of normal mental processes moderated such tendencies and led, in my view, to more enduring theories of involuntary experience. Edwards explained enthusiasm in terms of the role of "the secret and insensible

. . . influence of example and custom" in creating "impressions on the imagination." Sunderland emphasized the role of "sympathy" and "habit" in the generation of distinctive "mental states." Sunderland defined "sympathy" as the "tendency of one thing to act upon another." "Pathetism," which he preferred to "mesmerism," was deliberately coined from the same Greek root (*pathos*) that informed sympathy. He defined Pathetism, in parallel fashion, as "the Philosophy of Influences, in, or upon, the Human Mind." Moreover, he described quite precisely the everyday interplay between attention and dissociation whereby our "external senses" are suspended. Thus, he wrote: "We cease, for the time being, to hear, see, feel, for the reason that our minds are self-inducted, entranced, diverted, by some other object."

In my view, sympathy, suggestibility, and hypnotizability are better understood as abilities or capacities that can be discouraged or cultivated rather than as symptoms of mental weakness. Most anthropologists and many psychiatrists would agree that the capacity to dissociate is a psychobiological capacity of the species, although like other human abilities not necessarily one that is evenly distributed throughout the population or over the lifespan of the individual.[9] Empirical studies have found that dissociative ability correlates with hypnotizability, the latter following a normal (bell-curve) distribution in the general population. In some cases, dissociative abilities may be familially transmitted, both in families with a history of psychopathology and in families with a history of spiritual virtuosity.[10] For multiple "selves" to emerge both dissociative ability and a stimulus to use or develop that ability need to be present. Abilities that may emerge and take on a particular form in one context may take on different forms in other contexts.

If it is not a symptom of mental weakness, to what ability or capacity do sympathy, suggestibility, and hypnotizability point? Following Sunderland's lead, we could understand this ability in terms of the tendency of the mind to act upon or influence itself or others. In the West, the controlling aspects of this ability have often been stressed, as in the ability of a hypnotist to control a subject or the ability of a crowd to overwhelm the judgment of individuals (i.e., "mass hysteria").[11] In other cultures and traditions it has been cultivated to very different ends. This brings us back to the differences between Western and African performance styles. In African cultures, this ability has been cultivated in service of complex group interactions. A focus on African performance styles encourages us to shift our mode of viewing away from the actions of individuals or groups to the *interaction* among people in a group. Chauncy and Edwards, in typical Western fashion, explained enthusiasm by noting the interaction between the preacher and the congregation. From an African cultural perspective the constructedness of the rhythmic interaction and indeed the skill of the collective performance are not means of *explaining away* the action of the Spirit, but precisely the means whereby the dynamic rhythmic interconnection of individuals-within-a-group emerges and the Spirit is known.

An understanding of involuntary experiences as involving practical mastery or skilled performances implies, as with all acquired abilities, the possibility of more or less skilled performances. Levels of skill may be related to individual aptitude as well as socialization and training. Levels of skill tacitly underlie the *DSM-IV*'s emphasis on context and adjustment as criteria for distinguishing between patho-logical and nonpathological forms of what it refers to as dissociation or trance. The new edition of the *DSM* recognizes that trance or dissociation is a normal aspect of many of the world's cultures and understands it as nonpathological when it occurs in the context of a collective cultural or religious ritual and does not cause clinically significant distress or impairment. Most cultures view seemingly spontaneous and relatively unskilled performances as problematic and "treat" them in accord with the cultural "diagnosis" of the "illness." The most common "treatments" worldwide are exorcism or initiation. The first returns individuals to their original "healthy" state; the second transforms them into skilled performers. Unskilled performances around the world often consist in "falling unconscious to the ground."[12]

People can acquire or develop these skills under a variety of conditions. A basic list would include trauma (including physical or sexual abuse, torture, natural catastrophes), drugs and changes in body chemistry, self-inflicted pain (including various mortifications of the flesh), bodily deprivation (including reductions in food, sleep, and sensory stimulation), sleep and sleep-related states (including mental passivity and relaxation), heightened attention (including prayer and med-itation), and stimulation of the senses (including incense, chanting, music, and dance).[13] None of these phenomena are foreign to religious contexts. Many, in-cluding bodily deprivation and stimulation of the senses, have taken on specifi-cally religious forms within the various traditions. The cultivation of heightened forms of attention is central to many religious disciplines.[14]

CONTRIBUTION TO THE STUDY OF RELIGION IN PRACTICE

Theories, and the theoretical concepts that inform them, stand in various relations to practice. Some theoretical concepts are indigenous to a given tradition; others are foreign. Still others are indigenized. The Greek word *ecstasis* was indigenous to Christianity. Trance (the King James Bible's translation of *ecstasis*) and enthusi-asm were indigenous to Protestantism. Mesmerism, somnambulism, dissociation, and the subconscious were concepts foreign to Protestantism, although they were, as we have seen, indigenized to varying degrees. Religious traditions did not emerge or develop in isolation from surrounding debate, although some traditions distanced themselves from it longer than others. New religious movements were more exposed to competing interpretations and forced to assimilate them more quickly than were more established traditions. Thus, Adventism, Christian Sci-ence, Theosophy, and New Thought were forced to grapple with animal magne-tism, either demonizing it or appropriating it, much more quickly than was the camp-meeting tradition. For most of the nineteenth century, the camp-meeting tradition held this challenge at bay and continued to cast its disagreements over authenticity in the traditional language of enthusiasm and fanaticism.

Even within traditions, theories about religion stand in tension with religion in practice. This is nowhere more apparent than in evangelical Protestantism, which has insisted that true conversion involves experiential as opposed to simply theoretical knowledge. Theories, whether indigenous or foreign, may stand in tension with practice because they articulate a norm or ideal against which the theoreticians judge practice and to which theorists expect practice to conform. Such theories clash with and attempt to reform the theory implicit or explicit in the practices themselves. Even when stripped of such a normative agenda, theories of religion, James argued, stand in tension with living religion in the same way that concepts stand in tension with the "full facts" of experience. Whereas narratives of experience typically reflect indigenous theories about reality, foreign theories are present only insofar as they are being indigenized, that is incorporated into the narrative of experience. David Brainerd reflected Jonathan Edwards's theology in his narrative of his experience, as did Sarah Edwards. John Wesley and Ellen White grappled with the challenges posed by theories of animal spirits and animal magnetism, respectively. Those concepts were indigenized (as sinful or satanic) in their narratives of experience.

On the level of experience in practice, I have been particularly interested to show how practices often disparaged within Protestantism as "enthusiastic" or "fanatical" participated in traditions of discourse and practice built up and modified over time. I have tried to show something of the particularity of the experience of Methodists and their heirs in related denominations and the way in which their practice was at least implicitly informed by (theological) theory. I have focused on the construction of the individual and collective body as it developed in relation to Methodist-derived preaching, experience, and camp meetings. Wesley's reliance on biblically derived marks of the Spirit, his tendency to downplay the distinction between primary and secondary causation, and his willingness to lift up phenomena that were not "sure signs" of true religion distinguished him from Edwards. These theological emphases, combined with Wesley's decision to avoid enthusiasm through regulated lay-led experience meetings rather than a clerically led effort to distinguish between the natural and supernatural dimensions of experience, left Methodism relatively more open to the theological elaboration of involuntary experiences than the Presbyterian or Congregationalist traditions.

I began the book with a sense that the camp meeting was a crucial institution that linked early American Methodists and their heirs within the Adventist, Holiness, and Pentecostal movements; the importance of the Bible, especially typological exegesis, emerged in the writing of the book. In fact, only when researching early Pentecostal references to the Shekinah glory did I begin to realize that this was a tradition of typological exegesis relating to the Tabernacle which ran from the early camp meetings through the birth of Pentecostalism. The Tabernacle, as the dwelling place of God in the camp of the Israelites in the wilderness and in the Temple, prefigured God's presence or dwelling in Christ, in the Christian, and in the camp meeting. As such, it provided the basic mythos that informed the tradition's understanding of God's presence in the individual and collective body.

This tradition engaged in an extended debate over the meaning of Pentecost in relation to the "types" of the Old Testament that had direct implications for their understanding of Christian experience. The early camp-meeting tradition associated Pentecost with shouting in the presence of God based on the type of the Second Temple (where the people shouted with a great shout). The Methodist Holiness tradition associated Pentecost with sanctification based on the type of the First Temple (where the fire came down from heaven and consumed the burnt offering). The Pentecostal tradition associated Pentecost with a baptism of the Holy Spirit that followed sanctification based on a detailed typological exegesis of the structure and furnishings of the First Temple. They argued that sanctification took place at the "golden altar" prior to entering the Holy of Holies. There was, they pointed out, no altar in the Holy of Holies where the great Shekinah glory resided above the Ark of the Covenant.

The extension of typological exegesis beyond scripture lay at the heart of the more "enthusiastic" supernaturalist approach to involuntary experiences. Although orthodox "formalists" embraced typological exegesis, they were reluctant to extend it much beyond scripture itself. The mediating tradition, inspired by Andrew Jackson Davis's privileging of history (including historical criticism of the Bible) over theology, rejected typology as well as creeds in its desire to be free of the strictures of orthodoxy. In that sense, the mediating tradition prefigured both Protestant modernism's focus on the historical Jesus and its openness to historical criticism of the Bible. Modernists and mediators, however, viewed Jesus very differently. In contrast to the modernist conception of Jesus as moral teacher, Spiritualists viewed Jesus as a medium, Quimbyites as a clairvoyant, Christian Scientists as a demonstrator, Theosophists as an adept, and New Thought and Emmanuelists as a healer.

THE INTERPLAY BETWEEN THEORY AND PRACTICE

James's conceptual distinction between the science of religion (things made) and living religion (things in the making) corresponds to and furthers the distinctions between theory and religion-in-practice that inform the book. As James explains in more detail in *A Pluralistic Universe*, "when you have broken reality into concepts you never can reconstruct it in its wholeness. . . . But [he said] place yourself . . . inside of the living, moving, active thickness of the real, and all the abstractions and distinctions are given into your hand" (*PU*, 116). In short, James said, "What really *exists* is not things made but things in the making. Once made, they are dead, and an infinite number of alternative conceptual decompositions can be used in defining them" (*PU*, 117).

The closer we are to the experience in question the more we can see of the way it is embedded in and connected to other things. The more we abstract or disconnect "experience" from *the narrating of experience* in order that it may participate in more abstract discourses, the more it is fragmented or, as James says, "decomposed." First-person narratives allow us to focus on the narrating of experience and thus provide historians with our primary means of access to the experience-in-practice of an individual or community. Such narratives provide a means. of reconstituting the links between experience and the bodily knowledges, cultural traditions, and social relations that went into making or composing the experience. Third-person narratives are a step removed, although they often contain and rework first-person narratives. Theories of experience whether theological, spiritual, philosophical, sociological, or psychological, are the farthest removed and the most fragmented. Nonetheless, as we have seen, they inform the making and unmaking of experience at the level of narrative in varied and complicated ways.

Many phenomenologically oriented scholars of religion share James's comparative interest in the interplay between the general and the particular, that is, between theories of religion and living religions. As indicated in the introduction, however, most historians or phenomenologists of religion limit their comparisons to religious phenomena. Few share James's interest in comparing religious and nonreligious phenomena. Such comparisons shift our attention from the study of religion *per se* to the *processes* by which religious and nonreligious phenomena are made and unmade. I think this is a more interesting and fruitful question. However, in pursuing it we lose a sense of religion (or not-religion) as a substantive thing. Indeed, once we latch on to this question, it becomes clear that the question of "what is religion" (which really asks what is authentic or true religion) is disputed within traditions and not just between them. One locus for these disputes about "what is religion" clusters around "experience." Because of the disputes, both among insiders and between insiders and outsiders, the study of religion opens out at this point into the study of everything.

NOTES

1. My thinking about religious experience has been shaped in fundamental ways by the work of Wayne Proudfoot, *Religious Experience* (Berkeley: University of California Press, 1985), and J. Samuel Preus, *Explaining Religion* (New Haven: Yale University Press, 1989). My approach as a historian is similar to that advocated by Joan Scott in her article on "Experience" (in *Feminists Theorize the Political*, ed. Judith Butler and Joan W. Scott [New York: Routledge, 1992], 22–40). As she says of differences in experience:

> We know they exist, but not how they've been constructed; . . . we know that difference exists, but we don't understand it as constructed relationally. For that we need to attend to the historical processes that, through discourse, position subjects and produce their experiences. It is not individuals who have experience, but subjects who are constituted through experience. Experience in this definition then becomes not the origin of our explanation, not the authoritative . . . evidence that grounds what is known, but rather that which we seek to explain, that about which knowledge is produced. To think about experience in this way is to historicize it as well as to historicize the identities it produces (25–26).

While I agree with Scott that historians need to scrutinize "all explanatory categories usually taken for granted, including the category of 'experience,' " I resist locating agency in "history" rather than in subjects. Thus, with respect to the production of experience, I would say, paraphrasing Anthony Giddens, that subjects *simultaneously* constitute their experience and are constituted by it.

2. William Dean suggests that "reality itself might be conceived as comprised of chains of historical interpretations" ("An American Theology," *Process Studies* 12/2 [1982]: 124).

3. "Religion" in the traditional Protestant understanding of the term did not mean, as it does today, religion-in-general, but denoted the practical side of authentic Christianity. "Religion," understood as "true religion," referred to worship and practice, while "theology" referred to the theoretical side of the Christian enterprise, that is, to intellectual reflection on worship and practice (Richard A. Muller, *Post-Reformation Reformed Dogmatics*, vol. 1 [Grand Rapids: Baker Books, 1987], 113–21).

4. Robert A. Segal, *Explaining and Interpreting Religion: Essays on the Issue* (New York: Peter Lang, 1993), xii; Preus, *Explaining Religion*, xi; Ivan Strenski, *Religion in Relation: Method, Application and Moral Location* (Columbia: University of South Carolina Press, 1993), 2–3.

5. Wouter J. Hanegraaff makes a similar argument in his new book *New Age Religion and Western Culture: Esotericism in the Mirror of Western Thought* (Albany: SUNY Press, 1998), 442–61. I expect that this argument will be elaborated further in his forthcoming book, Antoine Faivre and idem., eds., *Western Esotericism and the Study of Religions*.

6. I am grateful to my colleague David Griffin for help in clarify the use of these terms.

7. American Psychiatric Association, *Diagnostic and Statistical Manual* [hereafter *DSM-IV*] (Washington, DC: American Psychiatric Association, 1994).

8. Many modern academic disciplines constituted themselves in part by taking stands in these controversies. In philosophy, Kant's foundational distinction between "sensible" and "non-sensible intuition" was intended to undercut the dangers of fanaticism. Chief among the "fanatical illusions" he opposed was the idea that humans could legitimately

claim to feel the "immediate presence of the Supreme Being" (Immanuel Kant, *Religion within the Limits of Reason Alone* [New York: Harper Torchbooks, 1960], cii–ciii, 162–63). Coleridge, leading the Romantic reaction to Enlightenment rationalism, took a different tack, recasting "enthusiasm," a derogatory term when applied to religious practitioners, as something positive when applied to poets. He, thus, legitimated inspiration in romantic poetry while continuing to denigrate it in religion (Jon Mee, " 'Babylon's Fall': Prophesy, Poetry and Politics in the 1790s," unpublished paper given at a conference on "Enthusiasm and Modernity in Europe, 1650–1850," Center for 17th and 18th Century Studies, Clarke Memorial Library, Los Angeles, May 3–4, 1996). Similar observations can be made about the rise of the social sciences. Durkheim, for example, linked religion to the dynamic process whereby individuals internalized the moral values of a society. This took place, he argued, in religious assemblies wherein a special "mental state" that he referred to as "collective effervescence" was induced. This state, he said, "might be described as *ecstatic*" (W.S.F. Pickering, ed., *Durkheim on Religion* [Atlanta: Scholars Press, 1994], 136).

9. Mikkel Borch-Jacobsen, *The Mimetic Tie: Psychoanalysis, Mimesis, and Affect* (Stanford: Stanford University Press, 1992), 98–99. Borch-Jacobsen writes: "You will call it 'animal magnetism,' 'waking somnambulism,' or 'transference' if you happen to be a psychotherapist; 'suggestion,' 'hysteria,' or 'modified state of consciousness' if you happen to be a psychiatrist or psychologist; 'trance' or 'ecstasy' if you are an anthropologist; 'demon possession' if a theologian" (99).

10. Jonathan Z. Smith, *Drudgery Divine* (Chicago: University of Chicago Press, 1990), 52; F.J.P. Poole, "Metaphors and Maps: Towards Comparison in the Anthropology of Religion," *JAAR* 54 (1986): 428.

11. Marilyn Robinson Waldman refers to such "more cumbersome multiword formulations" as "catchments." While there is nothing in Waldman's approach that would preclude the stipulation of catchments that include both religious and nonreligious phenomena, it is significant that she, like most scholars influenced by the phenomenological or "history of religions" approach to the study of religion, limits her comparisons to explicitly religious phenomena ("Inviting Prophets and Entertaining Comparisons," cited in panel presentations on Waldman's work, 1997 Annual Meeting of the American Academy of Religion, San Francisco, California). I am grateful to Tom Bremer for introducing me to Waldman's work.

12. Proudfoot, *Religious Experience*, 180–81.

13. The concept of "lived religion" is discussed in David Hall, ed., *Lived Religion* (Princeton: Princeton University Press, 1997). My use of the term differs from Hall's in that I explicitly specify that which is *not* "lived religion," juxtaposing "lived religion" or "religion-in-practice" with "theories of religion," including "theology" in its more abstract formulations. I do not mean to suggest that the two are unrelated; in fact, the book is devoted to an investigation of the interplay between them.

14. Michele Stephen, "Self, the Sacred Other, and Autonomous Imagination," in *Religious Imagination in New Guinea*, ed. Gilbert Herdt and Michelle Stephen (New Brunswick and London: Rutgers University Press, 1989), 47–48. This self-alien aspect of the experience has traditionally been highlighted by phenomenological studies of religion (cf. Rudolf Otto, *The Idea of the Holy* [New York: Oxford University Press, 1958], 11; Gerardus van der Leeuw, *Religion in Essence and Manifestation* [Princeton: Princeton University Press, 1986], 23–28; Mircea Eliade, *The Sacred and the Profane* [New York: Harcourt, Brace, and World, 1959], 11–13). When we attend, as Stephen suggests, to the subjective experience of the "native actor," we find a considerably higher degree of consensus among theorists with phenomenological and social scientific orientations. Durkheim, for example, recog-

nized this self-alien dimension of religious experience when he described "the man who lives according to religion . . . [as] above all a man who feels within himself a power of which he is not normally conscious, a power which is absent when he is not in the religious state" (Pickering, ed., *Durkheim on Religion*, 182). Feuerbach approached this self-alien dimension more psychologically when he claimed that "the ultimate secret of religion is the *relationship* between the *conscious* and *unconscious*, the *voluntary* and *involuntary* ['the I and the not-I'] *in one and the same individual*" (Ludwig Feuerbach, *Lectures on the Essence of Religion*, trans. Ralph Manheim [New York: Harper and Row, 1967], 310–11).

15. These descriptive phrases are loosely derived from the diagnostic terminology in the sections on Conversion and Dissociative Disorders in the *DSM-IV*, 452–57, 477–91, 727–29). I am extracting this terminology from the *DSM-IV* partly because of the care it takes in formulating descriptive language and partly because, like the turn-of-the-century psychologists of religion, I want to construct a "site for dialogue" between religion, anthropology, and psychiatry. Psychiatry has signaled a greater openness to such dialogue by recognizing both "conversion symptoms" (e.g. "falling down with loss or alteration of consciousness" and "visions") and "dissociation" as "a common and accepted expression of cultural activities or religious experience in many societies" rather than assuming that all such phenomena are evidence of psychopathology (*DSM-IV*, 454–55, 477). To test for hidden explanatory assumptions, I have mentally run this descriptive language past Jonathan Edwards, one of my most intellectually rigorous historical "informants." In deference to his desire to root authentic religious experience in a new "supernatural sense" entirely distinct from the natural senses, I have referred to *unusual* sensory experiences (that presumably could be understood as supernatural) rather than to *altered* (and thus presumably still natural) sensory perceptions or experiences.

16. The *DSM-IV* does not highlight the connection between dreams and dissociation, because of the traditional understanding of dissociation as pathology. Older terms, such as "somnambulism" and "trance," that attempted to name roughly comparable sets of experiences specifically located them in an intermediate space between sleep and waking.

17. Proudfoot, *Religious Experience*, 216–24; Segal, *Explaining and Interpreting Religion*, 1–2.

18. Theorizing, in other words, is dependent on its own sorts of practices, i.e., the practices associated with intellectual work (Pierre Bourdieu, *Homo Academicus* [Stanford: Stanford University Press, 1984]). Such practices may even involve involuntary experiences, as when authors describe themselves as inspired or possessed in the act of writing.

19. Pierre Bourdieu, *Outline of a Theory of Practice* (London: Cambridge University Press, 1977), 87; Paul Connerton, *How Societies Remember* (Cambridge: Cambridge University Press, 1977). Bourdieu cites Albert B. Lord's analysis of the training of the Yugoslavian *guslar* (bard)—a study that inspired analyses of the African American chanted sermon—as an example of this process (88).

20. On leveling the playing field between academic and other discourses, see Michael Jackson, *Paths Toward a Clearing: Radical Empiricism and Ethnographic Inquiry* (Bloomington: Indiana University Press), 4; and Dennis Tedlock and Bruce Mannheim, *The Dialogic Emergence of Culture* (Urbana: University of Illinois Press, 1995), 2–4.

21. Bernard McGinn has suggested that the "unhappy confrontation" between late-nineteenth-century French psychiatrists and Catholic theologians may help explain the "often hostile relations" between proponents of psychological and theological approaches to the study of mysticism during the present century (*The Foundations of Mysticism* [New York: Crossroads, 1991], 331).

22. Robert Fuller, *Mesmerism and the American Cure of Souls* (Philadelphia: University of Pennsylvania Press, 1982); James Hoopes, *Consciousness in New England: From Puritanism and Ideas to Psychoanalysis and Semiotics* (Baltimore and London: Johns Hopkins University Press, 1989); Robert Bruce Mullin, *Miracles and the Modern Religious Imagination* (New Haven: Yale University Press, 1996).

23. Nathan Hatch, "The Puzzle of American Methodism," *Church History* 63/2 (June 1994): 175–89.

PART ONE
FORMALISM, ENTHUSIASM, AND TRUE RELIGION, 1740–1820

1. Hillel Schwartz, *The French Prophets* (Berkeley: University of California Press, 1980), 17–19. The quote is taken from the title of one of Schwartz's sources, *A Relation of Several Hundreds of Children and Others that Prophesie and Preach in their Sleep* (1689).

2. Marc Vernous, *A Preservative against the False Prophets of the Times* (London, 1708), 23–24, quoted in Hillel Schwartz, *Knaves, Fools, Madmen, and that Subtile Effluvium: A Study of the Opposition to the French Prophets in England, 1706–1710* (Gainesville: University Press of Florida, 1978), facing p. 1.

3. Schwartz, *French Prophets*, 205–8, 288–89.

4. W. Reginald Ward and Richard P. Heitzenrater, eds., *Journals and Diaries, II (1738–1743)*, vol. 19 of *The Works of John Wesley* [hereafter *JW* 19] (Nashville: Abingdon, 1984), 33.

5. Schwartz, *French Prophets*, 202–7; Clarke Garret, *Spirit Poession and Popular Religion: From the Camisards to the Shakers* (Baltimore: The Johns Hopkins University Press, 1987), 79; Henry D. Rack, *Reasonable Enthusiast: John Wesley and the Rise of Methodism*, 2d. ed. (Nashville: Abingdon, 1993), 187.

6. Frank Baker, ed., *Letters II (1740–1755)*, vol. 26 of *The Works of John Wesley* [hereafter *JW* 26] (Oxford: Clarendon Press, 1982), 240–41, 231.

7. W. Reginald Ward and Richard P. Heitzenrater, eds., *Journals and Diaries, III (1743–54)*, vol. 20 of *The Works of John Wesley* [hereafter *JW* 20] (Nashville: Abingdon, 1991), 356, cited from another edition in Schwartz, *French Prophets*, 207.

8. See the OED, s.v. "Enthusiast," esp. 2.b. "One who erroneously believes himself to be the recipient of special divine communication; in the wider sense, one who holds extravagant and visionary religious opinions, or is characterized by ill-regulated fervour of religious emotion"; and "Formalist," esp. 3.b. "One who has the form of religion without the power."

9. *Spirituall Experiences of Sundry Believers* (1652), Epistle, and Jane Turner, *Choice Experiences* (1654), 202, quoted in Owen C. Watkins, *The Puritan Experience: Studies in Spiritual Autobiography* (New York: Schocken Books, 1972), 15. See also, the OED, s.v. "Experience," esp. 4.b. "In religious use: A state of mind or feeling forming part of the inner religious life; the mental history (of a person) with regard to religious emotion"; Geoffrey F. Nuttall, *The Holy Spirit in Puritan Faith and Experience*, introduction by Peter Lake (Chicago: University of Chicago Press, 1992), 38–42; and Nigel Smith, *Perfection Proclaimed: Language and Literature in English Radical Religion, 1640–1660* (Oxford: Clarendon Press, 1989).

10. Some historians trace enthusiasm from the classical era and/or early Christianity into the modern era. See, for example, Umphrey Lee, *The Historical Backgrounds of Early Methodist Enthusiasm* (New York: AMS Press, 1967), and Ronald Knox, *Enthusiasm* (New York: Oxford, 1950). Others have associated the rise of enthusiasm with the Reformation.

See for example, David S. Lovejoy, *Religious Enthusiasm in the New World: Heresy to Revolution* (Cambridge, MA: Harvard University Press, 1985), and Theophilus Evans, *The History of Modern Enthusiasm, from the Reformation to the Present Time* (London, 1757). Others read the late-seventeeth-century understanding of enthusiasm back into the early-seventeenth-century writings. Joe Lee Davis, for example, attempts to distinguish between "mystics" and "enthusiasts" ("Mystical versus Enthusiastic Sensibility," *Journal of the History of Ideas* 4 [1943]: 301–19). Schwartz and Stephen Gunter both suggest a possible connection between the new use of enthusiasm and the English Civil War (Schwartz, *Knaves*, 50, and W. Stephen Gunter, *The Limits of 'Divine Love': John Wesley's Response to Antinomianism and Enthusiasm* [Nashville: Kingswood, 1989], 119–20).

11. Robert Burton, *The Anatomy of Melancholy*, ed. Floyd Dell and Paul Jordan-Smith (New York: Farrar & Rinehart, 1927), 866–67, 896, 917–19.

12. Michael Heyd, in what is now the most comprehensive treatment of the history of enthusiasm, makes two significant points about Burton. He argues, first, that Burton was instrumental in bringing "the medical and philosophical tradition which linked enthusiasm with melancholy . . . [into] the vocabulary and contents of religious and ideological polemics in the seventeenth century" and, second, that "Catholics, Puritans, radical sectarians, and enthusiasts, were all gathered together by Burton under the rubric of 'religious enthusiasm' " (*'Be Sober and Reasonable': The Critique of Enthusiasm in the Seventeenth and Early Eighteenth Centuries* [Leiden: E. J. Brill, 1995], 64–65). Although I think the first point is well taken, I think that the second overstates the case. It is more accurate to say that "Hereticks . . . , Schismaticks, . . . Enthusiasts, &c." were all gathered under the rubric of "Religious Melancholy." He goes on to argue, "a long line of Anglican critics of enthusiasm in the second half of the seventeenth century" were deeply influenced by their reading of Burton (72), but it is they, not Burton, who actually foreground the category of "enthusiasm" (rather than "melancholy") as a catch-all term for religious excess.

13. George Rosen, "Enthusiasm: 'a dark lanthorn of the spirit," *Bulletin of the History of Medicine* 42/5 (1968):411–13.

14. According to Christopher Hill, twenty-two pamphlets were published in England in 1640 and 1966 in 1642 (*The World Turned Upside Down: Radical Ideas During the English Revolution* [New York: Viking Press, 1972], 49).

15. Watkins's bibliography lists eight autobiographies containing the word "experience" published in the 1640s and 1650s, six of them between 1651 and 1654; most of the other titles containing the word "experience" were published in the 1690s, many of them by Quakers.

16. In Umphrey Lee's bibliography (Historical Backgrounds, 161–69), see, for example, Dell (1641), Edwards (1645), Etherington (1645), Graunt (1645), Ministers of Yorkshire (1648), Pagitt (1645), *The Ranters Creed* (1651), *Take Warning* (1648), Taylor (1641).

17. I have found only two earlier uses of the term in titles (Umphrey Lee, *Historical Backgrounds*, 161–69). The word may have acquired closer associations with false inspiration in the American colonies, particularly in the wake of the Antinomian Controversy (see Lovejoy, *Religious Enthusiasm*, 87–110).

18. On divine inspiration, objective divine action, and personal encounter or inner experience as aspects of the larger subject of Christian revelation, see Keith Ward, *Religion and Revelation* (Oxford: Clarendon Press, 1994), 226–32.

19. Nuttall, *The Holy Spirit*, xxv.

20. Watkins, *Puritan Experience*, 95–97, 153–55.

21. Hill, *World Turned Upside Down*, 278–81.

22. Causaubon, *Treatise Concerning Enthusiasm*, 4–5, quoted in Rosen, "Enthusiasm," 414.

23. George Williamson, "The Restoration Revolt Against Enthusiasm," *Studies in Philology* 30 (1933): 597.

CHAPTER ONE
EXPLAINING ENTHUSIASM

1. On Hume as a philosopher of religion, see J.C.A. Gaskin, *Hume's Philosophy of Religion* (New York: Harper & Row, 1978); on Hume's place within the modern study of religion, see Preus, *Explaining Religion*, xiii–xiv, 84–103; and Peter Harrison, *"Religion and the Religious in the English Enlightenment* (Cambridge: Cambridge University Press, 1990), 157–72. In both the philosophy of religion and the history of the academic study of religion, the emphasis has been on Hume's later, more theoretical works on religion, i.e., *Dialogues concerning Natural Religion* and *The Natural History of Religion*. Rarely are his more historical or political writings (in which he discusses enthusiasm and superstition in the context of English history) integrated into an overall understanding of his views on religion. The various essays in *The Cambridge Companion to Hume* [hereafter *CC Hume*], ed. David Fate Norton (Cambridge: Cambridge University Press, 1993), provide a starting point for a more integrated view of Hume's thinking about religion. Peter Jones also provides a brief but more integrated overview (*Hume's Sentiments: Their Ciceronian and French Context* [Edinburgh: The University Press, 1982], 78–80).

2. Harrison, *"Religion" and the Religions*, 2–3, 120–26, 169; Frank E. Manuel, *The Eighteenth Century Confronts the Gods* (Cambridge, MA: Harvard University Press, 1959), 70–81, quote, 71.

3. For a classic account of the Puritan conversion experience see, Michael McGiffert, ed., *God's Plot: Puritan Spirituality in Thomas Shepard's Cambridge*, rev. ed. (Amherst: University of Massachusetts Press, 1994), 42–48. In addition to McGiffert's introduction, see especially Charles Lloyd Cohen, *God's Caress: The Psychology of Puritan Religious Experience* (New York: Oxford University Press, 1986); and David D. Hall, "On Common Ground: The Coherence of American Puritan Studies," *William and Mary Quarterly*, 3d series, 44 (1987): 193–221.

4. Chauncy provides a straightforward etymological definition of enthusiasm centering on inspiration in his sermon *Enthusiasm Described and Caution'd Against*. However, he does not limit his criticism, either there or in his later writings, simply to those who make such claims. Rather, building on the etymological definition, he defines "the *Enthusiast* [as] . . . one, who has a conceit of himself as a person favoured with the extraordinary presence of the *Deity*." In keeping with the broader connotations of "extraordinary presence," he includes anything that had been viewed as having supernatural origins within the purview of his discussion. Thus, phenomena such as fainting, swooning, and crying out at the time of conversion, insofar as they were granted supernatural significance by or in his sources, fall for Chauncy within the scope of enthusiasm (Charles Chauncy, *Enthusiasm Described and Caution'd Against* [1742], in *The Great Awakening: Documents Illustrating the Crisis and Its Consequences*, ed. Alan Heimert and Perry Miller [New York: Bobbs-Merrill Co., 1967], 230–31). On the conversion experience, see C. C. Goen, *Revivalism and Separatism in New England, 1740–1800* (Middletown, CT: Wesleyan University Press, 1987), 13–14.

5. Charles Chauncy, *Seasonable Thoughts on the State of Religion in New England* [hereafter *STSR*] (Boston, 1743; reprint ed., Hicksville, NY: Regina Press, 1975), 77.

6. Chauncy, *Enthusiasm Described*, 230–31, 234.

7. James Robe came to similar conclusions in Scotland, perhaps after reading Chauncy's "Letter to Wishart." Ironically, Robe, who was pro-revival, used the naturalism of the bodily effects associated with conversion to distinguish the Scottish converts from "enthusiasts" who claimed supernatural inspiration.

8. Norman Fiering, *Moral Philosophy at Seventeenth-Century Harvard* (Chapel Hill: University of North Carolina Press, 1981), 98, n. 76.

9. Katharine Park and Eckhard Kessler, "The Concept of Psychology," in Charles B. Schmitt, et al., eds., *The Cambridge History of Renaissance Philosophy* (Cambridge: Cambridge University Press, 1988), 455. For an English translation, see *Aristotle's Psychology*, trans. William A. Hammond (New York: Macmillan, Co., 1902).

10. Thomas S. Hall, *Ideas of Life and Matter: Studies in the History of General Physiology, 600 B.C.–1900 A.D.*, 2 vols. (Chicago: University of Chicago Press, 1969), 1: 193–96; Fiering, *Moral Philosophy*, 106–9; Katherine Park, "The Organic Soul," in Schmitt, et al., *Cambridge History of Renaissance Philosophy*, 464–69.

11. Park and Kessler, "Concept of Psychology," 456–57.

12. Fiering, *Moral Philosophy*, 110–14, 117–19, 138–44; quote p. 111.

13. Fiering discusses the mistaken tendency to attribute the discovery of the passions to Edwards (*Moral Philosophy*, 121–22); John Corrigan argues against the tendency to read Chauncy as hostile to the passions (*The Hidden Balance: Religion and the Social Theories of Charles Chauncy and Jonathan Mayhew* [Cambridge: Cambridge University Press, 1987], 30–33).

14. Chauncy, *Enthusiasm Described*, 248–49.

15. *The Philosophical Writings of Descartes* [hereafter, *Descartes*], vol. 1, trans. John Cottingham, et al. (Cambridge: Cambridge University Press, 1985), 108 (*Treatise on Man*); Thomas S. Hall, *Ideas of Life and Matter*, 1: 256; Gary Hatfield, "Descartes' Physiology and Its Relation to His Psychology," in *The Cambridge Companion to Descartes*, ed. John Cottingham (Cambridge: Cambridge University Press, 1992), 340–50; on automata, see also *Descartes*, 329; Thomas S. Hall, *Ideas of Life and Matter*, 1: 222–24.

16. *Descartes*, 99–100 (*Treatise on Man*), 330–32 (*The Passions of the Soul*).

17. *Descartes*, 340–41 (*Passions*).

18. *Descartes*, 342 (*Passions*); emphasis added.

19. G. S. Rousseau, "Science and the Discovery of the Imagination in Enlightened England," *Eighteenth Century Studies* 3 (1969): 114.

20. G. S. Rousseau, "Nerves, Spirits, and Fibres: Towards Defining the Origins of Sensibility," in *Studies in the Eighteenth Century, III*, ed. R. F. Brissenden and J. C. Eade (Toronto: University of Toronto Press, 1976), 144–52; John Mullan, "Hypochondria and Hysteria: Sensibility and the Physicians," *The Eighteenth Century* 25/2 (1984): 142–48.

21. G. S. Rousseau, " 'A Strange Pathology': Hysteria in the Early Modern World, 1500–1800," in Sander Gilman, et al., *Hysteria Beyond Freud* (Berkeley: University of California Press, 1993), 135.

22. Rousseau, "Strange Pathology," 140.

23. Rousseau, "Strange Pathology," 141–42; Mullan, "Hypochondria and Hysteria," 156–62.

24. Robe's observations suggest that among the common people fits were associated with epilepsy rather than hysteria. He wrote that "these convulsive effects [among converts], prejudiced many of the common sort against this blessed work—They know no other convulsions but the epilepsy, or what they call the falling-sickness—They know not that there are many sorts of convulsions, which are not the falling-sickness—or the fits, another name ordinary among them; and therefore whatever they hear called convulsions,

hysteric-fits, &c. they understand all in the worse sense" (James Robe, *Narratives of the Extraordinary Work of the Spirit of God, at Cambuslang, Kilsyth, &c. begun 1742* (Glasgow: David Niven, 1790), 197).

25. G. S. Rousseau, "Towards a Semiotics of the Nerve," in Peter Burke and Roy Porter, eds., *Language, Self, and Society: A Social History of Language* (Cambridge: Polity Press, 1991), 217.

26. Rousseau, "Strange Pathology," 222.

27. Charles Chauncy, "A Letter from a Gentleman in Boston to Mr. George Wishart . . . of Edinburgh . . .," in *The Great Awakening: Documents on the Revival of Religion, 1740-- 1745*, ed. Richard L. Bushman (Chapel Hill: University of North Carolina Press, 1989), 118–19.

28. Anthony Earl of Shaftesbury, *Characteristics*, 2 vols. (Gloucester, MA: Peter Smith, 1963), 1:39. This quote is from "A Letter Concerning Enthusiasm" and is derived, according to the editor's note, from Locke.

29. Manuel, *The Eighteenth Century Confronts the Gods*, 77–81. Trenchard's theory of contagion was based on the spread of "Effluviums" and "poisonous and melancholy Vapours" from one person to the next. See also, Schwartz, *Knaves*, 51–56.

30. Shaftesbury, *Characteristics*, 1: 13.

31. Here again he seems to be following Shaftesbury (ibid., 1: 31).

32. C. C. Goen, ed., *The Great Awakening*, vol. 4 of *The Works of Jonathan Edwards* in *The Works of Jonathan Edwards* [hereafter *JE* 4] (New Haven: Yale University Press, 1972), 48–54.

33. Robe, *Narratives*, 53–54.

34. In adopting a tiered model of the affections, Edwards was indebted to seventeenth-century works on the passions written by English Puritans rooted in a tradition that went back to Augustine (Fiering, *Moral Philosophy*, 159). The Puritans' underlying concern, as Fiering notes, was with "the problem of counterfeit religion or hypocrisy, the major theme in Puritan psychology for two hundred years" (161–62).

35. Vere Chappell, "Locke's Theory of Ideas," in *The Cambridge Companion to Locke*, ed. idem. (Cambridge: Cambridge University Press, 1994), 33, 53–54. Similarly, James Hoopes states, "Locke . . . believed that the way of ideas invalidated Antinomian claims of direct intercourse with the Almighty. . . . Even if the message was true, that did not prove that its appearance in the enthusiast's mind was owing to divine inspiration, for the enthusiast had empirical knowledge only of the idea or message, not of the substance that caused it" ("Calvinism and Consciousness from Edwards to Beecher," in *Jonathan Edwards and the American Experience*, ed. Nathan O. Hatch and Harry S. Stout [New York: Oxford University Press, 1988], 208–9).

36. Norman Fiering, *Jonathan Edwards's Moral Thought in Its British Context* (Chapel Hill: University of North Carolina Press, 1981), 35–40; Wallace E. Anderson, ed., *Scientific and Philosophical Writings*, vol. 6 of *The Works of Jonathan Edwards* [hereafter *JE* 6] (New Haven: Yale University Press, 1980), 16–26; and James Hoopes, "Jonathan Edwards's Religious Psychology," *The Journal of American History* 69/4 (1983): 849–65.

37. Hoopes, "Calvinism and Consciousness," 208–9; Fiering, *Edwards's Moral Thought*, 125–26.

38. Fiering, *Moral Philosophy*, 194–95.

39. Ava Chamberlain, "Self-Deception as a Theological Problem in Jonathan Edwards's 'Treatise Concerning the Religious Affections,' " *Church History* 63/4 (December 1994): 550–53. According to Chamberlain, "because sin distorted the [new spiritual sense], the saint . . . could not maintain an assurance unclouded by doubt. It is not, therefore, far

wrong to characterize Edwards as a theoretical antinomian and a practical Calvinist. . . . Christian practice [she concludes] was the locus of assurance because, in comparison with immediate experience, it was less liable to produce counterfeit convictions of grace" (552–53).

40. John E. Smith, ed., *Religious Affections*, vol. 2 of *The Works of Jonathan Edwards* [hereafter *JE* 2] (New Haven: Yale University Press, 1959), 200.

41. On Edwards use of Locke's terminology, see James Hoopes, "Religious Psychology," 859.

42. Fiering notes in this regard that Locke, "had he been alive, would undoubtedly have dismissed Edward's idea of a special sensation of divine things as 'enthusiastick' nonsense" (*Edwards's Moral Thought*, 125).

43. Ibid., 87.

44. Hoopes, "Religious Psychology," 859.

45. Ibid., 863–64.

46. Fiering, *Moral Philosophy*, 195; Fiering, *Edwards's Moral Thought*, 129–30, 131.

47. Ernest C. Mossner, *The Life of David Hume*, 2nd ed. (Oxford: Clarendon Press, 1980), 76–77.

48. John Biro, "Hume's New Science of Mind," in *CC Hume*, 39.

49. Mossner, *Life of David Hume*, 34, 51, 64–65.

50. David Hume, *A Treatise of Human Nature*, ed. Ernest C. Mossner (London: Penguin Books, 1969), 311.

51. Hume, *Treatise*, 313–14.

52. John Biro, "Hume's New Science of Mind," in *CC Hume*, 39.

53. Hume, *Treatise*, 312–13.

54. Hume, *Treatise*, 316.

55. David Hume, *A Kind of History of My Life* (1734) in *CC Hume*, 349; Mossner, *Life of David Hume*, 66–91.

56. David Hume to Henry Home, 2 December 1737, in *New Letters of David Hume*, ed. Raymond Klibansky and Ernest C. Mossner (Oxford: Clarendon Press, 1954), 2–3.

57. David Hume, *Essays: Moral, Political, and Literary*, ed. Eugene F. Miller (Indianapolis: Liberty Classics, 1987), 73–74.

58. David Hume, *The History of Great Britain: The Reigns of James I and Charles I* (Hammondsworth: Penguin Books, 1970), 673–74, 683.

59. David Wootton, "David Hume, 'The Historian,' " in *CC Hume*, 301–3.

60. Knud Haakonssen, "The Structure of Hume's Political Theory," in *CC Hume* 182–85; Hume, *Essays*, 78–79.

61. Haakonssen, "Hume's Political Theory," 183.

62. Mossner, *Life of David Hume*, 306.

63. Ibid.

64. Gaskin, *Hume's Philosophy of Religion*, 146; Hume quoted from *New Letters*, 12.

65. David Hume, *Dialogues and Natural History of Religion*, ed. J.C.A. Gaskin (Oxford: Oxford University Press), 139–40.

66. Hume, *Dialogues and Natural History*, 128, 143 (emphasis added).

67. Harrison, "Religion and the Religious," 158–59.

68. Hume, *Essays*, 76–78.

69. On the dispositions, see *CC Hume*, 15, 142; Hume, *Treatise*, 367–70. A thorough consideration of the implicit social dimensions of Hume's theory of religion would need to take into account not only his understanding of habit and custom, but also the various dispositions (e.g., to form bonded family groups, communicate feelings [sympathy], and form general rules) that gave rise to such social institutions as morality and government.

CHAPTER TWO
MAKING EXPERIENCE

1. Bourdieu, *Outline*, 87–89; Bourdieu and Loïc J. D. Wacquant, *An Invitation to Reflexive Sociology* (Chicago: University of Chicago Press, 1992), 126–27. This paragraph is shaped by my reading of Bourdieu, but the distinction between experience-in-practice and theories of experience, the connection between experience and practice, and the underlying concept of habit or habitus would have been readily understood by Edwards, Wesley, or, for that matter, Aquinas.

2. I am taking a little liberty in using the phrase "religious experience" here, since neither Edwards nor Wesley, as far as I know, used precisely that phrase. I do so because "religious experience" as such appeared in the titles of Methodist and Reformed narratives before the end of the eighteenth century, as an outgrowth of the language introduced by Edwards and Wesley.

3. Richard Sibbes, *The Complete Works of Richard Sibbes*, ed. Alexander B. Grosart (Edinburgh: J. Nichol, 1862–64), 4:412, quoted in Nuttall, *The Holy Spirit*, 39.

4. On the transatlantic awakening, see: Mark A. Noll, et al., *Evangelicalism: Comparative Studies of Popular Protestantism in North America, the British Isles, and Beyond, 1700–1990* (New York: Oxford University Press, 1994); Michael J. Crawford, *Seasons of Grace: Colonial New England's Revival Tradition in Its British Context* (New York: Oxford University Press, 1991); W. R. Ward, *The Protestant Evangelical Awakening* (Cambridge: Cambridge University Press, 1992). For my purposes, the most helpful have been John Walsh, " 'Methodism' and the Origins of English-Speaking Evangelicalism," in Noll, *Evangelicalism*, 19–37, and John Walsh, "Religious Societies: Methodist and Evangelical, 1738–1800," in W. J. Sheils and Diana Wood, *Voluntary Religion* (London: Basil Blackwell, 1986), 279–302. On Wesley and Edwards on religious experience, see: Robert Doyle Smith, "John Wesley and Jonathan Edwards on Religious Experience: A Comparative Analysis," *Wesleyan Theological Journal* 25 (spring 1990):130–46; Richard B. Steele, *'Gracious Affection' and 'True Virtue' according to Jonathan Edwards and John Wesley* (Metuchen, NJ: Scarecrow Press, 1994); Gregory S. Clapper, *John Wesley on Religious Affections* (Metuchen, NJ: Scarecrow Press, 1989), 138–49; and Richard E. Brantley, "The Common Ground of Wesley and Edwards," *Harvard Theological Review* 83:3 (1990):271–303. All these authors agree that there is a great deal of evidence to suggest that Edwards had a pronounced influence on Wesley. The most obvious and compelling is the fact that Wesley published abridged editions of all five of Edwards's revival treatises for the benefit of the Methodist wing of the evangelical movement (Steele, *'Gracious Affection,'* 157–58, 236–37). Apart from noting their predictable doctrinal differences with respect to predestination, free will, and sanctification, there has been little discussion of how, given their commonalities, they differed regarding the idea of religious experience. While Smith compares the conversion experiences of Edwards and Wesley, neither he nor the others attempt to account for the differences with regard to experience that emerged in the Wesleyan and Reformed traditions.

5. In doing so, he was referring back to a longstanding practice in some New England churches in which people gave an account of the saving action of God in their lives prior to being accepted as full members of the congregation. For traditional accounts, see McGiffert, *God's Plot*, 42–48, 149–225.

6. On the situation at Yale, see Norman Pettit, ed., *The Life of David Brainerd*, vol. 7 of *The Works of Jonathan Edwards* [hereafter JE 7] (New Haven: Yale University Press, 1985), 37–42.

7. In adopting the language of experience and experimental religion, Edwards appealed not only to his Puritan heritage, but to "experimental philosophy," that is, to the empiricism of Locke. This appeal, however, was made on analogical not epistemological grounds. That Edwards (and Wesley) appealed to Locke by analogy is not inconsequential, however, insofar as it made their approach to true religion sound empirical, while at the same time breaking with empiricism in radical ways (see note 11 below).

8. Albert C. Outler, ed., *Sermons I*, vol. 1 in *The Works of John Wesley* [hereafter *JW* 1] (Nashville: Abingdon, 1984), 274, 271.

9. Franz Hildebrandt and Oliver A. Beckerlegge, eds., *A Collection of Hymns for the Use of the People Called Methodist*, vol. 7 in *The Works of John Wesley* [hereafter *JW* 7] (Nashville: Abingdon, 1989), 74.

10. W. Reginald Ward and Richard P. Heitzenrater, eds., *Journals and Diaries, I (1735–1738)*, vol. 18 of *The Works of John Wesley* [hereafter *JW* 18] (Nashville: Abingdon, 1984), 145–46.

11. John Wesley to Rev. Samuel Wesley, Junior, Oct. 30, 1738 in Frank Baker, ed., *Letters I (1721–1739)*, vol. 25 in *The Works of John Wesley* [hereafter *JW* 25] (Oxford: Clarendon Press, 1980), 575.

12. Rupert E. Davies, ed., *The Methodist Societies: History, Nature and Design*, vol. 9 in *The Works of John Wesley* [hereafter *JW* 9] (Nashville: Abingdon, 1989), 35. As his theology developed, Wesley made a sharper distinction between justification (conversion) and sanctification (perfection). This distinction was central to later Methodist experience and is taken up in more detail in the next chapter.

13. Disagreement in the literature regarding Wesley's dependence on Locke parallels the disagreements surrounding Edwards. Outler argues that Wesley's epistemology was derived from "the intuitionist views of Christian Platonism." He argues, as I did in the last chapter with respect to Edwards, that this intuitionist theory of knowledge allowed Wesley "to follow . . . John Locke in his theories of empirical knowledge . . . and yet also to distinguish all such knowledge from our spiritual knowledge of God." Outler provides an extended discussion of Wesley's theory of knowledge and his debt to the Cambridge Platonists in a footnote to "The Witness of the Spirit, I" (see *JW* 1:276–77, note 46). In earlier comments on the "Witness of the Spirit" sermons, Outler notes that "by 'experience,' Wesley normally means *religious* intuition—not perceptions or feelings in general" (Albert C. Outler, *John Wesley* [New York: Oxford University Press, 1964], 209–10). See also, Gunter, *Limits of Divine Love*, 126–29.

Richard E. Brantley (*Locke, Wesley, and the Method of English Romanticism* [Gainesville: University of Florida Press, 1984]) wants to make a stronger case for Locke's influence on Wesley, rooting Wesley's emphasis on experience as much in Locke as in Pietism (and completely ignoring Puritanism). He does not go so far as to claim that Wesley's theory of religious knowledge was actually Lockean, but he does want to make the case that Wesley derived his methodology (specifically his emphasis on analogy) from Locke and that his language throughout was informed by a Lockean idiom (23, 29). He makes the important point that Wesley read Locke through Bishop Browne, who used Locke's analogical method to make a case for a spiritual sense *analogous to the natural senses* as understood by Locke and thus reclaimed a place for revelation and the witness of the Spirit (29–37). In his eagerness to have Enlightenment scholars pay attention to Wesley (18), Brantley, in my view, glosses over the radical distinction between the natural and spiritual senses and the role of conversion in acquiring the spiritual sense. As a result he is unable to comprehend why anyone would have charged Wesley with enthusiasm, dismissing the very idea with the comment that "he could hardly have been both an enthusiast and a follower of John

Locke" (16). Similar problems plague Brantley's more recent article, "The Common Ground of Wesley and Edwards," where again he tries to derive both Wesley's and Edwards's understanding of the (new) spiritual sense from their engagement with Locke without giving sufficient attention to where and why they break with him. In general, Brantley does not take seriously enough Norman Fiering's observation that Locke, "had he been alive, would undoubtedly have dismissed Edwards's [and, I would add, Wesley's] idea of a special sensation of divine things as 'enthusiastick' nonsense" (*Jonathan Edwards*, 125).

14. Clapper's analysis suggests the unsystematic nature of Wesley's thinking about the distinction between natural and religious affections and his tendency to read phenomena as supernatural, based on biblical precedent, that Edwards would have unequivocally categorized as natural (*John Wesley on Religious Affections*, 66–74).

15. John Wesley to Mrs. Elizabeth Hutton, August 22, 1744, *JW* 26: 113.

16. See Henry K. Knight, *The Presence of God in the Christian Life: John Wesley and the Means of Grace* (Metuchen, NJ: Scarecrow Press, 1992), 16–49. His second chapter, "The Means to the Christian Life," is divided into three sections: "The Religion of the Heart," "Against Formalism," and "Against Enthusiasm."

17. On the specific connection between the Witness of the Spirit sermons and the charges of enthusiasm leveled at Wesley, see Outler, *John Wesley*, 29, 209–10, and Gunter, *Limits of Divine Love*, 126–32. On charges of enthusiasm more generally, see Gunter, *Limits of Divine Love*, 118–37. On the "witness of the Spirit" in the various traditions, see *JW* 1:286, note 4. On the idea of the "witness of the Spirit" in Puritanism, and especially among the Quakers, see Nuttall, *The Holy Spirit*, 48–61. Wesley was influenced most directly in this regard by the radical wing of Pietism, specifically the Moravians, but perceptions of Wesley were heavily influenced by the Puritan, especially Quaker, associations his critics brought to their understanding of him.

18. Samuel Wesley was caught in this bind and protested to John: "release me from the horns of your dilemma, that I must either talk without knowledge, like a fool, or against it, like a knave[.] I conceive neither part strikes. For a man may reasonably argue against what he never felt, and may honestly deny what he has felt to be necessary to other" (*JW* 25:579; Gunter, *Limits of Divine Love*, 145).

19. Gerald R. Cragg, ed., *The Appeals to Men of Reason and Religion*, vol. 11 in *the Works of John Wesley* [hereafter *JW* 11] (Oxford: Clarendon Press, 1975), 63–64).

20. John Wesley, *An Extract of the Life of the Late Rev. David Brainerd, Missionary to the Indians*, 4th ed. (Dublin: Napper, 1812), 263–75. The net effect of Wesley's editing is (amusingly enough) to turn David Brainerd into a quintessential Methodist. Wesley's edited version begins with Edwards's first three paragraphs, minimally edited. These paragraphs, addressed to those who had fallen away after their conversion, emphasize that Brainerd's "pains and earnestness in religion were rather increased than diminished, after he had received satisfaction concerning the safety of his state." Wesley then replaces six deleted paragraphs addressed to the "high pretenders" with a new paragraph that states: "It appears plainly, from his [Brainerd's] conversion to his death, that the great object of the new sense of his mind, the new appetites given to him in his conversion, and thenceforward maintained and increased in his heart, was HOLINESS, conformity to God, living to God, and glorifying him. This was what drew his heart; this was the centre of his soul" (265). While Edwards did mention Brainerd's "longings after holiness" twice (501) and did refer to universal holiness at the end of his third paragraph, holiness would not strike most readers as the central theme of Edwards's original reflections. After Wesley edited the final sentence of Edwards's third paragraph so that the reference to universal holiness had more prominence and served as an effective lead-in to Wesley's new paragraph, Wesley's version flowed

seamlessly, leaving the reader with a new Brainerd for whom "holiness" was the point. Moreover, by leaving in the material defending Brainerd against charges of enthusiasm, while deleting Edwards's criticisms of "high pretenders," Wesley broadened Edwards's depiction of authentic religious experience and obscured precisely those points where he and Edwards parted company.

21. John Wesley to Rev. Samuel Wesley, Junior, Nov. 30, 1738.

22. W. Reginald Ward and Richard P. Heitzenrater, *Journals and Diaries, IV (1755–65)* in *The Works of John Wesley*, vol. 21 [hereafter *JW* 21] (Nashville: Abingdon Press, 1992), 223, quoted by Ward and Heitzenrater in the introduction to *JW* 18:48–49.

23. Gunter, *Limits of Divine Love*, 149–52; Rack, *Reasonable Enthusiast*, 194–97.

24. In a letter to the Countess of Huntington (March 10, 1759), he apparently had these phenomena in mind when he wrote: "Yet *we* thirst after something farther. We want to sink deeper and rise higher in the knowledge of God our Saviour. We want all helps for walking closely with him whom we have received, that we may the more speedily come to the measure of the stature of Christ" (quoted in note 45, *JW* 21:223–24).

25. *JW* 21:234, partially quoted by Ward and Heitzenrater (*JW* 18:48–49).

26. Watkins, *Puritan Experience*, 18, 25.

27. *A Letter from the Reverend Dr. Colman of Boston, to the Reverend Mr. Williams of Lebanon* (Boston, 1744), 4; Jonathan Parsons to Thomas Prince, April 14, 1744, *Christian History* 2:154, quoted in Goen, *Revivalism and Separatism*, 29–31.

28. *Diary of Joshua Hempstead*, 402–3, quoted in Goen, *Revivalism and Separatism*, 30.

29. Although the experiences to which Jonathan Edwards referred were described in Sarah Edwards's narrative, the qualifying comments quoted here were her husband's (Serano E. Dwight, *The Life of President Edwards* [New York: Carvill, 1830], 171–90.

30. Ibid., 176, 180, 186.

31. Robe, *Narratives*, 200–201.

32. Ibid., 200–203.

33. Leigh Schmidt, *Holy Fairs: Scottish Communions and American Revivals in the Early Modern Period* (Princeton: Princeton University Press, 1989), 117–18.

34. Ibid., 146; for Schmidt's discussion of this gap, see pp. 145–53. Schmidt also notes that the ministers sometimes let visionary experiences stand if they were presented with proper qualifications. Thus, if something was seen "with the eyes of [the] mind" or "by the eye of faith" as opposed to the "bodily eyes," it might be allowed to stand (148).

35. Umphry Lee argues that Wesley controlled enthusiasm practically, as, in effect, does Knight, *Presence of God*, 92–127.

36. On the distinction between church, sect, and society, see *JW* 9: 2–4.

37. Philipp Jakob Spener, *Pia Desideria* (1675) in Peter C. Erb, *Pietists: Selected Writings* (New York: Paulist Press, 1983), 32–33.

38. *JW* 9: 7–8; Ward, *Protestant Evangelical Awakening*, 118–44.

39. Walsh, "Religious Societies," 280.

40. Walsh, "Religious Societies," 284–85.

41. While phrases such as "sweet and lively," "ravishing," and "swallowed up" recur frequently throughout Sarah Edwards's original narrative, her husband suppresses her frequent references to God's presence, e.g., "a sense of his immediate presence" (Dwight, *Life of President Edwards*, 176), "God was present with me" (177). Nor does he mention her carefully qualified statements of visionary experiences, e.g., "I beheld them [the children of God] by faith in their risen and glorified state, with spiritual bodies re-fashioned after the image of Christ's glorified body, and arrayed in the beauty of heaven. . . . They appeared to my mind in all their reality and certainty, and as it were in actual and distinct vision; so

plain and evident were they to the eye of my faith" (178). Jonathan Edwards's account, in short, is a summary of his wife's narrative. It is broadly faithful to her account, while at the same time disguising her identity, casting her vivid account in more abstract theological language, and suppressing any potentially problematic details, such as visions or impressions on the imagination.

42. The images of being "ravished," "swallowed up," "sweetness," and "refreshment" were not new ones. Cf. the autobiography of Thomas Shepard (McGiffert, *God's Plot*, 84, 103, 108, 118), the author whom Edwards quoted more than any other (*JE* 2:53–57).

43. Brainerd, for example, indicated that he was using Solomon Stoddard's *A Guide to Christ* (Boston, 1742) in his devotions at the time of his conversion. This work, subtitled "The Way of Directing Souls that are under the Work of Conversion," provided a scripturally grounded framework for understanding the process of conversion. On devotional literature and the awakening, see Charles Hambrick-Stowe, "The Spirit of the Old Writers: Print Media, the Great Awakening, and Continuity in New England," in *Communications and Change in American Religious History*, ed. Leonard I. Sweet (Grand Rapids: Eerdmans, 1993), 126–40.

44. Charles E. Hambrick-Stowe, *The Practice of Piety: Puritan Devotional Disciplines in Seventeenth-Century New England* (Chapel Hill: University of North Carolina Press, 1982), 163.

45. "The Spiritual Travels of Nathan Cole," unpublished manuscript, Connecticut Historical Society, extract reprinted in Richard L. Bushman, ed., *The Great Awakening: Documents on the Revival of Religion, 1740–1745* (Chapel Hill: University of North Carolina Press, 1969), 68–70.

46. Ibid., 70.

47. Cole, quoted in Goen, *Revivalism and Separatism*, 138.

48. Letter of Charles Brockwell to the Secretary of the S.P.G., dated Feb. 18, 1741/2, in Goen, *Revivalism and Separatism*, 181.

49. Harry S. Stout, *Divine Dramatist* (Grand Rapids: Eerdmans, 1991), 39–40. Stout gives no citation for the quote other than the Anglican *Weekly Miscellany*.

50. Stout, *Divine Dramatist*, 93.

51. Quoted in Goen, *Revivalism and Separatism*, 179, and Albert J. Raboteau and David W. Wills, "Liturgical Style of the Radical Awakening," *Afro-American Religion: A Documentary History* [Working Draft (Dec. 1994)], vol. 2, ch. 5, doc. 24. I would like to thank Al Raboteau and David Wills for permission to use and cite this unpublished work-in-progress.

52. Diary of Joshua Hempstead, quoted in Raboteau and Wills, "Liturgical Style."

53. Goen, *Revivalism and Separatism*, 208–10. For a full discussion of the intricacies of church membership in relation to baptism and communion, see David Hall's introduction to Jonathan Edwards, *Ecclesiastical Writings*, ed. David D. Hall (New Haven and London: Yale University Press, 1994), 1–89; on the Separate Congregationalists in particular, see 47–50, 80–84.

54. Goen, *Revivalism and Separatism*, 182, 206–7.

55. John Broadus quoted in ibid., 180.

56. Gunter, *Limits of Divine Love*, 149–50. For another revisionist discussion of John Wesley's attitude toward "convulsions," see Rack, *Reasonable Enthusiast*, 194–97. Rack notes that while some of the earliest Wesley biographers allowed for the supernatural, "later biographers have found early Methodist supernaturalism embarrassing, and not least when Wesley believed in it" (195).

57. Gunter, *Limits of Divine Love*, 151. Despite Gunter's efforts to take these phenomena seriously, he still refers to them most frequently as "hysteria" or "hysterical" (138, 150–52) and occasionally as "ecstasies" (149, 151).

58. Wesley, *Journal* 4:471 (an older edition), quoted in Walsh, "Religious Societies," 288–89.

59. Ibid., 289.

60. J. Scott, *The Life of the Rev. T. Scott*, 6th ed. (London, 1824), 503–4, quoted in Walsh, "Religious Societies," 299.

CHAPTER THREE
SHOUTING METHODISTS

1. *The Chorus*, compiled by A. S. Jenks and D. S. Gilkey (Philadelphia, 1860), #241, quoted in Winthrop S. Hudson, "Shouting Methodists," *Encounter* 29 (1968):73.

2. The manuscript version of *Methodist Error* is at the Huntington Library, San Marino, California. A number of letters and reviews of the work bound in the volume establish the author as John Fanning Watson. Watson was for a time a bookseller (in Philadelphia from 1806 to 1814), a bank cashier (in Germantown from 1814 to 1848), a writer, and a local historian. He is best known as the author of the *Annals of Philadelphia and Pennsylvania, in the olden time; being a collection of memoirs, anecdotes, and incidents of the city and its inhabitants* (Philadelphia, 1830). Although he described himself as a "Wesleyan layman," Deborah Waters states that "while a bookseller, Watson pleased his mother by embracing religion, initially following his mother's Methodism, but remaining within the Episcopal Church" ("Philadephia's Boswell: John Fanning Watson," *The Pennsylvania Magazine of History and Biography* 98 [1974]:7–9).

3. [James Fanning Watson], *Methodist Error* (1814), 10; [Watson], *Methodist Error* (Trenton: D. & E. Fenton, 1819), 15. Hereafter *Methodist Error* will be cited in the text as either *ME*-1814 or *ME*-1819.

4. The Methodist ministers of Philadelphia, according to Watson, concurred with him "so far as *his main object* is concerned," but claimed that they could "manage *their objections* to these things, *with more discretion and moderation*" than Watson could (*ME*-1819, 193–94).

5. George Roberts, *The substance of a sermon (but now more enlarged) preached to, and at the request of the Conference of the Methodist Episcopal Church, held in Baltimore, March, 1807* (Baltimore: Henry Foxall, 1807), 29–30 (emphasis added).

6. The earliest Christians read the Septuagint (the Greek translation of Hebrew scriptures) as "prefiguring" Christian developments. In the New Testament itself, Paul depicted Adam as the "figure" or "type" of Christ and thus Christ as the "antitype" of Adam. Although the Protestant reformers rejected much of the more elaborate allegorical exegesis of the early and medieval church, even the most conservative Protestant exegetes recognized the legitimacy of the typologies instituted in the New Testament. The Puritan use of typology has been extensively discussed, but scholars have paid relatively little attention to the use of typology by nineteenth-century religious groups other than Mormons. On typology, see: Sacvan Bercovitch, ed., *Typology and Early American Literature* (Amherst: University of Massachusetts Press, 1972), 3–46; George P. Landow, *Victorian Shadows, Victorian Types: Biblical Typology in Victorian Literature, Art, and Thought* (Boston: Routledge & Kegan Paul, 1980), 1–64; Conrad Cherry, *Nature and Religious Imagination from Edwards to Bushnell* (Philadelphia: Fortress Press, 1980), 14–25. On typology in the early national period, see Mark A. Noll, "The Image of the United States as a Biblical Nation, 1776–1865," in Nathan

O. Hatch and Mark A. Noll, eds., *The Bible in America* (New York: Oxford University Press, 1982), 39–58. On the Mormon use of typology, see Philip L. Barlow, *Mormons and the Bible* (New York: Oxford University Press, 1991), 35–38, 66–69, 75–77, 83–84.

7. Most scholars acknowledge these touchstones in the history of the shout tradition, but it has been of particular interest to scholars of African American religion. The ring shout has received considerable attention from scholars concerned with slave religion and the survival of African traditions in the American context. In this regard, see, Albert J. Raboteau, *Slave Religion: The "Invisible Institution" in the Antebellum South* (New York: Oxford University Press, 1978); Melville Herskovits, *The Myth of the Negro Past* (Boston: Beacon, 1958); Sterling Stuckey, *Slave Culture: Nationalist Theory and the Foundations of Black America* (New York: Oxford, 1987), 3–97; and Robert Simpson, "The Shout and Shouting in Slave Religion in the United States," *The Southern Quarterly* 23/3 (1985):34–47. The origin of the music associated with the shout tradition has been the subject of extensive debate among musicologists over the years. For a review of the scholarship through 1959, see, D. K. Wilgus, *Anglo-American Folksong Scholarship Since 1898* (New Brunswick, NJ: Rutgers University Press, 1959), 345–64.

8. Mechel Sobel, *Trabelin' On: The Slave Journey to an Afro-Baptist Faith* (Westport, CT: Greenwood Press, 1979), and Walter F. Pitts, Jr., *Old Ship of Zion: The Afro-Baptist Ritual in the African Diaspora* (New York: Oxford University Press, 1993). Hudson emphasized the Euro-American and Methodist side of the tradition in "Shouting Methodists," 73–84. See, Ann Taves, "Knowing Through the Body: Dissociative Religious Experience in the African-American and British-American Methodist Traditions," *Journal of Religion* 73/2 (April 1993):200–22, for my initial attempt to present the Methodist side of the shout tradition in a way that did justice to both its European and African roots.

9. A number of dissertations and books have appeared since this was largely completed, including: Lester Ruth, " 'A Little Heaven Below': Quarterly Meetings as Seasons of Grace in Early American Methodism" (Ph.D. dissertation, University of Notre Dame, 1996); William C. Johnson, " 'To Dance in the Ring of All Creation': Camp Meeting Revivalism and the Color Line, 1799–1825" (Ph.D. dissertation, University of California at Riverside, 1997); Christine L. Heyrman, *Southern Cross: The Beginnings of the Bible Belt* (New York: Alfred A. Knopf, 1997); John H. Wigger, *Taking Heaven by Storm: Methodism and the Popularization of American Christianity* (New York: Oxford University Press, 1998). Deborah Vansau McCauley's *Appalachian Mountain Religion* (1995) is the most important study that has come to my attention since this was written. Working backwards from contemporary sources, McCauley attempts to construct a historical framework for the distinctive religiosity of the Appalachian region. She locates its roots in "pietism, Scots-Irish sacramental revivalism, Baptist revival culture during the Great Awakening in the mid-South, and plain-folk camp-meeting religion" (36). The analysis presented here is derived independently from (mostly) early Methodist sources. The emphasis on Methodist sources from the revivals in the mid-South in the 1770s and 1780s and in the mid-Atlantic in the 1790s and beyond illuminates Methodist and African American contributions to a tradition of camp-meeting religion that was not limited to either the frontier or the southern "high country." McCauley's work, taken together with the analysis presented here, begins to suggest the broader contours of an experiential tradition, which (with some distinctive variations) has been claimed as the distinctive center of both the religion of mountain whites and enslaved blacks.

10. I have found only a few disparate references to shouting or a shout prior to the Virginia revivals—one in the context of a sacrament Sunday at Edinburgh College (*Diary of Samuel Sewell*, 2 vols. [New York: Farrar Straus & Giroux, 1973], 1:352, quoted in Ward, *Protestant Evangelical Awakening*, 17) and another in an account of black conversions

on the Bryan Plantation in South Carolina in 1741 written by Salzburger immigrants. The latter refers to "those who love Christ . . . shouting and jubilating" (the relevant passage from the *Detailed Reports* of the Salzberger immigrants is quoted in Albert J. Raboteau and David W. Wills, "Slave Conversions on the Bryan Plantations [Nov-Dec 1741]," *Afro-American Religion* [Working Draft (Dec. 1994)] vol. 2, chap. 5, doc. 27).

11. Russell Richey, *Early American Methodism* (Bloomington: Indiana University Press, 1991), 50.

12. *Minutes of the Annual Conferences of the Methodist Episcopal Church for the Years 1773–1828*, vol. 1 (New York: Mason and Lane, 1840). In 1790 the circuits ringing the Chesapeake included Severn and Calvert on the western shore of Maryland; Cecil, Kent, Talbot, and Dorchester on the Delmarva Peninsula; and Portsmouth in Virginia. From the time racially differentiated statistics began to be kept in 1786 until 1790, more than half the members of the Calvert circuit were black (ibid.).

13. According to Leland, the ratio of blacks to whites in Virginia in 1788 was approximately six to seven (John Leland, "The Virginia Chronicle" [1790] in *The Writings of John Leland* [New York: G. W. Wood, 1845], 93).

14. I am adopting here what Mary Louise Pratt refers to as a "contact perspective." Such a perspective, in her words, "emphasizes how subjects are constituted in and by their relations to each other. It treats the relations among colonizers and colonized, . . . not in terms of separateness or apartheid, but in terms of copresence, interaction, interlocking understandings and practices, often within radically asymmetrical relations of power" (*Imperial Eyes: Travel Writing and Transculturation* [London and New York: Routledge, 1992], 7).

15. There is a large general literature on the revivals in Virginia, including Rhys Isaac, *The Transformation of Virginia, 1740–1790* (Chapel Hill: University of North Carolina Press, 1982); Wesley M. Geweher, *The Great Awakening in Virginia, 1740–1790* (Durham: Duke University Press, 1930); Mechal Sobel, *The World They Made Together: Black and White Values in Eighteenth-Century Virginia* (Princeton: Princeton University Press, 1987).

16. On the condensation of meaning, see John W. Work, *American Negro Songs* (New York: Howell, Soskin & Co., 1940), 9–10.

17. Eileen Southern, *The Music of Black Americans: A History*, 2nd ed. (New York: Norton, 1983), 15–20; John Storm Roberts, *Black Music of Two Worlds* (Trivoli, NY: Original Music, 1972), 168–74; LeRoi Jones, *Blues People: Negro Music in White America* (New York: William Morrow, 1963), 41–47; Brett Sutton, *Primitive Baptist Hymns of the Blue Ridge* (Chapel Hill: University of North Carolina Press, 1982), compares contemporary black and white congregational singing of the hymn tradition.

18. Southern, *Music of Black Americans*, 18–20.

19. LeRoi Jones, *Blues People*, 45–46. There is a large literature on the chanted sermon in both black and white contexts. See, for example, Gerald L. Davis, *I Got the Word in Me and I Can Sing It, You Know: A Study of the Performed African-American Sermon* (Philadelphia: University of Pennsylvania Press, 1985); William H. Pipes, *Say Amen Brother!* (New York: The William-Frederick Press, 1951); Bruce A. Rosenberg, *Can These Bones Live? The Art of the American Folk Preacher*, rev. ed. (Urbana and Chicago: The University of Illinois Press, 1988); on chanted sermons among white Baptists, see especially, Jeff Titon, *Powerhouse for God: Sacred Speech, Chant, and Song in an Appalachian Baptist Church* [recording] (Chapel Hill: University of North Carolina Press, 1982).

20. Olly Wilson, "The Association of Movement and Music as a Black Conceptual Approach to Music-Making," in *More Than Dancing: Essays on Afro-American Music and Musicians*, ed. Irene V. Jackson (Westport, CT: Greenwood Press, 1985), 10–11.

21. Southern, *Music of Black Americans*, 20–21.

22. See, for example, Raboteau, *Slave Religion*, 66–73; Stuckey, *Slave Culture*, 53–64, 83–98.

23. John Miller Chernoff, *African Rhythm and African Sensibility: Aesthetics and Social Action in African Musical Idioms* (Chicago and London: University of Chicago Press, 1979).

24. Raboteau and Wills, "Slave Conversions," in *Afro-American Religion*, vol. 2., chap. 5, doc. 17–24; Goen, *Revivalism and Separatism*, 90–91.

25. William Fristoe, *History of the Ketocton Baptist Association* (Staunton, VA: William Lyford, 1808), 21–22, quoted in Geweher, *Great Awakening in Virginia*, 109; John Leland, "Virginia Chronicle," 105.

26. The most notable exception to this is a journal kept by Separate Baptist John Williams during 1771; see John S. Moore, "John Williams' Journal: Edited with Comments," *Virginia Baptist Register* 17 (1978):795–813. Letters to Rippon's *Baptist Register*, which began publication in 1790, are also a source of first-hand materials, but since the Separates had largely lost their distinctive character by that time and blended in among the Regulars, these letters do not provide much first-hand documentation of the Separates.

27. For the South and especially Virginia, the most important sources are Morgan Edwards, *Materials Towards a History of the Baptists*, 2 vols., 1770–1792 (Danielsville, GA: Heritage Papers, 1984); Isaac Backus's diary entries relating to his travels through Virginia in 1789; Leland, "Virginia Chronicle" (1790); Fristoe, *Ketocton Baptist Association* (1808); Robert Semple, *History of the Rise and Progress of the Baptists in Virginia* (Richmond: By the Author, 1810); David Benedict, *A General History of the Baptist Denomination*, 2 vols. (Boston: Lincoln & Edmands, 1813).

28. M. Edwards, *History of the Baptists*, 2:90.

29. Leland, "Virginia Chronicle," 105.

30. Semple, *Baptists in Virginia*, 2.

31. Benedict, *Baptist Denomination*, 2:107.

32. On contemporary Primitive Baptists, see Sutton, *Primitive Baptist Hymns*, album notes, 16. Prior to the Civil War, according to Simpson ("Shout and Shouting"), such gatherings consisted of a "praise meeting" that included preaching, followed by "a 'shout.' " A "transition ritual of solemn handshaking" marked the transition between the two parts of the meeting (37).

33. Moore, "John Williams' Journal," 803–4.

34. On experience meetings in the context of slavery, see, for example, "The Religious Life of the Negro Slave," *Harper's New Monthly Magazine* 27 (1863):680–82.

35. Goen, *Revivalism and Separatism*, 296–7.

36. M. Edwards, *History of the Baptists*, 2:93.

37. William E. Montgomery, *Under Their Own Vine and Fig Tree: The African American Church in the South, 1865–1900* (Baton Rouge: Louisiana State University Press, 1992), 284, 310. See also, William E. Hatcher, *John Jasper: The Unmatched Negro Philosopher and Preacher* (New York, 1908; reprint New York: Negro University Press, 1969).

38. Leland, "Virginia Chronicle," 115.

39. Rack, *Reasonable Enthusiast*, 433.

40. In the British context, the preachers met in conference as "consultants" to Wesley during his lifetime; in the American context, beginning in the colonial period and more completely with the establishment of an independent church, authority was more firmly vested in the itinerants meeting in conference.

41. On quarterly conferences, see Ruth, " 'A Little Heaven' "; Richey, *Early American Methodism*, 21–32.

42. Rack, *Reasonable Enthusiast*, 336–38; Gunter, *Limits of Divine Love*, 222–26.

43. Rack, *Reasonable Enthusiast*, 340.

44. On sanctification, see Rack, *Reasonable Enthusiast*, 334–42, 397–401, 427–29.

45. "Account of Mr. Thomas Rankin," *Arminian Magazine* [London] 2 (1779):187–88, 193.

46. "Account of Rankin," 194–95.

47. Francis Asbury, *Journal and Letters*, 3 vols., ed. Elmer E. Clark, J. Manning Potts, and Jacob S. Payton [Nashville: Abingdon, 1958], 1:211–12]; Jesse Lee, *A Short History of the Methodists in the United States of America* (Baltimore: Magill & Clime, 1810), 50–53; Letter from McKendree to Bishop Asbury, 1803, quoted in Robert Paine, *Life and Times of William McKendree: Bishop of the Methodist Episcopal Church* (Nashville: Publishing House MEC, South, 1922), 34–35; John L.Peters, *Christian Perfection and American Methodism* (New York: Abingdon Press, 1956), 80–97.

48. Moore, "John Williams' Journal," 803–4 (emphasis added).

49. Leland, "Virginia Chronicle," 114–15 (emphasis added).

50. Asbury, *Journal and Letters*, 1:208, 210, 212.

51. Thomas Rankin to John Wesley, in ibid., 1:221.

52. R[ichard] Garrettson, "An Account of the Revival of the Work of God at Petersburg, in Virginia," *Arminian Magazine* [London] 13 (1790):302–4. There are at least three other accounts of this revival. See, "An Extract of a Letter from Philip Cox . . . to Bishop Coke, . . . Suffex-County, Virginia, July 1787," *Arminian Magazine* [Philadelphia] 2 (Feb. 1790):91–95; "Letter from [William] McKendree to Bishop Asbury [1803]," quoted in Paine, *Life and Times of William McKendree*, 34–35; and Minton Thrift, *Memoir of the Rev. Jesse Lee with extracts from his journals* (New York: Bangs & Mason, 1823; reprint ed., Arno Press, 1969), 94–98.

53. "An extract of a letter from Philip Bruce, elder of the Methodist Episcopal church, to Bishop Coke, dated Portsmouth, Virginia, March 25, 1788," *Arminian Magazine* [Philadelphia] 2 (Nov. 1790):563–64.

54. James Meacham, "A journal and travels of James Meacham, Part I, May 19–August 31, 1789," *Trinity College Historical Papers* 9 (1912):94, quoted in Dena J. Epstein, *Sinful Tunes and Spirituals: Black Folk Music to the Civil War* (Urbana: University of Illinois Press, 1977), 110.

55. Asbury, *Journal and Letters*, 1:210.

56. Ibid., 1:213.

57. Thomas Rankin to John Wesley, in Asbury, *Journal and Letters*, 1:221.

58. Jesse Lee, *History of the Methodists*, 51–52 (emphasis added); Rankin glosses over this visit in his journal (Asbury, *Journal and Letters*, 1:222).

59. Jesse Lee, *History of the Methodists*, 52.

60. R. Garrettson, "Revival of the Work of God at Petersburg," 303–4.

61. Ibid., 306.

62. "An extract of a letter from Philip Bruce," 563–64.

63. R. Garrettson, "Revival of the Work of God at Petersburg," 301–2, 303 (emphasis added).

64. Doris Andrews argues that the increasing differences in class among the Methodist membership that emerged during the 1790s meant that "many of the problems of authority in the movement had less to do with on-going conflict between 'preachers' and 'people' than among the people themselves" (Doris Andrews, "Popular Religion and the Revolution in the Middle Atlantic Ports: The Rise of the Methodists, 1770–1800" [Ph.D. dissertation, University of Pennsylvania, 1986], 301).

65. [William Colbert], "A Journal of the Travels of William Colbert, Methodist Preacher thro' parts of Maryland, Pennsylvania, New York, Delaware and Virginia in 1790 to 1838," 8 vols. (Garrett-Evangelical Theological Seminary, typescript version, 1:1–19). Segregated classes appear to have been established early on the Delmarva Peninsula as well. Ezekiel Cooper indicates that there were racially segregated classes as early as 1784 on both the Kent and Caroline circuits (George A. Phoebus, *Beams of Light on Early Methodism in America* [New York: Phillips & Hunt, 1887], 22–27).

66. Colbert, "Journal," 1:6.

67. [Benjamin Abbott], *Experience and Gospel Labours of the Rev. Benjamin Abbott* (New York: Emory and Waugh, 1830; originally published 1802), 5–30.

68. Robert Southey, *Life of Wesley*, 2 vols. (London: Oxford, 1925), 2:263.

69. *The Life Experience and Gospel Labors of the Rt. Rev. Richard Allen* (Nashville: Abingdon Press, 1960), 19.

70. Southey, *Life of Wesley*, 2:261; Abbott, *Experience and Gospel Labours*: "many fell . . . like dead men," 50, 77, 84, 86, 90; "Slain . . . all over the house," 50, 51, 59, 73, 86, 87, 93; falling and rising, 50, 51, 59, 73, 86, 87, 93; "shout in the camp," 50, 62, 82, 88, 91, 92, 95.

71. Ibid., 121.

72. Ibid., 131–32.

73. Asbury, *Journal and Letters*, 1:556 (Christmas Day, 1787, Virginia); Asbury, *Journal and Letters*, 2:204, 256, 257, 258 (1799–1800 in Virginia and Tennessee); Freeborn Garrettson, *American Methodist Pioneer: The Life and Journals of the Rev. Freeborn Garrettson, 1752–1827*, ed. Robert D. Simpson (Rutland, VT: Academy Press), 265. See also, Nov. 1789, a quarterly meeting at Choptank (Delmarva): "Great part of the saints brought out in loud ecstacies so that the whole house rang" (ibid., 264).

74. Asbury, *Journal and Letters*, 1:675. His entry for May 30, 1791 reads in part: "Our conference rose; and after love feast, the preachers dispersed. . . . Mr. Hammett's preaching was not well received; it was supposed to be aimed at our zealous men and passionate meetings: at the new church his preaching was still more exceptionable to those judicious persons who heard him. I expect some things will be retailed to my disadvantage."

75. Letter from Rev. Thomas Morrell to Rev. Ezekiel Cooper, Charleston, Feb. 20, 1792, in Phoebus, *Beams of Light*, 143–44.

76. John F. Watson, *Annals of Philadelphia, being a collection of memoirs, anecdotes, and incidents of the city and its inhabitants from the days of the Pilgrim founders*, 2 vols. (Philadelphia: Pennington & Hunt, 1844), 2:456 [this entire account is also in the 1830 ed., 397–98]. Henry Willis was appointed to Philadelphia at the Annual Conferences of 1791–1793 and thus would have been in Philadelphia through the spring of 1794 (Minutes for 1791–93). During his last year, Freeborn Garrettson and then Thomas Morrell were also appointed and may have taken over most of the responsibilities (Minutes, 1793).

77. Watson, *Annals* (1844), 2:456 [also in 1830 ed., 397–98].

78. Benjamin Abbott was assigned to the Long Island circuit at the 1791 annual conference, the Salem circuit in New Jersey at the 1792 annual conference (leaving in September 1793), and to the Cecil and Kent circuits on Maryland's eastern shore for the 1793 and 1794 conference years (Abbott, *Experience and Gospel Labours*, 311–12; Minutes, 1791–94). He spent the winter of 1795–96 in Philadelphia with friends and died during the summer of 1796. Since there was no Mr. Chambers assigned to Baltimore during this period, Chambers may have been a local preacher. If Abbott preached at St. George's while he was still stationed in Salem, New Jersey, as the passage suggests, this incident probably

occurred between the fall of 1792 and September 1793, some months after the "walk-out" and a year or so before the black members actually left to form the Bethel Church.

79. Doris Andrews, "The African Methodists of Philadelphia, 1794–1802," in *Perspectives on American Methodism: Interpretive Essays*, ed. Russell E. Richey, Kenneth E. Rowe, and Jean Miller Schmidt (Nashville: Kingswood Books, 1993), 147–48.

80. From the diary of Ezekiel Cooper, excerpted in Phoebus, *Beams of Light*, 287–89. For a reconstruction of the controversy, see Doris Andrews, "Popular Religion," 299–317.

81. Andrews, "Popular Religion," 309–13.

82. According to Cooper, "There were about sixty withdrew from the church, and about four hundred joined us, so that we lost nothing in numbers" (Phoebus, *Beams of Light*, 290, 291). Statistics for Philadelphia for 1801 indicate an increase of about 300 white members and 100 black, which came close to doubling the total membership in the Society.

83. Membership in the M.E.C., Philadelphia, by race, 1797–1803:

	1796	1797	1798	1799	1800	1801	1802	Acad.	1803
White	363	380	307	411	407	707	721	102	773
Black	181	163	184	211	257	448	456		522

84. Richard Allen and Jupiter Gibson to Ezekiel Cooper, Philadelphia, February 22, 1798 [for delivery to Francis Asbury] (Ezekiel Cooper Collection, Garrett Evangelical Seminary, vol. 15, #1); a portion of the letter is quoted in Phoebus, *Beams of Light*, 252–53. I am grateful to Ian B. Straker for providing me with a copy and transcription of the original letter. On Freeborn Garrettson and African Methodism, see Ian B. Straker, "Black and White and Gray All Over," unpublished paper presented at the American Academy of Religion, Nov. 1995.

85. Colbert, "Journal," 3:37, 42 (Charles Cavender was one of the itinerants appointed to Philadelphia that year).

86. Andrews's summary of the increase in new members admitted on trial to the Philadelphia society at the end of the 1790s suggests membership at the four chapels was divided along racial lines, such that while whites attended preaching services at the black chapels and often were converted in that context, they apparently did not join them (cf. Andrews, "Popular Religion," 298–99).

87. "From the Rev. Richard Sneath, to Dr. Coke" (Milford, Del., Oct. 1802), *Arminian Magazine* [London] 26 (April 1803):272–73 [emphasis added]. As in the South, prayer meetings played an important role in the revival at Bethel. Sneath indicates that they were "appointed immediately after preaching, [and] . . . were blessed in an extraordinary manner, especially to those under convictions" (ibid., 273).

88. Eileen Southern, "Hymnals of the Black Church," *The Journal of the I.T.C.* 14 (fall 1986):130–33; Southern, *Music of Black Americans*, 75–79.

89. Phoebus, *Beams of Light*, 290.

90. Freeborn Garretson to Catherine Garrettson, Philadelphia, June 17, 1809 (Freeborn and Mary Garretson Box, File # 14, Commission on Archives and History, Drew University, Madison, NJ). I am grateful to Ian Straker for providing me with a copy and transcript of this letter.

91. The itinerant apparently told Watson "he could raise or lower their spiritual efflata at his pleasure, and that he had actually made the experiment:—to paint the joys of religion was sure to raise them, and to speak of the practical holiness of their duties was sure to silence them."

92. Ezra Stiles Ely, "Review of *Methodist Error*," *Quarterly Theological Review* 2/2 (April 1919):229.

93. Rev. Robert W. Todd, *Methodism of the Penninsula* (Philadelphia: Methodist Episcopal Book Room, 1886), 81; Walter F. Pitts, Jr., *Old Ship of Zion: The Afro-Baptist Ritual in the African Diaspora* (New York: Oxford University Press, 1983), 11–33, 91–97.

94. Todd, *Methodism of the Penninsula*, 180–81.

95. Ibid.

96. Hymn #101 in Enoch Mudge, *The American Camp-Meeting Hymn Book. Containing a Variety of Original Hymns, Suitable to be Used at Camp-Meetings; and at Other Times in Private and Social Devotion* (Boston: Burdakin, 1818). I am grateful to Lester Ruth for bringing this to my attention.

97. Billy Hibbard, *The Life and Travels of B. Hibbard* (New York, 1825), 255. Again, I am grateful to Lester Ruth for bringing this to my attention.

98. There are descriptions of African-style circular dances in (apparently) non-Protestant contexts that are also referred to as "ring shouts." I am not making any claims about the meaning of "ring shouts" in other contexts. It would be interesting to trace the actual use of the term "ring shout." Although the Watson account is often cited as the earliest example of the "ring shout," none of the sources cited here actually makes use of the term. We have "praying circles," "social rings," and "shouting," but no references to the "ring shout" *per se*.

99. Todd, *Methodism of the Penninsula*, 38.

100. Zilpha Elaw, *Memoirs of the Life, Religious Experience, Ministerial travels, and Labors of Mrs. Zilpha Elaw* in *Sisters of the Spirit: Three Black Women's Autobiographies of the Nineteenth Century*, ed. William L. Andrews (Bloomington: Indiana University Press, 1986), 81.

101. Daniel Alexander Payne, *Recollections of Seventy Years* (Nashville: A.M.E. Sunday School Union Publishing House, 1888; repr. ed., New York: Arno Press, 1968), 253–54.

102. Most of the post–Civil War accounts of the ring shout do suggest that one or more persons were within the circle, although these persons are not usually understood to be mourners. In his description of the "negro-Methodist chants" performed by the men in his regiment, Thomas Wentworth Higginson stated that "inside and outside the inclosure men begin to quiver and dance, others join, a circle forms, winding monotonously round some one in the centre" (Thomas Wentworth Higginson, *Army Life in a Black Regiment* [Boston, 1900], 23–24). Fredricka Bremer describes women "dancing the 'holy dance' for one of the converted" (quoted in Stuckey, *Slave Culture*, 90). Simpson ("Shout and Shouting," 35), drawing on Epstein (*Sinful Tunes*, 232), claims that "a ring [is formed] around a singer."

103. Simpson, "Shout and Shouting," 37; H. G. Spaulding, "Under the Palmetto," *Continental Monthly* 4 (1863), in Bruce Jackson, ed., *The Negro and His Folklore in Nineteenth-Century Periodicals* (Austin: University of Texas Press, 1967), 67–68; and William Francis Allen, *Slave Songs of the United States* (New York: Simpson, 1867), xii–xiv.

104. Payne, *Recollections*, 254–56.

105. Charles A. Johnson, *The Frontier Camp Meeting: Religion's Harvest Time* (Dallas: Southern Methodist University Press, 1955; 2nd edition, 1985); Dickson D. Bruce, Jr., *And They All Sang Hallelujah: Plain-Folk Camp-Meeting Religion, 1800–1845* (Knoxville: University of Tennessee Press, 1974); John B. Boles, *The Great Revival, 1787–1805: The Origins of the Southern Evangelical Mind* (Lexington: The University Press of Kentucky, 1972). Most studies have noted, but not adequately explained, the virtual Methodist takeover of this institution within a few years of its emergence. For a critical perspective on this historiographical tradition, see Richey, *Early American Methodism*, 21–32.

106. On the Presbyterian sacramental meetings in Scotland and America, see Schmidt, *Holy Fairs*; on the continuity between Methodist quarterly conferences and camp meetings, see Richey, *Early American Methodism*, 21–32. There is little secondary literature on either

German pietist or Baptist "big meetings." For descriptions in primary sources, see *Rippon's Register* [1790]:105–6, which describes "big meetings" as "the common practice in Georgia, South and North Carolina, and in Virginia, in what we call the back parts of the country."

107. John McGee, "Commencement of the Great Revival," *Methodist Magazine* 4 (1821):190, quoted in Kenneth O. Brown, *Holy Ground: A Study of the American Camp Meeting* (New York: Garland, 1992), 18.

108. Rankin's account was originally published in J. P. MacLean, "The Kentucky Revival and Its Influence on the Miami Valley," *Ohio Archaeological and Historical Publications* 12 (1908):280, quoted in Brown, *Holy Ground*, 19. Others also comment on falling as "a new thing among Presbyterians" and one that "excited universal astonishment"; see "Extract of a Letter from the Rev. G. Baxter . . . to the Rev. Dr. Archibald Alexander," *Arminian Magazine* [London] 26 (Feb. 1803):88.

109. For accounts of such meetings, see *Rippon's Register*, 1009, 1104; Lorenzo Dow, *Extracts from Original Letters to the Methodist Bishops, Mostly from their Preachers and Members in North America* . . . (Liverpool: H. Forshaw, 1806), 10, 20–21, 24–25, 27, 30–31, 38–41, 52. Both Baptists and Methodists commented on the "extraordinary meeting" at Washaws, SC, in May 1802. It was organized by the Presbyterians around a sacramental meeting, with Methodists and Baptists invited to participate (*Rippon's Register*, 1104; Dow, *Extracts*, 20–21). The Methodist *Arminian Magazine* [London] published letters from Presbyterian ministers William Hodge, J. Hall, and Samuel McCorkle describing cooperative revivals in Tennessee and North Carolina (24 [June 1803]:268–85; see also reports from Methodists 26 [Sept. 1803]:418–19).

110. Richey, *Early American Methodism*, 31–32; Zachary Myles to William Myles, Jan. 11, 1803, *Arminian Magazine* 26 (June 1803):285.

111. Boles, *The Great Revival*, 94–100.

112. Charles A. Johnson, *Frontier Camp Meeting*, 50–51.

113. Dow, *Extracts*; Jesse Lee, *History of the Methodists*, 286–96.

114. Todd, *Methodism of the Penninsula*, 35; George White, *A Brief Account of the Life, Experience, Travels, and Gospel Labours of George White, An African* (New York, 1810) in *Black Itinerants of the Gospel*, ed. Graham Russell Hodges (Madison: Madison House, 1993), 54.

115. Dow, *Extracts*, 61; Elaw, *Memoirs*, 65.

116. On the Carolina meetings in the 1790s, see Brown, *Holy Ground*, 8; on the Delmarva Penninsula, see Todd, *Methodism of the Penninsula*, 179, 182; on meetings in Pennsylvania and New Jersey, see Elaw, *Memoirs*, 65. Both Charles A. Johnson (*Frontier Camp Meeting*, 46), probably following Todd, and D. Bruce (*And They All Sang Hallelujah*, 73), citing Gorham's *Camp Meeting Manual* (1854), confidently state that camp meetings were segregated with whites sitting in front of the preaching stand and blacks gathering at the back. The variability and complexity of interactions around separate and shared space is suggested by Richard Bassett, an itinerant stationed on the Dover circuit in Delaware, who referred to separate black and white love-feasts at the annual conference in 1802, but in the next breath described "twelve to fifteen hundred [who] came to the Lord's table, white and coloured people" (Dow, *Extracts*, 19).

117. Jesse Lee, *History of the Methodists*, 366–67; for Coate, see Dow, *Extracts*, 61–62, also the letter of Daniel Hitt in Dow, 57.

118. Elaw, *Memoirs*, 65–66.

119. Richey, *Early American Methodism*, 24.

120. Dow, *Extracts*, 55, 59, emphasis added; see also, 24, 28, 29, 31, 33, 37, 38, 43, 71.

121. White, *A Brief Account*, 53; Letter from McKendree to Bishop Asbury, 1803, quoted in Robert Paine, *Life and Times of William McKendree*, 37.

122. Sneathen in Dow, *Extracts*, 234; Baxter to Alexander, 1802, in Dow, *Extracts*, 91 (emphasis added).

123. For the sanctification experiences of Rebecca Cox Jackson (A.M.E.), Jarena Lee (A.M.E), and Zilpha Elaw (M.E.C.), see Jean McMahan Humez, *Gifts of Power: The Writings of Rebecca Jackson, Black Visionary, Shaker Eldress* (Amherst: University of Massachusetts Press, 1981), 76; Jarena Lee, *The Life and Religious Experience of Jarena Lee* in *Sisters of the Spirit*, ed. William Andrews, 34; and Elaw, *Memoirs*, 66–67.

124. White, *A Brief Account*, 58.

125. Fanny Newell, *Memoirs of Fanny Newell Written by Herself* [Kennebec: Hallowell, 1824], 81–82.

126. Examples from Dow, *Extracts*, include: "He shouted glory, glory to God for nearly four hours" and "the Lord's saints shouted aloud for joy" (44); "she rose and shouted glory to God! glory to God!" and "arose and shouted glory" (45); "shouting the praises of the Most High" (47); "the shouts of his people were heard afar off" (48); "cries of the distressed and shouts of joy" (54).

127. Southern, *Music of Black Americans*, 86–87; Jon Michael Spencer, *Black Hymnody: A Hymnological History of the African-American Church* (Knoxville: University of Tennessee Press, 1992), 4–7.

128. John Storm Roberts, *Black Music*, 162–75. Sutton provides excellent contemporary musical illustrations of the differences in black and white performance styles in a context where the words are, for the most part, taken from Isaac Watts.

129. D. Bruce, *And They All Sang Hallelujah*, 95. For reasons that are not clear, Dickson Bruce focuses exclusively on the tradition of "white spirituals" in the shape-note songbooks (96–122), ignoring the black spiritual tradition. Nonetheless, he says of the "white spirituals" that "the key word in the vocabulary of terms used to talk about God was . . . 'glory.' " The "plain-folk," as he refers to them, used the word in three ways: "First, they used it when they talked about the kind of praise they would give to God. Second, they occasionally used it to describe the power which had converted them. Finally, they used it to talk about heaven and the mode of existence which they, too, would achieve when they had finally realized salvation." Although Bruce does not refer to "shouts" or "shouting," a quick perusal of the shape-note songbooks that he used reveals an intimate connection between glorifying God and shouting. See, for example, in John G. McCurry, *Social Harp* (1855; reprint ed., Athens: University of Georgia Press, 1973): "When we all get to Heaven, We will shout aloud and sing, [Chorus] Shout glory, halle, hallelulujah" (42); "Streams of mercy never ceasing, Call for songs of loudest praise. [Chorus] Shout, oh, glory, glory, glory" (53); "Shout, oh, glory! praise the Lord on high"(81); "O, shout for joy, give God the glory" (104); *Shouting Song*, "Shout, oh, glory! sing glory, hallelujah!" (110); "Shout, oh, glory!" (111); "Shout on, pray on, we're gaining ground, Glory, hallelujah!" (158); also 37, 48, 106, 145, 184.

130. McCurry, *Social Harp*, 42, 53, 81, 110, 111.

131. Work, *American Negro Songs*, 180, 209. See also, "I'ntend to shout an' never stop" (47); "Pray on! Shout on!" (53); "Know you shoutin' happy" (65); "Shout, my sister, you are free" (137); "Shout for joy!" (173); "When I get to heaven goin' to sing and shout, Nobody there for turn me out" (176); "What is the matter the church won't shout" (248).

132. Both John Storm Roberts and Russell Richey point out that much that is today identified with black religion (or African American Christianity) had its origins in the inter-

racial traditions of the camp-meeting spiritual (Roberts, *Black Music*, 166; Richey, *Early American Methodism*, 60).

133. These are the only specifically denominational songs in the collections I have looked at.

134. Work, *American Negro Songs*, 219.

135. *The Chorus*, compiled by A. S. Jenks and D. S. Gilkey (Philadelphia, 1860), #241, quoted in Hudson, "Shouting Methodists," 73.

136. "Methodist and Formalist," in *Hesperian Harp*, compiled by William Hauser (Philadelphia, 1848), 454, quoted in Charles A. Johnson, *Frontier Camp Meeting*, 262–64.

137. Ibid. The complete text of the dialogue regarding scripture is as follows:

Formalist	. . . if this be religion
	I'm sure that it's something that never was seen,
	For the sacred pages that speak of all ages,
	Do nowhere declare that such ever has been.
Methodist	Don't be so soon shaken—if I'm not mistaken
	Such things were perform'd by believers of old;
	When the ark was coming, King David came running,
	And dancing before it, in Scripture we're told [II Sam. 6:14–15].
	When the Jewish nation had laid the foundation,
	To rebuild the temple at Ezra's command,
	Some wept and some praised, such noise there was raised,
	'Twas heard afar off and perhaps through the land [Ezra 3:1–14].
	And as for the preacher, Ezekiel the teacher,
	God taught him to stamp and to smite with the hand,
	To show the transgressions of that wicked nation
	To bid them repent and obey the command [Ezek. 21:16–17].
	For Scripture collation in this dispensation,
	The blessed Redeemer had handed it out—
	"If these cease from praising," we hear him there saying,
	"The stones to reprove them would quickly cry out" [Luke 19:37–40].
Formalist	Then Scripture's contrasted, for Paul has protested
	That order should reign in the house of the Lord . . . [I Cor. 14.40]
Methodist	. . . As Peter was preaching, and bold in his teaching,
	The plan of salvation in Jesus's name,
	The Spirit descended and some were offended,
	And said of these men, "They're filled with new wine."
	I never yet doubted that some of them shouted,
	While others lay prostrate, by power struck down;
	Some weeping, some praising, while others were saying:
	"They're drunkards or fools, or in falsehood abound" [Acts 2].
	As time is now flying and moments are dying,
	We're call'd to improve them, and quickly prepare
	For that awful hour when Jesus, in power
	And glory is coming—'tis now drawing near.
	Methinks there'll be shouting, and I'm not a-doubting,
	But crying and screaming for mercy in vain;
	Therefore, my dear brother, let us pray together,
	That your precious soul may be filled with the flame.

138. Charles A. Johnson, *Frontier Camp Meeting*, 264 (emphasis added).

139. I am grateful to my colleague, Marvin Sweeney, for help in piecing together the Biblical imagery underlying the sacralization of the camp.

140. White, *A Brief Account*, 54; James Jenkins to Rev. Dr. Coke, Dec. 10, 1804, *Arminian Magazine* 28 (Appendix), 573; Dow, *Extracts*, 41, 50, 51; see also, *Arminian Magazine* 27 [London] (March 1804):138; Brown, *Holy Ground*, xi.

141. Elaw, *Memoirs*, 65–66.

142. Dow, *Extracts*, 62–3.

143. Work, *American Negro Songs*, 143–45, 160, 226.

144. Elaw, *Memoirs*, 65.

145. Ibid., 65–66. *Zion's Walls:* "Come, fathers and mothers, Come, sisters and brothers, Come, join us in singing the praises of Jesus; O, fathers, don't you feel determined, To meet within the walls of Zion. We'll shout and go round, We'll shout and go round, We'll shout and go round the walls of Zion" (McCurry, *Social Harp*, 137). *Heavenly King:* "Children of the heavenly King, When we get to heaven we will part no more. As ye journey sweetly sing, When we get to heaven we will part no more. Friends, fare you well, Friends, fare you well, When we get to heaven we will part no more" (McCurry, *Social Harp*, 20).

146. Todd, *Methodism of the Penninsula*, 181–82.

147. Ibid., 182.

148. On hymnody, see Southern, "Hymnals," 132–33; Hudson, "Shouting Methodists," 84.

PART TWO
POPULAR PSYCHOLOGY AND POPULAR RELIGION, 1820–1890

1. William L. Stone, *Letter to Doctor A. Brigham on Animal Magnetism* (New York: George Dearborn & Co., 1837), 5–6.

2. G. Capron to Mr. Thomas C. Hartshorn, August 31, 1837, in J.P.F. Deleuze, *Practical Instruction in Animal Magnetism*, trans. Thomas C. Hartshorn (New York: D. Appleton & Co., 1843; repr. ed., New York: Da Capo Press, 1982), 233–34; Stone, *Letter to Brigham*, 10, 13–14; Alan Gauld, *A History of Hypnotism* (New York: Cambridge University Press, 1992), 180–83.

3. Stone, *Letter to Brigham*, 3, 7–8.

4. Jay Wharton Fay, *American Psychology Before William James* (Rutgers: Rutgers University Press, 1939; reprint ed., New York: Octagon Books, 1966); George Sidney Brett, *A History of Psychology; Vol. 3: Modern Psychology* (New York: Macmillan Co., 1921), 255–68; Edward F. Buchner, "A Quarter Century of Psychology in America, 1878–1903," *American Journal of Psychology* 14 (July-Oct. 1903):402–4; Daniel Walker Howe, *The Unitarian Conscience: Harvard Moral Philosophy, 1805–1861* (Cambridge: Harvard University Press, 1970), 31–44. The definition of mental philosophy appeared in "Importance of a Knowledge of Mental Philosophy to the Christian Minister," *Christian Review* 3 (Sept. 1838):430, quoted in Darius L. Salter, *Spirit and Intellect: Thomas Upham's Holiness Theology* (Metuchen, NJ: Scarecrow Press, 1986), 6. As Eugene Taylor points out, this approach ignored, among other things, "the burgeoning industry of folk psychology (phrenology, mesmerism, spiritual healing); the literary psychology of the transcendentalists, the medico-psychological movement—that is, the use of psychology by physicians such as George Beard, or the development of practical psychology in the state normal schools" (Eugene Taylor, *William James on Consciousness Beyond the Margin* [Princeton: Princeton University Press, 1996], 181).

5. William Hamilton, ed., *The Collected Works of Dugald Stewart*, 6 vols. (Edinburgh: Thomas Constable and Co., 1854), 4:147–61; Jane Rendall, *The Origins of the Scottish Enlightenment* (New York: St. Martin's Press, 1978), 102–22, 236–43; Daniel N. Robinson, *An Intellectual History of Psychology*, rev. ed. (New York: Macmillan, 1981), 207–44.

6. Daniel Steele, *Love Enthroned: Essays on Evangelical Perfection* (New York: Phillips & Hunt, 1884), 237–38; on Finney's use of academic psychology, see William G. McLoughlin, *Modern Revivalism: Charles Grandison Finney to Billy Graham* (New York: Ronald Press Co., 1959), 85–87.

7. Thomas Upham, *Elements of Mental Philosophy*, 2 vols. (3d ed., Portland, ME: W. Hyde, 1839), 2:382–91

8. Gerald N. Grob, *Mental Institutions in America: Social Policy to 1875* (New York: The Free Press, 1973), 137–38, 151–53; Nancy Tomes, *A Generous Confidence: Thomas Story Kirkbridge and the Art of Asylum-Keeping, 1840–1883* (Cambridge: Cambridge University Press, 1984), 74–75; Tanaquil Taubes, " 'Healthy Avenues of the Mind': Psychological Theory Building and the Influence of Religion During the Era of Moral Treatment," *American Journal of Psychiatry* 155/8 (August 1998):1001–7; Norman Dain, "Psychiatry and Anti-Psychiatry in the United States," in Mark S. Micale and Roy Porter, eds., *Discovering the History of Psychiatry* (New York: Oxford University Press, 1994), 417–18.

9. Amariah Brigham, *Observations on the Influence of Religion upon the Health and Welfare of Mankind* (Boston, 1835; reprint ed., New York: Arno Press, 1973), 252–59, 267–312, quotes 299, 304.

10. Michael J. Clark, "The Rejection of Psychological Approaches to Mental Disorder in Late Nineteenth-Century British Psychiatry," in Andrew Scull, ed., *Madhouses, Mad-Doctors, and Madmen: The Social History of Psychiatry in the Victorian Era* (Philadelphia: University of Pennsylvania Press, 1981), 301.

11. Hoopes, *Consciousness*, 95–97; Howe, *Unitarian Conscience*, 49.

12. Dain, "Psychiatry and Anti-Psychiatry," 421–22; Taubes, "Healthy Avenues," 1001–7.

13. For histories of psychiatry or psychotherapeutics that begin with Mesmer, see Henri F. Ellenberger, *The Discovery of the Unconscious: The History and Evolution of Dynamic Psychiatry* (New York: Basic Books, 1970); Gauld, *History*; Adam Crabtree, *From Mesmer to Freud: Magnetic Sleep and the Roots of Psychological Healing* (New Haven: Yale University Press, 1993). On Ellenberger's pioneering role in this regard, see Mark S. Micale, "Henri F. Ellenberger: The History of Psychiatry as the History of the Unconscious," in Micale and Porter, eds., *History of Psychiatry*, 112–34. On the shift from popular to professional, see Micale, "Ellenberger," 116–17; Fuller, *Mesmerism*, 61.

14. Two studies have specifically addressed the interconnections between mesmerism and American religion: Frank Podmore's *Mesmerism and Christian Science* (Philadelphia: G. W. Jacobs, 1909), and Fuller's *Mesmerism and the American Cure of Souls*.

15. I use the terms "academic" and "popular" to distinguish between the two tiers within the field of mental philosophy. La Roy Sunderland, who is described by Alan Gauld as a "professional magnetizer," described himself as a "mental philosopher," although as a former Methodist minister, he had neither an academic position nor a college education. This suggests that, as in the case of medicine, those who claimed the title of mental philosopher were quite varied in their background and that the academic mental philosophers, such as Thomas Upham, constituted an elite within the field. The word "psychology" began appearing in the titles of books published by academic mental philosophers during the 1840s. Likewise, Sunderland's *Book of Psychology*, a popular work, was published in 1854.

16. While overshadowed to some extent by rivals during his lifetime, Sunderland was later recognized as one of the most sophisticated theorists, American or European, in the era of animal magnetism. James Monroe Buckley wrote of Sunderland, "he alone of all the men of his time mastered the real cause of these phenomena, repudiating the absurdity of 'will power' and the mythical 'animal magnetism.' " ([Buckley], *Christian Advocate*, June 4, 1885, 358). Frank Podmore, a well-known late-nineteenth-century historian of spiritualism, commented that "Sunderland appears to have been one of the soundest and most cautious investigators of his time. He shared, indeed, with [the Englishman James] Braid the honour of having recognized in his later writings—and, it would seem, independently—that all the phenomena of the trance could be explained without fluid or aura or effluence of any kind, as being simply results of the subject's own mental reaction to suggestions supplied by the voice or gestures of the operator, or, in some cases, by the patient himself" (Podmore, *Modern Spiritualism*, 1:157). Gauld places Sunderland, along with James Braid and others, not among their chronological peers, the mesmerists, but in a special chapter devoted to "precursors of hypnotism." Gauld agrees with Podmore that Sunderland was "in many ways ahead of his time," but he singles Sunderland out more for the theories he rejected than for what he describes as the "idiosyncratic" theory he constructed (Gauld, *History*, 288–290, also, 184–85, 189, 193, 288; Crabtree, *Mesmer to Freud*, 222, 224–26, 229).

17. Eschenmayer, "Über Gassners Heilmethode," *Archiv für thierischen Magnetismus* 8/1 (1820):86–135, quoted in Ellenberger, *Discovery*, 54, 56.

18. Ibid., 62–63.

19. *Report of Dr. Benjamin Franklin, and other Commissioners, charged by the King of France, with the examination of the Animal Magnetism, as now practised at Paris* (London: Johnson, 1785), 25–27.

20. Gauld, *History*, 27–28.

21. Quoted in ibid., 41.

22. Ibid., 41–42.

23. A.M.J. de Chastenet de Puységur, *Détail des cures . . . par le magnétisme animal* in *Recueil des pièces les plus interessantes pour & contre le magnétisme animal*, vol. 1 (Lyon: n.p., 1785), 321–31, quoted in Gauld, *History*, 42.

CHAPTER FOUR
CLAIRVOYANTS AND VISIONARIES

1. La Roy Sunderland, *The Trance, and Correlative Phenomena* (Chicago: James Walker, 1868), 9–11.

2. Ronald Graybill, "Methodist Roots of the Adventist Tradition," unpublished paper, Loma Linda University, Department of Archives and Special Collections.

3. I use "adventists" in lowercase as a synonym for followers of William Miller prior to 1844 and as a general way to encompass both moderates and radicals after 1844. I modify adventist with terms such as moderate, radical, or "shut-door" when referring to various sub-groups within the movement after 1844. I capitalize Adventist only when used to refer to members of an adventist denomination (i.e., the Advent Christian Church or the Seventh-day Adventists).

4. On the connection between revivalism and abolition in the M.E.C., see, Donald Mathews, *Slavery and Methodism* (Princeton: Princeton University Press, 1965), 167. On the connection between adventism and revivalism, see Milton Perry, "The Role of the Camp Meeting in Millerite Revivalism, 1842–1844" (Ph.D. dissertation, Baylor University, 1994).

5. The two movements were not entirely opposed to one another. A number of prominent adventists supported abolition, including William Miller, and a number of prominent abolitionists, including Angelina Grimké, embraced the advent message. On the connection between abolition and adventism, see Ronald Graybill, "The Abolitionist-Millerite Connection," in *The Disappointed*, ed. Ronald L. Numbers and Jonathan M. Butler (Knoxville: University of Tennessee Press, 1993), 139–52.

6. La Roy Sunderland to Rev. R. H. Howard, 1872 (transcript of handwritten original, New England Methodist Historical Society Collection, Boston University School of Theology Library), 10–14; J. R. Jacob, "La Roy Sunderland: The Alienation of an Abolitionist," *American Studies* 6, no. 1 (1965):1–8; Lucius C. Matlack, *The History of American Slavery and Methodism from 1780 to 1849 and History of the Wesleyan Methodist Connection of America* (New York, 1849; repr. ed., Freeport, NY: Books for Libraries Press, 1971), 245–54; Mathews, *Slavery and Methodism*, 161–62; Edward D. Jervey, "LaRoy Sunderland: Zion's Watchman," *Methodist History* 6, no. 3 (April 1968):16–32.

7. Sunderland to Howard, 10–14; Jacob, "La Roy Sunderland," 1–8; John R. McKivigan, *The War against Proslavery Religion: Abolition and the Northern Churches, 1830–1865* (Ithaca: Cornell University Press, 1984), 46.

8. Mathews, *Slavery and Methodism*, 193–204.

9. On Storrs, see David L. Rowe, *Thunder and Trumpets: Millerites and Dissenting Religion in Upstate New York, 1800–1850* (Chico, CA: Scholar's Press, 1985), 121; and, Edwin Gaustad, ed., *The Rise of Adventism: Religion and Society in Mid-Nineteenth-Century America* (New York: Harper and Row, 1974), 168.

10. McKivigan, *War against Proslavery Religion*, 85.

11. Matlack, *American Slavery*, 332–33.

12. Rev. Stephen Allen and Rev. W. H. Pilsbury, *History of Methodism in Maine, 1793–1886* (Augusta: Charles E. Nash, 1887), 118; Graybill, "Methodist Roots," 5.

13. Allen & Pilsbury, *History of Methodism*, 121–22.

14. K. Dickerson, *The Philosophy of Mesmerism or Animal Magnetism, Being a Compilation of Facts ascertained by Experience, and Drawn from the Writings of the Most Celebrated Magnetisers in Europe and America* (Concord, NH: Morrill, Silsby & Co., 1843), 8–9. Although he drew huge large audiences, Gauld discounts Collyer's self-aggrandizing claims, highlighting Poyen's contributions and discussing Collyer as one among the many magnetizers who appeared on the scene beginning in 1840.

15. In addition to Sunderland, he mentions Dr. Gilbert of Boston; Rev. Mr. Dods, a Universalist clergyman, of Boston; Dr. Shattuck of Lowell, Massachusetts; and Mrs. Fergus of Boston.

16. Dickerson, *Philosophy of Mesmerism*, 9–10.

17. Ibid., 10; Robert Collyer, *Lights and Shadows of American Life* (Boston, 1838), 34.

18. Among the better-known professional magnetizers mentioned by Gauld, J. S. Grimes was a professor of medical jurisprudence, Dr. H. G. Darling was a former professor of physiology, J. R. Buchanan and Robert H. Collyer were physicians or had at least studied medicine, John Bovee Dods was a Universalist minister, and Sunderland, a former minister. The training or previous careers of the other three listed is unspecified (Gauld, *History*, 183–84).

19. La Roy Sunderland, *Book of Psychology* (New York: Stearns & Co., 1853), 41.

20. Amariah Brigham and La Roy Sunderland both refer to a Methodist revival in New England in 1823–25 (Brigham, *Observations*, 148–58).

21. Finney conducted his first revivals in 1824–25 in the small towns of western New York. On the Finney revivals, see Charles Finney, *Lectures on Revivals of Religion*, ed. William G. McLoughlin (Cambridge, MA: Harvard University Press, 1960), liii–liv.

22. Joseph A. Conforti, *Jonathan Edwards, Religious Tradition, and American Culture* (Chapel Hill: University of North Carolina Press, 1995), 17, 22.

23. Ibid., 10–61; on the eclipse of Methodism, see, Nathan Hatch, *Democratization of American Christianity* (Yale, 1989), 220–26 and Hatch, "Puzzle of American Methodism," 175–89.

24. Grant Powers, *Essay upon the Influence of the Imagination on the Nervous System, Contributing to a False Hope in Religion* (Andover: Flagg & Gould, 1828), 23–24.

25. Sometime in the early 1820s, Watson entered notes under the heading "Magnetism & Enthusiasm" in the back pages of the manuscript book for *Methodist Error*. The notes were drawn from his reading of the entry on "animal magnetism" in *Brewsters Encyclopedia*, along with "Bailly's Report" and relevant excerpts from Benjamin Franklin's memoirs. After summarizing the conclusions of the Commission, he wrote:

> If *natural* causes could thus excite *actions* in Mesmers &c cases, could not the *circumstances* of Camp meetings still more readily do it by *natural* means[?]. The only objection is that the People in them got converted. But might not *fright & concerns*, from such *unusual sensations*, lead men to *change* of their life & to consequent Conversion? How many fall off as if no change was induced by all their emotions? I merely put the question for information. (Watson, Mss. version of *Methodist Error*, n.p.)

26. On the early history of mesmerism in America, see Crabtree, *From Mesmer to Freud*, 213–18. Mesmer attempted to generate interest in animal magnetism in America in the 1780s through contacts with Benjamin Franklin and George Washington, neither of whom were particularly responsive. The Marquis de Lafayette was an enthusiastic promoter who visited with the Shakers in 1784. Apart from a brief flurry of interest during the 1790s in the "metallic tractors" of Elijah Perkins, a healing technique bearing some resemblance to that of magnetism, mesmerism seems, in Crabtree's words, "to have more or less slipped out of sight" until the publication of Powers's book in 1828 (ibid., 213–17).

27. Powers (*Essay*) quotes extensively from Watson on pp. 41–42, 55, 59–60, 65–66, 71–72, 75–77, 88–91, 93, 96, 98, 104–5 and Southey on pp. 35, 47, 50–53, 98–99.

28. Ibid., 86–87.

29. Ibid., 88–89.

30. John Bouvee Dods, *Six Lectures on the Philosophy of Mesmerism* (New York: Fowler & Wells, 1865), 62–63.

31. La Roy Sunderland, *The Book of Human Nature* (1854), 218.

32. Sunderland, *The Trance*, 9–17, quotes, 11–12. See also, Sunderland, *Psychology*, 41–47. Both incidents took place in Massachusetts in 1823.

33. Osian E. Dodge, *Boston Literary Museum*, July 21, 1849, quoted in Sunderland, *Human Nature*, xi.

34. [James Monroe Buckley], "La Roy Sunderland—II," *The Christian Advocate* 60, no. 23 (June 4, 1885): 358.

35. Sunderland, *Psychology*, 48–50.

36. La Roy Sunderland, *"Confessions of a Magnetizer" Exposed* [hereafter CME] (Boston: Redding & Co., 1845), 7; Dickerson, *Philosophy of Mesmerism*, 9.

37. *The Magnet* 1, no. 1 (June 1842): 2. Dr. John Elliotson, President of the Royal Medical Society of Edinburgh, was England's most prestigious (albeit much maligned) advocate of phrenology and mesmerism. On the controversy surrounding Elliotson, see Gauld, *History*, 199–203, 206–8.

38. "Sleep-Waking," *The Magnet* 2, no. 1 (July 1842):25.

39. It maintained a certain popularity, particularly in Francophone Europe throughout the course of the nineteenth century. Theodore Flournoy's *Des Indes à la Planète Mars*, a study of a Swiss medium published in 1899, was subtitled *Etude sur un cas de somnambulisme avec glossolalie*.

40. *The Magnet* 2, no. 1 (June 1843):3.

41. Charles Mais [stenographer], *The Surprising Case of Rachel Baker, who prays and preaches in her sleep* (New York: Whiting and Watson, 1814), 6.

42. "Sleep-Waking," *The Magnet* 1, no. 2 (June 1842):27. Sunderland notes that "the lady" referred to by Elliotson "was the celebrated 'sleeping preacher,' . . . Mrs. Baker," adding that he knew persons who had heard her preach (ibid).

43. Mais, *Case of Rachel Baker*, 12.

44. Ibid., 10; Several Medical Gentlemen, *Devotional Somnium; or, a Collection of Prayers and Exhortations, uttered by Miss Rachel Baker* (New York, 1815), 26–27.

45. "Trance," *The Magnet* 1, no. 10 (March 1843):224–25.

46. "Ecstacy," *The Magnet* 1, no. 11 (April 1843):248.

47. The word "trance" is used to translate the Greek *ekstasis* in Acts 10:10, 11:5, 22:17. The first two passages refer to Peter's vision of the "great sheet" ("he fell into a trance, and saw heaven opened") and the third to Paul's vision in the temple ("while I prayed in the temple, I was in a trance; and saw him [the Lord] saying unto me").

48. "Nomenclature," *The Magnet* 1, no. /9 (February 1843):201.

49. Dr. George Capron, a physician in Providence, commented: "the term Pathetism has also of late been proposed, and almost exclusively employed in the Magnet, a periodical published in New York, by La Roy Sunderland, and I am not philologist enough to discover any objection to the term itself, but I very much doubt the propriety of introducing any new terms, unless we are sure that they are not only better than the old ones, but also that they will be generally adopted" (Deleuze, *Practical Instruction*, 379).

50. "Nomenclature," *The Magnet* 1, no. 9 (February 1843): 201.

51. When theorists later reconceptualized this state as "trance" and even later as "dissociation," they broke the ties between this state and the sleeping-waking continuum. In reconstituting this state as dissociation, later theorists reconstituted it as a pathological state in which normal "associations" had been broken.

52. La Roy Sunderland, *Pathetism with Practical Instructions* (New York, 1843), v–vi.

53. He also mentions a number of works in French by Deleuze, Puisegur [sic], and others. He particularly recommends "Dr. Bertrand's excellent treatise *Du Magnétism Animal*." Those who read only English, he says, "should consult *Isis revelata*, a work just published in two volumes by Mr. Colquhoun of Edinburgh" (John Elliotson, *Human Physiology*, 5th ed. [London: Longman, 1840], note, p. 669).

54. Gauld, *History*, 245.

55. Elliotson, *Human Physiology*, 664.

56. Ibid., 665.

57. Joseph Ennemoser, *History of Magic*, 2 vols., trans. William Howitt (1854; repr. ed., New Hyde Park, NY: University Books, 1970), 1:iii, xiv, 26–27.

58. Ibid., 2:88–91.

59. Gauld, *History*, 144–46.

60. Gauld, *History*, 150–51; Ellenberger, *Discovery*, 79–81. According to Gauld, "with [Justinus] Kerner and his circle of friends—including Eschenmayer, Schelling, Schubert, Schleiermacher, Baader and Görres—the interplay of literary romanticism, nature philosophy, theology, and animal magnetism reached new heights" (*History*, 150). Jung-Stilling's

Theorie der Geisterkunde appeared in English translation in 1834; Kerner's *Seeress of Prevorst* was not translated until 1844. Justinus Kerner, remembered as a minor Romantic poet, was also a country physician and, according to Ellenberger, "one of the most important figures in the origins of dynamic psychiatry. . . . Historically, *The Seeress of Prevorst* represents the first monograph devoted to an in-depth study of a single patient. It retains its value today as a study of the 'mythopoetical function of the unconscious' and what it can do when given time and auspicious circumstances" (Henri Ellenberger, "Psychiatry and Its Unknown History," in Mark Micale, ed., *Beyond the Unconscious: Essays of Henri F. Ellenberger in the History of Psychiatry* (Princeton: Princeton University Press, 1993), 245.

61. "The Nature of Man," *The Magnet* 1, no. (December 1842):158–59.

62. Although Sunderland held at this time that "man has a faculty, or sense, independent of the physical organs," he did not equate this God-given "magnetic sense" with the soul or ascribe to it the sorts of mystical powers claimed by Jung-Stilling, "The Magnetic Phenomena," *The Magnet* 1, no. (July 1842):32. Sunderland also repeatedly cautioned his readers not to believe all the "marvelous stories" told about the magnetic state. He was particularly cautious when it came to claims of clairvoyance (*The Magnet* 1, no. [July 1842]:34).

63. Dickerson, *Philosophy of Mesmerism*, 5.

64. Dods, *Six Lectures*, 72.

65. Sunderland, *CME*, 26.

66. The most widely quoted American examples were Tennent's near-death experience (cf. Ennemoser, *History of Magic*, 2:429), and Rachel Baker's trance preaching (Elliotson, *Human Physiology*; Ennemoser, *History of Magic*, 2:442); Sunderland, *CME*, 105–7.

67. Sunderland, *CME*, 107.

68. Sunderland, *Psychology*, 46–48; Sunderland, *Trance*, 18. The first two accounts were written by Sunderland and published in 1854 and 1868; a third was written by James Monroe Buckley after interviewing Sunderland and published in 1885.

69. Because the last volume of *Zion's Watchman* is no longer extant, the nature of Sunderland's early experiments must be reconstructed from other sources. A testimonial letter signed by Sherwood, Fowler, Daniel Piexetto (president of the N. Y. Medical Society), a professor, and two ministers in March 1842 is reprinted in *The Trance*, 18–19, along with a brief description of the experiments; excerpts from the minutes of the experiments were published in *The Magnet* 1, no. 4 (September 1842):84–85; and *Pathetism* (1843), 77, 223–26. The surviving excerpts recount the subject's answers to questions about matters presumably known only to the experimenters (e.g., the contents of a vial, the recognition of objects held over her head, the contents of a newly published closed book, the ownership of objects held by the operator). The tests appear to be similar to those conducted by Dr. George Capron with Loraina Brackett. On the experiments with Brackett, see Gauld, *History*, 182; Deleuze, *Pratical Instruction*, 369–74; Stone, *Letter to Dr. Brigham*, 42–44.

70. Although Sunderland rejected phrenology entirely within the next few years, he was known in the early 1840s for blending phrenology and magnetism (*Psychology*, 50). On the popularity of "phreno-magnetism" in the early 1840s, see Gauld, *History*, 185.

71. "Medicinal Cases," *The Magnet* 1, no. 2 (July 1842):35–37 and 1, no. 3 (August 1842):58–59.

72. Ibid., 35.

73. In his narrative accounts of the events of this period published in the 1850s and 1860s, religion is arguably the central motif. This retrospective focus on religion reflected his growing interest in the psychology of religion and most specifically in bringing his past experience to bear on interpreting the Spiritualist movement.

74. *The Magnet* 1, no. 3 (August 1842):59.

75. "Pathetism," *American Millenarian*, reprinted in *The Magnet* 1/, no. 12 (May 1843):269–70.

76. Ibid., 270.

77. Sunderland, *Psychology*, 44–45.

78. Sunderland, *Trance*, 18.

79. [Buckley], "Sunderland," 358.

80. Ibid.

81. Sunderland, *Pathetism* (1843), 181.

82. Ibid., 181.

83. Ibid., 182.

84. *The Magnet* 1, no. 2 (July 1842):33, 35.

85. Sunderland, *CME*, 23. For Sunderland's early views on clairvoyance see "Caution," *The Magnet* 1, no. 2 (July 1842):34–35; "Magnetic Examinations," *The Magnet* 1, no. 4 (September 1842):83–85; "Clairvoyance," *The Magnet* 1, no. 5 (October 1842):97–99; *Pathetism* (1843), 211–30; *CME* (1845), 22–25.

86. Sunderland, *Pathetism* (1843), 190.

87. "Mr. Sunderland's Lectures," *Providence Evening Chronicle*, October 17, 1843, quoted in *The Magnet* 2 (1844):173.

88. "Mr. Sunderland's Lectures," *Boston Post*, November 23, 1843, quoted in *The Magnet* 2 (1844):177.

89. Sunderland, *Pathetism* (1843), 93.

90. "Pathetism," *Providence Chronicle*, October 21, 1843, quoted in *The Magnet* 2 (1844):174.

91. "Mr. Sunderland's Lectures," *Providence Evening Chronicle*, October 17, 1843, quoted in *The Magnet* 2 (1844):173.

92. Sunderland, *Psychology*, 47–48.

93. "Mr. Sunderland's Lectures," *The Boston Post*, November 23, 1843, quoted in *The Magnet* 2 (1844):177.

94. *The Magnet* 2 (1844):174.

95. "Pathetism and Music," *Boston Daily Mail*, November 27, 1843, quoted in *The Magnet* 2 (1844):178–79.

96. Sunderland, *Trance*, 197.

97. Phoebe Palmer, *The Way of Holiness* (52nd ed., New York: Palmer & Hughes, 1867), 74–75, in *The Devotional Writings of Phoebe Palmer*, ed. Donald Dayton (New York: Garland Pub., 1985).

98. Palmer, *Way of Holiness*, 33–39 (emphasis in original); Stephen Cooley, "The Possibilities of Grace: Poetic Discourse and Reflection in Methodist/Holiness Revivalism" (Ph.D. diss., University of Chicago, 1991), 78–81; Thomas C. Oden, ed., *Phoebe Palmer: Selected Writings* (New York: Paulist Press, 1988), 107–30; Harold E. Raser, *Phoebe Palmer: Her Life and Thought* (Lewiston: Edwin Mellon Press, 1987), 267–72.

99. Palmer, *Way of Holiness*, 38; see also, her diary account from 1846, quoted in Richard Wheatley, *The Life and Letters of Mrs. Phoebe Palmer* (New York, 1881; reprint ed., New York: Garland Publishing, Inc., 1884), 540–41.

100. Melvin E. Dieter, *The Holiness Revival of the Nineteenth Century*, 2nd ed. (Lanham, MD: Scarecrow Press, 1996), 25–26.

101. Palmer, *Way of Holiness*, 41–42.

102. Salter, *Spirit and Intellect*, 68–71; on the impact of the "consciousness concept" more generally, see Hoopes, *Consciousness*. Hoopes's focus on the New England tradition

in theology and philosophy limits his discussion to the Reformed tradition. When he concludes that "a great deal more might be done in exploring how the consciousness concept transformed Christian 'fundamentalism' from a religion of pious doubt into one of self-confident religious 'experience' " (277), the piety that he is referring to is Calvinist (not Methodist) in its origins. While Hoopes emphasizes the role of the consciousness concept in transforming traditional Reformed piety, the role of the Methodist tradition with its traditional emphasis on experience should be taken into account as well. For the Methodist tradition, the issue had less to do with the relationship between doubt and assurance than with the relationship between experience and faith, given Wesley's emphasis on the witness of the Spirit.

103. Patricia A. Ward, "Madame Guyon and Experiential Theology in America," *Church History* 67, no. 3 (September 1998):489–91, 495; John Wesley also published *An Extract of the Life of Madam Guyon* (London: R. Hawes, 1776) in his library of Christian classics.

104. Melvin E. Dieter, *The Holiness Revival of the Nineteenth Century* (Metuchen, NJ: The Scarecrow Press, 1980), 53; see also, 53–55, 88–90, n. 153–164; Darius Salter, "Mysticism in American Wesleyanism: Thomas Upham," *Wesleyan Theological Journal* 20, no. 1 (spring 1985):97–98; Cooley, "The Possibilities of Grace," 75–76.

105. Thomas C. Upham, *Life and Religious Opinions and Experience of Madame de la Mothe Guyon: Together with some account of the personal history and religious opinions of Fenelon, Archbishop of Cambray*, 2 vols. (1846; New York: Harper & Bros., 1851), 1:vi.

106. Upham, *Madame Guyon*, 387–89.

107. Thomas C. Upham, *The Life of Faith* (Boston: Waite, Pierce & Co., 1845), 359–60.

108. Upham, *Interior Life* (1843; 8th ed., New York: Harper & Bros., 1859), 288.

109. Upham, *Interior Life*, 288.

110. Salter, *Spirit and Intellect*, 185–86; Upham, *Outline of Disordered Mental Action* (1840; New York: Harper and Brothers, 1868), 91–93, 98–99, 106–7, 123–41; *Life of Faith*, 85–88, 143, 147–53.

111. Upham, *Life of Faith*, 84–88; Fay, *American Psychology Before James*, 97.

112. Upham, *Elements of Mental Philosophy* (Portland, ME: W. Hyde, 1839), 1:212, 214–15; 2:382–91.

113. See, Thomas C. Upham, *Abridgement of Mental Philosophy*, intro. Rand B. Evans (1861; reprint ed., Delmar, NY: Scholars' Facsimilies and Reprints, 1979), and Upham, *Outlines of Imperfect and Disordered Mental Action* (New York: Harper and Brothers, 1968). The quotes are from Evans's introduction to Upham's *Abridgement*, v.

114. John L. Peters, *Christian Perfection and American Methodism* (Nashville: Abingdon Press, 1956); Timothy L. Smith, *Revivalism and Social Reform in Mid-Nineteenth-Century America* (Nashville: Abingdon Press, 1957).

115. William C. Johnson has argued for a backlash against the more enthusiastic side of the tradition in the late 1810s and 1820s, but doesn't specially explore the impact of these reform efforts on the experience of sanctification (" 'To Dance in the Ring of all Creation,' " 127–55); see also McCauley, *Appalachian Mountain Religion*, 118–20. McCauley's claim (118) that "plain folk camp meeting religion" was thereafter "regionally specific to the mountains and foothills of Appalachia" strikes me as unlikely.

116. Kathryn Long, "Consecrated Respectability: Phoebe Palmer and the Refinement of American Methodism," unpublished paper. I would like to thank Scott Cormode for bringing this paper to my attention. On the transition from old-style to refined Methodism, see also, Richard L. Bushman, *The Refinement of America: Persons, Houses, Cities* (New York:

Vintage Books, 1993), 319–326; A. Gregory Schneider, *The Way of the Cross Leads Home: The Domestication of American Methodism* (Bloomington: Indiana University Press, 1993).

117. Upham, *Life of Faith*, 153, quoted in Salter, *Spirit and Intellect*, 186.

118. Perry, "Role of the Camp Meeting," 20–22. Based on the affiliation of 174 adventist lecturers in 1843–44, Everett N. Dick estimated the percentage of Methodists at 44%, Baptists 27%, Congregationalists 9%, Christians 8%, Presbyterians 7% (Perry, "Role of the Camp Meeting," 17). Other studies give little indication of the importance of the Methodist presence in the Millerite movement. David Rowe's study of Millerites in upstate New York, for example, is largely based on Baptist sources. According to Rowe, the Millerite movement went through three phases, an initial Baptist dominated phase centered in upstate New York, a second Christian dominated phase centered in New England, and a third phase, which he describes as a "mass movement" beginning in the 1840s (Rowe, *Thunder and Trumpets*, 35). The evidence provided by Dick and Perry suggests that it is this third phase that was particularly Methodist in its emphasis.

119. Perry, "Role of the Camp Meeting," 170–77, 207–8, 213–17, 236–66.

120. Ruth Alden Doan, "Millerism and Evangelical Culture," in Numbers and Butler, eds., *The Disappointed*, 118–22.

121. Three adventist "songsters" appeared between 1841 and 1843: *Millennial Musings* (1841), *Second Advent Hymns* (1842), and *Millennial Harp* (1843) (Perry, "Role of the Camp Meeting," 161–70).

122. "Jerusalem," which appeared in the *Millennial Harp* (1843) was, according to Perry, the song of choice for the closing of adventist camp meetings (Perry, "Role of the Camp Meeting," 214–15). Although Perry's discussion might lead one to believe that the adventists adapted this song from an Isaac Watts hymn, its appearance in a number of shape-note song books under the title "Never Part" suggests that it was a traditional part of the camp-meeting repertoire. See, "Never Part," McCurry, *Social Harp*, 94.

123. Formal "prayer tents" started to appear at Methodist camp meetings during the 1820s, perhaps replacing the more informal prayer circles and tent gatherings that had preceded them.

124. *Louisville Morning Courier*, October 1, 1844, quoted in Perry, "Role of the Camp Meeting," 256.

125. *New York Herald Extra*, 7, quoted in Perry, "Role of the Camp Meeting," 262.

126. Undated manuscript fragment attributed to Hiram Edson, published in Numbers and Butler, eds., *The Disappointed*, 214–15.

127. Perry, "Role of the Camp Meeting," 258.

128. Doan, "Millerism," 123–25.

129. Doan emphasizes what she refers to as the "radical supernaturalism" of the Millerites. She notes that while the exegetical emphases of the Millerites would be taken up by dispensational premillennialists late in the century, "the beliefs and assumptions—perhaps it would be accurate to say even yearnings—of radical supernaturalism found alternative expression in the related emergence of the Holiness and Pentecostal movements of the late nineteenth and early twentieth centuries" (Doan, *The Miller Heresy, Millennialism, and American Culture* [Philadelphia: Temple University Press, 1987], 214).

130. The classic scholarly study of Ellen G. White is Ronald L. Numbers, *Prophetess of Health: Ellen G. White and the Origins of Seventh-day Adventist Health Reform*, rev. ed. (Knoxville: University of Tennessee Press, 1992). In an afterword, Ronald and Janet Numbers discuss the question of EGW's mental health, concluding that "from youth onward she suffered from recurrent episodes of depression and anxiety to which she responded with somatizing defenses and a histrionic personality style" (203). In a recent essay, Jonathan

Butler interprets Ellen Harmon's illness and ecstasy in light of the anthropological literature of prophesy arguing that the role of the prophet relieved her illnesses rather than aggravating them ("Prophesy, Gender, and Culture," *Religion and American Culture* 6, no. 1 [1991]:15). Given that there were some, such as Southey, who questioned Abbott's mental health, to compare Harmon and Abbott is not necessarily to proclaim Harmon mentally healthy.

131. Ellen G. White, *Spiritual Gifts, My Christian Experience, Views and Labors* (Battle Creek: James White, 1860), 17–18.

132. White, *Spiritual Gifts*, 19.

133. Ellen G. White, "Experience and Views" (August 1851) in *Early Writings of Ellen G. White* (Washington, DC: Review and Herald, 1882),12; White, *Spiritual Gifts*, 20.

134. White, *Spiritual Gifts*, 21–22.

135. Ibid., 26–28.

136. Malcolm Bull and Keith Lockhard, *Seeking a Sanctuary: Seventh-day Adventism and the American Dream* (San Francisco: Harper & Row, 1989), 20.

137. Rowe, *Thunder and Trumpets*, 141.

138. Ibid., 141–50.

139. Ibid., 155.

140. *Proceedings of the Mutual Conference of Adventists held in the City of Albany, the 29th and 30th of April, and 1st of May 1845* (New York, 1845), 30, quoted in Ingemar Lindén, *1844 and the Shut Door Problem* (Uppsala: Uppsala University Press, 1982), 8.

141. I am using the terms "sabbath-keeping" and "sabbatarian" to designate those adventists who designated Saturday as the sabbath, rather than Sunday. This was to become a distinctive feature of the Seventh-day Adventists.

142. Numbers, *Prophetess*, 27–30; Butler, "Prophesy, Gender, and Culture," 19–23.

143. The prophetess, as depicted here, is clearly differentiated from the spiritualist mediums who emerged in the 1850s. While in trance EGW was profoundly separate from her "audience." She "left" them in trance, saw visions, and did not recount them orally or in writing until afterwards. Spiritualist mediums, by way of contrast, "departed" in trance so that the spirits could be present and interact with the "audience" either by speaking through the mouth of the medium or using her hand to write. While there is some effort made to distinguish EGW from spiritualist mediums, for simple chronological reasons this comes as something of an afterthought and is not as crucial to the formation of her religious experience as Methodism and mesmerism.

144. "Trial of Elder I. Dammon," *Piscataquis Farmer*, March 7, 1845, reprinted in Frederick Hoyt, "Trial of Elder I. Dammon Reported for the *Piscataquis Farmer*," *Spectrum* 17, no. 5 (1987):29–36; Numbers and Butler, eds., *The Disappointed*, 227–40; Bruce Weaver, "Incident in Atkinson: The Arrest and Trial of Israel Dammon," *Adventist Currents*, April 1988, 16–36. For discussions of the charges of mesmerism, see, Butler, "Prophesy, Gender and Culture," 13, 16; Numbers, *Prophetess*, 22–24.

145. *Portland Transcript*, November 1, 1945 [sic], quoted in Frederick Hoyt, "We Lift Up Our Voices Like a Trumpet: Millerites in Portland, Maine," *Spectrum* 17, no. 5 (1987):19–20.

146. Rennie Schoepflin, ed., "Scandal or Rite of Passage: Historians on the Dammon Trial," *Spectrum* 17, no. 5 (1987):39; Butler, "Prophesy, Gender, and Culture," 9.

147. Lindén, *1844*, p. 34, n. 40. Lindén also notes that two visionaries were said to have been called to the office as charismatic leaders before Ellen Harmon.

148. White, *Spiritual Gifts*, 40–41.

149. Lindén, *1844*, 50–51. Lindén indicates that moderate adventists had attacked Israel Dammon, John Moody, and Dorinda Baker by name as particularly fanatical and the *Day-Star*, a shut-door publication, had drawn the line at Dammon, admitting that he "was crazy, for everybody said so."

150. Numbers and Butler, eds., *The Disappointed*, 233.

151. The following passage from a published discussion of the trial transcript by a group of leading Adventist historians, indicates the extent to which the trial transcript forced a rethinking of EGW's relationship to "fanaticism" and gives a sense of what these historians found disconcerting *as Adventists*.

> *[Jonathan] Butler*: You cannot tell from this document that she had distanced herself from fanaticism.
> *[Ronald] Graybill*: That's right. It's just that she does say later on that she always condemned some of these practices. You can't tell that from here; this transcript certainly places her psychologically closer to the fanaticism than we had imagined. Part of it is just our feeling about the difference between a woman lying down on the floor, and a woman walking around having a vision.
> *Butler*: It is a striking difference. Here you have a young girl in repose, on her back on a pillow, and all around her, is this tremendous frenzy and turmoil. A few years later, you have a woman standing in trance, and the room is hushed; there is this solemn audience gathered and looking at her in rapt attention ("Scandal or Rite of Passage," 43).

152. Isley Osborn testimony in Hoyt, "Trial," 234.

153. Joel Doore testimony in Hoyt, "Trial," 235.

154. Testimony of Isley Osborn and George S. Woodbury in Hoyt, "Trial," 234–35.

155. Testimony of Loton Lambert and Joel Doore in Hoyt, "Trial," 230, 235. According to Lindén, the early EGW letters from the 1840s typically "include visions and direct 'messages' to various individuals" (Lindén, *1844*, 49).

156. George S. Woodbury testimony in Hoyt, "Trial," 235–36.

157. Lindén, *1844*, 16.

158. White, *Spiritual Gifts*, 39, 45.

159. Ibid., 50–51.

160. Ibid., 57.

161. Horatio W. Dresser, *The Quimby Manuscripts* (New Hyde Park, NY: University Books, 1969), 30–47.

162. White, "Experience," 21.

163. Ibid., 21–22; White, *Spiritual Gifts*, 57–58, 62–63; Numbers, *Prophetess*, 22–24. Numbers notes "White's . . . inability to distinguish empirically between her visions and those of her contemporaries. She distanced herself from other trance mediums not on the basis of physical evidence, but spiritual content" (214).

164. White, "Experience," 22; White, *Spiritual Gifts*, 58.

165. White, "Experience," 23.

166. White, *Spiritual Gifts*, 59.

167. Ellen G. White, *Early Writings* (1963), xxiii–xxiv.

168. Support for this would have to be gleaned from a careful analysis of what remains of the myriad of small sabbatarian broadsheets and newspapers published during the 1840s, as well as the secular press. Adventist historians Ron Graybill and Frederick Hoyt have been engaged in such research for some time.

169. Jonathan Butler makes this argument in Schoepflin, "Scandal," 45.

170. James White, "Preface" (1851) in Ellen G. White, *Early Writings*, vi.

171. *Review*, June 10, 1852 in Ellen G. White, *Early Writings*, 109. I am grateful to Michael Zbaraschuk for locating this reference.

172. *Review & Herald*, February 18, 1862, in [Ellen G. White], *Testimonies for the Church* (Mountain View, CA: Pacific Press, 1948), 1:290–91.

CHAPTER FIVE
EMBODYING SPIRITS

1. Most scholars, in keeping with later controversies within the movement itself, have brought dichotomous categories to their analysis of Spiritualism. This and the next two paragraphs indicate my approach to the three dichotomies most commonly used to interpret the movement: phenomenal vs. philosophical, Christian vs. anti-Christian, and religious vs. naturalistic. For a recent review of dichotomous approaches to the characterization of Spiritualists, see Bret Evan Carroll, "Unfree Spirits: Spiritualism and Religious Authority in Antebellum America" (Ph.D. dissertation, Cornell University, 1991), 17–18.

In identifying what I take to be the core idea of Spiritualism during the 1850s and 1860s, I am deliberately avoiding the distinction between phenomenal and philosophical Spiritualism. Much of the credit for this and other dichotomies that have been used to interpret the movement should go to Andrew Jackson Davis. Beginning in the 1870s, he made a sharp distinction between his "Harmonial Philosophy" and "Modern Spiritualism." He asserted in 1870 that the era of spiritual manifestations was "well-nigh over" and outlined a series of "errors and hurtful superstitions" that had come to pervade the Spiritualist movement. In a speech to the Spiritualists of New York City, delivered in March 1878, he indicated that "there are two very marked tendencies [in Modern Spiritualism]—the gradual formation of two wings, . . . one Rationalistic, the other Christian." Nine months later, he formed the first "Harmonial Society," in which he explicitly differentiated "Modern Spiritualism" from the "Harmonial Philosophy," not, in his words, because they disagreed on essentials, but because they are antagonistic "in the sphere of public uses," that is, with respect to social reform (Andrew Jackson Davis, *The Fountain; with Jets of New Meanings* [Boston: William White & Co., 1870], 210–19; Andrew Jackson Davis, *Beyond the Valley; A Sequel to 'The Magic Staff'* [Boston: Colby and Rich, 1885], 133, 143). As I show in this chapter, Davis's followers and indeed Davis himself were actively involved in making the connections between the Harmonial Philosophy and Modern Spiritualism in the early years of the Spiritualist movement. In fact in the early 1850s, Davis played an important role in interpreting and developing aspects of the movement that he later wanted to reject or deemphasize.

In distinguishing between a phenomenally oriented Spiritualism associated with circles and mediums and a more intellectually oriented Spiritualism associated with the thought of A. J. Davis, some scholars have been attempting to guard against reading the thought of elites into the minds of ordinary people (cf. Carroll, "Unfree Spirits," 16–17). While the latter aim is laudable, it has been overemphasized through assimilation to the phenomenal-philosophical dichotomy. I think it makes more sense to treat Spiritualism as we might treat any other religious movement where differences between elites and ordinary people, leaders and followers, and the more or less committed are both taken for granted and the subject of research. Moreover, that such differences are presumed to exist does not preclude the presence of commonalities of belief and practice across those differences, commonalities that, indeed, constitute the group or movement as such. This chapter is built around what I take to be the core of Spiritualist belief and practice, that which, in effect, defined Spiritualists as Spiritualists.

2. Howard Kerr and Charles L. Crow described Spiritualism as "a kind of 'historical hourglass' through which 'the sands of witchcraft, popular ghostlore, mesmerism, Swedenborgianism, and scientism [poured] . . . then to disperse into Theosophy and parapsychology'" (Howard Kerr and Charles Crow, *The Occult in America: New Historical Perspectives* [Urbana: University of Illinois Press, 1983], 4).

3. Janet Oppenheim, like many others, employs the distinction between Christian and anti-Christian Spiritualists in a dichotomous fashion in her account of British Spiritualism. She, however, recognizes the limits of this analytical construct and concludes that "the most fruitful approach suggests synthesis in place of dichotomy, an emphasis, not on the differences that separated the two branches of nineteenth-century Spiritualism, but on the profound similarities uniting them." Most significantly, she adds, "they shared important attitudes toward religion, improbable though such agreement may initially appear" and points to their common quest for a universal religion (*The Other World: Spiritualism and Psychical Research in England, 1850–1914* [Cambridge: Cambridge University Press, 1985], 63–110, quote, 107–8). Oppenheim, in my view, points in the right direction. My analysis of the first two decades of the movement begins with the idea of a continuum of views with respect to religion rather than two "camps."

4. When it comes to the dichotomy between religion and naturalism, scholars have tended to depict the movement as either religious or naturalistic. Laurence Moore, for example, questioned Emma Hardinge's claim that most nineteenth-century American Spiritualists regarded it "as a religion separate in all respects from any existing sect," suggesting that this was less a statement about Spiritualism as it was than "as she wished it to be" (Emma Hardinge [Britten], *Modern American Spiritualism: A Twenty Years' Record of the Communion between Earth and the World of the Spirits* [New York, 1870; repr. ed., New Hyde Park, NY: University Books, 1970], quoted in R. Laurence Moore, *In Search of White Crows: Spiritualism, Parapsychology, and American Culture* [New York: Oxford University Press, 1977], 42). A. J. Davis also claimed that Spiritualism was not a religion, but he did so in order to undercut the widespread belief that it *was* (*The Fountain*, 210–14). Both Hardinge's claim that Spiritualism was a religion and Davis's claim that it was not were published in 1870. Comparison of the two works suggests that, at least with respect to the first two decades of the movement, Hardinge's claim more accurately reflected the self-understanding of Spiritualists while Davis's claim reflected his own theological agenda. While Britten's *Modern American Spiritualism* was the Spiritualist equivalent of a "denominational" history, Davis's *Fountain* was theologically and not descriptively motivated. In his attack on the idea of Spiritualism as a religion, he conceded that "some of our best workers and most philosophical thinkers have strenuously advocated this error (of a medium-originated religion), as if it were the most solemn and momentous truth—adequate, when believed in and acted upon, to overcome all private human ills, and adequate not less to work in society universal redemption from every form of evil" (223). Moreover, he was quite clear that the reason he did not view Spiritualism as a religion was because it was diverging from what he viewed as *true* religion. Davis, in effect, recapitulated the familiar evangelical theological argument that experience alone cannot count as "true religion." True religion, for Davis, must bear fruit in practice (that is, progressive social reform). By 1870, he had decided that Spiritualism, as "a medium-originated religion," was not giving rise to "practical fruit" and *therefore* should not be considered as (true) religion (223).

Other scholars, such as Bret Evan Carroll, Ann Braude, Mary Farrell Bednarowski, and George Lawton, have argued that Spiritualism was a religious movement with a coherent worldview or theology (Carroll, "Unfree Spirits," 17–21; Ann Braude, *Radical Spirits: Spiritualism and Women's Rights in Nineteenth-Century America* [Boston: Beacon Press, 1989], 4,

12, 19, 32–55; Mary Farrell Bednarowski, "Nineteenth Century American Spiritualism: An Attempt at Scientific Religion" [Ph.D. dissertation, University of Minnesota, 1973], 20–23, 41–76; George Lawton, *The Drama of Life After Death: A Study of Spiritualist Religion* [New York: Henry Holt & Co., 1932]). The key here is recognizing, as Bednarowski argued, that Spiritualism as a movement was simultaneously religious and naturalistic (or in her words, scientific).

5. Emma Hardinge Britten, *Nineteenth Century Miracles . . . A Complete Historical Compendium* (Manchester & London: W. Britten, 1883), 124.

6. The connections between Spiritualism and liberal religion are widely recognized (see, for example, Braude, *Radical Spirits*, 44–49; Moore, *White Crows*, 48–65; Frank Podmore, *Modern Spiritualism*, 2 vols. [London: Methuen, 1902], 1:217–22). Although historians have focused on Spiritualism's difficulties forming formal institutional structures in the seventies, they have largely overlooked that fact that, beginning in the 1850s, Spiritualism possessed informal analogues to many of the traditional structures of Protestant revivalism. In addition to circles that functioned as analogues to Methodist class meetings, there were Sunday morning and afternoon lectures that functioned as analogues to Sunday preaching services, and Spiritualist "picnics" and grove meetings modeled on camp meetings. The *Spirit-Minstral*, one of the earliest Spiritualist songsters, was published in the early 1850s for use by "Meetings for Spiritual Intercourse" and others followed thereafter. Spiritualist mediums and lecturers, like Methodist itinerants, traveled extensively, visiting circles and giving public lectures. For a fuller discussion of Spiritualist organization efforts, see Bret E. Carroll, *Spiritualism in Antebellum America* (Bloomington: Indiana University Press, 1997), 152–62.

7. Hardinge [Britten], *Spiritualism*, 22–23. Frank Podmore (*Modern Spiritualism*), a highly skeptical member of the Society for Psychical Research wrote in 1902: "Historically, . . . Spiritualism is the direct outgrowth of Animal Magnetism. In America, the land of its birth . . . the embryo faith was incubated in the revelations of a 'magnetic' clairvoyant, and its first apostles were drawn mainly from the ranks of those who had studied and practised Animal Magnetism, or attended clairvoyant séances" (1:xiv). Continuity is also presumed in twentieth-century histories of Spiritualism and recent histories of psychology (cf. Oppenheim, *The Other World*, 219–21; Ellenberger, *Discovery*, 82–85; Fuller, *Mesmerism*, 69–104; Gauld, *History*, 214; Crabtree, *Mesmer to Freud*, 229–35). There is some disagreement regarding how much of a break Spiritualism represented relative to what had come before. Robert Fuller tends to blur the differences between interpretations of animal magnetism before and after the rise of the Spiritualist movement; Crabtree and Gauld, in their more recent histories of psychology, tend (as I have) to focus on the differences (Crabtree, *Mesmer to Freud*, 213–35; Gauld, *History*, 189–93).

8. Hardinge [Britten], *Spiritualism*, 22–23.

9. Ibid., 23.

10. Gauld identifies several ways in which Davis "paved the way" for modern American Spiritualism. First, "he accustomed a wide public to the idea that a clairvoyant somnambule might engage not just in medical diagnosis and travelling clairvoyance, but in the transmission of social, religious, and cosmological teachings." Second, he propounded "neo-Swedenborgian doctrines about the future state and the spirit spheres." Third, "he propagated the view that some new and stirring revelation was about to rock mankind" and "implied that this revelation would involve a bursting of the barriers that separate our world from the spiritual one" (Gauld, *History,* 191).

11. Andrew Jackson Davis, *The Magic Staff; An Autobiography*, 7th ed. (1864), 200–3.

12. Ibid., 93–94, 110–11, 200–3.

13. Andrew Jackson Davis, *The Principles of Nature, Her Divine Revelations, and a Voice to Mankind, by and through Andrew Jackson Davis, the 'Poughkeepsie Seer' and 'Clairvoyant'* (New York: Lyon and Fishbough, 1852 [1847]), ix–x, quotes are from William Fishbough's introduction.

14. Davis, *The Magic Staff*, 247.

15. James Stanley Grimes, *The Mysteries of the Head and Heart Explained* (Chicago, 1875), 359–61.

16. On Davis and his revelations see, Robert W. Delp, "Andrew Jackson Davis's *Revelations*, Harbinger of American Spiritualism," *New York Historical Society Quarterly* 60 (1971):211–334; Delp, "Andrew Jackson Davis: Prophet of Spiritualism," *The Journal of American History* 54 (1967):43–56.

17. Davis, *Principles*, xvii, 29. Ellen G. White's entrance into a similar deathlike state while she was "in vision" proved for her followers that her visions were *not* of mesmeric or spiritualist origin (John N. Loughborough, *Rise and Progress of the Seventh-day Adventists* [Battle Creek, MI: General Conference Association of the Seventh-day Adventists, 1892], 94–98).

18. Davis, *Principles*, 35–37.

19. George Bush, *Mesmer and Swedenborg; or, the Relation of the Developments of Mesmerism to the Doctrines and Disclosures of Swedenborg* (1847), 212–13, quoted in Crabtree, *Mesmer to Freud*, 230–31. On Swedenborg's influence on Davis, see Catherine L. Albanese, "On the Matter of Spirit: Andrew Jackson Davis and the Marriage of God and Nature," *Journal of the American Academy of Religion* 60, no. 1 (Spring 1992):1–18.

20. Davis, *Principles*, 514–66, quote, 559; Podmore, *Modern Spiritualism*, 1:170–71. Podmore does not say much about Davis's lectures on the Bible, but he provides a judicious assessment of the rest of the book (*Modern Spiritualism*, 1:160–69). According to George Bush and B. F. Barrett, "Davis['s] . . . work contains enunciations directly at variance not only with the teachings of Swedenborg, but with the creed of the whole Christian world on the great cardinal doctrines of the Bible, and in the character and claims of the Bible itself as revelation" (*"Davis' Revelations" Revealed* [New York: John Allen, 1847], 12–13).

21. Bush published a new English edition of Jung-Stilling's *Pneumatology* in 1851.

22. Eliab W. Capron and Henry D. Barron, *Explanation and History of the Mysterious Communion with Spirits, Comprehending the Rise and Progress of the Mysterious Noises in Western New-York, generally received as Spiritual Communications*, 2nd ed. (New York: Fowler and Wells, 1850), 15; Podmore, *Modern Spiritualism*, 1:179–81.

23. Hardinge [Britten], *Spiritualism*, 36–37.

24. Ibid., 36–37, 39; Braude, *Radical Spirits* 11–12.

25. Hardinge [Britten], *Spiritualism*, 39, 51–54; Werner Sollors, "Dr. Benjamin Franklin's Celestial Telegraph, or Indian Blessings to Gas-Lit American Drawing Rooms," *American Quarterly* 35, no. 5 (1983):465, 468. The earliest reference Hardinge gives is from 1849, when A. H. Jervis writes in response to verification of a spirit message that "God's telegraph has outdone Morse's altogether" (A. H. Jervis to E. W. Capron, n.d., referring to a statement that he made on April 10, 1849, quoted in Hardinge [Britten], *Spiritualism*, 51).

26. The distinction is evident in Emma Hardinge's own life. Although she functioned as a "clairvoyant and magnetic subject" for an occult society when she was a child, she was horrified when she first heard American Spiritualists talking incessantly of "their intercourse with '*Spirits of the dead*' " (Margaret Wilkinson, ed., *Autobiography of Emma Hardinge Britten* [London: John Heywood, 1900], 3–4, 15–16, emphasis in original).

27. Capron and Barron, *Explanation and History*, 80; Gauld, *History*, 192.

28. Hardinge [Britten], *Spiritualism*, 51–52, quote p. 52.

29. Eliab W. Capron, *Modern Spiritualism* (1855; reprint ed., New York : Arno Press, 1976), 113, 117.

30. Capron, *Modern Spiritualism*, 117–20; Carroll, "Free Spirits," 500–2.

31. Capron and Barron, *Explanation and History*, 6–7.

32. Ibid., 8; Moore, *White Crows*, 23–26.

33. Moore, *White Crows*, 7; Fuller, *Mesmerism*, 84.

34. Capron and Barron, *Explanation and History*, 19–26.

35. William Fishbough, *Univercoelum*, Feb. 3, 1849, quoted in Capron and Barron, *Explanations and History*, 31–32.

36. Davis, *Principles* [1847], 675, quoted in ibid., 35.

37. Ibid., 36.

38. Andrew Jackson Davis, *The Philosophy of Spirit Intercourse* (New York: Fowlers and Wells, Pub., 1851), 3, 46–47; on events in Stratford, see Podmore, *Modern Spiritualism*, 1:194–201, 204.

39. Davis, *Spirit Intercourse*, 24–26.

40. Ibid., 26–27.

41. Andrew Jackson Davis, *The Present Age and Inner Life* (New York: Partridge & Brittan, 1853), 76; Braude, *Radical Spirits,* 23–24.

42. Robert W. Delp, "A Spiritualist in Connecticut: Andrew Jackson Davis, the Hartford Years, 1850–1854," *New England Quarterly* 53, no. 3 (1980):346–47; Hardinge [Britten], *Spiritualism*, 70–75.

43. Hardinge [Britten], *Spiritualism*, 82–83.

44. *The Spiritual Telegraph* [hereafter *ST*] 1/1 (May 8, 1852): 4; *ST* 2/1 (May 7, 1853): 4.

45. Andrew Jackson Davis, *The Present Age*, 129–30, 161.

46. Davis, *The Present Age*, 30–31; the extract is from John Lacy, *A Relation of the Dealings of God to his Unworthy Servant, John Lacy, since the time of believing and professing himself inspired* (London, 1708).

47. Davis, *The Present Age*, 156–62.

48. Ibid., 187–97.

49. Rev. H. Mattison, *Spirit-rapping Unveiled! An Exposé of the Origin, History, Theology and Philosophy* (New York: J. C. Derby, 1855), 52–82, quotes pp. 70, 77, 75, 78, 72.

50. "List of Mediums," *Banner of Light* (hereafter *BL*), March 13, 1858.

51. Spiritualists were hampered as well by the absence of mechanical analogues for the more "developed" forms of mediumship; today they could have moved from the spiritual telegraph to the spiritual telephone or spiritual fax machine.

52. Fuller recognizes this shift when he observes: "The further spiritualism drifted toward mediumistic activity, the less likely it was to find mesmerism fit company. Trance mediums receive verbal communications from dead persons, not magnetic fluids" (*Mesmerism*, 99–100). In contrast to Fuller, and following Gauld and others, I include state-based theories within the family of mesmeric theories. This line of interpretation, as we saw in the last chapter, was descended from Mesmer's students Puységuer and Deleuze rather than directly from Mesmer himself.

53. "Lecturers' Appointments and Addresses," *BL*, January 5, 1867.

54. Expanding the traditional Protestant definition of trance as ecstatic and/or visionary out-of-body experience and the traditional mesmeric understanding of trance as a subset of somnambulism, he stated that "[trance] is a much better term by which to signify a

certain *state,* than that of *sleep,* which has often been used in its stead" (Sunderland, *Psychology,* 22–23).

55. The meeting took place on August 9, 1850. La Roy Sunderland, *Spiritual Philosopher*, vol. 1 (1850), 58, quoted in Capron, *Modern Spiritualism,* 209 (emphasis in Capron).

56. *ST* 2/44: 3/173, "New York Conference of Spiritualists," Feb. 21, 1854.

57. *BL*, April 11, 1857; April 24, 1858; October 2, 1858.

58. Carroll, "Free Spirits," 475–83.

59. Elizabeth D. Schull to First Congregational Church of Oberlin [1860], reprinted in *BL*, quoted in Hardinge [Britten], *Spiritualism,* 386.

60. Davis, *Principles,* 514.

61. Ibid., 548, 579, 557–58, 583–92, quote 583.

62. Ibid., 559.

63. Ibid., 559, 563, 566.

64. Ibid., 530–31.

65. Davis, *The Present Age,* 33–35, 42–43.

66. Mattison, *Spirit-rapping,* 89.

67. *ST*, February 18, 1854 and February 25, 1854.

68. At a convention of Spiritualists in Plymouth, Massachusetts, in 1858, it was resolved, among other things, that "Spiritualism and true Christianity are identical[,] . . . the natural Universe . . . is our 'Bible'[,] . . . [and the] evidences [of modern Spiritualism] are not surpassed in efficacy by those of historic Christianity." Dr. Gardner said, by way of elaboration, "I think and believe that the Bible is a beautifully inspired book of many truths; but it does not contain all truth, or but a small part of truth. I believe that the boundless Universe contains the word of God, and nothing is plenary, short of the whole" (*BL*, August 21, 1858).

69. Carroll distinguishes between Spiritualists who considered spirit communication as a replacement for the Bible, those who regarded the Bible itself as a spirit manifestation, those who viewed the Bible and spirit-communication as equally authoritative, and those who viewed the Bible as a higher authority than the spirits ("Unfree Spirits," note, 472–73).

70. J. D. Cox, *Modern Spiritualism compared with Christianity, in a debate between Joel Tiffany, Esq., of Painesville, O[hio] and Rev. Isaac Errett, of Warren, O[hio]* (Warren, Ohio: George Adams, 1855), iv.

71. Ibid..

72. "Mr. Thomas Gales Forster," *BL*, Sept. 24, 1857; "Through the Organism of Mr. Thomas Gales Forster, at the Music Hall, Sunday Morning, August 2, 1857," *BL*, Sept. 17, 1857. As the longest-lived and most widely circulated of Spiritualist periodicals, the *Banner* was, according to Ann Braude, decidedly "moderate" in its views ("News from the Spirit World: A Checklist of American Spiritualist Periodicals, 1847–1900," *American Antiquarian Society* 99, no. 2 [1989]:410).

73. "To the Thoughtful," *BL*, Sept. 3, 1857.

74. Edward Whipple, *A Biography of James M. Peebles, M.D., A.M.* (Battle Creek, MI: Published by the Author, 1901), 150.

75. James M. Peebles, *Jesus: Myth, Man, or God; or, The Popular Theology and the Positive Religion Contrasted* (London: J. Burns, 1870), 6, 88, 96. The Spiritualist Society of Louisville, Kentucky, formally incorporated as "The Friends of Progress and Free Religion," *Statement in relation the Opinions of Spiritualists as to the Fatherhood of God, the Brotherhood of all Men, Sin and Punishment, Infinite Progression, the Bible Sustaining Spiritualism, the Mediumship of Jesus, and the Good of Spiritualism* (Louisville, Ky.: Dearing, 1870), 1, 14. After

resigning from the Universalist ministry in 1856, James Peebles served as pastor of the "First Free Church of Battle Creek," a congregation of Spiritualists, Unitarians, Universalists, Quakers, and Free Thinkers (Whipple, *Biography of Peebles*, 70–71). The editors of *The Banner of Light* often referred to themselves as promoting the liberalization of Christianity or religion.

76. "Sabbath in Boston: Mrs. Hyser at the Melodeon," *BL*, July 17, 1858; "Meetings at the Melodeon [Sunday afternoon Spirit-Discourse]," *BL*, June 25, 1857; "Address of Thomas G. Forster [Spirit-discourse at the Melodeon on John 18:1]," *BL*, Sept., 10, 1857.

77. For a modern reading not unlike that generated by the Spiritualists, see Stevan L. Davies, *Jesus the Healer: Possession, Trance, and the Origins of Christianity* (New York: Continuum, 1995). Laurence Moore notes the difficulties that the Spiritualist reading of biblical miracles posed for their opponents, especially those Protestants who denied "modern miracles" while using biblical miracles to defend the authority of scripture (47–48). Little attention has been given to the Spiritualists' interest in Christian origins. The most extended treatment is in Bednarowski, "American Spiritualism," 54–58; see also, Moore, *White Crows*, 55; Oppenheim, *The Other World*, 222–23.

78. "Bible Evidence of Spiritualism," *BL*, July 2, 1857; "Spiritualism in All Things," *BL*, June 11, 1857; A. B. C., "Correspondence: Bible Spiritualism," *BL*, April 24, 1857.

79. R. P. Ambler, "'Spirits' through R. P. Ambler—Teacher," quoted in Mattison, *Spirit-rapping*, 89; *Opinions of Spiritualists*, 17–21; Editorial, "Spiritualism at Milford, and the *Christian Freeman*," *BL*, March 6, 1858.

80. "Telegraph, No. 34," quoted in Mattison, *Spirit-rapping*, 87; Editorial, "Spiritualism at Milford, and the *Christian Freeman*," *BL*, March 6, 1858.

81. "Spiritualism at the Music Hall and the Melodeon, June 28," *BL*, July 16, 1857; Editorial, "The Resurrection," *BL*, Feb. 6, 1858; "[*Spiritual*] *Telegraph*, no. 34," quoted in Mattison, *Spirit-rapping*, 86–87.

82. W. H. Porter, "Mrs. Henderson and Meeting at the Melodeon," *BL*, May 21, 1857.

83. Mattison, *Spirit-rapping*, 88.

84. "Address of Thomas G. Forster," Sept. 10, 1857; "Meetings at the Melodeon and the Music Hall, June 21," *BL*, July 21, 1857; *Opinions of Spiritualists*, 21.

85. Cox, *Modern Spiritualism*, v.

86. Ibid., 178.

87. Ibid., 182 (emphasis in original).

88. Ibid., 158, 200.

89. Ibid., 178, 182.

90. Message given by the spirit of John Hubbard, of Hanover, N.H., *BL*, April 18, 1857:6; "Laying on of Hands," *BL*, July 30, 1857.

91. Letter from B. S. Hobbs to the *Ambassador*, quoted in "Spiritualism in the Pulpit," *BL*, June 18, 1857.

92. "Our Admonitions Attested," *BL*, July 2, 1857.

93. J. M. Peebles, "Dr. Eli Ballou a Spiritualist," *BL*, Jan. 5, 1867, p. 8.

94. *BL*, Feb. 29, 1867, 3.

95. "New York Conference of Spiritualists," *ST*, Feb. 21, 1854; "Free Convention at Rutland, Vermont," *BL*, July 10, 1858.

96. William Howitt, *The History of the Supernatural in all Ages and Nations, and in all Churches, Christian and Pagan: Demonstrating a Universal Faith*, 2 vols. (London: Longman, et al., 1863).

97. Ibid., 1:115.

98. Ibid., 1:17–18.

99. Ibid., 1:224.

100. Ibid., 1:1.

101. James M. Peebles, *Seers of the Ages: Embracing Spiritualism Past and Present* (Boston: William White, 1869), 192.

102. Peebles, *Seers*, 180–81.

103. Ibid., 80. Peebles introduces the "mythic Christ" terminology in *Jesus: Myth, Man, or God*. In *Seers*, he refers, less intelligibly, to the "historic Jesus, copied from the Chrisna of India" (80).

104. Peebles, *Seers*, 81–82, 88.

105. Peebles, *Jesus*, 6.

106. William Howitt, "Anti-christian Spiritualism," *Spiritual Magazine* (Jan. 1870), quoted in Peebles, *Jesus*, 37, 39, 55.

107. Peebles, *Seers*, 94.

108. Peebles, *Jesus*, 103, 105. Peebles's formulation of the universals of religion parallels that of present day Unitarian-Universalists (minus the angels and spirits!) and suggests that far more of that denomination's heritage than it has heretofore acknowledged can perhaps be traced back to its involvement with Spiritualism. Stephen Prothero makes a similar observation about the parallels between Protestant liberalism (as manifest at Harvard Divinity School) and Theosophy, one of the later off-shoots of Spiritualism (*The White Buddhist: The Asian Odyssey of Henry Steel Olcott* [Bloomington, IN: Indiana University Press, 1996], ix–x.

109. Alex Owen provides a helpful analysis of the role of "mind passivity" in mediumship and an insightful discussion of the dynamics underlying the Spiritualist construction of reality (*The Darkened Room: Women, Power and Spiritualism in Late Victorian England* [Philadelphia: University of Pennsylvania Press, 1990], 213, 222).

110. In discussing the mechanism by which Spiritualists contributed to the liberalization of Protestant thought, I had in mind Ann Braude's argument regarding Spiritualism's contribution to women's rights.

111. "Meetings in Boston: Mr. H. B. Storer's Lectures," *BL*, May 1, 1858.

112. "Meetings at the Melodeon and the Music Hall, June 21," *BL*, July 2, 1857. For a fuller discussion of Hardinge's views, see Joscelyn Godwin, *The Theosophical Enlightenment* (Albany: SUNY Press, 1994), 202–4.

113. "Spiritualism at the Music Hall and the Melodeon, June 28," *BL*, July 16, 1857.

114. "Early Manifestations," *BL*, April 30, 1857; "Lectures Last Sunday," *BL*, May 22, 1858.

115. "Messages from an Arabian Prophet," *ST*, May 8, 1852.

116. Hardinge, *Spiritualism*, 481–82.

117. Ibid., 482, 489.

118. Ibid. Hardinge discusses her investigation of Western occult traditions in Hardinge Britten, *Miracles*, 436–43. Her book *Art Magic* was published in 1875, the same year that Blavatsky and Olcott founded the Theosophical Society. While Britten moved into the Western occult tradition, Theosophy was drawn more toward Asian religions. There was considerable overlap, however, as Hardinge indicates.

119. James Burns, "Human Nature," July 1, 1870, quoted in J. O. Barrett, *The Spiritual Pilgrim: A Biography of James M. Peebles* (Boston: William White and Co., 1872), 59–60.

120. Letter dated Nov. 12, 1861, quoted in Barrett, *Spiritual Pilgrim*, 77; Whipple, *Biography of Peebles*, 113.

121. Barrett, *Spiritual Pilgrim*, 104; Whipple, *Biography of Peebles*, 146; Peebles quote in Barrett, *Spiritual Pilgrim*, 106; Whipple, *Biography of Peebles*, 148.

122. Whipple, *Biography of Peebles*, 129.

123. Ibid., 503, quoted in Sally Jean Morita, "Modern Spiritualism and Reform in America" (Ph.D. dissertation, University of Oregon, 1995), 568–69. Morita provides the only extended discussion of Peebles that I have found in a secondary work on Spiritualism (cf. 511–85).

124. K. Paul Johnson, *The Masters Revealed: Madame Blavatsky and the Myth of the Great White Lodge* (Albany: SUNY Press, 1994), 78.

125. Thomas A. Tweed, *The American Encounter with Buddhism, 1844–1912* (Bloomington: Indiana University Press, 1992), 1–25, 48–77. On his characterization of esoteric Buddhists, see 50–51, 54. For a particular instance of the movement from Protestantism to Spiritualism to Theosophy to Buddhism, see Prothero, *The White Buddhist*, 14–61; on connections between Transcendentalism and Spiritualism, see Braude, *Radical Spirits*, 44–46.

126. Edward Tylor, *Primitive Culture*, 2 vols. (London: John Murray, 1871); reprinted as *The Origins of Culture* [hereafter, *OC*] (Gloucester, MA: Peter Smith, 1970) and *Religion in Primitive Culture* [hereafter, *RPC*] (Gloucester, MA: Peter Smith, 1970); *OC*, 156.

127. *OC*, 142; *RPC*, 10, 12.

128. *RPC*, 9–10, 83–84. In his discussion of rites and ceremonies—the practical side of animistic doctrine—Tyler also commented on revivalistic phenomena. He pointed to "ecstatic physical conditions," in particular, as having a "close alliance" with animistic religion. Such conditions, he said, are produced by interfering with the "healthy action of body and mind." Like Jonathan Edwards, Tylor singled out fasting as "among the strongest means of disturbing the functions of the mind so as to produce ecstatic vision" (ibid., 496). Other practices, such as "bodily exercises, chanting, and screaming," can also produce "ecstasy and swoon," he said. He identified "the practice of bringing on swoons or fits by religious exercises . . . [as] one belonging originally to savagery, [which] . . . has been continued into higher graces of civilization" (ibid., 505).

> In its morbid nature, [the phenomena of being "struck" down] . . . plainly correspond with the fits which history records among the convulsionnaires of St. Medard and the enthusiasts of the Cevennes. Nor need we go even a generation back to see symptoms of the same type accepted as signs of grace among ourselves. Medical descriptions of the scenes brought on by fanatical preachers at 'revivals' in England, Ireland, and America, are full of interest to students of the history of religious rites. . . . Such descriptions carry us far back in the history of the human mind, showing modern men still in ignorant sincerity producing the very fits and swoons to which for untold ages savage tribes have given religious import. (Ibid., 506–7)

129. George W. Stocking, Jr., "Animism in Theory and Practice: E. B. Tylor's Unpublished 'Notes on Spiritualism,' " *Man* 6, no. 1 (March 1971):89–91.

130. George W. Stocking, Jr., *Victorian Anthropology* (New York: The Free Press, 1987), 192.

131. A. J. Davis, "The Table of Explanation," in *The Present Age*, 197–98.

132. Davis, *The Present Age*, 145–46.

133. Joel Tiffany, "Psychological and Spiritual Phenomena," *BL*, June 26, 1858.

134. "New York Conference of Spiritualists," *ST*, Feb. 21, 1854.

135. Capron, *Modern Spiritualism*, 204–17; "Mrs. Margaret Evins Sunderland Cooper," *BL*, Sept. 4, 1858; Podmore, *Modern Spiritualism*, 1:204–6. Capron wrote of Sunderland in 1855: "That he was an enthusiast, none can doubt who knows his temperament, and has kept an eye on his course for the last twenty years. His ardent temperament would hardly

allow him to take a half-way, or even moderate, position on any subject" (*Modern Spiritualism*, 205).

136. Sunderland, *Human Nature*, 229–41, quote 229; Sunderland, *The Trance*, vii.

137. Sunderland to Howard, April 22, 1872, 25–26; James Monroe Buckley, "La Roy Sunderland," *Christian Advocate*, June 11, 1885.

138. Sunderland, *Psychology*, 42.

139. Sunderland, *Trance*, 9, 18; see also *Psychology*, 44–45.

140. La Roy Sunderland, "Letter to the editor," *BL*, Nov. 13, 1858.

141. See, for example, the chapter on attention in Dugald Stewart, *The Collected Works of Dugald Stewart*, 11 vols., ed. William Hamilton (Edinburgh: Thomas Constable & Co., 1854), 3:120–43.

142. Emphasis in quote one is added; emphasis in quote two is modified.

143. In his famous work on possession, Oesterreich distinguishes between "somnambulistic" and "lucid" possession. Sunderland's analysis can be described as limited to "somnambulistic possession," whereas Paul, and following him mainline Protestants, cultivated a form of conscious or "lucid possession" (Oughourlian, *The Puppet of Desire*, 96 makes this distinction drawing on Oesterreich [1927:56, 63]).

CHAPTER SIX
EXPLAINING TRANCE

1. Paul Starr, *The Social Transformation of Medicine* (New York: Basic Books, 1982), 82.

2. Starr, *Social Transformation*, 95, 102, 112–15.

3. George M. Beard, *The Scientific Basis of Delusions: A New Theory of Trance and Its Bearings on Human Testimony* (New York: G. P. Putnams' Sons, 1877), i.

4. Edward M. Brown, "Neurology and Spiritualism in the 1870s," *Bulletin of the History of Medicine* 57 (1983):563–64.

5. S. E. D. Shortt, "Physicians and Psychics: The Anglo-American Medical Response to Spiritualism, 1870–1890," *Journal of the History of Medicine and Allied Sciences* 39 (1984):344.

6. Beard, *Delusions*, i.

7. "Mme. Blavatsky. Her Experience—Her Opinion of American Spiritualism and American Society," *Spiritual Scientist* 1, no. 13 (3 Dec. 1874):148–49; Charles E. Rosenberg, "The Place of George M. Beard in Nineteenth-Century Psychiatry," *Bulletin of the History of Medicine* 36 (1962):245.

8. A. D. Rockwell, *Rambling Recollections: An Autobiography* (New York: Paul B. Hoeber, 1920), 183–85.

9. George M. Beard, "Psychology of Spiritism," *North American Review* 129 (1879):67, 70; Beard, *Delusions*, ii–v.

10. Beard, *Delusions*, 27.

11. Ibid., ii, vii, 19–21, 27–29. According to Beard, "this subjective theory of trance, and in conjunction with it the physiological law announced in this treatise, that no human being has any qualities different in *kind* from those that belong to the species in general, . . . is derived from all physiological observation. It is, more over, an inevitable deduction from the theory of evolution, according to which all new qualities are the result of slow development. If any human being were found to possess a sixth sense, the evolution theory, as now understood, would be entirely overthrown" (ii). He acknowledged that the normal senses may be heightened under trance and argued that "these exaltations of the normal

senses are the bases of many of the popular and professional delusions relating to 'second sight,' 'clairvoyance,' 'thought reading,' and the like" (21).

12. Ibid., 5.

13. Ibid., 6–7, 17.

14. Ibid., 14.

15. Ibid., 12–13.

16. Sunderland, *Psychology*, 13–14; Gauld, *History*, 363.

17. Beard, *Delusions*, 15–16; Azam was the first to develop a theoretical framework for understanding cases of double consciousness (Gauld, *History*, 363–69).

18. Gauld, *History*, 369.

19. J. Gordon Melton, "Christian Science-Metaphysical Family," *Encyclopedia of American Religions* [hereafter, *EAR*], 3 vols. [Tarrytown, NY: Triumph Books, 1991], 2:xx.

20. Horatio W. Dresser, ed., *The Quimby Manuscripts* [hereafter *QM*] (1921; reprint ed., New Hyde Park, NY: University Books, 1961), 78 (emphasis added). Despite referring to himself as "a medium," Quimby did not identify himself as a Spiritualist. He writes of himself during the 1850s: "He is not a spiritualist as is commonly understood, believing that he receives his power from departed spirits. But he believes the power is general and can be learned if persons would only consent to be taught" (*QM*, 83, 188).

21. Fuller argues that "[Quimby] moved mesmerism one step closer to modern psychiatry by specifically identifying faulty ideas—not magnetic fluids—as the root of all American nervousness (Fuller, *Mesmerism*, 121). He concludes that Quimby and his disciples set loose an ideological current which brushed aside concern for the mesmeric state of consciousness" (136). Robert Peel notes the importance of clairvoyance in Quimby's thought and gives the Dressers credit for obscuring it (Robert Peel, *Mary Baker Eddy: The Years of Trial* [New York: Holt, Rinehart and Winston, 1971], 208–9).

22. *QM*, 341 (emphasis added). Dresser inserted the word "organism." Dresser commented on this: "A mesmerizer or spiritist medium has, in Quimby's description, but one identity; while he, Quimby, when clairvoyant has two" (426).

23. *QM*, 191, 342.

24. Ibid., 189, 342.

25. Ibid., 341.

26. Ibid., 191.

27. Swedenborg referred to God as Wisdom and the idea was probably drawn directly or indirectly from him; on the influence of Andrew Jackson Davis and Swedenborg on Quimby, see Robert Peel, *Mary Baker Eddy: The Years of Discovery* (New York : Holt, Rinehart and Winston, 1966), 163.

28. *QM*, 201, 348.

29. Ibid., 409, partially quoted in Peel, *Eddy-Discovery*, 163.

30. *QM*, 198–99.

31. Ibid., 346, 369.

32. Ibid., 373.

33. Ibid., 347.

34. Ibid., 342. Dresser inserts "or intuitive" in brackets after "clairvoyant."

35. Ibid., 303.

36. Ibid., 305.

37. Mary Baker Glover, *Science and Health* [hereafter *SH*-1875] (Boston: Christian Scientist Publishing Co., 1875), 70.

38. Glover, *SH*-1875, 64–65 (emphasis added).

39. In later editions, Eddy refers to the "personal sense" as "corporeal, material, or physical" senses. I am basing my reading on a comparison of the 1875, 1881, and 1890 editions with the current edition.

40. Glover, *SH*-1875, 86.

41. Ibid., 80–81, 86, 100.

42. Ibid., 81–82.

43. *QM*, 245.

44. Glover, *SH*-1875, 124. Eddy refers to "imaginary self-hood" in *SH*-1875, 122.

45. Ibid., 121.

46. Ibid., 130.

47. "In the New Thought writers who went back to Quimby for inspiration the one common element is an emphasis on the 'God within' or the 'Christ within,' whereas Mrs. Eddy's writings constantly insist that God is not *in* man. . . . [In Quimby] God, Christ, 'scientific man,' and science are used as synonyms, and they all refer essentially to the higher processes of the human mind rather than to the 'Wholly Other' of Christian encounter" (Peel, *Eddy-Discovery*, 170).

48. Mary Baker Eddy, *Science and Health*, 3rd. ed., rev., 2 vols. [hereafter *SH*-1881] (Lynn, MA: Dr. Asa G. Eddy, 1881), 2:82, 86–87, 90–91; Stephen Gottschalk, *The Emergence of Christian Science in American Religious Life* (Berkeley: University of California Press, 1973), 20–21, 249–50.

49. Gottschalk, *Emergence*, 249–50.

50. Mary Baker Eddy, *Science and Health* (Boston: First Church of Christ, Scientist, 1994), xi, quoted in Gottschalk, *Emergence*, 216–17.

51. A. Farlow, "Historical Facts concerning Mary Baker Eddy and Christian Science," quoted in Peel, *Eddy-Discovery*, 212.

52. *QM*, 189.

53. Glover, *SH*-1875, 111.

54. Mary Baker G. Eddy, *Science and Health* [hereafter *SH*-1890] (Boston: By the Author, 1890), 256.

55. Stephen Prothero, "From Spiritualism to Theosophy: 'Uplifting' a Democratic Tradition," *Religion and American Culture* 3, no. 2 (summer 1993):204.

56. Bret E. Carroll, "The Religious Construction of Masculinity in Victorian America: The Male Mediumship of John Shoebridge Williams," *Religion and American Culture* 7, no. 1 (winter 1997):40.

57. Sunderland, *Human Nature*, 299, 317–18. On women and passivity, see Ann Braude, "The Perils of Passivity: Women's Leadership in Spiritualism and Christian Science," in Catherine Wessinger, ed., *Women's Leadership in Marginal Religions* (Urbana: University of Illinois Press, 1993), 55–67.

58. John Patrick Deveney, *Paschal Beverly Randolph: A Nineteenth-Century Black American Spiritualist, Rosicrucian, and Sex Magician* (Albany: SUNY Press, 1997), xxvii, 21–29; quote, 24–25.

59. Deveney, *Randolph*, 95–96 (emphasis added).

60. Ibid., 74–75.

61. Blavatsky, *Isis Unveiled*, 2 vols. (1877; reprinted, Pasadena: Theosophical University Press, 1976), 1:487–94; Helena Blavatsky, *The Key to Theosophy* (1889; reprint ed., Covina, CA: Theosophical University Press, 1946), 335–36; Deveney, *Randolph*, 283; Stephen Prothero, *The White Buddhist: The Asian Odyssey of Henry Steel Olcott* (Bloomington: Indiana University Press, 1996), 45–46; Prothero, "From Spiritualism to Theosophy," 203–4.

62. Deveney, *Randolph*, 111. Prothero argues that Theosophy represented an elite attempt to reform Spiritualism from above ("From Spiritualism to Theosophy," 198).

63. Henry S. Olcott, "Eastern Magic and Western Spiritualism [1875]," in Olcott, *Applied Theosophy and Other Essays* (Madras: Theosophical Publishing House, 1975), 242. I am grateful to Stephen Prothero for sharing copies of these obscure Theosophical sources.

64. Olcott, "Eastern Magic and Western Spiritualism," 207, 244, 219.

65. Paul Johnson, *The Masters Revealed*, 75–79; Prothero, *White Buddhist*, 62–75. Johnson describes the Spiritualist James Peebles as "one of the least-known yet most influential figures in Theosophical history" (75). Peebles was the unnamed friend described by Prothero (p. 63) as making the initial connection between Olcott, Blavatsky and their Asian correspondents.

66. Henry S. Olcott, "The Common Foundation of All Religions," *A Collection of Lectures* (Madras, 1883); reprinted in Olcott, *Applied Theosophy*, 45–46. Prothero states that Olcott located the "point of sympathy [of all religions] in history rather than psychology" (Prothero, *White Buddhist*, 149). I disagree with Prothero on this point and assume that he was unaware that Ennemoser's and Howitt's histories were psychologically informed.

67. Olcott, "Common Foundation," 51–54.

68. Ibid., 65, 69.

69. Ibid., 72, 74–75.

70. Blavatsky, *Key*, 7–9, 79–80, 369; see also, Blavatsky, *Isis Unveiled*, 2:337–40.

71. Blavatsky, *Isis Unveiled*, 2:33–34, 150, 201.

72. Blavatsky, *Key*, 79–80; Blavatsky, *Isis Unveiled*, 2:561.

73. Blavatsky, *Isis Unveiled*, 2:574; Blavatsky, *The Key*, 369.

74. Blavatsky, *The Key*, 67–68, 71, 323. Blavatsky corrected those Christian Theosophists who were identifying the Christos with either the Buddhi or with Atman (67), saying that technically it was equivalent to Buddhi, Mana and Atman (or "the abstract Spirit, . . . the Higher or reincarnating Ego, and the Universal Self") and thus the equivalent of the Christian Trinity, esoterically understood.

75. Blavatsky, *Isis Unveiled*, 2:558.

76. Julius Dresser, *The True History of Mental Science* (Boston: Alfred Budge and Sons, 1887), 20–21.

77. For later recountings of this history, see Horatio W. Dresser, *Health and the Inner Life: An Analytical and Historical Study of Spiritual Healing Theories, with an Account of the Life and Teachings of P. P. Quimby* (New York: G. P. Putman's Sons, 1906); Charles Braden, *Spirits in Rebellion: The Rise and Development of New Thought* (Dallas: Southern Methodist University Press, 1984) appropriates and extends this basic historical narrative.

78. John F. Teahan, "Warren Felt Evans and Mental Healing: Romantic Idealism and Practical Mysticism in Nineteenth-Century America," *Church History* 48 (March 1979):64–65.

79. W. F. Evans, *The Mental Cure* (1869), 252, quoted in Peel, *Eddy-Discovery*, 302.

80. Evans, *The Mental Cure*, 6th ed. (Boston: Colby and Rich, 1884), 177–79. Specifically, Evans says: "I do not refer to what is usually called clairvoyance, which is a much less spiritual state. They are not subject to what passes under the name of the trance, a magnetic sleep either self-induced or imposed upon them by another. They are not in a somnambulistic state, but in perfect consciousness and wakefulness. Yet they see with more or less clearness, either with the eye open or shut, in the light or in the darkness, hundreds of miles away, so that they can describe persons, and even places, with great particularity and exactness. . . . This state is far higher and more spiritual than ordinary clairvoyance" (178).

81. Evans, *Mental Cure*, 195–96.

82. Ibid., 263–65.

83. Ibid., 269.

84. Ibid., 269–70 (emphasis in original).

85. Ibid., 270, 76–77; W. F. Evans, *Soul and Body; or, The Spiritual Science of Health and Disease* (Boston: H. H. Carter, 1876), 93–94, 96–97.

86. Evans, *Soul and Body*, 1876.

87. W. F. Evans, *Esoteric Christianity and Mental Therapeutics* (Boston: H. H. Carter & Karrick, 1886), 14–15.

88. Evans, *Esoteric Christianity*, 16.

89. Peel, *Eddy-Trial*, 208–9.

90. See, for example, *QM*, 342.

91. H. W. Dresser, *Health and the Inner Life*, 247–49.

92. James Monroe Buckley, "Our New Vocation," *Christian Advocate* (June 3, 1880).

93. Buckley, "Faith-Healing and Kindred Phenomena," *The Century Illustrated Monthly Magazine* 32 New Series, no. 10 (May 1886–October 1886):221; reprinted as *Faith-Healing, Christian Science, and Kindred Phenomena* (New York: The Century Co., 1898).

94. Buckley, "Dealing with Spiritualism," *Christian Advocate* 57, no. 22 (June 1, 1882):1.

95. W. H. Daniels, ed., *Dr. Cullis and His Work* (Boston, 1885; reprint ed., New York: Garland Pub., Inc., 1985); Raymond J. Cunningham, "From Holiness to Healing: The Faith Cure in America 1872–1892, *Church History* 43 (1972):499–502.

96. "Faith Convention at Old Orchard," *Zion's Herald* 59, no. 32 (Aug. 9, 1882):253.

97. *Christian Advocate*, 57, no. 34 (Aug. 24, 1882):530.

98. Cunningham, "Holiness to Healing," 504.

99. L. T. Townsend, *"Faith-work," "Christian Science" and Other Cures* (New York: Phillips & Hunt, 1885), 28.

100. Buckley, *Faith-Healing*, 19–20, 28–32. Among the mental physiology texts he mentions are: Dr. Hack Tuke, *Illustrations of the Influence of the Mind on the Body* (1872); William Carpenter, *Principles of Mental Physiology* (1874); Henry Holland, *Chapters on Mental Physiology* (1852). They are discussed in Gauld, *History*, 199, 287, 298, 305, 348–49, 368, 463, 520–21. He describes two experiments that he conducted in 1868 designed to demonstrate that "the effects attributed to animal magnetism were the result of subjective mental conditions," one with a literary club comprised of the educated elite of Stamford, Connecticut, and the other at a public lecture to a thousand people at the City Hall in Dover, New Hampshire (*Faith-Healing*, 28–32).

101. Buckley, *Faith-Healing*, 38–41.

102. Ibid., 33–35. For descriptions of some of Buckley's cures, see, 22–24.

103. Ibid., 42.

104. Ibid., 22–24, 28–32. The letter quoted was from Professor E. A. Fuertes, Dean of the Department of Civil Engineering at Cornell University. It was written in January 1886 at Buckley's request and described what Fuertes recalled of the meeting in 1868.

105. On miracles, see, Bruce Mullin, *Miracle and the Modern Religious Imagination* (New Haven: Yale University Press, 1996), 101–7.

106. Buckley, "La Roy Sunderland," *Christian Advocate* 60, no. 23 (June 4, 1885):2.

107. Ibid., 60, no. 22 (May 28, 1885):1.

108. Ibid., vol. 60, no. 23 (June 4, 1885):2.

109. Buckely, *Faith-Healing*, 60–61; see also, Buckley, *History of Methodism*, 2 vols. (New York: Harper & Bros., 1898), 1:261–62.

110. Buckley, *Faith-Healing*, 61–64.

111. Mullin, *Miracle*, 143–78.

112. Daniels, ed., *Dr. Cullis*, 340–41.

113. Carrie Judd, "Ancient and Modern Spiritualism Considered in the Light of God's Word," *Triumph of Faith* 6, no. 10 (October 1886):231.

114. Ibid., 233. Judd is undoubtedly referring to a passage in Buckley's book where a reporter who attended at a demonstration conducted by Buckley was quoted as stating that *he* (the reporter) had been "at perhaps over a hundred séances of mesmeric, biologic, and so-called spiritual subjects or mediums" (Buckley, *Faith-Healing*, 31).

115. The Rev. W. T. Hogg, " 'Christian Science' Unmasked," *Triumphs of Faith* 10, no. 9 (Sept. 1890):198–99; see also, 10, no. 10 (October 1890):224–27; 10, no. 11 (Nov. 1890):252–55; 10, no.12 (Dec. 1890):265–68; 11, no. 1 (Jan. 1891):4–7. Other articles on Christian Science include: A. J. Gordon, " 'Christian Science' Tested by Scripture," *Triumphs of Faith* 6, no. 12 (Dec. 1886):276–80; The Rev. E. P. Marvin, "Christian Science (Not Christian and Not Science)," *Triumphs of Faith* 9, no. 3 (March 1889):52–54; Anna W. Prosser, "So Called 'Christian Science,' " *Triumphs of Faith* 10, no. 3 (March 1890):49–52. Edith Blumhofer indicates that the perception of Christian Science as a particular threat continued with the emergence of Pentecostalism. She comments: "The perception of Christian Science as an arch enemy suggests how close evangelical teaching on healing and Christian Science teaching were. When early Pentecostals listed their enemies, Christian Science usually led the list. Early Pentecostal periodicals contain many articles exposing the errors of Christian Science suggesting that they felt especially threatened by it" (Edith Blumhofer, *Restoring the Faith: The Assemblies of God, Pentecostalism, and American Culture* [Urbana: University of Illinois Press, 1993], 37, n. 32).

116. J.C.W., "'Faith-Healing and Kindred Phenomena,'" *Christian Science Journal* 4, no. 6 (Sept. 1886):137–38; Gottschalk, *Emergence*, 222–23.

117. Grant Wacker, "The Holy Spirit and the Spirit of the Age in American Protestantism, 1880–1910," *Journal of American History* 72, no. 1 (June 1985):48; Timothy L. Smith, *Called Unto Holiness* (Kansas City, MO: Nazarene Pub. House, 1962), 24–25; Jean Miller Schmidt, "Holiness and Perfection," *Encyclopedia of American Religious Experience*, 813–29.

118. A. McLean and J. W. Eaton, eds., *Penuel: or, Face to Face with God* (New York: W. C. Palmer, 1869; reprint ed., New York: Garland Pub. Co., 1984), 3–4, 12.

119. Ibid., 5–7.

120. Ibid., 5, 13.

121. D. Gregory Van Dussen, "The Bergen Camp Meeting in the American Holiness Movement," *Methodist History* 21, no. 2 (Jan. 1983):77–78.

122. B. T. Roberts, *Why Another Sect?* (Rochester, NY, 1879), 118, 121–22 and B. T. Roberts, *The Earnest Christian*, July 1861, p. 226, quoted in Van Dussen, "Bergen Camp Meeting," 86–87.

123. Long, "Consecrated Respectability," 28, internal quotes are from Elias Bowen, *History of the Origin of the Free Methodist Church* (Rochester, 1871), 20, 230, 231.

124. G. W. Henry, *Shouting in All Ages of the Church* (Oneida, NY: For the author, 1859; reprinted as *Shouting, Genuine and Spurious* [Chicago: Metropolitan Church Association, 1903]), 301, 289.

125. Henry, *Shouting*, 369–71.

126. Ibid., 22–23, 197–98. He includes a slightly different version of "The Methodist and the Formalist" under the title, "Good Morning, Brother Pilgrim!" (217–19).

127. Ibid., 225–28; his excerpts from Wesley continue, 330–48.

128. Ibid., 265–66, 268–73, 274–89.

129. Ibid., 290–357, quote, p. 349.

130. B. T. Roberts, ed., *The Earnest Christian*, Aug. 1860, 255, quoted in Van Dussen, "Bergen Camp Meeting," 86.

131. Galusha Anderson, *When Neighbors Were Neighbors* (Boston, 1911), 106, quoted in Van Dussen, "Bergen Camp Meeting," 87. See also, Roger Robins, "Vernacular American Landscape: Methodists, Camp Meetings, and Social Responsibility," *Religion and American Culture* 4, no. 2 (summer 1994):175.

132. Charles Edwin Jones, *Perfectionist Persuasion: The Holiness Movement and American Methodism, 1867–1936* (Metuchen, NJ: Scarecrow Press, 1974), 47–61. For a discussion of the conceptions of self underlying the divergent tendencies with the M.E.C., see A. Gregory Schneider, "Objective Selves Versus Empowered Selves: The Conflict over Holiness in the Post-Civil War Methodist Episcopal Church," *Methodist History* 32, no. 4 (July 1994):237–49.

133. W. McDonald and John E. Searles, *The Life of Rev. John S. Inskip* (Boston: McDonald & Gill, 1885; reprint ed., New York: Garland, 1985), 186, 196–97.

134. Quoted in John L. Peters, *Christian Perfection and American Methodism* (New York: Abingdon, 1956), 138.

135. McDonald and Searles, *Life of Inskip*, 218–72, 308.

136. On Dwight Moody's use of the tabernacle's in the seventies, see McLoughlin, *Modern Revivalism*, 223–25, 271.

137. William G. Rhind, *The Tabernacle in the Wilderness; The Shadow of Heavenly Things* (London, 1842); James Nisbet, *The Tabernacle: Its Literal Uses and Spiritual Applications* (London, 1853); Frank H. White, *Christ in the Tabernacle* (London, 1887); William Brown, *The Tabernacle and Its Priests and Services, Described and Considered in Relation to Christ and the Church* (Edinburgh, 1874); Richard Newton, *The Jewish Tabernacle and Its Furniture in their Typical Teaching* (New York, 1874).

138. William Cooke, *The Shekinah* (London, 1877), 15–16. I have tried to determine the extent and nature of Protestant interest in the Shekinah or "Shekinah glory." People with holiness or Pentecostal connections usually recognize the term. Both Edith Blumhofer and Greg Schneider told me of the Frances Ridley Havergal hymn, "Live Out Thy Life Within Me," the second stanza of which reads:

> Thy temple has been yielded, and purified of sin;
> Let thy Shekinah glory now shine forth from within,
> And all the earth keep silence, the body henceforth be
> Thy silent, gentle servant, moved only as by Thee.

Havergal was a British Protestant with Keswick connections. Blumhofer knew of it from a British hymnal with a Keswick slant; Schneider found it in an Adventist hymnal, dated 1864. Blumhofer thinks that "Keswick people (at least leaders) would not have countenanced claims to see Shekinah, but the language of Shekinah was fairly common among evangelicals" (email correspondence, April 26, 1998). According to Schneider, "Adventists made a lot of the Shekinah as the presence of God because of their heavy emphasis on the symbolism of the ancient Hebrew Temple" (email correspondence, April 30, 1998). Jonathan Edwards refers to "the Shekinah or cloud of glory over the mercy seat" in the tabernacle and temple (*A History of the Works of Redemption*, ed. John F. Wilson [New Haven: Yale University Press, 1989], 253–54). Wesley discussed it in terms very much like Cooke's in his *Explanatory Notes on the Old Testament* in conjunction with Ex. 13:21, 40:34–35 (John Wesley, *Wesley's Notes on the Bible* [Grand Rapids: Francis Asbury Press, 1987], 73, 93).

139. Cooke, *Shekinah*, 102, 158–59, 163, 165–67.

140. Ibid., 160–63.

141. William Brown, *Tabernacle*, 252–53, 258; Newton, *Jewish Tabernacle*, 303.

142. Cooke, *Shekinah*, x.

143. McDonald and Searles, *Life of Inskip*, 226 (emphasis in original).

144. Ibid., 235–36.

145. Steven Cooley, "Manna and the Manual: Sacramental and Instrumental Constructions of the Victorian Methodist Camp Meeting during the Mid-Nineteenth Century," *Religion and American Culture* 6, no. 2 (summer 1996):131–59; Cooley, "Possibilities of Grace: Poetic Discourse and Reflection in Methodist/Holiness Revivalism," [Ph.D. diss., University of Chicago, 1991], 110–21, 133–34).

146. Cooley emphasizes the variety of images that were elaborated in the context of Methodist-Holiness camp meetings. Images, such as Penuel, Beulah, Pisgah, and Bethany, were also popular. Penuel or Peniel was where Jacob wrestled with the angel and saw God face to face (Gen. 32.30) and reinforced the idea of God's presence in the camp (Cooley, "Possibilities of Grace," 154–57). Beulah was the new name given to Canaan in the time of glory. Bethany and Pisgah reflected the holiness movement's incorporation of divine healing and Palmer's altar theology. Bethany was where Mary anointed Jesus at the home of Simon the leper and where Jesus raised Lazarus from the dead. Pisgah was a mountain where altars were build and offers made (Num. 23:14) and the mountain upon which the Lord gave Moses two visions of Canaan (Deut. 3.27, 34:1).

147. McLean & Eaton, eds., *Penuel*, 5; Cooley, "Possibilities of Grace," 158–61, quote p. 159; Cooley, "The Methodist Ritual Cities of Urban Industrial America," unpublished paper.

148. Charles E. Jones, "Reclaiming the Text in Methodist Holiness and Pentecostal Spirituality," *Wesleyan Theological Journal* 30, no. 2 (fall 1995):167.

149. *Proceedings of the National Holiness Association, May 20–26, 1885* (Chicago: T. B. Arnold, 1885), 81–85; Cooley, "Possibilities of Grace," 166.

150. McLean & Eaton, eds., *Penuel*, 264–65, quoted in part in Cooley, "Possibilities," 58; Cooley, "Possibilities," 58–62.

151. McLean & Eaton, eds. *Penuel*, 476.

152. On Woodworth's positive regard for old-fashioned Methodism, see Wayne E. Warner, *The Woman Evangelist: The Life and Times of Charismatic Evangelist Maria B. Woodworth-Etter* (Metuchen, NJ: Scarecrow Press, 1986), 20–21. For others who made the comparison, see, for example: the man who compared Woodworth-Etter's revivals to "genuine, old-fashioned Methodist religion" and said he had not "witnessed the like since I attended the meetings of the poor black slaves in Kentucky, thirty years ago" (Warner, *Woman Evangelist*, 47); an editorial in the *St. Louis Post-Dispatch* that stated "[t]he so-called 'trances' and other forms of religious exaltation are of frequent occurrence wherever 'old-fashioned revivals' are held" ("Quackery and Emotional Religion," Sept. 3, 1890; "A Pastor on the Power," *St. Louis Post-Dispatch*, Sept. 8, 1890; "Science and Religion," *St. Louis Post-Dispatch*, Sept. 16, 1890). When children and adults were seized with the power at Trinity M.E. Church in St. Louis, the minister commented "nearly all of them had been at some time or other to the Woodworth meetings, but I do not think that could have had any serious effect, as the doings resembled very much one of the old-fashioned Methodist meetings" ("The 'Power' Was In," *St. Louis Post-Dispatch*, Oct. 13, 1890). I am grateful to Wayne Warner, Archivist for the Assemblies of God, for sharing copies of his newspaper files on Woodworth. Edith Blumhofer's statement that "Sister [Aimee Semple MacPherson] envisioned Pentecostalism as preeminently a personal experience best described in the vague but powerful cultural memory of old-time Methodist camp meetings" suggests the enduring power of this tradi-

tion (*Aimee Semple McPherson: Everybody's Sister* [Grand Rapids: Eerdmans, 1993), 387, also 220).

153. Maria B. Woodworth, *Life and Experiences* (Dayton, OH: United Brethren Publishing House, 1885), 19–27, quotes, 26–27, 33. Writing in 1890, Buckley indicated that while "[o]riginally she went into these trances herself, . . . now the whole thing is reduced to a system" (James Monroe Buckley, "Concluding Editorial Letter on the West," *Christian Advocate* (New York ed.) 66, no. 18 (April 3, 1891):1.

154. Woodworth, *Life and Experiences* (1885), 51, 57–58. In a later edition, she adds to this description the statement that "I had never seen anything like this. I felt it was the work of God, but did not know how to explain it, or what to say." At that point, "the Spirit of God" brought to mind an earlier vision of "falling sheaves," saying to her: "the falling sheaves is what you see here to-night, the slaying power of God. This is my power; I told you I would be with you and fight your battles; it is not the wisdom of men, but the power and wisdom of God that is needed to bring sinners from darkness to light" (Maria B. Woodworth, *The Life, Work, and Experience of Maria Beulah Woodworth, Evangelist*, rev. ed. [St. Louis, MO: Commercial Printing Co., 1894], 53–55).

155. "Victims of Hypnotism," unknown paper, Sept. 1, 1890; "She Will Be Tried," *St. Louis Post-Dispatch*, Sept. 2, 1890, p. 4; "Mrs. Woodworth's Mind," *St. Louis Globe-Democrat*, Sept. 2, 1890, quoted from unlabeled page; "The Civil Courts," *St. Louis Globe-Democrat*, Sept. 9, 1890; Warner, *Woman Evangelist*, 90–91. For a description of a typical meeting, see "Strange Scenes," *St. Louis Post-Dispatch*, Aug. 21, 1890.

156. "She Has No Fears," *St. Louis Post-Dispatch*, Sept., 2, 1890; "Science and Religion," *St. Louis Post-Dispatch*, Sept. 16, 1890.

157. "Religion of Hysteria," *St. Louis Post-Dispatch*, Sept. 14, 1890.

158. E.S.H., "Magnetic Phenomena," *St. Louis Post-Dispatch*, Sept. 21, 1890.

159. Ibid.

160. "Religious Trances," *St. Louis Daily Globe-Democrat*, Sept. 7, 1890.

161. James Monroe Buckley, "Concluding Editorial Letter on the West," *Christian Advocate* (New York ed.) 66, no. 18 (April 3, 1891):1–2; partially quoted in Warner, *Woman Evangelist*, 150.

162. "Quackery and Emotional Religion," *St. Louis Post-Dispatch*, Sept. 3, 1890; "Religious Trances," *St. Louis Daily Globe-Democrat*, Sept. 7, 1890.

163. "Strange Scenes," *St. Louis Post-Dispatch*, Aug. 21, 1890.

164. "The Woodworth Inquiry [editorial]," *St. Louis Post-Dispatch*, Sept. 2, 1890.

165. Christopher G. Goetz, Michel Bonduelle, and Toby Gelfand, *Charcot: Constructing Neurology* (New York : Oxford University Press, 1995), 196–98, 205, quote p. 209; Gauld, *History*, 306–15, 327. The conflict between Charcot and his rivals at Nancy is given extended treatment by Gauld, 297–362.

166. Mary James, "The Therapeutic Practices of Jean-Martin Charcot (1825–1893) in Their Historical and Social Context" (Ph.D. diss., University of Essex, 1989), cited in Micale, ed., *Beyond the Unconscious*, 279; Goetz, *Charcot*, 183, 276–77, 187; Jan Goldstein, "The Hysteria Diagnosis and the Politics of Anticlericalism in Nineteenth-Century France," *Journal of Modern History* 54, no. 2 (June 1982):209–39.

167. Mark S. Micale, *Approaching Hysteria* (Princeton: Princeton University Press, 1995), 275–76.

168. "Objects of the Society," *Proceedings of the Society for Psychical Research* [hereafter, *PSPR*] 1 (1883):3–4. On the census of hallucinations, see: Edmund Gurney, "Hallucinations," *PSPR* 3 (1885):151–89; Sidgwick, "An Address by the President on the Census of Hallucinations," *PSPR* 5 (1889):7–12, 429–35. On religious phenomena other than Spiritu-

alism, see: "Report on Phenomena Connected with Theosophy," *PSPR* 3 (1985):201–400; A. T. Myers and F.W.H. Myers, "Mind-Cure, Faith-Cure, and the Miracles of Lourdes," *PSPR* 9 (1893):160–210; Richard Hodgson, "Indian Magic and the Testimony of Conjurors," ibid., 354–66.

169. William James, "The Hidden Self," *Scribner's Magazine* 7, no. 3 (March 1890): 361–62.

170. Ibid., 362. According to James, "[t]he most recent and flagrant example of this is 'animal magnetism,' whose facts were stoutly dismissed as a pack of lies by academic medical science the world over, until the non-mystical theory of 'hypnotic suggestion' was found for them."

171. Ibid., 373, italics in original.

PART THREE
RELIGIOUS EXPERIENCE AND THE SUBCONSCIOUS, 1886–1910

1. Ellenberger, *Discovery*, 337–40.

2. Ibid., 339.

3. *L'Automatisme psychologique*, quoted in Myer's review, *Proceedings of the Society for Psychical Research* [hereafter *PSPR*] 6 (1889–90):196.

4. Gauld, *History*, 412. Gauld dates this "golden age" from the publication of Pierre Janet's *Automotisme psychologique* in 1889 through the publication of Morton Prince's *The Unconscious* in 1914. The articles on which the books were based appeared earlier, however, Janet's between 1886 and 1888 and Prince's between 1909 and 1910. For my purposes 1886 and 1910 are better markers, due to other events clustered around those dates.

5. Pierre Janet, "Les Acts inconscients et le dédoublement de la personnalité pendant le somnambulisme provoqué," *Revue Philosophique* 22 (Dec. 1886):577–91; Gauld, *History*, 369–75; Janet writes: "We have insisted on these developments of a new psychological existence, no longer alternating with the normal existence of the subject, but absolutely simultaneous" (quoted in Gauld, *History*, 372–73).

6. Most scholars have taken James's reference to 1886 as an allusion to the work of Frederic Myers. See, for example, William James, *Varieties of Religious Experience* [hereafter *VRE*], ed. John E. Smith (Cambridge, MA: Harvard University Press, 1985), 452, n. 190.17; Robert Charles Powell, "The 'Subliminal' versus the 'Subconscious,' " *Journal of the History of the Behavioral Sciences* 15 (1979):156; Eugene Taylor, *Consciousness*, 87; G. William Barnard, *Exploring Unseen Worlds: William James and the Philosophy of Mysticism* (Albany: SUNY Press, 1997), 173; Henry S. Levinson, *The Religious Investigations of William James* (Chapel Hill: University of North Carolina, 1981), 116. Although these scholars agree that James was referring to Myers, they do not agree on the particular publication that marked this discovery (John Smith cites Myers, "Human Personality in the Light of Hypnotic Suggestion," *PSPR* 4 [1886–87]; Powell cites Myers' long note appended to Gurney, Myers, & Podmore, *Phantasms of the Living* [1886]; Taylor, Levinson, and Barnard do not cite any text other than the *Varieties*). Moreover, both Smith and Powell recognize that 1886 was not the most felicitous date that James might have chosen to signal Myers's contributions to psychology, while Barnard ignores the 1886 date altogether and simply assumes James was referring to Myers's theory of the "subliminal self" (which appeared in 1892). Without diminishing the importance of Myers's work for James, I want to suggest that the reference in the *Varieties* was, in fact, a reference to Janet. In their exegesis of the James passage, these scholars have confused James's appropriation of Myers's particular understanding of the subconscious with the basic discovery upon which Myers premised his theory.

7. W. James, *Principles of Psychology* (1890; Cambridge, MA: Harvard University Press, 1981), 1213; see also, 200–209, 1208 and "The Hidden Self," 373. In 1892, James wrote: "Gurney shares, therefore, with Janet and Binet, whose observations were made with widely differing subjects and methods, the credit of demonstrating the simultaneous existence of two different strata of consciousness, ignorant of each other, in the same person" (William James, *Essays in Psychical Research* (hereafter *EPR*) [Cambridge, MA: Harvard University Press, 1986], 95). In 1903, James stated "[t]hat these other currents may not only alternate but may co-exist with each other is proved by Gurney's, Binet's, and Janet's discovery of subjects who, receiving suggestions during hypnosis and forgetting them when wakened, nevertheless then wrote them out automatically and unconsciously as soon as a pencil was placed in their hands" (W. James, "Review of *Human Personality and Its Survival of Bodily Death* by Frederic W. H. Myers," *PSPR* 18 [1903–4]:24). "Gurney, Janet, Binet and others" are cited in a review essay in 1896 as "prov[ing] that mutually disconnected currents of conscious life can simultaneously coexist in the same person" (William James, *Essays, Comments, and Reviews* (hereafter *ECR*) [Cambridge, MA: Harvard University Press, 1987], 527–29). Myers agreed with James on this point. In a review of French research, Myers referred to "the important point which M. Janet in France and Mr. Gurney in England have largely helped us to establish,—namely, the persistence of the hypnotic self, as a remembering and reasoning entity, during the reign of the primary self" (F. Myers, "French Experiments on Strata of Personality" *PSPR* 5 [1888–89]:377).

8. During this period, the term "subconscious" existed alongside the terms "subliminal" and "unconscious." Pierre Janet claimed he was the first to use the word subconscious (*actes inconscients*), while Frederick Myers proposed the term "subliminal" in the early 1890s. At the turn of the century, "the subconscious" was generally the broader of the two terms and did not necessarily connote acceptance of any one theory, whereas references to the "subliminal mind" generally connoted some allegiance to Myers's particular theory of the subconscious. The term "unconscious" was not widely used in the American context prior to Freud's lectures at Clark University in 1909 and, when it was, it was generally understood as a synonym for the subconscious. As psychoanalysis was more widely accepted during the 1910s, the unconscious came to be identified with the distinctively Freudian concept of repression. On Janet and the "subconscious," see Pierre Janet, "A Symposium on the Subconscious," *Journal of Abnormal Psychology* 2 (1907):58; Ellenberger, *Discovery*, 412, note 82; F. W. Myers, "The Subliminal Consciousness," *PSPR* 7 (1891–92):298–355; on Freud's concept of repression, see: Nathan G. Hale, Jr., *Freud and the Americans: The Beginnings of Psychoanalysis, 1876–1917* (New York: Oxford University Press, 1995), 168–69.

9. Janet described his *L'Automatisme psychologique* (1889) as "an essay in experimental psychology" (cf. Myers's review in *PSPR* 6 [1889–90]:186). The phrase "French experimental psychology of the subconscious" is from the forward to Binet's *On Double Consciousness* (1890), as noted in Eugene Taylor, "The New Jung Scholarship," *Psychoanalytic Review* 83, no. 4 (Aug. 1996):584, note 6.

10. Taylor, *Consciousness*, xii; Taylor, "The New Jung Scholarship," 547–68; Gauld, *History*, 389–400; for "Franglo-American," see 401, note 24. Recent scholarship on Jung tends to locate Jung intellectually in relation to this alliance rather than simply as a disaffected Freudian (Taylor, "The New Jung Scholarship").

11. On the most significant cases, see Ellenberger, "Psychiatry and Its Unknown History," in Micale, ed., *Beyond the Unconscious*, 239–53.

12. Micale, ed., *Beyond the Unconscious*, 57; Ellenberger, "Pierre Janet and His American Friends," in George E. Gifford, Jr., ed., *Psychoanalysis, Psychotherapy, and the New England Medical Scene, 1894–1944* (New York: Science History Pub., 1988), 63–72.

13. On the Boston school of psychotherapy, see Hale, *Freud and the Americans*, 116–24; on the British psychical researchers, see Alan Gauld, *The Founders of Psychical Research* (New York: Schocken Books, 1968).

14. James, *Principles* (1890), 1213.

15. Myers, "French Experiments," 387.

16. Gauld, *History*, 369–81, especially p. 379. Janet, like Charcot, equated hysteria and hypnotism. Their views were challenged by the research of Liébeault and Bernheim of the Nancy school, who claimed that virtually all hypnotic phenomena up to and including somnambulism could be induced in mentally normal individuals (Gauld, *History*, 327). Gauld gives extended treatment to the conflict between Charcot and his rivals at Nancy (297–362). F.W.H. Myers, his brother A. T. Myers, Edmund Gurney, and Morton Prince all visited Nancy (Gauld, *History*, 336). In his discussion of hypnotic trance in the *Principles*, James attributes it not to animal magnetism or "neurosis" (Charcot), but primarily to "suggestion" (Nancy), with the caveat that hypnosis did involve a change in the state of consciousness, i.e., "hypnotic trance" (Taylor, *Consciousness*, 38; Gauld, *History*, 352; James, *Principles*, 1199–1201).

17. Frederic W. H. Myers, "The Subliminal Consciousness," *PSPR* 7 (1891–92):301.

18. Myers, "French Experiments," 387.

19. William James, "Frederic Myers's Service to Psychology" (1901), in James, *EPR*, 198; James, "Address of the President before the Society for Psychical Research" (1896), in James, *EPR*, 132–33.

20. Myers, "Automatic Writing—IV," *PSPR* 5 (1889):523–24, emphasis in original.

21. F.W.H. Myers, "Multiplex Personality," *PSPR* 4 (1886–87):507.

22. Myers, "French Experiments," 396.

23. Myers, "Subliminal Consciousness," 299–300; Gauld provides the most extended discussion of Myers's idea of the subliminal consciousness, but does not root it firmly enough, in my view, in the research on secondary selves (Gauld, *Founders*, 275–99; Gauld, *History*, 393–400).

24. Myers, "Subliminal Consciousness," 301.

25. Ibid., 305.

26. In 1895, James wrote that when it came to theories of the mind, "no one . . . can be said to throw any more positive light than Mr. Myers or Janet" (James, *ECR*, 529).

27. William James, "The Hidden Self," 373; James, "What Psychical Research Has Accomplished" (James, *EPR*, 102, 98).

28. Myers, "French Experiments," 389.

29. Flournoy, *From India to the Planet Mars* (French ed., 1899), xv–xvii, 7–8; Myers, *PSPR* (1901), 385, quoted in Sonu Shamdasani, ed., *From India to the Planet Mars: A Case of Multiple Personality with Imaginary Language* by Theodore Flournoy (Princeton: Princeton University Press, 1994), xxx–xxxi.

30. Robert C. Le Clair, ed., *The Letters of William James and Théodore Flournoy* (Madison: University of Wisconsin Press, 1966), 90.

31. Ellenberger, *Discovery*, 150, 317–18, 781.

32. Reviews of Flournoy cited in Shamdasani, ed., *India to the Planet Mars*, xxvi–xxxi; reviews of Myers cited in Gauld, *Founders*, 293–94. Critical reviews of Myers include Frederic Harrison and W. H. Mallock, *The Nineteenth Century and After* 53 (1903):645–50, 628–44; G. F. Stout, *Hibbert Journal* 2 (1903):44–64.

33. Gauld, *History*, 412–16.

34. Hale, *Freud and the Americans*, 249; Taylor, *Consciousness*, 22–24.

35. "Symposium on the Subconscious," *Journal of Abnormal Psychology* 2 (1907):22–43, 58–89, quote p. 22.

CHAPTER SEVEN
THE PSYCHOLOGY OF RELIGION

1. Edwin G. Boring, *A History of Experimental Psychology* (New York: Appleton, 1929), 493–94. Boring tended to discount the "firsts" that could be attributed to James, i.e., that he was the first to teach the new scientific psychology in the United States (in 1875), the first to open a laboratory for student instruction (also in 1875), and the first to grant a Ph.D. in the new discipline, to G. Stanley Hall, in 1878 (Taylor, *Consciousness*, 9–10). For an extended discussion of the relationship between Hall and James, see: Eugene Taylor, "An Epistemological Critique of Experimentalism in Psychology; or, Why G. Stanley Hall Waited Until William James Was Out of Town to Found the American Psychological Association," in Helmut E. Adler and Robert W. Winkler, *Aspects of the History of Psychology in America: 1892–1992* (Washington: American Psychological Association, 1994), 37–61.

2. W. B. Selbie, *The Psychology of Religion* (Oxford: Clarendon Press, 1924), 4–5. Selbie's stress on Wundt seems to reflect his rejection of what he viewed as an overemphasis on psychopathology on the part of the "New Psychology" (4, 7–12). For the best early overview, see James Bissett Pratt, "The Psychology of Religion," *Harvard Theological Review* 1 (1908):435–54.

3. David M. Wulff, *Psychology of Religion: Classic and Contemporary Approaches*, 2nd ed. (New York: John Wiley & Sons, 1997), 25, 27; for similar assessment, see also, Eric J. Sharpe, *Comparative Religion: A History* (London: Duckworth, 1975), 97–118.

4. Wulff, *Psychology of Religion*, 28; emphasis added.

5. Boring, *History of Experimental Psychology*, 493; Eugene Taylor, "The Case for a Uniquely American Jamesian Tradition in Psychology," in Margaret E. Donnelly, ed., *Reinterpreting the Legacy of William James* (Washington, DC: American Psychological Association, 1992), 3–7.

6. James Leuba (at Bryn Mawr) was the only significant exception. Starbuck taught in the department of philosophy and psychology at the University of Iowa; James Bissett Pratt taught in the philosophy department at Williams College; Edward Scribner Ames held an appointment in the philosophy department (along with John Dewey and psychologist James Angell) at the University of Chicago; George Coe left the department of philosophy at Northwestern (where he taught psychology) for a position in religious education at Union Theological Seminary in New York.

7. For a general introduction to the pragmatism of James, Dewey, and Pierce and their followers, see David A. Hollinger, "The Problem of Pragmatism in American History," *Journal of American History* 67, no.1 (1980):88–107; for an account of James's evolutionary pragmatism, see Paul Jerome Croce, *Science and Religion in the Era of William James: Eclipse of Certainty, 1820–1880* (Chapel Hill: University of North Carolina Press, 1995). For James's positive commentary on the rise of "The Chicago School," see *The Psychological Bulletin* 1, no. 1 (Jan. 15, 1904):1–5. James Rowland Angell's article "The Province of Functional Psychology" (*The Psychological Review* N.S. 14, no. 2 [March 1907]:61–91) is often cited as signaling the birth of functional psychology *per se*. Angell was a member of the Chicago School and a younger colleague of Dewey's in the philosophy department. At Dewey's urging he went to Harvard to study with James in 1891, where among other things he

collated the American data for the census on hallucinations (Taylor, *Consciousness*, 73). Angell had a particularly strong influence on two of the psychologists of religion discussed here, Edward S. Ames, his student and later colleague, and George A. Coe.

8. Taylor, *Consciousness*, xii, 1, 9–10; Richard M. Gale, "John Dewey's Naturalization of William James," in Ruth Anna Putnam, ed., *Cambridge Companion to William James* (Cambridge: Cambridge University Press, 1997), 49–68.

9. Hanegraaff, *New Age Religion and Western Culture*, 384–513, provides a broader historical context for this claim.

10. Howard M. Feinstein, *Becoming William James* (Ithaca: Cornell University Press, 1984), 330–40; Taylor, *Consciousness*, 92–93, 104–8; for an extended discussion of the relationship between James and Münsterberg, see Daniel W. Bjork, *The Compromised Scientist* (New York: Columbia University Press, 1983), 39–70.

11. Edwin D. Starbuck, "Religion's Use of Me," in Vergilius Ferm, ed., *Religion in Transition* (New York: Macmillan Co., 1937), 221–25.

12. Starbuck, "Religion's Use of Me," 229–31.

13. Ibid., 231–32. On the rivalries between Harvard and Clark in the 1890s and Hall's attempts to dominate the field see, Dorothy Ross, *G. Stanley Hall: Psychologist as Prophet* (Chicago: University of Chicago Press, 1972), 231–50; and Taylor, "An Epistemological Critique," 37–61.

14. G. Stanley Hall, *Adolescence: Its Psychology and Its Relations to Physiology, Anthropology, Sociology, Sex, Crime, Religion, and Education*, 2 vols. (New York: D. Appleton & Co., 1905), 2:292, note 1.

15. Starbuck, *The Psychology of Religion* (New York: Charles Scribner's Sons, 1900), viii; Starbuck, "Religion's Use of Me," 226.

16. George A. Coe, "My Own Little Theatre," in Ferm, ed., *Religion*, 92, 96–102.

17. George A. Coe, "A Study in the Dynamics of Personality," *Psychological Review* 6 (1899):487–88.

18. William R. Hutchison, "Cultural Strain and Protestant Liberalism," *American Historical Review* 76, no. 2 (1971):410. Of the thirty-three "front-rank liberal leaders" examined, "7 percent had a sudden and emotional conversion; 27 per cent, some emotional elements prominent in decisions; *67 per cent, no identifiable conversion experience*" (emphasis added).

19. Coe, "My Own Little Theatre," 92–93.

20. Edwin Starbuck, *Psychological Review* [Nov. 1900], George A. Coe Papers, Scrapbook #1:52–53, Manuscript Group No. 36, Special Collections, Yale Divinity School Library.

21. James, *VRE*, 396 (note); George W. Wilson, *Methodist Theology vs. Methodist Theologians* (1904) quotes this passage from James in his flyleaf.

22. James to Bowne, March 31, 1901, in Warren E. Steinkraus, ed., *Representative Essays of Borden Parker Bowne* (Utica, NY: Meridian Pub. Co., 1981), 192.

23. William James, No. 64 (#4476), *Manuscript Essays and Notes* (Cambridge, MA, and London: Harvard University Press, 1988), 311–12; this note was written at "an early stage in the writing of the *Varieties* . . . James was working on Bowne in about March to May 1901" (352, n. 311.8).

24. Ralph Barton Perry, *The Thought and Character of William James*, 2 vols. (Boston: Little, Brown, & Co., 1935), 2:329.

25. Perry, *Thought and Character of William James*, 2:323–25; Mark R. Schwehn, "Making the World: William James and the Life of the Mind," *Harvard Library Bulletin* 30, no. 4 (1982):427; Feinstein, *Becoming William James*, 241–45. For a summary of scholarship through 1982 on James's young adult crises, see Schwehn, "Making the World," 440, n.

58. Louis Menand, "William James and the Case of the Epileptic Patient," *New York Review of Books* 45, no. 20 (December 17, 1998):81–93 provides a convincing analysis of how little we know about the context of James's "epileptic vision" (*VRE*, 134–35) despite the weight that historians have given it in their interpretations of James's early years.

26. Perry, *Thought and Character of William James*, 2:350–51 (emphasis added).

27. John Smith, editor of the critical edition of the *Varieties*, credits James with being the first to make "use of the expression 'religious experience' as a technical term" (James, *VRE*, xiii).

28. Ernst Troeltsch, "Empiricism and Platonism in the Philosophy of Religion," *Harvard Theological Review* 5, no. 4 (October 1912):401–2.

29. Ibid., 412–13.

30. Ibid., 409, 414.

31. James, *VRE*, 408; Troeltsch, "Empiricism," 411–12.

32. Micale, *Approaching Hysteria*, 272.

33. Levinson, *Religious Investigations*, 81–87; Sander L. Gilman, "Images of Hysteria," in Gilman, et al., *Hysteria Beyond Freud* (Berkeley: University of California Press, 1993), 367–77.

34. W.S.F. Pickering, ed., *Durkheim on Religion* (Atlanta: Scholar's Press, 1994), 123.

35. Steven Lukes, *Emile Durkheim: His Life and Work* (New York: Harper, 1972), 480–81, 455–77.

36. Emile Durkheim, *The Elementary Forms of the Religious Life* (New York: Free Press, 1965), 107; on animism, 86–87, on naturism, 99; cf. also Pickering, ed., *Durkheim*, 134.

37. Eugene Taylor, *William James on Exceptional Mental States: The 1896 Lowell Lectures* (Amherst: University of Massachusetts Press, 1984), 133.

38. Levinson, *Religious Investigations*, 76–81; Robert J. Richards, "The Personal Equation in Science: William James's Psychological and Moral Uses of Darwinian Theory," *Harvard Library Bulletin* 30, no. 4 (1982):399–405. On James's assimilation of Darwinism, see Croce, *Science and Religion*, 108–10, 147–48, 155–56.

39. Richards, "Personal Equation," 402–3, 405; Levinson, *Religious Investigations*, 76–81.

40. William James, "Myers's Service to Psychology" (1901), in *EPR* 199–200.

41. Ibid., 200.

42. Richards, "Personal Equation," 417; Levinson, *Religious Investigations*, 238–39; Croce, *Science and Religion*, 223; David Lamberth, *William James and the Metaphysics of Experience* (Cambridge: Cambridge University Press, 1999), chapter 4.

43. Levinson, *Religious Investigations*, 153–55. This, in other words, is a fuller statement of the distinctive function of religion prefigured in Lecture 2 (45–50), discussed above.

44. It is the phrase "or subliminally as Mr. Myers terms it" that in my view has led most scholars to confuse Janet's 1886 discovery of consciousness beyond the margin with Myers's 1892 theoretical interpretation of this discovery.

45. Eugene Taylor, "The Appearance of Swedenborg in the History of American Psychology," in Erland J. Brock, ed., *Swedenborg and His Influence* (Bryn Athyn, PA: The Academy of the New Church, 1988), 162.

46. Paul Jerome Croce, "Between Spiritualism and Science: William James on Religion and Human Nature," *Journal for the History of Modern Theology* 4 (1997):219.

47. Lamberth, *William James*, chap. 2.

48. The excursus begins with "And the first thing" (384) and ends with "For the moment let us pursue the analytic part of the task" (397).

49. On the development of his metaphysics of pure experience, cf. Lamberth, *William James*, chap. 2.

50. "Against the Medical Bill," *Boston Evening Transcript*, March 4, 1898.

51. William James, "Confidences of a 'Psychical Researcher,' " EPR, 374, quoted in Lamberth, *William James*, 197–98; see also, William James to Henry W. Rankin, June 16, 1891, quoted in Taylor, *Consciousness*, 90–91.

52. F.C.S. Schiller, "Idealism and the Dissociation of a Personality," *Journal of Philosophy, Psychology, and Scientific Methods* [hereafter *JPPSM*] 3, no. 18 (August 30, 1906):477–82; Willard C. Gore, "The Mad Absolute of a Pluralist," *JPPSM* 3, no. 21 (Oct. 11, 1906):575–77; William James, "The Mad Absolute," *JPPSM* 3, no. 24 (Nov. 22, 1906):656–57.

53. Perry, *Thought and Character of William James*, 2:326.

54. Joseph Jastrow, "The Status of the Subconscious," *American Journal of Psychology* 14 (1903):343; Irving King, "The Problem of the Subconscious," *Psychological Review* 13 (1906):36. The "pseudo-psychologist" in question was undoubtedly Myers, who acknowledged that his concluding speculations on spirit possession in *Human Personality* were likely to "suggest the medicine-man's wigwam rather than the study of the white philosopher" (Myers, *Human Personality* [1907 ed.], 333).

55. Joseph Jastrow, *The Subconscious* (Boston and New York: Houghton, Mifflin and Co., 1906), 535, 538.

56. King, "Problem of the Subconscious," 45, 47; A. H. Pierce, "Should We Still Retain the Expression 'Unconscious Cerebration' to Designate Certain Processes Connected With Mental Life?" *JPPSM* 3, no. 23 (Nov. 8, 1906):626–27.

57. A. H. Pierce, "Review of 'A Symposium on the Subconscious,' " *JPPSM* 4, no. 19 (Sep. 12, 1907):424, 428.

58. Morton Prince, "Professor Pierce's Version of the Late 'Symposium on the Subconscious," *JPPSM* 5, no. 3 (Jan. 30, 1908):69–75.

59. "Symposium on the Subconscious," *Journal of Abnormal Psychology* 2 (1907):22–43, 58–89, quote p. 22.

60. Ibid., 27, 32–33.

61. Frederick Morgan Davenport, *Primitive Traits in Religious Revivals: A Study in Mental and Social Evolution* (New York: Macmillan Co., 1905), 279–80.

62. Ibid., 13, 18, 19 (emphasis added), 21–22.

63. Ibid., 26, viii–x.

64. Lists of general psychologies of religion published in this period vary. Three other books that I might have discussed are: Irving King, *The Differentiation of the Religious Consciousness*, Monograph Supplement of the *Psychological Review*, 4, no. 4 (1904); James Leuba, *A Psychological Study of Religion: Its Origin, Function, and Future* (New York: Macmillan, 1912); George M. Stratton, *Psychology of the Religious Life* (London, 1911). Of these three figures, Leuba was the most important in terms of the psychology of religion. The volume cited here, the first in a projected series, dealt narrowly with issues of religion and magic and was ruled out for that reason. Coe's *Psychology of Religion* was perceived by many of Coe's colleagues in the psychology of religion as the first real textbook (see the letters and reviews by Ames, Pratt, King, and Starbuck in Coe Papers, Scrapbook #4, Manuscript Group No. 36, Special Collections, Yale Divinity School Library). Pratt's widely used textbook, *The Religious Consciousness*, was not published until 1920.

65. Edwin D. Starbuck, "The Varieties of Religious Experience," *Biblical World* 24 (1904):103–4, 109–10; see also, Starbuck, "Double-Mindedness" and "Intuitionalism" in *Hastings Encyclopedia*; and Starbuck, "The Feelings and Their Place in Religion," *American Journal of Religious Psychology and Education* 1 (1904–5):182.

66. James Bissett Pratt, "The Place and Value of the Marginal Region in Psychic Life," *Psychological Review* 13 (1906):56–57; Pratt, "The Subconscious and Religion," *Harvard Theological Review* 6 (1913):221–22, 227–28. (The latter article formed the basis for a chapter of the same title in *The Religious Consciousness* [New York: Macmillan Co., 1920], 45–67.)

67. James Bissett Pratt, *The Psychology of Religious Belief* (New York: Macmillan Co., 1907), 146–47.

68. Pratt, "Psychology of Religion," 451. In response to Coe, he writes (1920): "Yet I for one cannot feel that the danger of our becoming too emotional or too contemplative is really very great. . . . Will anyone who has been to church in the last fifteen years seriously affirm that the importance of mysticism and the 'spiritual life' is really being over-emphasized in our pulpits?" (*Religious Consciousness*, 478).

69. Edward Scribner Ames, *The Psychology of Religious Experience* (Boston: Houghton Mifflin, 1910), 9 (emphasis added). Ames was a student of John Dewey and James R. Angell at Chicago in the 1890s. He joined the faculty in the department of philosophy (which included psychology) along with Dewey, Angell, George Herbert Mead, James H. Tufts, and Addison Moore in 1900. The five men appointed by Dewey all shared his interests in philosophy, psychology, and education, although apart from Dewey they tended to specialize. Ames emphasized the psychology and philosophy of religion; Angell functional and experimental psychology (George Dykhuizen, *The Life and Mind of John Dewey* [Carbondale: Southern Illinois Press, 1973], 77–80). On Dewey's naturalistic reading of James, see Gale, "John Dewey's Naturalization of William James," 60–62.

70. Ames, *Psychology of Religious Experience*, 330–31 (emphasis added); Gale, "John Dewey's Naturalization of William James," 49; James R. Angell, "The Province of Functional Psychology," *Psychological Review* 14, no. 2 (1907):61–xx; James, "The Chicago School," *The Psychological Bulletin* 1, no. 1 (1904):1–5.

71. Ames, *Psychology of Religious Experience*, 28–29, 49, 168, 71, 134. On the psychology of habit, see 52–70. Ames argues, contra James, Frazer and others, that the primitive customs and taboos of which primitive ceremonials are a subset, arise not from ideas or systems of belief, as the anthropologists were suggesting, but rather "are reactions to felt needs and are non-rational. They develop into habitual activities, acquiring stability through repetition and efficiency, and gaining the powerful sanctions natural to long-standing habits." Ames felt that through the psychology of habit, "modern psychology had a significant contribution to make both to anthropology and the scientific study of the origins of religion" (54). Ames's approach was similar in some respects to that adopted by Durkheim in his *Elementary Forms* (1912). Durkheim derived the social nature of religion not from ceremonials generally, but from sacrifice in particular.

72. Ames, *Psychology of Religious Experience*, 291–94.

73. Ibid., 414.

74. George A. Coe, "Sources of the Mystical Revelation," *The Hibbert Journal* 6 (1907–8):364–66; George A. Coe to Anton T. Boisen, September 25, 1947, quoted in Anton T. Boisen, "Pioneer of Pastoral Psychology," *Pastoral Psychology* (Oct. 1952):64.

75. James H. Leuba, "Professor William James's Interpretation of Religious Experience," *International Journal of Ethics* 14 (1904):331; Coe, "Sources," 365–67.

76. James H. Leuba, "On the Psychology of a Group of Christian Mystics," *Mind* 14 (1905):25–26. Leuba noted that "what I have to say here will be much increased if you happen to have present in mind the views of Prof. William James on this point" (21–22).

77. Coe, "Sources," 367.

78. George A. Coe, "Religion and the Subconscious," *The American Journal of Theology* 13, no. 3 (July 1909):343–44.

79. Havelock Ellis, *Man and Woman* (4th ed., New York: Scribner, 1904; reprint ed., New York: Arno Press, 1974), 258–96, quote p. 292. Theoretically, Ellis relied primarily on Hack Tuke, a British physician, whose book *Sleep-Walking and Hypnotism* (1884) provided a physiologically based theory, dependent on the idea of unconscious cerebration, that linked the ostensibly pathological (hysterical somnambulism) with the ostensibly normal (sleep-walking) (Gauld, *History*, 348–49).

80. Ellis, *Man and Woman*, 292; Gloria Flaherty, *Shamanism and the Eighteenth Century* (Princeton: Princeton University Press, 1992); for references to competing terms, see p. 123.

81. George A. Coe, "The Mystical as a Psychological Concept," *JPPSM* 6, no. 8 (April 15, 1909):198.

82. Coe, "Mystical," 200–1.

83. Ibid.

84. George A. Coe, *The Psychology of Religion* (Chicago: University of Chicago Press, 1917), 119–51, 175–92.

85. Cultural evolution for Ames was primarily a result of biological adjustments or adaptations to economic changes internalized as new habits (Ames, *Psychology of Religious Experience*, 168–70, 194, 416). What this lacked, in Coe's view, was any awareness of the role of human agency or desire. As he put it, " 'adjustment' is his [Ames's] basal category, but just what is adjusted, and to what, does not distinctly appear" (Coe, *Psychology of Religion*, 30, n. 2). To correct this, Coe argued that a "functional psychology . . . should be first and foremost, a psychology of personal self-realizations" (ibid., 30–31).

86. Fred L. Brownlee, "Social Thought and Action," *Religious Education* 47, no. 2 (1952):80–81; Erwin L. Shaver, "Contribution to the Religious Education Association," ibid., 77; Lynn Euzenas, "George Albert Coe: Social Mystic," unpublished paper, May 14, 1993.

87. Douglas Clyde Macintosh to George A. Coe, November 25, 1922; George A. Coe to Douglas Clyde Macintosh, December 8, 1922, George A. Coe Papers, Correspondence, 1:1 (emphasis in original); George A. Coe, *Sadie Knowland Coe: A Chapter in a Life* (Privately printed, 1906).

88. Anton T. Boisen, "The Present Status of William James's Psychology of Religion," *Journal of Pastoral Care* 7, no. 3 (1953):155–56.

89. Boisen, "William James's Psychology of Religion," 156.

90. Ibid.

CHAPTER EIGHT
VARIETIES OF PROTESTANT RELIGIOUS EXPERIENCE

1. Mullin, *Miracles*, 185–88.

2. There is much scholarly debate over the origins of Pentecostalism. Both Charles Parham and William Seymour have been proposed as founders of the movement. On the debate, see Grant Wacker, "Travail of a Broken Family: Evangelical Responses to Pentecostalism in America, 1906–1916," *Journal of Ecclesiastical History* 47, no. 3 (July 1996):509 and Joe Creech, "Visions of Glory: The Place of the Azusa Street Revival in Pentecostal History," *Church History* 65, no. 3 (Sept. 1996):405–24.

3. Thomson Jay Hudson, *The Evolution of the Soul* (Chicago: A. C. McClurg & Co., 1904), ix–xi, 2–7, quote, 6–7. The New Thought tradition does not claim Hudson; see Braden, *Spirits in Rebellion*, and Dresser, *Health and the Inner Life*.

4. Hudson, *Evolution*, 3–5; Hudson, *A Scientific Demonstration of the Future Life* (Chicago: A. C. McClurg & Co., 1895), 292–95, 322–23.

5. "Notices of Books," *PSPR* 9 (1893–94):230–31.

6. "A Study of Personal Religion," *The* (Chicago) *Standard*, Nov. 8, 1902, Scrapbook 2:75; Rev. E. R. Lathrop, Hastings, MN, to George A. Coe, Nov. 13, 1902, Scrapbook 1; Rev. William D. Marsh, Pastor First MEC, Utica, NY, to George A. Coe, Dec. 4, 1900, Scrapbook 1, George A. Coe Papers, Manuscript Group No. 36, Special Collections, Yale Divinity School Library.

7. Of twenty-four leading Methodists asked to identify "The Most Helpful New Books for Christian Students and Workers," nine listed Coe's *Spiritual Life* among their six books ("Our Round Table," *Central Christian Advocate*, Dec. 5, 1900). In annual lists of best new books the faculty of Garrett and Boston University School of Theology both recommended *The Religion of a Mature Mind* as do two of eighteen "leading teachers of young preachers." Nine of the eighteen leading teachers list James's *Varieties* ("Wheat for the Preacher's Mill," *Central Christian Advocate*, Dec. 17, 1902). In a survey of "a number of our 'up-to-date' brethren" that produced nineteen lists of six new books that "every minister should read," Hall's *Adolescence* received one vote, Coe's *Spiritual Life* and *Religion of a Mature Mind* each received three votes, Schofield's *Unconscious Mind* one; and James's *Briefer Course on Psychology* one (Leonard W. Riley, "What Books Shall Ministers Read? Suggestions made by Pastors, Teachers and Editors," *The Standard*, May 20, 1905).

8. Dresser, *Health and the Inner Life*, 12, 242–43 (hereafter pages cited in the text).

9. Elwood Worcester, "Mental Healing," The Episcopalian Club of Massachusetts, Hotel Brunswick, Boston, May 13, 1907, typescript, Elwood Worcester Papers, Diocesan Library and Archives, Episcopal Diocese of Massachusetts, 20–21.

10. Elwood Worcester, Samuel McComb and Isador Coriat, *Religion and Medicine* (New York: Moffat, Yard, & Co., 1908), 7–8.

11. Ibid., 10–11.

12. "Science & Religion: Boston Agog over Its Newest Religious Fad," *Church Times*, Jan. 20, 1907. Newspaper articles related to the Emmanuel Movement are collected in the Emmanuel Movement Scrapbooks (B MS b123) and Isador H. Coriat Scrapbooks (B MS b254.1) at the Francis A. Countway Library of Medicine, Boston, MA.

13. Elwood Worcester, "Mental Healing," 8; Worcester, *Religion and Medicine*, 13.

14. For an overview of the movement, see E. Brooks Holifield, *A History of Pastoral Care in America* (Nashville: Abingdon, 1983), 202–9. Clergy-authored works promoting the movement included: Robert MacDonald, *Mind, Religion and Health with an Appreciation of the Emmanuel Movement* (New York: Funk and Wagnalls, 1908); Thomas Parker Boyd, *The How and Why of the Emmanuel Movement* (San Francisco: The Emmanuel Institute of Health, 1909); Oliver Huckel, *Mental Medicine* (New York: Thomas Y. Crowell, 1909); Charles Reynolds Brown, *Faith and Health* (New York: Thomas Y. Crowell, 1910); C. Bertram Runnalls, *Suggestions for Conducting a Church Class in Psycho-Therapy* (Milwaukee: Young Churchman, 1915).

15. According to Ian S. Evison, "[Cabot] rejected and thought Emmanuel should reject the 'theory of a separate and especially divine subconscious mind with a subterranean passage through it to god' " (Richard Cabot, "What Psychotherapeutic Methods Should Be Especially Developed at Emmanuel Church," Cabot Papers, box 71, folder: Misc. Writings,

quoted in Evison, "Pragmatism and Idealism in the Professions: The Case of Richard Clarke Cabot, 1869–1939" [Ph.D. diss., University of Chicago, December 1995], 274); Nathan G. Hale, Jr., ed., *James Jackson Putnam and Psychoanalysis* (Cambridge, MA: Harvard University Press, 1971), 13. In one of his Emmanuel-related lectures, Coriat stated that "there is nothing supernormal in subconscious activity" ("Sub-Conscious Activity," *Boston Transcript*, June 4, 1908.

16. Elwood Worcester, *Life's Adventure: The Story of a Varied Career* (New York: Charles Scribner's Sons, 1932), 90–94, quote 90–91.

17. Worcester, *Life's Adventure*, 45–46, 328–29.

18. "Science & Religion: Boston Agog," *Church Times*, Jan. 20, 1907.

19. "Clergymen Predominate," *Boston Transcript*, June 1, 1908; "Summer School at Emmanuel," *Boston Transcript*, May 27, 1908; "Mind Cure Pupils Meet at Emmanuel," *Boston Herald*, June 2, 1908.

20. "Healing Through Prayer: A Summary of Dr. McComb's Lectures on Psychotherapy," *Boston Transcript*, June 6, 1908; Samuel McComb, "Christianity and Health: An Experiment in Practical Religion," *The Century* 75 (1907–8):795. While Coriat did, indeed, agree that dissociation was not necessarily a sign of pathology, I have found no evidence that he viewed the subconscious in religious terms; see, for example, Coriat's chapter on "Diseases of the Subconscious" in *Religion and Medicine*, 199–217.

21. Hudson, *The Law of Psychic Phenomena* (Chicago: A. C. McClurg, 1895), 343–55; Samuel McComb, "Christianity and Health: An Experiment in Practical Religion," *The Century* 75 (1907–8):796–97.

22. Lightner Witmer, "Mental Healing and the Emmanuel Movement," *The Psychological Clinic* 2 (1907):243–44.

23. Ibid., 284–85, 294–95. Eugene Taylor notes that this was one of the most openly vitriolic rejections of James. See also, Anon. [Lightner Witmer], "Is the Psychology Taught at Harvard a National Peril?" *Current Literature* 46 (1909):437–38, cited in Taylor, *Consciousness*, 187.

24. Worcester, *Life's Adventure*, 276, quoted in part in Mullin, *Miracles*. 197.

25. Elwood Worcester and Samuel McComb, *The Christian Religion as a Healing Power* (New York: Moffat, Yard, and Co., 1909), 94–97; idem., *Religion and Medicine*, 338–68; Mullin, *Miracles*, 194–98.

26. Worcester, *Religion and Medicine*, 350–52, 354, 366.

27. Worcester, "Mental Healing," 21, 22–23, 25.

28. Worcester, *Life's Adventure*, 277–79 (emphasis added).

29. Ibid., 147.

30. Worcester, *Christian Religion*, 10–11.

31. "Healing Through Prayer: A Summary of Dr. McComb's Lectures on Psychotherapy," *Boston Transcript*, June 6, 1908.

32. "Worcesterism a Form of Hysteria, says Dr. Dercum," [Philadelphia] *North American*, Feb 5, 1908.

33. Worcester, *Life's Adventure*, 286–87; Worcester and McComb, *Healing Power*, 21–24.

34. Worcester, *Religion and Medicine*, 65–67.

35. Ibid., 67–68.

36. "'Moral-Healing' Service," *New York Evening Post*, Feb. 9, 1907.

37. "Remarkably Successful Results and Rapid Growth of Emmanuel Church Movement at Boston for Treatment of Nervous Disorders," *New York Times*, Jan. 5, 1908.

38. Untitled mss., 9–10, Elwood Worcester Papers.

39. Ibid., 15–16.

40. Ibid., 10–13.

41. "Remarkably Successful Results," *New York Times*, Jan. 5, 1908.

42. "Science & Religion: Boston Agog," *Church Times*, Jan. 20, 1907.

43. "As a Patient Sees It," Emmanuel Movement Scrapbooks [no newspaper named]; Lyman P. Powell, "Testimony of a Clergyman to the Application of the Emmanuel Plan in an Average Parish," Elwood Worcester Papers, Diocesan Library and Archives, Episcopal Diocese of Massachusetts.

44. J. V. Dittemore, Christian Science Committee on Publication for the State of New York, "The Real Teachings of Christian Science," Letter to the editor, *Buffalo Commercial*, Feb. 24, 1908.

45. "Emmanuel Movement under Criticism of New Thought Leader," *Bulletin* [North Dakota], Nov. 30, 1908.

46. "Emmanuel's Samaritan Record," *Boston Transcript*, Dec. 4, 1915.

47. Worcester, *Life's Adventure*, 287, 296.

48. *The Sunday Herald* (Boston), Dec. 27, 1908.

49. Sanford Gifford, "Medical Psychotherapy and the Emmanuel Movement in Boston, 1904–1912," in George E. Gifford, Jr., ed., *Psychoanalysis, Psychotherapy, and the New England Medical Scene* (New York: Science History Publications, 1978), 115.

50. Gifford, ed., *Psychoanalysis*, 115–16; Evison, "Pragmatism and Idealism," 290–99; Worcester and McComb, *Christian Religion*, 21–24.

51. "Emmanuel's Samaritan Record," *Boston Transcript*, Dec. 4, 1915.

52. "Emmanuel Movement Discussion," *Newark News*, Dec. 5, 1908; "To Found Hospital in Mental Healing," *Boston Herald*, June 22, 1908.

53. One of the clergy-authored books promoting the Emmanuel Movement described these four books as "immensely popular" among participants (Brown, *Faith and Health*, 149).

54. Elizabeth Towne, *Nautalus*, quoted in Michael Williams, "New America," *Van Norden Magazine*, 1908, 332.

55. William Sanday, *Christologies Ancient and Modern* (New York: Oxford University Press, 1910), v–vii; on Sanday, see Mullin, *Miracles*, 157–58, 161, 163–64, 165, 169.

56. Sanday, *Christologies*, 137–42.

57. Ibid., 152, 155–56.

58. Ibid., 155–56, 159.

59. Sanday, *Personality in Christ and Ourselves* (Oxford: Clarendon, 1911), 62–64, 73–74.

60. Coe, "Religion and the Subconscious," 338–39. For his introduction of the phrase, " 'psychic' theology," see, Coe, *Psychology of Religion*, 210, note 1; Sanday, whose relevant works appeared after Coe's 1909 article, was cited in the same note.

61. Charles F. Parham, *A Voice Crying in the Wilderness* (1902; 4th ed., Joplin, MO: Joplin Printing Co., 1944), 29, reprinted in Donald Dayton, ed., *The Sermons of Charles F. Parham* (New York: Garland Pub., Inc., 1985).

62. Dayton, ed., *Sermons of Parham*, 26–27.

63. "Pentecost Has Come," *The Apostolic Faith* (Los Angeles) 1, no. 1 (Sept. 1906):1; "Pentecostal Baptism Restored," *The Apostolic Faith* (Los Angeles) 1, no. 2 (Oct. 1906): 1; reprinted in E. Myron Noble, ed., *Like As of Fire: Newspapers from the Azusa Street World Wide Revival* (Washington, DC: Middle Atlantic Regional Press, 1995). Cited hereafter as *AFLA*.

64. *Topeka State Daily Journal*, July 26, 1906, quoted in James R. Goff, Jr., *Fields White Unto Harvest: Charles F. Parham and the Missionary Origins of Pentecostalism* (Fayetteville: University of Arkansas Press, 1988), 129.

65. Charles Parham, "A Note of Warning [Dec. 1, 1906]," *Apostolic Faith* (Jan. 1907), quoted in Sarah E. Parham, *The Life of Charles F. Parham* (Joplin, Mo.: Hunter Printing Co., 1930; reprint ed., New York: Garland Publishing, Inc., 1985), 168–69.

66. S. Parham, *Life*, 163–64; "Pentecost With Signs Following," *AFLA* 1, no. 4 (Dec. 1906):1.

67. Goff, *Fields White*, 128–46, 228 (note 55).

68. Ibid., 128–46.

69. C. Parham, *The Everlasting Gospel* (Baxter Springs, KS: Apostolic Faith Bible College, 1911), 27–28, reprinted in Dayton, ed., *Sermons of Charles F. Parham*; S. Parham, *Life*, 169.

70. C. Parham, *Everlasting Gospel*, 17 (emphasis added).

71. Scholars of Pentecostalism have not, in my view, given enough attention to the varieties of Pentecostal experience as they emerged in different theological and institutional contexts. The work of Edith Blumhofer and Joe Creech both point in this direction. In contrast to other, more monolithic interpretations of early Pentecostal experience, Blumhofer has argued that "at least two understandings of the nature and purpose of Pentecostal experience informed the convictions of the early Assemblies of God," the largest of the predominantly white Pentecostal denominations. One stressed Spirit baptism as a means of empowerment for missions and the other emphasized "a spirituality of being, rather than doing" (Edith L. Blumhofer, *'Pentecost in My Soul': Explorations in the Meaning of Pentecostal Experience in the Early Assemblies of God* [Springfield, MO: Gospel Publishing House, 1989], 9–10, 18–25). Joe Creech has argued that while Azusa Street provided the movement with a symbolic, and theologically significant, point of origin, it was only one of a number of points of origin and, thus, played a more limited role in the movement's historical development than has often been recognized. Even those who did "experience Pentecost" at Azusa brought their experience back into preexisting religious structures, which, Creech argues, gave "early pockets of pentecostal revival theological leanings, institutional structures, and a sociocultural ethos often quite different form" (Creech, "Visions of Glory," 407, 411, 413).

72. Edith L. Blumhofer, *The Assemblies of God* (Springfield, MO: Gospel Publishing House, 1989), 17–66; Robert Mapes Anderson, *Vision of the Disinherited: The Making of American Pentecostalism* (New York: Oxford University Press, 1979), 28–46.

73. "A Chicago Evangelist's Pentecost," *AFLA* 1, no. 6 (Feb.–Mar. 1907):4.

74. Ibid.

75. Ibid.

76. Frank Bartleman, "How Pentecost Came to Los Angeles" (1925), reprinted in *Witness to Pentecost: The Life of Frank Bartleman*, ed. Cecil M. Robeck (New York: Garland, 1985), 64, 87; "Bible Pentecost: Gracious Pentecostal Showers Continue to Fall," *AFLA* 1, no. 3 (Nov. 1906):1; "Pentecost in Middle States," *AFLA* 1, no. 6 (Feb.–Mar. 1907):3; "Portland Is Stirred," *AFLA* 1, no. 5 (Jan. 1907):1; "In the Last Days," *AFLA* 1, no. 9 (June–Sept. 1907):1.

77. Steven Barabas, "Keswick and Its Use of the Bible" (Ph.D. diss., Princeton Theological Seminary, 1948), 177–78, 180–81, 198; Andrew Murray, *The Full Blessing of Pentecost* (New York: Fleming H. Revell Co., 1908), 65–73, quoted in Barabas, "Keswick," 222–23.

78. Barabas, "Keswick," 215–16; F. B. Meyer, *The Call and Challenge of the Unseen* (London: Morgan & Scott, Ltd., n.d.), 67–71, quoted in Barabas, "Keswick," 229–30.

79. Bartleman, *Pentecost*, 71–72.

80. Ibid., 73–74.

81. C. H. Mason, "Tennessee Evangelist Witnesses," *AFLA* 1, no. 6 (Feb.–Mar. 1907):7; on Mason, see Hans A. Baer and Merrill Singer, *African-American Religion in the Twentieth Century: Varieties of Protest and Accommodation* (Knoxville: University of Tennessee Press, 1992), 150–55.

82. "Holiness Bible School Leader Receives Pentecost," *AFLA* 1, no. 6 (Feb.–Mar. 1907), 5 (emphasis added).

83. "In a Divine Trance," *AFLA* 1, no.8 (May 1907):3

84. Charles Parham, "Editorial," *AFLA* (Oct. 1912):6, quoted in Edith L. Blumhofer, *Restoring the Faith: The Assemblies of God, Pentecostalism, and American Culture* (Urbana and Chicago: University of Illinois Press, 1993), 68, n. 81.

85. "Counterfeits," *AFLA* 1, no. 4 (Dec. 1906):2.

86. Letter from J. M. Peebles to "Rev. Dwight L. Moody, Brother in Christ," San Diego *Vidette*, Feb. 12, 1899, quoted in Whipple, *Biography of Peebles*, 511–15.

87. Bartleman, *Pentecost*, 60.

88. Ibid., 69–70.

89. For New Testament based arguments, which generally followed the Keswick teachings, see: "Sanctified Before Pentecost," *AFLA* 1, no. 4 (Dec. 1906):2; "Tongues as Sign," *AFLA* 1, no. 1 (Sept. 1906):2; "The Enduement of Power," *AFLA* 1, no. 4 (Dec. 1906):2.

90. "The Way into the Holiest," *AFLA* 1, no. 2 (Oct. 1906):4.

91. "The Baptism with the Holy Ghost Foreshadowed," *AFLA* 1, no. 4 (Dec. 1906):2.

92. "Type of Pentecost. II. Chron. 5," *AFLA* 1, no. 7 (Apr. 1907):3.

93. "Salvation According to the True Tabernacle," *AFLA* 1, no. 10 (Sept. 1907):3.

94. "The Baptism with the Holy Spirit," *AFLA* 1, no. 11 (Oct.–Jan. 1908):4

95. J. M. P. Otts, *Christ and the Cherubim, or, The Ark of the Covenant A Type of Our Saviour*, introduction by Francis R. Beattie (Richmond, VA: Presbyterian Committee of Publication, 1896), 7, 10–11.

96. Beattie in Otts, *Christ*, 13–14.

97. Anton T. Boisen, "The New Evangelism," *Chicago Theological Seminary Register* 25, no. 2 (1935):9; Boisen, "The Holy Rollers Come to Town," *Chicago Theological Seminary Register* 29 (Jan. 1939), 5–6.

98. Ibid.

99. Robert L. Kelly, *Theological Education in America: A Study of One Hundred Sixty-One Theological Schools in the United States and Canada* (New York: George H. Doran Co., 1924), 142–43.

100. Kelly, *Theological Education*, 142–43.

101. In 1920, there were no courses in pastoral counseling and religious educators were "cast as the 'psychologists' within the seminaries and churches" (Holifield, *History of Pastoral Care*, 226).

102. Kelly, *Theological Education*, 143–44.

103. Ibid., 98.

104. Coe's major textbooks were *Education in Religion and Morals* (1904); *The Psychology of Religion* (1916); *A Social Theory of Religious Education* (1917). Coe was offered a position at the University of Chicago in 1908 and shortly thereafter at Union in New York. Coe accepted Union's offer because it gave him "a twofold opportunity that Northwestern could not provide, namely: exclusively graduate teaching, and concentration upon religious education and the psychology of religion, in which I desired to do original work" (George A. Coe to J. Roscoe Miller, President of Northwestern University, Feb. 26, 1950, Coe Papers, Manuscript Group No. 36: I:2:19). On Coe's centrality in this process, see H. Sheldon

Smith, *Faith and Nurture* (New York: Charles Scribner's Sons, 1941), 26–32; Jack L. Seymour, *From Sunday School to Church School* (Washington, DC: University Press of America, 1982), 79–101, 127–54; James E. Kirby, Russell E. Richey, and Kenneth E. Rowe, *The Methodists* (Westport, CT: Greenwood Press, 1996), 231–41.

105. Edward Scribner Ames, *The Psychology of Religious Experience* (Boston: Houghton Mifflin Co., 1910), 5 (emphasis added).

106. Smith, *Faith and Nurture*, 1–2.

107. Ames, *Psychology of Religious Experience*, 26–27. On the functional approach to theological education, W. Clark Gilpin, *A Preface to Theology* (Chicago: University of Chicago Press, 1996), 99–105. Gilpin depicts the psychology of religion as the curricular link between the social history of the early church and the social focus of the contemporary church at the University of Chicago Divinity School during the early twentieth century. On the modernization of the theological curriculum in the context of the new university, see Gilpin, *Preface*, 81–112; on Union in particular, see Younglae Kim, *Broken Knowledge: The Sway of the Scientific and Scholarly Ideal at Union Theological Seminary in New York, 1887–1926* (Lanham, MD: University Press of America, 1997), and Robert T. Handy, *A History of Union Theological Seminary in New York* (New York: Columbia University Press, 1987).

108. Arthur C. McGiffort, "Democracy and Religion," *Religious Education* 14 (1919): 157–58, quoted in Shelton Smith, Robert T. Handy and Lefferts A. Loetscher, *American Christianity*, 2 vols. (1960–63), 2:428.

109. Smith, Handy, and Loetscher, *American Christianity*, 2:429. For similar comments from the perspective of pastoral counseling, see Paul Johnson, "Pastoral Psychology in the Christian Community," *Spiritual Life* 15 (1969):58–64, quoted in *Clinical Handbook of Pastoral Counseling*, vol. 1, ed. Robert J. Wicks, Richard D. Parsons, Donald Capps (New York: Paulist Press, 1983), 18.

110. Clarence Abel, Pastor, Trinity Methodist Episcopal Church, Chicago to George A. Coe, March 3, 1903, Scrapbook 2:160–61, Coe Papers.

111. Rev. J. N. Dingle to Rev. Clarence Abel, Scrapbook 2:161, Coe Papers.

112. Coe, *Psychology of Religion*, 42, 142–43, 320; for the parallels between Coe's ideas and those of George Herbert Mead, see, Mead, *Mind, Self, and Society* (Chicago: The University of Chicago Press, 1934), 164, 227, 238–41, 253, 326.

113. George A. Coe, *The Core of Good Teaching: A Sunday-School Curriculum, The Completely Graded Series* (New York: Charles Scribner's Sons, 1912), 10–16.

114. Ibid., 12.

115. William Byron Forbush, *The Intermediate Teacher: The Life of Jesus*, Charles F. Kent and George A. Coe, Consulting Editors (New York: Charles Scribner's Sons, 1912), vi, xiii–xiv.

116. Ibid., vi, xv.

117. William Byron Forbush, *The Life of Jesus* (New York: Charles Scribner's Sons, 1912), 111, 123, 225.

CONCLUSION

1. Preus, *Explaining Religion*, xi; Segal, *Explaining and Interpreting Religion*, 1–2. Although in his earlier essays he described "religionists" as interpreters and "social scientists" as explainers of religion, Segal has suggested more recently that the confrontation between religionists and social scientists is "over *how*, not *whether*, religion is to be either explained or interpreted." For a critique of the dualistic typology of Preus and Segal from a contemporary

"mediator," see David Ray Griffin, "Religious Experience, Naturalism, and the Social Scientific Study of Religion," unpublished paper, and Griffin, *Religion and Scientific Naturalism* (New York: Oxford University Press, forthcoming).

2. The life and religious experience of Mme. Guyon is the only Catholic title. Among the Protestant authors, we find Methodists, Quakers, Baptists, United Brethren, and Adventists. "Religious experience" did not always appear in the titles of pious memoirs, but was one among several stock phrases that signaled such an account. *The Memoirs of the Life, Religious Experience, Ministerial Travels and Labours of Mrs. Zilpha Elaw, An American Female of Colour* captures the flavor of such titles. "Religious experience," here positioned between her "Life" and her "Ministerial Travels and Labours," referred to her experiences of conversion, sanctification, and call to the ministry. Although there are a few collections of religious experiences, they did not cross denominational lines.

3. Ian Hacking (taking "trance" as an unproblematic term) writes that in "our ignorance about trance, and our wish to make it pathological, . . . we colonize our own past, destroying traces of the original inhabitants. That is, we read multiple personality into other uses of trance, those that appeared in earlier European societies, and find it very hard to see them as they were seen then, not as precursors of multiple personality disorder, inadequately diagnosed, but as cultural uses of trance with their own *integrity*" (Ian Hacking, *Rewriting the Soul: Multiple Personality and the Sciences of Memory* [Princeton: Princeton University Press, 1995], 146). What Hacking refers to as "colonizing our own past" is another way to talk about "retrospective diagnosis," a practice roundly criticized by William James (Micale, *Approaching Hysteria*, 272).

4. Sunderland, *Trance*, 104-5, 107-8; for more recent discussions of cueing, see Rouget, *Music and Trance*, and Morton Marks, "Uncovering Ritual Structures in Afro-American Music," in Irvin I. Zaretsky and Mark P. Leone, *Religious Movements in Contemporary America* (Princeton: Princeton University Press, 1974), 6--134.

5. Connerton, *How Societies Remember*, 72-73. This way of speaking of experiences as constituted and reconstituted in connection with chains of associated or dissociated memories avoids the dualisms associated with the contemporary debates over "recovered" and "false" memories.

6. Ann Taves, "Feminization Revisited," in Brereton and Bendroth, *Women and Twentieth Century Protestantism* (Urbana: University of Illinois Press, forthcoming); for a discussion of sympathy as a unifying theme among mid-nineteenth-century evangelical and liberal Protestants, including abolitionists such as Sunderland, see Elizabeth B. Clark, " 'The Sacred Rights of the Weak': Pain, Sympathy, and the Culture of Individual Rights in Antebellum America," *Journal of American History* 82, no. 2 (Sept. 1995):463-93.

7. Chauncy, "Letter to Wishart" in Bushman, ed., *The Great Awakening*, 118-19.

8. Elizabeth Reis, "The Devil, the Body, and the Feminine Soul in Puritan New England," *The Journal of American History* 82, no. 1 (June 1995):15-36. I am grateful to Cathy Brekus for bringing this article to my attention.

9. Ernest R. Hilgard, *Divided Consciousness*, exp. ed. (New York: John Wiley & Sons, 1986); Erika Bourguignon, ed., *Religion, Altered States of Consciousness, and Social Change* (Columbus: Ohio State University Press, 1973), 12; Colin Ross, *Multiple Personality Disorder* (New York: John Wiley & Sons, 1989), 177-89.

10. Philip M. Coons, "The Differential Diagnosis of Possession States," *Dissociation* 4, no. 4 [Dec. 1993]:214); Carol S. North, et al., *Multiple Personalities, Multiple Disorders: Psychiatric Classification and Media Influence* [New York: Oxford University Press, 1993], 177-78).

11. Elaine Showalter, *Hystories: Hysterical Epidemics and Modern Culture* (New York: Columbia University Press, 1997).

12. *DSM-IV*, 729; *Transcultural Psychiatric Research Review* 29, no. 4 (1992):289, 319–30; Rouget, *Music and Trance*, 40–46.

13. Arnold M. Ludwig, "Altered States of Consciousness," in Charles T. Tart, ed., *Altered States of Consciousness*, 3rd ed. (San Francisco: Harper San Francisco, 1990), 19–22.

14. *Encyclopedia of Religion* (New York: Macmillan, 1987), s.v. "Attention."

God, power and presence of (cont.)
   and, 236–40; Woodworth revivals and, 241–
   42, 246
—among Pentecostals: at Azusa Street, 333,
   337–40. See also biblical typology; shekinah;
   shouting

habit: Ames on, 297–99, 425n.71, 426n.85;
   and bodily knowledge (Connerton), 10,
   372n.1; Hume on, 42, 45, 46; Sunderland
   on, 203–204, 357; Watson and, 77
hallucinations: census of (SPR), 248, 257,
   422n.7. See also visions
healing: Buckley on, 228–29; Coe on, 302;
   Eddy on, 217–18; and the Emmanuel movement, 316–17; Evans on, 223–24; and the
   holiness movement, 226–32, 241, 243; James
   on, 189; and New Thought, 310, 312; and
   Pentecostalism, 328; Quimby on, 213–15
heaven, experiences of: adventist, 155; Congregationalist (New Light), 32, 69–70; holiness,
   239; Methodist, 85–86, 87, 109, 114–15,
   144; Presbyterian, 137; and mesmeric demonstrations, 144, 147; Pentecostal, 332
hell, 24, 34–35, 62, 87, 160
higher power, 247, James on, 286, 288
histories, 6, 349–50; of enthusiasm (false religion), 18, 139–40, 180, 192; of magnetism
   and magic (false religion), 139, 180, 192; of
   spirits and the supernatural (true religion),
   180, 191–94, 198, 221
History of Great Britain, The (Hume), 21, 43–44
History of Magic, The (Ennemoser), 140, 191,
   221
History of the Supernatural, The (Howitt), 191,
   221
holiness movement: and the camp meeting tradition, 232–40; Coe on, 268–69; faith healing
   and, 207, 226–32; Palmer and, 122, 148–53;
   Woodworth and, 241–47
holy spirit. See spirit, holy
How Pentecost Came to Los Angeles (Bartleman),
   331
hymns and spiritual songs: Adventist, 153; African influences on, 80; and African Americans, 77; and camp meetings, 76, 77, 109–
   14; Pentecostal, 332; Separates, 71, 83; Spiritualist, 177; as testimony, 75; Watson on, 77,
   109; Watts, 110; ; C. Wesley, 110
hypnosis: 357; Borch-Jacobsen on, 8; Coe and
   Ellis on, 301; experimental psychology
   (French), 247, 253, 420n.16; Myers on,
   255–56, 258; and Pentecostalism, 329; and
   Woodworth, 242–43

imagination, 138, 145, 355–56; Chauncy on,
   23, 26, 28, 33; the Commissioners' Report on
   animal magnetism, 122–24, 126, 133, 136;
   Edwards on, 35, 39, 40, 50, 56, 61–62, 66;
   Hume on, 42, 45; Wesley on, 74
inspiration, 15, 23, 32, 35, 43, 125, 174; Coe
   on, 302; Wesley on, 51
inspiration, false. See enthusiasm
intuition, 52, 123, 299, 373n.13; in New
   Thought, 224–25; in Theosophy, 221

Jerusalem (biblical), 115, 239; as type of
   heaven, 153–55; Jesus entry into, 111, 113,
   234; Jesus: as adept (Blavatsky, Evans), 222,
   224–25; as clairvoyant (Quimby), 214–15; as
   demonstrator (Eddy), 215–17; as medium
   (Spiritualism), 182, 185, 187–88, 194; as
   mystic (Sanday), 326; as physician (Emmanuel), 318; as psychic scientist (Hudson),
   310; as teacher and revolutionist (modernist),
   304, 346
journalists: and the Emmanuel movement, 314,
   324; and the Woodworth revivals, 242–47
joy, 24–25, 61, 87, 144

Keswick movement, 332, 334

Law of Psychic Phenomena, The (Hudson), 310,
   313, 316
Life of David Brainerd, The (Edwards), 49, 61
Life of Madame Guyon, The (Upham), 150
Life of Wesley, The (Southey), 134
living religion. See Hall, David; James, William;
   religion in practice

Magnet, The (Sunderland), 130, 135, 136, 140,
   141, 142
Medical Superintendents of American Institutions for the Insane, Association of: 123. See
   also physicians, asylum
medicine, professionalization of, 208
mediums, Spiritualist: Beard on, 210–11; development of, 200–202; Eddy on, 316; Flournoy on, 258; Quimby and, 213; and signs
   and wonders, 189–90; Theosophists on,
   219–20; and trance, 177–80
melancholy, 17, 23; Hume on, 41–42, 44;
   James on, 273, 275
memory: bodily, 255, 233, 354; chains of, 255–
   56, 301, 355, 433n.5; recovered and false,
   433n.5; and trance, 205, 211–12
mental action, disordered: 150–51
mental weakness, 23, 28, 122, 124, 307, 356–
   57. See also nervous instability